WHEAT COUNTRY RAILROAD

WHEAT COUNTRY RAILROAD

THE NORTHERN PACIFIC'S SPOKANE & PALOUSE AND COMPETITORS

PHILIP F. BEACH

WSU PRESS

Washington State University Press
Pullman, Washington

Washington State University Press
PO Box 645910
Pullman, Washington 99164-5910
Phone: 800-354-7360
Fax: 509-335-8568
Email: wsupress@wsu.edu
Website: wsupress.wsu.edu

First printing 2018

Library of Congress Cataloging-in-Publication Data

Names: Beach, Phil, author.
Title: Wheat country railroad : the Northern Pacific's Spokane & Palouse
and competitors / Philip F. Beach.
Description: Pullman, Washington : Washington State University Press,
[2018]
| Includes bibliographical references and index.
Identifiers: LCCN 2018015310 | ISBN 9780874223613 (alk. paper)
Subjects: LCSH: Northern Pacific Railroad Company--History. | Spokane and
Palouse Railway Company--History. | Columbia and Palouse Railroad
Company--History. | Railroads--Washington (State)--History--19th
century.
| Railroads--Idaho--History--19th century. | Railroads--United
States--History--19th century.
Classification: LCC HE2791.N855 B43 2018 | DDC 385.09795--dc23 LC record
available at https://lccn.loc.gov/2018015310

On the cover: Engine NP No. 673 is probably about to leave Lewiston's first depot with train No. 10 for Spokane. *Photograph 032521, Bancroft Library, University of California, Berkeley.*

Contents

Illustrations and Maps

The Northern Pacific Railway
continues to live through
The Northern Pacific Railway Historical Association

Acknowledgments

My greatest debt is to Jerry Masters who located a great deal of correspondence and documents, particularly the correspondence of James J. Hill. I consulted with Marc Entze on railroads in eastern Washington. Robert Clark, editor in chief of Washington State University Press, encouraged and supported this work. Chelsea Feeney prepared the final map images based on research and drafts by the author and Mike Bertenstein (maps 1, 5, and 6). My son David C. Beach helped produce and correct some primary sources. I have a debt to the staffs of several archives and libraries, particularly the Minnesota Historical Society, the Archives and Special Collections of the University of Montana Library, the Washington State Library and the State Archives, the Oregon Historical Society, the Connell Heritage Museum, and the Manuscripts, Archives, and Special Collections of the Washington State University Library. Other organizations from which I drew materials are in the list of abbreviations. Unmentioned in the abbreviations are county public works departments and assessor offices, and Washington State and Idaho State revenue offices: Whitman County, Washington, and Latah and Nez Perce Counties in Idaho.

Friends who were of assistance include: Walt Ainsworth, Verne Alexander, Thomas Burg, Clive Carter, Dan Cozine, Paul Curtiss, Jim Davis, Jim Dick, Jim Frederickson, Thomas Hillebrant, Hudson Leighton, Jim Mattson, Gary Miller, John Phillips, Ray Poindexter, Ed Sherry, Chuck Soule, Lorenz Schrenk, Gary Tarbox, Jan and Bill Taylor, Thornton Waite, Jim West, and others.

In the end the author is responsible for all errors, omissions and misinterpretations.

Abbreviations

Railroad and related company's initials as used in the text (associated with):

BN: Burlington Northern, Inc.

BR: Bitter Root Railroad Company (ORN).

C&P: Columbia and Palouse Railroad Company (O&T/NP/ORN, later ORN).

CB&Q also "Burlington": Chicago, Burlington and Quincy Railroad Company (merged into the BN, 1970).

CP: Canadian Pacific Railway.

CRN: Coeur d'Alene Railway and Navigation Company (independent, later NP).

CSL: Clearwater Short Line Railway Company (NP).

CSP: Camas Prairie Railway (CSL/ORN; NP/UP).

CV: Columbia Valley Railroad (ORN/UP).

CW: Central Washington Railroad, predecessor to Washington Central (NP).

CWV: Clearwater Valley Railroad Company (ORN).

EW: Eastern Washington Railway Company (independent, later S&P).

EWA: Eastern Washington Railroad (SCRRN).

GN: Great Northern Railway (merged into the BN, 1970).

ICMT: Idaho, Clearwater and Montana Transportation Company.

IE: Inland Empire Railroad (SCAP).

IT: Idaho Transit.

LNPE: Lewiston, Nez Perce & Eastern Railway.

LSE: Lewiston & Southeastern Railway Company.

Manitoba: St. Paul, Minneapolis and Manitoba Railroad, later GN.

Milwaukee: Various all having Chicago, Milwaukee and either St. Paul or Puget Sound in their names.

ME: Moscow and Eastern Railroad, later Railway Company.

MIP: Montana, Idaho & Pacific Railroad Company (ORN).

NI: Nez Perce & Idaho Railroad Company.

NC: North Coast (Railway) Railroad Company (OWRN).

NP: Northern Pacific Railroad (in 1896, became Railway) Company (merged into the BN, 1970).

NPI: Northern Pacific and Idaho Railroad Company (S&P).

NW: The Northwestern Railroad Company (ORN).

OI: Oregon Improvement Company (OT).

ORE: Oregon Railway Extensions Company (ORN).

ORN: Oregon Railway (in 1896, became Railroad) and Navigation Company (later OSL, OWRN, UP).

OSL: Oregon Short Line Railway (in 1897, became Railroad) Company (1889-1897, Oregon Short Line and Utah Northern Railway Company (OSLUN) UP).

OSN: Oregon Steam Navigation Company (became ORN company).

OT: Oregon and Transcontinental Company.

OWT: Oregon and Washington Territory Railroad Company (independent, later WCR, then NP).

OWI: Oregon, Washington and Idaho Railroad Company (ORN).

OWRN: Oregon-Washington Railroad and Navigation Company (UP).

P&L: NP Palouse and Lewiston Branch.

P&S: Portland and Seattle Railway (SPS).

PSE: Palouse and Spokane Electric Railroad.

PLCR: Pullman, La Crosse and Columbia River Railroad.

SCRRN: Spokane & Columbia River Railroad & Navigation Company (NC).

S&I: Spokane and Inland Railway (SIE).

SIE: Spokane and Inland Empire Railroad (IE).

S&P: Spokane and Palouse Railway Company (NP).

SCAP: Spokane, Coeur d'Alene and Palouse Railway (GN).

SFI: Spokane Falls and Idaho Railroad Company (NP).

SLSE: Seattle Lake Shore and Eastern Railway Company (NP).

SPS: Seattle, Portland and Spokane Railway (merged into the BN, 1970).

SRV: Snake River Valley Railroad Company (ORN).

SST: Spokane and Southern Traction Company.

UF: Union Flat Railroad Company (ORN).

UP: Union Pacific Railway (in 1897, became Railroad) Company.

WC: Washington Central Railroad, successor to CW (NP).

WCR: Washington and Columbia River Railway, successor to OWT.

WI: Washington and Idaho Railroad Company (ORN).

WIM: Washington, Idaho and Montana Railway Company.

WPR: Wallula Pacific Railway (ORN).

WW&CR: Walla Walla and Columbia River Railroad Company (ORN).

Archives:

Baker: Baker Library Historical Collections, Harvard Business School.

Bancroft: Bancroft Library, University of California, Berkeley.

BFA: Billings Family Archives, The Woodstock Foundation, Inc. Woodstock, Vermont.

IDSHS: Idaho State Historical Society.

ISHS: Iowa State Historical Society, Grenville M. Dodge Collection.

JJH: James J. Hill Library, St. Paul, MN (since when most of the documents in this work were gathered the Hill collection moved to the Minnesota Historical Society).

MCL: Multnomah County Library, Wilson Room, Portland OR.

MHS: Minnesota Historical Society.

OHS: Oregon Historical Society.

NARA-P: National Archives & Records Administration, Pacific Alaska Region (Seattle).

UI: University of Idaho Archives.

UWS: University of Washington Special Collections.

UMT: University of Montana Archives.

Whitman College: Northwest Archives.

WSU: Washington State University Manuscripts, Archives, and Special Collections.

Newspaper Abbreviations and *Short Titles*:

CG (*Gazette*): Colfax *Gazette* (successor to PG).

IS: *Idaho Signal.*

LT (*Teller*): *[Lewiston] Teller.*

LTR (*Tribune*): *Lewiston Tribune.*

NYT (*Times*): *New York Times.*

PB (*Boomerang*): Palouse City *Boomerang.*

PG (*Gazette*): *Palouse Gazette*, published at Colfax, WA (predecessor to CG).

PH (*Herald*): *Pullman Herald.*

PN (*News*): *Palouse City News.*

OS (*Sun*): *Oakesdale Sun.*

ROR: *Rosalia Rustler.*

SR (*Review*): *Spokesman-Review (beginning 6/29/1894) and predecessors; Spokane Falls Review* SFR, *Spokane Falls Daily* SFD, *Spokane Falls Evening Review* SFEV, *Spokane Falls Morning Review* SFMR, *Spokane Falls Weekly Review* SFWR, *Spokane Review* SR, *Morning Spokesman, Spokane Spokesman.*

SS (*Spokesman*): *Spokane Spokesman.*

ST: *Spokan(e) Times.*

TN: *Tacoma Daily News.*

WSJ: *Wall Street Journal.*

WWJ (*Journal*): *Walla Walla [Daily] Journal.*

WWU (*Union*): *Walla Walla Union (beginning 3/29/1893) and predecessors; Walla Walla Daily Union* WWDU, *Walla Walla Weekly Union* WWWU, *Walla Walla Morning Union* WWMU, *Walla Walla Union-Journal* WWUJ.

Journal and Magazine Abbreviations:

C&F: *The Commercial & Financial Chronicle.*

NW: *The Northwest Magazine.*

PNQ: *Pacific Northwest Quarterly.*

RA: *The Railway Age.*

RAG: *Railway Age Gazette.*

RG: *The Railroad Gazette.*

RR: *The Railway Review.*

RW: *Railway World.*

WS: *The West Shore.*

Other:

WSDOT: Washington State Department of Transportation.

Chronology of the Northern Pacific Railroad, Oregon Railway & Navigation Co., and the Union Pacific Railway in the Palouse, 1860–1910

Date	Event
1860 Dec. 16	Initial charter of Oregon Steam Navigation Company (OSN) in Washington Territory.
1868	First British ship from Portland to Liverpool with Pacific Northwest wheat and flour.
1869	Northern Pacific (NP) engineer W. Milnor Roberts crossed Palouse, also 1878, NP Ward also 1872.
1870 May 31	NP 1864 congressional charter amended, main line to Portland and hence to Puget Sound with branch over Cascades.
1871 Mar. 19	NP begins construction at Kalama, Washington Territory, operation to Tacoma begins Dec. 16, 1873.
1872 April 5	NP purchased OSN.
1873 Sept. 18	Jay Cooke & Co. failed. NP lost control of OSN. Portland directors regained control of OSN.
1879 June 13	Henry Villard chartered Oregon Railway & Navigation Co. (ORN), majority of the directors required to be from Oregon. ORN acquired OSN 3/31/80 (Villard bought in May 1879). June 19 ORN directors agreed to construct into Palouse..
1879 Sept. 22	NP directors learn a line over Bitterroot Mountains not feasible. October NP begin construction east from Ainsworth, Columbia-Snake River confluence, to Lake Pend Oreille, Idaho Territory.
1880 Oct. 20	Villard-NP Traffic Agreement: NP and ORN to interchange at Wallula; ORN build from Wallula to Portland; except for line to Wallula NP not to build south of the Snake; except for Texas Ferry to Farmington the ORN not to build north of the Snake. The NP not precluded from building on the north bank of the Columbia nor the Cascade branch.
1881 Feb. 25	Buyout of NP by Villard announced. Villard elected NP president Sept. 15, 1881.
1881 June 28	Villard formed Oregon & Transcontinental Co. (OT) to hold about a third of NP stock and a majority of ORN stock.
1881 June 30	ORN annual report revealed extensive projected routes in the Palouse.
1881 Dec. 4	ORN operating from Walla Walla to south bank of Snake at (South) Riparia opposite Texas Ferry (Riparia).
1881 June 14	NP reaches Spokane Falls from Wallula.
1882 June 29	Villard charters Columbia & Palouse Railroad (C&P) to build from NP (MP 51, from Wallula, Palouse Junction, later Connell) to Colfax with branches to Moscow, I.T., and Farmington, W.T.
1882 Aug. 17	Supplementary Contract, ORN gave up lines in the Palouse.
1882 Nov. 20	ORN begins operating from Portland to Wallula.
1883 Feb. 23	ORN and Union Pacific (UP)/Oregon Short line (OSL) agree to connect at Huntington, OR.
1883 July 10	Tripartite Contract between the C&P, NP, ORN & OT: OT to finance C&P; NP to construct and operate for the benefit of ORN. NP and ORN each own half of C&P stock.

1883 Dec. 13 O&T Executive Committee recommends that Tripartite Agreement be modified to turn C&P over to ORN.

1883 Dec. 17 Villard resigns from boards and presidencies of ORN and OT.

1884 Jan. 1 C&P officially opened to Colfax.

1884 Jan. 4 Villard resigns from NP board and presidency. NP Board consents to annul Tripartite Agreement and loss of C&P. OT subsequently sold C&P stock and bonds to ORN.

1884 Jan. 17 Robert Harris, NP president.

1884 March Elijah Smith, OT president, and July 17 ORN president.

1884 June 15 NP board agrees lease of ORN might be desirable. 27th ORN Executive Committee authorizes the president to lease or make traffic contract with NP. Neither consummated.

1885 May 5 ORN President Smith rejects NP lease terms. NP and UP negotiate with ORN for a joint lease. NP board approves joint lease July 23. Negotiations continue.

1886 Mar. 1 NP charters Spokane & Palouse Railway (S&P). Operated by NP under lease until 8/15/93. Begins construction from Marshall April. February, 1887, ORN begins surveys paralleling S&P.

1886 Mar. 4 Oregon & Washington Territory Railroad (OWT) incorporated, constructed 1887 to 1889 south of Snake.

1887 Jan. 6 NP rejects joint lease. Jan. 21 UP President Charles Francis Adams writes Smith negotiations with NP "are off."

1887 Jan. 24 James J. Hill expresses interest to Elijah Smith to make connection with ORN at Missoula.

1887 April 25 OSL leases ORN in behalf of UP; lease dated January 1, 1887. Provision made for NP to join lease. Negotiations with NP begin, break down in 1889.

1887 May 13 NP Harris writes UP Adams inquiring Adams' interest in adjusting differences. Negotiations to June 1889 of Joint Lease of ORN to NP and UP and Arbitration Contract.

1887 May 26 Smith sues to stop all construction on S&P, construction continued. Suit dismissed October 26.

1887 Aug. 27 Smith appeales to Villard to save OT and ORN from bankruptcy. Villard raised $5,000,000 in 36 hours.

1887 Sept. 15 Villard elected to NP board. Harris forced out as president 9/20/88, remains on board as chairman. Thomas F. Oakes president 9/20/88. Harris forced off board 10/17/89.

1887 Sept. 28 NP and UP memorandum to divide the interior territory and payoff Elijah Smith. Sept. 30 NP favored joint lease. Oct. 3 Adams rejected NP terms. Oct. 20 a "Memorandum of Agreement" among ORN, UP, OT, OSL, and NP to divide territory at Snake River. Oct. 21 Smith seeks modifications.

1887 Dec. OWT comes under control of NP director and former president, C. B. Wright.

1888 Feb. Oregon legislature outlaws lease of an Oregon railroad by a parallel line, i.e., the NP.

1888 Feb. 18-19 Joint lease of ORN agreed to by NP and UP and New York directors of ORN, Portland directors opposed. Late March Adams and Villard meet delegation from Portland that demand that Portland be favored over all others. Adams says NP not acting in good faith regarding the OWT; Adams prepared to invade NP territory north of Snake.

1888 April 14 S&P track laid to Genesee, IT; service begins July 1, Marshall to Genesee, 103.66 miles.

1888 May 27 Operation through Stampede tunnel begins, giving NP direct connection to Puget Sound.

1889 February Arbitration contract drawn up establishing a neutral zone within which relations of parties would be regulated. According to Villard the arbitration contract substantially approved by executive committees of OSL, UP, and NP subject to OT's ORN stock placed in the hands of a trustee.

1889 April 9 Bridge across Snake at Riparia completed, giving ORN physical connection with its lines north of Snake.

1889 April	By middle of the month agreement that joint lease and arbitration contract would not be approved by all parties. Competition and distrust among the railroads, mutual dislike among Adams and Smith and Villard and opposition of Oregon interests too much to overcome.
1889 June	To control the OT Villard agrees to sell OT's majority of ORN's stock to UP and Hill interests—UP fears that NP will gain control of OT and the stock to break the UP lease of ORN or to maintain 6 percent interest payments that UP had agreed to 1/1/87. Smith loses his connections to the ORN, which both NP and UP desired.
1889 Sept. 16	James J. Hill reorganizes the St. Paul, Minneapolis & Manitoba Railroad into the Great Northern Railway (GN); next month orders surveys for westward extension from Montana.
1889 Oct. 7	ORN reaches Spokane from Farmington.
1889 Nov. 15	OSL (UP) buys OT's interest in ORN.
1890 May	Construction of S&P's Lewiston extension begins.
1890 Oct. 13	GN's Hill and UP's Adams, following discussion begun in Sept. 1889, agree that GN and ORN to connect at Spokane and ORN will haul GN traffic to Portland.
1890 Dec. 10	S&P begins service from Belmont to Farmington, 6.1 miles.
1891 Sept. 15	S&P, Pullman Junction to Juliaetta, 37.9 miles, turned over to operating department.
1892 Aug. 4	Washington & Columbia River Railroad (WCR) chartered. Acquires OWT 10/5/92 begins operation 11/5/92. Deeded to NP 5/24/95.
1892 Aug. 17	GN begins daily passenger service Spokane to St. Paul. GN completed to Everett 1/6/93.
1893 June 21	Villard resigns as NP chairman and director
1893 Aug. 15	NP receivership begins.
1893 Oct. 10	Receivers for S&P appointed, and discharged 11/17/94, NP receivers retroactively leased S&P from 8/15/93.
1893 Oct. 13	UP receivership begins. Caused in part by cost of ORN lease and payment to Villard for ORN stock.
1894 July 3	ORN receivership begins. Traffic agreements with UP gives GN access to Portland.
1895 Mar. 27	C&P ceases operating Washtucna to Connell, 29.73 miles.
1896 April 2	J. P. Morgan & Co., Hill, and Deutsche Bank agree NP should be independent of GN, but the two "shall form a permanent alliance...protecting the common interests of both Companies." They will seek to keep ORN independent. On 3/16/96 they agree they will establish a voting trust of NP stock controlled by Morgan Co.
1896 Aug. 17	Oregon Railroad & Navigation Co. (ORN) (chartered 7/16/96) acquired Oregon Railway & Navigation Co. A majority of the board of new company required to be Oregon residents. 19th voting trust controlled by Morgan Co. gives holders of ORN preferred stock 2/3rds ORN directors. The NP, GN, and UP hold preferred stock jointly.
1896 July 25	Northern Pacific Railway (NP) acquired Northern Pacific Railroad (NP). The new company begins operation 9/1/96. S&P operated by NP from 9/1/96 to 2/21/99 when sold to NP.
1897 Feb. 2	Oregon Short Line Railroad (OSL) incorporated and takes possession March 16. Company independent of UP.
1897 Feb. 15	The NP, GN, J. P. Morgan & Co. and Kuhn, Loeb & Co. (UP interests), agree that NP and GN will each acquire 1/4th of ORN preferred stock, remaining 1/2 held in trust by finance companies for reorganized UP. The contract states that NP and GN desire that ORN have a full and ample opportunity, without preference, to secure for its lines the freight and passenger business of NP, GN, OSL, and UP on terms equitable for all five companies. GN and NP invest approximately $1.1 million in ORN stock. Hope that conflicts between NP, GN, and ORN will be settled before UP and OSL acquired stock being held.

1897 May 17 A. L. Mohler, former GN manager, vice president and manager of the ORN, becomes president 9/3/97.

1897 July 1 Union Pacific Railroad (UP) purchases the Union Pacific Railway (UP) 11/1/97 and takes possession of main line 2/1/98. Beginning October 1897, the UP buys OSL stock and in Dec. has over a 1/3 of capital stock reorganized OSL and April 1898, three UP men replace Morgan representatives on OSL board. The OSL owns majority ORN common stock, but UP, NP, and GN jointly own controlling interest of preferred stock.

1897 Aug. 5 ORN and NP agree in "Portland Protocol" to avoid competitive building, take no action impairing each other's revenues without consultation. NP can complete its Lewiston extension but neither to acquire WCR without consultation. NP will seek to prevent WCR from manipulating rates on competitive business with ORN. ORN will interchange eastbound business at Wallula rather than Spokane.

1897 Aug. 12 Charles Mellen, second vice president of the New Haven, elected over objections of Hill, president and director of NP effective September 1.

1897 Dec. 6 Edward Henry Harriman elected to first board of reorganized UP and 5/23/98 elected chairman of executive committee. Oct. 1898, UP captures OSL board, Harriman elected to board. OSL stockholders January, 1899 agree to exchange OSL stock for UP common stock.

1898 January Construction resumes on S&P Lewiston extension, operation Marshall to Lewiston, 138.9 miles, begins 10/1/98.

1898 Jan. 28 Following this date GN and NP ORN stock was to be delivered to UP at cost.

1898 Feb. 17 Through Northwestern Improvement Co., NP purchases from C. B. Wright stock and bonds of WCR, deeded to NP 6/18/07. NP President Mellen proposes same day that WCR belong to ORN which should have all lines south and west of Snake River and NP lines north and east; NP and GN have trackage over ORN from Wallula to Portland and the GN trackage over NP from Spokane to Wallula; NP and UP should jointly lease ORN with latter operating lines to Portland and south of Snake River. He thinks all of this should be done before UP regains control of OSL and thus ORN. In March the ORN Executive Committee decides not to take up proposal.

1898 Mar. 3 ORN charters Snake River Valley Railroad (SRV) with support of Hill. Opened to traffic, Wallula to Grange City Junction, Dec. 1, 1899.

1898 Mar. 17 Mellen asks Mohler whether ORN would "consider the sale to us of your line from Connell to La Crosse, or a lease of the same for a term of years?" No agreement.

1898 April 4 Hill writes: "The Great Northern must have access to the Palouse country and the Walla Walla country, either by the lines of the Navigation Company or of the Northern Pacific Company, on fair and equal terms, or it would be compelled to build a line of its own into that country."

1898 June 1 S&P Supplementary Charter projects line from Pullman to near La Crosse to Connell and from Pullman-La Crosse to Colfax.

1898 Nov. 1 Harriman and Charles Coster, Morgan Co., meet and thereafter exchange correspondence on settlement in Pacific Northwest. Discussions break off mid-November. ORN wants lines east and south of Lewiston, NP wants use of ORN west of Lewiston.

1898 Nov. 9 NP charters Clearwater Short Line (CSL). Constructed: Potlatch Junction (Arrow) to Stites, opened traffic 5/15/00; and Lapwai Junction (Joseph, Spalding) to Grangeville, opened traffic 12/22/08. Numerous surveys and acquisition of rights of way south and west of Pullman and west of Lewiston, no construction.

189 Feb. 21 S&P conveys by deed to NP. Becomes Palouse & Lewiston, Genesee, and Farmington branches.

1899 July 14 Following agreement by J. P. Morgan & Co. and Harriman, ORN voting trust of August 19, 1896, dissolved, control passed to common stockholders, principal one was OSL.

1899 Aug. 7 A six month truce in the Clearwater country between NP and UP/OR&N put into effect.

1899 Oct. UP acquires ORN. About same time UP in an exchange of stock acquires OSL.

1900 Jan. 12	Harriman and Mellen agree to continue truce of 8/7/99 with certain exceptions. On April 1, 1901, the two parties agree to extend January 12 agreement indefinitely subject to a thirty days notification by either party.
1900 Nov. 12	Announcement that NP Voting Trust of Dec. 1, 1896, will be dissolved Jan. 1, 1901 (rather than Nov. 1, 1901). Three principal stockholders of GN, James J. Hill, John S. Kennedy, and Lord Strathcona are three largest holders of NP stock.
1903 Aug. 8	ORN chartered Oregon, Washington & Idaho Railroad (OWI). Riparia to Lewiston, opened to traffic 7/7/08.
1905 May 23	NP President Elliott agrees to Harriman proposal to build joint line from Riparia to Grangeville on Camas Prairie. 10/31/05 Elliott withdraws from Mellen-Harriman agreement 1/12/00, but no effect on joint line Riparia to Grangeville agreement.
1906 Nov. 9	Spokane & Inland Empire Railroad chartered. Operation begins from Spokane to Colfax 8/1/07 and to Moscow 9/15/08. Ultimately controlled by GN/NP and then solely GN.
1907 Oct.	The Washington, Idaho & Montana Railway began regular service from Palouse, Washington, to the end of the line at Bovill, Idaho.
1909 May 3	NP begins operation Snake River Junction to Riparia.
1909 Sept. 9	E. H. Harriman dies.
1909 Nov. 4	Camas Prairie Railroad (CSP) incorporated implementing contract of 9/1/09 between OWI (ORN), NP and CSL. 12/3/09 begins operating Riparia to Lewiston (OW&I) and Lewiston to Grangeville (CSL-NP).
1910 Nov. 23	UP charters Oregon-Washington Railroad & Navigation Co. (OWRN).
1910 Dec. 23	OWRN acquires all ORN lines. Ayer Junction to Spokane opened to traffic 9/15/1914.

Introduction

Railroad development and competition in the Palouse of eastern Washington State and northwest Idaho allowed settlement and agricultural development to flourish. The principal protagonists were the alliance of the Oregon Railway & Navigation Co. (ORN) and Union Pacific (UP) opposed by the Northern Pacific Railroad's (NP) Spokane & Palouse Railway (S&P). Our primary focus will be on the S&P until roughly 1910, by which time the issues of railroad development and competition were largely settled. There has been no comprehensive history of the S&P. We shall also provide a history of the Columbia and Palouse Railroad (C&P) up to the 1980s.[1] The C&P was the NP's first railroad in the Palouse, and its loss to the ORN was a major factor in the NP's construction of the S&P. The C&P became a major component of the ORN's Palouse lines.

The S&P built into one of most productive grain growing regions in the world, and the railroads believed that great profits would be made in the Palouse. But they also recognized the dangers of over-building their competitive infrastructure. For a quarter of a century the NP and ORN/UP struggled, in an atmosphere of distrust and competitive zeal, to find an outcome in which each would, from its perspective, be guaranteed an acceptable share of the traffic without excessive construction. The struggle was intensified by Palouse residents seeking competition between the railroad companies in order to reduce freight rates. They lobbied for at least two railroads everywhere, competitive routes to tidewater, and competition among ports.

Portland, Oregon, established itself early as the monopoly exporter of Palouse grain. Portland interests controlled the ORN into the early twentieth century, and those interests fought every threat to its dominance. Whenever there was a prospect of peace between the railroads, Portland interests generally viewed it as a threat. On the other hand, the NP was oriented toward the Puget Sound ports in Washington State, but not as intimately tied to them as the ORN was to Portland.

The Spokane and Palouse should not be treated as an isolated railroad. It was born in a monopolistic environment and was one side of the oligopolistic competition between the NP and the ORN/UP. In addition to railroad development on the Palouse, in this history the personalities, thoughts, and behavior of an array of powerful railroad leaders can be seen. The best known include Henry Villard, who created a monopoly with the ORN and defended it by gaining control of the NP, formed an early holding company, the Oregon & Transcontinental (OT) and lost control of all three largely because of his poor management; Charles Frances Adams, president of the UP who gained a lease of the ORN, achieving a share of the grain output of the Palouse and an outlet to tidewater, at the expense of bankrupting the UP, and battled Villard and Elijah Smith president of both the ORN and OT; James J. Hill, "the Empire Builder," president of the Great Northern (GN), who sought to force his way into the Palouse without building a railroad; and Edward H. Harriman, who built a successful railroad empire based on the Union Pacific and Southern Pacific companies, stabilized control of the ORN, developed a relationship with Charles Mellen, president of the NP, which might have brought railroad peace sooner to the Palouse except for the meddling of Hill. It was in the wheat fields of the Palouse that Hill and Harriman first came into personal and organizational conflict, a conflict that played out, both in the Pacific Northwest and on Wall Street.

But what about the Palouse? The Palouse Plateau, stretching south across eastern Washington and portions of Idaho and Oregon, is cut into north and south sections by the deep canyon of the Snake River. On the north side of the river, the plateau is largely drained by the Palouse River and to a smaller extent the Potlatch River. The plateau, underlaid by basalt rock thousands of feet deep, has a surface composed of wind-blown loess soil, "steeply yet smoothly rolling terrain...[with a] dense dendritic network of shallow creeks." The loess soils stretch from northeast Oregon north almost to Spokane and from the NP's Pasco-Spokane mainline east into Idaho. Originally covered with bunch grass, farmers quickly discovered that where bunch grass grew, wheat and other grains did exceptionally well.[2] The Palouse country was and is the principal source of Washington State wheat. In 1908, in the time of this account, the U.S. Department of Agriculture credited Washington State with 1.5 percent of the total wheat acreage in the United States. Kansas had the largest wheat acreage (19.1 percent). But the value of

Washington wheat per acre averaged $17.77 in the prior 10 years, Kansas, $11.06. Washington's average exceeded every other state by at least $5.00 per acre.[3]

The S&P entered the Palouse Plateau from the north. Henceforth "the Palouse" refers to the land north of the Snake River; "the Palouse Plateau" and "the Palouse country or region" refers to both sides of the Snake River and "the Walla Walla country" refers to the lands south of the Snake River. The division of north and south is important because most of attempts to control competitive over-building used the Snake River as a divide between the NP to the north and ORN to the south of the river.

While secondary sources are used in this account, the backbone of the work is found in internal railroad correspondence and documents, most of which are absent from prior railroad histories of the region. The available NP records are very extensive, primarily at the Minnesota Historical Society (MHS) and the University of Montana (UMT). The ORN/UP records available to the author are less extensive. The letters of James J. Hill, now at MHS, are also an important primary source. The chief value of the correspondence is that it is a record of the mostly nonpublic thoughts and interactions among the principals. The other major primary source are contemporary publications, particularly regional newspapers found on microfilm, mainly at the Washington State Library. The value of the newspapers is that they reveal public sentiments and fill in some gaps in information. Newspapers are unreliable at times and the sentiments, as well as the news, are what the editors select.

Because of the myriad of companies, references, characters, and complex chronology, the reader is referred to the lists of abbreviations and the chronology at the front of this work.

Railroad Beginnings in the Palouse Country, 1864–83

A. Early Surveys and Projections in the Palouse

In 1864 Congress chartered the Northern Pacific Railroad to build a railroad from the Great Lakes to Puget Sound, with a branch to Portland, Oregon. The NP charter was amended in 1870, making Portland the termination of the main line. Puget Sound would be connected via a branch over the Cascade Mountains. As long as the Cascade branch was incomplete, the accompanying land grant remained under threat from Puget Sound interests wanting the grant for their own railroad and from Portland interests wanting the grant forfeited so that the Cascade line would not be built.[1]

The Columbia River connected the interior Pacific Northwest to tide water. The Oregon Steam Navigation Company (OSN) was initially chartered in Washington Territory in 1860 and re-chartered in Oregon in 1862. By early 1863 the OSN monopolized Columbia River traffic by its control of the portage railroads at the Cascades of the Columbia and Celilo Falls. The result was very large profits. In 1868 the first British ship with a full cargo of Pacific Northwest wheat and flour sailed from Portland to Liverpool.[2]

W. Milnor Roberts in the employ of Jay Cooke & Co., the Northern Pacific Railroad (NP) financier, was sent west in June 1869 to investigate the feasibility of the NP route. He crossed the Palouse and "found that grass grows every where, 'covering' all the hills and valleys without exception wherever we have come...and as far as the eye could see on either side." Beginning in August 1870 the NP made "a rapid preliminary survey of the North Bank of the Columbia River from Vancouver [opposite Portland] to [Priest] Rapids, a distance of about three hundred miles." In October 1870 the NP filed a map in Oregon City, Oregon, land office of a projected main line on the north bank of the Columbia west to Vancouver, Washington Territory, and then northward to Puget Sound. Portland was on a branch from Vancouver. Surveying on the north bank continued in 1872. By 1871 some 200 Americans had settled on Union Flat in the Palouse, just north and almost 2,000 feet above the Snake River, but with no access to a market they were feeding their wheat crop to their hogs.[3]

In 1871 the NP began construction from Kalama, Washington Territory, on the Columbia River below Portland, to Puget Sound. Operation to Tacoma, Washington Territory, began December 16, 1873. The line was isolated from the remainder of the NP for over 13 years until a switchback line over the Cascades was opened, July 2, 1887.

Threatened by the NP's interest in building down the Columbia River, the owners of the OSN in 1872 renewed an offer to sell a controlling interest in their company to the NP.[4] On April 5, 1872, for $2,000,000 in gold, Jay Cooke & Co. bought three quarters of the OSN stock, half in cash and half in NP stock. The Portland directors of the OSN retained the other quarter and management of the company. Jay Cooke & Co. failed in September, 1873. The OSN stock was part of the bankruptcy estate, despite an attempt by the NP to retain control of the company the OSN stock was distributed in mostly small lots among numerous creditors in part settlement of claims. The company was unknown and the stock had a low price in the market. This enabled the Portland directors to buy back the stock. By the spring of 1879 they and their friends held four-fifths of the stock.[5] We cannot know what the course of railroad development in the Pacific Northwest would have taken if the NP had retained control of the OSN, but it is clear the loss changed the dynamics of railroad development and competition.

In the 1870s the NP examined three routes from Montana to the Columbia River. None of them directly crossed the Palouse. In early 1878 W. Milnor Roberts, now the NP's chief engineer, again crossed the Palouse country and again reported favorably on its potential. In May 1879 there were reports that a route through Colfax, the county seat of Whitman County in the heart of the Palouse, was being considered.[6] On August 28, 1879, the directors adopted the location of the mainline from Ainsworth, Washington Territory, on the Columbia River near the mouth of the Snake River to Spokane Falls and thence to Lake Pend Oreille in Idaho Territory. This route was west of the Palouse. But the resolution also said that route would be used only if a preferable route could not be found via Lewiston and Washtucna Coulee. The coulee provided a route through Colfax and the Palouse.[7] Clearly at this early date the NP directors recognized the traffic potential of the Palouse.

The Lewiston *Teller* had long argued that NP's early surveys had been incomplete. The NP surveyor H. M. McCartney had left Mt. Idaho, near present-day Grangeville, on July 16 with a party of six "to test the great question of an easy transit across [the Bitterroot] divide." The newspaper editor encountered McCartney in Lewiston August 26 and learned from him that no pass under 6000 feet had been found and that "the approach to the summit was abrupt and precipitous." The "Ska-ka-ho" pass that the Lewiston press championed was not found. The editor blamed the failure on McCartney's guides. McCartney's report contains no criticism of his single guide. The newspaper's critique of the survey said that he was 75 to 80 miles south of Lolo Pass and that he had not been on the Lolo Trail. If McCartney's report had been favorable, NP surveyors would have had the same difficulty that the NP had in 1890 in finding a route from the Palouse Plateau down 2,000 feet to the Snake/Clearwater River at Lewiston. On November 28 the editor of the *Teller* wrote,

> Never did a company commit a greater blunder than did the N. P. company when they finally determined to run from the mouth of the Snake to the Pond'Oreille with their main line. If it had become necessary they had better tunneled twenty-five miles though the crest of the Bitter Root mountains and taken the Clearwater route than to have allowed any other company to have secured any portion of the country north of Snake river for a competing line.[8]

For years thereafter the newspaper regularly reminded the NP of its "blunder."

McCartney's telegram was read to the board on September 22. A year later, September 28, 1880, the NP adopted the definite location of the railroad from Wallula on the Columbia to Spokane Falls. The NP main line from Wallula to the Snake River and from north of the Snake River at Ainsworth to Spokane Falls were completed in 1882. The *Palouse Gazette* reported in March 1880 that "Marshalltown," seven miles from Spokane Falls and on the NP survey, had come into existence. It was from Marshall that the Spokane & Palouse began construction in 1886.[9]

While the NP considered its options, others saw opportunities in the Palouse. The Seattle and Colfax Railroad Company was organized in 1875. The next year it was succeeded by the Seattle and Walla Walla Railroad & Transportation Co. An 1877 Territorial Legislative act authorized several counties to subsidize the company. Whitman County was authorized to contribute $60,000. In the same year the *Palouse Gazette* reported the organization of the Palouse Valley Railroad. This line was to be built from the Snake River up the North Fork of the Palouse River to the mountains. "This road will make a market to the seaboard at all seasons of the year for eastern Washington, which can never be interfered with by any other line, and it will pay large dividends from the day of its birth." The *Gazette* claimed it could be built for $10,000 per mile.[10]

Henry Villard took his first trip up the Columbia River in May 1876.

> I perceived the practical monopoly which the control of the lower and upper portages gave to the navigation company [OSN]. This strong grip upon the natural outlet of the vast, fertile, but hardly touched regions drained by the Columbia and Snake rivers influenced my thoughts with enticing visions of the empire that could be built upon such resources.... The excursion strengthened my belief in my scheme of consolidation with the navigation company into a firm resolution to attempt its realization as soon as possible. Indeed, it was at that early date that a plan arose distinctly in my mind which remain ever present with me until it was carried out through the organization of the Oregon Railway & Navigation Company.[11]

The *Gazette* reported in late June 1878 that OSN President Captain J. C. Ainsworth said that the OSN intended to build a narrow gauge line to feed OSN steamboats from some point on the Snake River, perhaps Texas Ferry, toward the mountains, perhaps to Colfax or Palouse City. In early January 1879 the *Gazette* was of the opinion, "A railroad from Colfax to Snake river will be built and put into operation by the people of Whitman county within the next five years."[12]

In the spring of 1879 a report on a visit to the Palouse called Colfax, "the largest and much the most citified of the new towns of country.... Like most towns of Eastern Oregon and Washington, Colfax is situated in a hole in the ground.... An ascent of four hundred feet carries us above Colfax to the ordinary level of the prairie. The best land in this immediate vicinity has been already taken. But there are still thousands of acres right around Colfax which will sometime be worked."[13]

B. The Oregon Railway & Navigation Company

In May 1879 Henry Villard[14] acquired the OSN, which had in 1878 acquired Dorsey Baker's narrow gauge Walla Walla and Columbia River Railroad Company (WW&CR),[15] at the time the only railroad in eastern Washington. It began operation between Wallula and Walla Walla in 1875. NP Chief Engineer W. Milnor Roberts wrote in 1878 that the line was "a perfect gold mine," earning "not less than $1,000 per day clear profit—perhaps considerably more."[16] In June Villard offered to share control of the OSN with the Union Pacific, but the UP did not invest, probably because of "the adverse attitude" of C. P. Huntington of the Central Pacific. Villard, with the aid of German investors, raised the necessary capital.[17] The *Walla Walla Union* reported in October that OSN Vice President S. G. Reed commented after returning from his first trip to the Palouse that had he "visited that country before, the O. S. N. Co., would never have sold out."[18]

On June 13, 1879, Villard chartered the Oregon Railway and Navigation Company (ORN) to control the OSN.[19] The charter required that a majority of the directors be from Oregon, in practice this meant Portland. The charter included building railroads from Portland to Wallula and Boise and from Walla Walla to the Snake River and "[f]rom a point on the Snake river...near the mouth of the Palouse river, along the valley of the Palouse river in a North easterly direction, to the head waters of the Spokane river." The principal office of the company was Portland. Two days after the charter was filed the ORN directors agreed to construct "a new line through the so-called Palouse country north of the Snake River."[20]

With the incorporation of the ORN, Ficken wrote that Villard "immediately became the dominant business leader of the Pacific Northwest, exercising more influence over the development of Washington Territory than any other individual." Lewty, assessing the situation and quoting from Villard's *Memoires*, commented,

> Villard's objectives in forming OR&N were to secure control of the Columbia Gateway and its eastern approaches, perpetuate the monopoly previously enjoyed by the Oregon Steam Navigation Co., and funnel all the traffic of the northern transcontinental railroads into Portland on his own terms. He expressed relief the Union Pacific had withdrawn from the scheme, admitting that his preference all along had been to "...proceed upon an independent basis until the Oregon Railway & Navigation Co. had secured absolute control of the Columbia Valley and of the approaches there to, so that it could command its own terms of connection with any through line coming either from south or north."[21]

The ORN, as well as the OSN, became what would be called a hundred years later a "cash cow." The necessity that it remain so was an important influence on subsequent events. The ORN took up the OSN monopoly from the interior to tidewater. But it also had the same vulnerability as the OSN: that another company would also connect the interior to tidewater. Portland was vulnerable if the connection avoided Portland. The management of the ORN, particularly after Villard, did what it could to hinder these threats.

In June 1879 it was reported that ORN Chief Engineer Hans Thielsen had four survey parties in the Palouse. He said, "that the company would surely build so as to tap this great wheat country either with their main road or its branches." One of his surveys was from Walla Walla to Colfax and another from Genesee, Idaho, to the Snake River opposite Grange City. Thielsen in July wrote Villard of the NP threat in the Palouse, "It is country well worth fighting for,...let us be the aggressive party, and forthwith and ahead of them build that portion of our contemplated lines that will prevent them from occupying any portion of the much desired Palouse country." A month later Thielsen wrote Villard stating his belief that the NP could get a better line down the Clearwater River than the line from the mouth of the Snake River to the Spokane River. "In view of all these facts and possibilities, I think it...to be our true policy to let me drop everything else and let me get our road up Union Flat and from thence if possible even some distance over into the Clearwater country located, with right-of-way secured, and even commence work on it, before the other party can make preparations or is aware of what we are doing."[22] At the time the NP was seriously considering a route similar to Thielsen's recommendation.

In late September NP President Frederick Billings wrote a letter to an Olympia newspaper which advocated that the NP build directly across the Cascades to Puget Sound rather than along the Columbia River. In response Villard suggested that the NP and ORN share in advertising the Pacific Northwest. Soon he suggested that the railroads share routes and traffic. Billings did not take Villard seriously. The NP board on November 19, 1879, appointed a committee to negotiate with the ORN jointly building from the month of the Snake River down the south bank of the Columbia River. The NP offered to lease the ORN. Billings reported to the NP executive committee January 12, 1880, that the negotiations with the ORN "were either in suspense or at an end."[23]

Colfax was the largest town north of the Snake River in the early 1880s. No evidence can be seen of the Columbia & Palouse in the distance, and thus it was taken prior to late 1883. Looking south on Main Street toward the hills that surround the town and were major obstacles for railroads entering the canyon. *Historical Photographs printed by Alex Blendl, #1409.*

C. The ORN Begins Construction in the Palouse

In summer 1879 two ORN survey parties were dispatched to the Palouse. The *Palouse Gazette* urged the citizens of Colfax to act: "It is time for the citizens of Colfax and vicinity to awake to the importance of taking prompt action in this important matter." And later, "The ORN indicates that a railroad will be built from Texas Ferry to Colfax if the right of way is guaranteed. Citizens of Colfax should act promptly in this important matter." In late December 1879 it was reported that the ORN had rails and equipment for 200 miles of standard gauge railroad. Fifty miles of rails would be used to extend from Walla Walla to the Snake River, and 50 miles would be used to build from Texas Ferry into the Palouse. A meeting January 10 in Uniontown would consider right of way terms in Union Flat for either the ORN or the NP. The organizer of the meeting argued that a narrow gauge railroad could be built in Union Flat for $5,000 per mile and that cost would make it feasible for wheat alone to support the line. A survey of land owners in Union Flat found that all but two would donate right of way to the ORN. The *Gazette* over the months expended a great deal of paper and ink assuring the people of Colfax that their town had the strategic location in the Palouse and could not fail to attract a railroad if the people looked after their interests.[24]

An ORN map from probably early 1880 shows a line from approximately the location of Connell on the NP mainline to the Palouse River, essentially the future location of the Columbia & Palouse Railroad. The map shows a line from Grange City across the Snake River to Texas Ferry, up Alkali Flat and Willow Springs Creek to Union Flat Creek, east on Union Flat to a point several miles southwest of Colfax, south of the route later built on Rebel Flat Creek to Colfax. The map also shows a branch running from Union Flat northeast to a point southwest of St. John, roughly the south end of the route of the Pleasant Valley Branch built in 1888–89. In addition the map shows the WW&CR and projected lines south of the Snake River.[25]

S. G. Reed, now a vice president of the ORN, wrote the citizens of Colfax January 29, 1880, "that at the present time the railroad is located only between Texas Ferry and Union Flat. Our engineer will probably be in your vicinity sometime during the coming summer and may confer with you. We shall be happy to have your co-operation and...if it is deemed advisable to continue the road to [Colfax]." Late in February it was reported that the ORN had secured right of way from Texas Ferry, 30 miles, to Union Flat, and the railroad would be in Colfax in a few months. The next month it was learned that the line would be standard gauge rather than narrow gauge. In April Thielsen asserted that work on the Texas Ferry-Union Flat line would begin in "a very short time." The ORN would survey from Union Flat to Colfax and from there to the mountains.[26]

Villard's agent in Walla Walla, Thomas R. Tannatt, wrote Villard in May and June that he thought the line should be pushed north beyond Colfax and to Farmington. He also had information that Dorsey Baker, the builder of the WW&CR, had purchased land in the Palouse. Newspapers reported that the ORN was extremely busy with surveys in the Palouse in the summer of 1880. In June the NP directors agreed to confer with the ORN about the Texas Ferry line.[27]

In late June 1880 "a final" survey was made into Colfax, which included a more than 2 percent grade down to the Palouse River in the town. A month later the railroad was still hunting for a route into Colfax; the line would be built to Colfax if it helped the railroad toward Moscow and Farmington. ORN ambivalence is understandable. Colfax was at the time the most important town north of the Snake River, but in a canyon, while both Moscow and Farmington were on the plateau and could be reached without entering the canyon. A letter from Portland on August 3 stated that the grading from Celilo to Wallula on the Columbia River was nearly completed and that the entire force would be moved to grading 33 miles from Texas Ferry to Union Flat.[28]

In a circular to ORN stockholders dated August 1, 1880, George M. Pullman and William Endicott Jr. reported on a trip to Oregon and eastern Washington. "It can, indeed, be safely said that nowhere else in this country does rich soil and mild climate combine to the same degree in insuring such extraordinary results of almost every agricultural pursuit, as regards quantity, quality, and regularity of yield.... Our examination of the Company's business and property justify us in congratulating you upon the ownership of what we do not hesitate to pronounce one of the most promising transportation enterprises in the United States." The visitors recommended the completion of the railroad line from Wallula to Portland and building a line from Walla Walla via Grange City and Texas Ferry to Colfax and Farmington, with branches to Pataha and Dayton and a line over the Blue Mountains to the Grande Ronde Valley.[29] Villard undoubtedly viewed the eight page report as money well spent.

In early September Thielsen was in Colfax. He led the newspaper to believe that the ORN would construct to Colfax and eventually from there to Moscow and to Farmington. The paper went on to say, "Before this plan is definitely adopted, the company expects the citizens of Colfax, Moscow, and Farmington, and people living along the lines of the roads to take steps toward guaranteeing the right of way in whole or in part, and also to make arrangements for the donation of depot grounds.... Let us all then work in unison, and place our shoulders firmly against the car of progress and assist and encourage an enterprise from which, if successfully carried out, innumerable benefits will result."

In January 1881 a bill was introduced in Congress to allow the ORN to build a Snake River bridge at Texas Ferry. In a speech in St. Paul in July 1881, Villard said that the ORN had in 1880 transported to San Francisco 170,000 tons of freight, 110,000 tons of which was wheat.[30] How much of the wheat was from the interior is unknown, but regardless it had to go by boat from Wallula to Portland.

D. Henry Villard Gains Control of the Northern Pacific Railroad and Pushes Palouse Construction

The NP began construction northeast from Ainsworth in October 1879, and in March 1880 it began construction of a 12-mile extension across the Snake River from Ainsworth to Wallula.[31] Villard asked that the latter construction be stopped and when that did not happen he made a parallel survey. Wallula was the western terminus of the ORN's WW&CR and the OSN's principal landing in eastern Washington Territory. Wallula was also the eastern point of ORN's construction to Portland. The NP opposed the ORN building north of Wallula. Villard initiated negotiations with the NP. Villard wrote later,

> When the determination to build [the NP] line was announced and confirmed by the arrival of construction material for transportation by us up the Columbia, I had become at once impressed with the danger of a conflict for the control of the Columbia Valley, on the one hand, and the great advantage it would be to us, on the other hand, if our river road became the recognized outlet of the new

Northern Pacific line. I was perfectly conscious that I had usurped the right to build along the Columbia, which had been granted to the Northern Pacific by an act of Congress; and, while we had occupied the left bank, there was nothing to prevent the other company from running a parallel line down on the right bank. If the Northern Pacific had then been as strong financially as it became soon afterwards, or if its management had had more foresight and had been more resolute, we should never have been allowed to take undisputed possession of the valley. I am sure, if positions had been reversed, I should have made a determined fight to prevent it.

On March 1, 1880, Villard and NP President Frederick Billings met and "Billings received word from Milnor Roberts that the NP should go over the Cascades via Snoqualmie Pass." Villard proposed that the ORN lease the NP's Pend Oreille Division (Ainsworth east into Idaho), "effectively annexing the Palouse country." This was rejected. In the Villard files there is a hand written draft of an agreement dated "July ___ 1880" under which the ORN would complete a line from Wallula to Portland by December 31, 1884, the NP business from the east would be turned over to the ORN at Wallula and the ORN would construct for the NP a line on the north bank of the Columbia west to The Dalles. On August 18, 1880, Billings reported to the directors that he had ordered surveys, profiles and estimates of a line from The Dalles to Wallula.[32] Such a line would push the interchange with the ORN further west. On September 9, 1880, Villard wrote ORN Vice President Thomas F. Oakes that, "I shall have so much to do with the financing of NP if my plans work out that I will be able to prevent them from constructing on the Columbia or across the Cascades so long as necessary in our interest."[33]

Negotiations eventually led to the October 20, 1880, Traffic Agreement. Most of the provisions of the agreement pertained to the division of freight revenues and will not be discussed here. Under the agreement the ORN would build within three years a standard gauge line from Wallula to Portland on the south bank of the Columbia River (it had begun a narrow gauge line), and that the NP could run trains on it at a fixed rate per mile. The NP and ORN agreed to interchange traffic at Wallula. They also agreed that except for the Wallula line, the NP would not build south of the Snake River, and the ORN would not build north of the Snake River, "except that…[it] may complete and operate its proposed and intended branch via Texas Ferry on Snake River, thence in a northwesterly direction to Rebel Flat, thence in an easterly direction to Colfax, and thence in a north[easterly] direction to its terminus at or near Farmington." It also noted that one of the intended branches of the NP "is to be constructed into and beyond the 'Palouse Country,' and thus reach territory and traffic common to it and the said proposed branch of the Oregon Company to Farmington." The NP was not precluded from building on the north bank of the Columbia or the Cascade branch over the mountains to Puget Sound. The ORN executive committee approved the agreement October 21. The NP directors approved the agreement December 16, 1880. According to Rigdon the UP perspective was that "the traffic contract operated satisfactorily between the companies" until Villard's financial problems in 1883–84. After that the management of the NP did not hold themselves bound by the agreement."[34]

At best the traffic agreement was a temporary roadblock to NP ambitions which threatened the ORN's and Portland's monopolies: The NP could build down the Columbia and/or across the Cascades.[35] Villard's attorneys were of the opinion that the contract could not be enforced in the courts.[36] The Snake River division between the NP and ORN was much cited over the years by both roads when it suited their respective convenience. In less than a year the ORN was aggressively surveying and building north of the Snake River and never did recognize on the ground the agreement's prohibition on the ORN.

At the time of the agreement, the NP did not have the funds to build its transcontinental line. Villard offered to form a syndicate to raise the funds, but he was turned down. On November 17 Villard wrote Oakes, "My real object is to use ORN money to buy NP stock. This we shall attempt to do under any circumstances…perhaps a pool. $20 million would get control." At the time of Villard's death the *Spokesman Review* gave an explanation of Villard's strategy:

Portland had grown rich off its control of the interior commerce. These fortunes were in danger. The Northern Pacific was menacing Portland. It was threatening at one time to make Kalama, on the Columbia river, its terminus, and again it frightened the Portland capitalists with the prospect of a great city on Puget sound. Villard grasped the situation. He played on the fears of the Portland millionaires, and then came forward as their friend and protector. He met them in quiet council, and bared a portion of his plans. He showed them with a limited millions he could control the railroad situation of the Pacific northwest. A little 'blind pool' would do the work, and into it they threw their millions. The essence of the blind pool was childlike trust in Villard.[37]

In December 1880 a syndicate of American and European bankers had agreed to buy $40 million in NP bonds. After commissions, this assured the NP $36 million for construction which was assumed to be sufficient to build and equip the entire main line. Villard wrote,

"This great financial success had immediately changed the disposition of the Northern Pacific management, and signs appeared of an impending determination to resort to aggressive construction against us." In addition to the Columbia River surveys, the NP actively sought a route over the Cascades. By early January 1881 the NP had constructed a temporary line between Wallula and the Snake River and had laid over 40 miles of track from Ainsworth. Villard quickly organized the "blind pool" to fund buying control of the NP. The *Oregonian* knew what was happening, reporting on February 21: "The part which Portland will play in this development is apparent. This city will be the main depot of the vast resources of the northwest. It will be the chief point of concentration for the prodigious energies which the new era will awaken and develop. Mr. Villard's success in this great undertaking identifies the Northern Pacific with Oregon and with Portland, as never before." In March the *New York Times* said the ORN would control the NP and its interests would be subordinate to the ORN. Villard denied in an April 1 letter that the acquisition of the NP was to stop construction across the Cascades, "in order to make it tributary exclusively to the Oregon Railway & Navigation Company. I pronounce this allegation unqualifiedly false." The *Walla Walla Union* printed the letter, but was not convinced. The NP board May 19 elected Villard associates Thomas F. Oakes and Artemas H. Holmes directors. Oakes resigned his position as vice president and general manager of the ORN. Holmes was an ORN board member. Villard at the meeting "as a large stockholder" stated that "he was not and never had been opposed to building [the Cascade branch], nor was he opposed to the building of any branch or to any policy which was for the pecuniary interest of the Northern Pacific stockholders." In June it was reported that Villard had spent about $16 million dollars for NP common and preferred stock, mostly the latter. On June 9 A. H. Barney replaced Billings as NP president. Billings remained on the board. Villard later wrote, "Mr. Oakes, however, was practically the chief executive." Barney remained president until Villard became president on September 15, 1881. Oakes was the same day elected vice president.[38]

The Spokane Times, March 10, 1881, probably spoke for many in eastern Washington, when it commented,

> The report that Villard has obtained the controlling interest in the N. P. railroad cannot be received with any degree of pleasure by residents...his interests are not identical with our own.... [It] would probably be to his advantage to make the Northern Pacific simply a branch line and feeder to a trunk line down the Columbia river to Portland. Half the best lands in Eastern and Western Washington have been donated to an enterprise which promised us a road direct to Puget Sound. We still want that road; and the sooner it is built the better satisfaction it will give.

The *Lewiston Teller* on April 21 saw that the ultimate purpose of Villard was to delay the Cascade branch until the time when the ORN had perfected its control of traffic to Portland.

> If Villard is successful in this, whether by fair means or foul it makes no difference in the results, we of Eastern Oregon and Washington and North Idaho will be left a long series of years completely at the mercy of the O. R. & N. Company respecting freight and passage between this and sea board without means of escape, whose tender mercies have been foreshadowed by a list of rates of transportation averaging much higher than were those of the O. S. N. Co. during the last three years of their administration.

A week later the newspaper took the view that Oregon would oppose Washington statehood until the ORN and Portland had secured control of the traffic from the interior.[39]

In May 1881 Villard placed about a third of NP stock and a majority of ORN stock into his new holding company, the Oregon and Transcontinental Co. (OT). Subscribers to the pool received stock in the OT in portion to their contribution to the pool. Incorporated in Oregon June 28, the OT was chartered to build 12 railroad lines mostly in Oregon and Washington, but as far east as Minnesota. The lines included from Walla Walla to the Snake River and Lewiston, and from the Snake River up the Palouse River to the headwaters of the Spokane River and branch lines as necessary. The charter also called on the company to assist and contract for the construction of other lines. The principal office of the company was Portland. Villard served as president and Thomas Oakes, vice president.[40]

In a June letter to a close associate Villard said that the OT was the "corner stone" of his endeavors. In July Villard wrote to Oakes, "I need hardly tell you that my supreme control of the Northern Pacific is absolutely recognized by everybody now, and we shall be able to manage every thing hereafter as suits our views." Hedges' assessment is the same: "It is difficult to conceive of a strategic site for a line of rail or water communication in the Pacific Northwest which was not anticipated in the articles of incorporation of the Oregon and Transcontinental Company. No point of vantage had been overlooked. The execution of this comprehensive program would mean the concentration in the hands of a single corporation, of all the transportation interests of the

Far Northwest." Hedges went on to say that it was not Villard's fear of an NP line to Portland "which impelled Villard to adopt his drastic measures for control of that company.... It was, rather, the obstinate persistence with which the Northern Pacific clung to plans to build to the sound which forced Villard to his policy of complete domination." During the winter of 1879–80, the port of Portland was suspended for a time due to ice on the river. At that time Oakes wrote Villard that if the NP built the short distance from Kalama to Portland to take the grain to the sound in the winter it would eventually result, with a line over the Cascades, in the divergence of the both the west and east ward trade from Portland to Puget Sound. Hedges says, "It was in the face of this danger that Villard acquired control of the Northern Pacific."[41]

A circular from Villard to the NP stockholders dated August 25, 1881, justified control of the NP on the basis of his control of the ORN. If the two railroads were not under the same control, "[t]he situation...was fraught with the danger of a ruinous conflict between the two Companies...that the best means of avoiding this danger was to create an identity of interests that would result in mutual protection instead of destruction." Once control of both companies was secured "it was further deemed best to concentrate it in a third corporation." The OT would benefit the stockholders of the NP by insuring it the business of the ORN, worth five million dollars gross annually to the NP, and by providing it the construction of some 1,500 miles of branch lines to prevent the encroachments of rival interests.[42]

In October 1881 in speeches in Tacoma, Seattle, Walla Walla and Portland, Villard set out his position that Seattle and Portland should be connected and that grain could be brought from Portland to the sound more cheaply than across the Cascades, although the latter line would eventually be built. Portland would be the focus of 2,000 miles of local lines and the terminus of a system from Chicago, and within a year have an unbroken rail link to Puget Sound. In Hedges' view, the tone of Villard's statements were that he was adopting a comprehensive policy to promote the development of all the rival cities rather than artificially aiding one at the expense of the others. Despite Villard's heavy investment in Portland, she could not expect discrimination in her favor. In the face of the reality of greater competition from the Sound, Portland interests intensified their efforts to have the river improved. From 1883 onward systematic improvements of the bar and channel were on-going.[43]

In meeting with the Walla Walla Board of Trade Villard heard of concerns about rate discrimination against the interior. He assured the listeners that was not the policy of his administration. He further said that the great Trinity of the OT, NP and ORN "will furnish the country east of the Cascades with lumber and coal at reasonable prices and carry away its surplus products for a cheap freight [rate]." The NP line to Puget Sound would be built when it can be a paying proposition. "I have said we should endeavor to be a *benevolent monopoly* and I am free to say it is a good thing for you that there is a monopoly here, because you would not otherwise have as many lines built to-day and you would not receive the liberal treatment you have received. This combination of transportation interests will enable us in the future, upon the strength of the advantages it will afford, to make sacrifices upon local lines, and to build them in advance of actual wants." Villard told an audience in Tacoma that the territory between Walla Walla and Tacoma was not sufficiently developed for a railroad, which the Lewiston *Teller* dismissed as confusing cause and effect. It went on to say, that Villard's program was to "force all the business down the Columbia.... How do the people like the programme?" Ficken's assessment of Villard's intentions is similar: abandon immediate plans of building across the Cascades and in the interim, and as he told Portland merchants, build up Portland and take possession of the Puget Sound towns "best adapted to shipping grain or products of the country."[44]

On March 10, 1881, it was reported that the ORN had awarded a contract to grade 60 miles of road between Texas Ferry and Colfax and that the ORN had, after considering proposals for the stone work for the Snake River bridge at Riparia, decided to do the work itself. The bridge would be 1740 feet long, and except for an iron draw span, the spans would be Howe wood trusses. The story concluded, "the bridge will be finished this year, and will cost from $300,000 to $320,000." In August the contract for the bridge was let, 33 miles of grading was completed north of the Snake River, and the contractors were at work on Rebel Flat west of Colfax.[45]

The ORN was not content to restrict itself to the 1880 agreement regarding lines north of the Snake River. A May 1881 map shows three lines violating the 1880 agreement. The June 30, 1881, ORN Annual Report listed five Palouse lines on which construction had been definitely decided, three were clearly violations of the agreement, 81 miles out of 146; Colfax to Farmington allowed by the agreement was absent from the report.[46] The map in the NP Annual Report of September 15 shows the ORN from Riparia to Moscow with branches to Sprague and north of Farmington. In a letter of the 30th NP Vice President Oakes asked the NP General Land Agent to obtain from Thielsen, chief engineer of the ORN, tracings of several lines. Among them were four in the Palouse, three outside of the agreed upon limits. Oakes goes on to say that a contract between the NP and the ORN provided that the NP "shall furnish right of way through its lands for any of the lines above referred to...to the extent of one hundred (100) feet on each side of the located line with such depot grounds as are required and marked on said tracings."[47]

On July 27, 1881, articles for the Idaho, Clearwater and Montana Transportation Co. (ICMT) were filed at Lewiston. If the projections of this company had been built, Lewiston would have emerged as the railroad center of the area. The primary interest of the ICMT was a line from Lewiston up the Clearwater River and across the Bitterroots and a branch into the Camas Prairie. A second line was projected from Lewiston north to the NP main line east of Spokane. There was also a line from Lewiston to La Grande, Oregon. This company, particularly its eastward surveys, generated considerable interest in Lewiston for several months. At an April 1882 meeting the stockholders heard reports on Snake and Clearwater Rivers progress and that the company had been working with farmers in the Genesee and Potlatch sections to make them tributary to the railroad.[48]

The *Gazette* reported in early October that the contractor expected to have completed grading from Riparia to Colfax by the middle of November. There were four camps on the grade, about five miles apart. In mid-October 1881 Villard said the Snake River bridge at Texas Ferry had been abandoned in favor of a ferry and the NP bridge being built at Ainsworth. A line would be built from the NP mainline up Washtucna Coulee to connect in Union Flat with the grade to Colfax. In the meantime the railroad from Walla Walla would be extended from Grange City east to Texas Ferry. Once across the Snake travelers could take the stage to Colfax. Also in October Villard said that the NP would shortly build from Spokane Falls south up Hangman Creek through Farmington to Moscow. Thus Villard identified in general the two routes which would be built into the Palouse by the Columbia & Palouse and the Spokane & Palouse. A week later the *Gazette* reported that the ORN was surveying west from the Riparia-Colfax line to the NP main line. Later in the fall, Villard said that the ORN would build into the Clearwater country "and it will be done soon." One of the possible routes was south from Colfax and another was up the Snake River from Texas Ferry. A month later in an interview, Villard said the Cascade branch would be built but the route had not been chosen. During this time the ORN made at least three reconnaissances up the Clearwater toward a crossing of the Bitterroot Mountains at Lolo Pass.[49]

At a meeting in Colfax, November 23, 1881, the ORN engineer said he was there under the instructions of Thielsen "to find the best possible grade into town, and to ascertain what the people were disposed to do" in regard to the right of way and depot grounds. He "was informed by the unanimous vote of the assemblage that the company was guaranteed the right of way through Colfax and depot grounds within the city limits, and that a deed would be executed as soon as the people were assured that the road would be built and equipped."[50]

On December 4, 1881, ORN service began from Walla Walla to the south bank of the Snake River at Texas Ferry (South Riparia). The ORN then had a continuous line of 200 miles via Walla Walla from The Dalles to the Snake River. It was not until November 20, 1882, that service began from the Snake River to Portland (287 miles). With completion of the NP in September 1883, Portland gained a transcontinental connection at Wallula. Puget Sound did not have a direct transcontinental connection until the opening of the NP switchback over Stampede Pass in July 1887.[51]

In early January 1882 the *Teller* carried an editorial from the Portland *Standard* responding to the report that the ORN in December had a net earnings of $234,300 on a gross of $458,300. "What better argument for legislative interference can our people want? To make profits so fabulous for the Eastern magnates we are all taxed from the bread we eat to the clothes on our backs. How in the name of common sense could profits so immense be made, considering our meager population, without exorbitant and oppressive charges!" The newspaper claimed that the nine dollar a ton on wheat from The Dalles to Portland was the same as the charge from the upper Mississippi to Liverpool. The claim that the difference was because of the higher volume in the latter case had no merit because the ORN could not haul all the wheat that was available east of the Cascades.[52]

The ORN stockholders meeting June 19, 1882, approved construction from Texas Ferry to Lewiston. The ORN Annual Report of June 30 said that for the year $5,927,347 had been spent on railroad construction and a grand total of $15,764,605 had been spent on construction and equipment since July 1, 1879. Completed were 203 miles of the 243-mile main line from Walla Walla to Portland, 60 miles connecting Walla Walla to Texas Ferry and Dayton, 44 miles of the 174 mile Baker City Branch and the Wallula to Walla Walla line had been changed to standard gauge. The net earnings of the ORN for the year, exclusive of taxes (which were $67,675) were $2,403,114 on a gross revenue of $4,947,980 (which excluded the WW&CR) and $1,296,000 in dividends were paid; the ORN like its OSN predecessor was extremely profitable. In the report Villard gloried in the ORN monopoly, "The commanding position of this line is unique. There is no other like it in the United States representing as it does the Western end of the great new transcontinental line and the only practicable outlet to the Pacific Ocean of all the vast nation between California and Nevada, on the South, British Columbia on the North, and Idaho on the East."[53]

NP Eastern Counsel George Gray warned Villard May 8, 1882, that the Cascade branch needed to be definitely located before Washington became a state. Statehood would reduce the land grant per mile from 25,600 acres to 12,800 acres. NP Chief Engineer Adna Anderson, September 13, 1882, notarized a map showing a north bank route on the Columbia River from the Snake River to Vancouver where one line stayed on the north bank to Kalama and another crossed the river to Portland and down the south bank to opposite Kalama. In early August 1883 word came that the NP had "started in earnest" on the Cascade branch. The *Union* reported later in the month that the NP had contracted for 125 miles of the Cascade branch from Ainsworth to Yakima City, which was as far as the branch had been definitely located.[54]

The ORN, UP and affiliates, and the NP agreed, February 23, 1883, to set the point of connection between the ORN and the Oregon Short Line at Huntington, Oregon, and to establish a division of rates.[55] Completion of this line would end the NP's monopoly to the east.

E. Land Sales[56]

To help pay for construction, the Northern Pacific Railroad received in 1864 the largest land grant given to any railroad in the United States. In the territories the NP received for constructed railroad the odd-numbered township sections 40 miles on either side of the track. To compensate for sections already occupied the railroad could apply for unoccupied odd numbered sections in the indemnity area, often referred to as lieu lands, ten miles beyond the limit of the grant. The land grant and claimed occupancy, often based on the Homestead Act of 1862 that allowed a person to claim 160 acres of government land based on occupancy and improvements, created a great deal of litigation. Whether purchased from the railroad or the government, titles to the land were often uncertain, sometimes for decades. Many of the disputes took years to settle.[57]

Beginning in November 1879 until January 1881 the NP advertised over 175 townships in which there were odd numbered sections for sale in eastern Washington Territory. The townships ran diagonally from southwest to northeast, from almost as far south as Walla Walla to north of Spokane Falls and from west of the Columbia River to the Idaho Territory boundary, but much of the best land in the Palouse was excluded, particularly east of Colfax and in Union Flat. The Federal government sold land for $2.50 an acre. The NP sold the advertised land for $2.60, the 10 cents covering the NP expenses of surveying, bookkeeping, and administration. The NP offered to sell on credit at four dollars an acre with a down payment and four equal subsequent payments at 7 percent interest. Thus one could buy 160 acres of railroad land for cash at $2.60 per acre, a total of $416, or on time for $724. The prices charged by the railroad changed with time, reaching eight to ten dollars an acre in Whitman County. Up to mid-June 1880, the NP Land Office in Colfax sold 37,830 acres, receiving $112,643 in tracts averaging 178 acres. On November 17, 1880, the Interior Department recognized a map of definite location of the NP between near Wallula to near Spokane Falls. The United States commissioners, on November 4, 1881, accepted the NP mainline from Wallula into Idaho. The NP could then make formal claim to alternate sections in much of the Palouse. Between 1880 and 1890 the NP subsidiary Northwestern Improvement Company sold, mostly on credit, more than $7 million worth of Palouse farmland.[58]

The OSN, beginning in 1879, used the NP land office in Colfax as one of its four land offices.[59] The October 20, 1880, Traffic Agreement provided for the sale to the Oregon Improvement Co. of 300,000 acres of NP land in the Palouse near the ORN's projected line.[60] Prior to that agreement the NP board of directors had approved the sale to the Improvement Co. of odd sections in ten townships in the Palouse for $2.60 per acre. A few days later Billings reported the sale of four additional townships to the Improvement Co., at the same $2.60 per acre, the gross price to be determined when the company's actual possession could be determined. A contract of October 20, 1880, for the sale of 149,011 acres for $387,429 to Henry Villard, trustee of the Oregon Improvement Co., was approved by the NP board. The contract reserved to the NP rights-of-way not exceeding 100 feet wide for any railroad the NP should choose to build and in any 10 miles of line a site not exceeding nine acres was reserved to the NP for depot, side tracks and other railroad purposes. If the United States Government survey were to show that the acreage was less than specified, the NP would either convey additional lands or refund at $2.60 per acre. If the survey showed there were additional acres, the NP would be reimbursed at $2.60 per acre. Nine of the townships were outside of the advertised land and laid west and north of Colfax, and was on average better land than that advertised by the NP.[61] These lands subsequently became part of the settlement transferring the Columbia and Palouse Railroad to the ORN (see chapter II).

In July 1882 the Colfax land office burned and all the records were destroyed.[62] The land office was moved to Spokane Falls. Marshall Field, the Chicago department store magnate, bought 35,000 acres of NP Palouse land at $2.65 per acre. In 1887 he offered to sell for 10 bushels of wheat per acre per year for a term of six years, a value of $30 per acre. In 1888 he was selling for 12 bushels per acre per year for six years, a value of $36 per acre. During 1888 the sales of government lands at Walla Walla and Spokane totaled approximately 549,000 acres. During the same year the NP sold about 147,000 acres in eastern Washington. The NP reported sales of a half a million acres in eastern Washington in the year ending June 30, 1898; more than sold in the previous six years.[63]

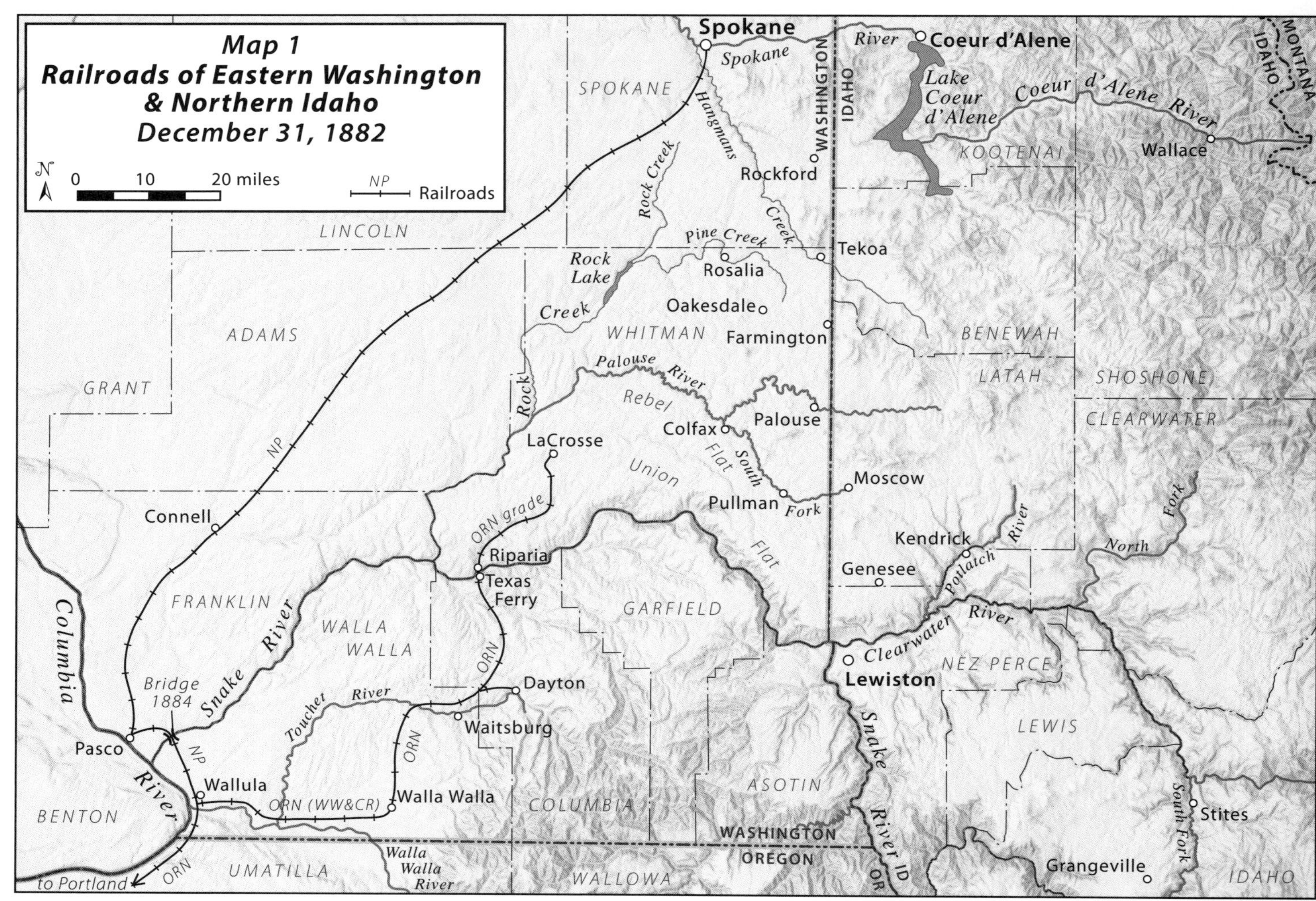

Map by Mike Bartenstein, Mike Walker, 1998, and Philip Beach. Drawn by Chelsea Feeney, www.cmcfeeney.com.

The Columbia and Palouse Railroad to 1886 and the Fall of Villard

The creation of the Columbia and Palouse (C&P) is the prime example of Villard's policy of coordination among competitive railroads. When Villard was forced out, the coordination ended and territorial conflict ensued between the NP and ORN. The conflict continued for over two decades.

A. The Tripartite Contract and the Organization of the Columbia & Palouse Railroad

In February 1882 the *Palouse Gazette* reported a rumor that the ORN would abandon the grade from Texas Ferry to Rebel Flat and instead connect Colfax to a point on the NP. NP Vice President Oakes said in late March, "a branch is under construction diverging from the main line of the Northern Pacific at a point 50 miles north of Wallula and running eastward to Colfax.... The policy of the company in constructing branches is to let about a year intervene between the grading and the track laying. During the year's delay settlers come into the country on the assurance of the early completion of the branch, and thus by the time it is opened for business there is traffic to sustain it."[1]

In March a survey party was working from Sprague, on the NP mainline, to Endicott, on Rebel Flat Creek. But two months later it was clear that Palouse Junction (which in 1888 became Connell, Washington), at the mouth of Washtucna Coulee, 51 miles north of Wallula, would be the point of connection to the Palouse Country. In May the *Gazette* was full of anxiety that the ORN would not build into Colfax because of the necessary grades, but it expressed confidence that the citizens of Colfax would stay put and build "a nicely graded and graveled wagon road" to the railroad.[2]

The NP directors, on April 20, 1882, resolved to renegotiate the 1880 Traffic Agreement because of "changed circumstances." On August 17 the board accepted a Supplementary Traffic Contract, signed by ORN President Villard and NP Vice President Oakes. In exchange for NP concessions, the ORN agreed to abandon construction of the Farmington branch via Texas Ferry and Colfax, to proceed no farther than Texas Ferry on the Snake River, and to concede to the NP all traffic in the Palouse Country and the territory east thereof.[3] It was not long before the ORN ignored the 1882 contract as it had the 1880 agreement.

On May 9, 1882, the NP executive committee agreed to a Tripartite Contract under which the Oregon & Transcontinental would build unspecified NP branch lines. The third party in the contract would be corporations formed to build one or more branch lines. Henry Villard would hold branch lines' first mortgages issued at $20,000 per mile constructed. Because of its charter and finances NP was restricted in its ability to build branch lines. The contract was used to build several branches in North Dakota and Minnesota.[4]

On June 29 Villard incorporated the Columbia and Palouse Railroad Company (C&P) to build a railroad from Palouse Junction, near milepost 51 on the NP mainline from Wallula Junction to Colfax, a branch from about three miles west of Colfax to Moscow, and a branch from at or near the mouth of Rebel Flat Creek to Farmington. Survey work for the line had begun in March 1881. Initially Villard held the 10,000 shares issued by the company. The company was organized at Walla Walla July 1 and C. H. Prescott, an official of the ORN, was elected president. On November 14 the stockholders, with Villard holding all the shares except the one share held by each of the five other stockholders, agreed to build the road, for which $350,000 had already been expended.[5] Six days later the ORN line from Wallula to Portland began operation thus connecting the NP to Portland.

The Oregon & Transcontinental (OT) annual report for the year ending June 30, 1882, said that the resources of the company would be devoted to providing branch lines for the NP which "appear indispensable for the protection and development of its traffic and the enhancement of the value of its land grant." Among those selected was the C&P "to the beautiful and well settled portions of eastern Washington Territory, known as Palouse Country." About 75 miles were to be built in 1883, affording an outlet for a very large wheat crop. Thirty-seven miles of the C&P had been graded from Palouse Junction toward Colfax. *Railway Age* reported that in June OT stockholders were offered $6,000,000 in OT bonds to be used, at the rate of $20,000 per mile, to purchase and construct several NP branch lines including the C&P. OT Supplementary Articles filed in July 1882 added a branch from about three miles west of Colfax, through Colfax and thence up the north fork of Palouse River to its head. An additional line was to be from Cheney on the NP mainline southeasterly to a connection with the line to Farmington. The proposed C&P construction now totaled about 230 miles. The NP Annual Report of September 21, 1882, noted that the grading of the Palouse branch from Palouse Junction to Colfax was nearly completed and that track was expected to reach Colfax and possibly Farmington by the end of the year.[6]

In April 1883 the Walla Walla Board of Trade endeavored to enlist the support of Lewiston in pushing for the line from Walla Walla to Colfax via Texas Ferry. The Lewiston *Teller* saw no advantage to the line; Lewiston wanted a line down the Snake River to Ainsworth. The newspaper was optimistic that the Union Pacific's Oregon Short Line (OSL) would build down the Snake River from Huntington, Oregon, to Lewiston, and that the Utah Northern would build across the Bitterroot Mountains to Lewiston and into the Palouse. That month Lewiston suffered a letdown to hopes for a railroad. Lewiston learned in early April that Villard would arrive by steamboat on the 26th. The residents prepared an impressive welcome. A large delegation of Lewiston businessmen went down to the docks to greet Villard. Villard did not leave the boat and did not meet with the residents. The next day he took a short tour of the town and had a short interview with the *Teller*. He said that surveyors had found that routes from Pataha Creek and up the Snake River to Lewiston to be unfeasible. Villard promised Lewiston nothing and thought it was well served by steam boats. He said that he would endeavor to complete the line to Moscow that season. The purpose of his visit was to learn what the OSL was up to on the Snake River.[7]

On June 26 the C&P directors agreed to a contract with the OT and Henry Villard to authorize $30,000 per mile for the first mortgage of 6 percent gold bonds and to credit Villard $23,000 per mile of constructed road to cover part payment of his stock subscription.[8]

The May and June actions of the NP and C&P lead toward the July 10, 1883, Tripartite Contract between the C&P, the first part, the NP and ORN, the second part, and the OT, the third part. The C&P, with NP help, was to construct, maintain and operate a railroad from Wallula Junction to Colfax and from there to Moscow and Farmington, to be completed by January 1, 1886, to the satisfaction of the chief engineers of the NP and ORN. The C&P was to feed traffic to the NP and be operated by the NP in a manner to "furnish a large amount of business to and greatly increase the earnings of" the ORN. The NP agreed it needed the assistance of both the ORN and the OT. If the NP built to Portland or Puget Sound the contract would be modified. All earnings from C&P traffic would be divided among the three railroad companies on a mileage basis, with the actual mileage on the C&P doubled. The annual net earnings of the C&P would be guaranteed by the NP and ORN to be at least $2,100 per mile for interest, principle payments, and sinking fund. To pay for the road, the C&P had executed the mortgage agreement of June 26 (noted above) giving "all of its property, privileges, and franchises," to Henry Villard and Artemas H. Holmes to secure payment of principal and interest on its bond. After three years a sinking fund would be established into which the C&P would annually deposit an amount equal to 1 percent of the amount of all the bonds. The stock of the C&P would be issued to Villard and held in trust for the OT, in the meantime voting rights on the stock and dividends would be divided equally between the NP and ORN. When the NP and ORN had paid or guaranteed the first mortgage and fulfilled the provisions of the contract, the stock of the C&P would be distributed equally between the NP and ORN. The contract was signed by C. H. Prescott, C&P president, and H. Villard, president of the NP, the ORN and the OT.[9] The essence of the contract was that the OT would finance the building of an NP branch for the benefit of the ORN and the C&P would have resources to pay the mortgage. The contract implicitly gave recognition of the territorial division at the Snake River as agreed to in the 1880 and 1882 agreements. Of the several tripartite agreements this was the only one that included a third railroad in addition to the NP and the branch line company. The OT Annual Report of June 30, 1883, explained the contract with NP & ORN, but had no mention of Villard's central role. The ORN Annual Report, of the same date, includes a map showing the line from Palouse Junction to Farmington and Moscow as an OT and NP branch. The NP Annual Report of September 20 map shows the C&P as an NP branch (the NP Annual Report the year before shows the line as an OT branch). No mention is made of the Tripartite Contract.

B. Construction to Colfax

Grading began at Palouse Junction May 22, 1882. On July 14 the *Gazette* commented, "Palouse Junction is the name of the commencement of the grade to Colfax which is the first road undertaken by the Oregon and Transcontinental company, which is but another name for the ever changing railroad chameleon that holds possession of the industrial interests of the Pacific." A correspondent from the Waitsburg *Times*, visiting Palouse Junction in July wrote, "it is a waterless, sandy region, fit only for the abode of rattlesnakes and cayotes [sic]. At present there is a camp of railroad men here employed grading." Most of the labor was Chinese. "Drivers and white men generally are very scarce." The Chinese were being taught to drive teams. They went on strike for higher pay and their wages were raised to $1.50 per day. "White men receive but $2.00 and teams are paid $4.00 per day."[10]

On November 4, 1882, ORN Assistant Chief Engineer H. B. Thielsen wrote his father that 54 miles would be graded before the ground was frozen; only three miles to Colfax would remain. Shortly thereafter it was discovered that the 20 miles of rail at Palouse Junction was iron, not steel. The *Gazette* February 9, 1883, referred to the C&P as "the Northern Pacific and Oregon Transcontinental railway system." The contractor estimated that the Farmington branch could be constructed via Colfax and Silver Creek for $100,000 less than any other route (this was the route ultimately constructed). But the *Gazette* said, "The Moscow branch will probably be built from Rebel Flat via Plainville, still there is a possibility of the branch running through Colfax."[11]

The NP's Western Auditor wrote Oakes February 1883 that the C&P accounts "have been kept distinct" and that payments were being made by the ORN on account of the OT. "We present bills promptly to the O. R. & N. Co. for expenditures incurred on this account."[12] The fact that the ORN was directly paying for construction rather than the OT, as originally planned, was a major determinate in the subsequent ownership of the C&P.

The C&P Trustees February 13, 1883, adopted location maps, Palouse Junction to Moscow, 112.4 miles, and from Plainville to a point approximately five miles east of Rosalia on Pine Creek and about 25 miles north of Colfax. In what is probably a later survey, Bureau of Land Management (BLM) maps show a C&P survey from about three miles northeast of Garfield, running north to the same township as the 1883 line. In early March maps showed the definite location of the C&P for 46.43 miles east of Palouse Junction.[13]

According to the Walla Walla *Union* the "necessary limit" for railroads in eastern Washington was a line from Texas Ferry to Colfax. The western end of the Palouse branch and the NP mainline north of Wallula Junction "is practically a desert, utterly incapable of ever supporting a population great enough to furnish local traffic of value." A line north to Spokane Falls from Riparia would pass through a country of "marvelous" agricultural resources." The editorial then went to the heart of the matter, "Unless the track is laid on the road bed already graded between Snake river and Willow Creek and the necessary facilities for crossing the river at Riparia provided, Walla Walla will lose the trade of the Palouse country." The *Palouse Gazette* in Colfax had a different view; it reported that Villard had written that "his counselors are unanimous in advising against the building of the line from Texas Ferry to Colfax." The editor added, "Under this arrangement the Palouse country will not be tributary to Walla Walla, for which Mr. Villard has our sincere thanks." In late June the *Gazette* reported that grading would be completed that week to the point where the new line intersected the old grade from Texas Ferry and that the track layers were at work.[14]

By June 13, 1883, Robert E. O'Brien, OT chief engineer and ORN assistant manager, was so unhappy with the performance of the Thielsens, father and son, that he wrote Oakes, "If Mr. Villard insists on retaining these gentlemen as my assistants, I will give them entire control and will give them advices whenever asked for, but must decline all responsibility for their actions and their work." Regarding supervising them, "As life is too short and I am too busy to waste my time in this way, I decline." One of his complaints was that he had to divert a party he had hired for other purposes to complete the location of the Palouse branch. Thielsen wrote Villard, June 25, 1883, saying that Oakes had promised that interference from O'Brien would cease. In the same letter Thielsen reported that on May 25 track laying had stopped because the iron rails taken up between Umatilla and Castle Rock had not arrived. On July 17 O'Brien wrote to both the senior Thielsen and Oakes. The former he placed in charge of the Baker City and Walla Walla branches "which are the only construction work of the O. R. & N. Co. now in progress." Son Henry was put in charge of engineering work on the finished road. He concluded, "Hoping that this arrangement will be satisfactory to you and secure the desired harmony in our operations." In the letter to Oakes he enclosed the letter to Thielsen saying, "you will observe that I have settled [t]his matter in the manner suggested by you.... By the time I get through with my experience upon this Road, I think I will have acquired considerable diplomatic talent."[15]

O'Brien was in Colfax the first week of July for the purpose of definitely locating the railroad and depot. O'Brien said that the main line would pass through the north end of the town and on to Farmington. The Moscow branch would leave the main line about seven miles west at Rebel Flat Creek (approximately at the proposed town of Plainville). The railroad was to be pushed ahead as fast as money and men could do it and Colfax would have a connection in the fall. The only difficulty was the shortage of labor. Town residents sought to persuade O'Brien that the line to Moscow should leave Colfax, rather than Plainville, and go up the South Fork of the Palouse River. O'Brien "after discussing the proposition in all its bearings, promised the desired location on condition that the citizens of Colfax furnish the right of way to Pullman." This was agreed to. In addition to the right-of-way, the company was to receive 240 acres in the north end of town for the depot and shops. The following day, "O'Brien, representing the company, entered into a written agreement with the citizens of Colfax, binding each to the faithful performance of the contract." By the middle of the next week a committee from the town had secured the right-of-way. The newspaper concluded, "A new era has dawned upon Colfax and every branch of business feels the impetus."[16]

On the same trip O'Brien was in Moscow to locate sites for railroad buildings and an elevator. Citizens of Moscow donated 470 acres of land and 96 town lots (subsequently reduced to 82). The company intended to carry the year's crop "if no extraordinary obstacle interferes." O'Brien told the citizens the elevator company had a contract for lumber and would have it completed in time to store grain in the fall, provided the necessary teams can be obtained for hauling the lumber.[17]

Plainville, at the intersection of several roads and near the junction with the proposed Rebel Flat line to Moscow, was plated by the Oregon Improvement Co. under the direction of Thomas R. Tannatt. It was to rival Colfax by attracting businessmen from Walla Walla, but it created such hostility in Colfax that Tannatt offered owners of lots in Colfax corresponding lots in Plainville. The *Gazette* noted at the end of August that Plainville had been abandoned and money would be refunded to those who bought lots. A post office application was made for "Plainview" June 6, 1883; it claimed that the post office would be a thousand feet from the depot. No depot was built. The post office closed December 5, 1884. Undoubtedly "Plainville" and "Plainview" are the same place.[18]

In early August O'Brien assured a *Gazette* interviewer that the Moscow line would go up the South Fork of the Palouse, but the location of the Farmington branch had not been established. He expected the line to Colfax to be completed by the middle of October. The right-of-way had been satisfactorily arranged for lands out of town, "but within the city limits, no. It is important that your citizens should take this matter in hand at once." A week later the *Gazette* reported, "All the ground between the summit and Colfax has been broken. About one third of the summit cut is finished. One hundred and fifty teams are at work every day, and fifty more are waiting for drivers. The force is divided

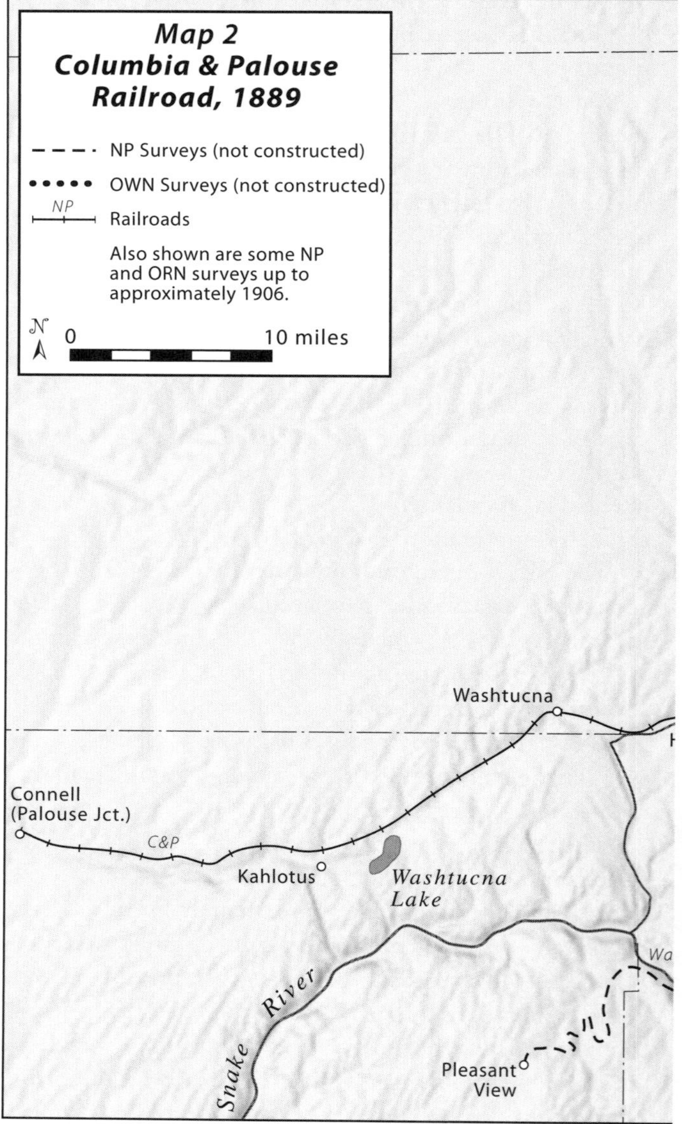

into eighteen different gangs and stretched all along the work from the summit to this city.... Work up the South Palouse will be commenced to-day or to-morrow." The same issue reported an *Oregonian* interview with O'Brien. Building the Moscow line from Colfax "will necessitate a longer line and heavier grades than if Colfax was left to one side and a branch built to it, but as there was an implied promise to build to Colfax, which was the basis of rebuilding the town after the last fire, the company adopted the more expensive line, both as regards construction and operation." The *Gazette* reminded readers that Villard a year earlier had promised Colfax railroad facilities. He kept his promise and now he has made Colfax "the principal railroad center of Eastern Washington Territory. It will be a cold day when the people of Colfax lose confidence in Henry Villard or forget his kindness toward them."[19]

On August 16 NP Chief Engineer Adna Anderson reported to Oakes that track laying was slowed to a half mile a day by bridge building. The summit cut above Colfax was three quarters done and the trestle over Wood's gulch would be 50 feet high and 600 feet long. Work was being pushed five or six miles up the South Fork of the Palouse toward Pullman. Beginning the 21st, 60 men and teams were grading between Moscow and Pullman. The *Union* reported that a preliminary survey was being made east from Moscow into the Potlatch country.[20]

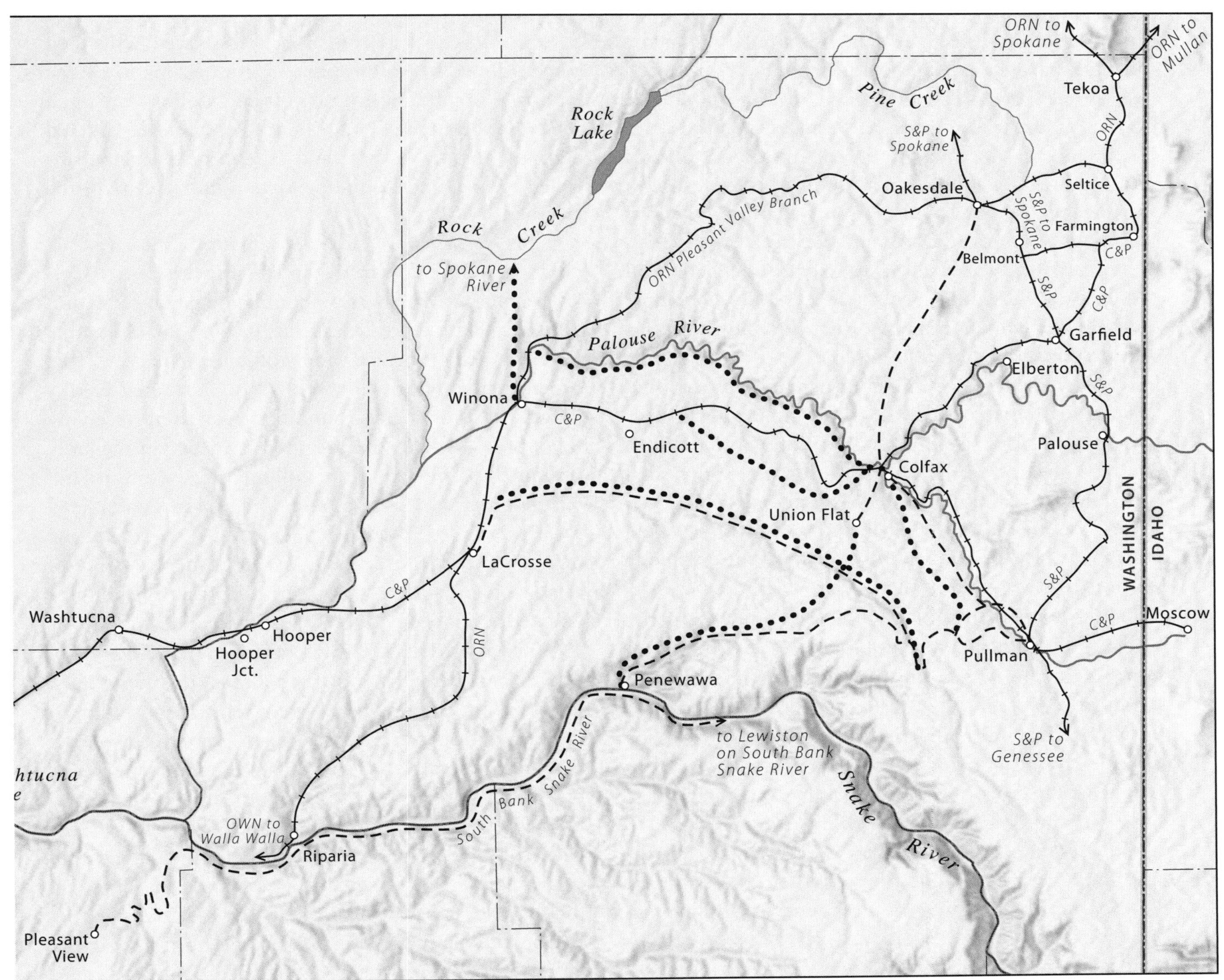

Primary source NP map 1906, MHS 132.1.4.4., redrafted by Philip Beach and drawn by Chelsea Feeney, www.cmcfeeney.com.

On September 3, 1883, the NP main line from Lake Superior to Wallula, Washington Territory, was officially opened to traffic.

On Oregon Improvement Co. letterhead, Tannatt wrote Villard September 28 that he and Thielsen had examined the line from Palouse Junction to Colfax and thence to Moscow and "in the direction of Farmington." He said that the line from Palouse Junction to two miles from Colfax was "in excellent condition." At that point "the line is thrown down into canyon by a torturous route." The depot grounds in Colfax he had seen twice under six feet of water. The line from Colfax to Moscow would require 17 truss bridges in six miles and the entire line would be under water at times. "Personally I am willing to stake my reputation as an engineer and even my connection with your interests on this question.... The O. I. Co. is seriously injured.... The O. T. Co. is building a line that cannot meet the demands at a large expense and one that will not be operated one year, throwing away money and doing little good to a most valuable section." Tannatt also sent a telegram: "line into Colfax and thence to Moscow...[w]ill cost one million more than old line.... Order suspension of work on Moscow line until reports reach you. The whole farming interests of Palouse Country are against line as projected." O'Brien in an October 2 letter to Oakes rejected the claim that the location via Colfax would cost $1,000,000 more than via Plainville. He claimed that the line via Colfax would actually be $50,000 cheaper than the Plainville line. O'Brien wrote November 3 that Thielsen said that Tannatt did not go over the line from Colfax to Moscow with him and so far as Thielsen knew Tannatt did not go over that portion of the line at all; his statements were from hearsay not observation. O'Brien concluded, "Even if they were based on his own observation, they are so absurd as hardly to warrant the time in making any reply to them."[21]

"The master stroke of Mr. Villard's genius was the Oregon Transcontinental company...." So began an editorial in the *Gazette* in mid-October. The NP and ORN stock were both protected from the "vicissitudes" of Wall Street. The operating officials of the railroads were free to focus their attention to traffic. "[T]he force of a centrifugal organization which has no equal in the history of railroads, together with the firm and precisely confident guidance of Mr. Villard, are enough to answer once and forever the question whether the Northern Pacific and its combining systems are secure to the present management." The grade to Colfax was practically finished. The Wood Gulch trestle was going up slowly. "The boss track layer" was confident that the road would be finished to Colfax in three weeks and in the next week there would be 50 "Chinaman" on the track through Colfax. The grade toward Pullman was completed for four miles, and between Pullman and Moscow the grade was "practically completed." The turntable at Endicott was about completed.[22]

Saturday, November 10, 1883, was a big day for Colfax: tracks were completed to the north end of town that afternoon and "the first train of the Columbia and Palouse Railroad Company steamed within the city limits." In a month the depot would be completed. The new station agent said that the line would be turned over to the operating department in three weeks. Until then passengers and freight would be taken daily in mixed trains leaving for the junction each morning and arriving each evening. Two weeks later notice was given that the rate on wheat from Colfax to Portland would be seven dollars per ton. Two car loads of Palouse wheat were scheduled to be shipped to Minneapolis as an experiment. By the end of November both Endicott and Colfax were open to regular business. The ORN on December 28 ordered all construction to cease and all contracts legally cancelled. "Give cause to public on account severity of the weather."[23]

The *Gazette* reported that on January 1, 1884, the NP began running daily trains from Palouse Junction to Colfax leaving for Colfax at 3:30 am and arriving at 9 pm. The line would be known as the "Palouse and Columbia River Branch of the NP" and would be managed by the superintendent of the Idaho Division, headquartered at Sprague. All of the surrounding towns were receiving freight via Colfax. The locomotive to be permanently stationed at Colfax to aid in pulling up the westward hill to Crest arrived December 31. Grading was completed for most of the 25.5 miles to Moscow. A week later the newspaper had bad news: A study on the feasibility of establishing grain elevators concluded that the country was not developed enough to justify their erection.[24]

When construction was discontinued in the vicinity of Colfax, those employed by the railroad, including track layers and bridge builders, were given transportation to Portland. The construction company employees were left to fend for themselves. Over 200 of them were in Colfax on Sunday, January 12, expecting the railroad company to give them passes to Portland. The City Hall was provided for their lodging, and they decided to take the train on Monday. They boarded the train and refused to pay their fares or to vacate. They were persuaded to leave the cars on Tuesday afternoon after the mayor promised that he would try to get them passes to Portland. The train pulled out and the men went to City Hall where they were provided supper and breakfast. On the 16th the train left 12 hours late. The next day O'Brien telegraphed that the railroad would take them for half fare, but the train would not return until the railroad was guaranteed protection. The mayor telegraphed that the town would do its best to provide protection. The men were told the contents of the telegram and that the town would no longer provide them food. Ten deputy sheriffs protected the train, and it came and went without incident. About 40 of the men took advantage of the half fares and left for Portland, and 20 to 30 left for the mines and logging camps. When the newspaper went to press on Friday about half the men remained and were quiet and peaceable.[25]

In late January the *Gazette* reported that trains would run tri-weekly, leaving Colfax on Mondays, Wednesdays, and Fridays and arriving on alternate days. There was no objection to this for passengers and freight, but "A tri-weekly mail is inadequate to the demands of business in this section." The Post Office wanted mail service six days a week beginning February 11. A day later the Post Office responded that the C&P would be paid pro rata for service performed less frequently than six days a week. Mail cars began on February 11.[26]

O'Brien in Colfax said that work on the Moscow extension was discontinued because of icy conditions which had caused several injuries in bridge construction. Work would begin at "the earliest possible moment" and should be done in two months. The amount of money required to finish the branch was nominal compared to amount already spent. O'Brien commented, "I regard [C&P] as the most valuable piece the company owns and think it will make a better showing than any other." The depot buildings were held up by a shortage of lumber.[27]

C. Villard Forced Out and the ORN Gains Control of C&P

One of Villard's first acts when he gained control of the NP in 1881 was to declare a dividend on the preferred stock of the NP. His rationale was that since 1875 the railroad had used surplus earnings for construction rather than dividends. The over $4.5 million in dividends paid ultimately contributed to Villard being forced out of the presidencies of the NP, OT, and ORN in late 1883. Daggett wrote, "the Northern Pacific had been and was in so precarious a condition that not a dollar of its resources could safely have been alienated." By early August 1883 there was increasing concern about the financial condition of the NP. Villard was absent from the September stockholders meeting, but he remained a director and president. The NP deficit was nearly $9.5 million by October and Villard said another $5.5 million would be needed.[28]

On November 27, 1883, William Endicott Jr. wrote Villard that he understood that the ORN would guarantee one half of the C&P bonds at $30,000 per mile on 117 miles ($1,755,000 on the distance to Moscow). Endicott pointed out that the OT credit was poor and the NP's doubtful, but the ORN's was strong and its guarantee would help sell the bonds. Under the Tripartite Agreement the OT was responsible for the bonds. Ignoring the agreements of 1880 and 1882, Endicott wrote, "As this road is mainly in ORN territory" and the NP might not be willing to guarantee its half of the OT bonds, "it might be well for the ORN to take it off their hands, with proper arrangements for permanent use of N. P. tracks to connect with ORN.... The sale of 3,500,000 at 97.5 would help the OT a long way out of its Slough of Despair." "What do you think of this?" Villard responded the next day, "If $3,510,000 bonds could be disposed of in this way it will of course bring immense relief to the [OT].... I affirm my belief that a [complete control?] of that line will not be a burden upon, but beneficial to the O.R. & N."[29] On December 12 Frederick Billings wrote in his diary of apparently his first awareness of the debts of the OT, "The notification of a debt of $19,000,000 was an awful shock.... I fear the Co. will go into the hands of a Receiver... I cannot stand Villard."[30] Villard wrote Endicott December 15 that excluding claims against the NP, the floating liabilities of the OT were a little over $16,000,000.[31] In January the OT sold 30,000 shares of Northern Pacific Preferred stock, 30,000 shares of Northern Pacific Common stock, and 10,000 shares of Oregon Railway & Navigation Company stock and borrowed $1,200,000 for a total of about $3,510,000.[32]

The ORN executive committee on December 13 recommended that the Tripartite Contract of 1883 be modified so that the ORN could assume all the obligations of the C&P, provided that the OT and NP agreed. The OT executive committee agreed; since the ORN had expressed the desire to assume all the obligations of the Tripartite Contract, it "thereby became entitled to acquire all the capital stock..." of the C&P. On the 31st the ORN's Eastern directors and the executive committee recommended that additional first mortgage bonds be issued at 5 percent for 40 years to, among other things, acquire the C&P.[33]

On December 17, three and half months after the completion of the NP transcontinental line, Henry Villard resigned from the boards and presidencies of the ORN and OT. Endicott became president and Prescott vice president and treasurer of the OT (Prescott was also president and manager of the Oregon Improvement Co., president of the C&P and vice president of the ORN), and T. Jefferson Coolidge, former president of the Santa Fe Railway, became president of the ORN.[34] On January 4 Villard resigned from the board and presidency of the NP. That day the NP board of directors passed a resolution finding that it was in the interest of the NP to "be released from the obligations of the...Tripartite Contract," the Company consented "to the abrogation and annulment of the...Tripartite Contract" and that the NP would make agreement with the ORN and C&P for use of the NP to Wallula. The price of NP stock, a major asset of the OT, fell.[35] Villard's perceived strength was finances, not management, and when confidence in that eroded, he was a liability.

Initially the office of NP president was vacant. Oakes was vice president and acting general manager. On January 17, 1884, Robert Harris, who had been on the NP board since 1879, was elected president. Harris, who had been president of the CB&Q and vice president of the Erie Railroad, was according to Hedges, "altogether subservient to C. B. Wright...one of the dominant figures in the Tacoma Land Company." Based on reading his correspondence I do not think Harris "was altogether subservient" to Wright; in any case Harris was highly regarded in railroad circles. Elijah Smith became president of the OT in March 1884, and succeeded Coolidge as president of the ORN July 17, 1884. Smith, a Boston investor and financier, was "abrasive" but had extensive railroad experience, including a year on the NP board of directors beginning September 1881. There remained some overlap in the boards of directors of the three companies.[36]

A special committee was appointed by the OT executive committee to examine the holdings of the OT. The committee report, December 31, 1883, said that Villard's "absence, in consequence of severe illness, during the examination has greatly interfered with the committee's labors, and has prevented their making a report as satisfactory in detail as they would have desired." They found among the assets 152,027 ORN shares, 153,700 NP preferred and 147,934 NP common shares. No mention was made of the C&P bonds and stock held in trust for the NP and ORN which subsequently were turned over to the ORN. The Oregon Improvement Co. was listed as an asset of $514,000, however as noted below the Oregon Improvement Company (OI) owed the ORN a larger amount. The OT liabilities amounted to over $11 million.[37]

On January 5 Oakes wrote Prescott that the NP was prepared to turn the C&P over to the ORN, but the NP was waiting action by the OT to cover any deficit the NP had in operating the C&P. On January 10 agreement was made for the OT to deliver to the ORN all the stock and bonds of the C&P. On the 31st the ORN executive committee approved the use of $2,700,000 of the new 5 percent bonds to purchase the bonds and entire capital stock of the C&P held by the OT, "provided that a suitable contract shall be made...giving this company the use of the NP from Palouse Junction to a connection with its own main line."[38]

On December 31, 1883, the ORN eastern directors and executive committee recommended securing the Improvement Co. lands adjacent to the lines of the ORN and the Columbia & Palouse and that "the sale of which lands, in small tracts to actual settlers, would be advantageous to the passenger and freight traffic of this Company, and would also enable the Oregon Improvement Company to pay its large indebtedness to this Company." According to Meinig, an examination of the annual reports of the OI and ORN reveals that the ORN received 112,408 acres of the 149,011 acres of the OI's original holdings. Coolidge reported to the ORN executive committee July 10 that when he became president, the Improvement Co. owed the ORN $600,000 and that debt had been settled by purchase of the Improvement Co.'s Palouse lands. The OI in September 1886, reported a profit of $142,456 on the sale of land to ORN.[39]

On January 7, 1884, Villard wrote Endicott he was glad "that earnest efforts are now being made for a definite regulation of the relations between the O. R. & N. and the Northern Pacific by lease and otherwise." He hoped the negotiations would yield something satisfactory to both companies. "Knowing that you have the interests of the O. R. & N. Co., great at heart, I feel sure that you will make no undue concession, unwarranted by the circumstance of the case. The O. R. & N. Co. being my particular creation it would cut me to the quick to see any unnecessary sacrifice imposed upon it." He went on, "I beg further to make an earnest appeal in behalf of the [Oregon] Improvement Co. of which as you know, I am unfortunately the largest stockholder, largely through your instrumentality."[40]

At the time of his resignation as ORN president, Coolidge wrote, "I found things in a much greater state of confusion than I expected."[41] Coolidge commissioned George S. Morison to examine and report on the condition of the ORN. Morison's report of February 11, 1884, said that the C&P line was built and in operation from Palouse Junction to Colfax, 89 miles, that track was laid another five miles and that grading was nearly completed to Moscow, 113 miles. One hundred and nine miles of original 56-pound iron rail was taken from the main line of the ORN between Celilo and Wallula for use on the C&P. "[T]he road is very fairly located and in-expensively built; while not first class, it is apparently quite as good as the circumstances of the case demand." Section houses and water tanks were erected where needed but no station building had yet been erected. From Endicott eastward "it is a thoroughly first rate farming country." Morison found comparatively little population and Colfax with about 800 people was the only town of importance. "Little profit can be expected from this road for the first year or two, but the country may be expected to settle up rapidly and, after a few years, the business from Whitman County will be a very valuable one." The land purchased by the OI from the NP was in the center of Whitman County along the line of the C&P in the best part of this country. He concluded that because of the more favorable grades, it would be expedient to arrange with the NP to handle the business between Palouse Junction and Wallula rather than build the Texas Ferry line.[42]

The NP board approved a resolution February 21, 1884, to repeal the Tripartite Contract while preserving the contract of October 20, 1880, and its supplement of July 1, 1883.[43]

Oakes wired NP President Harris on February 29, 1884: "The Palouse branch is badly washed and considerable outlay will be necessary to put it in order...it was understood this branch would be turned over to ORN and thus far I have been operating the branch for their account if there is any change in the program I would be glad to know as the branch is not at present paying expenses." Oakes the next day reminded Harris that neither the ORN nor the NP had formally accepted the C&P.[44]

Gill's valuation report to the ICC gives March 4, 1884, as the date service ended and the last day of NP operation of the line. On the 5th according to Oakes two miles were under two feet of water 29 miles from Palouse Junction and Washtucna Lake was still rising. "[T]here is no business between junction and Lake and very little beyond, not enough to pay for transferring. I suggest abandonment of Columbia & Palouse for present...until an estimate can be made of cost to change line." Harris thought that probably by the time the water had subsided and the C&P could be operated, a decision would be reached whether the C&P continued under the Tripartite Contract or transferred to the ORN. On the 7th Harris wrote Coolidge that pending a new agreement, the Tripartite Contract governed and the NP would join the ORN in carrying out its provisions.[45]

Harris wrote Oakes on March 10, "there has been too much irregularity as to the manner in which the N. P. has entered upon the C. & P. I fail to see by any provision of the Tripartite Contract that the O. & T. Co. can be held for any expenses incurred upon such portions of the road as have been completed in accordance with the contract. The only thing that the O. & T. is responsible for is the interest on the bonds for two years from the time of its acceptance." Oakes wrote Harris on the 12th that there was slight damage to the line on either side of the lake, but at the lake the water had stood two feet over the track.

> From the testimony of residents it appears that the lake is gradually rising and extending from year to year; should it continue to do so about three miles of the track will be permanently submerged in present location. In fact it would [?] that an inexcusable blunder in location has been made at this point,—It being alleged that the original locating engineer was shown by the informant a high water mark about eight feet above the present grade. The legend is that the lake gradually fills from a large spring, having been relieved on the last occasion (some 30 years ago) by a sub terrain [?] outlet. Surveys have determined that its utterly impracticable to drain the lake and the only feasible alternative deemed to be the relocation of the line at the point in question, placing it upon the first bench above the lake out of reach of any possible high water from that source.

Oakes on the 14th wrote Harris that the NP had been operating the C&P for the OT and ORN at the request of OT Chief Engineer O'Brien, "for the reason that they found themselves with 90 miles of Road, without any operating force to handle it." Oakes said that he would at once begin negotiations with Prescott to turn over the C&P to the ORN.[46]

On March 21 Harris told Coolidge that it was his understanding that the OT was not responsible for the $20,000 needed to place the C&P in operating condition. As a result he asked that the ORN agree to advance half of the needed funds to the C&P and pay the NP the remainder when the C&P was turned over to the ORN. On the 22nd Coolidge agreed that the OT "is not responsible after acceptance of the road. We should not have accepted it but having done so I think we are bound to repair it." But he was not prepared to agree that the ORN pay the whole expense. On the 25th Harris responded, "If Contract is abrogated the profits and benefits will accrue to the O. R. & N. wholly, and hence any outlay for reconstruction should be paid wholly by O. R. & N. Co." Oakes' view on the 27th was that the NP had no obligation to pay for the repairs to the line.[47]

President Coolidge reported to the ORN executive

committee on March 24 that all the C&P stock, except that held by the directors, had been received from the OT. The ORN purchased the C&P for $2,489,520 which included securities having a par value of $3,829,000, consisting of $1,000,000 in capital stock and $2,829,000 in first mortgage 6 percent gold bonds at $30,000 per constructed miles or 94.3 miles (the total track miles of the certificates of completion, 12/01/83 and 01/19/84). The ORN paid $26,400 per constructed mile. The ICC Valuation Report on the UP gives the OT construction cost as $1,935.779 or $20,528 per mile. As a result the OT netted approximately $890,000 on the sale of the bonds and no longer had obligation to pay interest on them. The ORN financed the purchase of the C&P 6 percent bonds with 5 percent bonds, and by virtue of owning all the C&P bonds was freed from paying the 6 percent interest, but the OT was still dependent on the ORN paying dividends on the ORN stock.[48]

Coolidge informed Harris, April 4, that the ORN bought the stock and bonds of the C&P and would assume running the C&P, if Harris agreed. Harris was willing that the ORN take over running the C&P at once, provided that the existing contract stayed in effect until it had actually been abrogated and the substitution made. While Harris was "perfectly clear" in his mind that the NP should not participate in the expense of reconstructing the C&P; he was willing to take it to arbitration if Coolidge disagreed. On April 14 Oakes expressed concern that the Union Pacific would use the C&P to extend into the Coeur d'Alene mining district. "I confess to a good deal of anxiety about our future relations with the O. R. & N. company." Oakes wrote Harris on the 16th that he had received communications from ORN Assistant to the President George O. Manchester and C&P President Prescott, demanding that the NP pay half the cost of putting the C&P into order. Oakes concluded, "I think however we have them so thoroughly tied up with contracts there will be no difficulty in bringing the management to an equitable recognition of the real situation." Harris telegraphed the next day, "If the O. R. & N. takes full possession of the Palouse road before contracts are signed it should be without any reservation about cost of reconstruction. We will be willing to leave to arbitration that question if we cannot agree."[49]

ORN officials in Colfax assured the town that rail connections would be restored as soon as repairs could be made. Two weeks later the water was about three feet over the tracks and had risen nearly six inches in two weeks. On May 2, 1884, the *Gazette* said that in the Walla Walla *Union*'s opinion that despite the grades on either side of the Snake River, the Texas Ferry line should be used rather than the C&P to Palouse Junction The Texas Ferry line would require little work, the rail could come from the abandoned portion of the C&P and a transfer boat could be used on the Snake River. The *Gazette* responded that the Palouse was content with the C&P and did not want Walla Walla as a middle man. It had no objection to the Texas Ferry route so long as the C&P remained open.[50]

On June 6, 1884, Oakes wired Harris, "We are turning over to O. R. & N. people yesterday and today the Palouse Branch without conditions." The 1884 and 1885 NP Annual Reports are silent on the change of C&P ownership. The 1887 Annual Report said that the transfer was an "apparent mistake."[51]

According to the *Gazette*, July 4, "It is hardly probable that the trains will run into Colfax before August first." But things looked better a week later when an advance agent for Cole's Circus said that railroad would lose "a large forfeit" if it failed to get the circus to Colfax for a performance on July 28. Two weeks later the *Gazette* reported that the track had been laid around the lake and that cars could pass despite the lack of ballast and surfacing. Repairs to bridges were being made east of the lake and the rumor was that the train would arrive in Colfax the 27th. Whether the circus arrived is unknown. Officially train service was restored to Colfax August 1. Trains left Palouse Junction at 6 a.m. on Mondays, Wednesdays and Fridays, arrived at Colfax at 11 a.m. and returned on alternate days at 2 p.m., arriving Palouse Junction at 7 p.m. The Walla Walla *Union*'s general assessment of the C&P: "the first 60 miles are entirely in the wrong place; and the road, as a whole, is a monumental piece of stupidity."[52]

D. The Collapse of Villard's "Consolidation" Strategy

In negotiating to purchase the Oregon Steam Navigation Co., Villard, May 11, 1878, wrote John C. Ainsworth, who represented the OSN, that he wanted a "consolidation" which would "retain the separate organization of the participating companies."[53] In the Palouse Villard consolidated four companies: the ORN, NP, OT and C&P. The ORN was the "cash cow" and his primary purpose was its protection and promotion. He gained control of the NP to protect the ORN from competition to tide water and to provide a friendly eastern connection. The OT was to protect the NP and ORN from other financial and commercial influences. When Villard decided that the Palouse branch of the ORN should be reached by the NP's bridge at Ainsworth rather than an ORN bridge at Texas Ferry, it made sense to divorce the branch from the ORN, to which it was not physically connected, and put the NP in charge. The Tripartite Agreement was a consolidation. It transformed the Palouse branch into the C&P, which the OT financed, NP constructed, was jointly owned by the NP and ORN and operated by the NP for the benefit of the ORN. In the 1882 supplemental agreement to the traffic contract of 1880 the ORN gave up a right to build north of the Snake River and thus reduce the NP's incentive to compete with the ORN south of the river. Mention should also be made of Villard's acquisition in 1880 of the Seattle & Walla Walla which, aside from the NP, was the most immediate threat to the ORN's monopoly to tidewater. The acquisition also meant that he had some control of Snoqualmie Pass, one of the routes considered by the NP for its crossing of the Cascades. Early in 1883 he stopped the UP from building west of Huntington, Oregon, which would give the ORN a second connection to the east rather than a competitor to Portland.

But all of this was at best a holding action. He surely knew that eventually a company he could not control, or make agreement with, would challenge the tidewater monopoly and that company or others would enter the Palouse. As long as he could forestall this, his "benevolent monopoly"[54] was guaranteed to be a success.

The first official manifestation of pending collapse of consolidation in the Palouse came December 13, 1883, when the OT executive committee recommended that the C&P be turned over to the ORN. Four days later Villard resigned from the presidencies and boards of the OT and ORN. On January 4, 1884, the day Villard resigned from the NP presidency and board, the NP board consented "to the abrogation and annulment of the...Tripartite Contract" so that the ORN could take responsibility for the C&P. It is difficult to imagine that these actions would have occurred over the strong objection of Villard. The letters cited above between him and Endicott suggest that Villard supported, if he didn't initiate, the board's action in order to deal with the precarious financial condition of the OT. Participants in the "Blind Pool" were heavily invested in the OT because they received OT stock rather than NP stock. The only internal significant source of money was the ORN which had cash and borrowing capacity. Endicott saw a transfer of the C&P, in his view "mainly in ORN territory," as a device for using the ORN to save the OT. The Palouse land of the Oregon Improvement Co. was also transferred to the ORN to help satisfy OI debts, which ultimately the OT would have to underwrite.

According to Gill, "The joint ownership of this line had not given satisfaction" and the transfer "was carrying out a purpose of Villard's."[55] Gill does not tell us what the dissatisfaction was, nor Villard's purpose. The C&P was not turned over to the NP operating department until January 1, 1884. The actual operation of the C&P by the NP could not have been the source of dissatisfaction. Nothing has been found in NP correspondence or in limited ORN correspondence or in newspaper accounts to tell us the source of the dissatisfaction. But we do know the purpose of the transfer.

The purpose of the transfer was to reduce the debt of the OT at the cost of consolidation. It is reasonable to believe that both the ORN and OT were more important to Villard than the NP. Villard gained control of the NP to protect the ORN and used the OT to avoid distributing NP and ORN stock to investors who might be tempted to sell. This view appears to be supported by letters from Elijah Smith, as president of both the ORN and OT, to Villard prior to the lease of the ORN to the UP. Those letters, quoted in part in chapter IV, tell Villard that in building the Cascade branch the NP was acting in manner of material harm to the OT and ORN. Presumably Smith had reason to believe that Villard was sympathetic to the argument and might therefore use his influence to stop the NP. If Villard sought to do so, it was unsuccessful. When Villard returned to active involvement in the affairs of the NP and the two Oregon companies, consolidation still motivated his actions, but he failed to achieve it.

Another explanation is found in President Harris' deposition in an 1887 OT suit which sought to block expansion of the Spokane & Palouse Railway. Harris testified that the ORN and OT requested that the July 10, 1883, tripartite contract be rescinded. On April 5, 1884, the NP agreed, "being influenced, in part, by the uncertainty then attending its efforts to construct its Cascade branch, through the construction of which branch alone could the defendant [NP] equally participate with the [ORN], in the advantages and profits accruing from the construction of the [C&P]." Harris does not identify the other influences. By itself, this explanation is not, at least in hind sight, very convincing. On the other hand, it does help give a justification for the building of the Spokane and Palouse, a matter he sought to justify in his testimony.[56] As we have noted above, the NP's 1887 Annual Report declared that the transfer was an "apparent mistake."

What we do know is that the transfer of the C&P to the ORN severed the mutual interest of the NP and ORN in the C&P, placed the ORN north of the Snake River and set the stage for the NP reentering the Palouse and eventually entering ORN territory south of the Snake River. As Hedges writes, when Villard "had ceased to be the actual directing force in the three companies, their interests became more specialized and conflict resulted."[57] Some of the resulting conflict is seen in the next section which considers the efforts of the NP and ORN to reach an agreement about C&P traffic between Palouse Junction and Wallula.

E. Traffic Contract Negotiations and Rescinding the 1883 Tripartite Contract

ORN President Coolidge notified NP Vice President Oakes, January 31, 1884, that as of that date the ORN would decline to honor terms favorable to the NP in the Traffic Contract of October 20, 1880. Two days later he reminded Oakes that under the Tripartite Contract the ORN had "a right of track over your road between the Palouse Junction and Wallula for Palouse Branch traffic." Coolidge pointed out that the Tripartite Contract provided that the NP's right to use the ORN from The Dalles to Portland included payment of double the actual cost of maintenance and that the first year payment would be 70 cents per train mile. He proposed that it was reasonable to have the same rights, terms, and conditions from Palouse Junction to Wallula. He thought it unlikely that the ORN would actually exercise the right in preference to interchanging traffic, but he wanted the contract to recognize the ORN's right. He indicated a willingness to drop the double mileage granted to the C&P in the Tripartite Contract to one and a half miles. Oakes wrote Harris that from Palouse Junction to Wallula the NP should receive the same constructive mileage as the C&P and that the NP should receive five dollars per car, loaded or empty, and 50 cents per passenger for the use of the Snake River bridge. He had no objection to a new contract so that the ORN could either use trackage or agree on a division of rates. Oakes concluded by noting that Coolidge could not abrogate the contract by "mere notice."[58]

On February 11 Harris wrote Coolidge, "This company cannot recognize such notice, or any right on your part, without the consent of the other contracting party, to decline, at your pleasure, in any arbitrary or other manner, to comply with the terms of this contract." Harris for the NP, Coolidge for the ORN, and Endicott for the OT traded traffic agreement proposals for several days in February. On February 20 Harris for the NP and Assistant to the President George O. Manchester for the ORN agreed to recommend to the respective boards (1) the NP receive 20 percent of the rates on all business between points on the C&P and Portland, the ORN to fix the rates; and (2) at its option the ORN to have trackage between Palouse Junction and Wallula Junction for all business between all points on the Palouse branch and all points on the ORN at the rate of 70 cents per train mile, Snake River bridge counting as 40 miles; rate per mile after first year to be adjusted annually by mutual agreement or by arbitration. The NP board of directors on the 21st agreed to have a contract prepared based on the 20th agreement and to repeal the Tripartite Contract, but preserve the contract of October 20, 1880, and its supplement, July 1, 1883. On April 14, 1884, Harris sent Coolidge a draft contract between the NP, ORN and C&P largely based on the Manchester-Harris memorandum. While he and Manchester had not discussed business to and from the C&P and the east, an article regarding that business was in the draft. "I think the provisions are fair to both parties and I hope will be satisfactory to your company." The proposed contract was not formally adopted. Presumably business was interchanged at Palouse Junction and Wallula rather than the ORN operating under trackage rights. On April 20 NP's Snake River bridge at Ainsworth was opened to traffic.[59]

The *Gazette* reported that in the first 26 days of November 1884, 400 carloads of freight were shipped from Colfax, of which 376 were wheat. The *Union* claimed that the Colfax grain dealers had 25,000 tons of wheat in their warehouses and the railroad was carrying away only what was brought in daily. "The prospects for getting their grain to market soon are not brilliant." The *Gazette* complained in January 1885 that "When the railroad was completed, our people thought delayed mails and freights things of the past, but they were mistaken." By late January Washtucna Lake had risen three feet in the recent thaw and was as high as it was the spring before when the track was flooded.[60]

Harris wired Oakes on January 6, 1885, that the Tripartite Contract "has practically been abrogated by all parties, and the one under consideration is the same as my memorandum last Spring [April 14] so far as division of rates is concerned." The 22nd Oakes wired Harris: "John Muir [ORN traffic manager] notifies Hannaford [NP general freight agent] in writing abrogating agreement regarding traffic with Columbia & Palouse RR. I have instructed him not to recognize Muir's authority and to demand continuance present arrangement until change shall be mutually agreed upon between you and [Elijah] Smith [now ORN president]."[61]

Frederick Billings, NP Director and former president, arrived in Colfax on a special train, June 18, 1885, to inspect the C&P and determine its value in case the line was leased by the NP. He listened carefully to complaints of a citizens' committee about the lack of settlement of the NP's lieu lands, "exorbitant" freight rates, the impracticability of shipping livestock and wool because of "the exactions" of the ORN. "He fully understood that this clashing of interests was detrimental to both the people and the company and said there was no reason why it should be permitted to exist." The *Gazette* concluded: "Mr. Billings is a pleasant and agreeable gentleman, easily approached, and in him we believe the Palouse country has a true friend."[62]

In October a rumor circulated that the ORN had decided to complete the road from Texas Ferry to the C&P near Endicott and to then take up the track from that point to the NP.[63]

Harris wrote Oakes, November 24, 1885, that the ORN notified the NP that it desired to abrogate the Tripartite Contract of July 10, 1883. Muir on December 4 informed Hannaford, "No notice has been received at this end in regard to the abrogation of the tripartite contract." On December 22 the C&P Stockholders and Trustees abrogated the contract of July 10, 1883. On the 26th Hannaford wrote Oakes that Smith appeared to have neglected to notify his people and "This leaves us in the same confused state in regard to divisions that has prevailed for the past year or more."[64]

Harris wrote March 29, 1886, that the ORN has "wanted the privilege of building a connection from Texas Ferry and in as much as the Nor. Pac. is relieved wholly from obligations upon Columbia & Palouse Bonds we were willing they should cut off the connection at Palouse Junction if they should desire. The essential point is that the Nor. Pac. incurs no expense or liability in consequence of Columbia & Palouse Road." By April 24, 1886, all four parties to the Tripartite Contract of July 10, 1883, had rescinded it. The consolidation strategy with respect to the C&P was formally dead. On June 26, 1886, the C&P paid a 5.5 percent dividend, $55,000, to the ORN.[65]

On May 8, 1886, Harris wrote Oakes that he discussed the C&P traffic contract with ORN's C. J. Smith. He stressed that the Snake River Bridge should be the equivalent of 40 miles and that any arrangements should be retroactive to the beginning of operation of the C&P. Harris asked Oakes to have a contract prepared. Harris reported to Oakes that the NP board on "June 17 authorized the execution of a contract for the interchange of business with the Columbia & Palouse R. R. Co. on the terms named in the memorandum enclosed in yours of May 24th." Six months later on December 17, 1886, Harris wrote Elijah Smith enclosing a draft of the contract on the C&P business prepared in the summer.[66] No evidence has been found that any formal agreement was made on a Palouse Junction to Wallula traffic contract. Shortly thereafter the ORN and UP entered into serious negotiations for the lease of the ORN to the UP (see chapter III).

From September 1, 1885, to June 15, 1886, Knapp Burrell & Co. shipped 12,423 tons of wheat, oats, barley and flax from six railroad warehouses (Colfax, Diamond, Guy, Pullman, Moscow, and Pampa) and eight river warehouses. The railroad warehouses accounted for almost 90 percent of the total. Wheat was the predominate grain shipped, with Colfax accounting for 39 percent of total tons of all grains and the largest share of wheat, oats, and barley. Pullman was second, accounting for 25 percent of the total tons and was the principal point for flax. Flax tonnage was more than twice that of oats, but less than half the tonnage of barley and about a twentieth of wheat.[67]

F. Construction to Moscow

In a speech in Portland, April 1883, Villard said, "We shall endeavor to complete [the] line to Moscow this season if possible. That line I consider is of great importance, because its opens up a beautiful and extremely fertile country." When the road to Colfax was opened in January 1884, five miles of track had been laid toward Moscow and beyond extensive grading had been done. In mid-September a contractor thought the Moscow extension would be completed in the fall. The line to Huntington, Oregon (the OSL/UP connection with the ORN), was completed and so they would be able "to devote their whole force and energy to the Moscow branch." The assumption was so strong that Moscow would immediately have a railroad that the *History of Idaho Territory* published in San Francisco in 1884 stated that Moscow had a railroad.[68] It would be almost a year before work resumed.

The *Gazette* said in April 1885 that the ORN would

probably accept Moscow's wheat subsidy proposition. Apparently Portland business interests would provide construction money for a percentage of the freight receipts. A month later the newspaper reported that the ORN had raised freight rates on NP construction material for the Cascade branch. In retaliation the NP refused to haul ORN cars with construction material for the Moscow branch.[69]

The Portland *Oregonian* reported that Elijah Smith in June said the Moscow branch "ought to be built at once." It would be built that season if the funds could be raised. A July report in the Walla Walla *Union* said that Moscow farmers had agreed to ship at least 30,000 tons of grain the first year to Portland and pay an additional dollar surcharge on the seven dollar per ton rate. The economy of Moscow had boomed in 1883, but when the railroad did not come it stagnated.[70]

On July 21 a construction train arrived in Colfax with 200 workmen, two-thirds of whom were Chinese. Most of the work would be between the end of the track and Pullman, where there was heavy rock work and 16 bridges to be built. The construction from Pullman to Moscow would consume 15 days. Rather than a subsidy, the line would require a dollar surcharge per ton on the grain from all points above Colfax.[71] The next five issues of the *Gazette* reported construction in full swing. The number of workers employed were said to be 500. The tri-weekly train was unable to handle all the construction materials, as a result daily train service began. The *Daily Journal* reported that track laying reached Pullman September 9.[72]

The first regular train arrived in Pullman on September 16, 1885. The first train arrived in Moscow September 23. A warehouse was initially used as the Moscow depot which was still under construction October 23. According to the *Gazette* the Moscow extension was turned over to the operating department Saturday, September 26. The first shipment of Moscow flax, nine cars, left the following Wednesday. The Moscow turntable was in order on Sunday and the water tank was shipped in the same day. The extension from Colfax to Moscow was 27.8 miles long with re-measurement addition of .76 miles in Idaho.[73]

On October 29, 1885, the Walla Walla *Journal* said the Moscow extension had taken some freight from the Snake River boats. A year before Almota had shipped 10,000 tons and it was predicted that in 1885 it would be much less. The *Gazette* reported December 11 that the first wheat shipped in bulk, rather than sacks, from the Palouse country was sent the week before to Portland from the elevator at Moscow. In February 1886 the *Journal* reported that 200,000 bushels of wheat had been shipped from Pullman since the branch was completed. It was reported in 1886 that the rate on wheat in 1885 was $8 a ton and that year it was $7 "and if the junction is made with Riparia, avoiding the payment of $1 a ton for the 52 miles of the N. P. haul, the rate will be $6." The Moore brothers in Moscow secured land for a depot and erected very extensive warehouses, but insisted that they have exclusive warehouse privileges in exchange for the depot land. Mr. Beacon, a prosperous farmer heard of this, and donated the 20 acres where the depot was built. The newspaper concluded, "The result is, that farmers, through healthy competition, have not been subjected to excessive charges for warehousing and carrying their grain." The *Journal* had earlier lauded the ORN for rejecting a request from outsiders to have an exclusive privilege to erect warehouses and platforms on the Moscow branch.[74]

G. Construction to Farmington

The *Gazette* said in early October 1885 that ORN President Smith was "making strenuous efforts" to get the money to build the Farmington branch. The following week, in response to rumors that the NP would enter the Palouse, "the prospect for an early commencement of work on Farmington branch is good." On the 24th a "railroad meeting" was held in Colfax "for the purpose of publicly inviting railroads to enter the country and to urge the construction of contemplated lines, especially the Farmington branch." The next day surveyors arrived in Colfax to survey to Farmington.[75]

On November 26 the *Oregonian* reported that a committee formed by George W. Truax had pledges for all the right-of-way between Silver Creek and Farmington. In a letter in the *Gazette* President Smith said he favored "putting in the branch in the spring, and am in favor of doing such preliminary work as we can do this year, taking into consideration the lateness of the season and what we have to do elsewhere." A week later it was reported that Smith did not know when construction would begin. ORN General Manager C. H. Prescott assured visitors that the branch would go directly to Farmington, no matter where the junction was located. The *Gazette* concluded, "From this, it would appear that the point of junction is not definitely located, and it behooves Colfax to be up and doing." Two weeks later: "Good. The O. R. & N. surveyors have received orders to cross-section the route surveyed between this city and Farmington."[76]

From Lewiston December 9, NP Assistant Engineer J. B. Alexander wrote NP Chief Engineer Adna Anderson that the ORN conductor "at Moscow told me they do not haul a bushel of wheat from any point west of Endicott." He went on that ORN had surveyed east of Farmington toward Coeur d'Alene Lake. "Their object...is thought to be the mining trade of Coeur d'Alene Mts., and the grain raised by the Indians, which is estimated at 100,000 bushels this year. A spur from Rathdrum to the Foot of the Lake would interfere with that scheme."[77]

A January 11, 1886, letter to Prescott reported that three surveys had been run from points on the C&P to Farmington. The first left the C&P at the mouth of Rebel Flat following a route, except for the east end, that was essentially the route subsequently built by the ORN as the Pleasant Valley branch from Winona to Seltice in 1888–89 (see chapter VII). The second left the C&P at the Colfax depot and was the route built to Farmington. The third, which was never built, left the C&P nine miles east of Colfax, on the South Fork of the Palouse River, up Four Mile Creek to Palouse City and north along the Washington-Idaho boundary. Regarding the latter route Alexander had reported to Anderson January 2 that it was rumored that the ORN would adopt the line so as to obstruct the southward progress of the Eastern Washington Railway Co. (the predecessor to the Spokane and Palouse) and compel a junction at Palouse City.[78]

The Walla Walla *Journal*, March 12, said that with the ORN on its way and the NP certain to act, the farmers at Farmington were cultivating every possible acre. The ORN was paying a fair price for land which farmers would not donate. The *Gazette* concurred that the ORN was making "liberal" payments for right-of-way. By April 16 surveyors had cross sectioned nearly to Garfield from Colfax.[79]

The ORN executive committee, April 21, 1886, authorized building from Colfax to Farmington, the sale of sufficient bonds to cover the cost of the Farmington branch and to reimburse the company for earnings used in the construction of the Moscow and Pomeroy branches.[80]

Prescott wrote Elijah Smith May 11 that bids on the Farmington branch were so high the ORN would do the work itself. But that day Nelson Bennett, the NP contractor on the Cascade branch, came in and made a bid that was so low that "I hardly think we can do the work ourselves.... We asked Bennett how he could afford to give us these figures. His answer was that certain parties...had been circulating stories that he had the inside track on the N. P. and could not get a contract on any other railroad and he thought he would show them that he could get a contract and that he had just $20,000 to lose on this job. I hardly think he will be out a great deal, but I feel quite sure there is no margin of profit in it for him."[81]

On May 19, the Walla Walla *Daily Journal* in a lengthy article on the Farmington branch said Bennett had sublet a portion of the contract, principally track work, to George W. Hunt of Corvallis, Oregon. Two thousand Chinese and 200 carts would be used. Chinese could be hired for 70 cents a day at Portland. Four or five hundred Chinese from Portland camped at Starbuck for nearly three months awaiting work on the Farmington branch. Doing nothing, they had run up a considerable debt with the ORN. The ORN wanted to keep them organized at Starbuck, but would not employ them until work commenced on the branch. "Two or three times they have gathered in large crowds and proceeded to their companies' agents here, and vented their indignation on them in the most vociferous manner imaginable." Violence was apparently limited to "violent gesticulations." On the 15th, orders came for them to move to Endicott via the Snake River crossing. The Chinese refused to move because they would have to walk several miles and they feared this was a ruse to get them further from Portland. Their contract was that when the Pataha (Pomeroy) branch was completed, they would be returned to Portland and if they allowed themselves to be taken elsewhere it would invalidate that contract.[82]

The *Gazette* reported May 21 that the contract with Bennett called for completion of the branch by October 1, with trains running by November 1. Two days earlier Bennett arrived in Colfax with a force of 150 white men and was followed the next day "by a gang of Chinamen." The *Daily Journal* reported that work commenced on the 21st. On May 28 the *Gazette* reported that the first grading was done about four miles above Colfax.[83]

In early June the Chinese were working off an $8,000 board bill owed to Portland contractors. A Howe truss would be used to cross the South Palouse River at Colfax. The next week the newspaper reported that "White laborers are paid $1.75 per day. Chinamen receive 80 cents." Teamsters struck the week before for four dollars a day for four horse teams, an increase of 50 cents a day. They had not yet returned to work. On June 18, the *Gazette* reported about 650 white men and 450 Chinese were employed. Hunt's scraper work was completed for six or seven miles above Colfax. The next day the Walla Walla *Union* said that, "It has been necessary to engage more white men, as a great many of those that came first were nothing more or less than Portland bums and hoodlums. Train men are being troubled by them, as they are breaking into sealed cars, their intention being to steal a ride to Portland, where opium and cheap beer abound."[84]

On June 25 the *Gazette* reported grading into Farmington. "They are tearing up the race track, much to the dissatisfaction of the Indians." It was reported that S. M. Wait, who had founded Waitsburg and three other towns, including Dayton, had purchased over 400 acres on the North Palouse at the mouth of Silver Creek, on the Farmington Branch, 12 miles above Colfax, where he proposed to build a town called "Evergreen." The site was subsequently named "Elberton." Almost a year later the *West Shore* reported that a saw mill was in operation and a large roller-process flouring mill was under construction. The June 1887 issue of the magazine had a full page advertising the opportunities at Elberton.[85]

President Smith was so impressed with Farmington that he ordered the line, stations, etc., to be completed by August 15. Preparations were being made to connect Garfield and Belmont with a stage line as soon as the Spokane & Palouse was completed to Belmont.[86]

Track laying began Tuesday, July 20. Material for 10 miles of road was stored in Colfax. About August 1 the *W. H. Besse* with a cargo of rails for the branch was lost on the Columbia River Bar. The ORN found enough rails in inventory to complete the line. In mid-August all the grading between Garfield and Farmington was expected to be completed. The grading between Colfax and Garfield was done except for two cuts. A week later track laying had been delayed by a rock cut a short distance west of Garfield.[87]

The first train arrived at Garfield on Saturday, August 21, 1886. The track was laid around the uncompleted rock cut. The work of the ORN engineers at Garfield would soon be completed. "The boys will be missed, as they have been here so long they seem like residents." The population of Garfield was estimated at over 500. Noon, Monday, August 30, 1886, tracks were laid into Farmington. In September the Walla Walla *Journal* reported that the railroad station at Farmington was already enclosed.[88]

Gill's report to the ICC said that Colfax to Farmington was 27.20 miles with a re-measurement adding .28 miles. The line was opened September 19, 1886. Construction was done by the ORN in the name of the C&P. It wasn't until May 24, 1887, that the C&P directors approved maps of the constructed line.[89]

The Walla Walla *Journal*, November 23, 1886, pointed out that with the C&P in Farmington and the S&P only six miles away, travelers could go from Colfax to Farmington, spend the night and next morning take the train from Belmont to Spokane Falls. Workers in Farmington were erecting a water tank and making ready for a roundhouse. The *Gazette* reported that the carpenter work on the Garfield depot was completed on November 30, and the workmen were going to Pullman to put up the depot there.[90]

The story of the C&P continues in chapter XVII and more on the railroad is found in Appendix II.

Chapter II Appendix

1. C&P Track Laying Record, Palouse Junction to Moscow, 1883–85

Date	Distance from Palouse Junction	Sources and Notes
May 25, 1883	27 miles	Thielsen letter to Villard, June 25, 1883, ran out of rails 5/25/83, when replenished unknown (MHS, 137.H.4.1.B).
Aug. 16, 1883	32 miles	Anderson letter to Oakes (MHS, 137.H.3.7.B).
Sept. 15, 1883	55 miles	Turned over to the operating department. Accepted by NP executive committee 11/10/83 (NP Papers).
Oct. 3, 1883	75 miles	Anderson certified 20 additional miles bringing total to 75 (MHS, 137.H.3.9.B).
Oct. 12, 1883	82 miles	Certified completed and ready for operation (MHS, 137.H.3.9.B).
Nov. 10, 1883	[88.8 miles]	Tracks completed to north end of Colfax (PG 11/16/83, 3).
Dec. 29, 1883	90 miles	Certified completed, 1.2 miles beyond Colfax station, completed C&P according to provisions of agreement of 1883 (OHS, 299, Box 85, ORN Executive Committee Minutes, 126–30).
[Dec. 31, 1883]	94.3 miles	Certified completed 1/19/84 (MHS, 137.I.19.6.F). The point is about 4 miles up the South Fork Palouse River from Colfax.
July/Aug, 1885		Track laying began again.
Sept. 9, 1885	[107.4]	Track laying reached Pullman (WWDJ 9/14/85, 3).
[Sept. 23, 1885]	[116.8] Total length of branch from Colfax 28.56 miles	First train arrived Moscow (Lecompte 1988, 24–25; Gill 1916, 5).

2. C&P Track Laying Record, Colfax to Farmington, 1886

Date	Distance from Palouse Junction	Sources and Notes
July 20, 1886	[88.8 miles]	Track laying began at Colfax (PG 7/23/86, 3).
[Aug. 21, 1886]	[106.4]	First train arrived Garfield with temporary track at a cut (PG 8/27/86, 3).
Aug. 30, 1886	[115.8] Total length of branch from Colfax 27.48 miles	Tracks laid to Farmington (PG 9/3/86, 3; Gill 1916, 5).

The Northern Pacific Prepares to Return to the Palouse, 1885–86

The Palouse commercial potential was large. The Northern Pacific could not ignore it, but having lost its presence in the Palouse, it needed to organize a company and determine a route.

A. NP Surveys and the Eastern Washington Railway Company

In February 1885 it was rumored that the NP would build from Spokane Falls into the Palouse and perhaps extend to Genesee and Lewiston in Idaho Territory. In July the Spokane *Evening Review* opined, "There is not a locality anywhere that holds out a more promising investment for capitalists than a railroad from Spokane Falls, tapping the rich Palouse country." That month ORN General Manager C. H. Prescott wrote ORN President Elijah Smith about rumors that people were endeavoring to secure a railroad from Spokane Falls to Farmington. "I understand that Mr. James McNaught of Seattle, who, you know, is Attorney for the Northern Pacific, O. R. & N., and Oregon Improvement Cos., has just returned from that part of the country and was much interested in the scheme in behalf of the Northern Pacific Co." He warned, "If this road is built, it will not stop eventually at Farmington." He told Smith that McNaught told the Farmington people that the branch would be built as soon as finances could be arranged.[1]

A meeting was held in Palouse City October 16 to encourage some railroad to construct into the town. They preferred the NP, but if that failed they would try to induce the ORN to build from the mouth of Four Mile Creek on the Colfax-Moscow line. The *Evening Review* reported that there was a large audience at the meeting and a resolution was unanimously passed seeking "speedy building of a railroad to Spokane Falls" and pledging "substantial aid in labor and material and in providing an advantageous right of way."[2]

F. Louis Clark, who worked in Spokane, apparently attended the meeting of the 16th while visiting Farmington and Palouse City. He wrote to relative J. G. Clark, associated with Wheelwright, Clark & Co., of Bangor, Maine, "The people of that section feel very hard against the ORN Co, but if we had not been there, I think the Co's Agent would have succeeded in getting a great deal of aid for the construction of an extension to take the wheat West, and away from us. As it was we had two hours to impress upon them the greater advantage of a R.R to Spokane." He said that a resolution that he furnished "was adopted with a unanimous shout" with the ORN agent present. Two thousand dollars was then raised in a few minutes. Several farmers between Palouse City and Farmington offered 10 cents a bushel subsidy, the difference between the price at Colfax and at Spokane Falls. It was estimated that in a 10-mile-wide strip in the 70 miles from Spokane Falls to Palouse City via Rockford and Farmington there was a half million bushels of wheat and a large amount of barley and oats. Because no more than a quarter of the occupied land had been broken, farmers told him that if there was a railroad they would raise four to five times as much grain. "If your friends do not take hold of it somebody will because the people are aroused and will give large bonuses in labor and material to anybody who will accept their aid in building the Road."[3]

In late October the *Evening Review* carried an editorial from the Palouse *News* which estimated that there was 76,800 acres in grain for export between Palouse City and Spokane Falls. This would yield conservatively 51,200 tons, and at a rate of $8 per ton to haul east the NP would gross $368,000. The editorial concluded, "Taking these figures to be correct...the N. P. R. R. Co. cannot afford to neglect this golden opportunity, which, in the course of another year's delay may be plucked from its grasp." The next day it was reported that a meeting in Rockford had urged a railroad from Farmington to Spokane Falls via Rockford. On October 29 a large crowd assembled in Glover's Hall in Spokane Falls to adopt resolutions in support of several NP branch lines from Spokane Falls. A. M. Cannon, chairman of the board of trade and Mayor of Spokane Falls, 1885-87, appointed a committee to draft the resolution; copies were sent to the NP directors, the Superintendent of the NP Idaho Division, and to Farmington, Moscow, Rockford, Palouse City, Colfax, and Cheney. On October 30 the Review said, "The sudden activity of the O. R. & N. has awakened the N. P. officials to a sense of their danger in remaining passive while a strong competing line reaches out and secures control of the most valuable grain country on the Pacific slope." Another meeting was held in Rockford to examine routes for connecting with Spokane Falls. In addition to the grain, businessmen in Rockford believed that it and Spokane Falls would be the chief supply points for the Coeur d'Alene mines in Idaho. The Palouse City *News* was quoted to the effect that while Cheney claimed the branch would extend from it, Palouse City preferred Spokane Falls, but "we want the road, no matter where it comes from."[4]

An NP surveying party began locating a line from Cheney via Spangle to Rosalia and Farmington toward the end of October. Two weeks later the *Gazette* reported that NP President Robert Harris said that the company would soon build to Farmington whether the ORN did so or not. The response of the ORN was to begin surveying from Colfax to Farmington. J. M. Buckley, Assistant General Manager, Western Divisions of the NP, sent Harris November 9 Articles of Incorporation for the "Northern Pacific, Spokane Falls and Southern Railroad Company."[5]

The *Evening Review* on November 12, 1885, announced that papers for the "Eastern Washington Railway" Company were ready to be filed. Construction would "commence as soon as the surveyors now in the field have located the most feasible line. C. B. Wright [Jr.] and A. A. Newberry [sic] have left our city for the front. They will follow the surveyors and will determine on terminal points and other matters connected with location." Wright was reported as saying that the new road would be completed in time to move the crops of next year and that work on the roadbed would begin as soon as the frost was out of the ground.[6]

James McNaught, NP legal Department, Seattle, the next day wrote NP President Harris of his September examination of the country between Spokane Falls and Farmington. He found it better wheat, barley, and flax country than either Walla Walla or Dayton. A line to Waverly, about 35 miles, would have two million bushels of wheat tributary to it. He said that the ORN was making a survey from Colfax to Rosalia. He went on,

> Marshall Field of Chicago owns along the Hangman [Creek] about 18,000 acres of land. Doctor Baker of Walla Walla about 10,000 acres. I have had some conversation with Miles Moore, Dr. Baker's son-in-law, and believe that I could get Dr. Baker to take a large amount of stock and bonds in this proposed road. And it occurs to me that Marshall Field might be induced to do the same thing. It would certainly double the value of his land. I think I could have a large block of stock taken at Spokane Falls. I feel very confident that the road would pay interest on cost of construction right from the date of its completion.
>
> If the O. R. & N. builds to Rosalia and from thence to Waverly or Latah, that road would practically control the wheat fields of Washington Territory east of your line of road, unless this piece of road is constructed.[7]

On November 15, 1885, the charter of The Eastern Washington Railway Company (EW) was filed with the "Commissioner of Deeds etc. for the Territory of Washington in Philadelphia."[8] The charter specified that company would build a railroad, from a point on the NP, between MP 145 and the Idaho Line, in Washington Territory to a point in Washington Territory on or near the Snake River. The capital stock was to be $1 million. The initial seven trustees would manage the company until April 1, 1886. The foreign trustees were T. F. Oakes, St. Paul, Minnesota; Nelson Bennett, Deer Lodge, Montana; and Charles B. Wright Jr., Philadelphia, Pennsylvania. The domestic trustees were Anthony M. Cannon, Paul F. Mohr and A. A. Newbery, all of Spokane Falls; and Joseph Jorgenson of Walla Walla. The EW was never organized.[9] Later sworn testimony claimed that the NP had nothing to do with either the organization or incorporation of the EW, and that Harris had no prior knowledge that such a company was being formed. The involvement of Oakes and Wright was said to be at the insistence of the local incorporators and was done for the purpose of enhancing the financial prospects of the company.[10]

The day after the EW charter was filed in Philadelphia, Oakes wrote Harris:

> It is a foregone conclusion that the O. R. & N. Co. purposes the immediate construction of a line from Colfax to Farmington, and there are some indications pointing to a still further extension; that is, they have surveyors in the field locating a line from Farmington north to Rosalia, seeking evidently to control the grain traffic of Hangman Creek country, as well as that of the Palouse, and it is more than probable they intend to still further extend a line in the direction of, if not actually to, the Coeur D'Alene country.
>
> In view of the fact that the Columbia and Palouse branch

> was originally constructed in the joint interest of both companies, and that subsequently this company waived its right to ownership therein, a condition of things exists that otherwise could not occur; that is, the O. R. & N. Co. to-day is in possession of a line traversing a territory that properly belongs to the Northern Pacific co., and strictly speaking I presume that company would have the right to complete so much of the system as was originally contemplated. In other words, they would have the right to complete the line from Colfax to Farmington. But I think they should be at once notified that any extension beyond that point into our territory will be looked upon as an unfriendly act, and in order to be in a position hereafter to check-mate any further aggressive movement into our territory, arrangements should be made for the speedy construction of a branch line from Spokane Falls or Marshall southeastward to Farmington, and perhaps to [P]alouse city. The people of Spokane Falls have for some time past been alive to the plans and movements of the O. R. & N. Co's management, and foreseeing the effect upon their trade, of the extension to Farmington, have organized a local Railroad Co. for the purpose of building to that point and to Palouse, with a branch towards the Coeur D'Alene country. In order to have a voice in the management of this organization, with a view to its control hereafter..., it was arranged while Mr. Wright was here that he and I were to take a three-fifths interest in the enterprise.... The movement has not progressed far enough to enable me to give any intelligent opinion as to the desirability of adopting the plans in full, of the people who have it in charge. Of the value of a line to Farmington I have no doubt; as to whether a branch to the Coeur D'Alene mines may be desirable or not remains to be determined.
>
> The shipment of wheat this year of the Columbia and Palouse line will aggregate 275000 tons. Of this amount fully one half originates in the territory immediately adjacent to Farmington, and the country between Farmington and Spokane Falls.... Our shipments of wheat this year east bound from Washington Territory, will aggregate over 500,000 bushels. This is the country from which the Cascade division will hereafter draw the larger part of its traffic, and the branch I have suggested will be a step in the right direction for providing traffic when the division is opened to Tacoma.

Oakes concluded that if the ORN extended beyond Farmington the NP should immediately build branches in the Walla Walla region.[11] Oakes in this letter proposes the response taken by the NP to ORN inclusions into the Palouse and implies that Harris was not involved in the establishment of the EW.

The Spokane *Morning Review* of the 19th quoted at length from the Portland *Standard* of the 17th:

> Charles B. Wright, Jr., of Philadelphia, son of the director of the Northern Pacific railroad company, arrived in this city to-day. The object of his visit to this region is connection with the proposed branch of the Northern Pacific into the Palouse river country, and for the past few days he has been making a personal examination of the different routes proposed into the country. Two or three surveys are being made now to ascertain which is the most feasible route for the railroad to follow. Mr. Wright states that it is the intention of the Northern Pacific people to have the proposed road from the Palouse river country built to one of three points, Cheney, Marshall or Spokane Falls, in time to take out next season's crops.... This settles the question as to whether there was any foundation to the reports which have been circulated quite extensively of late about such a branch being built by the Northern Pacific.... [T]he present visit of Mr. Wright will undoubtedly settle the matter. The building of such a branch by the Northern Pacific indicates that that company will not allow the O. R. & N. company to secure supreme control of the grain traffic of rich and growing regions commonly known as the Palouse country.[12]

The threat to Portland was laid out.

The NP board of directors, November 19, 1885, directed the president to procure or build a railroad from Spokane Falls to Farmington. On November 20 President Harris wrote J. G. Clark, of Bangor ME, that he took pleasure in informing Clark of the board's decision.[13]

McNaught of the legal department wrote Harris November 20 that he had dictated the articles of incorporation for the Northern Pacific, of the Spokane and Southern Railroad Company. He goes on,

> Mr. Buckley has undoubtedly advised you of the fact that articles of incorporation have been prepared and probably signed by this time by Mr. Oakes, C. B. Wright Jr.... and...others, for a road I believe called the Northeastern, for the same section of the country. I have never seen the articles of incorporation.... My understanding is that Mr. Oakes permitted his name to be used in these articles for the purpose of being fully advised as to what they were doing and checkmating any erroneous move.
>
> If it is thought advisable to attempt to get any aid from Spokane Falls, would be pleased to have you advise me early. The city of Spokane intends to obtain a new charter from the present Legislature convening early in December, and it will be necessary for us to look after it a little so as to see that it has power to vote aid and issue bonds.

Harris responded that he did know that Wright and others had arranged for the EW. "We shall go ahead under it." He went on to say that he was opposed to cities and counties voting aid to railroad companies, "sooner or later it makes trouble."[14]

J. G. Clark, of Bangor, Maine, telegraphed President Harris sometime in November: "The new Oakes Wright Cannon Company are surveying to Farmington. Does Harris know this. Are Harris and Oakes in sympathy. Shall we secure right of way against Oakes. Please wire them instructions." Harris wrote Clark on November 30:

> I have telegraphed Clark & Curtis as follows: "Northern Pacific Co. will cooperate with Eastern Washington R. R. Co. I send this message at request of J. G. Clark."
>
> When Mr. C. B. Wright was at St Paul, he arranged with Mr. Cannon and his associates to join them in organizing the Eastern Washington R. R. Co. Articles of Incorporation were filed in the office of the Secretary of the Territory last week. The Northern Pacific Co. will cooperate with that Co[mpany] in causing a Railroad to be built from a point on the Northern Pacific near Spokane Falls Southerly to Snake River.... Wherever the connection is made Spokane must necessarily be the real commercial terminus. Without doubt it will be the most considerable city in Eastern Washington. Whatever advantages any other point may have, Spokane will have these in addition to its splendid water power.[15]

The Spokane *Morning Review* had a report from the Palouse *News* of November 20 that NP surveyors under Paul F. Mohr had reached Palouse City on the 18th after running a 65-mile line from Marshall. Mohr "is well pleased with the entire line of the survey, and will undoubtedly make a favorable report. Don't be surprised to see a locomotive in Palouse City within a year."[16]

ORN President Elijah Smith wrote General Manager C. H. Prescott on November 29:

> I have written you of the fact that the Northern Pacific Board passed a vote authorizing the construction of a road to Farmington, and the general tenor of Mr. Harris' talk is to the effect that he did not propose to have the O. R. & N. Co. put out its branches and drain the whole of that country as it has the Walla Walla territory. How far they will go I do not know. While they have no right to build Branches I suppose it can be done an indirect way by aiding local people in doing so. He produced considerable of a sensation in the Board as I understand...stating that we were proposing to build into their country. Mr. [J. H.] Hall stated to the Board and I have stated...that nothing had been discussed except the three Branches, two of which would be done at once and Farmington Branch as soon as possible, but it occurred to me since that your efforts in securing the right of way to the Coeur d'Alene mines may be going outside of our territory as described and limited in the contact between our Co. and the Northern Pacific Co. we want to be careful about this as that is the agreement which keeps them from building or aiding in building a road into Walla Walla. It is possible the organization and other action reported in the newspaper...about immediate construction of Spokane Falls to Farmington may not indicate immediate prosecution of the work although my idea is that it does and we may as well contemplate it in that view.[17]

Oakes wrote Harris on December 2 that he had heard that the ORN intended to bridge the Snake River at Riparia, connect to the C&P and extend to Farmington and thence to the Coeur d'Alene district. Harris replied that he had discussed the matter with Smith and was assured that the ORN had no intention to extend north of Farmington.[18]

Writing from Lewiston on December 9, Assistant Engineer J. B. Alexander reported to NP Chief Engineer Adna Anderson that he went with Mohr to examine Mohr's surveys south of Spokane. He thought the Marshall Creek route was better than the Hangman Creek route in that it required no bridging and had moderate grading. It appeared to him that the line via Marshall, Spangle, and Rosalia to be satisfactory given the character of the country. They continued south to a point about a mile southeast of where Oakesdale was subsequently located. From that point a survey went generally easterly to Farmington, "where Mohr says it runs into the mountains and stops with no change to 'advance' south, except backwards." The next day they went from Palouse City to Moscow and via Uniontown to Lewiston. Alexander was inclined to think a possible route south from Palouse City would run to the South Palouse at Pullman and from there to Moscow.

> The ridge between here [Lewiston] and Uniontown I make by aneroid to be 2115 feet above the river. The distance by the wagon road which zig-zags down the mountain is 4.73 miles from the summit to the river. The country is the worst tumbled up of all I ever saw, to be an agricultural country. The land is extremely rich, and they plow it to the tops of hills 100 feet high. From Palouse City to the bluffs near the river, it is all taken up and fenced, and much of it under cultivation.... The Conductor of R.R.& N. at Moscow told me they do not haul a bushel of wheat from any point west of Endicott.[19]

On December 11, 1885, NP President Harris wrote the senior Wright that parties friendly to the NP be requested to complete the organization of the EW and make surveys, estimates, and construction under the supervision of the NP, that the road be leased to the NP at a rental sufficient to pay interest and retire the construction bonds and that the NP would have full voting power and dividends, if any. Wright responded on the 14th. He agreed and wrote, "So far as I am concerned, I care very little about having anything to do with the project if there are others who will under take it who are in the interests of the N. P. R. R." Anderson wrote on the 30th that he had gone over the maps and profiles of the EW and estimated that a road as good as the C&P could be built with 56 lb. steel rail at inside of $12,000 per mile and might exceed $11,000 by very little.[20]

On January 2, 1886, Alexander wrote a lengthy report to Anderson on the country south of Spokane Falls. The report contains commentary on the weather, topography, elevations, stream sizes, timber, soil, cultivation and crops, income from crops (mostly wheat), settlement, roads, grain warehouses, grain "chutes" from the plateau to the Snake River, Snake River navigation, freight rates on the river and from Colfax, the amount of wheat shipped, total freight shipments into Colfax, and populations of towns. At the northern end of the proposed line, Alexander found it impracticable to use Spokane Falls as the terminal. In addition to Marshall, the line could be built out of Cheney, but Spokane would be the principal city of the region, so Marshall should be preferred. He found Mohr's line from Marshall, through Spangle, Rosalia, and Garfield to Palouse City to be "quite direct and is as practicable as the country will admit of." He thought the objective of the line should be Genesee rather than Palouse City, but it was impracticable to run a line directly from the latter to the former, thus he recommended that the line run south west from Palouse City to Pullman and hence to Union Flat to Genesee. If this line was built a branch could be built from Oakesdale to Colfax. He noted that the ORN had surveyed from Colfax to Farmington via Garfield, if the ORN did not build the line, the Colfax branch could diverge near Garfield and occupy their survey and save three miles. Alexander explored Steptoe canyon from Colton to the Snake River. He found it to be steep, narrow, crooked and rocky. "It is therefore out of the question." He next explored Penawawa Canyon as a route from Union Flat to the Snake River. In association with Almota Creek, he thought that this would be a very desirable route to the river. It would be less difficult to build and operate and would be in wheat most of the way and the business from south of the Snake would justify its construction. His recommendation was that the line be built south from Palouse City rather than Colfax because of the lumber mills at the former. ORN engineers had run a line from Colfax to Palouse City along Four Mile Creek. "It was rumored in the country that the O.R. & N. Co. would adopt this line instead of the one by Garfield so as to obstruct the southward progress of the E.W. Co. and compel a junction at Palouse City. There is room enough however for two roads down Four Mile Creek."[21] Alexander's recommendations largely were followed in building the Spokane & Palouse (S&P) to Genesee.

The NP executive committee on January 13, 1886, set the location of the railroad from a point at or near Marshall, southerly to a point about two miles southeast of Oakesdale and three miles northwest of Belmont, a distance of about 43 miles. The remainder of the resolution dealt with financing which was subsequently altered. Subcommittees of the NP executive and finance committees met February 3. Harris submitted Alexander's report. August Belmont, of the finance committee, expressed doubt about undertaking the 43-mile railroad, but he was willing to refer it to the executive committee for a decision. Cannon and Mohr were present the next day at a meeting of the executive committee. They said that if the railroad was from Spokane Falls, its citizens would contribute $50,000, $25,000 in cash and $25,000 in real estate. The terms the committee recommended to the board included: "That its corporate name be changed to 'The Spokane Falls and Southern Railroad Company'; that the citizens of Spokane Falls shall give aid in the amount and form as stated; that the road shall be constructed under this Company's supervision and to its satisfaction." The remainder of the terms were financial which were subsequently changed. Cannon and Mohr agreed to the terms.[22]

On February 18, 1886, the NP directors passed a resolution "referring to The Spokane Falls and Southern Railroad Company, heretofore, 'Eastern Washington'."

> That a legally organized corporation being, or to be immediately, lawfully empowered to build the railroad from a point on the Northern Pacific Railroad, near Spokane Falls, southwardly, to a point in Township 19, North Range 44 East, and estimated distance of forty-three miles, for the construction of said railroad, the said firm will advance all the money required, not exceeding the amount of 85 percent on $16,000 per mile, and to take therefore the bonds of said Spokane Falls and Southern Railroad, (by whatever name the same shall be know) to an amount, which at the rate of 85 per cent on the par of the principal will pay the actual cost of the construction of said railroad; the said bonds to run for the period of fifty years, and to bear interest at six per cent, per annum, payable semi-annually...to be secured by a mortgage on all the property, present and future, franchises and privileges of the company, the mortgage to provide for a sinking fund sufficient to redeem the bonds at or before maturity, and to commence ten years after the date of the bonds—that a traffic contract between that corporation and this company for the interchange of traffic, and this company shall guarantee the payment of the interest on the bonds and the installment to the sinking fund as provided in the mortgage.

> Messrs. August Belmont & Co. to be entitled to bonds for each ten miles as the same shall be completed...
>
> ...the entire of the capital stock of the said Spokane Falls and Southern Railroad is to be...assigned to this company as full paid, non-assessable stock; but until the bonds of that company...shall have been fully paid or redeemed, or their redemption adequately provided for by the sinking fund, the said stock shall be deposited with, and in the name of, a trustee to be agreed on by the parties; but in the meantime the voting power and the right to dividends on said stock shall be in this company.[23]

The Spokane *Morning Review* reported February 21 that a party of surveyors would leave Spokane the next day to cross-section the railroad. The newspaper commented, "Many thought that the original organization of this company meant nothing, but the rapidity with which it has been materialized and made a tangible fact proves conclusively that the men who took hold of the project knew what they were at."[24]

On February 5 Harris wrote Frederick Billings and C. B. Wright, "Would not Spokane and Palouse be better and more suggestive name than Spokane & Southern? The term Palouse suggests rich country already well known and highly esteemed." On March 1, 1886, Supplemental Articles of Incorporation of the Eastern Washington Railway Company were filed with Washington Territory. They had been filed February 9 at Philadelphia, Pennsylvania, with the Commissioner of Deeds for the Territory. The first provision was to change the name to the "Spokane and Palouse Railway Company." The purpose was to build and operate a railroad from a connection with the main line of the NP at or near the town of Marshall to some point on or near the Snake River, all in Washington Territory and to build branch railroads to other points or places in Washington Territory. The incorporators were Thomas F. Oakes, Charles B. Wright, E. J. Brickell, and Watson C. Squire. The trustees in addition to Oakes were Charles B. Wright Jr., Nelson Bennett, Anthony McCue Cannon, Paul F. Mohr, A. A. Newbery, and Dr. Joseph Jorgensen.[25]

On February 24 Harris asked Anderson, "Would it not be well to ask Bennett to make proposal for grading, bridging, tying and laying track Spokane & Palouse Road. We wish to start work as early as possible." Harris also telegraphed Anderson to ask Cannon to have the S&P adopt a resolution authorizing construction of 43 miles and to issue to the NP 6,880 shares of stock as compensation for guaranteeing interest on bonds and sinking fund. He said as soon as his instructions had been carried out, contracts would be prepared and sent to Cannon for execution. On the 26th Harris wrote Wright that there was disappointment among the Washington based S&P trustees about "the outcome of the Spokane and Palouse project...but that of course there was nothing for them to do but to concur." Harris wished the road to be completed by July 1.[26]

On March 2, 1886, the Cheney, Palouse and Snake River Railroad was incorporated to build from Cheney to the Snake River on the Idaho border. It was not constructed.[27]

B. The Organization of the Spokane & Palouse Railway

Mohr's report of June 30, 1886, to Anderson summarized the work accomplished. Prior to the organization of the EW, Mohr made reconnaissances in 1885, south of Spokane Falls, to find "the most available route" as due south as possible to or near the Palouse River. "I explored every available route between the points named. I placed a party in the field about November 1, 1885, and made such instrumental surveys as were necessary to ascertain the route which combined the most favorable grades, the lightest curvatures, and the most equal division of the grain belt." The surveys were completed December 3. He organized a locating party and put them in the field early in March. The location of the line to a mile southeast of what would be Oakesdale was completed in early April and location for five additional miles (probably to Belmont) was made in early May. The preliminary surveys under the EW amounted to about 260 miles of line. About $6,000 was spent on the preliminary surveys, incidental expenses of organizing the company and obtaining right-of-way.[28]

The S&P Trustees met at Spokane Falls on March 9, 1886, and adopted by-laws which stated that the annual meeting would be in Spokane Falls. Cannon was elected president, Wright, vice president. The executive committee authorized the officers to take steps to immediately construct a railroad from the NP, at or near Marshall, to a point in the vicinity of Oakesdale on the line adopted by the trustees as its definite location. The authorized capital stock of the S&P was $1 million divided into shares of $100 each. The trustees authorized the issuance of 9,930 shares to the NP for its guarantee of interest and the funded debt of the S&P; 70 shares were issued to the S&P trustees.[29]

On March 10, the Spokane *Morning Review* reported

on the trustees' meeting in the company offices on the second story of the Van Valkerberg building. Mohr was elected chief engineer. The paper said the road was under Mohr's control and that he had done effective work for Spokane Falls. Construction would commence as soon as surveys from Marshall to Rosalia and up Hangman Creek to Waverly and Latah were completed. "It is not improbable that the route up Hangman creek will be selected on account of the easy grades, which may offset the somewhat more expensive work of construction. Spokane Falls has cause to be jubilant."[30]

Anderson wrote Harris March 13 about the trustee meeting, "There was a good deal of soreness felt on the part of the parties who had worked up the former arrangement, but Mr. Cannon took at once a decided stand that the present arrangement with the Road was better than any other without it, to which the others at length assented, and passed the proper resolutions." The location work would probably be finished in early April. Bennett and another contractor had examined the work. Until the right-of-way was secured over the entire 43 miles, Anderson thought it advisable to keep matters as quiet as possible. The ground was extremely muddy but construction would commence in three or four weeks. He would endeavor to complete and have running the 43 miles by August 1. He thought this could "be done without difficulty."[31]

On March 27 Mohr reported to Anderson that the road had been located to south of Rosalia and that he had two parties in the field, one locating and the other cross sectioning. Suitable timber for ties and piling were not available along the route of the railroad. The *Gazette* said the Montana Improvement Company, an NP company, had been accused of stealing timber from public lands. "In order to avoid responsibility the Montana Improvement Company recently changed its name, and with a view of giving color to the pretense of cutting timber only for mining purposes.... It has been extending its operations and now ships lumber cut from the public domain as far east as St. Paul."[32]

Anderson wrote March 23, Harris that, "The only difficulty I anticipate is in obtaining ties and timber, and in the steel for track coming forward with sufficient promptness. The local work is comparatively light, and a strong contractor can complete it in sixty to ninety days." Anderson would talk to Cannon and Wright in regard to their compensation as officers of the S&P. Anderson concluded,

> I have arranged with Mr. Mohr to conduct the surveys and location of the road, as he seems to be fully competent to do so.
>
> He has received no compensation, whatever, for his services in the surveys and approximate location, made last fall. Both he and Mr. Cannon think that the time they were employed in getting up the road, inasmuch as they failed to secure their share, should not be thrown away, and I suggest the propriety of a certain amount being allowed them; at least to Mr. Mohr, for services which the present Company would have been obliged to pay, had it taken hold of it at first.

Harris agreed that Cannon and Mohr should be paid for services to the NP.[33]

Anderson wrote Harris April 26 enclosing an agreement made October 26, 1885,[34] among Newbery, Mohr and Cannon about their reimbursement for work on the EW. The agreement called for a $10 per diem compensation for time spent away from Spokane Falls for surveys, right-of-way business or any other necessary business connected with and for the benefit of the company. The agreement concluded, "That the parties [Newbery, Mohr and Cannon] subscribing to and entering into this contract shall share equally in any stocks, bonds, benefits, or other profits growing out of said enterprise." Anderson recommended that they be paid their per diem for organizing the company, obtaining right-of-way, etc. Anderson continued,

> When I last saw Mr. Cannon he made this point: That all of them spent several weeks last fall in securing the right-of-way. It cost them little or no money, but occupied their time; and through their personal influence and efforts they obtained releases for right-of way over a large portion of the line now about to be occupied by the road. Mr. Cannon suggested that a mode of compensation to himself and associates might be found by the Spokane & Palouse Railway Company paying them for this right-of-way, which otherwise the S. & P. Rwy. Co. might or might not have obtained without payment of money.

On July 29, 1886, Harris wrote Anderson that he had arranged to have Cannon compensated "in full for services to Oct. 1st, 1886, $3100."[35]

In a mid-March from Palouse City, the Palouse *Gazette* reported, "Every day our town has some new assurance that the Spokane & Palouse R. R. will be completed to Palouse City this summer. A prominent official of the proposed line assured our people that the road would be built in time to transport the next crop. We hope this great enterprise is no delusion, as one of our neighbors would have us believe."[36]

The S&P executive committee met in New York City March 23, 1886. Harris and Belmont were present, Cannon absent. Harris was authorized to contract for the S&P with Bethlehem Iron Company for 2,300 tons of 56-pound steel rails of the NP standard pattern to be delivered at the mill in April and May for 35 dollars per ton of 2240 pounds and $2.25 per ton delivered to Buffalo.[37]

The Spokane Falls *Morning Review* editorialized March 27:

> From A. M. Cannon...we learn that all arrangements have been perfected and the line is an assured fact...there now being several railroad contractors and builders in the city who will make bids for doing the work.... It is the intention to complete and have in running order fifty miles of road by the latter part of August.... In spite of all the obstacles that outsiders have attempted to throw in the way of the construction of this road, it is bound to be built and its completion will not only a great benefit to Spokane Falls but it will be a long hoped for blessing to that vast scope of rich and productive agricultural lands extending to the south of us.... The scheme is one of great promise to the country and marks a new era of prosperity for this immediate portion of eastern Washington.[38]

Cannon wrote Harris, March 29, that "The work on the road is being pushed forward to the best of our ability, and, fortunately, we are being favored with very fine weather." On April 1, the first meeting of the stockholders of the S&P was held in Spokane Falls. Cannon, Mohr, Newbery, Buckley, Wright Jr., Belmont, and Harris were elected trustees, each receiving 6,887 votes. The NP held 6,880 shares; the remaining shares were held one each by the stockholders, all of whom were elected trustees. On the same day the trustees met and elected Cannon president and Wright vice president. Cannon, Harris, and Belmont were selected as the executive committee. Harris and Belmont were absent at both meetings.[39]

Apparently there was some consideration of stopping construction a mile south of Oakesdale for on April 7, Cannon wrote Anderson arguing that the construction for the year should be extended four or five miles further south. "This would not carry us beyond the limit of the territory which may be considered as the natural domain belonging to and tributary, to the Northern Pacific Railroad Company." Anderson telegraphed Harris the 15th endorsing Cannon's argument. Harris was apparently persuaded because on April 20 Anderson wrote Harris that the road would be extended 43 miles "to the point Mr. Cannon designates." Harris telegraphed Cannon on June 3 instructing him to call a board meeting to adopt a route to the 43rd mile. On June 5 Harris wrote S&P Treasurer G. S. Baxter authorizing him to open an S&P account at Cannon's Bank of Spokane Falls, "not having on deposit at any one time more than $2,000."[40]

The NP board of directors approved the 999-year S&P lease to the NP June 17, 1886. Cannon and Newbery signed for the S&P on June 29 at Spokane Falls and filed with the New York Commissioner of Deeds for Washington Territory July 21. Under the lease the Trustees of the S&P were obligated to finance the mortgage. For all the capital stock of the S&P, the NP would pay a rent equal to 6 percent on the bonds, and after 10 years the amount necessary for the sinking fund. Until the redemption of the bonds, The Farmers' Loan and Trust Company would hold the stock as Trustee. After the bonds had been paid, purchased or redeemed the NP would pay a rental agreed to by the NP and the S&P. The S&P agreed to construct the railroad and as each 10-mile section was approved by the NP, it became subject to the lease. The NP would pay all costs and taxes associated with the maintenance and operation of the S&P.[41]

The S&P trustees June 24, 1886, authorized the execution of the mortgage, the issuing of bonds for construction and the lease of the S&P to the NP. The first mortgage of May 1, 1886, to The Farmers' Loan and Trust Company was for an estimated 43 miles of road financed by 6 percent gold bonds, payable semi-annually for 50 years, not to exceed $16,000 per mile ($688,000 total) of main track and branches in Washington Territory. Beginning November 1, 1895, a sinking fund would be established and payments made into it sufficient to redeem all the bonds, at or before maturity, at a price equal to par plus 5 percent annually. President Cannon and Secretary Newbery signed the mortgage in Spokane Falls June 29, and Farmers' in New York July 12. The mortgage was filed in Spokane July 20. The New York Stock Exchange listed on September 22 "688 First Mortgage Sinking Fund Six Per Cent Gold Bonds" of the S&P dated May 1, 1886, and due May 1, 1936.[42]

On July 1, 1886, the S&P stockholders approved a trust agreement that provided the 10,000 shares of S&P stock would be transferred to Farmers' Loan and Trust Company except a sufficient number of shares would be used to qualify S&P directors. The NP retained the sole power of voting and receiving dividends on the stock. When the mortgage was adequately provided for, Farmers' would transfer all the stock to the NP.[43]

Harris, in response to an earlier letter, wrote a Mr. Jackson in Middletown, CT, on July 23, 1886, that he thought the bonds on the S&P "good." He went on to say,

> but until the country tributary to it has become well filled up, its pro rata proportion of joint earnings with the Northern Pacific will probably not be enough to meet its fixed charges, but when the adjacent country is well settled, I will expect the net profit off the Road to be enough for that purpose. Taken in connection with the Northern Pacific as a feeder to it, I have not hesitated to advise the construction of the Branch feeling well assured it will give a good account of itself.[44]

Lease Negotiations, 1881–1887

The desire to consolidate the railroads in the Pacific Northwest did not die with the fall of Villard and the ORN's control of the C&P. Negotiations regarding lease of the ORN to the NP, to the UP, or to both jointly were influenced by several conflicting circumstances: (1) Portland's physical shortcomings as a port compared to Puget Sound; (2) the revenues needs of the ORN; (3) the NP goal of reaching Puget Sound over the Cascades; (4) the agricultural and commercial shipping needs of the interior; and (5) competition between the NP and ORN/UP for grain traffic and the potential to overbuild branch lines.

Portland, more than 100 miles from the mouth of the Columbia River and with a dependable river channel depth of only 10 feet, was physically disadvantaged compared to Puget Sound deep water ports. The Columbia bar was both exceedingly dangerous and subject to high wind and fog. Portland's major advantage was a water level rail route east along the river, while Puget Sound looked east to the mountainous wall of the Cascades.

The ORN had a pressing need to protect and maximize its revenues because of its bonded debt, the shoddy construction of its south bank line along the Columbia River, and its branch line construction program. The OT was dependent on high dividends from the ORN. Its revenue prospects were tied to its monopoly to tidewater through Portland. The ORN was a Portland company and its management was sensitive to the interests of Portland. Through most of 1886, ORN's profitability was enhanced by its monopoly in the Palouse and Walla Walla grain regions. An NP entrance into the grain regions and completion of its line across the Cascades threatened both the ORN and Portland. After the UP leased the ORN in January 1887, it was in the same position.

The NP was chartered to cross the Cascades to Puget Sound. Building over the mountains would result in a large land grant, free the NP from dependence on the ORN to reach tidewater, and enrich NP officials who had invested in the Puget Sound region, particularly Tacoma. To reach its traffic potential to Puget Sound, the NP needed a presence in the grain regions of eastern Washington.

Interior Pacific Northwest economic development and well-being depended on low freight rates, particularly on grain. Railroads were the key to achieving low rates. The Columbia River in its natural state was navigable, but at relatively high cost. Low rates were unlikely if a single port or railroad had a monopoly. The people of the interior wanted choices among railroads and ports.

In the search for traffic neither the NP nor ORN/UP could ignore the grain regions. Territorial "invasion" was inevitable. Neither railroad built as much line as they surveyed, or to which they acquired right of way, but the tit for tat kept both companies on edge regarding what the other was doing.

A. Regional Resentment toward the ORN and Portland

Regional shippers of agricultural and commercial goods resented the control of rates by the ORN and Portland. As mentioned in chapter I, in October 1881 Henry Villard spoke of the "benevolent monopoly" that he had created. In February 1883 the Walla Walla *Union* lauded Henry Villard in an editorial which concluded:

> When Mr. Villard, in one of his addresses, styled the O. R. & N. Co., 'a benevolent monopoly,' few had faith enough to believe that his company would ever do less than take from the producers and consumers, furnished with means of transportation by the company, 'what the freight will bear.' And yet within three years the company has expended many millions of dollars in increasing its capacity for business and reduced the freight charges on the products of the country three dollars and a half a ton. We challenge the production of a parallel instance.[1]

By early 1884 the perception of a benevolent monopoly was gone. The regional newspapers documented the dissatisfaction. There was some dissatisfaction with the NP, but most of the ire was directed at the ORN and Portland, and came predominately from south of the Snake River. After the NP established itself north of the Snake, criticism increased and the NP and the Great Northern, as well as the ORN, were targets.

In 1884 the Walla Walla *Union* claimed it cost five dollars less per ton to ship from Chicago to Portland and then back to Walla Walla than to ship directly to Walla Walla. In Colfax the *Gazette* printed a table of rates from Chicago to Portland comparing Chicago to Walla Walla to prove the point. Some examples show agricultural implements to Portland, $2.35, to Walla Walla, $2.85; boots and shoes, $5.00 and $6.10; and fancy goods, $10.00 and $11.10. The *Gazette* repeated a story from the Walla Walla *Journal* that the rate on a car load of flour from Walla Walla to Thompson Falls, Montana Territory, was $267; from Chicago, three times as far, the rate was $110.[2]

"Portland is seldom completely happy." So begins an editorial in the *Union* on June 7, 1884. "Heretofore it has been denied that Portland dealers had special contracts and claimed that they were all compelled to pay the regular published tariff rates. The complaints we have copied from the commercial paper proves the contrary to be true." Four and half months later, NP President Robert Harris in response to complaints of Portland merchants said, "It is absurd to suppose that I could have guaranteed Portland merchants rates so low as to enable them to compete with New York manufacturers. How could I know whether Portland could compete with New York?" Harris said he had been misquoted so as to imply that special low rates had been given to Portland.[3]

The *Union*, on January 24, 1885, noted that so far as the newspaper could determine new freight rates treated the interior and Portland equally. But the Portland *Journal of Commerce* complained that the rates threatened Portland as a wholesale center. To the *Union* this demonstrated that the old rates were arranged for the benefit of Portland. A week later after examining the new rates, the *Union* decided that the new rates were an improvement over the previous rates, but still discriminated in favor of Portland.[4]

The *Daily Journal* reported June 11, 1885, that Charles Francis Adams, UP president, said in Portland that no railroad should discriminate even if it makes a fortune doing so. He went on to say, "Therefore, it is not part of the policy of the Union Pacific, as now managed, to seek to build up Portland or other cities." The newspaper went on to ask why the railroad then charged 94 cents per hundred pounds more from Chicago to Walla Walla than it did to Portland. "If it is not to build up Portland at the expense of Walla Walla and other inland towns, it must be to enrich the Union Pacific by methods not approved by its president, or he does not mean what he says."[5]

The interior's complaints of high and discriminatory rates, as well as under-capacity for harvest shipments, went on for years.

B. The NP's Cascade Branch and the ORN Lease Negotiations

While not necessarily responsive to the complaints of their customers, the railroads sought to better their own situations by exploring various means of sharing revenue, leasing arrangements, and building new track. Even before the NP transcontinental line was completed and the Oregon Short Line (OSL), the UP line in Idaho, made a connection with the ORN at Huntington, Oregon, the railroads were considering a shared traffic contract. As early as January 13, 1883, Robert E. O'Brien, OT chief engineer and ORN assistant manager responded to a letter from NP Vice President Oakes regarding traffic relations of the ORN with the OSL/UP and the NP. He assumed that the ORN would be neutral with regard to through traffic to all points on the ORN west of Umatilla to the eastern termini of the UP and NP. He thought "pools" should be formed to "ensure & maintain harmony between the competing roads." A proposed "Portland Pool" would cover all traffic from and through Portland and west of Umatilla to the eastern termini of the UP and NP. Estimated traffic revenue of $1,800,000 in 1884 and $3,000,000 in 1888 (with two-thirds from freight) would be divided with half to the NP and UP, the other half to the ORN, with the latter credited with an extra 100 miles above actual distance. O'Brien concluded, "The whole matter requires considerable study." A traffic contract between the NP, ORN and UP, pertaining to the UP's share of the transcontinental traffic, dated February 23, 1883, was printed. Whether the agreement was actually implemented is unknown, though the NP approved a supplementary agreement regarding the Huntington connection in June 1884.[6] Those who shipped freight saw the printed contract as evidence that rates would remain uncompetitive.

The NP executive committee on August 15, 1883, authorized the modification of the Traffic Contract of October 20, 1880 by executing a Second Supplementary Traffic Contract with the ORN. The committee recognized that when the ORN made connection with the OSL, it would have about 411 miles of haul from Portland to Huntington, but only about 214 miles for interchange with the NP at Wallula. The purpose of the modification was "to induce [ORN] to interchange the larger part of its traffic to and from the East with [the NP] instead of with the Oregon Short Line and the Union Pacific companies." In general the inducement was to give the ORN a greater share of the earnings on traffic interchanged at Wallula. The new contract was to be dated July 1, 1883.[7]

With the prospect of a new eastern connection with the completion of the Union Pacific's Oregon Short Line, the ORN notified the NP January 31, 1884, that as of that date it would decline to allow both constructive mileage and the bonus for interchanged business given to the NP in the Traffic Contract of October 20, 1880. The advantages were given to acquire the NP right of way on the south bank of the Columbia River. Negotiations followed.[8]

Hedges thought that the ORN, with its monopoly to the coast and, in the near future, two connections to the east, it was in a superior bargaining position with respect to the NP. Asay does not share that view:

> It was far from certain, given the shoddy construction with which Villard had endowed the ORN, that the railroad could survive head to head competition with the Northern Pacific. It was also unclear whether Portland could survive the threat posed by Tacoma. The primary question facing ORN's new leadership at this critical point was whether ORN should forego independence and seek safe harbor with the NP, or if it should strike out in a new direction under the guidance of the expanding Union Pacific system. As it turned out, the desires of the City of Portland played a major role in shaping the outcome.

According to the *Oregonian*, March 14, 1884, the ORN earnings could not justify more than a 5 percent dividend on the stock, the branch lines were unprofitable, the river boats were run at a loss to keep out competitors, the boats on Puget Sound were too expensive to operate and there was the possibility that the Southern Pacific/Central Pacific would enter Portland and take some traffic.[9]

In the meantime, the NP continued work on the Cascade branch to Puget Sound. Portland interests and others lobbied Congress to deny the NP the land grant from the construction of the Cascade branch. Harris wrote March 7, 1884, that the immediate construction of the branch was so dependent on what Congress did that session he was unable to form an opinion on whether to proceed. The April 4 issue of the *Gazette* published an editorial from the Walla Walla *Union* which is representative of the interior sentiment toward Portland's actions:

> In the light shed by the recent actions and explanations of the railroad officials in regard to freight rates it is easy to see why the *Oregonian* urges the forfeiture of the grant for the Cascade branch. The new freight rates are declared by the railroad officials to have been devised and established in the interest of Portland and Portland alone. They are an attempt to force inhabitants of the interior to contribute to the wealth of the fresh water seaport. If the grant for the Cascade branch is declared forfeited the declaration will fasten the present freight rates on the interior for very many years. If the grant is extended the Northern Pacific will speedily build a road over the mountains to Puget Sound and become independent of the O. R. & N. Co.; and be placed in a condition to fix rates to the interior from the east and from the west.... The construction of a road over the Cascade range would deprive Portland of its monopoly, decrease its prosperity and diminish its wealth.[10]

In 1884 negotiations of a lease of the ORN began. They would continue for more than two years. The ORN executive committee, May 20, 1884, appointed ORN President Coolidge and William Endicott to negotiate a lease or traffic contract with the NP, UP or another corporation. On June 15 the NP board expressed the opinion that a lease of the ORN was desirable, but before agreeing to it, more information was needed on the liabilities and assets of the ORN. The ORN executive committee June 27 authorized the president to lease the line to the NP or make a traffic agreement with the NP on all but the future OSL connection. Suggested terms were: the ORN would complete the connection with the OSL, pay all unfunded debts, turn the property over free; the NP to pay all taxes and most rentals. Harris said that the 8 percent dividend that the NP would be obligated to guarantee was the equivalent of 10 percent when the "water" was taken into account. "Still I think the Northern Pacific would not lose anything the first five years, and I hope that business will be large enough after five years we would lose nothing at 8%." In Harris' opinion an advantage of the lease would be that the NP would get aid from both Oregon and Washington in holding the land grant for the Cascade branch.[11]

On July 10 the ORN executive committee recommended modifications in the proposed lease to the NP. At that same meeting President T. J. Coolidge presented his letter of resignation which included a draft recommendation of a traffic contract with the NP. The draft said that the NP would not construct the Cascade branch and all Puget Sound traffic would be routed via Portland on the ORN. As Asay says, these conditions were unlikely to be agreed to by the NP; "Coolidge was out of his element in these negotiations." The directors accepted the resignation on July 17 and elected Elijah Smith president. Smith, a Boston financier and early investor in ORN, who was known as the "Prophet," slowed down negotiations to await completion of the OSL connection and because ORN's earnings were not strong enough to make a higher rental price attractive. Smith later also became president of the OT. For both positions his goals were to look after the OT's substantial investments in the NP and ORN and to insure that the NP would use the ORN line to Portland rather than a line to Puget Sound.[12]

On July 25 the *Gazette* reported that NP President Harris informed an *Oregonian* reporter that the NP would take over the ORN the latter part of August by means of a 99-year lease. He said that the lease would have no effect on the building of the Cascade branch. July 26 the *Union* reported that Elijah Smith said that the ORN directors had decided to lease the company to the NP. It was the newspaper's opinion that the lease would result in the Texas Ferry line not being constructed, but it would open up Puget Sound to interior grain. The *Union* claimed that as long as Villard was in control freight rates did not discriminate in favor of Portland, but once he lost control the rates were changed in March and Walla Walla merchants, who had primarily purchased from Chicago, New York, and other eastern markets, were forced "to go to the small semi-wholesale houses in Portland for supplies.... We are certain that if the discriminating freight rates are abolished and the freight and regulation in force prior to March last restored, the happiness and prosperity of the people will be very materially increased, enemies will be converted into active friends and the income of the Northern Pacific will be greatly enhanced." Two weeks later the *Union* said, "When freight rates are arranged so that Walla Walla and other points can trade with St. Paul upon the same terms that Portland does there will be ample cause for rejoicing by the merchants and consumers of Eastern Washington. Speed the day."[13]

On July 29 Harris telegraphed directors J. P. Morgan, B. P. Cheney, and F. Billings that after spending 10 days on the line, he was satisfied that it was in the best interest of both parties that the lease as proposed be arranged. The NP board on September 9, 1884, received the negotiating committee's draft agreement with the ORN. The board resolved that the railroad could not pay the interest rates in the draft. The subject was referred back to the committee.[14]

Elijah Smith sought to divert the NP from building the Cascade branch. The lease of the ORN to the NP, with the NP guaranteeing fixed dividends on ORN stock, would give the NP an incentive not to harm the ORN. Smith also pointed out that with the OT having about 200,000 shares of common and preferred NP stock, it should be represented on the NP board by three directors, Smith and two others. In the election of NP directors on September 18, Harris and C. B. Wright blocked Smith's attempt to gain representation on the NP board. Smith having failed to gain sufficient control to stop the NP from building the Cascade branch, sought other means.[15]

The *Union* reported that the NP directors meeting October 2 did not take up the lease; Oakes said there was no agreement on terms and the desire of some ORN officers and stockholders to operate the road independently. Because of the tripartite agreement among the NP, UP, and ORN to maintain rates and division of the business equitable and just to all parties, the importance of the lease of the ORN "was greatly exaggerated." Should either the NP or UP lease the line they would have to carry out the tripartite agreement. "The day for disregarding or ignoring contracts of this kind is passed." A broker identified with the NP said that NP officials had been considering whether it was worthwhile to combat the UP. If the UP leased the ORN, "you will see a new tack taken, Portland will be, in effect, abandoned by the prompt completion of the [Cascade] line." Oakes said the broker "is evidently a well-informed source." Oakes said that so far as the NP was concerned it contemplated using the track from Wallula to Portland.[16]

Harris wrote Cheney October 24 that his attempts to take up the lease with Smith had come to nothing. The ORN sought to defer the matter claiming that future earnings of the ORN would be better; they "seemed to expect much greater results from the connection with the OSL (Oregon Short Line) than we think there is any ground for." Harris had been advised that a switch back over the Cascades was practicable pending completion of the tunnel. This would enable the NP to complete the road to Puget Sound in 1885, which would be an important factor in dealing with the ORN lease. "Without doubt some of the O.R. & N. people may think that the N.P. can be greatly embarrassed by the lack of hearty cooperation with us—which feeling if it exists will give way when they see we can get beyond their control in so short a time." Both the NP and ORN were in no hurry regarding the lease.[17]

Oakes had written Harris October 4, 1884, that since the ORN-OSL connection was nearing completion, thought should be given to a pooling contract which would enable rates to be maintained and a proper division made of the business on a money basis. The same day Harris wrote UP President Charles Francis Adams Jr. suggesting that the NP and UP agree to a division of the west bound business. Otherwise the UP (and presumably the NP) would be forced to cut rates on west bound business to get a corresponding proportion of the east bound business off the ORN. He pointed out that the ORN may wish to show the NP that it needed to lease the ORN to protect its interchange at Wallula from ORN favoring the

UP interchange at Huntington. Harris wrote Oakes that he had an interview with Adams, "and I think we will find the U.P. disposed to consider matters fairly." A pooling agreement was signed by the UP, OSL, and NP April 14, 1885, and was effective as of December 1, 1884.[18]

The last spike was driven connecting the ORN with the OSL at Huntington, Oregon, on November 25, 1884. The ORN began service to Huntington December 1. The ORN was no longer dependent on the NP for an eastern connection, but the NP was still dependent on the ORN connection at Wallula to Portland and a ferry across the Columbia River to its Tacoma line.[19]

The *Gazette* had long opposed abandoning the west end of the C&P and using the Texas Ferry route. But now that the ORN had connection with the Oregon Short Line the objection became "groundless. In fact, the anticipation that such a course on the part of the O. R. & N. would force the N. P. to build into the Palouse country is a strong reason why the people of this section should favor the move. We want opposition and strife between the railroad companies and the country, tapped by as many roads as possible." The *Union* responded to the *Gazette* editorial, "it is very plain that the ORN will, in self defense, be compelled to take up the track from Palouse Junction to Willow creek and connect the Palouse system with the main line of their road at Texas Ferry."[20]

There was increasing interest in the Walla Walla area to break the ORN monopoly by building a connection with the NP at Wallula or Ainsworth. In mid-January 1885, Harris told its advocates that the NP would not build the line. He concluded in one letter, "I feel very confident that by the time the Cascade Branch is completed there will be found a way for the people of your section of the Territory to transact their business with the Sound by the direct Road without building another Road from Walla Walla to the Columbia River. When that time comes, and no other way is found, will it not be then early enough to build the other Road?"[21]

The NP directors February 19 agreed to enter into a lease of the ORN for 999 years, and would pay, in addition to fixed charges, dividends of 5 percent for three years and 6 percent thereafter on the $24,000,000 of the capital stock of the ORN. The agreement was contingent on verifying the ORN business and income. The ORN had proposed that the NP pay interest on the ORN bonds plus a 6 percent dividend on the ORN stock the first year, 7 percent the second year, and 8 percent thereafter. The ORN did not immediately respond.[22]

In March 1885 UP President Adams wrote Harris that Elijah Smith had come to see him about making a deal if the NP did not. Adams told Smith that he was ready to come in as a joint party under any arrangement that Har-

NP engine No. 2, at Troy in 1908. This and one other Class M, 2-10-0, were built by Baldwin in 1886 for use on the temporary switchback line over Stampede Pass. After the Stamped Pass tunnel was completed the NP used them on other locations of steep grades requiring slow speeds. The 2.2 to 2.4 percent grade from Kendrick to Howell fit those requirements. No. 2 was scrapped in 1933 (Schrenk & Frey 2013, 67-70, 225). *Herb V. Banks Photographer, R. V. Nixon Collection RVN06905, Museum of the Rockies, Montana State University.*

ris would make. Adams wrote, "Under no circumstances, I assured him, would we enter into any agreement except with a distinct understanding that the Northern Pacific could come into it on practically equal terms, and those terms the Northern Pacific must have assented to."[23]

At an April 29 meeting of representatives of the UP, ORN, and NP, the NP asked for a positive response to the NP's proposal of February 19. Smith responded May 5 that the ORN board would not approve the NP's proposal for a lease on the basis of 5 percent for three years and 6 percent thereafter on the capital stock of the ORN. Smith informed Harris that the ORN would accept a joint NP-UP lease on the basis of 5 percent for one year and 6 percent thereafter, and that after five years the ORN would receive 7 percent, if earned. On May 21 the NP board of directors by a divided vote (Wright and Bullitt against) agreed to a joint lease of the ORN for 5 percent for three years and 6 percent thereafter provided that the ORN was responsible for all floating debt, suits, claims, and that the ORN would use its Palouse and Baker City lands and Villard's New York house to settle those responsibilities and that the fixed charges would not exceed the amount (not stated in the resolution) in the negotiating committee report.[24]

At a May 28, 1885, conference between Sidney Dillon, former president of the UP, ORN and OT President Elijah Smith, Billings, and Harris agreed to recommend a joint lease. The next day Dillon telegraphed Adams,

> Lease agreed upon yesterday, substantially as follows: Rental 5 for 3 years, and 6 thereafter, to commence July 1st if practicable; lessee to receive all assets of every kind including lands; Villard property, and interest in hotel at Portland; $1,000,000 of 5% bonds to be set aside to pay specified indebtedness, amounting to about $750,000. Any surplus of bonds to be returned. Any other claims, if any, to be paid by lessee out of the rental due O. R. & N. Co. I think this is a good arrangement.

According to Asay, minor details needed to be worked out; one was Smith's insistence, likely forced by the Portland directors, that the NP not construct the Cascade branch. A story in the Philadelphia *Press*, May 30, said that neither the UP or ORN were legally capable of entering into such a lease. This and other reports from Philadelphia were likely inspired by C. B. Wright, who owned property in Tacoma, for the purpose of getting better terms or derailing the lease entirely. But a New York story of May 31 said, "The joint lease of the O. R. & N. properties is acknowledged by Union Pacific officials to [have] been consummated."[25]

Harris told Cheney June 6 that to protect the NP, if the UP for whatever reason did not pay its share, the lease should provide that each party was responsible for only one half of the payments. The NP board June 18 approved a memorandum on the lease as it appeared to settle the outstanding issues. The *Union* quoted the Portland *Journal of Commerce*:

> [T]here is no doubt that the general effect of this lease will be in favor of Portland. The only real harm which the Northern Pacific could do this neighborhood was the building of the Cascade branch. This difficulty is now removed, as, under the circumstances, the enormous expenditure for this work would be unnecessary and unwise. The people of the Yakima valley, however, may thank their stars that this lease and the cessation of construction has not occurred sooner. The subject has been in the balance just long enough to enable the completion of the road into the rich country about Yakima City and Ellensburg, and the stoppage of construction at these points make them supply depots for interior Washington for an indefinite time to come.

From St. Paul June 23 Harris was quoted as saying the lease was "virtually decided upon" and the report that the ORN was opposed was "without foundation." According to Harris the ORN declined to make a lease with the NP alone because of a threat of an independent line connecting the UP to Portland. Harris went on to say that the lease would not affect the building of the Cascade branch.[26]

Under the lead "A Death Warrant," the Walla Walla *Union* on June 27 offered a long editorial on the joint lease:

> No one can see anything but harm for the Inland Empire in the lines of the lease. Of course it will be necessary for the leasing companies to make their leased property pay the rent, and to that end the present system of low rates from the East to Portland and high rates to all inland places will be continued...it is evident from the utterances of the *Oregonian*, which seems to speak by authority, that the rates on the products of the country will be maintained and arranged in such a manner that they must seek a market by way of Portland, or, in the language of a railroad official, "rot on the farms." The organ of Portland declares:
>
> "The policy of the lessees must of necessity by what railroad men call a 'rail policy,'.... It will...prevent the proposed transportation of wheat over the Northern Pacific for water shipment at Duluth, for the Union Pacific, having no water termination at its eastern end, will demand that the wheat of our 'inland empire' by shipped west by the 'mutual line,' and it will have the power to enforce this demand."

The Walla Walla *Daily Journal* had a different view:

> It is a mistaken idea...that Portland railroad influence is in favor of discriminating rates, while the eastern stockholders would make all our transportation lines benevolent monopolies but for the malign influence of wicked partners out west. The truth is, that the reduction of one dollar per ton on wheat last year was made by the Portland directors, in opposition to the wishes of the eastern directors, and that Portland influence is now in favor of a further reduction and unanimously in favor of putting flour on the same schedule rates with wheat. The eastern idea is to earn dividends; the western idea to increase value through a liberal policy of development.[27]

The *New York Times* reported that C. B. Wright July 3 sent a circular letter marked "confidential" asking for proxies in favor of himself or Robert Harris to be voted at the stockholders meeting in September. Wright was opposed to the lease, partly because the guaranteed payments would make the NP common and preferred stock secondary to the payment of interest on the ORN stocks and bonds. The *Times* concluded, "It is surmised that Wright is opposed to the NP entering into such a lease individually or jointly, because it would possibly retard the completion of the Cascade branch, in the building of which he is personally interested."[28]

Harris had a lease drawn up and presented it to the NP board July 23, 1885. A resolution approving the proposed lease was adopted by a vote of 8 to 2. Wright and Bullitt again voted against the lease. The next day Harris sent Adams and Smith copies of the lease approved by the board and asked for the UP's and ORN's early approval. In an interview by a St. Paul *Pioneer Press* reporter in late July, ORN President Smith said that the lease had not been approved. He didn't think the ORN would gain much from the lease, but the lease was a good idea because it would serve to stop railroad building to the coast by the NP and UP.[29]

At the next meeting of the board, August 20, Harris read letters from Smith and Adams objecting to provisions of the joint lease. On September 1, 1885, the *Journal* reported that ORN President Smith was lukewarm to the lease and dissatisfied with the terms. On the 5th the *Union* in an editorial, "That Objectionable Lease," noted that based on a $25,000,000 valuation of the ORN, the lessees would pay an annual rental of $1,200,000 the first three years and $1,440,000 for the remaining 996 years of the lease. Dorsey Baker, the early railroad builder in Walla Walla, and a large holder of NP stock, instructed his proxy to vote against the lease and sent a strong argument against the lease to the stockholders' meeting. The Portland holders of NP stock favored the lease because it would delay, if not prevent, the completion of the Cascade branch.[30]

The *Times* on September 16, the day before the NP directors' meeting, said that there were two factions competing on the board. The followers of Brayton Ives and J. P. Morgan favored the completion of the Cascade branch and the reelection of Harris as president. Elijah Smith and the followers of Billings favored the lease of the ORN and a new president. At the directors meeting, with Oakes voting no, the board voted to receive a letter from Elijah Smith, as president of the OT rather than ORN: "That in view of the large holding of stock in the Northern Pacific Railroad company by this Company, and with the belief of the managers that the prosecution of the work on the Cascade Branch so called is unwise and unnecessary, and likely to prove disastrous to the Northern Pacific R. R. Cos. Securities, the President is hereby authorized and directed to express the views of this Company to the officers of the Northern Pacific Company, and to protest against the further progress of the work at the present time." The *Times* reported that Smith gave up his battle when he could not get a court order against Morgan voting 120,000 shares of NP stock held in trust for the OT. Smith wrote a similar letter to Villard on November 9 that the directors of the NP were "jeopardizing the stocks and bonds of [the] company in pursuing an enterprise and scheme which inures to their private interests at Tacoma." Hedges adds that Smith would have been more correct if he had said the stocks and bonds of the OT and ORN. Smith considered seeking an injunction against the letting of contracts for the Cascade branch, but was advised against it.[31]

On October 31 Harris wrote Adams that nothing was done about the lease at the last board meeting, because "there was nothing to do except to wait for any communication the [ORN] might make." Adams wrote Harris, November 24, 1885, "I do not believe in fighting, I do not believe in wasteful construction. I do not believe in destroying business by foolish competition. We are coming to all these things with considerable rapidity." The *West Shore*, December 1885, commented, "That the spectacle presented of the O. R. & N. Co. and Northern Pacific surveying rival lines into the Palouse country is of itself a sufficient evidence that the long-talked-of lease will not be made." The *Northwest Magazine*, the same month, saw the joint lease negotiations collapsing as the ORN was showing more vigor by branch line building and possibly cutting the C&P off from its connection with the NP. The completion of the Cascade branch was seen as necessary for the well-being of the NP.[32]

In 1886 the ORN was receiving 28 cents per hundred pounds on the 213 miles from Wallula to Portland on through freight from Chicago, while the NP was receiving the same amount on the 1,699 miles from St. Paul to Wallula. If the NP didn't comply with the ORN it would divert eastward traffic to the UP. Hedges observed, "Whatever chance...the Northern Pacific would forego the right of building the [Cascade] branch was destroyed by the growing selfishness of the Oregon Company. In the absence of a harmonizing leadership, old rivalries reasserted themselves, and the company in control of the Columbia gateway, endeavoring to capitalize on a moment of advantage, helped to keep alive the perennially disturbing problem of Puget Sound competition."[33]

By January 1886 Smith was resigned to the NP under Harris and Wright building the Cascade branch. He wrote Villard January 22 that the OT had two courses of action, secure control of the NP or sell out and tie the ORN to the UP. Under the head line "Glorious News" the Walla Walla *Union* in late January reported that the contract for the Cascade tunnel had been let to Nelson Bennett. While the tunnel was under construction a switchback would be built and grain would move to Tacoma before December 1. The *Gazette,* quoting an unnamed Wall Street man, said that the decision to build the tunnel "was in the nature of a death warrant, and the last of the Villard. They staved off letting the contracts as long as they could, to save the Oregon Railway and Navigation, but the influences of the board are dead against them nowadays." The *Union* reported on March 6 that the NP directors were divided 11–2 on letting the tunnel contract. The two negative votes were those of the OT and ORN directors.[34]

In May 1886 there was an attempt to remove Elijah Smith as president of both the ORN and OT by OT and NP director Brayton Ives. A group of UP stockholders, seeing advantage in the OT charter for branch line construction, formed a pool to gain control of the OT to prevent a possible attempt by the NP to gain control of the ORN through the OT. As a result UP President Adams obtained Smith's agreement that the UP would be represented on the boards of the OT and ORN, and that the ORN would be leased exclusively to the UP. UP representatives were placed on the boards of both the ORN and OT. Adams saw an alliance with the NP giving way to an alliance with the ORN. Adams wrote his assistant, "I regard it myself as one of the most significant developments that have taken place since I have been in control." Villard's associate Artemas Holmes told him that "Ives lost his courage" and that Villard could have won it for Ives. Harris wrote June 10, 1886, that the executive committee had declined to authorize the proposed lease and that he was unable to resume negotiations unless instructed by the committee.[35]

On June 19 the *Union* saw the re-election of Elijah Smith as the president of the OT as the death of the NP lease of the ORN. "We are glad Smith triumphs." The *Gazette* saw things somewhat differently. It asked June 18 "in whose interest was it to delay the Cascade Branch?" It claimed that the ORN made annually $2,000,000 which should be in the pockets of the producers. "With the completion of the Cascade branch they will lose the greater part of this great fortune, and our people will reap the benefit." The *Gazette* favored the NP leasing the ORN, which it thought was a forgone conclusion. "In such a case the benefits accruing to this country will be large."[36]

Portland interests and others had lobbied Congress to seek forfeiture of the NP land grant on the ground that it had failed to complete all its chartered lines. The *Journal* quoted the St. Paul *Pioneer Press,* that NP officials had said that no matter what Congress did the Cascade branch would neither be abandoned nor delayed. The *Gazette* saw things differently. It quoted a telegram from Harris to Oakes stating that if the forfeiture became law "the company will have no choice" but to stop work. The *Gazette* concluded, "And this is the way forfeiture is to benefit the people of eastern Washington." The *Union* had a similar view. The next week it reported that at the urging of the *Oregonian,* the ORN, and the OSL, the Portland Board of Trade on June 29 expunged a June 24 resolution opposing the forfeiture. The editor believed for some time that Portland was an enemy of the Cascade branch and supported it only when its construction was in the future. The editor was pleased that Portland had shown its true nature.[37]

Adams wrote G. M. Dodge, September 2, 1886, asking him how he thought the UP should direct its development. On October 27 Dodge responded that to give the UP a line of its own to the Pacific coast it should gain control of the ORN either by purchase or lease. If there was no agreement with the ORN, then the UP should immediately standard gauge the Utah Northern, build to Lewiston and down the north bank of the Columbia River. He concluded by saying that the development of the territory west of the Rocky Mountains "should be intelligently handled by the U.P. and N.P. roads under agreements as to territory so that any competing lines should be avoided and the capital planted in the country made to feed continuously both lines of Road east and west."[38]

At the NP board meeting, November 18, 1886, Harris reported that the committee on relations with ORN had made progress on a lease. Before accepting the report Director Billings said while he opposed the original lease he was now strongly in favor of a joint lease: "it would be a grievous mistake on the part of the Northern Pacific directors, and one to result in great injury to the stockholders, to allow the control of the [ORN] company's lines to be held solely by the Union Pacific company." Five other directors indicated their support for the joint lease. The *Railroad Gazette* reported November 19 that the UP was willing to meet the ORN's insistence on 6 percent on the stock, but that the NP refused to give more than 5 percent.[39]

In an attempt to avoid a rate war, UP President Adams discussed a joint lease with Harris November 26. Harris wrote Adams on the 27th referring to the conversation the day before regarding NP participation in the proposed contract between the UP and the ORN on the basis of a guarantee by the UP of the fixed charges and 6 percent on the capital stock of the ORN. He wanted to restate the basis of the participation of the NP:

> That the Northern Pacific lease to the Union Pacific the right of trackage on its road between Portland and Tacoma at three per cent. on an agreed valuation of that piece of road: that the O. R. & N. lease to the Northern Pacific the Columbia and Palouse road, at six per cent on an agreed valuation of it: that the O. R. & N. withdraw from the country north of the Snake River: that the Northern Pacific keep out of the territory south the Snake.

The remainder of the response concerned the division of the business to and from north and south of the Snake River and other details never adopted and which Adams objected to on the 30th. Adams did not recall agreeing that all the business between north of the Snake and the Sound should be exclusively NP. His recollection was that business would be free to go to the Sound or Portland as might be its interest. He also did not recall that business between points on the ORN and the East should be pooled equally. If the NP had the territory north of the Snake exclusively and then the business south of the Snake was to be pooled, "it would seem to me that the contract would resemble a jug with three handles, of which the Northern Pacific grasped two, while the Union Pacific had a feeble hold on one." He dared not present these terms to the UP directors. Nevertheless he did not want to shut the door to further discussion.[40]

On December 2 Elijah Smith wrote Prescott, enclosing a copy of a letter, probably that of the 27th from Harris to Adams. Smith summarized the Harris letter and wrote,

> I hardly think the territory division will be agreed to by the Union Pacific. I am very sure that it will not by this company. The territory north of Snake River includes the Palouse country, the Coeur d'Alene mines, the vast agricultural country in the great bend of the Columbia, possible extension and development of the Kootenai country, the opening of the Colville and Moses reservations and all the Yakima and Kittitas valleys, whatever they may amount to. This particular territory is one that will in the near future absorb the largest portion of the emigrations and will be the most rapidly developed. The country south of Snake River, along the Walla Walla River and the Pass of the Blue Mountains, is at present very largely in a state of cultivation, and while we have not by any means obtained the maximum business that could be expected from this country, yet its growth in proportion to the territory north of Snake River must be very small percentage.

Smith wrote Adams not to surrender the Palouse so easily because it was "worth vastly more for future development than the Walla Walla country."[41]

In his response to Adams, Harris attempted to clarify his suggestions regarding pooling of traffic and earnings. He defended his plan, "It seems to me the plan is a very fair one to both Co.s. provided both Companies participate in the guarantee." Nevertheless, at this point the issue of pooling was dropped because the Interstate Commerce Act of 1887 outlawed pooling. The central issue of discussions became the division of territory north and south of the Snake River which "encountered the determined, even violent, opposition of business men of Portland and western Oregon" because of the potential loss of the Palouse and access to the Coeur d'Alene mining district. Those south of the Snake were also opposed because there was no prospect of relief from ORN freight rates.[42]

On December 16, 1886, the NP committee on relations with ORN reported to the NP directors that it had met with representatives of the ORN on November 23 to consider NP participation in a lease already agreed to by the ORN and UP, the terms of which were a guaranteed payment of an amount equal to the fixed charges of the ORN and 6 percent per year on the ORN capital stock; the ORN would retain assets amounting to approximately $1 million. Smith said that the ORN was willing for the NP's joint participation in the contract and that he would use his influence to procure the consent of the UP if the NP desired to make such an arrangement. Following a general debate on a 6–5 vote the NP directors approved a joint lease or traffic contract "substantially in accordance with the letter of President Harris of Nov. 27th...and that the executive Officers of the Company be directed to ascertain if this be practicable and report to the Board."[43]

On December 31, 1886, Harris responded to Adam's letter of the 29th (which has not been found) on the proposed lease of the ORN. With a couple of exceptions he agreed to the contents. On the same date, Harris wrote August Belmont, "The proposed division of territory does not vary much from what I suggested at our former conference and is a division that I think the Northern Pacific could accept." He also solicited the views of Oakes on Adams' letter. Oakes thought the proposed terms were open to criticism on a number of grounds. His main argument against the lease was that the NP ought not enter into a supplemental agreement with the UP, but "should participate in the lease upon equal terms in every respect."[44]

The NP directors met January 6, 1887, to receive a letter from Belmont stating that while he favored the lease, he thought it advisable to investigate the ORN's assets. Harris reported on conferences with UP officials. The basis for the lease should be that the NP would not in any case be responsible for more than one-half of the rental and that division of the business be based on north and south of the Snake River, with the NP having the former and the ORN the latter. Harris concluded his report by saying that he thought the rental was "acceptable" and the proposed division of the traffic was "reasonable and fair." Billings read a letter from Oakes who examined the earnings of the ORN and concluded that the railroad was profitable and probably could be made more profitable, but the river and Puget Sound maritime business earnings were questionable. A lengthy assessment by Brookman on the value of the ORN was read to the board (not placed in the minutes until January 27). He found numerous things "misleading" in the reports of the company including charging to construction operating costs and "paying dividends not earned." He did not think that when the Cascade branch was completed that the ORN would be able to charge the current rates and the importance of Portland would decline as a shipping point. Brookman challenged the view that the NP-UP could operate the ORN at less cost. "Is it possible, when as is evident, a respectable portion of the cost of operation is now charged to construction account?" If the UP leases the ORN, "The very weight of its obligations will naturally make them anxious to deal fairly with us; but if not we will be in a position to compete with them." He concluded, "The increased tonnage of the territory now tributary to the [ORN] will be more than taken by the Northern Pacific and other competing lines." Billings moved that the board request the executive officers continue to negotiate a lease. A recess was taken before voting. The motion was defeated; Billings, Hall, and Stackpole voted yes, and Wright, Ives, Brookman, Fargo, and Bullitt voted no. The board then considered a resolution that it was not "expedient" for the NP to participate in a joint lease, but negotiations should continue with the UP "for the purpose of securing an equitable division of traffic and a continuation of harmonious relations." The resolution passed by the same division of the members as the preceding motion. Harris had been at the meeting prior to the recess, but did not vote on either resolution. Harris, Belmont, and Cheney had voted in favor of continued negotiations at the December 16 meeting of the board. If they had voted, it is possible that negotiations on the lease would have continued.[45]

Harris wrote Adams on the 7th reporting the board's decision not to enter into the lease, but to continue discussions on a division of the traffic. Harris indicated his desire to meet with Adams once the UP had taken possession of the ORN. He concluded, "Our views are so nearly alike in the matter, that I do not anticipate any difficulty in coming to an arrangement that will be satisfactory to both." On the 21st Adams wrote Elijah Smith, "All negotiations with the Northern Pacific are off. They will remain off until your company and this company tie up. After we are tied up it will be ample time to talk with the Northern Pacific people." In the meantime the press had many rumors as to what was happening.[46]

C. Oregon Railway & Navigation Co. Leased to the Union Pacific

The UP and the ORN were naturally drawn together by the former's need to assure itself of access to the Pacific Coast and the latter's need to protect itself in competition with the NP's Cascade branch. During the 1886 negotiations on the joint lease, Harris confronted Adams with the 1880 traffic contract. Adams came to understand that the traffic contract made the ORN at the mercy of the NP once the Cascade branch was completed. Adams wrote to an associate October 15, 1886, "If my understanding of this contract is correct, you will see at once that the Navigation Company must break it." Adams wrote Sidney Dillon on November 16 that agreement had been reached with the ORN,

> the Oregon Short Line is to lease the Navigation Company, at its fixed charges and six per cent on its stock; the Navigation Company binding itself to construct as large an amount of railroad as the [UP] shall require...in Idaho, eastern Oregon, and, if necessary, in Washington.... The Short Line system will thus receive complete development at a very low cost, as this additional road can be built on five per cent bonds sold at par, and consequently the fixed charges upon it will not exceed $750 per mile per annum, instead of $1500 which we pay on the Oregon Short Line.

The lease to the Oregon Short Line (OSL) was to avoid legal constraints on the UP. The UP directors approved the lease December 15, 1886. A Walla Walla *Journal* correspond had earlier commented that, "The greater part of our people feared only evil from a joint lease..." but a lease to the UP alone would encourage competition in eastern Washington.[47]

The ORN executive committee received a draft lease March 14, 1887. Elijah Smith wrote the 21st:

> I want them [ORN Executive Committee] to vote that if Union Pacific are not prepared to present to the O.R.N. Lease to their Annual Meeting with President's and Directors' recommendation, we may as well call it off.
>
> J. J. Hill is here and I have had correspondence with him and while I would only take his Road if we can get it because we cannot button up the Union Pacific, I would rather open negotiations with him than to await the results of the Investigating Committee. If it is a good thing to do for the two properties, let us do it and face the music and fight the next step when we have to take it. We cannot take but one step at a time and if we keep looking ahead and try to consider what difficulties will occur if we take the first one we will make but slow progress. Matters have assumed such shape now that we cannot wait.
>
> The Northern Pacific have decided to build an extension of their Spokane and Palouse branch in the direction of Lewiston and Harris stated to his board that it was in harmony with the UP and Mr. Adams if they took the O. R. & N. property. If they go ahead with it we must build some Branches and Extensions; and if the Union Pacific take the Road and Property they should properly direct this business, and I want them to get into position to do so, or, else give up the matter and let us go it on our own hook, or with other parties. The O. R. & N. and O. & T. people will insist on soon coming to a crisis. They have... got an idea that Adams is lacking in courage to come to a head. I don't agree with them, I believe he wants the Lease because he believes they ought have it and I don't believe when it comes to the point he will hesitate, but I agree with our people that he ought now to be prepared to present it and recommend it at his annual meeting or drop it, in fact matters are in such shape now as to compel us to take that Position.[48]

The ORN executive committee May 10, 1887, approved a 99-year lease dated January 1, 1887, but entered into on April 25 in New York. The lease was signed by Adams for the OSL, Dillon for the UP, former Oregon Governor Hawley for the ORN, and Elijah Smith for the OT. The lease recognized that the ORN operated and owned substantially all the stock and bonds of the C&P. The ORN was allowed to issue 5 percent bonds to pay for 600 miles of branch lines in Washington, Oregon, and Idaho, not to exceed $25,000 per mile. The OSL was to pay the ORN $1,440,000 per year, 6 percent on the $24,000,000 shares of the ORN, the cost of certain obligations of the ORN, and the cost for its operation. The OSL and UP, with the consent of the ORN, at their discretion, could enter into any agreement not inconsistent with the terms of the lease with the NP or any other person or corporation. There had been a question whether the ORN could make the lease under Oregon law. On February 10, 1887, the Oregon Legislature adopted an amendment allowing the lease. The U.S. Congress soon after allowed the lease. In February 1888 the Oregon Legislature enacted a statute forbidding the leasing of parallel or competing lines. The Cascade branch of the NP fell under this provision.[49]

Interior newspapers were optimistic about the future now that the UP controlled the ORN. Portland and ORN creditors and stockholders were pleased with the lease. But the UP was obligated to pay over $2.2 million annually for the lease and interest. According to Asay, "Consequently, the UP could ill afford any serious head-to-head competition with the NP for wheat and other business in eastern Oregon and Washington. Yet that was exactly what the NP had in mind." The payments were an important contribution to the bankruptcy of the UP in 1893.[50]

The NP Annual Report, September 15, 1887, took note of the lease of the ORN to the UP.

> The first effect of this change is naturally a loss to the Northern Pacific of some portion of its Portland business, and also of its California business formerly received by the steamships of the O. R. & N. Co. We are also threatened with invasion by the Union Pacific of that part of the productive territory north of the Snake River, now tributary to the Northern Pacific Road, and which would be exclusively in our traffic belt had it not been for the apparent mistake of transferring four years ago the Northern Pacific interest in the Columbia and Palouse Railroad to the O. R. & N. Co. In case such an invasion is made, the Northern Pacific Company should be able to more than compensate for any loss of traffic which may result, by throwing branches into the highly fertile [lands] south of the Snake River now exclusively occupied by the Union Pacific.[51]

Meanwhile unhappiness with the ORN south of the Snake River persisted. Walla Walla continued to seek a direct connection with the NP. Hope raised when the Oregon & Washington Territory Railroad (OWT) was incorporated in Oregon, March 4, 1886, for the purpose of building a railroad from Pendleton to Wallula. On November 8, 1886, Harris wrote that whether the system would be in concert with the NP depended on the new company building where the NP preferred. On May 9, 1887, Harris wrote Oakes that he thought it "very desirable" that the NP gain control of the OWT. "On what terms could it be acquired." In the same month arrangements were made with NP director C. B. Wright and his Philadelphia business associates for the issuing of OWT bonds. Supplementary charters authorized a line from Wallula to Dayton via Walla Walla and other branch lines. Construction began by George W. Hunt May 20 at Wallula toward Pendleton. Hunt, who became manager of the OWT, built 163 miles of road in Umatilla County, Oregon, and Walla Walla and Columbia Counties in Washington between May 1887 and July 1889. Wright's involvement and suspicion that the NP was supporting the OWT's invasion of what had been exclusively ORN territory darkened subsequent negotiations with the ORN/UP.[52]

In the meantime the NP began construction of the Spokane & Palouse into the heart of the Palouse. Writing Oakes from Palouse Junction, July 1886, the NP associated writer and publisher, Eugene V. Smalley, said,

> Prescott says the building of our Palouse Line is a violation of the old Villard agreement that the traffic of Washington belongs to the O.R. & N., that an outside company can be organized to build branches for the O. R. & N. as well as one for the N.P.; that if the N.P. builds to the Coeur d'Alene mines, there will be two roads there; that there may be an O. R. & N. line to Spokane Falls; that the Moscow Branch will go on to the Potlatch Country & e. These are, I presume Elijah Smith's views; as also some talk about the O. R. & N. postponing dividends for a year or two, if company to fight the N.P.[53]

Further attempts to negotiate a consolidation of railroads in eastern Washington are described in chapter VIII.

The Spokane & Palouse Begins Construction: Marshall to Belmont, 1886–87

Bids for constructing 43 miles from Marshall were received in early April 1886. Nelson Bennett's bid of $82,389 for grading, track laying and surfacing, although not the lowest, was accepted and the contract was drawn up April 9. S&P President A. M. Cannon explained the award to NP President Harris on April 12,

> While Mr. Bennett was some fourteen hundred dollars higher than the lowest bidder, we [Cannon and NP Chief Engineer Adna Anderson] felt that he was best able to accomplish the work, within the short time at our disposal, to enable us to take out the coming crop; his entire outfit being close at hand [on the Cascade branch contract], his financial responsibility being unquestioned, and, furthermore, he being the only bidder who undertook to do the work upon all specifications—thus avoiding all excuse (by reason of the possible non-performances of others), for the non-completion of the work by the time specified. The time set for the completion of the contract is August 1st.[1]

The *Gazette* noted that Marshall was incorporated by the town site company. "The building of the Spokane & Palouse railroad will generate quite a boom at Marshall." ORN President Elijah Smith was informed that on the 16th Nelson Bennett moved his men from the Cascade Tunnel to Spokane Falls. S&P Engineer-in-Charge Paul F. Mohr wrote Anderson that Bennett commenced grading on the 20th and work would be underway all along the line when additional men arrived.[2]

NP Assistant General Manager J. M. Buckley forwarded Harris a January letter that claimed a survey showed that a route from Cheney, approximately four miles southwest of Marshall on the NP mainline, into the Palouse was shorter and less costly to build and operate than from other locations. Harris wrote Anderson on April 3 quoting at length a letter boosting Cheney and offering several reasons for changing the route. It claimed a line from Farmington via Cheney to the Grand Coulee of the Columbia, about 120 miles, had only a 260 foot elevation variation in the whole distance. Marshall was not a suitable location to begin the S&P because it was 300 feet below Cheney and below the agricultural country. Freight from the S&P to Tacoma would have to be doubled from Marshall to Cheney; from Cheney the line would be 2.5 to 5 miles shorter. And the line at Cheney would create a sale of $5000 worth of NP lots in Cheney. Harris asked Anderson, "Do you know of anything to change your views as heretofore expressed that 'Marshall was the best point, all things considered, for the northern terminus of the Spokane & Palouse Road rather than Cheney?'" Mohr wrote Anderson April 23 that a route from Cheney would be quite expensive to build, but the distance was shorter and that might justify the expense. Mohr sent Anderson profiles of the two routes to a junction at Plaza. The Cheney line had drainage problems and the first five miles from Cheney south was over basaltic ridges and tule lakes and in seven or eight miles crossed three divides and would necessitate heavy work and steep grades. The total elevation against westward traffic on the Cheney line was nearly double that of the Marshall line. It would be easier to reach Cheney from Spangle, but the same rocky country and tule lakes would be encountered. "I am convinced it would be money thrown away to attempt any cut-off line over the country in question." On the 27th Anderson responded to Harris, enclosing the report from Mohr. "I have no doubt we have the best line the country affords, for economy and facility in working, and also in cost." He added, "The line from Marshall to the common point has a steady and quite regular ascent. On the Marshall line there are no grades exceeding 65 feet per mile against the traffic, while on the Cheney line grades of 120 feet to the mile would be necessary to overcome some of the summits."[3] Consideration of a line from Cheney to the S&P reappeared for several years, all with the same result.

Mohr wrote Anderson on April 27 that a construction engine would be needed in a few days. Bennett had been using 2-6-0 Engine 457 for his track-laying machine on the Cascade branch and wanted to know if the same engine and crew could be made available. Mohr went on to say that Oakes and Wright had visited that day and Oakes suggested that a portion of the depot expenses at Marshall be charged to the NP. The question of a joint depot for the NP and S&P in Spokane was discussed. The depot in Spokane was inadequate in inclement weather.

Mohr reported May 4 that grading for the first seven miles was "very nearly completed." The main difficulty was in obtaining steel or iron for side tracks and other iron material. By the end of May there had been grading through mile post 39 and in June grading reached the end of the line at mile post 43.[4]

The *Gazette* said May 7 that there was no doubt the S&P would be built to Palouse City, "as Bill Turnbow has agreed to furnish all the whiskey that is necessary for its construction, regardless of local option." A meeting the week before at Palouse City adopted a resolution pledging to secure for the S&P the right-of-way from that city to Garfield on the same terms given by the citizens of Spangle. It was claimed that Palouse City could load 26 cars of wheat per day and that there was enough timber for lumber loading of one car every hour for about 26 years. The next week the newspaper reported that the citizens of Garfield had offered $50,000 to the NP to make Garfield the terminus of the S&P. They would if necessary raise the amount to $100,000. Mayor Cannon wrote the Spokane Falls city council in mid-May that he had received Oakes' request for a donation of lots for a depot and yard. In return the NP promised that Spokane would "be the perpetual terminus" of the S&P. As it then stood the purchase of the lots would require private subscriptions without delay. The city charter needed to be amended to allow a subsidy to the railroad.[5]

On May 24 Bennett claimed an extension on his contract because work had been delayed for 10 days because of failure to provide a locomotive and other equipment for track laying, cars to transport sawed timber to Marshall, and the lack of bolts and spikes for trestles and culverts. Mohr wrote Anderson,

> We have had a great deal of difficulty in getting cars; and which it would, of course, be difficult to prove that these delays were intention, yet, such little attention has been paid to our demands for cars that it certainly looks peculiar. What reason Mr. Buckley can have for working against us is entirely beyond my ability to fathom, although, perhaps, I might make a shrewd guess. The work of construction has gone on very smoothly and expeditiously, except for where we have come to contact with Mr. Buckley's department. It is a somewhat strange commentary upon the management of the freight depart that Mr. Bennett should have been compelled to haul freight by wagons from Spokane Falls to Marshall! Yet such has been the case.

Mohr's opinion was that Buckley resented being denied participation in the railroad when first projected. On the 28th Mohr wrote Anderson that the tie contractor was in default because of the lack of transportation. Because ties were otherwise available the S&P would not be harmed. NP Attorney McNaught advised Mohr to make an amicable settlement with the tie contractor because he had turned over records pertaining to the government's $99,000 suit against the NP regarding cutting government timber in Idaho and "furthermore, that he expected valuable assistance from him in the matter of the frauds at Sprague." Mohr wrote the contractor that because of the failure to deliver 60,000 ties on or before June 1, the contract was null and void.

In late May the *Gazette* reported that a new town was to be laid out about 12 miles north of Garfield. James McCoy, the land owner, said the S&P had selected the town site. McCoy proposed to lay out 100 acres and give alternate lots to the railroad. According the Hitchman, the town of McCoy was platted July 14, 1886, but a movement was already under way to change the name to Oakesdale. Mohr wrote Oakes: "We think of naming our best town 'Oakesdale.' We don't expect the erection of Universities, or other public edifices. Do you consent?"[6] Apparently Oakes consented.

Mohr wrote Anderson June 4 that the new steel rails would only lay a few miles. Grading would be finished in a few days. It was necessary to expedite the taking up of the old rails which were to be used, "I would respectfully suggest the utmost haste in that matter." Bennett's track laying crew was idle for the want of ties and it was difficult to find a financially responsible tie contractor. On the 9th Mohr informed Anderson that a tie contractor had withdrawn his bid because the government had seized a large quantity of the logs he expected to use for ties. Two days later Mohr telegraphed Anderson that Bennett had 60,000 ties on the Yakima Division which he would sell cheap if the government would allow them to be moved. By July 1 the tie problem had been resolved and there would be no further delay by a shortage of ties. Mohr explained to Anderson that a tie subcontractor was trying to sell directly to the S&P and was hindering the work of the tie contractor. The subcontractor "is such an utterly irresponsible character, and has the reputation of being such an inveterate liar, that I disliked very much any dealings with him direct."[7]

The Spokane *Morning Review* reported that the terminus of the S&P would be "Belmont," in honor of August Belmont. The company would erect a depot, freight house, roundhouse and other "necessary complements of a terminal point." While numerous applications for business locations had been received by the S&P, it had been decided to reserve all lots until the whole plat had been put on the market. The post office at Belmont was established in November 1886 to serve a claimed 60 people.[8]

Because of uncertainty about whether Congress would take back the land grant on the Cascade branch, Oakes June 17 telegraphed Harris that Anderson said if work was suspended on the S&P, he could probably lay 10 to 15 miles on the Cascade branch in two or three weeks. Oakes did not think suspending work on the S&P would be a "detriment to our interest." Harris responded the same day in cipher, "Do not in any way delay Spokane Branch at present. In a few days we will be able to tell whether we can gain anything by laying track on Cascade at once." Rails and associated hardware remained in short supply.[9]

Mohr wrote Anderson the 24th that the S&P was to be charged $27 a day for Engine 311 and crew and that Engine 458 and crew would be put on the S&P payroll. He wanted a telegraph operator assigned to the S&P; NP operators had given NP business preference and S&P telegrams had lain over as long as 15 hours. Two days later the arrangement on Engine 311 was $7 per day plus NP expenses.

Mohr reported to Anderson on construction to June 30, 1886, saying in part, grading was almost finished and track laying had reach 13 miles. There had been delays in furnishing ties because "of the unusually exacting attitude of the Government in relation to the cutting of timber for the construction of railroads; and partly by reason of the unfortunate quarrel between the members of the Operating Department of the N. P. R. R. and the tie contractor, which threatened, at one time, to seriously delay us in the completion the work."[10]

On July 2 Mohr wrote that J. McNealy, owning land between Spangle and Rosalia, proposed to fence off the line to prevent track laying. In the absence of an injunction Mohr proposed to "go right on." The track should be laid "with utmost speed, and if he makes any move to tear up our track, have sufficient force of men there to prevent his doing it. This man proposes to act as 'ugly' as he can." Condemnation papers would be ready in a few days.

The S&P bought four engines from the NP for $20,000. On July 7 Mohr wrote Portland to send Engines One and Two to Spokane Falls. On December 9, 1886, Mohr reported that S&P #1 began service on the S&P July 15, #2 on July 16, #3 and 4 on August 16. Number two moved to the NP's Spokane & Idaho (S&I), November 1, #3 on September 1, and #4 from October 6 to 31.[11] On August 15 Mohr wrote F. P. Weymouth, Idaho Division Superintendent, complaining about the use of an S&P locomotive for switching at Rathdrum (S&I). Such use was interfering with completing the road to Belmont by the 25th and would Weymouth issue instructions which "will obviate this difficulty."

It was anticipated that the S&P would use springs for its water needs, but Mohr wrote Anderson July 13 the springs were almost dry. Four water stations with wells and tanks of 36,000 gallons capacity were necessary; in each case the water was within six to eight feet of the surface. On the 14th Mohr wrote Anderson that NP depot standard plans had inadequate freight capacity for the S&P. As a result new plans were drawn with larger freight capacity and smaller waiting rooms. The depots would be inexpensive.

On July 17 Anderson sent Harris a certificate that 20 miles of the S&P was complete and ready for operation, extending just south of Plaza. In response to Harris's report on track laying progress for the week ending the 17th, Belmont wanted to know how long it would take to complete the road, when the bonds would be sent and what would be the earliest date for the first installment on the bonds. Harris responded that Anderson said that ten more miles would be ready August 1 and the entire 43-mile line would probably be completed by August 15 to 20th. "All difficulties seem to be overcome, but there is extreme scarcity of labor." The line had been delayed by labor troubles at the mills producing the rails and the tie supply had been interrupted by "unexpected" rulings by the Commissioner of the General Land Office. He concluded, "I will give close attention to the matter and push the work to completion and the issue of the Bonds at the earliest practicable moment." On the 23rd Harris telegraphed Anderson asking if completion of S&P "be hastened by using Cascade Branch rails?" Anderson responded the same day that he did not think that would speed up completion of the line. Sufficient rails for the time being were available from the operating department.[12]

On July 24, 1886, the Washington Railroad and Transportation Co. was incorporated to build from Genesee, Idaho Territory, to connect, via Colfax, with the S&P in the McCoy/Rosalia area. Also mentioned was a crossing of the Snake River at Central Ferry,[13] never constructed.

On August 7 Anderson telegraphed Harris,

> About eight miles of track material remain to be received to complete Spokane and Palouse RW they are coming forward from the mountain grades and I think will all be on hand by the fifteenth to twentieth. The recent delay in laying track came from using one of the old [M]arent trestle spans [from Montana] when it was erected some essential iron parts were missing and had to be procured new from Portland before bridge was safe to pass. There is extraordinary scarcity of labor contractors paying 2 ½ per day but cannot get men.

The next day Anderson telegraphed Harris the material for the hundred-foot truss bridge (bridge 49) at

South Pine Creek was available, "after this bridge there is no obstruction and unless some accident occurs there is no doubt of completing track before end this month."[14]

Mohr telegraphed Harris on August 26 that track was laid to Belmont 43 miles at two p.m. that day. He said it would take a week to get the track in good shape. Anderson sent the certificate of completeness the next day. The *Review* September 1 said, "The Spokane and Palouse road may be modest in its dimensions, but it is a very important addition to the transportation facilities of the territory" and in a short time "will be one of the most important feeders" to the NP. Operation on 42.96 miles between Marshall and Belmont began October 15, 1886, but construction continued until March 1, 1887.[15]

Harris wrote the Belmont Company September 10 that he would take steps at once to have the S&P bonds listed. On the 13th Harris telegraphed Oakes asking when operation would begin and an estimate of the grain traffic on the line that year. Oakes telegraphed Harris that the S&P would be turned over in several days because it was not yet surfaced. The road would haul out two thousand car loads of wheat during the fall.[16]

The *Review,* September 29, carried an interview with Mohr. "With his usual courtesy, Mr. Mohr answered our inquiries and briefly informed us of the objects of the company." The company wanted to finish by winter,

> a network of side tracks for the use of the main lines and branch east of Howard street [Spokane], but the most important improvement...is the company will put up a round-house, repair shops and car yards on the flat on the large block bounded by McClellan and Washington streets and Railroad avenue and Second streets.... The shops and round-house will be substantial structures, of large capacity, and will give employment to a good force of skilled mechanics...it is proposed to erect a large and handsome union depot that will be a credit to the city and of a size to correspond with the promises held out for the future growth of the Falls. This edifice is to be put up for the accommodation of the main line, the Palouse branch and the Idaho branch. The union depot will occupy the site of the present passenger depot, but will be a great improvement in every respect. The present depot will probably be removed to Marshall.... This movement on the part of the railroad company insures for Spokane Falls the real terminus of both the Palouse and Idaho branches, and all future feeders.[17]

On October 1, 1886, the *Gazette* quoted the Spokane *Chronicle:* "We understand that the Spokane & Palouse road has made a rate of $1.50 per ton for wheat from Belmont to Spokane and $9.50 from Belmont to Duluth, giving Spokane the benefit of the through rates. This will give Spokane a great advantage in supplying her mills the year through and make the milling business

Rosalia, Washington, looking east, photographed by F. Jay Haynes, May 1889. From left to right along the S&P tracks are: A typical grain warehouse, outhouse, combination depot, section house, water tank, Haynes' car in front of what appears to be a small warehouse. *Photograph: H-2048, Montana Historical Society, Haynes Foundation Collection.*

of our city one of heavy proportions." The Walla Walla *Union's* response to the announced rate was: "Walla Walla must have independent connection with the Northern Pacific."[18]

Cannon wrote Harris, December 7, 1886, that a stockholders meeting was held the day before. The old board and officers were elected as Harris had instructed; Harris and August Belmont Jr. were elected to the executive committee. The trustees elected were August Belmont Jr., J. M. Buckley, Anthony M. Cannon, Robert Harris, Paul F. Mohr, A. A. Newbery, and F. P. Weymouth. The officers of the company were: Cannon, president; Harris, vice president; Newbery, secretary; G. S. Baxter, treasurer; and J. M. Barker, auditor.[19]

The front of the Rosalia depot in the 1970s with few changes in 90 years. The front of the depot has not been lengthened. There are curtains on the agent's residence windows. Photograph by Roy Ramey, the Rosalia agent. *Ray Poindexter photograph.*

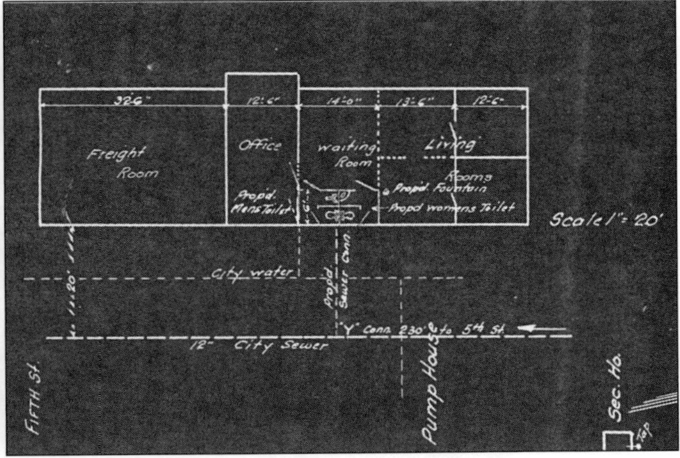

The back of the Rosalia depot (1962) and a 1922 floor plan of the depot. At the near (north) end is the agent's residence door and windows with curtains. Next are the two windows for the restrooms, which replaced the outhouse in 1923. The depot was replaced in 1978 with a Modular Frame Bldg 24′ x 80′. *The photograph, Roy Poindexter; the plan from NP Authorization for Expenditure (AFE) 1996-22.*

On December 13 Mohr informed Anderson that the country was "utterly stripped of building materials." A list on the 15th, for insurance, contains depots at Marshall, Spangle, Rosalia, Oakesdale, and Belmont; water tanks and pump houses at Marshall, Spangle, Rosalia, and Belmont; section houses and tool houses at Spangle, Rosalia, and Belmont; roundhouses at Belmont (2 stalls) and Spokane Falls (3 stalls). The latter also had a 60-foot turntable and a warehouse for construction materials. The total value listed was $37,375. From a report on the 25th it is learned that not all of these facilities were actually completed. In that same report Mohr described problems with some of the rails:

> The work of curving rails where not properly curved by Bennett, and which work is being done for Bennett's account, is being pushed as rapidly as possible. It is impossible to get some of the second-hand rail which came from the Mullen and Evaro grades, into any satisfactory shape, it is so kincked [sic] up that with our appliances we cannot do much with it. It ought to be replaced with a portion the new rail ordered. You will remember that at the time the track was laid we were very short of rail, and used all the rail we had, good bad, or indifferent, with the idea of replacing it as soon as new rail could be obtained. Such portions of the track laid with old rail as are impossible to get into good shape with new rail, I am simply putting into the best shape circumstances will admit of.

On January 3, 1887, Mohr telegraphed Oakes that the S&P ought to have the mail business. The post office was using a stage route. The next day Mohr advised William Spangle at Spangle, that to get regular mail service the people should get a petition extensively signed as soon as possible and send it to the Post Office Department. On the 15th Mohr wrote to conductor Dan Crowley at Rosalia that he had just received a new schedule of wages for the S&P, effective January 1; conductors would receive $90 per calendar month and brakemen, $80, both for 12-hour days. No extra time would be allowed except for emergencies and authorization from the superintendent or engineer-in-charge.[20]

On January 27 Mohr sent Anderson a report on work on the S&P from November 1 to date. Due to an "extreme scarcity of labor" and a shortage of track materials, Nelson Bennett's work was delayed, as a result when the road was turned over to the operating department on October 15 material for side tracks and full spiking was still missing and the road bed was in need of much work. Mohr reported that,

> A gang of Italians was employed Nov. 1st. numbering 60 men, but very little could be done with them..., I discharged the whole lot...but valuable time was lost with them; and by the time we got in thorough working

The Rosalia section house in 1971. The section house was built in 1886 as a one and a half story 20′x 26′ frame building. A one story 13′ x 26′ addition to the back was built later and a 9′ x 10′ extension, lighting, and toilet were added in 1954. The section house was retired in 1976. *Roy Poindexter photograph.*

order with a good gang of men, heavy rains, and alternate frosts and thaws interfered materially with the work.... The material in the cuts through McCoy's and Fellows Divides composed of indurate clay, which was so hard last Summer that powder had to be employed in loosening it, became soft and 'soapy' under the influences of rain, frost and thaws, occasioning a miserable road-bed and causing slides which completely filled up the ditches throughout the length of these cuts. The surface soil composing many of the embankments also became liquid mud in many places, necessitating the use of gravel ballast. In several places small springs made their appearance, of which there was no sign before that, and which had to be provided for.... There is still some work to be done to place the track in first class shape; but as the ground...is frozen very hard, so that in order to raise the track the material would have to be removed from between the ties with picks, the original ballast would have to be removed, and its place supplied with gravel. As soon as warm weather would set in; it would simply necessitate going over the work twice as the frozen chunks of earth under the track would have no stability whatever. I have therefore concluded, after correcting the worst points, to discharge the crew next Saturday, Jan. 29th. If you should decide that it is proper for the Construction Department to do this remaining work after warm weather sets in, it can be done in about two weeks, at a cost of about $2,000.00.

Work had been completed on the wye at Belmont, 16 miles of track had been surfaced, given proper elevation at all curves and rails had been curved and rail braces put on wherever necessary at an average cost of $220 per mile. Requisite ditching had been done on 10.5 miles at an average cost of $100 per mile. One hundred twelve cars of mud had been removed from roadbed and ditches and 76 car loads of gravel were placed in track at the same points.

About 200 bent rails have been removed and replaced with new steel. 56 carloads of rip-rap have been put in place. 493 carloads of earth have been hauled an average distance of one mile, and placed in track. 351 carloads of gravel have been hauled an average distance of 17 ½ miles and placed in track.... The cattle guard fences in number 54 have all been put in; the sign posts of various kinds have been painted, and are ready to put in the ground as soon as it thaws out. All the buildings have been completed between Spokane and Belmont, except the coal-shed at Belmont, and the Round-house, which lacks the smoke jacks which have not arrived from the shops.[21]

Oakes on January 26, 1887, wrote Harris that complaints on passenger rates between Belmont and Cheney were substantially correct. "It was deemed advisable to put a lower rate in effect between Belmont and Spokane Falls to accommodate the farming community around Belmont, the facilities for trading, banking &c., being so limited at that point that people were in the habit of going to Farmington or Colfax, on the O. R. & N. Not understanding that there was any call for such tickets to Cheney, no action was taken in that direction. We have, however, now made a round trip rate to Cheney the same as that to Spokane Falls." In early February the *Review* in story from Rosalia reported that the increase in passenger business on the S&P was very noticeable. Those wishing to go west from Colfax and Moscow are taking this route in preference to the ORN route through Walla Walla because "[t]he accommodations are better and the time is much shorter." The *Gazette* on the 18th reported that the stage line between Garfield and Belmont was well patronized and nearly all the travel between Spokane Falls and Colfax was going via Garfield. Later in the year a notice in the *Review* proclaimed that Garfield had first class hotel accommodations, "second to none in the Palouse country." The notice suggested that S&P passengers for Colfax take the first class stage from Belmont to Garfield, stay in the hotel, and the next morning leave on the 8:20 a.m. train for Colfax. A story reported in March 1888 had a different view: On the advice of a fellow drummer a commercial representative took the S&P to Belmont expecting to go to Walla Walla. When he reached Belmont he learned he would lose three days having to take stages, steamers, and more trains to reach Walla Walla. "The return train to Spokane found him in the seat nearest the front door of the forward coach, and it was the general opinion that his wicked informant would do well to secure a berth in the local hospital in advance." The *Gazette* was of the opinion that "it would be an excellent thing if the train would make connection with the train to Colfax."[22]

On May 5th Harris wrote Anderson about expenditures at Spokane Falls for a roundhouse:

This was a distinct Spokane & Palouse expenditure, and had it not been made at Spokane Falls, must have been made at Marshall. The question is whether Spokane & Palouse expenditures proper should be charged to the Northern Pacific? The question is determined by the articles of incorporation of the Spokane & Palouse Ry Co. which provide that the road shall be from Marshall to a point at or near the Snake River. Clearly we cannot expend the proceeds of bonds of that Company in any other locality than between the points covered by its articles on incorporation.[23]

With respect to the Spokane Falls depot, Mohr wrote NP Superintendent F. P. Weymouth, May 3, 1887, that he had heard that Lewis, the contractor, had not allowed Daley, inspector of bridges and buildings, a Weymouth subordinate, to inspect his work. Mohr stated that Daley's attempted inspection could not have emanated from Weymouth, because Weymouth did not have "the remotest authority to cause the inspection of buildings for the [S&P] construction department." Mohr reminded Weymouth that he had asked to have Daley inspect the building in Mohr's absence, but that he wanted to see Daley prior to his absence and Weymouth had responded that he would send Mr. Daley to Mohr.

> Not hearing from you before I left, I did not notify Mr. Lewis that Mr. Daley would inspect or superintend the building, I am not surprised, therefore, that Mr. Lewis objected (if he did object) to having some man utterly unknown to him as being in authority, give him orders.
>
> The claim made by you, that Mr. Cannon or I, prevented the inspection, is consequently false in every detail, and particular.
>
> As a conclusion, I will say, as I said in the beginning, that I will be much pleased now, as I have always been, to have Mr. Daley inspect the Depot in question, and that notification to that effect, will result at once, in his being the Inspector of that Depot, Lewis to the contrary, notwithstanding. My affairs are open at all times, to the inspection and criticism of those whose business it is to do so, and I trust that in the future, you will contain yourself with the limits of your own jurisdiction, and will not encroach upon mine.[24]

On August 1, 1887, Anderson reported that to June 30, 1887, 43.75 miles of track had been laid on the S&P from Marshall to a little beyond Belmont. Laid on the main track and sidings were 949 gross tons of old steel rail from the Mullan and Evaro grades on the NP main line. The remainder of the road was laid with new 56-pound steel rail, NP standard. The cost of the road somewhat exceeded the estimate because of additional side tracks at Marshall, Spangle, Rosalia and Belmont, more "commodious" depots built at the same stations and because interest on the bonds was charged to construction.

In August 1887 the *Review* printed a glowing letter from Oakesdale. Last year before the S&P, 148,000 bushels of grain, 97,000 pounds of wool, and 60,000 pounds of fruit were shipped from Oakesdale. In 1887 it was expected that 500,000 to 600,000 bushels of grain would be shipped. Laboring men were in short supply and the wages were $2.00 to $4.00 per day and carpenters were unavailable at any price.[25]

In a letter to Belmont on November 7, 1887, Harris said the earnings of the S&P through September 30 were $37,991, the expenses were $72,112 (operating expenses $31,872, taxes $680 and guarantee on bonds $39,560) for a deficit of $34,121, but the main line revenue from S&P was $85,068.[26]

Oakesdale, Washington, NP combination depot, north side, 1962. The depot was built in late 1886, 24′ wide and lengthened 38′ to 105′ total in 1903. The depot was removed in 1983. Except for its dormer, the Oakesdale depot was similar to the Rosalia depot. *Roy Poindexter photograph.*

Appendix: Track Laying Record, Marshall to Belmont, 1886–87

1886	Distance from Marshall	Sources and Notes
May 28	Well short of MP 1	(2) Track laid between Marshall and Bridge 1. Mohr said that track laying began May 30th (6).
June 1	Two and a half miles	(5)
June 9	Between MPs 4 & 5	(2)
June 12	Five miles, 1,749 ft.	(1) For the week ending on 12th, two miles, 4,835 ft. laid.
June 14	Between MPs 7 & 8	(2)
June 19	Nine miles, 3,628 ft.	(1) For the week ending on 19th, four miles, 1,880 ft. laid.
June 20	10 miles completed	(6)
June 21	Between M.P's 10 & 11	(2)
June 26	13 miles, 972 ft.	(1) (2) For the week ending on 26th, three miles, 2,624 ft. laid. Ending point just beyond Spangle.
July 3	14 miles, 5,192 ft.	(1) For the week ending on 3rd, one mile, 4,220 ft. laid.
July 7	MP 16	(2)
July 10	17 miles, 2,152 ft.	(1) For the week ending on 10th, two miles, 2,240 ft. laid.
July 12	Between MPs 18 & 19	(2)
July 14	Between MPs 19 & 20	(2) Approximately Plaza.
July 15	20 miles completed	(6) (1)
July 17	20 miles, 702 ft.	(3) For the week ending on 17th, two miles, 3,840 ft. laid.
July 24	21 miles, 4,432 ft.	(1) For the week ending on 24th, one mile, 3,720 ft. laid. At approximately mile 21.9 "Hardman's" (2).
July 31	24 miles, 1,672 ft.	(1) For the week ending on 31st, two miles, 2,520 ft. laid.
August 7	28 miles, 1,752 ft.	(1) (2) For the week ending on 7th, four miles, 80 ft. laid. About a mile and half beyond Rosalia.
August 10	30 miles completed	(6)
August 11	30 miles, 492 ft.	(1) 6300 ft. laid on the 11th.
August 18	34 miles, 2,083 ft.	(1) 3900 ft. laid on 18th.
August 21	38 miles, 1,363 ft.	(1) For the week ending on 21st, six miles, 3,020 ft. laid. 4,500 ft. laid on 20th. A little more than a mile beyond Oakesdale.
August 22	38 miles, 4,569 ft.	(1) 3,100 ft. laid on 22nd.
August 24	41 miles, 5,046 ft.	(1) On the 24th, 8,200 ft. laid.
August 26	43 miles	(4) Laid to Belmont at 2:00 p.m.
August 28	43 miles	(1) For week ending on 28th, four miles, 3,917 ft. laid. (8) Total 42.96 miles.
1887		
January 27		(7) Mohr wrote Anderson that the line had been extended at Belmont 2,260 ft. since August 31. (9) Anderson 8/1/87, total 43.75 miles.

Sources: (1) MHS, 137.H.4.8.F (telegrams from Anderson to Harris); (2) MHS, 134.L.18.8.F (Construction Profile) (3) MHS, 137.H.10.10.F; (4) MHS, 137.H.4.10.F (telegram Mohr to Harris); (5) PG 6/4/86, 3; (6) MHS, 136 K.12.3.B (Mohr's 1/27/87 report to Anderson—the report is not consistent with other sources above, for example it states that 43 miles were completed August 25th); (7) UMT 128/370/514; (8) NP 1933; (9) MHS, 137.H.6.6.F #57.

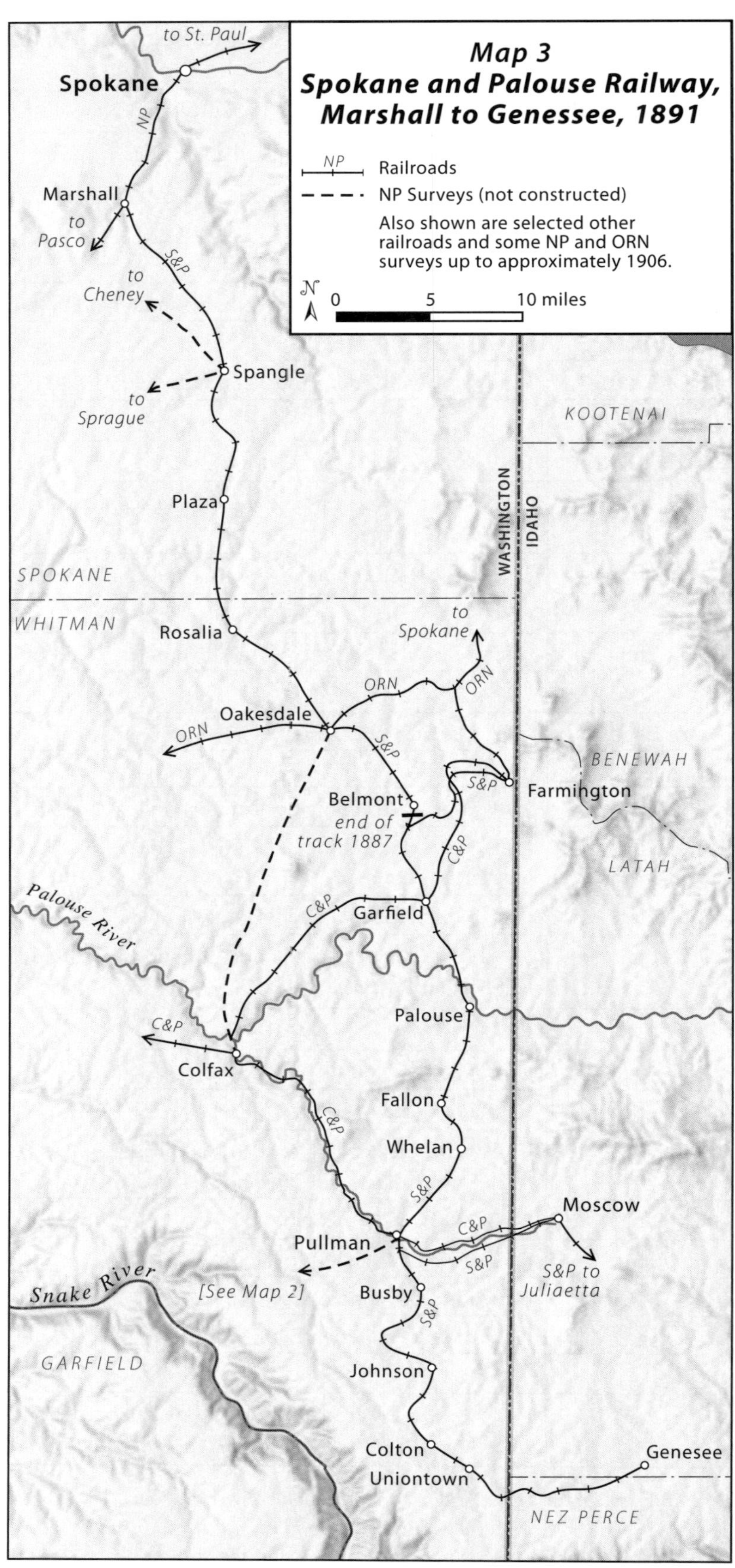

Primary source NP map 1906, MHS 132.1.4.4., redrafted by Philip Beach and drawn by Chelsea Feeney, www.cmcfeeney.com

The Spokane & Palouse Extends to Genesee, 1886–88

In August 1886 during construction to Belmont, NP President Robert Harris wrote Vice President and General Manager Thomas Oakes, "I think the time is come for us to locate the extension of the Spokane & Palouse Road from Belmont to Palouse City." He continued that the ORN and NP ought to agree on a plan to avoid unnecessary duplication "but at present there is very little encouragement that we can agree with them as to any plan that does not, in effect, surrender to them all of the valuable and productive country." Oakes responded that he thought that the line should be deferred until completion of the Cascade branch. So far NP construction should not be construed as an invasion of ORN territory, but construction south of Farmington might be so construed.[1]

At the same time the ORN was strengthening its commitment to the Palouse. In October the ORN executive committee authorized construction from Texas Ferry, on the Snake River, to the C&P. November 4 Harris telegraphed Chief Engineer Adna Anderson to locate from Belmont to Genesee and to secure the right-of-way. The survey work began on the 20th. S&P surveyors arrived in Palouse City on the 28th to find "the people are very much elated over the new developments, as they were entirely unexpected."[2]

S&P Engineer-in-Charge Paul F. Mohr pointed out to Harris in early December that the S&P charter only provided for a railroad in Washington Territory; adding Idaho Territory to the charter would help to secure right-of-way over public lands in Idaho and to cut timber for the railroad on government lands in Idaho. Earlier the S&P had been denied the right to cut such timber because the charter only specified Washington.[3]

Mohr initiated a survey to be made from Oakesdale to Colfax on December 8. On the 10th the *Gazette* reported that Garfield was excited at the prospect of the S&P and the right-of-way agent had "secured a great part of the distance from Belmont to Palouse City." On the 17th the newspaper said that Colton gave the S&P 20 acres for depot purposes and the citizens of Uniontown and vicinity had guaranteed right-of-way from the Idaho line to Colton. On the 18th Mohr reported that the preliminary survey to Genesee had been finished. The distance was 65 miles and the route was "very good." The NP board of directors, December 16, 1886, set in motion work on an extension to Genesee in Idaho.[4]

In a letter on December 22, 1886, Mohr instructed right-of-way agent A. P. Curry that in

> the matter of securing the assistance of residents of small towns or villages, in...obtaining right-of-way, it is of course desirable to enlist every influence that can be obtained, without thereby binding us to obligations what may turn out in the future to be a greater burden than the free right-of-way is worth. I think it is perfectly feasible to enlist the assistance of residents upon the simple basis of the general good to that entire section of the country, and to make no promises beyond the simple statement that if it be the interests of the Company and the people who are to be served (that is, the farmers) a station or depot will be located upon town-sites already established; but that where it may subsequently appear that town-sites are not wisely chosen, the Company reserves the right to place its depots or stations where it will be to the best interests of all parties concerned.... What I particularly wish to avoid is to get any right-of-way conditioned upon selecting such and such places as depot grounds.[5]

In the meantime the ORN was busy. ORN General Manager C. H. Prescott on January 19 informed President Elijah Smith that surveys would be made "at the earliest possible moment" in the Potlatch and Camas Prairie countries and that from Pullman through the area being surveyed by the NP "shall have full investigation." On the same day the surveyors were on Union Flat 10 or 11 miles from Pullman.[6]

In letters from January 18 to 23, 1887, Mohr laid out for Anderson issues in the location of the line to Genesee. The ORN was locating a line four to seven miles distant paralleling the C&P's Farmington branch. Mohr thought the S&P line should go through Palouse City and Pullman, rather than Colfax or Moscow. He wanted Anderson to consider whether the actions of the ORN justified a change in route. The ORN could not be "fenced" south of Belmont. If the S&P were to run from Moscow to Genesee, the road from Pullman to Colton would be at the mercy of the ORN. "There is no doubt that the line we have just run, and which in the main follows Assistant Engineer, J. B. Alexander's 1885 reconnaissance, controls as much business as any single line through this country can command." Heavy grades could be avoided if the line was not run to Palouse City, but it was an important town with several large lumbering mills and should not be avoided. A decision was needed as soon as possible on whether to go via Palouse City. He and S&P President Cannon thought they should run a line from Colfax to a junction with the preliminary at Colton to obtain right-of-way and "mystify...the ORN people who were anxiously watching every move we made and in several cases interfering with our R. of Way man's work." In regards to a line from Moscow to Genesee, Mohr believed that Alexander had gone over the ground very carefully and he did not consider himself justified in varying from the instructions sent him to go via Pullman.[7]

On February 8 Mohr sent a map, profile, and estimate to Harris. The map and the accompanying letter included a number of alternatives to the recommended route. For the recommended route the preliminary cost estimate was for 63.6 miles, $12,881 per mile, $820,155. The map from Mohr included two lines not built, but are of importance in future events: (1) from Spangle southeast to Hangman Creek thence to south end of Coeur d'Alene Lake, up the Coeur d'Alene River to the South Fork and up the S. Fork to Milo (Evolution), into the Coeur d'Alene mining district (the Milo branch was surveyed); and (2) a line from Union Flat to Penawawa on the Snake River.[8]

By mid-February nearly all the right-of-way was secured. Locating the line was slowed because of snow. On March 4 the *Gazette* reported that S&P engineers were surveying from Belmont to Farmington. A week later it was reported that a location party was working on Cow Creek east of Uniontown.[9]

On February 23, 1887, the NP engineer office in St. Paul received Mohr's 29-page printed report of surveys and reconnaissances he had made in Umatilla County, Oregon, and in Walla Walla, Columbia, and Whitman Counties, Washington Territory, in November 1886, at the instruction of Anderson. Included was a survey from Texas Ferry along the Snake River to Penawawa Creek and up the creek to Union Flat thence to a connection with the Genesee extension.[10] The surveying south of the Snake River, an area that the ORN thought was theirs, was particularly extensive. The ORN was undoubtedly aware of Mohr's activities and they probably contributed to Elijah Smith's determination to respond to NP actions in the Palouse. He wrote Prescott, February 23:

> I have yours of 15th inst, relative to lines out of Pullman to the [Genesee] and Potlatch countries. I am greatly disappointed to hear the N.P.RR. have gone in ahead of us and had obtained bonds for right of way for the only practical route. Our race is now a tail-race where with our knowledge of the country and the available routes we should have been first. We must lose no time now. Put Engineers in the field now and survey every practicable line where opposition may be expected. *If we run over the same line* used by the N.P.RR. and can get right of way I should do so....follow the N.P.RR. line 10 miles to [Genesee]. If that is a good route and you can get bonds or deeds for right of way use it. If we have opposition we must make it a bitter and destructive one...[emphasis in the original].
>
> ...I also enclose a map of the Palouse country on which I have drawn desirable both from point of revenue and of stopping competition. I would draw your attention more particularly to the one standing from a point near Endicott and running to the forks of the Hangman. This will go through a good country all the way, cut the N.P. line in two, and make a direct connection with the line to the Coeur d'Alene mines by which the ore can go to Portland without being dragged up down hill at Colfax.
>
> I wish you would have engineering parties placed in the field at once.... On the heels of the engineer parties send the right way agent to get bonds for right of way if possible.
>
> If there is a pass or Canyon which forms the only practical route, buy the right of way if necessary....
>
> We want to cover every available line no matter if we parallel our own line within a ten mile limit. We need [not] build unless we see it to our advantage hereafter, but we must have our surveys and preliminary work in such shape that we can act at once. I fear we have allowed valuable time to escape us already, but we must do our best now.[11]

By March 11 ORN surveyors were running a preliminary survey from the top of the hill west of Colfax into the Genesee country. "They are very reticent as to the intentions of the company, but the general impression is that the O. R. & N. Co. proposes building...to gain an advantage over the N. P." Two weeks later the ORN surveyors were in Union Flat.[12]

On March 11 Anderson telegraphed Harris in cipher asking, "Has an arrangement been made for extending Spokane & Palouse it is desirable to commence at once in order to get ties down the Palouse river on the spring freshet." On the 17th the NP board agreed to extending the S&P to Genesee. Harris telegraphed Anderson, "Extension Spokane & Palouse authorized. Please go ahead. Will there be any difficulty to complete by September first?" On the 19th the Spokane Falls *Review* reported the decision and saw the new road as a great enhancement.[13]

Anderson telegraphed Harris, "ORN are paralleling our lines in Washington territory & avow their purpose of building alongside them whether this bluff or business I don't know." Harris responded, "What new mischief is up." On the 19th Harris telegraphed Anderson in cipher, "You should have contractors at work between the crossing of Moscow Branch [C&P] and Genesee at the earliest moment you can get them there. Do not let O.R&N take possession of any part of your location. How soon can you get to work on it. Answer." Anderson telegraphed contractor Nelson Bennett on March 22, "Do you want to build road from Belmont south, and if so how soon can you get at work there, and at what price will you do work." Bennett responded the same day from Helena, "I will do work same prices as work on same line last year.... Can commence at once with large force." Anderson responded on the 31st, "I will accept your proposition for grading on extension of Spokane & Palouse R. R. Before deciding on bridging and other matters, will have personal conference with you."[14]

The *Gazette* reported April 1 that the ORN surveyors had run a line from Uniontown to Genesee paralleling the S&P survey and had run a line from Uniontown up Thorn Creek to Moscow. On the same day the Walla Walla *Daily Journal* reported an interview with Anderson in Minneapolis on March 26, the line would be to Genesee by December 1. He would say nothing about the ORN paralleling the S&P, "becoming a profound agnostic when closely questioned." On April 8 the *Gazette* said there were three corps of engineers in Pullman and the town was looking forward to becoming the railroad center of eastern Washington.[15]

The *Daily Journal* reported on the 13th that graders were scattered from Belmont to Garfield. The newspaper carried a Bennett advertisement seeking men and teams. Geo. Truax informed Elijah Smith on the 17th, "The N. P. has got their men and tools at Belmont, ready to commence work south to Genesee." The Lewiston *Teller* said April 21 that with encouragement from the people, it had been assured that the S&P would extend to Lewiston if a route down to the river could be found.[16]

On April 28 Mohr reported to Anderson that,

> The O.R. & N. Co. party were cross-sectioning their line between Colton and Uniontown while I was there. Their location crosses and recrosses our line in many places. McClellan, their Chief Engineer was personally on the ground, superintending the work. He told Mr. Gable of Uniontown that they proposed to change their line from the confluence of Thorn Creek and Union Flat, and instead of going to Genesee, to go up Thorn Creek...so as to cut us off as much as possible from wheat which is raised in large quantities in the Potlatch country west of Little Potlatch Creek. Their tactics seem to be: First, to get between our line and Snake River, where the body of land embraced between the two, is considerably greater than at Colton, and where they would deprive us of all the wheat between Union Flat Creek and Snake River...at the same time covering a part of the ground which a branch from our line to Penawawa was destined to control, with the object of "fencing us out". Beyond Colton, where the belt of wheat land between our line and Snake River, is quite narrow, they aim to get between our line and their Moscow branch, to cut us off from the wheat North of their line and to divide the wheat between their line and our line, and furthermore to be near the head-water of Potlatch creek to get the wheat coming from that country....
>
> The survey which was made by the O. R. & N. people a month or six weeks ago, paralleled our line all the way from Pullman to Genesee, and these moves now communicated, have only been made during the last two weeks, and as they are making a definite location and cross-sectioning it, I anticipate that this will be the route built,—if built at all....
>
> The sentiment of the people all the way from Pullman to Genesee, is most enthusiastically in favor of the Northern Pacific. While we are getting almost all of our right-of-way gratis, as well as depot grounds, the O. R. & N. right-of-way Agent Mr. Watt, is obliged to pay the heaviest prices for his right-of-way, and many of the people threaten to enjoin them from entering upon their lands with, a view of delaying their work. I have been told that Mr. Watt is paying as high as a thousand dollars per mile, to get through some of their property....
>
> I was told that the O.R. & N. had several car loads of scrapers and plows at Pullman ready to be used as soon as we commenced work below that point, and that in the meantime their instructions were to await our movements.

He also reported, "Bennett's men are industriously at work grading between Belmont and Pullman.[17] Anderson forwarded Mohr's letter to Harris, who responded that he had written UP President C. F. Adams calling his attention to the October 1880 contract and the August 1882 supplementary contract where by the ORN agreed, that except for Farmington and Moscow, not to build north of the Snake River. In a construction report for the year ending June 30, 1887, Anderson wrote that the ORN had "paid very high prices for right-of-way, with the effect of causing farmers to evade their agreements with the [S&P], and thus increasing the cost."[18]

Grading began in May at several locations between Belmont and Pullman. The newspaper reported on May 6 that S&P surveyors were camped north of Colton, "apparently ready for a flank movement of some kind from the opposition folks.[19]

NP Director Billings recommended to Harris, April 23, 1887, "based on information...so direct and positive," should send someone to Spokane Falls to make an examination of the construction department.[20] On the same day Harris directed M. P. Martin, assistant general auditor, to go to Spokane Falls to "carefully examine the construction accounts of the Spokane and Palouse.... Your examination should be thorough, with a view to determining whether the prices paid by the Company for all work and materials used in construction have been fair: whether there have been any intermediate profits paid to any one; and if any what?"[21] On May 3-4, 1887, Mohr wrote similar letters to General Manager Oakes and General Auditor J. A. Barker, stating that he was being "investigated." He wanted to know who "the mainspring" of the investigation was. "The coming of this inquisition was busily heralded by our friend [F. P.] Weymouth [NP Superintendent at Sprague]...I have not the slightest objection" to an investigation, but he did object to "a zealous detective, prejudiced to the brim" seeking to find "wholesale theft and corruption." He believed that his business and other affairs were of such prominence that Martin did not need to seek information "among disgruntled contractors or down right enemies" including "a criminal" who did not receive a contract. Martin investigated the contract with Bennett, which was made by Anderson when Mohr was absent. "Not a single contract was let without Anderson's full understanding and approval." If Martin's report is truthful and fair and based on the facts, Mohr would have no objection, but he did object to the report "being embellished with the outpourings of disgruntled contractors chronic enemies." He asked Oakes "to prevent injustice being done," but he asked for no favors. He did regret that he had lost his temper when Martin "went to work as a man who was determined to find something 'crooked'" and when Martin criticized work which was outside of Martin's jurisdiction and accountable to Anderson. He closed his letter to Oakes by saying he could make five times as much more pleasantly than fighting Weymouth and Assistant General Manager J. M. Buckley "who want my place for themselves or some friend."

Martin's report to Harris was mailed May 11. In Spokane Falls he confined himself to examining contracts and bids "as Mr. Mohr would produce, and to investigating the charges already presented to you.... Mr. Mohr told me with considerable passion in replying to questions I had asked, that he did not care to be questioned as if he was on a witness stand." Martin found that the ties for the Marshall to Belmont line in 1886 were furnished by three contractors. Significantly more was paid per tie to the H. S. Davis & Co. than to the other two contractors. Martin in part wrote,

> H. S. Davis is dead, but I learn he was a man of no financial responsibility, the "co" of the firm was B. H. Bennett, son-in-law to Mr. Cannon and cashier of his bank. June 28th, three days after the date of the contract, Davis assigned all his right, title and interest therein to B. H. Bennett and the assignment was witnessed by A. M. Cannon. Mr. Mohr states he had no knowledge as to who composed the firm of Davis and Co. until after Davis' death about November 1st 1886...
>
> It may be proper to date that during the months of July and August, Davis the contractor was also employed for twenty four days as Timber Inspector at a salary of $100 per month.

Martin found that the buildings along the line of the S&P were erected under contract and in each instance where he saw the bids the contract went to the lowest bidder. He did not know whether the contract with J. W. Lewis to build the Spokane Falls station went to the lowest bidder; Mohr failed to show Martin two bids that Martin knew were received for the station. Several friends of the NP in Spokane told Martin that Cannon, Mohr, and Lewis were "to a certain extent partners," but Martin said he could find no confirmation.

> The contract for extension from Belmont (65 miles) has been let to Nelson Bennett at same rates as his last contract, no other bids were asked or received. The contract to furnish ties was also let to Nelson Bennett without competition at $900 per mile, a little more than 34 cents per tie. Other contractors wanted to bid, but were not allowed the opportunity. One of them John H. Stone is now under contract to Mr. Bennett to furnish from 100,000 to 125,000 ties at 24 cents each. This contract was let by Messrs Cannon and Mohr (hastily I think) and approved by General Anderson, but it is my opinion that the General was not in possession of the exact facts when his approval was obtained.
>
> Few of the contracts are formally executed before work is commenced, in fact Bennett's contract is not yet drawn up, although work has been in progress for thirty days or more.
>
> In performing the disagreeable duty assigned me, I have earnestly tried to be fair and impartial, omitting everything that seemed to me to be an error of judgment or trivial in its nature, being careful to make no statement that is not substantiated. Mr. Mohr in his letters to Messrs Oakes and Barker attached hereto, has tried to forestall anything I may say by maligning me, but this might be expected of a man who has quarrels with nearly everyone with whom he comes in contract. No one in Spokane knew from me my business, except the officers of the Spokane and Palouse Railway, I talked with no one in

regard to Mr. Mohr or his work, except the employees of the two Companies, Mr. Stone, a reputable man whom I have known for many years, and one other whose name I am not at liberty to use at this time. A service of more than seventeen years with the Northern Pacific Railroad ought to enable me to judge its friends and enemies as accurately as can Mr. Mohr.

In regard to townsites along the line of the Spokane and Palouse, I understand they have been assigned to the original promoters of the Eastern Washington Ry. And that neither the Northern pacific nor the Spokane and Palouse have any interest therein.

Mr. Bennett's bid for the first 43 miles of the Spokane and Palouse was, all things considered, as favorable as any offered, and I think the contract was properly awarded to him.

On May 22, 1887, Anderson telegraphed Harris in cipher:

I have Martin's report to you relative to matter into which he was instructed to make private inquiry. I have accidentally learned the source of C. B. Wright's information which he gave to you. It came from most vicious enemy of in all Eastern Washington Terry. So far as I can now judge from my knowledge of the man and circumstances error of judgment may have been made but I am unable to discover evidence of wrong intention and am not satisfied that anyone personally connected with Spokane & Palouse wrongfully made one cent from contractor or otherwise. Martin appears to have got most of his information from associates of C. B. Wright's informant and political enemies of A. M. Cannon when you come to Helena I propose to have Cannon and Mohr meet us there and explain if they can please treat this as entirely confidential.[22]

At roughly the same time Mohr had a dispute with the NP Land Department about a lot in Spokane Falls that he believed he was promised at a certain price. In the end Mohr lost an appeal to Harris on this matter.[23]

In early May Anderson wrote Harris that if steel arrived before the end of May, track-laying would begin at once and was expected to progress at about 20 miles per month. About the same time Mohr wrote Harris, that in the absence of Newbery, the land agent, that he had secured nearly all of the way-of-way from Belmont to Genesee without costing the company a cent. For what the ORN had been paying, the land was worth over $40,000.[24]

On May 11 Julius Galland, secretary of ORN's Washington & Idaho Railroad, wrote President Smith,

The Spokane & P. people are having considerable trouble with Right of way matters from Palouse City South. As is sometimes usual, Mohr, Cannon, Houghton and the S&P officials have associated together as Palouse Land Improvement Co., to which...all lands and bonuses are given, particularly townsites and it may not be wrong to assume that they play the old game of having the improvements made in leveling streets and fixing up the town property of the Improvement Co. charged up to Construction acct. of S&P.

Down in Palouse City & Genesee & also in Pullman where previously prominent citizens upon the verbal assurance of the Rt of way man (who just at the proper moment resigns his position) that the road would run to those towns, and had no outside town interests, had as a committee procured agreements covering right of way from the Farmers along the line they *now* asked to make up large cash amounts, or not get the road—in all the above cases road going to the side say 1 to 2 miles and new towns talked of being stacked by the Palouse Improvement Co—This has aroused the ire of a good many of the best men in the section and they may yet considerable trouble in getting through. This I have from prominent merchants in the country [emphasis in original]....

Weather here the last month has been the worst ever experienced at this time the year and in consequence not much work is being done by the S&P on extension.[25]

On May 24 the NP board of directors accepted August Belmont & Co.'s offer for the Genesee extension bonds at a rate not exceeding $16,000 per mile, that the contract be similar to the March 13, 1886, contract on the earlier S&P bonds, but that instead of 85 percent being allowed to the NP, that 95.5 percent be allowed and that any proceeds of the sale of bonds above par be divided equally between the NP and the Belmont company.[26]

The S&P Trustees May 28 in Spokane Falls approved supplemental articles, a supplementary lease, and adopted a map of the general route of the extension. The articles of incorporation authorized the company to construct lines to the "Clearwater River in Idaho Territory, or any other places or places in Idaho Territory, or Montana Territory." The articles were filed in Washington Territory June 13, 1887. The lease of the S&P to the NP corrected a "clerical" error in the lease of May 1, 1886, by changing the 43 mile estimated length to an estimated length of 110 miles. The lease was dated June 1, 1887 and filed in Whitman County January 7, 1888. The map extended the line from Belmont to approximately Leon, Washington Territory, on the Washington-Idaho boundary, to a point near the Snake River in Washington Territory, and a branch from Leon terminating approximately three miles southeast of Moscow, Idaho.[27]

On May 27 the *Gazette* reported that the ORN was paying cash for right-of-way and that ORN surveyors were eight miles east of Moscow. The S&P had about

300 men at work. Early June S&P surveyors were cross sectioning near Colton, graders were busy at Pullman, and about five miles of road bed between Palouse City and Pullman was finished. On the 1st an S&P contractor and his foremen were arrested for trespass on the land of A. F. Keys, farmer, two miles from Palouse City. The next day the remaining 42 members of the grading crew were arrested. A few days after work had begun on his property Keys was offered $125 for right-of-way, which he refused, demanding $400. Work continued. Keys was offered $250, which he refused. The right-of-way agent said he would have the land condemned and work proceeded until the arrests. The issue was settled on the 2nd when Keys accepted $400 for right-of-way, $50 for damages and $50 for attorney fees. Other farmers were interested in how it might affect right-of-ways through their property. By June 10 cross sectioning between Uniontown and Genesee was about completed. On the 24th the newspaper said that arrangements were being made to commence grading from Pullman to Genesee and that the NP Elevator Co. had been making arrangements in Pullman to build an elevator. The *Morning Review* reported that the company was constructing an elevator at Garfield and intended to build elevators at every station between Belmont and Genesee.[28]

Thomas J. Potter, vice president and joint manager of the UP and ORN, on June 14, 1887, sent Elijah Smith a "Memoranda for New Lines." It contained 13 recommendations, two of which were:

> 7. As soon as the party that is now locating from Moscow to the Potlatch country has finished survey, have it filed, and in event of the Northern Pacific attempting to go into that country, build the line, distance to be agreed upon hereafter when we get more information with reference to that country....
>
> 13. ...recommend that we discontinue procuring any right of way on the line from Pullman to Genesee, believing that it will not pay to construct a line in that country, it being in competition with other lines of ours...

On July 26 the ORN executive committee adopted the 13 recommendations. On August 17 the C&P filed a Second Supplemental Articles of Incorporation which included a line from a point at or near Pullman to Genesee, about 35 miles. The ORN executive committee March 26, 1888, received various expenses including the Pullman and Genesee branch, $3,931. Between then and November no additional expenses were recorded.[29]

Elijah Smith was president of both the ORN and OT. The OT claimed to own 136,081 shares of NP stock and a controlling interest in the ORN. The OT on May 26, 1887, brought suit in the United States Circuit Court in New York to restrain the NP from issuing more stock or bonds or providing any means for the payment of interest on bonds issued for the construction of the S&P. The injunction also sought to stop all construction on the S&P and to forbid the NP from controlling the S&P. The complaint charged that the NP had no right to construct the S&P because the OT was not consulted and the new road was against the interests of the OT in that it would saddle the NP main line with debt. An additional injunction was sought against the construction of the Oregon & Washington Territory Railroad. The Spokane Falls *Morning Review* reported June 9 that Harris said that he, "thought the matter very weak and frivolous, and hardly likely to receive serious consideration in court." On the 15th Cannon informed Harris that in order to keep work progressing, Cannon would personally advance money for right-of-way deeds and if the injunction was made permanent Spokane interests would construct the remainder of the Spokane and Palouse and form a new organization to make a traffic contract with the NP. On the 17th Anderson telegraphed Harris in cipher that Bennett could arrange to carry the S&P provided that he had assurance that it would be made good in a few months. Anderson told him that it would be made good. On the 20th the court issued a restraining order on the NP until July 8 when a hearing on the OT amended bill of complaint would be held. In the meantime the NP and all of its officers were enjoined from giving financial or material aid to the S&P.[30]

In response to Harris, Mohr wrote that no track had been laid south of Belmont because no steel had yet arrived. On June 22 Harris wrote John P. Vollmer assuming he had heard about the injunction to prevent the road being built to the bluffs near Lewiston, but "I think we will get there notwithstanding." A special meeting of the S&P Trustees on June 28 accepted Harris' resignation as vice president and trustee. On July 15 Oakes informed Harris that the four engines sold to the S&P had been taken back for $5,000 each.[31]

On July 2 a pile driver driving piles for the Palouse River bridge above Palouse City fell into the river. Four members of the crew went into the water, one man breaking his leg. On the same day the machine was recovered and on the day of the newspaper report the machine was working on the last bridge crossing the river. On July 4 in Palouse City, Peter Olsen, a subcontractor on the S&P, was shot dead by W. S. Reader, constable and deputy marshal. The shooting occurred about 11:00 p.m., following the request of a saloon keeper for officials to clear his saloon of railroad workers who were demanding liquor without being able to pay. Following the shooting the railroad workers searched for Reader unsuccessfully.[32]

On July 7 Anderson telegraphed Harris in cipher asking that authority be given for the sale, to some outside party, of 6.160 tons of track supplies for use on the S&P. On the 12th he again telegraphed Harris in cipher that Cannon was willing to advance money to the S&P, but there must be some definite arrangement for reimbursement and interest. Cannon had advanced $7,000 to $8,000 for right-of-way, pay to engineers, and other purposes. Harris, in cipher, told Anderson to go ahead with construction; the president and treasurer of the S&P should be authorized by the S&P Trustees to sell bonds not exceeding $16,000 per mile at not less than 95 percent and to borrow not exceeding $200,000 at 6 percent, payable in four months using Company notes. On the 13th the Trustees at Spokane Falls carried out Harris' instructions.[33]

On July 15 both the *Railroad Gazette* and *Railway Age* reported that the OT suit had been held over. The next day Harris wrote the editor of the *Gazette* that the NP had not since the time when the OT dominated the management of the NP, built any branch which "saddles the Company with debt, or burdens this Company in any respect." The motivation behind the suit was not that the OT was a large holder of NP stock, but because the OT held a majority of the stock of the ORN, a rival company.[34]

On the 26th Harris telegraphed Anderson that there should be at Marshall 2,000 tons of rails and fastenings "subject to order of whomsoever it may concern." The next day Harris telegraphed Anderson to do nothing about the rails until further advice. Harris explained, "I do this so as not to give any ground, however slightly for the OT to claim nonobservance of the injunction. Perhaps Mr. Cannon will know in a few days what arrangements he can make for buying the rails and fastenings." Harris telegraphed Cannon that the NP could not act because of the injunction. He concluded, "I think parties will make you a bid for bonds in few days."[35]

The construction profile shows grading from Pullman to Genesee beginning in several locations in July. In late July the S&P graders were working on either side of Pullman, but the location of the Pullman depot was still uncertain. Thirty miles of grading from Belmont was practically completed and 17 miles of bridge work was done. Ties for 25 miles were on the ground and rails would arrive within the week. The railroad was expected to be operating to Pullman by the middle of September.[36]

On August 3 Anderson telegraphed Harris in cipher, that it was necessary that something be done about financing the S&P. Bennett wired that he needed money or he would close down. He had advanced over $100,000 and Cannon about $30,000. Bennett was growing nervous about the delay in placing securities. Harris responded that if Bennett was unable to get S&P notes discounted and if Harris could not get friends to advance the money to lay 20 miles of track and if other arrangements could not be made, work would have to stop. He thought he could get 2,000 tons of rails from Bethlehem with S&P acceptances for four months at 6 percent. If Bennett could get the notes discounted for his work, they could get the bonds as soon as 20 miles of track were laid, then Bennett could be paid from the bonds. Harris asked Anderson what he thought of completing the first 20 miles south of Belmont as soon as possible and then stopping all work. He pointed out that the S&P had no means to pay until track was laid and the bonds issued. Anderson wired Harris suggesting that if the S&P bonds were sent to Spokane Falls, $200,000 could be raised on the coupons. The rails arrived in time to have 10 miles of track laid by September 29.[37]

In early August the *Review* reported that farmers were "unanimously…indignant" over the attempts of the ORN to block the S&P and would drive their grain to Belmont and "the highest prices paid over the Palouse country." The NP Elevator Co. was highly regarded by the farmers and three or four teams were engaged daily for over two weeks bringing grain from the ORN warehouses in Farmington to the NP Elevator Co. in Belmont. One of the NP engines which carried the name "Spokane & Palouse" had been repainted and re-lettered at Sprague and was now NP no. 36. It was understood that S&P nos. 2, 3 and 4 were to be re-lettered NP. The passenger coach was full most evenings when it arrived in Belmont.[38]

The *Gazette* said August 19 that S&P officers were "out" with Pullman because they could not get the donation of land they expected for a depot. The short item concluded, "This dabbling in town sites is a mighty small business for a railroad company, nevertheless as it is a custom of the Northern Pacific and its allies, it is not good policy for a small country town to buck against it." In early September work on the 500-foot rock cut opposite Pullman was "progressing energetically. Rocks fly through, over and on to the town with uncomfortable freedom." At least two buildings were damaged. A week later the newspaper reported that track laying had begun on the S&P.[39]

On Sunday morning September 10 the S&P worked as quickly as possible at Garfield putting in a crossing of the C&P Farmington line. A little after noon an ORN official arrived and told the S&P superintendent that he had instructions to the remove the crossing, but the ORN was outnumbered, withdrew, and the crossing was completed before night and a guard of 40 to 75 men was posted. About three o'clock, while the S&P men were having a good time, 25 ORN men arrived and began removing the crossing. They were discovered and being outnumbered they removed themselves. The S&P increased its force to 110 men on Wednesday night, the day force being smaller. The track laying forces were expected to arrive on the 16th. The S&P was spending $500 a day to guard the crossing. The NP's Anderson went to Portland to apologize to W. H. Holcomb, ORN General Manager. On September 15 the S&P agreed to bear all the costs of construction and maintenance of the crossings at Garfield and Pullman to the specifications of the C&P, that if a flagman was necessary the S&P would pay the costs of persons of C&P choosing and any signals and gates. C&P trains would have priority over S&P trains of the same class and passenger trains would in all cases have priority over freight trains. The C&P Trustees agreed November 22, 1887, to the conditions and that for the sum of one dollar each to allow the S&P to cross the C&P at Garfield and Pullman. The 1887 contract continued to govern both crossings to at least 1929.[40]

A certificate of the completion of precisely the first 10 miles of track was signed by Anderson October 1. On the 3rd Harris asked Anderson when he might expect the certificate for the second 10 miles. Anderson responded that Bennett was nearly crippled for money and so work was slow. On the 10th Anderson telegraphed to say it would be 12 or 15 days at least. There was "extreme difficult[y] of getting timber anywhere in the country and escape government seizures is one of serious troubles."[41]

E. W. Cowgill, Bennett superintendent, and John Tobin, tracklaying boss, were arrested for trespass on the field of J. G. Potter, near Garfield. On September 21 they were fined $25 and costs in Colfax. The S&P appealed the court decision. Potter lived on a disputed claim and had put a wire across the S&P right-of-way and Cowgill cut the wire. November 9 Mohr wrote Anderson that the land claimed by Potter was also claimed by a Mr. Lawrence who had given the right-of-way gratis. U.S. Land Office decided against Potter. Mohr had Potter arrested for obstruction and had him placed under a $2,000 bail that Potter could not raise (the newspaper said he raised a $1,000 bond for his release). "This case had a very salutary effect upon other similar cases."[42]

On October 7 it was noted that the NP Elevator Co. would build elevators at Four Mile Creek [Fallon], Branham [Whelan], and Pullman. A farmer told the *Gazette* that 500,000 bushels of wheat would be hauled to Garfield instead of Colfax because the lower freight rate was worth five cents a bushel. The Pullman tank and pump house were completed by November 25 on Missouri Flat near the location of the depot.[43]

Mohr wrote Anderson October 11 that the shortage of laborers was so great that even paying a premium did not get sufficient workers. Even if Bennett were paid what

Palouse City, Washington, February 1890. Behind the caboose (lower left) is the combination depot built in 1887, 108′ x 20′, lengthened 50′ in 1892. To the right is "Haynes Palace Studio" car, a water tank, and warehouses. To the right of the depot middle distance is the wagon bridge across the Palouse River. *Photograph: H-2373, Montana Historical Society, Haynes Foundation Collection.*

he was owed it would not necessarily speed up the work. On the other hand, "Bennett is himself hard-pressed by those to whom he owes money, that he cannot very well be blamed for lack of energy." He concluded that there was enough rail to lay 18 2/3rds miles and that ties were not a problem. On the 20th he wrote Bennett that he would accept bids for the Palouse River Howe truss bridges. Mohr assured D. L. Staley on the 22nd that the line would reach Staley's station on or before December 1 and therefore Staley should go ahead and erect his warehouse.[44]

On October 11 Harris wrote Billings that he had learned that the OT executive committee had voted to dismiss the S&P suit until the lease of the ORN was settled. On the same day Harris telegraphed Anderson to tell Bennett that the payments "will be adjusted in a few days and all hands will have easy sailing.... Any such action [to attach property at Spokane] by Bennett is unnecessary and damaging & will delay and not force the payments. Everything is all right if he will be patient a few days longer." The S&P owed Bennett $117,120. The injunction was dissolved and suit dismissed on the 26th.[45]

Mohr wrote T. T. Hughes of Palouse City October 25 offering $500 to settle a dispute even though Hughes did not have title to the land in question. The dispute had gone on too long and Hughes was unreasonable. "Should you in any way interfere with our track-laying, I wish it distinctly understood that this offer is withdrawn and null and void." This was one of several disputes about right-of-way claims. The ORN may have been involved in provoking some of the disputes. One dispute in Palouse City began in 1887 and finally ended in 1907 when the United States Supreme Court gave for the second time an opinion against the NP.[46]

Mohr wrote Wm. Moir, master mechanic at Sprague November 2 that he was willing to trade engines provided the new engine would arrive before the one he had was given up. "We are so closely pushed for work now that we cannot afford even half a minute's delay." On the 4th Mohr wrote that he was anxious to have the track finished to Palouse City the next day and the main track and side tracks were to be properly surfaced and lined.

On November 3 Mohr wrote Oakes asking for advice on right-of-way, between Marshall and Fellows' Divide, obtained from citizens of Spangle; it was worth at least $5,000, but the citizens refused to deliver the deeds. The operating department had been stopping trains at a point not acceptable to Spangle citizens. Mohr thought a compromise might be arranged if the operating department would agree not to stop at the point in question except for the purpose of removing wheat during the shipping season. On the same day Mohr wrote three Palouse City residents in regard to an unpaid $2,750 that Palouse City residents had agreed to provide for right-of-way between Garfield and Four Mile Creek. Mohr said he was willing to compromise, "What is the best you can do?"

On the 4th Mohr ordered another engine, caboose, and crew for an additional material train. The distance to the front had grown such that two trains were necessary. This would be in addition to the two engines with the track laying machine, one hauling surfacing material and another materials. The new engine would switch at Belmont and take wheat out of Four Mile Creek, Palouse City, and Garfield. The warehouses were full and from 10 to 15 empty box cars were needed per day. He wrote Cowgill that because of the necessity of taking wheat from warehouses at Garfield and Palouse City, he would accept track as soon as it reached Palouse City. On the same day Mohr wrote that because of "the exceedingly treacherous nature of the soft clay cuts...it will be necessary to have the ditches deeper and wider than is usually the case." Mohr was anxious to finish the track laying so that Genesee could be reached before the heavy snows. Bennett would increase the track laying and surfacing forces provided material was received as needed. As a result Mohr had arranged to have track materials distributed along the Spokane Falls & Idaho (where Mohr was also the engineer-in-charge) to be delivered to the S&P.

On November 9 the NP elevator at Four Mile, filled with wheat, collapsed and was reported a "total wreck." Wheat was piled up outside of warehouses and in Pullman it was a serious problem. "It is to be hoped that the N. P. is better supplied with cars than the niggardly O. R. & N." By December 17 the Pullman NP Elevator was ready to receive grain. Track laying continued until snow fell and was beyond Staley in late December. At that point the McConnell, Chambers & Co. warehouse was receiving a large quantity of grain.[47]

On November 17 Mohr wrote J. R. Clark at Belmont that cabooses would have to be turned over to the operating department. "They will furnish us lumber cars with doors at each end and which we will have time to fit up with stoves and seats before cabooses are taken away." He told Clark he could not send another engine. A double crew should be put on Engine 223 or any other engine Clark had. "By taking out wheat at night and putting on double crew on other engines, you must get along the best you can." Wanting to replace Clark, Mohr inquired of Buckley on November 24 "[c]an you recommend to me a first class man who can take charge of all Construction trains and all matters relating to the moving of material to the front, and of wheat from Pullman and other points to Belmont. He must be a thoroughly competent man accustomed to handling train men. I will pay him whatever salary you deem proper, and agreed in with him. The job will last about two months." On the same day Mohr wrote Cowgill, "I propose to put a man in charge of this whole business, who will either exact obedience from trainmen or get some who will." Under the label "Personal" Mohr wrote Assistant Engineer Lewis on the 25th, that the last two times he had been at Belmont a large part of the force were sleeping at eight in the morning. "if there is any superfluity of time, the matter can be corrected by dispensing with the services of some of the employes [sic]...I will be pleased to have you ascertain as accurately as possible, what the causes of the confusion and delays in the matter of forwarding material etc., by trains, have been.... It seems that [Mr. Clark] does not possess sufficient force of will or understanding of the requirements, to be exacted from train men, to preserve proper discipline."

On the 28th Mohr wrote a lengthy letter to S. G. Fulton, assistant general freight agent, Portland, about the problems of moving wheat. There was a shortage of motive power which he had been unsuccessful in remedying. He tried to double the crews, work each crew 12 hours, and to run trains at night. When this was done the crews resigned because they were no longer making overtime, which they could make on the main line. During the day track laying required all the available motive power. When motive power could be temporarily spared, no cars were available to move the grain. "I will also state here that I do not receive the slightest assistance from Mr. Weymouth; from an inbred and hereditary opposition to the Construction Department he is rather pleased than otherwise to see us in hot water." He doubted his authority to raise the pay of train men to what they would make with over time on the main line. This increase in pay would be chargeable to the construction department which gets a "very small compensation" from hauling grain. If the operating department would furnish more motive power at their expense and if he were given the authority to adjust the pay, "matters can no doubt be readily arranged." There was nearly 500,000 bushels awaiting movement between Pullman and Genesee in addition to that between Belmont and Pullman. The great misfortune was the injunction, if work could have been done in the summer, the line would be completed and "all the difficulties avoided." On the same day Mohr wrote Anderson enclosing a copy of his letter to Fulton. He noted that Bennett objected to interruptions in his work because of wheat traffic and that they did not want to delay Bennett. He said he did not want to increase the costs of the construction department to accommodate the operating department without Anderson's consent. On December 3 Mohr wrote Weymouth, requesting that he not hire crews who have resigned from construction on account of being confined to a 12-hour limit.

Paul Schulze telegraphed Harris on November 29 that he had been credibly advised that Mohr had been working with Seattle, Lake Shore and Eastern interests while they were in Spokane Falls and they left with Mohr on the S&P to the Snake River.[48]

On the 28th Mohr had responded to a telegram from S&P Treasurer Baxter blaming Mohr's office for delays in payments to Bennett. "While I regret, exceedingly, to deprive anyone of the comfortable sensation of a fulfilled duty, and that greater comfort still of feeling that it is always 'the other fellow' who is at fault, I am nevertheless obliged in justice to myself, to make a modest denial of the liability of your charge." Mohr gave in some detail the timeliness of the estimates sent from his office and reasons when there were delays. He concluded, "I do not mention this with the slightest spirit of resentment, because I am confident you did not consider, carefully, the facts when you made the claim which it is the object of this to controvert."

Having time to think about it, Mohr on December 2 wrote a second letter to Baxter. The letter is more temperate and is revealing in how Mohr saw his and the S&P's situations. He did not want the controversy seen "only a little squabble as to the question of our respective promptness in the discharge of official duties." The freight department, the Northern Pacific Elevator Co., farmers, Anderson, and Harris were all pushing to get the work done. "All along our proposed stations, thousands of tons of wheat lie stacked up in sacks, along the road side, exposed to the weather; whose owners are clamorous for relief." Mohr had promised the farmers who used the Snake River for transport that the railroad would reach them for removal of the harvest, but it did not because of the nonpayment of Bennett's estimates and the slow arrival of material.

> Being short of money they of course must sell their wheat, they can now neither ship it over our line, neither can they, on account of the bottomless condition of the roads, haul it to Snake River points.... By the time the injunction proceedings were dissolved, and payment of estimates could be partially resumed, Bennett, on account of the strait in which he was placed for want of money, had lost a large part of his force, a number of his sub-contractors deserted him, the Fall rains softening up the material, the days became very short...; hard frosts solidified the soil, and of the force remaining, many quit work on account of the inclemency of the season.... [W]e were not able to supply either cars or motive power in sufficient quantities

to enable the work to progress as it should. If work is delayed until the roads are permanently frozen, shippers and farmers will in their disgust, haul the largest part to the nearest O. R. & N. points, or to Snake River.... The Company was owing Bennett on the 20th of November, about $100,000.00.

Mohr telegraphed E. L. Cowgill on December 1, "Just received telegram from Robert Harris that track must positively reach eighty third mile post by December tenth; & Idaho line—December 24. This must be accomplished at all hazard." On December 3 track was laid to Pullman (approximately MP 76). On the 12th Anderson telegraphed Harris that it was imperative to operate as far as Uniontown, 95th mile. He was informed that there were 100,000 bushels of wheat south of Pullman waiting transportation. Laying track in the winter would cost $1,000 to $2,000 more per mile than in the spring. Anderson telegraphed on the 24th that it was imperative to reach Genesee as soon as possible. The farmers there had held 500,000 bushels for the arrival of the railroad.[49]

Harris had separately telegraphed Anderson and Cannon, September 12, 1887, that he had heard from Oakes that Mohr had taken steps in Genesee "to locate depot with view to town site speculation and in a place inconvenient for the interest of the Railroad Company and the public. It would be suicidal for us to antagonize the people interested in Genesee." The depot should be located for the best interests of the people and the railroad and "without any regard to the profits of a townsite."[50] On December 6 citizens of Genesee wrote several letters and petitions to Harris claiming that although the citizens of Genesee had secured right-of-way and had donated 40 acres for depot purposes, etc., local officers of the company had changed the railroad location to a new town site about a mile west of the town. "That change will utterly destroy the Old Town...we do not believe the Managers of the Company endorse this speculation and at a cost to themselves and injury to the Old settlers hence we ask protection and relief at your hands." The citizens claimed that their depot site, for which they were willing to donate 50 acres, was higher and better located with respect to roads than the new site, the Evans property. They said that the new site was deeded to Paul Mohr and four friends, all residing in Spokane Falls. Harris responded he would look into doing what was practicable to protect the interests of the citizens of Genesee.

Mohr on December 14, 1887, wrote P. Joy, agent at Belmont, "Bennett claims he has a car of powder and other material, at Belmont, which, owing to your action, he cannot get. Is it not possible for you to straighten this out with Bennett, as the powder is needed on the work." Bennett telegraphed Harris on the 28th: "It is utterly impossible for me to make any headway on S and P work owing to delays caused at Belmont by an obstreperous agent we shall be compelled to quit work unless some remedy devised have stood this imposition long as we can." The same day Bennett sent a second telegram to Harris:

> Agent Joy has used every possible technicality to obstruct the delivery of supplies. Both President and Engineer reported him I have repeatedly done so and finally by advice of Gen Anderson I moved my headquarters away from Belmont to secure harmony and he still holds my supplies at Belmont under any and every pretext. Weymouth and Buckley seem to hold some animosity toward Mohr and will offer no relief. My burden in that work has not been light and I ought not be subject to the pranks of an irresponsible agent.

On the same day Anderson also telegraphed Harris:

> Station agent at Belmont is charged by Bennett & his Superintendent as being Cranky and taking pleasure in putting obstructions in the way of doing their work. Bennett is aggressive and hot headed. There has been a good deal of trouble with this agent all through season but operating department have declined to change him. Have sent message to see if peace cannot be restored. I presume both are more or less to blame.[51]

On December 20 Mohr inquired from Cowgill why no track was laid the day before. The "weather was fine and ground in good condition." In a second letter he pointed out that a number of right-of-way and depot contracts were conditioned on reaching Colton by January 1. He asked if the crews could work Sundays and Christmas for extra pay. Mohr told Lewis December 22 that if necessary, he should put in an additional side track at Palouse City for empty cars. The next day Mohr wrote Harris that the weather had been unusually bad that winter, softening the roadbed to the consistency of mush, holding neither men nor track. Heavy trains of wheat had passed over the line before the banks had a chance to settle. The paramount interest of the company has been to move an estimated million and half bushels between Pullman and Genesee. "The...contractors who are undoubtedly losing money, would be only too much pleased to get into a quarrel and stop work, necessitating the exercise of a good deal of policy in handling them." He concluded, "I am exceedingly anxious to have the road finished, myself, as I have some business engagements that I wish to enter on as quickly as possible." Harris responded that he had asked Buckley to go over the line with Mohr to determine whether to continue track laying or wait for spring. It was reported in Portland that Bennett told Cowgill to work until the 24th and then to pull out.[52]

Harris telegraphed Anderson December 19 to appoint NP Principal Assistant Engineer H. S. Huson as chief engineer for the Spokane and Palouse to take effect January 1. The S&P stockholders elected January 6, 1888, trustees: Cannon, Schulze, Buckley, Huson, A. A. Newbery, J. H. Mitchell, Jr. and F. P. Weymouth. The trustees meeting immediately elected Cannon, president; Buckley, vice president; Geo. S. Baxter, treasurer; and Newbery, secretary. Newbery reported the results to Harris adding that Huson replaced Anderson as trustee because the latter had severed his connection with the NP on January 1.[53]

Buckley telegraphed Harris January 8 that there was about 14 miles of track yet to be laid. He recommended that the track be laid then rather than let the construction forces go. It would cost about $125 more per mile to lay the tracks then than in the spring. Tracks laid in the winter could be surfaced by the construction department and there would be no need to incur the expenses of reassembling a construction crew. The tracks south of Belmont should not be used for traffic until surfaced. In any case without a Columbia River bridge at Kennewick there was no way to get additional wheat to the coast. The ferry at Kennewick, which was in bad shape and could fail at any time, was only able to haul construction materials. There was ice at Kennewick and the ferry was not running. Huson wrote Harris on the 11th agreeing with Buckley that the remaining 14 miles should be laid by February 1. Surfacing had been done to Pullman, 32.6 miles, and about three miles of the 28.4 miles from Pullman to Genesee. It was not possible to do surfacing at a reasonable cost in the winter and the Belmont to Pullman track would need to be gone over again. After the track reached Genesee there would remain "a small amount of finishing to do" on trestles and the three Howe spans across the Palouse River, and on buildings, many of which were up. It was "very necessary" that the Howe Trusses be erected before spring so as not to lose the false

This location was given five different names by the S&P/NP. "Johnsons" on the combination depot was the name from approximately 1891 to 1908. It was Johnson, Washington, from 1915 to the abandonment of the Genesee Branch in 1984. The 20′ x 81′ depot was built in 1902. *Photograph 99-150, Manuscript and Special Collections, Washington State University Library.*

work. Huson recommended that the Spokane Falls office be closed, except for the chief clerk, February 1. Both Mohr and Bennett had been told to rush the track to Genesee and abandon efforts to surface.[54]

On January 13 Harris wrote Mohr saying, "It looks to me as if it would be May before the track is laid and ready for business." He did not want to take the responsibility of advising farmers to hold their grain for shipment on the S&P. On the same day Harris wrote Huson that Mohr wanted to finish his S&P responsibilities as soon as possible; Huson should "meet his convenience in this respect." Huson responded that he had notified Mohr that he could go after February 1.[55]

On the 17th Harris telegraphed Huson asking the cost of laying three quarters of a mile of track on S&P the week before. Huson responded, "Impossible to answer your inquiry as to cost of track laying spokane & palouse with any degree of accuracy, the expense has doubtless been very high. The weather has been extremely cold and unfavorable & no fuel for engines except green wood at five dollars cord. For these reasons I recommend that the work be stopped at once and all forces discharged except the station organization." Harris on the 20th ordered Huson to stop construction and informed Cannon of his decision. Harris thought Huson should proceed with the bridge and building work. On the 21st, Cannon telegraphed Harris:

> Mr. Mohr is dismissing all men returning motive power to Sprague & stopping work generally I was in hopes we could lay to 93rd mile post before quitting so as to give us the bonds for the 5th section of 10 miles but the snows are so severe I fear it would be impossible we need proceeds to 5th 10 miles to pay up contractors can you arrange payments with this & could not bonds be issued on 8 miles now completed on 5th section.

Harris responded that the bonds could not be issued on less than ten miles, but he would arrange to pay contractors. The next day Cannon telegraphed saying that mild weather had set in and that Bennett telegraphed that now that the worst of the winter was over Bennett could finish the work more cheaply then than by stopping and recommencing work later. Harris on the 25th telegraphed Oakes about Cannon's recommendation and concluded "Do you see any reason for changing programme [sec]?"[56]

S&P Secretary A. A. Newbery, January 10, wrote Harris, enclosing a clipping from the Spokane *Chronicle* of that day reporting that Mohr was asked whether his situation with the railroad changed since he was no longer a director. Mohr was reported to have responded, "The recent election has no relation whatever to my position as engineer in charge, my position and duties remaining precisely the same as heretofore." He said his position would terminate with the completion of the railroad and that he "hoped to have the road finished in about two months." Mohr said he had resigned from his director position. "The only truthful statement is that P. F. Mohr will be at least *two months* laying the few miles of track between Colton & Genesee" [emphasis in original]. Huson, after inspecting the line with Buckley, told Newbery that if he had been in charge the line would have been completed two months ago. Huson also said, "that Mr. Mohr displayed absolute ignorance of the work during the trip." Newbery said he asked Huson "why he didn't make a clear sweep of the S. & P." The response was that that Anderson "wanted Mohr retained & that he was afraid to dismiss him." Newbery continued:

> Mohr is paying no attention whatever to the work—went East this morning with Mr. Gilman of the Seattle, Lake Shore & Eastern Road—in fact he is giving more attention to the interests of the Lake Shore than the S. & P.—his only desire to remain in charge of the S. & P. is to work his townsite schemes—particularly at Genesee where it is proposed to work a similar town moving scheme as Yakima only of course on a smaller scale.... It is an outrage & should not be permitted—"Engineering difficulties" is the plea made by Mohr but that is simple rubbish there are no engineering difficulties—and if the S. & P. is built into the present town of Genesee the Company can get liberal donations of land—otherwise the town will have to move & Mohr Cannon et al get the benefits. There is no reason why the Spokane & Palouse Ry. Co. should not have the benefit of all the donations & concessions of land & town lots on the Extension from Belmont to Genesee.... I presumed they would be obtained in the Company's interest—instead however there has been an outside land company formed by Mohr, Cannon & others not in anyway connected with the S. & P. Ry Co who are about to reap the benefits which properly belong to the Company—all these concessions & gifts have been made in consideration of the building of the road—in some cases the line has been charged at great expense to the R. R. Co. to reach some special tract of land upon which a depot has been built or located & a townsite acquired by the outside land Co.—A great deal of this property can yet be saved to the S. & P. if Mohr is removed and someone authorized to take charge of the matter in conjunction with Mr. Huson. If Mohr remains in charge it is a safe wager that the line will not be completed to Genesee by March 1st—"

Newbery included a hand written note for Harris listing town sites south of Belmont with the "value of lots given to Land Co." totaling $39,500. Mohr claimed that the original Genesee railroad site was a marsh. On January 17 Harris wrote Oakes instructing him to have a "proper" person look into the matter. Apparently before

Oakes acted, G. W. Bird, traveling auditor, was instructed on the 20th by the assistant general auditor to go to Genesee to "thoroughly investigate." Bird submitted his report January 28. Bird, probably relying too much on a local land owner whose offer of land was rejected by Mohr, found that Mohr benefited, as did John H. Evans, a local land owner, in changing the site, "There is no doubt in my mind but that the old town site & original survey is far preferable to the one chosen." A majority of the merchants were there for years and drew trade from 22 miles east and 10 miles both north and south. All were opposed to moving. They were still willing to donate land for the depot site. The new site is nearly as high as the old, but the "Y" track was in a marsh.[57]

Mohr telegraphed Harris on January 23 that he thought it in the interest of the public and the company for the operating department to accept the road to Staley, 39 miles south of Belmont. The expense of operating from Spokane to Staley would be about the same as operating to Belmont. On the 24th Harris referred the matter to Oakes. Oakes' response came in two telegrams, the first on the 25th: "Huson will be at Spokane tomorrow or next day & will make necessary changes all things considered. I think we should close the work & get rid of present management substituting an economical staff & resuming work soon as we get rid of present outfit will let you know what Huson thinks when I hear from him." The second on the 30th: "Huson has closed all work at front on [S&P] discharged forces except train crew & few men gathering scattered material. [S]pokane office reduced to two men. Mohr given to Feby first to straighten up and get out. Perhaps we can do some business on the line after current force is cleaned out."[58]

W. H. Wrightman,[59] assistant engineer, wrote Huson on February 19 the first of a series of reports on conditions south of Belmont. Lewis had laborers clearing cuts and digging ditches. In all of the deep cuts the earth had slid and partially covered the tracks. The line had been surfaced from Belmont to about five miles south of Pullman, but beyond little surfacing had been done and the track was not completely tied. Logs had damaged the false works at the first and third crossings of the Palouse River. He was going to place men at the bridge sites to protect the false work from logs being put into the river about 15 miles above the third crossing. As soon as the road was sufficiently dry he would put about five gangs of 10 men each to surface track and thoroughly ditch all the cuts. Laborers were being paid $2.00 per day and bridge men $3.00. A week or so later the worst of the cuts between Palouse and Pullman had been cleared. Section crews had been put in place, the line was occupied from Belmont to Pullman. From Pullman to the end of the line the track gang would look after the line. A train was running daily between Belmont and Staley. Track laying could probably begin as soon as the rail arrived.

On February 21 Bennett telegraphed Harris that he had not received payments since November and he could not get an answer from St. Paul. Harris responded the same day that payments had been arranged and on the 23rd Bennett thanked him for his prompt reply. Harris telegraphed Oakes that it was desirable to resume track laying as soon a practicable so the S&P could sell its bonds and pay its debts. Harris wrote Oakes that the board had authorized the return of the $100,000 bond Bennett deposited in Helena. Bennett thanked Harris and said he would submit a claim for extra cost, namely interest on borrowed money and work done in the winter on a summer contract. Bennett closed saying, "I am exceedingly sorry the necessity arose for this action, but I cannot see why I should be made to carry a burden of this nature without recompense."[60]

In early March men were working south of Pullman and Wrightman expected the track laying outfit to leave in the morning for the front. Four cars of 100-foot span timbers arrived as had four cars of 161-foot span timbers. In a later letter he thought that they could lay a half mile of track a day, but that might be delayed by six inches of snow in the proceeding 24 hours. They were taking about 15 cars of wheat a day to Belmont. In 15 days or so trains would be running to Colton. There would be considerable local business in lumber, wood, and produce in addition to passenger, merchandise, and grain. A daily train south of Belmont would be possible if the train from Spokane arrived at Belmont at nine in the morning. He said a train would start from Colton arriving at Belmont in time to arrive at Spokane at a reasonable time. A construction train left Belmont daily in the morning for Staley. He thought ballasting, buildings and bridges would be completed July 1.

Oakes instructed Huson to visit Genesee, which he did on February 23. On March 15 he wrote Oakes that he had met with Evans and other leading citizens to talk the matter over.

> The topography of the country shows that it was impossible, either now or in the beginning, to run a line past the old town without locating the station upon the grounds of Mr. Evans… in the beginning Mr. Evans was willing to give these grounds to the Company…it became known that unless the people of the old town bestirred themselves Mr. Mohr would make an arrangement with Mr. Evans to go to the new place.…[Mohr had three offers of land including that of Evans]…You can readily see the opportunity which Mr. Mohr had, and which he undoubtedly took advantage of, to make the most for himself.

> Originally the location could been made...through the old town, just as easily as where it has been placed. Mr. Evans would have been contented at that time to have given right of way for stations grounds. At the present, of course he is unwilling to do so, as he has got a better thing in the new town, and will of course, not give it up. It is not practicable to locate the sidings at the old town, except upon grounds owned by Mr. Evans. We could of course condemn, but in order to do so we would have to abandon about $8,000 worth of work which has been expended in grading sidings at the new town, and spend in addition about $8,000 more in grading at the old town, besides making about half a mile longer line.
>
> ...There is little at the old town...There is no question in my mind but what the people of the old town would peaceably move to the new. Under the circumstances, I advocate remaining where we are...
>
> I called the citizens together and explained to them that in my opinion the act of the representative of the Company in establishing a new town in their midst was reprehensible. For this action on his part the man who was to blame had been removed, and was no longer connected with the Company. I explained to them it was too much now to ask us to expend additional money necessary in order to go to the old town to accommodate [the offer of] Mr. Levy who, from the beginning to end had acted in an illiberal manner, and that even if we attempted to go we would have to enter into a long condemnation suit with Mr. Evans. The citizens acknowledge the force of my argument, and seemed in the main to be satisfied, and friendly to the Company.
>
> As regards the dryness of the two towns, there is no difference.... The wagon roads at present time do not go to the new town, but it will cost but a small sum to put them there, and when done the new town will be as accessible as the old. I have been much edified by the report of Mr. Bird which shows great painstaking. It has helped me a great deal in forming my conclusions. There are however, engineering questions which enter into the subject which, of course Mr. Bird could not be expected to understand.
>
> In view of all the facts, allow me to suggest that while a wrong has been done in that community, we are not in shape to right it without great expense.

Oakes sent Huson's report to Harris, saying "I concur with him in the position taken and think this subject can be considered as ended." On April 2 Harris wrote Oakes that the executive committee had endorsed Huson's report.

In mid-March the S&P was ballasted and the passenger train was running to Johnson (south of Pullman). Oakesdale had in less than two years grown to 200 inhabitants, and 300,000 to 400,000 bushels of wheat, oats, and barley were to be shipped from four grain warehouses.[61]

Wrightman wrote that track laying recommenced on March 13. The track laying was slowed by slides in the cut at the end of the track. Shippers in Colton were nearly ready to load wheat. He expected that starting the 25th they would take a train a day from there. *The West Shore* described the cut at Colton:

> At the time of the suspension of work last winter, the track had reached the deep cut within about one and one-half miles of Colton. Several springs course this cut, making the road bed a complete mire of muck. On account of this, the track laying was attended with difficulties and progressed slowly. After the track had been laid through the cut, and it became necessary for the engine and heavily loaded cars to pass through, the ties and track would sink with their heavy burden as much as a foot. This trouble is now avoided, and the work of construction will be pushed as rapidly as possible.

Track was completed to Colton on March 19, the first freight was received on the 21st, and first passenger train on the 25th. It was reported that 200,000 bushels of grain were waiting at Colton. There was complaint in Rosalia of the use of Chinese labor on that section of the S&P; it was considered to be "very unfair to honest white labor."[62]

Cannon, March 19, 1888, tendered his resignation as S&P president and director to Harris. He would have done so sooner if not for the injunction. S&P contractors were overdraw at his Bank of Spokane and could not repay because they had not been reimbursed. He enclosed his bill for services to February 6 when Oakes assumed control. He thanked Harris for his "kindness, the courtesy, and justice which you have always shown in your dealings with me." The Spokane Falls *Morning Review* reported that Cannon had resigned to turn his attention to getting the Seattle, Lake Shore and Eastern into Spokane (see chapter XIII). Cannon pointed out that the S&P was practically completed and his position would be "minimal." His relations with the NP "were of the most cordial nature." On the April 19 the S&P trustees accepted Cannon's resignation and elected Harris president. On June 18 Harris wrote Cannon that he had approved the bill sent March 19 and he should hear from the treasurer "in due time."[63]

In late March Wrightman reported that about 45 men were laying track and another 25 or so were ditching between Staley and Colton. Tracking laying would resume after an 18-span bridge was completed. In early April track was almost to Genesee, but two 17-span bridges needed to be constructed, which would take about five days. Later in April the tracks reached Genesee. All buildings were well advanced except those at Genesee. General work of surfacing had not begun. Soon about 50 men would be surfacing at Belmont and a smaller crew at Genesee. Erection of a 101-foot span bridge would begin shortly. A through train would begin taking freight to Genesee April 17. An Odd Fellows excursion from Pullman to Spokane Falls and return would on the 27th. On the 22nd Wrightman wrote that ties and spiking had been completed to Genesee and that the track laying force was moving to Belmont to begin surfacing. Heavy rains would delay ballasting.

In May farmers around Rosalia were unhappy that the NP elevator was not paying the same prices as were being paid at other points on the S&P. There was talk of erecting a farmers' warehouse. In Oakesdale there were 40 cars of wheat on the side track, the warehouses were about full and no cars to ship grain. One to three thousand bushels of grain were arriving daily. "If they cannot move it now, what will they do this fall?" In mid-May President Harris made his first S&P tour of inspection. "He stated that his expectations were more than verified and expressed his surprise upon finding such an extent of rich farming lands."[64]

In May Huson made overlapping certificates of completion: from mile post 83 to mile 97 1/3, at the Washington and Idaho territorial boundary; mile 93 to mile 97 1/3; and mile 93 to 104, the end of the line. The reason for the overlapping certificates was uncertainty whether bonds could be issued on less than 10 miles and whether Farmers' Loan and Trust would bond the Idaho portion.[65]

In early May Wrightman wrote that surfacing was completed to within four miles of Palouse. By May 20 ballasting was complete to Palouse and in several places beyond, leaving about 36 miles to ballast. Until ballasting was completed the line should not be turned over, by which time the depot at Genesee would be completed and all other buildings necessary for immediate use would be ready. The trusses for the three Howe spans were up, but floors and some cribbing needed to be done. If there were sufficient cars probably 20 to 25 could be shipped per day. On May 27 Wrightman wrote that except for a mile and half still remaining at Palouse ballasting had been completed to about two miles south of Four Mile Creek. The weather had been fine and "work was going along well." He had not yet made leases for warehouses.

Towns along the S&P were talking about hiring a man to work trains at Spokane Falls for immigrants. The NP immigration agent informed the *Gazette* that the NP

The Uniontown, Washington, combination depot, 20′ x 71′, was built in 1888. In 1959 lumber from this depot was used by the Colton agent to enlarge his depot between Johnson and Uniontown on the Genesee Branch. The engine is NP 697, 4-4-0, class C-3, built in 1882 and offered for sale, but not sold, in 1910. *Photograph 87-058A, Manuscript and Special Collections, Washington State University Library.*

Waiting for the train in Genesee, Idaho. The combination depot, 20′ x 116′, was built in 1888. The three Genesee Branch depots pictured in the book are similar, although this depot has the freight room at the opposite side of the agent's bay as compared with the other depots. *Photograph: 6-3-21, Latah County Historical Society.*

would make special efforts to divert immigration to the Palouse country. Pullman, about 300 people, was the largest grain depot in Washington Territory, shipping wheat, barley, oats, and flax from the 1887 crop.[66]

Wrightman's June 3 letter reported that ballasting was completed to about a mile north of Pullman and considerable work had been done in the vicinity of Uniontown and Genesee. Most buildings were completed and the bridges would be done in a day or two. The track would be ready for the operating department on the 20th, but work might need to be done after that and the stock yards needed completion. The ORN competed for the wheat business at every station south of Belmont and the limited warehouse facilities on the S&P meant that the NP needed to furnish transportation or lose considerable business. He returned one engine; the two remaining could haul out 18 to 20 cars a day. On June 11 Wrightman estimated that there were 202,000 bushels of wheat in warehouses from Garfield to Genesee and another 485,000 "in country." On the 24th about five miles of ballasting needed to be done. The engine house at Genesee and the painting of bridges would be completed in a few days. The warehouse leases for Garfield, Uniontown, and Genesee were completed.

Harris wrote Oakes June 11 that Bennett wanted a settlement on his S&P work: Bennett had stood by the S&P and the NP ought to do whatever was right in the matter. The NP Finance Committee June 27 authorized the NP to accept S&P drafts, not to exceed $100,000, to pay contractors; the NP to be reimbursed by the S&P.[67]

In the year ended June 30, 1887, the NP shipped 1,823 cars of wheat to Portland; in 1888 2,763 cars went to Portland and 1,622 to Tacoma. In addition there had been considerable movement of wheat from Washington to Duluth, but with the completion of the Columbia River bridge and Stampede tunnel this had declined. "[T]o avoid complications with the [ORN], it was considered necessary to raise the rate upon wheat from Washington Territory to eastern terminals, resulting in almost entirely stopping shipments in this direction. It is more profitable for this Company to encourage such shipments to the Puget Sound market."[68]

On July 1, 1888, the Belmont to Genesee line, 60.66 miles, was turned over to the operating department. From Marshall to Genesee the line was 103.66 miles long. Augustus C. Bowman was the engineer on the first train from Genesee to Spokane Falls. According to Bowman, in 1910, the train consisted of three cars: combination mail and baggage car, smoker, and day coach. At Genesee he, and conductor Thomas F. Garvin, were issued the following order:[69]

Order 20 Sprague July 1 88
Garvin & Engr.
Leave Genesee at five-5 o'clock a.m. and Run to Spokane Falls on the following special time card; avoiding regular trains.

Genesee - Lv 5 am
Uniontown - " 529 "
Colton - " 539 "
Johnson Siding - " 552 "
Staleys - " 601 "
Pullman - {Arr 621 "
{Lv 641 "
Whelan - " 658 "
Four Mile - " 713 "
Palouse - " 733 "
Garfield - " 805 "
Belmont - " 828 "
Oakesdale - " 842 "
Rosalia - " 910 "
Plaza - " 929 "
Spangle - " 952 "
Marshall Jct - " 1025 "
Spokane Falls - Arr 1050 "
Do not pass Belmont Without Getting Orders
12 FPW
13 Garvin SPO. & Bowman[70]

Probably the first S&P timetable for the completed line from Spokane to Genesee appeared in the *Review* July 11, 1888: eastbound the unnumbered passenger train departed Genesee daily at 5:00 a.m. and arrived Spokane at 10:50 a.m.; westbound the passenger departed Spokane at 1:25 p.m. and arrived Genesee at 7:05 p.m. The freight train departed Spokane at 7:30 a.m. and Genesee at 5:30 a.m.[71]

On July 2 Wrightman reported that ballasting was completed. To complete rip rapping and ditching would take seven or eight days. The stockyards would be completed at about the same time. Since February 25, 819 cars of grain were taken out and during the fall and early winter 283 cars were taken out, making 1097 cars to June 30. In addition to grain and hay, stock and flax were taken out and 202 cars of merchandise received. He estimated that there were still 850 cars to go.

The NP immigration commissioner said that the elevator and warehouse capacity for wheat at Spangle, Plaza, Rosalia, Oakesdale, Belmont, Garfield, Palouse City, Four Mile [Fallon], Whalen, Staley, Johnson, Colton, Uniontown, and Genesee would aggregate over 2,000,000 bushels. The Northern Pacific Elevator Co. had 18 warehouses in Washington Territory and were making arrangements for six more. There were nine warehouses in Tacoma with 45,000 sq. ft., all covered with wheat seven sacks high.[72]

Trains were delayed in September 1888 by a burning bridge north of Rosalia. On October 8 a new railway postal service began from Spokane Falls to Genesee. From Rosalia: "No cars to carry off our grain." Early November 1888 a correspondent to the *Review* wrote: "boarded the train at Uniontown and found that the grain warehouses clear to Spangle filled with grain and still more coming in; in fact the warehouses are blocked for want of cars."

> Palouse City is booming, the good price, being paid for grain and the saw mills being the chief cause of lively times. ...Oakesdale, things look prosperous. It is reported that the S. & P. can safely depend on having to haul a half million bushels of grain out of the town, and it is really surprising where this vast amount comes from.... The North[ern] Pacific is taxed to its utmost in handling all the freight offered, but it is equal to the occasion.... I cannot close this letter without saying a word of praise in favor of the North Pacific, for having placed such excellent facilities at the disposal of the traveling public. The whole distance from Genesee to Spokane and return is made in one day, giving one an excellent opportunity for seeing this truly great inland empire. The passenger train is in charge of Conductor Tom McGovern, who takes especial delight in making one feel at ease while aboard his train.

In November it was reported that an extra S&P freight train was put on to move the grain. That month 742,000 pounds of grain was shipped from Garfield on the ORN. The previous November's total was 510,600.[73]

At the December 3, 1888, meeting of the S&P stockholders were Farmers' Loan & Trust Co., 9993 shares and one share each for Harris, Buckley, S. G. Ramsey, Paul Schulze, J. H. Mitchell Jr., H. S. Huson, and Newman Kline. Harris had requested that C. H. Prescott (late of the ORN/C&P) be substituted for Kline; the remainder of the trustees were reelected and NP Chief Engineer J. W. Kendrick was appointed chief engineer of the S&P.[74]

On November 26, 1888, a north bound freight went onto the ground eight miles north of Pullman in the "summit cut." The accident was caused by spreading rails. The engine and one car passed safely, but six following loaded cars went into the mud almost over their wheels. Passenger trains were delayed until the next evening. Engine No. 70 on the train to Spokane December 27 struck a band of horses south of Marshall and the small snowplow on the pilot nearly cut two of the animals in two.[75]

During the last six months of 1888, the S&P shipped 10,459,598 pounds from Pullman and received 3,157,618. The ORN shipped 11,673,626 pounds from Pullman and received 2,659,189 for a grand total of 27,950,031 pounds at Pullman. The information was provided to the *Herald* by the S&P agent E. F. Crawford and the ORN agent H. H. Brown. From April 19 to December 1, 1888, the revenues of the S&P at Uniontown were $50,613.88.[76]

Genesee, Idaho, from the south in 1908 looking toward the "relocated" site of the town (see p. 73). From the left is a grain warehouse with the wagon unloading ramp visible to the right. Across the street is the depot with a train at right end of the building, railroad west end. *Photographer G. W. Hanson: 77-95.1/E, Idaho State Historical Society.*

Appendix: Track Laying Record, Belmont to Genesee, 1887–88

1887-88	Distance from Marshall	Sources and Notes
Sept. 9		Report that track laying had begun (PG 9/9/87).
Sept. 29	Near MP 53, 10 miles from Belmont.	(1) (2) Profile shows 9/29/87. Certificate of precisely 10 miles completed signed October 1.
Oct. 31	Between MPs 59 & 60.	(1) Between bridges 124 & 125, west of Palouse City.
Nov. 5	64 miles, 2,487 feet.	(3) Over five miles beyond Palouse City. Week ending 5th, six miles, 562 feet main track laid.
Nov. 12	66 miles, 4,447 feet.	(3) Week ending the 12th, one mile, 1960 feet main track laid.
Nov. 19	71 miles, 4,719 feet.	(3) Week ending the 19th, five miles, 272 feet laid.
Nov. 26	75 miles, 211 feet.	(3) Pullman. Week ending the 26th, four miles, 772 feet laid. Profile (1) shows track beyond MP 76 at about ORN crossing.
Dec. 3	76 miles, 1,131 feet.	(3) Week ending the 3rd, one mile, 920 feet laid.
Dec. 10	76 miles, 1,491 feet	(3) Week ending the 10th, 360 feet laid.
Dec. 17	78 miles, 2,385 feet.	(3) Week ending the 17th, two miles, 894 feet laid.
Dec. 24	MP 83.	(3) Fortieth mile from Belmont reached.
Dec. 31	Near east of MP 89.	(1) West of "Gibbson's Divide."
Jan. 2	Near east of MP 90.	(1)
Jan. 14	90 miles, 3,847 feet.	(4)
Mar. 13		(7) Track laying recommenced.
Mar. 19	MP 92.2.	(6) Colton
Mar. 21	93 miles.	(5) Certificate for the fifth 10 miles from Belmont signed.
April 9	Between MP 100 & MP 101.	(1)
April 14	MP 104.	(5) Completed to Genesee. Certified April 24. (1) Shows end of track at 2732 feet beyond MP 104.

Sources: (1) Construction Profile; (2) From Anderson MHS, 136.K.12.3.B; (3) From Anderson MHS, 137.H.5.1.B; (4) From Huson MHS, 137.H.5.2.F; (5) From Huson or Kendrick MHS, 137.H.5.3.B; (6) LT 5/3/88, 1; (7) From Wrightman UMT, 128/370/513.

Oregon Railway & Navigation Projection and Expansion in the Palouse, 1884–90

The ORN was the principal competitor of the S&P. Recall the Oregon Short Line (OSL), on behalf of the Union Pacific Railway, leased the ORN April 1887, effective the first of that year.

A. The Washington & Idaho Railroad (WI), S&P, and the Coeur d'Alene Mining District[1]

In February 1884 A. M. Cannon, later president of the S&P, wrote NP President Harris recommending that the NP build from its main line near the Idaho-Washington boundary to Coeur d'Alene Lake. Construction was urged as a gateway to the mines in the Coeur d'Alene District and to defend against another company moving into the area.[2]

In mid-November 1885 NP General Manager Oakes wrote Harris that if the ORN persisted in its design to extend beyond Farmington a plan should immediately be developed for a system of branch lines in the Walla Walla region "that can be speedily and cheaply constructed." That possibility was on the mind of ORN President Elijah Smith when he wrote General Manager C. H. Prescott, in the same month, "it occurred to me since that your efforts in securing the right-of-way to the Coeur d'Alene mines may be going outside of our territory as described and limited in the contact between our Co. and the Northern Pacific Co. we want to be careful about this as that is the agreement which keeps them from building or aiding in building a road into Walla Walla.[3]

Oakes wrote Harris in early December that he heard indirectly that D. P. Thompson of Portland had quoted John Muir of the ORN, that the purpose of the company was to build from the Snake River to a connection with the C&P and to extend the latter to Coeur d'Alene Lake. "Rumors of this kind have been afloat for some time, but this is the first information that has reached me in definite form purporting to emanate direct from any officer of that Company." The matter should be taken up with Smith as to their plans and "to show him that an offensive measure of this kind will result in the construction of lines into the WW country that would deprive his Company of far more business than they could secure by extensions to the Coeur D'Alene country." Harris responded that he had discussed the matter with Elijah Smith, and "he assured me that there was no intention on the part of the ORN to extend the Road North of Farmington." On the same day Harris wrote Smith, quoting from Oakes' letter asking, "Will you be so kind as to confirm by letter that it is not the intention of the ORN to cause the extension of any Road North of Farmington and oblige?" On the last day of 1885 Chief Engineer Anderson sent Harris a newspaper clipping on the Coeur d'Alene mines, which he said did not exaggerate, and noted that the ORN was busy surveying in that section.[4]

In his December 9 report on potential Palouse routes, Assistant Engineer J. B. Alexander wrote that the ORN had surveyed from Farmington toward Coeur d'Alene Lake. "Their object in going east of Farmington is thought to be the mining trade of Coeur d'Alene Mts., and the grain raised by the Indians, which is estimated at 100,000 bushels this year. A spur from Rathdrum to the Foot of the Lake would interfere with that scheme."[5]

In mid-December Prescott wrote Smith that D. P. Thompson was interested in building smelting and refining works in Portland and wanted an all-rail route from the Coeur d'Alene region. Thompson in talking to Coeur d'Alene people, "has gone beyond any assurances that have been given to him here and, in stating that the O. R. & N. Co. would build beyond Farmington, he has done so without any authority." Prescott noted that Thompson had stated in writing that what he said was entirely his responsibility. On the 28th Smith wrote Harris enclosing Prescott's letter. The following April Thompson wrote Smith urging the ORN to build to Farmington "this season" and from there to the Coeur d'Alene mines. He was "deeply concerned" that the NP would divert ores to either Tacoma or Duluth. A month later Thompson wrote Muir that S&P Chief Engineer

Paul Mohr had told him that the NP would survey from Farmington to the Coeur d'Alene mines.[6]

Mohr informed Anderson May 4, 1886, that he understood that the ORN was engaged in securing right-of-way through the Indian reservation to Lake Coeur d'Alene. "I presume, however, that this is simply a 'demonstration.'" In mid-May S&P President Cannon wrote Oakes relating that he had formed a small committee of men influential with the Coeur d'Alene Indians to prevent Chief Saltese from going to Washington on behalf of the ORN. He and Mohr would start that week to make a reconnaissance. He was of the opinion that a route from the Palouse to the mining district was preferred over from Rathdrum, which was preferred by the Helena people. A route from the Palouse would get all the wheat in the 'Rockford country', have light grades and have sufficient income that the investment would be returned even if the mines failed. Cannon later sent Harris Mohr's reconnaissance of June 11 from Spangle to "Milo" (near what is now Kellogg, Idaho) on the South Fork of the Coeur d'Alene River, about 81 miles. Mohr wrote that the line on its western end would traverse "exceedingly rich agricultural" lands and on the eastern end "magnificent forests" together yielding 100,000 tons per year. The line would not exceed $1,225,000 or a little over $15,000 per mile. In comparison the line from Rathdrum would be 92 miles and involve "almost continuous heavy rock cutting" along the lake. The lake was frequently closed for four or five months by ice and the need to break bulk from rail to boat and back to rail, made the lake not a practicable alternative. In addition, the Rathdrum line had little traffic resources and would leave the country south of the lake exposed to the ORN. Mohr wrote,

> There seems to be a question of our right to enter upon the Coeur d'Alene Reservation for the purpose of making surveys, and the Indian agent has notified me that a party entering the reservation for the purpose of surveying or for any other purpose would be treated as trespassers unless the Indians, themselves, were favorable. A great fete will take place on the 22nd. Inst at the old mission, at which all the tribes and their chiefs will be present, and I have made arrangements with Father Jacquet to be there. The priests are favorable to the railroad, and claim that the Indians would cheerfully give their consent. We have succeeded, I think, in heading off the O. R. & N. people, who have made themselves very unpopular with the Indians by the action of their agent, General Tannatt.

Mohr wrote Indian Agent Benjamin P. Moore on the 11th asking whether a preliminary survey through the Coeur d'Alene Indian Reservation starting at Spangle and ending at Milo would conflict with the rules and regulations of the Interior Department. The Palouse *Gazette* in late June said that both the NP and ORN were surveying in the vicinity of Rathdrum.[7]

On June 15 the United States Land Office in Coeur d'Alene wrote Oakes that the ORN would build from Farmington to the mining district and recommended that the NP find a suitable route from Thompson Falls, Montana Territory. Oakes telegraphed Harris that he had learned from D. C. Corbin that the ORN "has very positive designs on the Coeur d'Alene country" via a line from Farmington. "Of course, you understand how desirable it is to forestall them if practicable." Mohr informed NP Chief Engineer Adna Anderson July 1 that he would begin surveying from Milo to Spangle the next day.[8]

The *Gazette* reported in early July an ORN preliminary survey from Farmington had found an easy route around the south end of the lake to the mines. The ORN had also decided to build from Texas Ferry to the C&P. "This will almost surely send the Spokane and Palouse branch on south through Colfax."[9]

On July 7, 1886, the ORN filed a charter for the Washington and Idaho Railroad Company (WI) with the Secretary of State of Washington Territory. The initial trustees were all from Farmington. The objectives were to build from Farmington to Spokane Falls, a branch line from the forks of Hangman Creek generally northeast across the Coeur d'Alene Indian Reservation to Wardner, Idaho Territory [near present day Kellogg], and another branch from near Spangle to the mouth of the Coeur d'Alene River.[10]

Corbin considered it too long and expensive to build from the S&P. He and others, including Sam T. Hauser, a Montana entrepreneur, filed July 1, 1886, in Montana a charter for the Coeur d'Alene Railway and Navigation Company (CRN). The company projected a narrow gauge line of 140 miles from Thompson Falls, Montana Territory, to the mining district and thence down the Coeur d'Alene River to the Cataldo Mission where steam boats would be used to Coeur d'Alene City. Grading and bridging contracts for the CRN were awarded August 4 and construction began east from Mission.[11]

In early July Cannon wrote Harris that he and Mohr had explored the territory from Spangle to Milo and had found that the St. Joseph and St. Mary's rivers navigable and that "the mountains are densely covered with the most magnificent timber I have ever seen." He reported that officials of the ORN, including Smith and Prescott, had traveled the country from Spangle. "Should the O. R. & N. push their road into this country from the south it would be exceedingly difficult for us to recoup the advantages lost." If the NP was involved with Corbin in the proposed line from Milo to the lake he did not want to tread on their toes. He pointed out that from the NP mainline near the Idaho border to the Spokane River was only four miles and offered navigation to any point on the lake. "We have the verbal consent of the Coeur d'Alene Indians to cross the reservation with our surveys; so that difficulty is disposed of."[12]

NP associated writer and publisher Eugene V. Smalley wrote Oakes in mid-July that Prescott told him that the S&P violated the 1880 Traffic Agreement and that the ORN might respond by building to Spokane, the Coeur d'Alene district, and the Potlatch country east of Moscow. Smalley urged the NP to occupy the good country of eastern Washington as soon as possible. Later in the month Mohr wrote, "While we have the tacit consent of the Coeur d'Alene Indians to cross the Reservation with our surveys, we ought to conclude...some definite and formal arrangement which would give us the right to build across this Reservation, should it become desirable or necessary to do so. I am informed by the Indian Agent...that but one right will be given." Mohr wrote Harris July 20 that the WI was securing right-of-way between Farmington and the Idaho border and seeking consent of the Indians to cross the reservation. He warned that if the ORN meant business it was questionable how long the NP could retain preference with the Indians. Harris responded that with respect to ORN right-of-way, "We shall try to forestall them."[13]

Although the possibility of a line to the mines from the S&P remained alive for several additional months, in retrospect, the proposal was precluded July 22, 1886, when the NP board of directors authorized construction from the NP mainline to Coeur d'Alene Lake. A party under Mohr was withdrawn from the S&P to survey the line. The Palouse *Gazette* reported construction commenced August 31 with Mohr as engineer-in-charge. On October 24 the Spokane Falls and Idaho Railroad Company (SFI) was incorporated in Spokane on the same day that operation began from Hauser Junction, Idaho Territory, on the NP main line east of Spokane, to Coeur d'Alene City, 13.64 miles. The SFI shared its offices and shops in Spokane Falls with the S&P, and Cannon, Newbery, and Mohr were on the boards of both companies.[14]

From Farmington, A. S. Watt, ORN land agent, wrote Prescott August 4, 1886:

> Am informed by [George W.] Truax that Chief Seltice and Stephen Liberty, his interpreter were here yesterday. They say the Spokane & Palouse and N. P. People were trying to get the same privileges of surveying across the reservation that had been granted by the Indians to the Washington & Idaho Company. The engineer, Mohr, had told them that three or four thousand dollars would be nothing if they wanted money and that he would take as many of them to Washington City as wished to go. Seltice replied that he had already agreed with the other company and declined to entertain any proposition from them. Mr. Truax says Seltice desires very much to go to Washington and as an Indian cannot be expected to be very much better than a white man—the temptation may be too great for him. Unless he can be promised the trip by Mr. Smith he possibly may undertake to go back on his agreements. The Indians have removed the N. P. surveyors from the Reservation. It is reported they had gotten down the Coeur d'Alene from the Old Mission to within about ten miles of its mouth when they were removed.
>
> Seltice also desires very much to see Mr. Smith and have a "talk" so that if he comes up it would be well to have the Chief notified so that he can meet him here. Whilst it is not best to create the impression among the Indians that they are of so very great importance, still, as these other people are using all possible means to acquire equal privileges with the W. & I. Company, it is best not to ignore their desires or disregard their customs—one of which, and one they recognize on all occasions, is for the Chief to have a "talk."

The *Gazette* reported that on September 2 the WI began surveying from Farmington to the Old Mission. In October the WI was cross sectioning between Farmington and Wardner. The right-of-way had been obtained. It was expected that work would begin next season.[15]

In mid-October the Acting Secretary of the Interior wrote the Commissioner of Indian Affairs that if the Indians gave their consent, that no harm would be done by allowing the WI, as the S&P had been allowed, to survey across the Coeur d'Alene Indian Reservation. That this be done "with the express understanding that no steps shall be taken by either Company towards the construction of a road prior to the final action of Congress." On November 10, 1886, WI supplemental articles added an extension in Idaho to Mullan. Truax wrote Elijah Smith the end of November that the maps across the reservation had been sent to Portland and that the survey to Spokane would probably be done in two weeks. It was important that if the Indians went to Washington that someone go with them. In places there was room for only one railroad and the narrow gauge had surveyed some of them. He recommended that some men be placed on those places before the other party knew anything about it.[16]

Mohr wrote Indian Agent Moore, December 9, that he had received a telegram from Newbery, in Washington, D.C., that the Indian Commissioners did not want Chief Saltese to go to Washington. Shortly thereafter, Mohr learned that Saltese did not want to leave for Washington for a week or 10 days and might not go at all. Truax and Steve Liberty were urging strongly that he go and that they would accompany him. Mohr wrote Anderson that a friend of the NP would arrange to accompany Saltese if he went to Washington. He reminded Anderson that Liberty, Saltese's "man of business is 'for sale'..." and that Liberty had come to Mohr "with an offer to fix Saltese 'for our interest' for a sum of $1,000.00." Later Mohr wrote Anderson that Moore had sent a message to the resident agent stating that under no circumstances should Saltese go east. Moore, while friendly to the NP, did not want to appear to be taking sides.[17]

Truax wrote Smith in late December that Saltese had received orders from the Secretary of the Interior not to go to Washington and the Chief was told not to tell anyone. Truax thought that Newbury or Indian Agent Moore would charge that the Chief has been bought by Truax. "I never gave him one cent.... It is my opinion that Mr. Newbury will get down to anything to beat us.... I think it would be advisable to have some one keep track of what Newbury does." He went on the say he would take the Indians to Washington after Congress adjourned and "have them ask the President grant the right-of-way by Executive Order."[18]

On December 15 the St. Paul, Minnesota and Manitoba surveyor, A. B. Roger, wrote James J. Hill about his examination of routes to Missoula and from there into the Coeur d'Alene, Palouse, and Clearwater drainages. On January 24 Hill wrote Smith expressing interest in making a connection with the ORN at Missoula. Smith wrote March 21 "J. J. Hill is here and I have had correspondence with him and while I would only take his Road if we can get it because we cannot button up the Union Pacific." The May *Northwest Magazine* speculated that "the real instigators" of the WI was the Manitoba system. The evidence was that the WI was being extended east to the mines and thus could meet the Manitoba at Missoula. Missoula "undoubtedly is where Hill is quietly working to spring his line on the Northwest, and likely by the Seattle, Lake Shore & Eastern to the Sound."[19]

Mohr wrote Oakes in mid-January that Moore was going to Washington, D.C., at his own expense, except for transportation, and would be of considerable assistance to Newbery in Washington. Moore had written the Interior Department that the S&P would be of more importance to the Indians than the ORN and his influence prevented Chief Saltese from accompanying Truax to Washington. Later in the month Elijah Smith wrote United States Senator J. M. Dolph, Oregon, that the WI was ready to build from Farmington to Mullan as soon as the Congress and the Interior Department gave permission to cross the Coeur d'Alene Indian Reservation. The line had been surveyed and $10,000 had been expended for right-of-way from Farmington to the Indian reservation.[20]

On February 8, 1887, Mohr sent Harris a preliminary map of the S&P extension from Belmont to Genesee, which included a line from Spangle southeast to Hangman Creek thence to the south end of Coeur d'Alene Lake, up the Coeur d'Alene River and up the S. Fork to Milo, Idaho. The cost of construction of the S&P as of June 30, 1887, included the Milo Branch survey, $11,620, same as reported to the ICC in 1916.[21]

Oakes telegraphed Harris April 4, 1887, that the ORN had commenced grading from Farmington through the reservation and that Elijah Smith was working with the Interior Department to keep others from interfering. On the same day Harris wrote D. M. Sweat, of Portland, Maine, instructing him to go to Washington, D.C., "and block this little game of the O.R. & N. It needs prompt attention." On the 17th WI President Truax wrote Smith, that "We have made it so disagreeable for Indian agent Moore that he has resigned so we will not be bothered with him much longer." In early May the UP chief engineer reported that both the ORN and NP had unsuccessfully applied in the last session of Congress for right-of-way across the Indian Reservation; both were likely to get it in the next session. "If the Northern Pacific people should also threaten to build from Rosalia, it should not deter us from going on, unless we could succeed in making a contract with them for the use of a joint line." Mohr on May 20 telegraphed Harris that the ORN was purchasing right-of-way from Farmington to the Spokane River, east of Spokane Falls, and could use the river at Post Falls for navigation to the mission and thereby avoid crossing the reservation.[22]

Interestingly, Thomas J. Potter in his June 14, 1887, "Memoranda for New Lines" did not mention a line to the Coeur d'Alene mines and Spokane (see below and chapter VIII). A second supplemental articles for the WI, July 2, added a line from Mullan to Missoula and a line from Endicott (on the C&P) northeast to connect with the main line at the forks of Hangman Creek, about 12 miles north of Farmington. On July 15 C. C. Van Arsdol was instructed by the WI Secretary to survey to Missoula, but it should not be known that he had come from recent UP service. On December 11 Van Arsdol reported that the Missoula survey was completed. In the meantime in September Van Arsdol was reported by a Lewiston newspaper to be working two miles from Lewiston on the north bank of the Snake River after having surveyed from the Coeur d'Alene down the Potlatch to the Clearwater River and hence to the Snake River.[23]

In July the WI received permission from the Coeur d'Alene Indians to cross the reservation. That month, Truax took Chief Seltice and several elders to Washington, D.C., by special train. They met with President Cleveland and received his support in principle for a line across the reservation.[24]

WI right-of-way agent C. M. Stearns in Spokane Falls in July said that he was getting right-of-way to Mullan and Spokane Falls. The only exception was Spokane Falls where excessive prices were being asked. At least 60 men were grading the Farmington to Mullan line. The NP was working on the other side of the Bitterroot Mountains along the St. Regis River toward Coeur d'Alene. The Walla Walla *Daily Journal* reported in September that Stearns stated that the railroad would push its line from Farmington to Spokane Falls at once. The Spokane Falls *Morning Review* quoting from the *Oregonian,* said that the ORN was using the WI to build to the Coeur d'Alene so as not to be in violation of an agreement five years earlier among the ORN, NP, and UP not to invade each other's territory. H. S. Huson, NP principal assistant engineer, revealed in an interview by the Seattle *Post Intelligencer,* that Corbin had secured an injunction against the ORN encroaching on the CRN right-of-way and that as a consequence the ORN "force has broken up and gone away." The Lewiston *Teller* in its continuous quest for a Lewiston railroad had a helpful suggestion for the ORN; if it built up the Snake to Lewiston it could from there go up the Clearwater River to the Potlatch River and thence north to the Coeur d'Alene and avoid the Indian reservation (but it would have to cross the Nez Perce reservation east of Lewiston).[25]

On January 17, 1888, the ORN executive committee heard provisions of the proposed joint lease of the ORN to the UP (OSL) and NP in which the NP was to be given nearly exclusive control of the territory north of the Snake River and the OSL-ORN south of the river. President Smith reported to the ORN executive committee that the NP had agreed February 1 to pay $65,270 for the organization and construction of the WI. The ORN sought an additional $4,730.[26] The joint lease never came into existence.

On February 2 Senator Dolph introduced in Congress a bill granting the WI right-of-way across the Coeur d'Alene Indian Reservation. On May 18 the bill became law and on that day the WI franchise was transferred to the ORN. The ORN directors on May 31 approved a proposal by the Oregon Short Line (OSL) to construct the WI from Tekoa (on the line to Rockford) to Mullan, 90 miles, $1,620,600. Disagreements with the Indians held up right-of-way settlement until November. The secretary of interior approved the map of definite location on December 7. At the apparent instigation of the NP, the U.S. Attorney-General issued an opinion that the secretary did not have the authority to permit construction until the amount of compensation to Indians had been fixed. On February 8, 1889, permission was granted by the secretary. During that time, the WI worked on either side of the reservation.[27]

In the meantime, construction on the narrow gauge CRN continued. Track reached Wallace September 10, 1887, but an injunction gained by the WI did not allow operation until it was dissolved October 29. The first regular train arrived in Wallace November 2. On June 14, 1888, Oakes informed Harris that Corbin had been invited to Portland by ORN interests to confer about purchasing the CRN; Oakes urged that the NP purchase or lease the CRN. The NP leased the CRN, October 1, 1888. On March 24, 1889, the CRN reached Mullan. Truax wrote Elijah Smith on the 25th that the NP had not yet made a definite location across the reservation. Engineers and contractors had looked over the WI line east of Mullan. He was fearful that the NP would "jump in there with a big force." In January 1890 the NP began construction of a standard gauge line from Missoula to the mining district. The first freight train reached Wallace August 14, 1891. The narrow gauge was removed from Mission to Mullan between 1891 and 1902.[28]

It was reported June 14, 1889, that WI track laying from Tekoa across the Coeur d'Alene Indian Reservation would begin as soon as the track from Winona to Seltice Junction was completed (see Oregon Railway Extensions Co. below). The WI line from Tekoa, on the Farmington to Rockford line, 93.77 miles, began operation to Mullan March 30, 1890. A branch from Wallace to Burke was opened to traffic January 10, 1891. The lines from Wallace to Mullan and Burke were destroyed in floods June 1894. The Burke branch was restored to joint NP-ORN operation. The Mullan extension was not rebuilt but the ORN accessed Mullan over the NP.[29]

B. The Washington & Idaho to Spokane Falls[30]

The *Review* reported December 15, 1886, that the WI was surveying a line from Farmington to Spokane via Rockford. WI President Truax assured the newspaper that trains would be running to Spokane Falls before December 1, 1887. In May 1888 the *Gazette* reported "On good authority" that the ORN would enter Spokane that year. That month the NP became aware of ORN activity in the Palouse including apparent preparation to build from Farmington to Spokane Falls. Harris wrote UP President C. F. Adams inquiring whether he had any information explaining the activities of the ORN. Oakes telegraphed Harris on the 26th that the ORN had let contracts for a Spokane extension. Adams responded on the 28th that the ORN activities were fully justified in light of the Oregon & Washington Territory Railroad organizing a line from Wallula to Walla Walla.[31]

On the 31st ORN Directors approved an OSL proposal to construct the 1887 WI located line from Farmington to Rockford, 33 miles, $528,000. According to the *Gazette*, work commenced June 4 with 175 men. Truax purchased the right of away and the OSL supervised the work. By mid-August grading was completed between Farmington and Rockford. Track laying was delayed because cars were needed to haul grain. Construction was completed to Rockford, December 7, 1888. The first regular train reached Rockford in mid-December.[32]

It was asserted in November 1888 that if Spokane citizens would donate depot grounds and procure the right-of-way between Rockford and Spokane, the ORN would build at once. ORN surveyors were running a line north from Waverly. Articles were filed in Spokane May 3, 1889, for the Spokane Falls & Rockford Railroad. The railroad was organized by the ORN and Spokane Falls businessmen and was subsequently built under the WI charter. The Spokane incorporators included A. M. Cannon, former S&P president. He told a reporter, "The company means business, and it is expected that work will begin within fifteen days, and to be pushed to speedy completion, thus affording Spokane Falls another outlet, east and west." The extension was financed by Portland, and as the *Oregonian* was quoted, "Let no one fail to notice that Portland is not only up and coming, but that Portland is in the lead of the great development of the Northwest." The people at Farmington were anxious that the line to Spokane be completed because the lack of a connection between the S&P and ORN at Garfield meant that merchandise from Portland arrived as quickly as that from Spokane.[33]

Grading on the Spokane Falls line began in mid-June 1889 and continued to early September. The ORN comptroller reported in early August that little work had been done on the line, "They have had difficulty in procuring laborers and teams." Tracklaying began at Rockford August 30. The NP was reluctant to allow the WI to cross at grade east of Spokane. The NP line was on a 1 percent grade eastbound and trains would have to stop at the crossing. On September 19 the two railroads agreed that the ORN would pay to reduce the NP grade to half a percent.[34]

The Farmington to Rockford, 33.7 miles, was constructed June to December 1888, and opened to traffic December 15, and the Rockford to Spokane, 26.7 miles, was constructed June to October 1889, and opened to traffic October 7.[35] In 1899 the ORN constructed a branch on the line of 4.76 miles from Fairfield, Washington, to Waverly, to serve a sugar beet mill. The line opened July 7, 1899, and was pulled up in 1913 in response to failure of the sugar beet promotion in the Palouse.[36]

B. The Texas Ferry/Riparia Bridge and the Oregon Railway Extensions Co.[37]

As mentioned in chapters I and II, the ORN built from Walla Walla to Texas Ferry and had surveyed a line from Texas Ferry to Colfax in 1881, but the partially completed grade was abandoned when it was decided to build the Columbia & Palouse from the NP at Palouse Junction (Connell). Dependence on the NP to access its lines north of the Snake River was not satisfactory to the ORN. Construction from Texas Ferry to a connection with the C&P was delayed in part by the lease negotiations. In the fall of 1885 rumors were circulating that the ORN had decided to complete the road from Texas Ferry to the C&P near Endicott and to then take up the track from that point to Palouse Junction. A transfer ferry would be used until a bridge across the Snake River was built.[38]

The ORN Directors approved a map for Texas Ferry to La Crosse on September 13, 1886. The October estimates from Texas Ferry (South Riparia) to the 53rd mile post of C&P, 24 miles plus two miles of sidings: $237,596 using old rail and $272,355 for new rail. On December 17 the *Gazette* quoted the Portland *Mercury*: "Rumor says that the grade between Texas Ferry and Willow Creek soon to be railed, thus cutting the country off from a connection with the N. P., and making them entirely tributary to the Union Pacific branches." The *Gazette* editor responded, "To speak plainly the people of this section don't take kindly to the idea of being tributary to one system of railroads."[39]

The *Gazette* reported January 14, 1887, that the ORN had finished surveying the inclines on either side of the river and was revising the line from Riparia to Pampa. The

Walla Walla *Daily Journal* did not think that the ORN would take up the tracks to Palouse Junction when the Riparia line was completed, pointing out that there was business to be developed along that part of the line and if it were torn out the NP would quickly occupy the route and establish a S&P connection with the main line. Two months later the *Journal* understood that the ORN would take up the tracks and put a boat on the Snake River to supply the country the branch would abandon.[40]

On June 14, 1887, Thomas J. Potter sent his "Memoranda for New Lines" to ORN President Smith. The first recommendation was:

> have the inclines at Texas Ferry located and order material for their construction. At the same time Mr. Potter will open negotiations with the Northern Pacific Railroad Company for train mileage from Palouse Junction to Wallula Junction. Should we get into a fight with the Northern Pacific, or should they not be willing to make reasonable arrangement with us for above mentioned train mileage, then complete the line from Texas Ferry to the 53rd mile post on the Palouse Branch. Distance about 25 miles and it will cost with the inclines at Texas Ferry about $350,000.00.

In late June ORN Superintendent Rowe received orders to locate the incline at Riparia and order material for its immediate construction; he had no knowledge of the company's further intentions. The Walla Walla *Union* took the view that as a result of Smith's failure to gain control of the NP, the ORN must build the line from Riparia. The NP had a rate of five dollars a ton on wheat from all points in Washington to Tacoma. The ORN was compelled to pay the NP a dollar a ton on wheat between Palouse Jct. and Wallula, leaving it with only four dollars a ton to Portland. The only way to avoid the payment was to finish the link. Portland interests claimed that the grain traffic between Palouse Junction and Wallula was 20 cars a day and thus at a dollar a ton the ORN had already paid 10 times the sum of money needed to build the Texas Ferry line.[41]

The ORN executive committee February 15, 1888, received estimates for building from Riparia to the junction of the Snake and Clearwater Rivers opposite Lewiston, 71.5 miles; railroad $1,684,569, bridge at Riparia $387,289, for a total of $2,071,858. The board

The steamer *Almota* at the Texas Ferry-Riparia transfer between rail and water. In 1881 the ORN completed a line from Walla Walla, Washington, to Texas Ferry on the south bank of the Snake River. In the same year the ORN stopped grading a line from Riparia on the north bank to Colfax. There were no trains on the north bank until 1888 when the ORN completed a line from Riparia to La Crosse on the Columbia & Palouse Railroad. A permanent bridge completed in 1889 eliminated the need to ferry on the north-south route, but from the transfer Lewiston, Idaho, received most of its ORN freight and passengers until 1908 when the Riparia-Lewiston line was opened. If the photograph was taken between 1881 to 1888 it is on the south side of the river at Texas Ferry. From 1888 to 1908 it could be on either side of the river. The *Almota* was built in the 1870s by the Oregon Steam Navigation Co. *Manuscript and Special Collections, Washington State University Library, Photo Collection 2, Box 33, folder 7.*

of directors March 12, 1888, adopted a map from the west boundary of the Nez Perce Indian Reservation to Riparia, 77.7 miles.[42]

On March 6 UP President Adams asked Harris to have the NP directors approve a resolution passed by the OSL directors requesting the ORN under the (proposed) joint lease of January 20, 1888, to make nearly $4,300,000 in expenditures for equipment and construction. The construction included the Riparia bridge and the line to the junction of Snake and Clearwater Rivers. The resolution also requested the ORN issue $4,000,000 in 5 percent bonds to finance the expenditures. Harris responded that the executive committee would submit a recommendation to the board on the 15th.[43]

On the 15th ORN manager W. H. Holcomb wrote a UP official strongly urging construction of the Texas Ferry to C&P line. "I think if the owners of the O. R. & N. Co. could be out here for a while and see the trouble and annoyance and expense we have in handling this business via Wallula and Palouse Junction they would consider it wise to construct this piece of line." In mid-April ORN surveyors were surveying from the C&P at about Endicott to Farmington. Another report said the surveyors were running a line from near Endicott to

The Texas Ferry-Riparia bridge completed in 1889 and photographed from the southwest, c. 1950s or '60s, for U.S. Army Corps of Engineers in preparation for the construction of Lower Monumental Dam on the Snake River. Riparia, Washington, is on the north bank, the ORN depot is just beyond the south end of the cut of cars aligned for the bridge. The depot sits between the bridge to La Crosse line (extended to the left the track following Alkali Creek, seen flowing into the Snake beyond the bridge) and the bridge to Lewiston line which circles around to the east. The line paralleling the river from left is the NP line from Snake River Junction to Riparia, and continuing to the right the ORN/CSP to Lewiston. (See photograph p. 234 for ground level view of trains and Riparia depot.) *Photograph 77-95 0128, Corps of Army Engineers, "Lower Monumental Reservoir" folder, National Archives & Records Administration, Pacific Alaska Region (Seattle).*

Hangman Creek and thence to Spokane with a branch separating at the forks of Hangman Creek going to Coeur d'Alene. At the same time ORN engineers were boring in the Snake River for bridge foundations.[44]

On May 25, 1888, the ORN incorporated the Oregon Railway Extensions Co. (ORE) in Oregon. The incorporators were all residents of Portland. The company was to build several railroad lines including from Texas Ferry northeast to the WI line from Farmington to Rockford where it crossed Dutch Flat [Seltice]. The ORN directors May 31 approved a proposal by the OSL to construct from MP 63 on the C&P (Winona) to the WI at Dutch Flat, 51 miles, $765,000. The line is often referred to as the Pleasant Valley branch. According to Lewty, the branch was built primarily to boost sales of the land acquired from the NP as a result of the traffic agreement of October 1880. On the same day the directors also approved proposals by the OSL to construct a bridge between Riparia and Texas Ferry, $387,289, and to construct Texas Ferry to milepost 53 on C&P, 25 miles, $300,000.[45]

A day earlier construction had begun on the Riparia to C&P line with about 30 teams repairing the old grade and filling washouts. A few days earlier the contractor had loaded their grading outfit on cars at Prescott to be moved to Endicott. The move put an end to ORN building to Eureka Flat in Walla Walla County. The next week the *Gazette* commented, the ORN "began in earnest this week and will be continued until that company's lines penetrate every section of Eastern Washington and Northern Idaho that promises to yield a reasonable amount of traffic. It is evident that the joint lease has been declared 'off,' and each company is now at liberty to push lines wherever thought desirable." By early June the contract for the Riparia bridge had been let; a temporary bridge would be erected for the 1888 crop. Track laying began on the C&P June 15.[46]

In late July graders were at work on the Pleasant Valley branch and track was laid east from Riparia 15 miles. On August 20, 1888, the ORN board of directors accepted the act approved by Congress July 9 authorizing construction of railroad bridges across the Snake and Clearwater Rivers. Also they adopted location maps and plans for the Riparia Bridge and directed that approval of the Secretary of War be sought.[47]

As will be discussed in chapter VIII an injunction was issued July 27, 1888, against ORN construction north of the Snake River. But the *Gazette* reported that in early August construction crews were increased on the Riparia and Pleasant Valley lines and "The injunction has not delayed work any." Holcomb said that he expected to see passenger trains with Pullman palace cars "and all the modern conveniences" running on the Riparia line to Farmington in two weeks. Work was progressing on the central pier and the shore abutments of the Riparia bridge. By mid-August only six miles of rail remained to be laid from Riparia to the C&P. The temporary bridge at Riparia was completed on the 23rd with the first regular train crossing on the 26th.

> On Tuesday morning, August 28, at 10:15 o'clock the first through train over the new line from Portland to Farmington arrived at Colfax. It comprised two coaches and the Pullman sleeping car Walla Walla, and was drawn by engine No. 79. A large number of citizens and the Colfax brass band, assembled at the depot to celebrate the occasion, and the scene was an animated one as the train swept down the grade and alongside the depot. The transfer of mails and baggage took but a few minutes, the Moscow mail car was switched off, and the regular train backed down to the switch and started for Farmington. The new system had been inaugurated.

So began the Palouse *Gazette's* report on the 31st. Over the new line through Riparia, Colfax was 346 miles from Portland. The junction of the C&P with the Riparia line was La Crosse, and the line from La Crosse Junction to Palouse Junction would be called the Pampa branch. A mixed train would be run from Palouse Junction to La Crosse to connect in both directions with the regular Colfax passenger train.[48]

Gill's report to the ICC gives the mileage from (South) Riparia to La Crosse Jct. as 24.6 miles. Construction was by the ORN in its own name. The line began on the south bank of the Snake River and ran to La Crosse. Between Hay and Jerita, three miles, the northbound grade was 1.7 percent. As of September 30, 1888, expenditures for the branch were $289,194. On August 28 it opened to traffic with the establishment of daily through passenger service from Portland to Farmington via Pendleton. The east bound train left Portland at 2:40 p.m., passed Walla Walla at 3:30 a.m. and arrived at Farmington at 11:15 a.m. West bound the train left Farmington at 12:30 p.m., Walla Walla at 8:15 p.m. and arrived at Portland, 8:55 a.m.[49]

Because of ice in the river in early January 1889 the temporary bridge at Riparia was deemed unsafe to move more than one freight car at a time. On January 19 the last of 36 cars were pulled across by cable. In the meantime passengers and mail were carried via Palouse Junction. By the 25th the bridge had been repaired and traffic resumed. On the south side of the river, the first steel span for the bridge was in place by the 21st.[50]

On the Pleasant Valley line service on the east end between Seltice and Oakesdale began in October 1888. By

January 18, 1889, three miles of track had been completed at the Winona end and by February 15 track laying had passed St. John and was 17 miles from Oakesdale. In May work was being pushed on the ORN's five warehouses and grain elevator at Oakesdale with a total capacity of over a million bushels. After a delay because of the lack of rails, track laying began again in mid-June at St. John to fill the gap to Oakesdale. It was expected that they would lay two miles a day with the track laying machine.[51]

The permanent bridge at Riparia was completed April 9, 1889. It consisted of two 325-foot fixed truss spans and one 325-foot manually operated swing truss span. Prior to the 9th the NP began running a steamboat to Lewiston. Passage at Riparia had been blocked by the ORN's temporary bridge, which the ORN now took out.[52]

The Pleasant Valley branch, Winona Junction to Seltice, was turned over to the operating department July 25, 1889, with regular service August 15. The ORN issued a circular on August 19 that said the line was completed, 47.94 miles. Seltice was 383.8 miles from Portland. The first regular passenger train passed through Oakesdale December 23, 1889. The construction period of the Pleasant Valley branch was June 1888 to July 1889. The branch began at Winona Junction and ended at Seltice, and crossed four major summits with seven of the eight approaches exceeding 1.00 percent grades with a maximum of 1.58 percent. The ORN directors declared January 8, 1890, that the ORE from Winona to Seltice was constructed at the expense of the ORN under the OSL lease of January 1, 1887, as modified November 7, 1889. The operational history of the ORE varied only slightly from that of the WI reported in note 35 above.[53]

In 1909 ORN relocated the line from Hay to Riparia to ease the curves and follow one side of the creek. The Pleasant Valley branch, in October 1910, became the first line north of the Snake River to receive a gas motor car service. The motor car left Tekoa immediately after the train from Spokane departed for Colfax and met the same train at Winona. It returned after meeting the train from Pendleton at Winona and arrived in Tekoa to meet the same train bound for Spokane.[54]

The Joint Lease and the Arbitration Contract Negotiations, 1887–89

Although leased to the Union Pacific (UP), through the Oregon Short Line (OSL), the Oregon Railway & Navigation Co. (ORN) was not owned by the UP/OSL, and thus often acted as an independent corporation. The negotiations among the UP, Northern Pacific (NP), and ORN over railroad development in the interior Pacific Northwest continued for over two years while both the NP and ORN were competitively expanding in the Palouse. Complicating the UP/ORN-NP relationship was the construction of the Oregon & Washington Territory Railroad (OWT) in territory the ORN considered exclusively theirs. As we have seen, Elijah Smith, president of both the ORN and Oregon & Transcontinental (OT) fought back by seeking an injunction against the NP aiding the construction of the Spokane & Palouse (S&P). At the same time the NP completed a temporary line over Stampede Pass and on July 4, 1887, began sending eastern Washington grain to Puget Sound. The UP and ORN believed threats to the ORN would be reduced if the NP was in a joint lease of the ORN with the UP. A majority of the NP directors were willing to explore the possibility of a joint lease, however competition and animosity worked against agreement.

A. The Joint Lease

On May 13, 1887, NP President Robert Harris wrote UP President Charles Francis Adams inquiring whether Adams was interested in adjusting their differences. In a telegram to NP General Manager Thomas Oakes Harris said, "I do not expect any other conclusion than that each Company may promote branch roads as it thinks best. On this basis I feel, sure we can keep up with the procession." At the NP board meeting of the 24th Harris read a letter from Adams wondering whether the NP would adhere to the agreement not to build into each other's territory. The board resolved that the railroads should "endeavor to effect a division of the territory or business in Eastern Washington" (a similar resolution passed June 16). On the same day Harris received notice that the OT intended to sue to restrain construction of the S&P. Harris wrote Adams the next day that the suit "was not quite consistent with the friendly manner in which I was endeavoring to adjust this matter." He would not negotiate under duress. He was sure that Adams could bring the suit to an end. On July 21, the NP directors voted to enter into a traffic agreement with the OWT for interchange at Wallula and on the same day voted to discharge the committee on negotiations with the UP.[1]

The Walla Walla *Union* claimed that a "Special Spy of the Interior Department" at the instigation of Elijah Smith concluded that the NP was illegally cutting timber. On September 14 suit was filed asking for an injunction against NP timber cutting and up to $2,000,000 for unlawfully cut timber since July 4, 1879. It was alleged that timber was used illegally on the line from Wallula to Spokane Falls, the Kennewick bridge, the S&P and on the OWT from Wallula to Pendleton as well as the Cascade Tunnel and snow sheds. On October 6 an injunction was granted against the NP, Nelson Bennett and others from cutting timber in the Cascades for the Kennewick bridge and the OWT. The court decision announced in November said that the injunction applied to the Kennewick bridge, OWT, and for snow sheds on road already accepted by U.S. Commissioners. Timber could be taken for the tunnel, switchback, and snow sheds on not yet accepted road.[2]

Harris and Frederick Billings met with Adams on June 29. They suggested that the ORN lease the Columbia & Palouse (C&P) to the NP and that the ORN wholly withdraw from north of the Snake River. Adams suggested that the NP's Cascade branch be leased to the ORN.[3] On July 2 supplemental articles of the ORN's Washington & Idaho (WI) added a line from Mullan, Idaho to Missoula, Montana, and a line from Endicott (on the C&P) northeast to connect with the main line at or near the forks of Hangman Creek, about twelve miles north of Farmington. On the 26th the ORN executive committee adopted recommendations which constituted an aggressive program north and south of the Snake by the UP-ORN.[4]

The OT owned a majority of ORN stock, but the actual control of the ORN was in the hands of its bondholders and the seven Portland directors appointed in compliance with Oregon law. The OT also owned a large block of NP stock. The ORN had five million in debentures reaching maturity April 1, 1887. In 1886, Elijah Smith had arranged loans to finance new ORN construction and to refinance maturing bonds, but less than 20 percent of the bonds sold. The OT was forced to borrow $3,300,000 to pay for unsold bonds.[5]

OT President Elijah Smith invited UP officials and directors to form a pool to buy NP stock to elect NP directors favorable to the joint lease. The Walla Walla *Journal* reported that Harris when asked about an expected contest between the NP management and Smith, responded that the OT controlled 235,000 of NP's 870,000 shares, "and you can bet your hat that until they control more than that they cannot manage the Northern Pacific." The *Journal* reported August 3 that Elijah Smith and the UP would seek three positions on the NP board of directors. Smith claimed he had a majority of the stock. In the meantime the market for OT stock fell and it had loans due which it could not finance. Also the ORN had insufficient earning to cover the 6 percent that the UP had to pay annually for the lease. Smith appealed to Henry Villard August 27 to save the two companies he had created. If Villard provided five million dollars for the OT to cover the call on 70,000 NP shares it had purchased, Smith offered ORN bonds held by the OT, twenty thousand shares of ORN stock, control of both the OT and ORN, and enough proxies to choose his own NP board. Villard in thirty-six hours raised five million dollars from his European connections and paid off the OT loans and bought three million in 5 percent bonds of the ORN to replace 7 percent bonds held by the OT, thereby saving both the OT and ORN from embarrassment and probable bankruptcy. In addition Villard gained control of the OT. Adams declined Villard's offer of a place on the NP board. There was also an effort to place Smith on the NP board. Adams left the choice of directors to others, "insisting only that 'it is understood the lease is to be made with no further nonsense.'"[6]

In addition to the joint lease, Adams had other concerns. James J. Hill was pushing the St. Paul, Minneapolis & Manitoba Railway (Manitoba), the future Great Northern (GN), steadily westward. Adams saw the UP, NP, and ORN as all over capitalized compared to the Manitoba, thus paying higher interest charges. If the three companies could be "brought into line at this time" things would be manageable, but "the companies are now drifting as fast as they can into a conflict."[7]

The Walla Walla *Union* editorialized September 3, 1887,

> It is our deliberate opinion that if Elijah Smith succeeds in his attempt to capture the management of the Northern Pacific, that work on the Cascade tunnel will be stopped, that the construction of the extension of the Spokane & Palouse and the Pendleton & Wallula [OWT] will be indefinitely suspended and strong efforts made to kill every attempt to secure another road between Walla Walla and Wallula. The success of Elijah Smith in this present effort would be a very heavy blow on the prosperity of the Inland Empire.

On September 20 the *Journal* quoted two letters from the St. Paul *Pioneer Press*. The first, the 12th, was to Villard from C. B. Wright supporting Villard for the NP board because Villard could do more to bring about "harmonious relations between the Northern Pacific... and other corporations west of the Rocky mountains..." than any other person. On the 15th Villard responded that he could "hardly decline to serve the Northern Pacific...to bring about harmonious relations between it and the Union Pacific...I feel confident that a satisfactory solution lies in a joint lease of the [ORN] by the Union Pacific and Northern Pacific."[8]

Villard was elected to the NP board September 15, 1887. Villard was partially successful in gaining a board interlocked with the OT and UP. Villard voted 365,799 of the 754,193 shares that elected five new members and retained eight. Two of the new members, Colgate Hoyt and John B. Trevor, were associated with the UP. The Palouse *Gazette* commented "Villard is expected to act as a mediator between opposing railroad factions, and it is predicted that his wise counsel and sense of fairness will secure to all northwestern points an equal share of advantages... The management of the Northern Pacific, since his retirement, has not been satisfactory... The people of the northwest have faith in Henry Villard." Villard declined the NP presidency. Buss from his extensive analysis of Villard, the financier, concludes, "In the years after 1887 Villard can only be described as a promoter of the Northern Pacific Railroad." But an argument can be made that Villard's primary interest remained the OT and ORN, not the NP. Villard in his *Memoirs*, in its third person account, said of the election "he always looked upon it as the greatest mistake he ever made."[9]

Harris and Oakes, representing the NP, and Adams and Thomas J. Potter (vice president and joint manager of the UP and ORN), representing the UP, met September 28. The views of the NP were in a "Memorandum of Conversation and understandings reached," but it was conceded that "the Union Pacific might or might not accede" to NP's view. The specifics of the memorandum included the usual items—division of territory, access to Puget Sound, and rights to specific lines. At the NP board meeting September 30, Vice President Oakes reported several points of agreement reached by the three companies, but all depended on the NP and UP reaching an agreement on a joint lease of the ORN. The Board passed a resolution that the NP join the UP in a joint lease of the ORN at 6 percent a year of the $24,000,000 capital stock of the ORN. Eastern Washington opinion soured at the prospects of agreement. The *Gazette* commented, "The Inland Empire can now hope for no further relief arising from competition. The railroads have us in their power, and it remains to be seen whether Villard will exert his influence, which is undoubtedly very great, to secure a reasonable reduction of the present excessive freight rates." The report from Portland in the *Teller* said that Portland interests were very unsettled by the agreement, particularly the loss of the C&P. The *Union* viewed the agreement to be bad for Walla Walla, the only consolation being that Portland would also be adversely affected.[10]

Adams wrote Villard October 3 that the NP proposed joint lease was not acceptable and would not be recommended to the UP directors. The NP and ORN would receive large benefits from the lease, the UP much less so; the UP wanted a reduction in the 6 percent rental. Nevertheless, the UP side had a financial incentive to keep the lease negotiations going in a positive public atmosphere. The pool had invested heavily in NP stock, which had a weak market; the stock dropped on negative reports about the lease negotiations, thereby triggering fresh margin calls. Adams claimed that he lost over three hundred thousand dollars as a result.[11]

On October 20 the committee on relations with the UP and ORN, Villard chairman, Billings and Colby, presented the NP board a "Memorandum of Agreement" among the ORN, UP, OT, OSL and NP. The NP would enter into the lease of the ORN by the UP and OSL dated January 1, 1887. The provisions of the agreement were similar to the provisions, elaborated below, in the joint lease agreed to by the NP and UP in January 1888. Elijah Smith wrote Adams October 21 that he signed the memorandum under protest and did not do so until assured that an ORN proposal regarding the C&P would be included: that the company assuming control would have the net earnings and pay a rental equivalent to the interest on all the bonds of the C&P and extensions. He enclosed other modifications he wanted in the agreement.[12]

On the 22nd Harris wrote a Walla Walla resident assuring that with the proposed lease, "there is no occasion in this for the people of Eastern Washington to be alarmed lest they may be called upon to pay exorbitant rates." Rather than parallel roads in the country, there would be "a system of Roads that will give the largest service at the least expense." While the principle of competition applied to most all kinds of businesses it did not apply to railroads. "After the contracts have been properly executed and put into operation, I think that the people of the Territory will see that there is no cause for complaint." The same day Harris wrote Colby that if each party to the understanding were to wait for the others to act, nothing would be accomplished.[13]

The Walla Walla *Journal* on December 1, 1887, reported that the OWT had been sold to George Washington Hunt and C. B. Wright. Potter telegraphed Adams on the 6th, "Hunt...returned to Portland, and tells Ladd, one of our directors there, that he has sold out his road to Mr. Wright...no lease should be signed until Wright lets us have that road at cost." Adams wrote Harris that "it would be useless to continue negotiations for a joint lease until the matter of the Hunt roads were disposed of." On December 13 Harris wrote Adams, "I have no doubt that a satisfactory arrangement in regards to the Wallula and Pendleton Road will be reached." The NP board met on the 15th and appointed a special committee of Villard, Billings and Ives to deal with the "misunderstanding" that had arisen regarding the OWT. At the Board meeting on December 29 the proposed lease was read, fully considered and "materially amended" and postponed to be printed, submitted to the UP and then to be taken up in a special meeting called by the president.[14]

Potter wrote Adams, January 12, 1888, that he would pay Wright $100,000 more for the OWT than it cost rather than let the NP have it. On the 16th Potter wrote that the UP should not agree to anything unless the OWT was turned over to the ORN without conditions. He went on, "The Northern Pacific people are an uncertain quantity. You cannot tell where to find them. I find this is so in dealing with them in traffic matters. We have got to keep watch on them all the time, and they are continually doing something which is not the right thing to do, so that I have no patience with them and would rather fight them than compromise." Hedges' conclusion, and the author's, is that Wright acted in a personal capacity in his financing of the OWT, but the effect was the same as if the NP was directly aiding the line.[15]

On January 17 the ORN executive committee agreed to have the joint lease replace the OSL lease. The lease came to the UP board on January 18. Potter and Frederick L. Ames opposed it unless there was a definite commitment that the OWT would be turned over to the ORN. Adams wrote Sidney Dillon and others, "It was only after I had explained in the most elaborate manner that any action on our part hanging up this lease would throw the whole game into the hands of Messrs. Wright, Hunt, and others, that our directors ratified the instrument." Subsequently certain ORN Portland directors protested the joint lease.[16]

The NP directors on January 19 received a report on the joint lease. The NP committee had accepted some minor amendments proposed by the other companies and was submitting the lease contract in its final form and requesting that it be ratified at that meeting, which was done. The Joint Lease of the ORN, between the ORN, OSL, UP and NP, is in the minutes of the directors dated January 20. Provisions of the lease included: For one dollar the OSL and UP would convey to the NP an undivided half interest in the lease of the ORN by the OSL on January 1, 1887. The NP and OSL would each assume half of the obligations of the OSL to the ORN, including the 6 percent dividends on the ORN stock. The UP continued to be the guarantor of the obligations of the OSL. The obligation to pay interest on the bonds would continue even if the earning of the ORN were not sufficient to make the payments. If one of the parties to the lease became in default, the other would be obligated to pay that part and would be the sole leaser. The OSL would prepare and deliver to the NP authenticated schedules of the all the properties and obligations of the ORN as of July 1, 1888. The C&P would be operated by and at the expense of the NP. The NP would retain the earnings of the C&P and would be solely obligated to pay the interest on the bonds issued by the ORN for C&P construction and for any construction made by the ORN at the request of the NP. The amount of such bonds was given as $3,529,164 at 5 percent per year. The NP agreed that the rates would be same on all freight traffic to or from Portland or Tacoma on the NP main line, any present or future tributaries, including the C&P, between the Snake River and Lake Pend Oreille, and unless specifically consigned all such traffic would be consigned to the ORN. Traffic to or from the OWT and Portland or Tacoma would have equal rates per mile which ever route it took and that the NP would account monthly for traffic with the OWT. The ORN had the right to acquire the OWT "without any hindrance or interference by" the NP and that the NP would not seek to control or acquire any part of the OWT. If the ORN acquired the OWT it would be considered as a part of the ORN property under the lease. In general there was to be no discrimination against either the NP or UP/OSL on rates or consignment of traffic to the ORN. The NP was, except within fifteen miles of the C&P, to have exclusive control of railroad lines north of the Snake and Clearwater Rivers and south of the NP mainline. The UP/OSL was to have exclusive control south of the Salmon River and east of the Snake River and south of a line running from Huntington west to the summit of the Cascades. In the territory between the two jurisdictions, the ORN was to have exclusive control and to construct such lines as requested by the two leasing parties. The NP agreed not to construct any railroad within fifteen miles of the C&P, and the ORN would construct any extensions of the C&P requested by the NP. By joint request, the ORN could construct railroad lines in any of the territory mentioned in the lease. The contracts with the NP dated October 20, 1880 and August 17, 1882, would be in abeyance while the joint lease was in effect.[17]

Adams wrote Harris January 23, "the thing will not hold together unless the most absolute good faith prevails between the parties. If there is the slightest attempt on one side or the other to take undue advantage a quarrel and consequent catastrophe will come about at a very early day. We shall have difficulty enough to hold our subordinates in anyhow. You know how jealous and suspicious railroad subordinates always are of each other."[18]

The Spokane Falls *Review* quoted extensively from the *Oregonian* on the lease:

> This will be a virtual consolidation of the Union and Northern within the territory west of the Rocky mountains. Its effect will be to prevent competitive rates and, extension of railroad facilities to new points; it will trammel up the commerce and industries of the country, will check private enterprise and public growth, and will bring about a still deeper hostility to the railroads on the part of the people than that which now prevails. The instinct of the people seize the fact at once that these combinations are opposed to the public welfare, and hence their attempts to meet and countervail them by severe legislation, which, though it may seldom accomplish what is intended, nevertheless compels respect as an effort of the people to protect themselves.

The Walla Walla *Journal* commented on Portland's opposition to the lease, "The foregoing sounds quite neighborly and it's a great pity, that friendly feelings from the representative people of the metropolis of the great Northwest was not manifested toward the people of the great Columbia basin and the Inland Empire long ago," The Walla Walla *Union* saw that Portland's loss would be

Walla Walla's gain by cheaper rates to Tacoma. The *Teller* commented that the lease would give the interior a choice of ports and, "Being no longer bound, by chains of iron, to Portland's rapacity, our products would naturally flow to the magnificent ports on Puget Sound."[19]

The NP objected to ORN plans to build on the north side of the Snake River from Wallula to Lewiston. Adams called it a "cool attempt on the part of Harris, this blundering gas-bag, to cheat me!" Adams in his response cited the Memorandum of the conference of September 28, 1887, in which it was agreed that the ORN could build up the Snake River to Lewiston and beyond Lewiston to the Little Salmon where it would meet the OSL building down the Snake River and "has always been a project which the directors of this company have had clearly in mind...and my assurances in this respect were one of the considerations which led to their action on the joint lease." Harris responded that this was "a preliminary conversation which subsequently dropped out of sight and an agreement entered into a contradictory character by the territory north of the Snake was set off to the Northern Pacific; that the two arrangements were inconsistent." As far as Adams was concerned the September 28 agreement underlay the January 20 lease and was a part of the lease. "It does seem to me as if I can rely on nothing which is not down in black and white." The lease was modified to allow the ORN to build from Wallula to Lewiston along the north bank of the Snake River.[20]

On February 9, 1888, Smith reported to the ORN executive committee that the NP had agreed to pay $65,270 for the organization and construction of the WI. The ORN sought an additional $4,730. Smith sent a telegram to A. Dolph, a Portland director: "Consummation of joint lease is considered of great importance. Executive Committee is unanimous that it cannot now be delayed without making trouble. We are sure if fully understood Portland people would concur." Gill says that "the lease was fully concurred in by Elijah Smith."[21]

The NP signed the joint lease and on February 13 Adams signed the lease, including a supplementary agreement of February 10 for the UP and OSL in the presence of Villard in the law offices of A. H. Holmes. Holmes wrote a memorandum saying Adams "put his signature thereto with the understanding that unless good faith was kept by the Northern Pacific Company in regard to the various matters contained in the Joint Lease he did not regard the lease as binding or operative upon his companies." Holmes' memorandum continued that Harris came into the office and was asked if he wished to assent to the same condition and he did. On the same day Adams dictated a memorandum on the signing of the joint lease, that the NP would make no objection to the UP building a line up the Snake River on either bank as engineering requirements might make most advantageous and for the present the ORN was to incur liabilities only up to $2.5 million. Holmes certified that the following was "a correct summary of what transpired in my presence on the occasion referred to.... Adams stated in front of Villard that Villard and he had agreed... that Villard would be responsible for the actions of the NP board and that it would be within the power of the Union Pacific to break the joint lease at any time when it was persuaded that the Northern Pacific was not carrying out this policy in perfect good faith." Holmes attached Adams' memorandum to the joint lease and his certification. The joint lease was ratified by the UP board on February 18 and by the NP and the New York directors of the ORN on the 19th.[22]

The joint lease was bitterly opposed by the Portland business community. The ORN Oregon directors wrote February 16 to the president and executive committee that the "pending joint lease should not be signed." They raised several considerations and objections, generally the same as those in the Dolph to Smith letter quoted below. The executive committee took no action. Adams responded that he supported the lease and opposed duplicate construction. The Oregon legislation which had enabled the OSL lease the year before, in February passed a measure prohibiting the leasing of parallel or competing railroads, thereby prohibiting a lease to the NP. John R. Dillon, the UP general solicitor, held the opinion that while the form of the joint lease did not come strictly under the prohibitory language of the Oregon statute, it was "within the mischief."[23]

On March 1, ORN Portland attorney and director C. A. Dolph wrote Elijah Smith that he learned that Harris wanted two of the ORN eastern directors to go to Portland to authorize the execution of the lease. The other four Portland directors were opposed to the lease. Dolph did not want to vote on the lease unless it involved all the directors. He summarized many of the Portland arguments against the lease:

> While I do not propose to question the wisdom of the management of either of the companies in the transaction...the effect of transferring the whole production of the Palouse country to the Northern Pacific Railroad Company, making tidewater at Puget Sound its destination, and making equal rates upon all grain shipped to Portland as high as to Tacoma, a greater distance, will have the effect to take away the principal part of the shipping theretofore done at this port. This, of course, will deprive Portland of a large amount of trade now held with the

> country thus made tributary to Puget Sound...people residing here have recently invested a large amount of money in the Coeur d'Alene mines which they have developed under the expectation that they would soon be able to ship their ores direct to Portland. They see plainly that this, in case the lease is entered into, will be impossible.
>
> ...in case this matter is carried out, transportation by water upon the Columbia River, so far as the Oregon Railway and Navigation Company is concerned, will be largely if not completely discontinued. The settled opinion, however, is that the Northern Pacific does not propose to continue bound by the joint lease longer than is necessary to get complete control of that portion of the country which can be made tributary to its lines. This I can hardly credit, but so much discussion has been had over this question, as to greatly disturb the business community, and is sure, in my judgment, to control legislative action....
>
> [I]s it fair to ask me to place myself in such a position that when business interests hereafter suffer by reason of the loss of a trade they have so long enjoyed, I alone of the resident directors, should be held responsible?[24]

Meanwhile an injunction against the ORN aiding the NP to become a joint owner of the OSL lease was filed in an Oregon court by Van B. De Lashmutt, mayor of Portland, a prominent banker, largely interested in the Coeur d'Alene mines and an ORN stockholder, as of February 13, when Portland director Corbett transferred 50 shares to him (both De Lashmutt and Corbett denied collusion). Relief was sought on the grounds that the NP was in competition with the ORN and the lease was against public policy and the laws of Oregon. The injunction was granted. Villard's view was that when the people of Portland "properly understood the question involved the opposition would quickly die out."[25]

The *Railroad Gazette*, March 9, had an extended commentary on the joint lease. The charter of the ORN required that a majority of the thirteen directors be Oregon residents. Three of the Oregon directors were employees of the ORN, representing eastern investors, the other four were stockholding directors. "These latter are said to be in sympathy with the citizens of Portland and are using every means...to put obstacles in the way of the lease being ratified...this opposition arises indirectly from the opening up of transportation facilities between the Eastern states and the interior towns of Oregon, Washington and Idaho, and more directly from the completion of the [NP] across the Cascade Mountains to Puget Sound." Prior to 1883 all commerce between the interior and the world was tributary to Portland. "That Portland exacted toll from all the back country is vouched for by the people who bore the burden, and is indirectly attested by the claim now made by the residents of Portland that their city is wealthier per capita than any other in the United States." Beginning in 1883 people in the interior could trade with Chicago, St. Louis, and New York without going through Portland. "There still prevails a sentiment among [the people of Portland] that the territory west of the Rocky Mountains somehow belongs to Portland, and should be tributary to their city." Portland's business had been sustained by lower rates to it than to interior points. The opening of the Cascade line of the NP meant that Tacoma and Seattle, deep water ports and not dependent on a tug and pilot like Portland, could compete for the principal commodity shipped from Portland: wheat. Dealers in Tacoma were able to offer about two cents per bushel more than Portland dealers. Under the lease wheat rates to Portland and Tacoma, regardless of origin, would be the same. Under those conditions much of the wheat would naturally flow to Tacoma.[26]

Hedges summarized an editorial in the March 19 *Oregonian*: Portland was entitled to lower rates from the interior than Tacoma because of its water-grade route; a cheaper rail rate would counterbalance the higher shipping costs on the Columbia and enable Portland to get a fair share of the grain traffic; under the lease the ORN would be managed in the interests of the NP which would divert traffic to the Sound because of the equalized rail rates and the higher Portland river costs; and eastern ORN stockholders were indifferent to Portland's situation because they were granted a fixed percentage of the value of the ORN without reference to its earnings.[27]

In late March Adams and Villard invited representatives from the Portland Board of Trade to New York. The Portland delegation submitted six demands. The first three were: first, the rail rates from the interior should discriminate in favor of Portland, if not the ORN service from the sea to Portland and return should be at a cost not exceeding those from the sea to Tacoma and return. Second, the ORN should be permitted to build from Riparia to the C&P and to build from Farmington to the Coeur d'Alene district and the C&P was to be operated as a "residue" of the ORN. Third, the ORN would control the OWT. (The second and third demands meant that the ORN would be north of the Snake River, but the NP would not be south of the river.) Hedges comments, "The extraordinary character of these demands is apparent. Equal treatment was not even to be considered by Portland. She must have the advantage on every point." Nevertheless, Villard and Adams agreed to the first and third demands. Villard, soon to leave for Germany to make financial arrangements, expressed hope that the injunction would be discontinued. In Adams' opinion the joint lease would prevent a rate war and would safeguard the interests of Portland and the ORN. According to Rigdon both Villard and Adams assured the delegation that the lease would not be ratified until they were advised "and the reorganization of the management of the Northern Pacific had been effected." When the committee returned to Portland the board of trade adopted a resolution expressing confidence in Villard and his policies.[28]

On March 28 Villard reported to the NP executive committee the results of the meetings with the Portland delegation. He said that the Portland opposition to the lease would end if the ORN provided navigation assistance between Portland and the bar of the Columbia River. He said that Adams favored this arrangement. The committee minutes did not mention other conditions the delegation insisted upon. Villard reported the strong desire of Adams for the UP to acquire the OWT. The committee agreed to the ORN issuing two million dollars in bonds provided that none of the money would be used for the construction of branch lines unless the NP and the OSL agreed.[29]

Elijah Smith wrote March 30 that he did not believe that the Portland delegates had in any important way changed their minds about the undesirability of the lease or the bad motives of the NP. "The Portland directors of the O. R. & N. Co. declined to discuss the removal of the injunction suit at all as they said they had no hand in it and no control over it, which I believe to be true. It is hard to tell what will be the result I am inclined to think it will remain as it is for the present." The injunction continued and the ORN board delayed action on the bonds contracted to Villard for sale in Germany. For Villard, "This sad business is hourly getting into a worse mess." Adams blamed Smith, "Foolishness should stop and the prophet if he will neither fish nor cut bait, must go ashore."[30]

On March 30 Oakes wrote Harris that he had heard from E. V. Smalley in Portland that two Manitoba contractors had arrived to bid on ORN branch work. Oakes quoted Smalley on the situation in Portland:

> The feeling here is intensely hostile to the joint lease. It amounts almost to a popular craze, and is skillfully worked up by the 'Oregonian'. That paper is talking so much about our Cascade grades and our 'unnatural route to the sea' that I am going to write it a letter showing that, except in the immediate vicinity of Walla Walla, all the grain coming to Portland over the O. R. & N. must first be handled over grades as heavy as those on the Northern Pacific before it reaches the 'Water level route.' You know what a tremendous grade there is from Riparia to the top of the hill over the line to Walla Walla. All the grain from the Snake River country and from Pomeroy and Pataha must be hauled up that hill. Then there are the Blue Mountain grades for grain from Grande Ronde and the Powder River Valley to go over.

The Walla Walla *Weekly Union* objected to Portland's assertion that it was cheaper to haul grain to Portland than Tacoma "the O. R. & N. Co. road down the Columbia is, by reason of the sliding character of its roadbed, its great sand drifts and remoteness from fuel, a very expensive road to operate." The paper claimed that the NP had none of these handicaps and that once the tunnel was completed "it will not cost any more to haul a train from Wallula to Tacoma over the [NP] than it will to haul a like train from Wallula to Portland. It is nothing but unmitigated selfishness which causes Portland to demand that more shall be charged to haul wheat to Tacoma than is charged to haul it to her warehouses."[31]

In the meantime there were more tangible developments. The Walla Walla *Weekly Union* reported March 24, 1888, that track laying had begun on the OWT and that the road would reach Centerville, Oregon, in twenty-five days. On April 13 the first train crossed the NP's Columbia River bridge at Kennewick. From July, 1887, when the switchback was opened, to the end of March, Tacoma received 1184 cars of wheat, 105 came from Portland. The Walla Walla *Journal* referred to G. W. Hunt, the builder of the OWT as "our Moses and second Henry Villard." Stampede Tunnel opened to traffic on May 27.[32] In two months the competitive situation for the ORN and Portland had become potentially worse.

Adams became aware that certain members of the NP board were giving assistance to Hunt and the OWT. Adams informed Villard that the UP would have to take measures to protect itself if something was not done. According to Adams, Villard agreed. Adams drew up plans with ORN General Manager Holcomb for the construction of lines from Riparia to Lewiston and into the Coeur d'Alene. Adams conferred with Villard in New York in early April and showed him, with Holcomb present, maps of the proposed lines. According to Adams and Holcomb, Villard agreed, an assertion he later denied. On April 4, 1888, Oakes wrote Harris that the ORN Portland offices had a profile for the Riparia to Lewiston line and that bids were being solicited.[33]

The NP directors April 19 received a letter from Oakes concerning the ORN proposal to build from Riparia to Lewiston. The proposed road was parallel to and mostly less than fifteen miles from the C&P and S&P, but nearby productive land was closer to the latter. The productive territory tributary to the line was small compared to its length. Oakes noted that the C&P and the S&P plus the ORN lines south of the Snake River had reduced the tonnage moving on the river. The proposed line was economically unjustified, as boats owned by the ORN could handle traffic via the Columbia most of the year. "The building of this road would be a waste of money...much more so for the Northern Pacific when it is to be held responsible for one half of the fixed charges of the [ORN]." The NP board voted against construction of the road. From the point of view of the UP and ORN, the NP was thus insincere in entering into the lease. A few days later when asked in Portland whether the NP would build any branches that year, Harris was quoted as saying, "Yes, we will build a few branches in Washington Territory, just to kept up with the procession, you know."[34]

In mid-May the NP became aware of ORN surveying in the Palouse and Potlatch countries and quietly negotiating with contractors. The NP executive committee requested Harris to write Adams for an explanation. Harris wrote Adams May 26. Adams responded on the 28th he was not aware of ORN movements in the Potlatch country. In his view movements in the Palouse were fully justified in light of Hunt organizing a new line from Wallula to Walla Walla with the full knowledge and financial support of certain NP directors. The actions in the Palouse "are made with a careful view to the probable execution of the joint lease. They are also being so made that, in case the joint lease shall fall through" the ORN would be compensated for the injuries received from Hunt. "In this matter I am acting with the full knowledge and concurrence of Mr. Villard." Adams supported the joint lease, but as long as there were questions about its implementation, it was his duty to protect UP interests. After being asked by Adams, the ORN Portland directors on May 31 approved plans for $3,600,000 of construction on 199 miles in the Palouse, including a bridge between Riparia and Texas Ferry. In October 1888 the ORN executive committee authorized the construction of the lines.[35]

The construction plans were probably moved along by OT developments. Prior to Villard leaving for Germany in April, he and Adams agreed that in order to secure the joint lease, re-composition of the NP and ORN boards was necessary. They would seek control of the OT in order to exclude Smith and others on the boards who opposed the lease. Villard would enlist aid from German bankers to buy a large amount of OT stock. In late May, after Villard's departure, Adams discovered that Charles Colby and Colgate Hoyt, whom Villard had left in charge of OT affairs, had agreed to elect to the boards of the OT and ORN persons whose primary interests were the NP. These included Brayton Ives and C. B. Wright. Adams suspected a plot to replace Smith with Ives "who of all men living is most offensive to him." Adams sought to delay the ORN election. Adams sent Gardiner M. Lane to Europe; Adams demanded that the present board continue until the joint lease was agreed upon. Lane in early June was confident that Villard's plans had not changed and that nothing would be done until his return to New York. About June 1 Villard was told that Elijah Smith had gone to Boston to arouse Adams against the joint lease. Villard's account of Lane's visit was that the UP would not ratify the lease without certain modifications. He thought these unimportant and cabled to recommend concession. "The reply came that it had already been made, but that the Union Pacific had backed out of the agreement altogether." The Walla Walla *Union* viewed this as "good News."[36]

Wheat and flour shipments from Portland continued to increase after Stampede Pass tunnel was opened and were still above those from Puget Sound in 1894, but the proportion of the shipments going through Puget Sound ports increased substantially: in 1888 Puget Sound shipped 15.1% of the wheat and 15.5% of the flour; in 1894 the percentages were 42.8 and 48.0 respectively. Ficken places the completion of the Cascade branch into a larger context:

> The key factor making Washington eligible for statehood was completion of the Northern Pacific Railroad over the Cascades to Commencement Bay on Puget Sound. The immigration of large numbers of people from the East instantly became possible, as did the selling of lumber and wheat on a west-to-east basis. Directly linking...Spokane Falls...with Tacoma, the Palouse and the Coeur d'Alene with the Sound and the Strait of Juan de Fuca, the railroad broke the Columbia River monopoly on cross-regional trade, fatally undermining Portland's economic leadership of the Pacific Northwest. The advantage in a long struggle for mastery shifted dramatically from Portland to Puget Sound, from fresh water to salt water.[37]

Oakes wrote Harris June 4 that the ORN had formed an "Extension Company" to build to the Coeur d'Alene that year. A director of the ORN was asked if this action would not conflict with the terms of the joint lease, to which he responded that he would like to be as certain of living thirty years as he was that the lease would never go into effect. On the 11th Harris wrote that he had received notice from Adams that the UP and OSL voted on the 2nd to reconsider the January joint lease contract. Oakes responded, "In view of the action taken by [UP] in regard to ORN lease in my opinion we should no longer keep up the semblance of friendly traffic relations with ORN but cut entirely loose and do our own business in and out of Portland Via Tacoma."[38]

The *West Shore* in June celebrated the failure of the joint lease announcing that the ORN had begun construction to the Coeur d'Alene mines and the Texas Ferry line to the C&P. "These are the natural fruits of the failure of the joint lease project, and the beginning of these improvements shows that the managers of the O. R. & N. Co. have been aroused to the situation, and appreciate how nearly the road came to being 'bottled up.'"[39]

On June 18 Hoyt's faction installed Villard as president of the OT and Ives as vice president. On the same day Adams joined with Elijah Smith to retain Smith as president of the ORN. Villard intended to remove Smith as the ORN president, but the old OT board voted its stock in the ORN election. In general, the newspapers in eastern Washington were pleased with the re-election of Smith because it meant, as they saw it, a continuation of branch building. At the end of June it was reported that the ORN would put tug-boats on the Columbia River bar and reduce the charges to and from Portland to the bar by nearly $2,000 on a 1,200 ton wheat ship, about four and half cents a bushel.[40]

The June 30, 1888, ORN annual report said that the opening of the NP Cascade branch "and the construction by it of branch lines into territory hitherto tributary to the lines of this Company, will probably divert some the business heretofore controlled entirely by us, but with a fair and proper regard for the maintenance of rates and territorial rights, there will be sufficient business for both roads at remunerative figures." The report also said the joint lease by the OSL and NP was not likely under the terms agreed to because of legal action.

On July 27 Brayton Ives and others secured in New York a temporary injunction against the ORN building a bridge at Riparia, a branch line from Riparia to the C&P and from Farmington and Endicott to Spokane Falls and to the Coeur d'Alene mining district. The complaint argued that the UP, OSL, NP and ORN had entered into a joint lease which would have taken effect on July 1 except for the UP and ORN backing an injunction in Oregon against the lease. Instead of carrying out the lease, the UP and ORN were building lines which were in violation of the joint lease provisions establishing an equitable division of the territory. Elijah Smith's affidavit said that he refused to execute the lease until the ORN board had acted on it in Portland and that the Portland members refused to give authority to execute the lease. Adams in his affidavit stated that the NP or persons acting in its interest had aided in building lines which were prohibited by the joint lease and that the OSL board had reconsidered making the lease before the lease would have become operative.[41]

Villard returned to the United States in late July. A. H. Holmes wrote Adams on August 1 that Villard disapproved of the Ives suit, but he could not control it. Holmes wrote, "Elijah Smith is so much of a red flag to him, apparently, as Ives is distasteful to you." Adams conferred with Villard August 1 and the next day wrote Villard that the UP and OSL withdrawal from the lease was not a change in policy, but was necessitated by the attitudes of the people of Oregon and the actions of Hunt in the Walla Walla region. "We concluded that a careful revision in several essential points of the proposed joint lease was necessary." (Adams wrote in his diary on August 1, "In this Oregon business I have in truth got myself out of my depth. I have not known my own mind clearly." Adams blamed Villard and Smith for the fix he was in: "a vagabond Teuton and a Yankee swine.") Villard thanked Adams for his explanation of the withdrawals but, "I cannot consider these explanations, however, as sufficient and satisfactory, and I am more especially at a loss to conceive how any understanding I had with you could justify the attempt to withdraw on the part of your companies." Adams wrote the same day, reminding Villard that he had agreed to the ORN construction before Villard left for Europe and then inserted a copy of the letter he sent Harris on May 28 (above). Adams admitted that he had not appreciated the public opposition in Oregon to the lease. In view of these conditions and the actions of Hunt he could "not see how the formal withdrawal of the Oregon Short Line from the instrument as it then stood could have been avoided...I am now...ready to take the question up with you and endeavor to reach some result which shall be reasonably satisfactory to the people of Oregon, and yet shall preserve the properties we represent from impending disaster..." Villard responded on the 7th that he was prepared to buy for his German friends $2,000,000 of ORN bonds, but he would not do so except under the joint lease and for purposes the NP had agreed to. He went on,

> Now you come and claim that I constituted myself both a fool and a knave by consenting, or seeming to consent, whichever way you may put it, to a course of action, that is, the construction of the two lines, described north of the Snake River, with the proceeds of two millions of O. R. & N. consolidated bonds, directly contrary to my above-mentioned record. I must beg leave to denounce this as an absolutely unwarranted piece of perversion and grossly insulting to me. I feel very strongly on this point because you not only ventured to make this imputation to me in your letter, but you also conveyed it in your letter to President Harris, which you quote, and of the existence of which I have until now been in ignorance.

Villard said that he had agreed that Holcomb should take measures needed to defeat Hunt, he favored the Coeur d'Alene line being built under the joint lease, but denied supporting the Texas Ferry line. As for the Portland interests, Adams had told the Portland delegation that great corporations could not be managed to satisfy local interests and the joint lease was the only means to prevent war between the UP and NP to the lasting injury of the ORN and Portland. Adams returned Villard's letter on the 13th saying that he had read only the first three pages and declined to read the remainder, "if I did so it would be impossible that either business or personal relations could hereafter exist between us." Adams said he was willing to meet with Villard to take up questions of business between the two companies, "but this must be upon the distinct understanding that no reference then or hereafter is to be made to the matters to which the communication herewith returned relates." Rigdon says that Adams never again had direct dealings with Villard and communicated with him only through intermediaries. Klein says about Adams, "Humiliation was for him at once a sackcloth and a vendetta, yet he told Lane with a straight face that 'temper has nothing to do with business. For myself I can truthfully say that I do not feel the slightest degree of irritation over all these charges.'" The personal feud did not end until Adams and associates were able to force Villard out of the affairs of the ORN and OT. In Hedges' view, given the consistent opposition of Portland interests, the joint lease would never be executed and that Adams "had ample reason for terminating the lease. As to the manner in which he terminated it, particularly his alliance with Elijah Smith and the perpetuation in control of the Navigation Company of the anti-Villard group, his case is not so strong."[42]

Villard had seen the joint lease as a way to bring justice to all. With the end of the joint lease, Villard and his German backers feared that the UP with Elijah Smith would attempt to secure control of the OT, the NP's largest stockholder. The Deutsche Bank had thirty million in bonds of the ORN and NP and did not want the UP to control the situation in the Pacific Northwest. A syndicate was formed to purchase 75,000 shares of OT. The principal property of the OT was the ORN, which was controlled by Smith. As Hedges says, "But any policy which promised a square deal to C. B. Wright and his Tacoma interests must meet the hostility of Smith" and Portland.[43]

On August 9 Harris wrote Wright about a meeting with Adams, Ames, and Villard the day before. Adams expressed a desire for a joint lease, but thought that the one agreed to would be difficult to work under. Villard pressed Adams to rescind the June action canceling authority to make the lease. Adams responded he was not well enough informed on the OWT and he was going to Oregon the following week. When he returned he would take up the matter. Adams suggested that preferable to the joint lease would be to place the ORN, C&P, OWT, and the NP branches south of the NP main line in Washington Territory under an administration similar to the Montana Union and operated by agreement between the NP and UP. At the August 10 meeting of the NP directors Villard responded to Adams' letter of May 28 that claimed that the UP's actions north of the Snake River were undertaken with the knowledge and consent of Villard, "was absolutely unfounded and false."[44]

UP general solicitor John R. Dillon wrote Adams August 10 that the NP had no legal authority to enter into the lease: there was no legal power in its congressional charter and the Oregon act of 1887 made the lease contrary to the laws of Oregon. The sentiment in Oregon would prevent execution of the lease and if executed it would be invalidated by the Oregon courts or legislature. "The only thing left that seems to me at all practicable is to call the joint lease off, but negotiate, if possible, for a division of territory." He was not optimistic; the ORN was an Oregon chartered company and Oregon sentiment was against a division of territory. After his trip of inquiry on the ORN and NP, Adams wrote August 30: "Mr. Holcomb is unalterably opposed to the old joint lease, and I also am satisfied that it was a mistake; it could not have stood. It was well that we abandoned it as we did in deference to the public opinion of Oregon."[45]

A special committee recommended to the NP board of directors August 16 that Vice President Oakes negotiate with G. W. Hunt to turn over to the NP the stock and bonds of the OWT and that Hunt be contracted to complete the railroad. There was no recorded opposition to the recommendation. The *Palouse Gazette* had reported that the Northern Pacific Elevator Company was putting up warehouses along the OWT and would erect an elevator in Walla Walla. In early September under the influence of Oregon's United States Senator Dolph, the committee on public lands reported favorably a bill forfeiting all NP lands except right of way and station grounds.[46]

The New York Supreme Court heard the Ives suit September 18. It was argued that Smith and certain UP officials violated the injunction by continuing to build branch lines, the Riparia bridge, and transferring $1,200,000 from Farmers' Loan & Trust Co. On

December 4 the injunction was made permanent on the grounds, "that the building is in violation of contracts in 1880 and 1882, and of the joint lease of 1888, which apportioned certain territory, and also that the expenditure of $3,600,289 in building this bridge and new roads was 'squandering' the bonds of the [ORN] in useless building." The judge was not prepared to rule the lease void or as a violation of the Interstate Commerce Act. The judge found that the OWT construction did not justify the ORN construction because the OWT work was known before the joint lease was agreed to. The UP's counsel was confident that the injunction would be overturned on appeal, but since the decision only bound those within New York and could not reach the Oregon directors, the decision was not appealed. Adams, using the ORN Oregon directors and OSL funding, was able to proceed with the projected lines (see chapter VII).[47]

On September 20, 1888, J. C. Bullitt was added to the NP board of directors. Immediately after the stockholders meeting the directors accepted the resignation of Robert Harris as president, but elected him chairman of the board, at the same salary as the president, $20,000 per year. Villard was nominated for the presidency, but declined. Vice President and General Manager Thomas F. Oakes was unanimously elected president. C. H. Prescott, recently the general manager of the ORN, was elected second vice president. The *Palouse Gazette* said, "The election of Mr. Oakes means the complete ascendancy of Henry Villard to the control of the [NP]...It is less than five years since Mr. Villard's disastrous failure. Yet he has won his way up again in the face of all opposition, and furnished the world with another striking example of what enterprise may do which coupled with indomitable perseverance and energetic will."[48]

B. The Arbitration Contract

UP officials perceived Villard's objective was to use OT's minority but substantial interest in the NP to gain control of the NP and then use OT's majority of ORN stock to break the lease with the OSL and to operate the ORN in conjunction with the NP. Adams opened negotiations with Harris, Billings, and Oakes to devise a plan to accomplish the same objectives as the joint lease. At the same time Adams determined that if the NP could not be induced to join an equitable and amicable arrangement,

> We propose to introduce both the Utah & Northern and Hill's Manitoba road as aggressive competitors into the heart of the Northern Pacific territory. We propose to put the Northern Pacific into bankruptcy after these lines are opened, if we can do it, and we think we can. Once in bankruptcy, it at least will not be able to construct... [competitive lines].
>
> In addition to all this, we propose to protect our lease of the Navigation Company through the machinery of the courts and legislature of Oregon. Although the lease may be attacked, it will take three years at least to break it. During that time it is our intention to fortify ourselves in the laws and courts of Oregon and in the local opinion of Portland, so that if our lease ever is broken, the Navigation Company would still be independent.[49]

During the fall of 1888, Adams, Oakes, and Harris had several discussions; they agreed that a war of competitive construction would be wasteful and could be disastrous. Adams insisted upon the right of the ORN to occupy territory north of the Snake River and build to the Coeur d'Alene district. It was agreed that all the lines under construction would be operated in the common interest under an "Arbitration Contract." At the NP executive committee meeting November 28 Oakes and Harris said an agreement with the UP "can be reached." UP interests in early December bought OT stock to put pressure on the NP. Adams wrote Sidney Dillon, December 4, the negotiations "were rapidly brought to a satisfactory conclusion...Taken together, it was by far the most gratifying experience I have ever had in such matters...no threats used; no talk to what either company could do by itself, regardless of the other." On the same day the Ives suit for an injunction against ORN construction north of the Snake River was upheld (see above). December 11, Oakes submitted to the NP executive committee a draft arbitration contract between the NP and OSL/UP. An amended draft was referred to Counsel. Oakes and Harris were instructed to confer with the executive officers of the OT about acquiring the OT's ORN stock. At the NP board meeting December 20, Villard, OT president, stated that OT's ORN stock would not be sold at any price unless the NP was fully protected against the UP.[50]

In response to the injunction, Smith and the ORN Portland directors sued to restrain the OT from interfering in ORN's management. Villard suggested to Adams that the new agreement should include dumping Smith and the Portland directors from the board. Adams wanted to get rid of Smith, but Smith provided protection for UP interests. The solution was for the UP and NP to jointly buy the OT's ORN stock.[51] It was reported in mid-December that the NP and UP had agreed to buy the OT's ORN stock at nearly $15 a share, enough to pay the company's debts, which in November 1888 were $5.8 million. This would also free the UP from its guarantee of dividends on the ORN stock. The OT would retain its NP stock and other assets. On January 21, 1889, the NP Directors adopted a draft Arbitration Contract. Harris wrote Adams that the board approved the contract provided that the stock of the ORN was deposited with trustees and held for the equal benefit of the UP and NP. The contract was described by a NP director as "an agreement to operate all their lines together, jointly, and for joint benefits. It is an agreement for harmony instead of war and rivalry." The OT directors appointed a committee to arrange the sale of the stock. The *Railway Review* reported that conferences between Adams and Oakes justified the hope on Wall Street that the NP would join the lease of the ORN. "The most that was accomplished was an agreement to leave questions about branch lines and division of territory to arbitration, if the companies themselves could not agree. As this has been the principal obstacle to the joint lease, the progress made at the conference is regarded as substantial."[52]

In February 1889 the arbitration contract was drawn up establishing a neutral zone within which the relations of the parties would be regulated. The boundaries of the zone were from the mouth of the Columbia River to the NP mainline river crossing at Pasco, following the mainline northeast to the eastern boundary of Idaho, along the east boundary to the forty-fifth parallel (south of the Salmon River) to the west bank of the Snake River, south to the latitude of Huntington, then to the Pacific coast and north to the mouth of the Columbia River. Within the zone all railroads lines, present and future, "shall be controlled, managed and operated on the basis of absolute impartiality" for the benefit of the NP, UP/OSL. Portland and all Puget Sound ports were to be common points and the UP was to have trackage from Portland to Puget Sound on the NP. In order to insure impartial administration a board of five managers would supervise. The presidents of the NP and UP were to be members of the board as well as two members nominated by concurrent action of the boards of the NP and UP. The fifth manager was to be named in the contract and his successor named by the remaining managers. All differences regarding the construction of lines in the zone would be submitted to the managers for settlement. The NP would pay one-half of the rental of the ORN and the UP and OSL would guarantee the other half. The UP and OSL would transfer "rights, title, and interests in or to the capital stock" of the WI and ORE to a trust company in New York. The NP was to do likewise regarding the CRN, S&P, and Spokane Falls and Idaho Railroad. The sole power of voting and receiving dividends thereon was to remain with the managers. No mention was made of the OWT. According to Villard the arbitration contract was substantially approved by the executive committees of the OSL and UP and the NP subject to the OT's ORN stock being placed in the hands of a trustee.[53]

The execution of the contract was subject to the acceptance of a financial plan to be drawn up at the same time. The essence of the plan was that for $12,000,000 the OT would sell its ORN stock equally to the NP and UP. The stock would be held in trust until the companies could buy the stock. The OT would issue mortgage bonds against the stock at 5 percent. The NP and UP would pay 6 percent on the ORN stock, 5 percent to the OT and 1 percent into a sinking fund to pay off the bonds in about 40 years. According to Villard, "the only obstacle in the way of carrying the plan into effect immediately...was the attitude of opposition assumed by Elijah Smith and some of his fellow directors of the [ORN]; they declined, either to assist in this plan of settlement or to resign their positions in the Navigation Company, and to permit others to succeed them with whom it would have been possible to negotiate." To give time to work out details of the agreement and because of the unfriendly relations between the NP and OT on one side and the ORN on the other, the agreement would become effective July 1, 1889, after the June annual election of the ORN.[54]

On March 1 Harris wrote Billings that Wright and Bullitt were strongly against 6 percent rent. Adams said the UP deficit on the ORN guarantee the last year was $300,000. On March 19 the UP executive committee endorsed the arbitration contract. The NP and OT were slow to act and Adams thought Villard was stalling. Villard accused Adams of plotting with the Portland ORN directors against the OT. Villard fell ill in April 1889.[55]

Newspapers reacted negatively to the prospect of an agreement. Typical was the Lewiston *Teller*: "arbitration contract, if consummated, will bode no good to the shippers, that it will make the rates of freight continue as high and perhaps higher than they have been, that there cannot or will not be any chance of competition, till a competitive through line from the east built and is [in] operation."[56]

Rigdon pointed out the complex situation. Adams, in view of the greater security of the ORN under a joint guarantee, proposed that the rental be reduced to

5 percent. The NP and OT disagreed. The UP/ORN were pushing construction north of the Snake River. The OWT was expanding. "Bitter enmity had developed between Elijah Smith and Henry Villard...." UP interests and the ORN management were in conflict: Smith refused to comply with terms of the lease to sell ORN bonds to pay for WI and ORE construction, which forced the UP to advance nearly $2,500,000. Adams and the UP board were unanimous that a change in ORN management was essential. The danger was that at the annual meeting in June the OT would vote its majority of ORN stock for a board subservient to Villard and the NP. Adams was advised that a suit in Oregon might prevent the OT from voting its stock; therefore a majority of the minority could control the election. But such an injunction might cut both ways; Villard's lawyers also knew of this possibility.[57]

The New York *Times* carried a report April 8, 1889, that the UP had instructed its agents to issue through tickets from the east to points north of Portland. NP traffic manager J. M. Hannaford responded, "The Union Pacific is trying to force its way into that part of the Northwest, but so far as I see it can do absolutely nothing...We have made no such arrangement with the Union Pacific, and if it wants to issue through tickets it can only do so by taking these up at Portland and giving the passengers in return a regular NP ticket, bought and paid for at ordinary rates. We will not recognize any tickets issued by it under any circumstances." The dispute went on into at least late 1892.[58]

Adams wrote Sidney Dillon April 10 a history of what had transpired and what the UP proposed to do. The NP had "been very careless in their observance of agreements of late, and have been making frequent incursions into our territory in utter disregard of all agreements." On the 3rd Adams had told Harris that because Villard proposed to make changes in the management of the OT and ORN in June, the UP would not wait any longer for an agreement. "Under these circumstances, I told him that the time for delay was over, and we now proposed to take care of ourselves." Adams suggested that an agreement could be reached on the basis that the OSL construct from Rockford to Spokane Falls and each company have trackage over the other to competitive points. Adams thought Harris was favorable to the idea. The NP board was to meet on the 18th, if the NP agreed there was time to reach an agreement. Adams told the ORN Portland directors, with Harris present, if the NP did not agree to the arbitration contract then those parts of the ORN which were under injunction as a result of the Ives suit would be separated from the remainder and sold to the UP. The ORN would be reimbursed for every dollar it had spent on the separated lines. The NP would be turned out of Butte and Anaconda and a close alliance would be made with Hill and the Manitoba road. The Portland directors "were very favorably impressed with this idea, but wished to communicate with their friends." Following the meeting Holcomb was told to put surveyors in the field between Rockford and Spokane Falls. Adams concluded his letter to Dillon: "The whole question, therefore, rests in the hands of Mr. Ives and friends, representing as they do, both the Transcontinental and the Northern Pacific. If they choose to accede to the perfectly fair, businesslike and equitable arrangement I have offered to Mr. Harris, peace will be restored in 24 hours. If they do not, we propose to take care of ourselves."[59]

The OT board became aware of Adam's proposal and on April 11 appointed a committee, Villard, Ives, and Bull (directors of both OT and NP) to facilitate negotiations on the arbitration agreement, including the 6 percent rental. The OT directors pledged "their best efforts to induce the Northern Pacific Company to approve all the features of the agreement." Ives and Bull telegraphed Adams about the resolution and urged that he not take any "hasty action." Adams responded on the 12th, the day Villard later said that the presidents had substantially reached agreement,

> The directors of the Union Pacific do not propose...to take any 'hasty action' in these matters...during the last six months, this company has lost no occasion to press the board of the Navigation Company and the board of the Northern Pacific to some conclusion which would secure friendly relations between our companies in Washington and Idaho...we have failed completely, having been met by litigations of the most vexatious character, by a series of intrigues and obstructive measures, unnecessary to characterize,- all ending in a systematic procrastination which I will frankly confess has finally exhausted the patience of our directors, and practically taken the control of events out of my hands...
>
> I notice in your telegram you say that the directors of the Oregon & Transcontinental who have also seats as directors in the board of the Northern Pacific, five in number will use their utmost efforts to secure from the Northern Pacific the adoption of the arbitration agreement 'on the six per cent basis'. On the part of this company, I must say at once that we object to this limitation...I do not see why the Navigation Company should receive as a pure bonus the large increase in value which will come to its stock, if this arbitration agreement is carried out, without making any concessions to secure it...The Navigation, as you are aware, has hardly earned its operating expense during the current year. It will probably, from present appearances,

> run a million behind its rental before the year closes. This is largely due to the construction of the Cascade Division of the Northern Pacific...The directors of the Union Pacific would unquestionably object to your making the 6 per cent basis an ultimatum in this negotiation...
>
> ...the long and provoking delays to which this negotiation has been subjected have probably already committed the Union Pacific to action which heretofore might have been avoided. I must further add that I am under distinct instructions from the directors to delay none of the preparations which are now being made to enable the Union Pacific in any event which may arise, to protect its own interests...
>
> The present discouraging aspect of affairs, I must say again, is wholly due to the delays, obstructions, and vexatious litigation to which this company has during the last ten months been subjected, and personally I am no longer responsible for results.

In Villard's view this letter signified the abandonment of the settlement, "which was in no sense the fault of the [OT], made it necessary for the mangers of that company to devise some other plan of funding its indebtedness and establish its financial policy upon a wise and permanent basis." Adams wrote Harris April 12 that the UP directors were filled "with uneasiness lest the Northern Pacific has some plan in hand which does not appear on the surface, and is merely deferring action month by month until it is in position to refuse to negotiation further...They say, and very truly, that they do not see why the Northern Pacific cannot act now."[60]

Adams had favored ownership of the ORN, but as he wrote his assistant Gardiner M. Lane, April, 17, 1889,

> I have become more and more uneasy about the financial futures of the Navigation Company, as also about the legal position in which the ownership of the stock would place us...The heavy falling off in the traffic of the Navigation Company I am more and more convinced is due to a permanent cause not be removed by any single harvest, that cause being the competition of the Northern Pacific to Puget Sound points by way the Cascade Division, and the Oregon & California by way the Shasta Route, between Portland and San Francisco. This falling off of traffic leads me to entertain very grave doubts as to whether it would be safe for the Union Pacific to commit itself to so large an investment as is involved in buying half of the stock of the Railway & Navigation Company. I do not feel as if I could recommend it to our board of directors...

This conclusion lead to the proposal to sell the NP permanent trackage on ORN, "thus avoiding the necessity of further construction like that of the Hunt roads." Similarly the sale of NP trackage to the UP would avoid duplicating construction to Coeur d'Alene and Puget Sound. Harris favored the plan and so did certain members of the NP board. "Under this plan...each company would be responsible for the fixed charges, rentals, etc., of its own branches or leased lines. All questions of valuation, joint payment of rental, division of loss, etc., would thus be avoided.[61]

At the NP board meeting on April 18, 1889, Harris reported Adams' suggestion that the ORN and NP lease to each other trackage on the interior branch lines and from Portland to Puget Sound. Adams wrote, "Without some joint arrangement, the duplication of roads will be inevitable, the debt or obligations of both companies will be increased, the tendency of rates downward will be hastened and the public will not be as well served as is practicable under such arrangement as that recommended." Harris estimated that under the arrangement proposed by Adams the net profit to the NP April 1, 1888, to April 1, 1889, on the S&P would be $295,637, and from the ORN lines $318,000, for a total of $613,637 (as against $650,753 without the trackage leases). Harris wired Adams that the proposed lease of trackage was not taken up, but he thought it would have favorable consideration by the directors as a reasonable and practicable plan for avoiding unnecessary duplication of roads.[62]

A related issue for Adams was the OT's majority of the ORN stock. The UP board had concluded that the UP position in the northwest depended on elimination of Villard and the OT as controlling factors. If Villard gained control of the ORN board in June, the ORN would break the lease to the OSL and join the ORN to the NP. But control of the OT would commit the UP to the 6 percent rental. On the other hand if trackage rights were secured the OT would be of no value to the UP. On April 23, when he could not get agreement among UP directors to his plan, Adams dropped it and agreed to allow directors Sidney Dillon and Grenville Dodge (and Elijah Smith) to try to seize control of the OT and oust Villard. Dodge told Adams, the UP should buy control of the OT, the NP had no intension of treating the UP fairly and was attacking "us and our subordinates in every sneaking, intriguing way, trying to demoralize them. They have done this especially against Mr. Holcomb, whom I know they fear because of his knowledge, and who, I think, is doing his level best to take care of his properties."[63]

The NP board April 25 considered a Villard substitute motion which alleged that the UP had acted in bad faith while negotiating with the NP; thus the UP should demonstrate its desire for good relations with the NP for any further negotiations. The minutes conclude,

"After full discussion, the original resolution offered by Bullitt to rescind approval of the arbitration contract was adopted." This outcome the *Herald* said, "means a rate war and fierce competition that the people will look to with pleasure."[64]

Despite misgivings about control of the OT, Adams stood aside of the attempt to buy a controlling interest in the OT. The purchase of OT stock raised its price, alerting Villard. Villard's response was the OT directors May 10 voting to issue 100,000 shares of unsubscribed preferred stock in the OT treasury. The stock had full voting power, 6 percent dividends guaranteed and would be held in trust for Villard to vote as he pleased. Dillon and Lane, UP directors, were removed from the executive committee of the OT. The $10,000,000 to be realized from the OT stock would enable Villard to buy full control of the NP and reconstitute its board to his liking. To prevent Villard from controlling the OT board and thus the ORN board, UP parties considered legal action to liquidate the OT or appointing a receiver on the grounds that the OT was in violation of Oregon law and contrary to public policy. The receiver could vote the OT's ORN stock for directors favorable to the UP. According to Brayton Ives, who had resigned from the OT board and was cooperating with the UP parties, Villard had a majority of OT stock. Ives urged that proceedings begin at once on liquidating the OT. It was said that Ives, Billings, and Harris had given their personal assurances that they were in harmony with Adams and could be depended upon. Aware that the OT holding of ORN were a continuing source of conflict, Villard attempted to sell the stock, but the stock was inactive and he was unable to get a fair price for a large block of stock.[65]

On May 16 Dodge wrote Adams of a meeting he had that day with NP people (apparently including Harris, Oaks, Bullitt, and Billings). "My conclusion is that they are yet undecided whether it is best to negotiate with us with the O. T. in our hands, or in the hands of Mr. Villard." Both parties agreed that Villard's holding of the OT could prevent any agreement made among them. "What they will do I don't know, but it seems to me during the whole conversation that they were afraid of Villard." They thought it fair that a trackage agreement would send business by the shortest railroad to its destination. Dodge thought the proposed agreement was biased in favor of the NP. Adams sought to reassure Dodge, explaining that the year before there was a tendency for grain to go to Puget Sound because of lower rates, but under the agreement the business lost from the interior would be more than made up by the UP getting into Puget Sound on the same terms as the NP. As Adams saw it the UP was trading away a four hundred mile grain haul for an eighteen hundred mile haul from Omaha; the NP "shall make 50 cents on the wheat traffic from Washington to Puget Sound, [while] we can make $2.00 on the east and west business from Omaha to the same points." Portland has advantages, but these will not be realized as long as "Portland stands upon its traditions and does not go into a struggle to maintain its own business...What Portland people desire is to make us fight their battle against Puget Sound. We cannot afford to do so. Unless Portland will assume its fair share of that fight, we had better make up our minds to go Puget Sound points ourselves, and compete with the Northern Pacific for the interior business to those points."[66]

Elijah Smith fearing that the new OT preferred stock would be used in the coming director's election, procured May 17 a temporary injunction against issuing the stock. Villard denied that its purpose was to influence the election; it was to be used to reduce the floating debt of the company. In addition, Villard alleged, based on the April 12 letter above, that Adams sought to have the UP and OSL join forces with the NP to force a reduction in the 6 percent rent. Villard believed that Adams' statement that the ORN earnings were insufficient to cover the rent was a misstatement of the facts. The OT received over $720,000 a year and thus it was vitally important that the rent be maintained. Villard also maintained that negotiations on the arbitration agreement were suspended by Adams in April. Action on the suit was suspended by both parties.[67]

Villard and associates issued a circular to OT stockholders May 18 soliciting proxies, first to prevent the recurrence of difficulties existing between the NP, UP, and ORN as a result of the withdrawal of the UP from the joint lease and arbitration agreement; second, to oppose attempts to reduce the ORN rent and to resist control of the ORN by the UP and the Manitoba; and third, to fund the indebtedness of the OT. The UP, ORN, and Manitoba interests sought proxies to reduce the rent and to gain control of the NP using the OT's 25 percent interest as a nucleus. The same day Harris wrote Adams that the NP board approved a memorandum by Harris and Adams on trackage which was referred to the executive committee for action.[68]

Adams wrote Dodge that the traffic agreement with the NP ought to remove all the difficulties between the UP and NP, "Everything which could have been gained by a control of the Transcontinental will then have been gained by another process." He went on, "We never will have peace or quiet until the Transcontinental is liquidated." The OT should be attacked in two quarters, first on grounds of public policy and second "its value must be destroyed by legal steps taken to prevent its voting the stock it holds at the election of any corporation...On both these points, the law is with us, public opinion is with us, and the legislatures will be with us." He was sorry that the attempt to gain control of the OT had failed, "On your account, I wish it had turned out differently. On my own account, I am not dissatisfied with the result. I am dreadfully afraid that if we had succeeded, Elijah Smith would also have succeeded in keeping the Transcontinental alive...Now we can go for [liquidation]."[69]

J. M. Thurston, UP general solicitor, who was working with ORN attorney C. A. Dolph, to lay the ground work for an attack on Villard in Oregon, wrote Adams from Portland, May 20:

> The situation here, so far as public opinion is concerned, is the very best we could have desired. 'The Oregonian'... is urging the public Prosecutor to bring action to destroy the Transcontinental organization...Mr. Smith is strongly of opinion that suit should not be commenced until it is clearly evident that Villard's party has control, and in this opinion I fully concur. There are several reasons for it:
>
> ...public expectation will be worked up to believe that the destruction of the O. & T. Co. will leave the Navigation Co. free to reduce existing rates upon its system, as well as through rates to and from the east. If this expectation should be met there is no saying how far the popular demand might be carried. We are breeding an anti-monopoly storm which it will be impossible to still...
>
> ...the Transcontinental should be wound up. Its existence is a continued menace to the O. R. & N., and it certainly is to the Union Pacific interests now held under the lease, but it would be so much better to wind it up under the supervision of a favorable board of directors than through the harsher process of a court...
>
> The more I study the legal question the more I am convinced that the courts of Oregon will put an end to the corporate existence of the O. & T...this would induce many [stockholders] to throw their stocks upon the market, and the effect might be very disastrous to the market price of the stock. If therefore you become satisfied that you have no chance for control I venture to suggest that yourself and those whom you represent might wish to delay the commencement of proceedings until you could unload your O. & T. stock at prevailing quotations...
>
> The present injunctions in New York and Oregon restraining the O. & T. from disposing of the Navigation Co. stock, supplemented by an injunction restraining it from voting the stock, would keep it in the treasury of the O. & T. Co. and leave it there until the ligation over it was ended. In the meantime you would be control of the Navigation Co's affairs through the present friendly board of directors.[70]

In a lengthy interview in the *New York Times*, May 21, Villard said he opposed the Smith faction gaining control of the OT because that would put the UP on both sides of the table regarding any modification of the ORN lease. "The interest of the [OT], as the chief owner of the [ORN], is that the terms of the lease should not be modified to its disadvantage and...that its interests shall be represented by its owners and not by the lessees of the property." There was no basis for the attempted injunction, the proposal to issue preferred stock was not a secret and all Smith needed to do was to ask, but neither Smith nor any of his associates asked a single question on the subject. The purpose of the suit was to stampede stockholders of the OT into selling their stock. "I think that the record of transfers will show that the entire ownership of the stock has changed with the last three weeks...the old stockholders...[became] victims of the bluff game, that seems to have been thus deliberately played upon them."

> I have known, moreover, that the [UP] and [Manitoba] had begun months ago to arrange traffic combinations against the [NP]...For I am sure it will arouse every independent holder of [NP] stock to the moral perils that would befall the company if James J. Hill acquired control over it. I don't wonder that his appetite has been whetted in that direction, for while the [NP] earnings have shown a steady increase in the last two years, those of his own company, as everybody knows, have undergone an enormous decease since last fall. To divert traffic from the [NP] system to his own would, of course, be a very easy and effective means of making up his losses. It is no wonder, considering the recent decline in the [UP] earnings, that it is also hungry for the same prey.[71]

Elijah Smith replied on the 31st:

> The difference between the intentions of Mr. Villard relative to the [OT], and of those who have joined me in asking for your proxies, is that we propose to secure to the [ORN], an additional customer, viz.: The [Manitoba], and thus prevent the completion of another line to the Pacific Coast, while he has assumed an attitude of antagonize to all except the [NP]; to harmonize all interests in the Pacific Northwest by considering all of them as factors in the situation and to provide for the unfunded debt of [OT] without increasing its capitalization and fixed charges which Mr. Villard has already attempted to do. Taking Mr. Villard at his word, there is no difference in our respective attitude toward the present lease of the

[ORN], nor in the determination to maintain the dividend now guaranteed on the stock of that company.[72]

Adams sent a draft trackage agreement to Harris, who responded May 28 that the executive committee had considered the draft and with a few modifications had approved it conditioned upon the road being constructed from Rockford to Spokane Falls be turned over to the NP to complete and the ORN given trackage. On the 29th Adams declined to accept the proposal, "In case the agreement we are now making ever were broken...the O. R. N. would find itself in the air at Rockford, and compelled to seek its way into Spokane Falls through the worst kind of duplicate construction." Adams wrote Dodge that his intention was to let the trackage negotiations "drift" until "our presence in Spokane Falls [is] an established fact, to be accepted as such." Dodge responded, "I know that you have great confidence in this traffic agreement, but I do not change my mind. I do not think that the Northern Pacific has any idea of making that agreement, or any other until they are absolutely forced into for their own protection." Adams responded, "In this again I think you are wrong. The Northern Pacific is disposed to favor the trackage agreement because they think they will have the best of it."[73]

In late May the UP directors found themselves in a quandary regarding their plan to liquidate the OT. As Adams wrote, "They found that they had the wolf by the ears." If the OT was speedily liquidated, "[it] would probably put into bankruptcy several of my friends... they had so loaded themselves up with stock, exactly as Mr. Villard...if a move to liquidate were to knock the stock...down 10 or 15 points thereby, their margins would be wiped out, and they wiped out with them." Villard in Portland probably realized the UP was in control of the situation in Oregon and could bring about the liquidation of the OT. The UP lease could not be broken and, given the ORN construction in eastern Washington, OT's ORN stock did not protect the NP.[74]

Meantime, on June 1 it was announced that Villard had proxies for a majority of the OT shares. Thurston and Dillon could find no law prohibiting a minority of the stockholders from voting when the majority could not. So an injunction was sought to prevent the OT from voting its majority of the ORN stock. Dodge's advice on the 2nd was that UP interests should buy ORN stock to achieve a majority of the remaining stock, so as to control the ORN election.[75]

For help in soliciting proxies for the ORN election, Villard in early May employed Charles Fairchild of Lee Higginson & Company of New York, a firm which did business with Adams. Villard said he wished to act with the full knowledge and consent of Adams. A May 27 Fairchild letter containing what Villard was willing to do regarding the ORN was passed on to Adams: the eastern directors were, except for Villard, to be neutral, not on the NP or UP boards; Elijah Smith was to be removed as a director and president; the OSL lease was to be modified to agree with the terms of the joint lease or the arbitration contract; the ORN would accept the joint lease, arbitration contract or trackage, as Adams might prefer, and Villard would use his influence with the NP board to secure its approval; the ORN branches north of the Snake River would be recognized; the ORN would acquire the OWT if it could be bought; injunction suits would be withdrawn; and Villard would support modification of the 6 percent rental. Adams on the 28th replied that he could agree to the proposed settlement, except that Villard should not be on the ORN board. The same day Adams sent Dodge the Fairchild letter:

> Under these circumstances...we ought to close this business up before we stir up any more...popular feeling...it seems to me we are playing with fire to a most dangerous extent, and ought to stop it if we can....We cannot afford to continue this fight, in order to pull Elijah Smith's chestnuts out of the fire...Mr. Smith is too deeply interested in the Transcontinental to carry on the contest at any great risk to himself. He would have to accede to reasonable terms.

Adams wrote to another associate about Villard:

> The impudent rascal has absolutely stolen my thunder, and is to rattle it all around the skies. As you doubtless know, Harris and I have been working on a system of trackage exchange between the Union Pacific and the Northern Pacific...It is unnecessary for me to say that it is not the habit of my mind, when a person offers me all I ask for, to reject it for the reason that offer comes from an enemy. If Mr. Villard wants this cheap glory he is welcome to it.

In a second letter to Dodge the same day Adams said he thought the lease's value was overestimated; the UP transferred to the ORN two passengers for every one received; regarding freight so far as Adams could find the ORN gave to the UP only some wool that went beyond the Missouri River, the remainder was for points on the UP west of the river; and the freight turned over to the ORN came from east of the Missouri, which the UP had to compete for, lease or no lease. Adams estimated that the OSL did not make $200,000 per year on the lease while it cost $500,000 per year. "Under the circumstances, I have no disposition whatever to disturb the lease.... On the other hand, I cannot go off into paroxysms of terror over the idea of this lease being broken on the other side. *They never will dare to break it on God's earth* [emphasis in original]." Under the circumstances Adams thought the composition of the ORN board was not of much importance. "I would rather have Villard and eight clerks upon it than the board we had last year." When the UP gained possession of the WI and ORE and made a connection with the Manitoba nothing the NP or the ORN might do made much difference. He concluded "For myself therefore I am perfectly willing you should make any arrangement with Oakes which commends itself to your judgment." On June 4 an agreement signed by Adams and Oakes provided that all the ORN stock which they controlled or could influence would be used to select directors agreed upon by Villard for the NP and Grenville Dodge for the UP. The lease rental of the ORN would be maintained. The ORN would assume responsibility for the WI and ORE. All litigation between the ORN and OT would be dismissed. The OT's ORN stock would be sold. It was agreed that the final conclusions of the negotiations would be left to later in the month in Portland. Regarding the ORN line from Rockford to Spokane Falls, Adams said the matter should be disposed of in the trackage contract. He wrote, "Of course we will not give up the exclusive ownership of road to Spokane."[76]

Adams put Dodge in charge of negotiating with Villard in Portland. On June 5 Adams wrote Dodge to keep in mind that the UP was in possession of the situation in Portland. The ORN was in their hands and an agreement with Smith placed the WI and ORE under the control of the UP. Without the WI and ORE, the ORN could not earn more than its fixed charges nor earn anything for its stock and if the lease was broken ORN stock would fall and hang there. "I think you will find Villard very conscious of [the ability of UP to liquidate the OT] and disposed therefore to do everything in his power to reach such a settlement with us as will enable him to make a market for [OT and NP]. Unless I greatly mistake the situation, he will have just two objects in view. One, to increase his control in the Northern Pacific board, and the other to 'boom' the [NP and OT] stocks, including in the latter the Navigation Company." Adams was sure that Villard would concede everything to obtain the two objectives. An objective of the UP should be to get out of the OT even if it is not liquidated. Villard should be made to understand that unless terms in that respect were satisfactory, "we propose to tie O. T. up so that he can do nothing with it." Even if the legal actions the UP might take were not legally sound, the UP could cause a temporary delay which would upset his plans. Adams said further,

> accordingly do not propose to press the trackage contract any further until we hear the results of your negotiations at Portland...I have not the faintest idea of yielding any interest in the line between Rockford and Spokane, or to give another company a veto power over our use of it... the Manitoba is the strongest card in our hands. I do not propose to put ourselves in any position which would hamper us in dealing with that company or establishing the closest possible relations with it. If these two cardinal points of policy are understood as adopted by us, and at the same time construction is being pressed rapidly forward to Mullen and Spokane Falls,—which are the keys of the situation in that region,—I do not see why we are not perfectly in position to wait and let time play our game for us.[77]

The *Oregonian* wrote June 10:

> The criticism by Portland of Mr. Villard has simply been a protest against his effort to hamper or strip the Oregon road for the benefit of the Northern road. This is a policy that would render the Oregon road powerless, would injure the business of Portland and of Oregon, would leave the great country north of the Snake river to the Northern without competition...Since the [OT], in the hands of Mr. Villard, is the instrument of this policy, it is the enemy of Oregon, and to a large degree of the Northwest, and as it was created by...Oregon's authority, it ought to be disincorporated and dissolved. Mr. Villard's opposition to the extension of the [ORN] lines into the Northern territory, while the Northern has been entering the Navigation territory at all possible points, is regarded here as the touchstone of his policy.

Hedges comments, "It was ironical that the man who, more than anyone else, had taken a large and disinterested view of the situation and had worked to harmonize the rival interests, should have received more of the odium from both side than anyone else." In an interview with a man "high up in the councils" of the NP, "The Northern Pacific road is going to gobble up the O. R. & N. Co. That is what the Oregon Transcontinental election means...Villard is acting in this matter for the Northern Pacific company. C. B. Wright and his friends who are pulling strings, are perfectly willing to have Villard put to the front as a figure head in this matter. The Wright crowd know what they are about."[78]

Lane wrote Adams from Portland, June 12, that it was peaceful in Portland and "All matters now satisfactorily disposed of excepting the Oregon Transcontinental O. R. & N. stock. Villard is evidently much afraid of attacks from us or Elijah Smith. Of course impossible to say what

Smith might may do on arrival." Two days later, "Elijah Smith arrived this evening. He was at first belligerent but later calmed down somewhat. He can defeat agreement if he wishes. Important to bring all influence to bear to induce him to accept agreement." On the 15th Lane wired that Villard agreed to buy all the UP's controlled OT stock at cost and sell at 90 all the OT's ORN stock. The annual meetings of the OT and ORN occurred June 17. In letters to Dodge that day, Villard agreed to the OT disposing of its ORN stock, 120,027 shares, at a price below par. At the OT meeting Villard's directors were elected and they gave Villard authority to sell its ORN stock to local and Eastern capitalists, including Portland bankers, UP and Manitoba interests. At the ORN meeting a compromise board agreed to by Villard and Dodge was elected. The new ORN board pledged to complete its lines north of the Snake River and to open up to all connections from the East including the NP and the Manitoba. The lease of the ORN was to continue at 6 percent. Dodge reported to Adams, the NP assumed the bonded debt and obligations of the OT. Villard "was willing to concede anything to get O. & T. in shape."[79]

In Adam's view the agreement was a complete success. Control of the country north of the Snake River was conceded and the lines to Coeur d'Alene region and Spokane Falls recognized. ORN securities were to be used to defray the costs of construction. The parties were to cooperate to secure trackage for the UP to Puget Sound. The OSL lease of the ORN was to be maintained but the burden of the OSL was reduced by a special fund in the ORN treasury to be used for the benefit of the property. All litigation was to be dismissed. All of the OT stock bought by friends of the UP would be sold without loss. Elijah Smith did not give up his ORN directorship, presidency, or injunction suit without "aggressive persuasion." Dodge and Lane agreed to protect Smith's investment in OT stock. All of the terms of the Dodge-Villard agreement were eventually carried out except for the trackage agreement. The *Oregonian* saw the agreement as "a complete victory for Portland...The most favorable feature of the [ORN] election was that the seven Portland directors were elected unconditionally."[80] Hedges comments, "The closing scene of the story of the connection of Henry Villard with the railroads of Oregon was his appearance [June 14] before a rather hostile assemblage at a Board of Trade meeting in Portland, in June, 1889. At this meeting he was severely criticized in regard to his attitude toward various aspects of the railroad question.... All in all, it was not an entirely fitting termination of Henry Villard's relations with the city for which he had done so much."[81]

Elijah Smith wrote ORN stockholders June 25, defending the alliance with the UP as "natural" because of a common opponent, the NP, "with which Company, it is not believed that any agreement for future relations can be made on terms that would preserve the integrity of your property and its income." He also sought cooperation from the Manitoba road capitalists. The compromise reached prior to his arrival in Portland on the 14th would have given control of the ORN to the UP and NP and a "majority of the new directors would been susceptible to...[Villard's] influence. This development proved to me most conclusively that the representatives of the Union Pacific company were not to be implicitly trusted with the protection of your interests." The alternative to the compromise was "protracted and expensive litigation." He hoped for modifications in the ORN board when the OT ORN holdings passed into other hands. The OT "has always been a menace to the best interests" of the ORN. He announced his retirement from the ORN presidency "which I would have yielded to others before, had I been convinced that our common interest would have been promoted by such action."[82]

On July 1, 1889, the directors of the ORN elected Edmund Smith president to succeed Elijah Smith. Asay's appraisal of the Smith presidency: "His term in office had been stormy, and certainly he had incurred the wrath of Villard and Adams from time to time. Yet he protected the interests of his company above those of the UP or NP, and in so doing enabled Portland to maintain its presence in eastern Washington and Oregon."[83]

The *Railroad Gazette,* July 5, thought that while the UP had a deficit of $350,000 in 1888 on the 6 percent ORN stock dividend guarantee, the dividend was not unreasonable. The UP had netted over a half million dollars on the interchange traffic and the traffic was sure to grow. "If the greater part of this present and prospective traffic can be carried over the [ORN] lines impartially, the future of that property ought to be assured." [84]

On July 30 Dodge wrote Lane that Elijah Smith refused to agree to anything and that an agreement could be made with Hill for trackage from Montana to Spokane. Hill's directors had given him authority to spend $5,000,000 to build to Mullan. Holcomb wrote Dodge August 5 that he would try to convince Adams that "we cannot successfully operate the O. R. & N. Company without treating Hill as a factor."[85]

Dodge wrote Elijah Smith, August 1,

> I have made every endeavor to have you carry out your agreement made with me in Portland, Oregon, so as to enable me to carry out my agreements based upon your

> promise. I am convinced you do not intend to do it, but simply hold it to trade upon. I therefore notify you unless you dismiss the injunction suit in New York and Portland and withhold all opposition to carrying out my agreements made in Portland with Mr. Villard by Monday, August 5th, by three P. M. all agreements written or verbal, and all understandings with you are at an end at that time and date.

Lane on the 2nd wrote, "Smith now threatens to bring a suit against the Oregon & Transcontinental Co. restraining it from disposing of any of its assets except by distribution pro rata to its stockholders. This injunction, if obtained will probably prevent our purchasing the O. R. & N. stock held by the O. & T. Co." Smith to Dodge on the 5th, "The intimation contained in your letter of bad faith on my part is not warranted and entirely without foundation." On the 9th Lane informed Dodge that Smith had agreed to all the terms of the agreement and had signed it.[86]

On August 14 Lane wrote Adams,

> We must begin construction to the Sound at once, or, better still, join with the Central Pacific and Manitoba in such construction. The Northern Pacific will never come to terms until we do this. Oakes is opposing us in the matter and is attempting to excite his co-directors to such an extent (by stories of our wickedness and unfairness) that they will refuse to consider the agreement. Harris is still with us, but he can never carry the agreement through the board with Oakes opposing it.
>
> I am sure that Harris, if he were in our position, would approve the course outlined above. Oakes is fair spoken, but I am convinced that General Dodge and Mr. Holcomb have been right in distrusting him. He cannot be moved by fairness. He can only be moved by brute strength [emphasis in the original].

Dodge shared Lane's view and advised Adams on the 21st to induce Hill to "cover" the line from Missoula to Mullan, assume control of the Montana Union, and arrange to reach Seattle. Adams reached a tentative agreement with Hill which would give the Manitoba trackage over the ORN into Portland. Adams wrote Lane the same day:

> If it were worth while, I could make out a much stronger case in favor of Mr. Oakes and the Northern Pacific direction than you seem disposed to allow…I am unable to conceal from myself that the course of the Union Pacific, and my own course, during this long negotiations, has not been above criticism. More than once we have made propositions, and even entered into contracts, and then receded from them…Moreover, we are the aggressors, as thing now stand, in the matter of the Puget Sound traffic. Our own arbitrator decided that question against us, and we refused to abide by his decision…While he [Oakes] has seen us withdraw—as we did withdraw—from a joint lease which we had ratified; and subsequently kick over—as we did kick over—a joint management arrangement which we ourselves had proposed—do you think it wholly unreasonable in him to reach the conclusion that we are not in earnest, especially in view of the fact that we refuse to abide by the decision of our own arbitrator in a most import traffic question?
>
> I am aware that many of our friends have thought that Mr. Oakes and the Northern Pacific management were playing with me, and merely working for delay. The delay, as I understand it, has all worked in our favor. We have been occupying steadily during the past year the whole debatable territory north of the Snake. Our lines are being pressed forward to Mullen and Spokane Falls. We have bridged the Snake at Riparia.[87]

R. Suydam, a banker and UP stockholder, wrote Adams September 10 of a conversation he had with Oakes. Hunt refused to sell the OWT, but the NP would be obliged to eventually buy it. Oakes said there would be no progress on trackage until the UP agreed to hold the Rockford-Spokane line in joint ownership. It was suggested that if that were the only obstacle, Adams and Oakes could work out their differences. Oakes replied "Look here, you have been talking peace a long time to me; suppose you go to your Union Pacific friends and talk peace to them; they are doing the fighting, not me." Oakes said that the NP would not grant trackage west of Garrison as Hill had proposed. "If Mr. Hill wishes to get into that country he must build his own line: our company will never take him there. … [T]he true way to deal with Mr. Hill was for the Union Pacific and Northern Pacific to combine and crush him, and then take him in; instead…the Union Pacific has pursued the policy of giving his line trackage rights on terms which could not be profitable, but which divided the business at many points in Union Pacific territory." Rigdon says that Adams was not able to bring the negotiations to a conclusion. "Oakes played hide-and-seek with him…the Northern Pacific people had only been temporizing, and did not intend to make any joint trackage agreement whatever." Adams wrote Dodge September 21 that he had signed an agreement with Hill. "It seemed to me to leave the thing in very satisfactory position, as we committed ourselves to absolutely nothing except giving Hill power to fight the Northern Pacific at his own expense as much as he liked. I cannot see how it would hurt us in the slightest degree if he should make terms with them."[88]

On September 19, 1889, the NP directors rejected Villard's proposal for refinancing the NP as "too indefinite. It offered loopholes for bad management, or worse…. It gave too much leeway, particularly for 'commissions' and 'premiums' for [financing] the gigantic mortgage." At the NP annual meeting, October 17, 1889, Villard was in complete control and was elected chairman of the board, replacing Harris. Oakes remained president. Robert Harris and three others were removed as directors. Wright remained the only director from the pre-Villard era. Over three-fourths of the preferred stock was voted for Villard's proposed mortgage. In his testimony in the proceedings brought by the NP directors against the receivers in 1894, Oakes said that Villard had been in fact the NP president, presiding at the meetings, appointing the finance committee, and controlling the treasurer, leaving Oakes with little to say.[89]

The October 17, 1889, NP Annual Report did not mention negotiations with the UP but said:

> The aggressive attitude of the Union Pacific Company, through its subordinate organizations in Washington and Idaho Territories, has perhaps been the most troublesome element in our territory on the Pacific Slope. While it has not, as yet, cut any important figure in our traffic movement or earnings, it stands as a menace to the maintenance of rates, and with the prospective early completion of that Company's new lines we shall undoubtedly soon suffer a further division of the business afforded by the Coeur d'Alene mining district and the thriving city of Spokane Falls....We have derived much benefit from the co-operation of the [OWT] in securing to us participation on favorable terms in the wheat tonnage of southeastern Washington.[90]

Beginning August 1, 1889, the Oregon Short Line and Utah Northern Railway (OSL&UN) operated the ORN under the lease of January 1, 1887. This continued until October 13, 1893, when the receivers of the Union Pacific System began operation of the ORN.[91] A special meeting of the OT stockholders, November 5, 1889, authorized the dissolution of the company. On the 15th the OSL&UN purchased from the OT a majority of the stock of the ORN. The purchase was to be partly financed by a $13,000,000 OSL&UN mortgage dated September 2, 1889; in November 1890 nearly half of the collateral trust bonds remained unsold. To pay for the ORN stock the UP increased its floating debt and short-term notes. Adams, unable to weather the financial crisis at the UP, was succeeded by Sidney Dillon as the UP president on November 26, 1890. Adams was able to eliminate the floating debt he inherited, but as a result of the ORN purchase the UP's floating debt was in 1890 substantially the same as when Adams became president in 1884. In addition to floating debt other woes fell on the UP, all contributing to Adams' downfall and the 1893 bankruptcy of the UP. The 1889 wheat crop was poor, the winter of 1889-90 was severe, and the enormous crop of 1890 could not be moved (see chapter X). The earnings of the ORN fell short of the rental about $350,000 in 1888, $736,000 in 1889 and were likely to be $1,500,000 in 1890. A few days before his fall, Adams wrote Oakes asking that the NP raise its eastbound wheat rates from fifty cents to sixty-five cents. Oakes refused to do so. If he had agreed, it probably would have resulted in more wheat moving westward on the ORN. The combination of a falling ORN stock price and tight money made it more and more difficult to borrow money on the collateral trust bonds which had only stock as security.[92]

Hedges concluded his study of Villard in the Northwest by pointing out that when Villard returned to activity in 1887 he did not have a personal interest in any of the companies, but he was the agent for German capital which was invested in the NP, ORN, and OT,

> and for that reason could have no object in sponsoring a policy which would injure any one of them. Probably no railway promoter in the Pacific Northwest ever strove so earnestly for the good of all as did Villard, from 1887 to 1889. Creative organizer that he was, he turned to a policy of compromise and attempted by various means to bring about a condition of harmony and fair competition.
>
> For a time, through his joint lease plan, he seemed to be on the verge of success...But such an arrangement was doomed to failure almost with its inception. Years of rivalry and animosity had developed a host of complications and, finely conceived as the plan was, it is not surprising that it failed. A contest so rooted in the actual physiography of the region could not be adjusted at a stroke, however well directed. The war for the control of territory continued.... Millions of dollars were expended in this premature building until competitive construction was brought to a halt by the financial collapse of both the Union and Northern Pacific, and the disputed areas were crisscrossed with grass-covered railway tracks.

Villard made another effort to bring some harmony in the Northwest. Villard attempted to buy control of the Manitoba in the interest of the NP, but Hill backed out at the last minute.[93]

Having failed to gain access to the NP's Portland-Puget Sound line, Adams and James J. Hill agreed July, 1889, to form the Portland & Puget Sound Railroad to construct an independent line. Some grading and bridging, including work on a Columbia River bridge at Vancouver, was done. In August 1891 the UP and GN agreed that all expenditures for the project should be stopped.[94]

At the beginning of 1890 there was no longer any attempt to work out a grand strategy by the NP and UP to accommodate each other in the Northwest interior (such attempts would return later in the decade).

The ORN, controlled by the UP through the lease, but under the influence of its Portland directors, had strengthened its position north of the Snake River. The NP was locating lines to Lewiston and Colfax, both in ORN territory. South of the Snake River, Hunt's OWT, still independent, but with a traffic contract with the NP, competed with the ORN and had solicited a subsidy from Portland for an extension to that city. Hunt was also making preparation for building a line to Grays Harbor; thus the OWT was a threat to both the NP and ORN. Over the horizon was James J. Hill's Manitoba, shortly to be the Great Northern Railway (GN), posed to extend to the coast; another threat to both the NP and UP. The NP built into the Big Bend Country west of Spokane, both to compete with the likely route of the GN and to hinder the building of the Seattle, Lake Shore & Eastern; both the NP and GN considered acquiring the latter. The NP ultimately did so in 1890.[95]

Early Projections of the Spokane & Palouse to Colfax and Penawawa, 1885–92

When the NP lost control of the C&P in 1884, Colfax was the most important town in the Palouse. The NP's interest in Colfax continued off-and-on for two decades. Colfax would have welcomed the NP. But building into Colfax was physically challenging and the NP always seemed to have more important projects. Penawawa Gulch, west of Pullman and southwest of Colfax, is the only feasible route west of Riparia from the Palouse Plateau to the Snake River. The NP for two decades made extensive surveys in Penawawa.

On July 10, 1885, NP President Robert Harris, accompanied by his chief engineer, general manager, and land agent, arrived in Colfax. He was told by several citizens of "the disadvantages under which this section was laboring, consequent upon discrimination in freights, the high price at which railroad lands are held and the uncertain position occupied by settlers on lieu lands." Harris was attentive, but made no promises. Eighteen months later people in Colfax were still pushing for an NP connection.[1]

The NP made a preliminary survey in November 1885 beginning at approximately Oakesdale south through Colfax to Union Flat west of Pullman and up the flat to the Washington-Idaho border. On January 2, 1886, Assistant Engineer J. B. Alexander wrote a lengthy report to NP Chief Engineer Adna Anderson in which he made recommendations about reaching Colfax and the Snake River. The *Gazette* in July 1886 reported that the ORN had decided to build from Texas Ferry to the C&P. "This will almost surely send the Spokane and Palouse branch on south through Colfax." The same month Mohr wrote Anderson that he met with a group of Colfax business men who proposed that if the S&P surveyed to Colfax via Dry Creek and if the estimated cost of grading and ties did not exceed the average cost of similar work on the S&P main line, they would perform the work and if provided the steel they would turn it over to the S&P. Mohr asked Anderson whether he should make the survey; building south from Colfax was feasible, but Palouse City was preferred. Anderson agreed that a continuation of the main line south from Colfax was not desirable. The end of July the *Gazette* reported that articles of incorporation for the Washington Railroad and Transportation Company had been filed in Whitman County by people from Colfax and Uniontown. The company proposed three routes: from Colfax southeasterly to Genesee via Spring Creek and Uniontown; from Colfax northeasterly to near McCoy on the S&P; and from Colfax to the Snake River.[2]

On August 21 Harris wrote Vice President and General Manager Thomas Oakes that he thought it time to locate an extension of the S&P from Belmont to Palouse City rather than to Colfax. Oakes agreed. Mohr wrote Assistant Engineer Lewis December 8 that, after completing the survey to Genesee, a survey from Oakesdale to Colfax on to a junction with the Genesee line should be run. Early in January a reasonably graded line from Oakesdale to Colfax via Conway Gulch and Dry Creek was identified.[3]

On February 23, 1887, the NP engineer office in St. Paul received Mohr's 29-page printed report on numerous surveys and reconnaissances he had made in November 1886. From Texas Ferry he investigated a line east along the Snake River to Penawawa Creek and up the creek to Union Flat thence to a connection with the S&P Genesee extension. "This line affords the only available and practicable route from the Snake River to the plateau north of it." Mohr estimated that the route would control about half the wheat business between itself and the Snake River; only about 30 percent of the good wheat land in that vicinity was under cultivation. His estimate for a north bank line from Riparia to the S&P via Penawawa was 64.75 miles, $966,000, $14,919 per mile.[4]

Late January 1887, Harris in response to a letter from John P. Vollmer of Lewiston, reported that the track over the Cascades should be completed in April and "We… will be in a position to do a part of the grain business of Snake River in the fall if there were any boats that could be used for this purpose." Harris inquired of Anderson about boats on the Snake River. Anderson responded that between Riparia and Ainsworth navigation was generally restricted to from May to the middle of July. This had been investigated at the time of building the Ainsworth Snake River bridge. The stone for the piers came from above Riparia. Alexander about a year earlier in his explorations for S&P "examined the subject very thoroughly." On the north bank of the river the table land some two thousand feet high was broken in only two places below Lewiston, at Riparia and Penawawa. The only feasible way to reach the river from the S&P was from somewhere near Pullman and required about 30 miles of construction. This would give the NP the same opportunities for river traffic as the ORN. Along the table land, on both sides of the river, were numerous chutes used to slide grain down to river warehouses and hence to boats. The ORN boats were said to do a very good paying business. The line to Penawawa could be built that season for about $400,000 to $450,000, without rolling stock or any interest on the bonds. The boats could readily be built at Kennewick but hardly in time to get them up river that season unless there was a temporary flood in the fall. On April 1, 1887, Harris telegraphed Anderson in cipher, "We cannot say anything more to Vollmer just now. Let us get breath and we will tackle Penawawa Branch." The NP annual report of September 15, 1887, commented, "The question of the expediency of building from some point on the present completed line in southwesterly direction to Colfax, and thence to the Snake River, is worthy of careful consideration. By the aid of steamboats on the river a large grain tonnage could be obtained for the Northern Pacific."[5]

Rumors were abundant in 1889. In February there was a rumor that the NP would build from Rosalia to Colfax. The Canadian Pacific was reported to be looking into a line from British Columbia to Colfax. As the editor of the *Gazette* said "Let not a railroad escape." In March there was a rumor in Palouse City that Colfax would build a line to an NP connection at Palouse City. In June, "It is now positively asserted on good authority that the Northern Pacific will build to Colfax this summer." In August committees were formed in Sprague and Colfax to push for a railroad line between the two points. From Garfield in September, if the ORN did not let the NP use their track between Garfield and Colfax, the NP would build to Colfax in retaliation of the ORN building into NP territory. In December it was reported that the NP was surveying a route from Oakesdale west of Steptoe Butte to Colfax and thence south to the Snake River. A few days later the report was that the line was located. "It is said to be the intention of the Northern Pacific to push this branch to a junction with Hunt's road [O&WT]...at a point north of the Snake river." The Oakesdale *Sun* reported December 13 that NP surveyors were looking for a route from Cheney to Colfax.[6]

The desire for the NP in Colfax was fueled by ORN freight rates according to the Colfax *Commoner*, from the Walla Walla *Union*, July, 1889:

> The producers of the Northwest will no longer sell their grain for five cents a bushel less, simply in order that it may go to Portland, unless where they can not help themselves. Such was the case last year, along the line of the O. R. & N., that where they could not get their grains to the Northern Pacific, farmers were compelled to dispose of their grain at five cents less a bushel. It is in consequence of this marked difference in rates on the two roads that a wide spread feeling has been inculcated though the farming districts of Eastern Washington against the O. R. & N. road and in favor of relief, in some manner or other...
>
> It has seemed to be a policy of Portland and the O. R. & N., which has been long pursued, to get all they possibly could out of the northwest, without any reference whatever to the welfare of the people, or the development of the country.

In November the ORN rate from Elberton to Colfax, 13 miles, was seven dollars per hundred on lumber. The rate from Elberton to Spokane, 65 miles, was five dollars, the same rate as the NP from Palouse City to Spokane. "There is no competition into Colfax; hence, the charges are placed at the pleasure of the O. R. & N. Must it always be thus?"[7]

Based on a January 3, 1890, report by NP Assistant Engineer C. C. Van Arsdol (recently of the ORN), Division Engineer Huson sent Chief Engineer Kendrick a report of a survey from Oakesdale to Colfax. The estimated cost was $13,000 per mile and grades 90 feet to the mile. "The country through which this line passes is very good, and together with the town of Colfax will probably justify its construction." Huson advised against a line from Rosalia to Colfax, 13 miles longer and "would not develop much new country." On February 28 the S&P trustees adopted a definite location from Oakesdale to Colfax, 25.37 miles. Bureau of Land Management maps show an S&P survey from southeast of Oakesdale running southwest to the northwest side of Steptoe Butte, from there following more or less the route subsequently built by the Spokane & Inland Empire in 1907 through what is now Steptoe and on to Colfax.[8]

Farmers in southern Whitman County wrote Oakes January 1890, that they had learned of the NP survey from Colfax up Spring Flat across Union Flat and down Penawawa Creek to the Snake River. "We...urge that immediate steps be taken to complete this road the coming season, as it will undoubtedly be a paying investment and will relieve the farmers of their present inconveniences." Accompanying the letter was a list of farmers and how many acres would be planted if the railroad were built. They estimated that 24,541 tons would be produced without the railroad and 29,189 with the railroad. They wrote again in April.[9]

On February 1 Van Arsdol reported on the survey from Colfax to the head of Penawawa. The maximum grades from Colfax to head of Penawawa Creek were 90 feet to the mile. He found that the grade down the Penawawa would be 2.6 percent for two miles, but might be reduced to 2.2 percent. The cost of grading and bridging would be from 20 to 30 percent more per mile than from Oakesdale to Colfax. On April 19 Kendrick wrote Oakes that from Colfax to Penawawa on the Snake River, 62 miles, would have an average cost of $16,000 per mile. The day before the NP land agent in Colfax strongly urged construction of the line and from Penawawa up the Snake River to Lewiston. A line could easily and cheaply be built on the north side of the river through valuable fruit farms. Kendrick wrote, "The project commends itself...I have directed Huson to send a man to look over the line from Penawawa to Lewiston, and hope that the Company will be in condition to build the line from Oakesdale to Penawawa, and if desirable to complete the same to Lewiston." The farmers in the area preferred a connection with the NP because the UP had enjoyed a monopoly and "made rates upon the basis of what the traffic could stand." On May 1, 1890, Oakes responded, "We will let Penawawa extension rest for present." This was the same day that Oakes authorized Kendrick to award the contract for the S&P Lewiston extension.[10]

A mass meeting in Colfax in May protested UP service and considered forming a local organization for the purpose of obtaining right of way and surveying a line to the S&P. The *Gazette* said: "[ORN] have charged exorbitant freight and fare rates. Such as not another line in the United States dare do.... We need the Northern Pacific and we ought to have it." Early May the *West Shore* reported that in addition to the Oakesdale-Colfax-Snake River line, a line was proposed from Sprague to Pleasant Valley via St. John and to Colfax and beyond. The *Gazette* carried "A special dispatch" May 22 from Sprague that combinations of business men in Sprague and Colfax were "being quietly formed" to grade a railroad between the two places and sufficient stock had been subscribed to insure success. "By request the names of the prime movers are suppressed for the present." A week later the *Gazette* said the proposed railroad would run from Lewiston to the Seattle, Lake Shore & Eastern (see chapter XII) via Colfax and Sprague. People in Lewiston, Colfax, and Sprague were involved and the articles of incorporation, of this yet to be named railroad, had been drawn up.[11]

On July 11, 1890, Kendrick wired Oakes that a delegation from Colfax had urged a line from Rosalia to Colfax, a distance of 28 miles, through fine country. The receipts at Colfax the previous year had been $250,000. If the line was constructed that year they promised free right of way and station grounds and to extend all assistance possible during construction. Kendrick believed "it should be carried out if practicable." Oakes responded that if the people of Colfax would in addition to giving right of way and depot grounds, grade the line, "I think we can arrange to lay rails this year otherwise not."[12]

The October 16, 1890, NP annual report map includes a line from Oakesdale to Colfax (map was repeated in the next report). The *Gazette* reported January 23, 1891, from the Oakesdale *Sun*: "We believe the Northern Pacific stands ready to build a branch line from Oakesdale to Colfax and only waits for the encouragement from those alone the route. A guarantee of the right of way, is certainly all they would ask."[13]

The Alliance Railroad Company was incorporated at Colfax, July, 1891, by wheat farmers west of Pullman to build a railroad from a point near Pullman in a westerly direction to the head of Penawawa Creek and then down the creek to the Snake River. "There was considerable activity in securing right of way...and an effort to interest other railroad companies in the construction of the line." On July 30 Van Arsdol wrote Principal Assistant Engineer E. H. McHenry thanking him for information on a position with a company being organized at Colfax.

He thought McHenry's idea of building to Colfax from Oakesdale rather than Rosalia was correct. "Rosalia would give a longer and more expensive line to build and to operate, having two additional summits and would secure but little additional traffic." On August 5 Van Arsdol reported that he had met with the Colfax people; they had no organization but had decided to incorporate to raise funds. They had some kind of understanding with the NP that if they graded the line, the NP would complete it and repay them with a traffic agreement. They expressed the desire that Van Arsdol take charge of the engineering work.[14]

On August 20 McHenry wrote Kendrick that there had been considerable agitation in the past months about the S&P building to Colfax. To McHenry it was "unquestionably" justified on the basis of the business available and the fact that the NP would in a short time have to compete not only with the UP, but also the GN for traffic in the region. If financing could be arranged he thought that the NP should occupy the region in the vicinity of Colfax, southeast of Colfax and extend eastward following the general course of the Clearwater River. The citizens of Colfax and vicinity had agreed to donate free of charge all the right of way required between Oakesdale and Colfax, including depot and terminal grounds. They would also advance sufficient money to complete grading and bridges and pay for ties. The company would pay them in bonds for the amount expended at a rate of 87 percent. "All things considered, I think this is a very fair proposition for the Company, and results in enabling us to construct a very much needed branch at a time when the maximum of business it is offering, and the conditions are most favorable for building the road at the least cost. Our right of way will cost us nothing, and at this time we are not liable to interference from the U. P., on account of their condition, and we will forestall the Great Northern by a considerable time." Based on the estimate and the proposals for financing he estimated that the cash cost to the NP would be $105,090. Kendrick commented to President Oakes, "I think there is no doubt that the line from Oakesdale through Colfax to Penawawa would be remunerative." If the line were built, "I think that a cross line should be constructed from Pullman west, so as to make it practicable to run trains though Colfax to points on the Palouse Extension, and to Lewiston, if so desired." Kendrick wrote Oakes October 12, 1891: "In connection with the matter of the entrance of the Great Northern Company into Spokane Falls, I desire to call your attention to the certainty that Hill will, at an early date, proceed to construct a system of feeders into the Palouse and Potlatch regions. I know that it is impracticable for the Company to incur any expense at this time in the construction of additional mileage, yet I believe that it is a matter of great future importance that this extremely rich district should be more fully occupied."[15]

On March 13, 1892, Oakes was in Spokane and responded to a reporter's question about branch lines, "We shall build no more branches this year." The reporter asked him about the proposed branch from Palouse City to Colfax, Oakes responded, "If they build and equip it for us we will operate it." Oakes asked a Colfax delegation what inducements they had to offer. They responded that they would give free right of way, terminal grounds, or a cash bonus. Oakes asked them to find out how large a bonus they could give and he would take it up with the Board. The *Gazette* commented that the 16-mile road would cost about $350,000, an amount which should be easily secured, there being in each town several residents who were worth that amount. A Colfax committee raised the promised bonus of $40,000 and it was understood that there would be no problem in Palouse City raising its share. A definite proposal would be made to the NP, if it did not respond positively the business men of the two towns would build it themselves and try to sell it to the Union Pacific. It was learned on the 25th that the people of Palouse were not inclined to subscribe to the bonus, but the Colfax people were determined and $20,000 was readily subscribed and a committee was formed to raise additional subscriptions and to arrange a general project of assessing property in the town. Later the *Gazette* published a list of subscribers to demonstrate that the NP could have the required $50,000. Only two men refused to contribute, "and it happens that they usually are the loudest mouthed and longest winded on ordinary occasions when money is not needed." Van Arsdol wrote the NP land agent in Colfax, April 7 that if the company being organized in Colfax desired an engineer he was available "owing to the fact that the Northern Pacific has practically stopped all construction work I am now at leisure."[16]

Van Arsdol on April 19 wrote contractor F. D. Howell inviting him to look over the proposed Penawawa road. People on Penawawa were interested in a railroad and had obtained part of the right of way and were anxious to move that year's crop. Van Arsdol told them that Howell was able to handle the work if they raised sufficient subscriptions. He said that 22 miles of road would secure the business and could be built at about the average cost of Palouse construction. Howell was not interested in the work, but Van Arsdol attempted to get him to reconsider on June 20 by reporting that a subsidy of $60,000 could be raised plus 160 acres in town sites. At a meeting of the Alliance Railroad Co. Board of Directors held on November 7, 1892, the secretary was ordered to return subscription notes and contracts to their makers, and the Alliance Railroad Company thereby ceased to function.[17]

The NP's books as of August 31, 1896, carried an outlay of $5,712 for a survey described as "Colfax Extension."[18] The NP's interest in Colfax and Penawawa is continued in chapter XVIII.

The Spokane & Palouse and the Oregon Railway & Navigation Consider Routes to Lewiston, 1885–92

With the completion of the S&P to Genesee, the NP began to realize return on investment. More revenue was to be expected when the line reached Lewiston, the gateway to the Clearwater, Camas Prairie, and Potlatch countries. The ORN, having most of the business in and out of Lewiston on the Snake River, was not going to be left behind.

A. S&P Organization and Operation in 1889

The Northern Pacific Elevator Company warehouse at Pullman was full in early 1889 at 150,000 bushels. The Uniontown *Journal* claimed that that town was "the banner wheat station" on the S&P. The competition of the S&P and ORN at Garfield made it the most popular shipping point in the county. Wheat and barley for the past two seasons brought three to five cents more per bushel at competitive points such as Garfield. Considerable wheat was being shipped to Duluth and Minneapolis.[1]

This view appears to be of the newly constructed Palouse City Roller [Flour] Mill, c. 1889. The mill was located to the right, out of view, of the Haynes Photograph (p. 70). There were several flour mills on S&P. *Photograph 1987-1/168, Whitman County Historical Society.*

The Oregon Railway Extension Co. agreed January 4, 1889, that it would construct and maintain the ORE's crossing of the S&P at Oakesdale. In February the S&P proposed to furnish materials for fences if the farmers would set the posts and string the wire. In May a reporter for the Spokane Falls *Morning Review* took a trip over the S&P and reported many cattle along the line, and trains delayed by cattle on the tracks. The animals were frequently assisted off the line by the cowcatcher, but many were killed, particularly during heavy snow. Some of the encounters resulted in trains being derailed or damaged, and injuries to trainmen. The S&P was fenced with two strings of wire and a board on top from Uniontown to Genesee. By June 20 the line north of Rosalia was fenced. The *Gazette* reported from Palouse City *Boomerang* that, "A company will at once be formed with its headquarters in Palouse City for the early survey and construction of the Palouse Valley railroad, a line to branch with the S & P at this place and extend up the Palouse river, and eventually be extended to some point farther east."[2] Nothing came of the proposal.

The S&P and NP entered into a "Provisional Contract" February 15, 1889, that provided for a traffic agreement and a guarantee of the S&P bonds by the NP if the lease of July 1886 became inoperative. The contract was signed by Robert Harris as president of the S&P and James B. Williams as vice president of the NP.[3]

The NP appealed to reduce the road-bed assessment from $5,000 to $3,000 per mile. The Whitman County Commissioners upheld the $5,000 assessment. The *Gazette* commented, "Inasmuch as the road in this county is mortgaged for $16,000 a mile, the valuation of $5,000 a mile for assessment purposes is low enough. If the company wishes to have the assessment uniform throughout the territory, why not make it $5,000 a mile." The railroad then offered $3,500 a mile for 1888 and $4,000 for 1889 and a reduction of land assessment from 98 cents an acre to 89 cents. The county prosecuting attorney was of the opinion that the commissioners ought to accept the offer of the railroad.[4]

The 1889 NP annual report said that for the year ending June 30, 1889, S&P gross earnings were $176,716 (3rd of 23 NP branch lines); operating expenses, $147,785 (2nd of 23); taxes, $1,100; guarantee on the bonds, $93,420; total expenditures, $242,305 (3rd of 23); deficit, $65,589 (4th of 19); main line revenue from interchange business was $664,392 (2nd of 22). While there was a reduction in wheat traffic from the eastern section of the NP, "large crops were harvested in the Palouse and Walla Walla districts and the business was handled very satisfactorily via Cascade Division, as follow: 3,775 car loads to Puget Sound; 675 car loads to local intermediate milling points; and 312 car loads to Portland. In addition...about 900 car loads of Washington wheat were transported to eastern terminals."[5]

In early December a north bound passenger train was derailed by spreading rails about two miles from Palouse City. Several passengers were badly shaken up. The Spangle *Record* received "authoritative information" that the Cheney to Spangle "cut-off" would be completed the next year. The December 1889 S&P receipts at Pullman were double what they had been in December 1888.[6]

B. The S&P and ORN Search for a Route to Lewiston from the Palouse Plateau

With all the territory above the junction of the Snake and Clearwater rivers tributary to it, Lewiston was long viewed as an attractive railroad destination. It also was located on what appeared to be a feasible route via Lolo Pass from eastern Washington to Montana. Beginning in the 1870s Lewiston residents habitually thought a railroad was only a few months away. But the months became years. After much surveying extending into the twentieth century, no railroad was built over Lolo Pass. Lewiston lies almost 2,000 feet below the Palouse Plateau; finding a route down was a challenge. In 1898, Lewiston finally received a railroad from the plateau. Ten years later a line was completed up the Snake River from Wallula to Lewiston. When no railroad was built down the Snake River from Idaho or Oregon, Lewiston complained to the Interstate Commerce Commission about the omission, but the ICC refused to order the UP to remedy the situation.

The S&P filed supplemental articles in Washington Territory June 13, 1887, which allowed it to construct from any place on its line to any place or places on the Clearwater River in Idaho Territory or any place or places in Idaho or Montana territories. In mid-June Harris wrote John P. Vollmer in Lewiston assuming he had heard of the injunction preventing construction to the bluffs near Lewiston (see chapter VI), but "I think we will get there notwithstanding."[7]

In mid-June the *Teller* included an article from the *Oregonian* that said the real and concealed purpose for the S&P extension to Genesee was to build by "stealth" into the Potlatch country. The newspaper urged the ORN to immediate action. "Prompt action will secure permanently for Portland a rich district, while delay may give it into the hands of our rivals. We need not remind the new management that the interests of the city and of the railroad are identical in this matter."[8]

In late May the *Gazette* had reported that ORN surveyors were eight miles east of Moscow running a line to the Clearwater River. On August 17, 1887, the Columbia & Palouse filed second supplemental articles of incorporation in Washington Territory, adding three more lines to the charter (see chapter II): one line would run from Moscow to Potlatch Creek and down it to a point on the Clearwater River, a distance of about 40 miles. On October 18 C&P directors adopted a location map from Moscow to the Nez Perce Indian Reservation boundary, 22.6 miles. Bureau of Land Management maps show a C&P line east from Moscow paralleling as far as Joel, the subsequently built S&P extension to Lewiston and then down Middle Potlatch Creek to approximately Juliaetta.[9]

NP Division Engineer H. S. Huson informed Harris, January 17, 1888, that S&P Engineer Paul F. Mohr said that Moscow was the best point from which to reach the Potlatch Country. The route would be down the Little Potlatch to the Potlatch. It could also be reached from Genesee. "The whole Potlatch Country is very rough and two per cent grades would have to be used upon either route." Early February Huson wrote Harris that he had learned that W. H. Kennedy, ORN chief engineer, had complete notes on a survey run from Moscow down the Little Potlatch to the Potlatch. Perhaps Harris could get copies, which would save the expense of a survey. Harris responded that they would be able to use Kennedy's notes if needed.[10]

In early April the *Union* said the ORN had promised the people of Lewiston a railroad in 12 months provided the people guaranteed the right of way and depot grounds. On April 31, 1888, a few days after track was laid to Genesee, Mohr called Harris's attention to a map showing that a mile east of Uniontown there was a water course extending south toward Lewiston. Mohr said that a branch of about six miles was practicable almost to the point where the water course abruptly drops off the plateau 2,000 feet to the Snake River. Vollmer told Mohr that a short branch would capture a majority of the supplies going to Lewiston. A wagon road would be required, teams could make two trips a day "with ease." Harris wrote Chief Engineer Adna Anderson, "if Mohr's suggestion is a good one, perhaps it would be better to extend the main line to the point he suggests & let the piece of road from the point of junction to Genesee be a branch." Anderson responded that the road should be built. It would be within two or three "air line" miles of Lewiston with a wagon road of five or six miles. "I think it desirable, if not imperative, to build as near the edge of the plateau as practicable" with spur tracks beyond Genesee, perhaps to Moscow, "to properly secure the business of that region to the Northern Pacific."[11]

A map dated 1888, probably early that year, shows preliminary surveys of potential routes to Lewiston. "Line F" leaves the built line a little north of Uniontown and goes south, paralleling what is now U.S. 195, along Spring Creek to a divide on the bluffs of the Snake River about three miles north of the river (Mohr's recommendation?). "Line G" leaves the built line just east of the WA-ID boundary, crosses a divide and terminates about four miles north of Lewiston, also terminating on the bluffs. Lines "H" and "J" run north from Genesee eight or nine miles. While the two lines each increase the distance to Lewiston, they are approaches to the heads of the Little and Middle Potlatch creeks and the West Fork of Bear Creek. The latter two lines would facilitate reaching Moscow from Genesee.[12]

From June 23 into late November 1888, NP Assistant Engineer W. N. Wightman wrote NP Principal Assistant Engineer H. S. Huson a series of letters on surveys in the Potlatch country.[13] His letters reveal the difficulties of finding a route to the Clearwater River. Wightman included reports of ORN surveys in the same area. In one instance an ORN party working about two miles below Juliaetta, where they were stopped the year before at the Nez Perce Reservation, worked only a day before they were again ordered off.

On July 4 Wightman reported that, "The 'Potlatch Country' is large and very rich. An extension of 25 miles should give the first year of operation 2000 cars of grain, 150 cars of stock; and something like 250 cars of merchandise.... I earnestly hope that surveys may be made covering all this country this season." He said that if 10 miles of road were constructed that season, the NP would be in a position to construct though any canyon leading to the Clearwater before any other road could begin construction. The ORN at Moscow was in position to beat the NP to the choice of routes.

The *Union* reported that a practical route down Catholic Gulch had been found by S&P surveyors;[14] no reports of a NP survey in Catholic Gulch have been found. The gulch is west of all the forks of the Potlatch and flows directly into the Clearwater below the mouth of the Potlatch River; it is unlikely that it was found to be feasible by any serious survey. Or was this an attempt by the S&P to throw the ORN off as to its plans?

In mid-September the Lewiston *Teller* reported that both the S&P and ORN were surveying lines in the Potlatch country. In early October the newspaper reported that the ORN had been delayed crossing the reservation even after Congress had acted. After permission was again given, they surveyed down the Potlatch River to Hatwai Creek on the north bank of the Clearwater (about four miles east of Lewiston). The ORN was also seeking a route to the Camas Prairie.[15]

Wightman requested permission to cross the reservation but the response from the Indian agent was apparently not favorable. He thought that if a legal right could be secured to survey on the south side of the Clearwater they should do so without waiting for an act of Congress. If not then a line should be run from the Camas Prairie to Lewiston. "The ORN will soon have very accurate information of all this country and will have a decided advantage of the northern in case of any rivalry."

On October 31 Wightman wrote Huson that the right of way through the Branham estate at Whelan was unsettled. The estate would be in probate until spring, but Mrs. Branham would receive most of the land needed for right of way and she would deed it to the S&P. On November 1 Wightman sent a deed to Mrs. Rachel J. Branham for her children to sign for the part of the station site they would inherit. Wightman inquired whether the Whelan depot could be used for an office and residence. There was no suitable place at Genesee where he was then located and construction would likely start at Whelan. By November 22 he had moved to Whelan.[16]

Rumors flew: in November the S&P would extend to Juliaetta and possibly to the Camas Prairie in the spring; in January the ORN would in the spring make a permanent location from Riparia to Lewiston and into the Camas Prairie; and in February the ORN would shortly locate a line from Farmington to Deep Creek, thence to the Palouse river, thence down to the Potlatch country.[17]

Under the subject "S. & P. Surveys into Potlatch country," Huson on February 18, 1889, wrote a lengthy letter to Kendrick on five locations, with maps, profiles, and estimates.[18] Examination of the country gave two points, Cornwall and Juliaetta, which must be passed. Cornwall could be reached by all the routes thus far surveyed from Genesee and Whelan. "There is another good route from Pullman, which has not yet been surveyed and which I hardly think worth while to survey, as it will parallel the O. R. & N," Huson wrote. Estimates for the five locations: (1) Whelan to Cornwall [near present day Joel], 16 miles, $231,661, Moscow is "a considerable town" and "If built immediately, it will head off the O. R. & N. and will afford a remunerative trade" (Huson favored this over any other extension toward the Potlatch country); (2) Genesee to Cornwall, 14.75 miles, $184,937, 2.23 percent maximum grades against southbound traffic and 2.5 maximum grades against northbound traffic and requires a haul from Cornwall to Marshall Junction 32.5 miles longer than by way of Whelan, the grades opposed to the heaviest traffic are 2.5 percent as against 1.5 via Whelan; (3) Cornwall to Juliaetta via Middle Potlatch, 13.3 miles, $353,409, 3 percent grades and very heavy work, canyon not accessible by wagon roads and likely bring conflict with ORN over right of way; (4) Cornwall via Bear Creek to Juliaetta on the Potlatch River, 23 miles, $384,467, 2.5 percent grades, four stations can be located along the route, estimate makes only a $31,000 difference between this route and route via Middle Potlatch; and (5) Juliaetta to the Clearwater, 9 miles, $125,706, moderate expense. "Juliaetta will also ultimately become an important town." "I urgently recommend the construction of the line from Whelan by the way of Bear Creek to Juliaetta...Later on the line could be extended into Lewiston...but this much of the line will pay as well as any portion of the [S&P] already constructed and will keep the territory threatened by the O. R. & N."[19]

On May 14, 1889, Huson filed at the U.S. Land Office in Lewiston maps of definite locations of the five locations above, plus Genesee to a point on the Little Potlatch, 10 miles, the next day the S&P Trustees adopted the maps. The maps were approved by the land office July 11.[20] The map in the NP Annual Report, October 17, 1889, shows only a line from Genesee to Potlatch Creek.

Huson wrote NP Chief Engineer J. W. Kendrick June 8 reporting on his May trip into the Potlatch Country. In addition to grains he saw fruit of all kinds growing. "Its capabilities, to my mind, are the greatest of any section of country I have seen in the West." That year there would be about 15,000 tons of wheat to be taken out and the potential at 20 bushels to the acre was 123,000 tons when fully developed. He estimated that in the second year there would be 60,000 tons of wheat. This would generate $360,000 of revenue and that together with other freight and passenger traffic the line would generate $702,000 the second year of operation. He estimated the operating expenses to be $144,000 and the construction expenses at $616,127, about $15,800 per mile, for 39 miles (Whelan to Juliaetta via Bear Creek). If it were bonded at $20,000 per mile at 6 percent interest, finance charges would be $46,800 per year. The route selected was thought the only practicable one from Spokane Falls to Lewiston. "It is beyond doubt a much better proposition than the extension of the Central Washington [railroad west from Spokane Falls]."[21]

Kendrick sent NP President Thomas F. Oakes, January 30, 1890, his recommendation regarding a line to Lewiston. The first route suggested from Genesee was impracticable because of the character of the country and undesirable because it did not penetrate a good agricultural region. The best route was from Whelan via Moscow, Cornwall, and Bear Creek down to Juliaetta and to the Clearwater River. Kendrick quoted extensively from Huson's letters of February 18 and June 8, 1889 (both above). From Juliaetta a line was examined to Lewiston and up the Snake River to Asotin. Above Lewiston was the Camas Prairie containing fine grain land. The prairie could be reached by a line up Tammany Creek to Lake Waha, about 22 miles, which could be built "very cheaply, and such a line would control the wheat shipments of the entire plateau on that side of the river." On the Washington side near Asotin there were about 200 sections of tillable land. Until the Nez Perce reservation was thrown open, which he thought would soon occur, consent of the Indians would be necessary to build to Lewiston. He said he had received information that the ORN intended to build to Juliaetta in the spring; the NP should immediately construct from Whelan to Juliaetta. He enclosed an estimate of the cost of the line, same as Huson above, and a map of ORN and NP lines in the vicinity.[22] Kendrick went on to say that upon investigation he had learned that the S&P charter did not provide for building lines in Idaho and therefore the 7.1 mile portion in Idaho terminating at Genesee did not properly come under the charter and was not bonded. The surveys from Lewiston to Lake Waha were made with the intention of filing under the name of the Idaho Transit Co. (see below). He enclosed a copy of the company's charter and commented that it was not in a form of any value to the NP. "I believe that this matter should be taken in hand at once, and arrangements made to commence the construction of the line as soon as it is possible to do so in the spring."[23]

Huson wrote Kendrick February 21 that the Lewiston Board of Trade believed subsidies of $40,000 to $50,000 could be raised for building 25 miles up Tammany Gulch (see below). If the NP put steamers on the Snake River and constructed the Tammany Gulch line it would take all the wheat from back of Lewiston. It could be brought down to the Snake by railroad and transferred to boats. On February 26 Kendrick forwarded to Oakes Huson's information on the potential subsidy and suggested that station grounds be secured in Lewiston at once and that a definite location be made for a line from the head of Tammany Gulch and through Lewiston to the Indian reservation. The UP had obtained from Congress permission to cross the reservation. He closed, "if any subsidies are to be obtained, it behooves us to take steps indicating a purpose of constructing a line immediately."[24]

Kendrick estimated March 26 that the 68 miles of line and eight sidings from Whelan to Asotin and a five-mile branch on Tammany Creek to School House was $1,117,000. Oakes wrote NP Chairman Henry Villard April 3 that a bill granting the NP a 150-foot right-of-way through the Indian reservation had passed the House of Representatives. The UP had the consent of the Indians and the NP would need to do likewise after the bill became law. Oakes in Spokane Falls met with a committee from Lewiston. "[T]hey agreed to undertake to raise a bonus and to secure the necessary right of way and terminals on condition that the line should be completed ready for operation before January 1, 1891; and they would listen to no suggestion of a later date..." and if the NP was not prepared they would negotiate with the UP. The bonus would amount to $75,000 but Oakes thought $50,000 was more realistic. "The more valuable concession is the agreement on the part of the citizens to secure adequate right of way and terminals, under the direction of an agent of the Company." He concluded, "The success of this enterprise depends upon our taking prompt action... the Union Pacific are fully aware of the full value of the district, and are quite likely to extend their line to this point another year." Oakes telegraphed Villard on April 6: "Union Pacific people actively at work securing right of way from Walla Walla to Lewiston we should build immediately from Spokane and Palouse line to that point." On the 7th the NP directors authorized the president to make the necessary arrangements to construct from some point on the S&P a line of about 63 miles to Lewiston with an extension to Asotin and a branch up Tammany Creek for a total of 73 miles.[25]

Questions were raised whether the S&P mortgage covered construction in Idaho. An opinion of the NP Attorney's Office, April 15, 1890, said, "The original mortgage covers all branches the company may be authorized to build. The company is authorized by supplemental articles May 28, 1887, to build a branch into Idaho, hence the original mortgage covers that branch, and bonds to the amount of $16,000 per mile [at 6 percent] can be issued on that branch under the original mortgage."[26]

The Spokane Falls Board of Trade passed a resolution in early April urging the NP to extend the S&P to Lewiston. Writing on April 15 to Oakes, the board said, "The Spokane & Palouse Branch has been a very important factor in the growth of this city; and its extension into the valley of the Snake River and the Camas Prairie would open up a wide field for the ramification of our commerce. The Union Pacific Railroad are seeking to reach the country in question via the Snake River at Riparia, which would practically cut off Lewiston Valley from the trading of this section, unless the Spokane & Palouse was extended."[27]

C. The Idaho Transit Company[28]

John P. Vollmer claimed that the Idaho Transit (IT) was originally conceived in 1887 by him and other Lewiston and Asotin parties. Vollmer said that the NP was behind it from the first; he was the leader and main stockholder of the company and his understanding was that the IT franchises, rights-of-way, plats, and surveys would be transferred to the NP on condition that it would carry out Vollmer's plans to grade, build, and operate the line from Lewiston to Grangeville via Tammany Creek and Lake Waha, and would make Lewiston the end of the railroad division. When completed the road would be sold to the NP. The other stockholders were not aware of this. The NP wanted to get the road constructed and into its hands without inciting the ORN. Vollmer sent NP President Harris May 8, 1888, a copy of the articles of the Idaho Transit Co. "I have endeavored to cover the ground to comply with your suggestions. Let me know if you have any further wishes regarding this organization before I file the papers."[29] Apparently two days later an agreement was made between Harris and Vollmer to build from Lewiston to Grangeville.

The charter for the Idaho Transit Company (IT) was filed at Asotin, Washington Territory, June 9, 1888. Vollmer witnessed the charter but did not sign. Three residents of Asotin signed. It was capitalized at $500 and was to connect Lewiston to Asotin, Anatone, Uniontown, and Genesee with stage, freight, telegraph, and telephone lines. There was no mention of a railroad in the charter; perhaps not to alert the ORN. The existence of the IT was not mentioned in the Lewiston *Teller* until mid-November. The newspaper reported that the IT would belong to the NP, but would be built partly with NP money and private money. Surveying from Lewiston to the Camas Prairie via Lake Waha would begin immediately and within one month the line to Mt. Idaho, about 80 miles, would be completed. Rail and equipment would be brought to Lewiston by boat and construction would not wait for the S&P to be completed to Lewiston. In the section above is Kendrick's view in January 1890, that the IT charter was "not of any value to the Company."[30]

According to Vollmer, authority to begin work was issued October 15, 1888, and surveying began on November 8, and ended January 21, 1889. The survey was run from Lewiston to Asotin, and up Tammany Creek, a distance of 24.4 miles.[31] Shortly after that the NP announced its plans to build to Lewiston and to absorb the IT.

On April 13, 1889, Huson sent Kendrick maps and estimates for the Idaho Transit. The maps were in two sections: Lewiston to Asotin and mouth of Tammany Creek to Lake Waha. The estimate was $293,536. "Such a line will enable us to reach the entire wheat belt of that region, and give shippers as ready access to rail as water."[32] Vollmer said the NP "at once entered upon the work vigorously and in good faith and expended in the neighborhood of $50,000 in construction work along Snake river above Lewiston and Tammany Hollow towards Lake Waha."

Chapters XI and XVII continue the story of NP's and others involvement in building up Tammany Creek. The inability to get timely permission to cross the Nez Perce Indian Reservation and the 1893 NP bankruptcy stymied this effort as well as completion to Lewiston.

D. The Northern Pacific on the Snake River

As found in chapter IX President Harris corresponded with Vollmer and Ida Anderson in early 1887 about Vollmer's proposal to put boats on the Snake River. In early July Vollmer proposed to build and operate two steamboats and barges on the condition that his bonds of $40,000 to $50,000 be placed and that a satisfactory traffic contract for 10 or more years be made. Anderson said that he had learned from steamboat captains that a properly constructed boat could run between Kennewick and Lewiston most seasons except when closed by ice. At low water 75 tons, or 2,500 bushels of wheat, 13 car loads, could be transported on a round trip every two days or less. At high water, boat and barges could take 500 tons or 16,000 bushels or more. Harris wrote the 22nd asking Wright and Oakes what they thought about telling Vollmer to go ahead as long as it did not cost more than $50,000. On the 28th Harris telegraphed Anderson to tell Vollmer to go ahead. On August 5 David Wilson, on behalf of himself, Vollmer, and associates, telegraphed Anderson from Pasco a detailed proposal for a contract to build two boats and two barges at NP expense and a traffic agreement on grain shipped to Kennewick. The *Gazette* stated November 4, 1887, that "The Northern Pacific railroad company will in all probability establish a line of steamers between Ainsworth and Lewiston next summer, and also build a narrow gauge road from Lewiston to the great Camas prairie, a distance of sixty miles."[33]

In the summer of 1888 a contract was signed between J. J. Holland and the NP to build a large boat, 202.5 feet long, 38-feet beam, and 6-feet depth, to navigate the Columbia and Snake Rivers. Machinery from the transfer boat *Billings* would be used and the *Billings* would become a wharf boat. Holland claimed that the boat would be able to climb all the rapids on the Upper Columbia. Several days prior to April 12, 1889, the NP began running a boat to Lewiston which required the removal of the ORN's temporary bridge at Riparia. The permanent bridge at Riparia was completed that month. The author did not find any later account of regular NP operation of boats on the Snake River.[34]

In 1892 three boats, probably ORN, were engaged in moving wheat from above Riparia. A boat arrived each day at Riparia with 200 tons of grain. A wire ropeway was constructed at Deadman on the Snake River to transport grain from the plateau to the river. The ropeway was 6,200 feet long and descended 1,900 feet. Three men per hour could transport 138 to 148 sacks of wheat at a labor cost of 60 cents.[35] This was one of several facilities on the Snake River for moving grain from the plateau to the river.

Spokane & Palouse Operation, the Lewiston Extension Construction, 1890–93, and the Farmington Branch, 1890–1910

Only the decision to build into the Palouse in 1886 was more important to the S&P than the decision to build to Lewiston. Although the extension was not completed in the time period of this chapter, its completion remained high on the agenda of the NP. In 1893 the NP went into receivership and construction ceased.

Above left: Plaza, Washington, looking south as photographed by F. Jay Haynes, February, 1890. The 4-4-0 engine was built by Baldwin, 1879, as number 19, for service on the construction of the Pend d'Oreille Division. It was renumbered 310 and classified B-2 after the east and west ends of the NP were linked (L. P. Schrenk communication May 2, 2002.) Most of Haynes' photographic income was from portraits—this is probably the T. J. Johnston family. In Haynes' list of photographs the place is identified as Marshall, and Nolan (1983, 89) accepts the location. Those familiar with the terrain at Marshall know this is incorrect. Grain warehouses are on the right. At the time of the photograph Plaza did not have a depot, built in 1902. *Photograph: H-2115, Montana Historical Society, Haynes Foundation Collection.*

Above right: A 1993 photograph taken from approximately the same spot as the Haynes' photograph. Grain elevators have replaced the grain warehouses, and except for vegetation, not much has changed. *Photographer: Philip F. Beach, June 16, 1993.*

A. S&P and NPI Organization and Operation

Snow began falling Christmas 1889 and continued for five days. By January 5 Rosalia had had seven snow storms and drifts as high as 12 feet. The passenger train due at Spokane Falls at 10:20 a.m. on January 2 did not arrive until 10:15 p.m. on the 3rd. On the 4th the train from Spokane was canceled. A day later five engines and a plow failed to open the line to Rosalia, and at Plaza the plow collided with and destroyed three cars loaded with grain. On the 8th a passenger train went off the track between Colton and Pullman and on the 9th the passenger train to Spokane Falls was stopped south of Rosalia by deep drifts in a cut. In the meantime no ORN train had arrived in Spokane in over a week and there were wrecks at Winona and Tekoa. On the 21st the ORN was able to run a train from Spokane Falls to Pendleton. On the 23rd S&P passenger and freight trains and the snow plow were stopped in a cut between Pullman and Palouse City. By February 6 all trains were moving.[1]

In March 1890 it was reported that the S&P and ORN would connect at Pullman in response to the amount of transferring done between the roads and a Washington State constitutional requirement. In May the round trip fare from Oakesdale to Spokane Falls on the S&P was $2.80, the ORN, $5.60. Their passenger trains from Spokane Falls arrived in Oakesdale at the same time "and it's a run to which reaches the crossing first. So far the Union Pacific has been ahead."[2]

Because of favorable legislation that the NP had secured in Washington State, the NP General Counsel recommended in early May that any company organized for the Lewiston extension be done under the general laws of Washington. In New York City, May 19, 1890, the charter for the Northern Pacific and Idaho Railroad Company (NPI) was approved. The purpose of the company was to build a railroad from the S&P in Whitman County to Lewiston via Moscow, the west fork of Bear Creek and Big Potlatch to Juliaetta and from Lewiston to the mouth of Tammany Creek to Lake Waha, an estimated 91 miles. The capital stock was to be $2 million in 20,000 shares and the principal place of business Tacoma. The charter was filed in Washington State, June 4, 1890. It was not incorporated in Idaho.[3]

The Farmers Alliance Warehouse Co. of Palouse City was unable to procure land from the S&P to build a warehouse; if the ORN built from Elberton to Palouse City it would build a 200 x 40-foot warehouse on the ORN. The Alliance was building large warehouses at the mouth of Four Mile Creek and at Guy on the C&P/ORN. In response to a fire in Pullman in early July the NP announced it would carry building materials to Pullman at half rates.[4]

The assessed values for Whitman County were reported August 1. The NP value was $560,222, consisting of lands, $92,602; depots, stations, rolling stock, etc., $92,620; and tracks and sidetracks, $375,000. The ORN value was $1,204,585, consisting of lands, $99,210; tracks and sidetracks, $937,500; rolling stock $87,875; and depots, grounds, etc., $80,000. The total assessed value in the county was $8,793,634.[5]

The NP board of directors and the trustees of the NPI and S&P between June 2, 1890, and April 30, 1891, passed a series of resolutions regarding financing of the Lewiston extension. In the end they decided that the Idaho construction of the Lewiston extension and the constructed line from the Washington-Idaho boundary to Genesee (7.26 miles) would be financed by the S&P mortgage on the Idaho Division dated October 1, 1890, at $30,000 per mile. The 5 percent bonds, $1,218,000 (40.6 miles, construction through 1893), were payable October 1, 1940.[6]

The 1890 wheat crop was very large. The *Spokesman* reported an estimate that it would take 27,200 carloads of 30,000 pounds each to move the crop. "The through freights a year ago were generally composed of two sections, each with about twenty-five cars. Now they invariably have three sections of as many cars as a locomotive can haul." A large amount of grain was coming by wagon from St. John, on the ORN's Pleasant Valley branch, to Rosalia because of better rates on the S&P. But the Anderson Brothers of Rosalia were shipping over the ORN because of a shortage of cars on S&P. "There seems to be no immediate relief, and warehouses along the [S&P] will soon be filled." The NP rented cars from other companies and on October 1 car orders on the S&P were being promptly filled. Sparks from a freight train October 3 started a fire in stubble on Four Mile Creek that burned 40 acres of stubble, straw stacks, a house and buildings, about 1,000 bushels of wheat and several hundred rails. The NP Elevator Co. warehouse in Colton was full to the roof in October when the pressure caused one side to give way letting about 10,000 bushels out on the ground.[7]

In June wheat was selling for 85 cents a bushel in Chicago and in Spokane for from 58 to 62 cents; by early November wheat was $1.02 in Chicago, but in Spokane 50 cents. "The reason for this anomalous and unfortunate condition is easily found—a lack of transportation facilities." The *Review* editorial on November 12 said in part:

> the farmers of Eastern Washington...are not receiving a fair price for wheat, and for this loss the railroads are directly responsible. First, by charging rates on grain shipments to the seaboard that are considered extortionate and second by failing to provide adequate rolling stock and thereby preventing grain buyers from paying a fair price for the wheat they purchase. Whether or not the latter condition is due to a conspiracy between the railroad companies and their adjuncts, the elevator companies, or to the exercise of faulty judgment, the *Review* is not prepared to say at present.[8]

NP President Oakes wired 2nd Vice President Prescott, November 24, "Will you please publish fact that there is no foundation for story started in Washington to effect that railroad companies have combined with elevators to depress price of wheat. We are giving farmers of state every car we can furnish, notwithstanding large additions to our rolling stock in anticipation of large crop we find to our sincere regret that we did not provide sufficient number of additional cars." Two days later he wired W. S. Mellen, General Manager, that he had just received a dispatch from Rosalia complaining of the lack of facilities for handling wheat. "Have Barney and Smith delivered all their box cars?" On the 28th Oakes wired Mellen to "concentrate every facility upon Spokane and Palouse until they are relieved." Mellen in St. Paul on the 28th said,

> This question of cars has caused me more trouble than anything I have ever had come up. The fact of the matter is this: Washington has no storage facilities, and farmers expect the railroad to move in thirty days a large portion of the crop, which it so happens is enormous. The railroad is not to blame in any way. There is no collusion between railroads, nor with the Northern Pacific Elevator Company.... We have there cars enough, but they can't be moved. There are today 350 empty box cars in the Tacoma yards that we would like to send to the Palouse country, but there are no engines to move them, yet twenty-five engines have been taken from [the east] and sent to Washington in the past thirty days. It is a physical impossibility for any railroad to do more than the Northern Pacific company is now doing. Every wheat growing state... and every railroad has had, and always will have the same difficulty.

Farmers in Uniontown on the 24th said if the NP failed to move the grain an attempt would be made to interest the ORN or Great Northern to build, and failing that they would build a road of their own. "If the roads now in this country are not able to handle the grain let us have another, for many thousands of dollars have been lost by the wheat grower this fall by his inability to market his produce."[9]

In November the NP Elevator Co. wrote C. C. Van Arsdol, NP Lewiston extension engineer, that cars were being diverted to McConnell & Chambers for wheat loading by claiming the cars were for the construction company. The November and December reports on grain movement, or lack thereof, were numerous: 1,250,000 bushels stored in elevators on the S&P could not be moved and 1,200 car loads were on platforms; in Dayton and Waitsburg where the ORN and OWT competed grain was moved promptly; and at Pullman, where the S&P and ORN competed, "the absence of the great piles of sacked grain, covered by boards, awaiting cars, which are very noticeable at all other stations." The purchase of wheat had practically come to a standstill because of the shortage of space to store the grain: "every station in the Palouse country the elevators and warehouse are completely filled; stacks of wheat are piled upon platforms, and at places upon the ground also. About one-third of the season's yield is still in the fields." The NP stated that for the season ending December 1, 1890, the NP moved over 50 percent more grain than the year before: "The reason of the present delay is that this year's yield has been so much in excess of what was produced last season that we were not prepared for it." There were nearly enough cars available but insufficient motive power to move them and many loaded cars were standing 10 to 12 days before they were moved. During a week in December there was not a day in which fewer than 600 loaded cars were in the Pasco yard and some days the number went as high as 1,000.[10]

Shipments of wheat, oats, and barley on the S&P and OWT, August to November 1889 were 2,121 cars and in 1890 the same months, 3,672. A little over a third of the increase was in oats and barley, the remainder in wheat. On December 26 the *Gazette* reported "there is every indication that the [wheat] blockade has been broken...so far as Portland and Puget Sound shipments are concerned." But the price of wheat had fallen so low in Chicago that there wasn't much point in shipping to there. There was no wheat blockade at Sprague; as soon as a car left the car shops the local dealers would get a hold of it. They also made use of empty coal cars for wheat. Between the two sources they had 12 to 15 cars a day for wheat. Eventually, the agent at Sprague was told not to give wheat buyers any more cars for three weeks. On January 2, 1891, General Manager Mellen wrote Vice President J. B. Williams that the problem was unloading the grain in Tacoma. He noted that if Washington had the extensive storage facilities that Minnesota and North Dakota had there would have been no problem. From Tacoma it was reported that the port had 1,062,500 bushels, about 50 percent of the Washington wheat crop, being held for shipping.[11]

The receipts at Palouse City in December were $59,900, the best record on the S&P. Train No. 60 hit cattle on the Hangman Creek bridge the evening of January 5, 1891. The engine and several cars derailed, several cattle killed, but no fatalities. On February 18 the regular freight tried to pass an extra on the main line about three miles north of Rosalia and hit the caboose, destroying it and derailing several box cars. No one was hurt. The engine and baggage car of the May 8 night passenger train were derailed at Whelan. The engineer saw an open switch in time to slow the train. No serious damage was done. The conductor went to Pullman on a hand car to get the branch line train to bring the passengers to Pullman. On June 13 an NP car repairman was killed at Pullman when run over by the car he was working on.[12]

NP inspectors reported in April that the 1891 wheat acreage in Washington was a quarter larger than the year before and that a favorable growing season gave promise of an enormous crop. The NP ordered 75 additional locomotives and 2,000 box cars. The committee representing Whitman County in the determination of the location of the agricultural college agreed upon Pullman. The NP wanted Palouse City and the ORN, Colfax, so it was decided in May to place it where both railroads were located.[13]

S&P local freight No. 160 to Spokane Falls crashed through the trestle over Hangman Creek southwest of Spokane, July 13, 1891, killing one and seriously injuring another and mangling two cars of stock. On August 3 the regular passenger train was wrecked at Moscow. The train was backing from Pullman, the tender struck two horses, the engineer and fireman jumped. The tender was thrown about 15 feet from the track and engine was "upset" on the other side. There was a freight car between the engine and the passenger car and it was partly derailed and badly crushed. The passengers were severely shaken up but uninjured.[14]

The Whitman County commissioners uniformly assessed railroad roadbeds in 1891 at $10,000 per mile, double what they did in 1889. Both the NP and UP objected, but the commissioners refused to reduce the assessment. The NP said the assessment should be $5,500 per mile and the UP said $7,000. The county claimed the companies had the property bonded at $25,000 per mile and were paying interest at $40,000 per mile. The railroad companies by affidavit claimed that their lines in Whitman County cost only $6,000 per mile. The Washington State Board of Equalization reduced the assessed value of NP and UP to $5,300 per mile.[15]

Mellen reported to Oakes on July 15 that for the 11 months ending May 30, 1891, the wheat shipments and revenue from the interior Pacific Northwest amounted to 425,538,412 lbs. and $1,516,911.[16] The NP Annual Report of October 15, 1891, reported the car loads of wheat from Washington and Oregon were:

To	1890–91	1889–90	Increase
Puget Sound	7,121	3,525	3,596
Spokane, Sprague, &c	10,051	983	9,068
Portland	206	70	136
Minneapolis & Duluth	6,000	-------	6,000

"The east-bound movement of wheat was rendered possible by the unusual condition of the market."[17]

The NP and the UP had a conflict in Oakesdale in early November. As told by the Pullman *Herald*:

> Sunday last was a busy day in Oakesdale...It seems that the Union Pacific company had decided that the Northern Pacific road was getting the "lion's share" of the grain hauling from Oakesdale [one report said the NP handled about eighty per cent of the grain at Oakesdale] and despite their efforts to secure patronage the situation remained unchanged...At last driven to desperation the U. P. directors decided to secure a more equal division of the spoils at all hazards and consequently made an attempt to build a sidetrack to warehouses on the N. P. road...
>
> Despite the fact that the day was the blessed Sabbath on which men are commanded to do no work but to rest, etc., the U. P. men began to work bright and early and were making good headway at laying track when there arrived on the scene ...men who began to lay track too.
>
> As...the ground which both wished to occupy was identically the same, there was a conflict. The Union Pacific men would carry ties and place them on the ground preparatory to receiving the rails The Northern Pacific men, being greater in number, would immediately throw the ties aside and replace them with those of the Northern Pacific road. This thing lasted until after dark when lanterns were lighted and the work continued. Considerable liquor had been consumed by some of the men and it soon became evident that trouble was not far distant.
>
> About 8 o'clock p. m., the Northern Pacific men had about gained possession of the field and the Union Pacific men were getting desperate, J. A. Turner, section foreman on the N. P. at Garfield was standing on a tie when some of the U. P. men tried to take it away to be replaced by one of their own. To this Turner objected and kept his stand on the tie. This enraged J. C. Brannan, section foreman on the U. P., at this place, that he stepped up behind Mr. Turner and invited him to get off, in language more forcible than polite. Upon his refusal to comply Brannan struck him a wicked blow on the head with his lantern, badly cutting Turner's head and falling him to the earth. After striking Turner, Brannan started to run, closely followed by Turner's men who soon overtook him and felled him to the ground with a heavy crowbar. Eye witnesses say that Brannan would have been killed had not the men been taken off. As he was quite badly hurt. The Union men then withdrew and the Northern men worked all night and got their track laid and cars placed thereon effectually shutting out their opponents.
>
> Monday morning...Constable Largent arrested Brannan and brought him before Justice Fisk where he plead guilty [on a charge of assault and battery] and was fined five dollars and cost which he paid.
>
> It is not known what steps the U. P. company will take but they will probably drop the matter as it is not thought

A collision at Pullman, Washington, in the rock cut south of the depot, December 6, 1891. *Photograph 1989-10-23, Whitman County Historical Society.*

they can succeed. The warehouses are all built on the N. P. right-of-way as this company let the warehouse companies have the ground on condition that the grain be shipped over its road.

A. B. Jackson, NP traveling freight agent, as quoted in another newspaper,

> It is not a matter of much consequence anyhow. Our company has been getting nearly all the Oakesdale business and, of course, the Union Pacific did not like it. There is only one elevator on their track, so they decided to put in a side track to two of the warehouses on our line. Our officials learned of it and put in a spur themselves to block them out. After sparring around for two or three days, they got a track laid down outside of our track, the latter being kept covered with freight cars and an engine to prevent their pulling it up. On Saturday we had to cut our train in two to give the farmers access to the warehouse, and they took advantage of this to throw in a pile of cordwood and prevent the trainmen from backing up again. They then pulled up part of our track and connected theirs ...and they filled their track up with cars of their own.

Apparently the UP was able to get a restraining order against the NP. F. W. Gilbert, superintendent of the NP's Idaho Division, was quoted in late November,

> Yes, we go the worst of the Oakesdale fight. That is, we have had to tear up our tracks, but the Union Pacific has not gained much by it. Although they have entrance to the warehouses now, we had all the wheat in them bought before they got there, so they will have to wait another year before they will get much good out of it.[18]

There was a S&P collision at Pullman, December 6, 1891.

> Quite a serious collision occurred here at 10:30 this morning, in the cut close to the crossing where the passenger train stops for meals. The cut is deep and on a sharp curve. The local freight going south had just pulled out and was making slow time on account of the heavy curve, when the engineer saw about a hundred feet ahead the engine of the Lewiston branch freight bearing down upon him. Both trains were moving slowly, but with their great weight and the small space between them a collision was inevitable. The engineers had barely time to reverse before the engines came together with a crash. The smaller engine of the south-bound train was quite baldly demolished, having her pilot and nearly all her front stove away and her tender lifted off the tracks and driven back on a flat car loaded with lumber, driving the lumber through the end of a boxcar loaded with merchandise. The flat car was broken in two and the draw heads of several cars were broken to pieces. The huge engine of the north-bound train was

> lifted and held 18 inches above the rails, but to all appearances, except for...her pilot, only slightly damaged. None of the men received any serious injury, the only one hurt being a man in the caboose who was thrown on the stove and cut about the face. The blame for the accident seems to be placed on the conductor of the incoming train.

The S&P passenger train into Oakesdale the 27th was several hours late on account of spending the night in the snow between Palouse City and Pullman.[19]

From 1890 to 1891 the acreage under cultivation in Whitman County increased from 191,000 to 389,000, the taxable real property from $5,000,000 to $15,000,000 and the population doubled in two years. General Manager Mellen informed Oakes in 1892 that between August 1890 and May 1891 eastbound grain from Washington amounted to 73,838 tons with revenues of $737,942 (55 percent of the total tonnage was December to February). No wheat moved from Washington to eastern terminals from August 1891 to March 1892. While the total number of bushels of wheat exported from Portland and Puget Sound fluctuated from season to season there was a general annual increase from the 1881–82 to the 1891–92 season. The NP's Cascade line was completed in 1888. Prior to the 1888–89 season the grain shipped from Tacoma was a trifle compared to Portland, but in that season it amounted to about 36 percent and in the next three seasons Tacoma's share of the two ports' exports was not less than 41 percent each season. Acres sown to wheat in 1891 on the S&P was 185,721 and in 1892, 239,268. In 1892 the two stations with the most wheat acres were Oakesdale and Pullman with 27,622 and 27,000 respectively (the latter also had 1,000 acres in barley, 2,500 in oats, and 300 in flax). The average per acre bushel yield of wheat in 1891 on the S&P ranged from Plaza at 12 to 30–31 at five stations; the further south and east generally the greater yield. Palouse yields were greater than other NP lines in Washington. In 1892 the NP used ventilated refrigerator cars to haul fruit from eastern Washington, including Whitman County, east and to Puget Sound at reduced rates to compete with California fruit.[20]

On August 16, 1892, nearly all of Kendrick was destroyed by fire. In late September 1892 grain buyers in Pullman were complaining about the lack of cars. It was said that the scarcity was caused by a large shipment of shingles from the Sound which consumed all the surplus cars on the NP in Washington. The UP had cars, but as the new crop came in the UP had trouble supplying cars.[21]

In mid-November 1892, 400,000 bushels of wheat were stacked outside of warehouses and elevators in Palouse City. The Farmers Alliance elevator and the Northern Pacific and C. & C. warehouses were full. It was estimated that 600,000 bushels had already been shipped from Palouse and another 200,000 bushels were to come in from the country.[22]

It was reported in June 1893 that the wheat crop at Genesee was expected to be a million bushels, twice the 1892 crop. Some of this was accounted for by an expected 40-bushels to the acre yield and some from the rental of Nez Perce Indian Reservation land by ranchers. In late July a grain elevator in Genesee with 42,000 bushels was destroyed by fire along with three NP freight cars. By early October continuing rains were delaying harvest and destroying the crop; late that month it was estimated that the Palouse wheat crop would be between two and two and half million bushels instead of the earlier expectation of 10 million bushels. The NP moved about 3,000 empty cars west for the grain traffic. In early November two grain trains a day ran to Tacoma and about 100 cars a day were being unloaded there. In general east bound traffic except for shingles had "practically disappeared" and eastern roads would not furnish cars for shingles because the rates were so low.[23]

On August 15, 1893, the NP entered receivership; this will be taken up in chapter XII.

B. Construction to Juliaetta

A committee of the Farmers' Alliance and the Lewiston Board of Trade met February 19, 1890, and pledged $80,000 to $100,000 to the S&P if it would construct a line to Lewiston in time to take out the fall crop. The *Review* saw that it was in Spokane's interest that the S&P get to Lewiston before G. W. Hunt's Oregon & Washington Territory and thereby drain business from Spokane.[24]

The Pullman *Herald* March 1 reported a rumor that the S&P line to Moscow would leave from Branham (Whelan). A Pullman delegation complained to Chief Engineer Kendrick and Principal Assistant Engineer Huson in Spokane that the proposed extension would leave Pullman on a side track. Also meeting with Kendrick and Huson was a delegation from Lewiston, which was informed, "that if the citizens of Lewiston made a fair and liberal proposition to the railroad authorities, guaranteeing them right way and a cash bonus, etc.... the road would be extended to Lewiston on or before

January 1, 1891." April 24 the *Teller* reported Kendrick telegraphed that the extension was assured if the railroad received a $65,000 subsidy. The citizens got to work and a contract for $45,000 was achieved and would be paid January 1, 1891, or before, and an additional $20,000 would be paid a year thereafter. Kendrick telegraphed April 28 acknowledging the subsidy from Lewiston which he understood to be exclusive of the subsidies to be raised citizens of Tammany Gulch and Lake Waha. He commented, "I am not quite clear about the right of way through the Indian Reservation; that is whether conditions imposed will occasion any delay, but I think not." The next week Division Engineer C. C. Van Arsdol was in Lewiston working with the citizens to select right of way and depot grounds. The Lewiston citizens reaffirmed their support for the S&P and declined to make a similar offer to the ORN.[25]

On April 16 the Pullman Board of Trade agreed to give 10 acres in Pullman "for depot grounds or for any other purpose you may desire." They would also provide depot grounds in Moscow and right of way via the South Palouse River. The board claimed that the South Palouse route would gain 8,000 to 10,000 more tons of grain and other traffic than the Whelan route. Furthermore, "Pullman is the most important shipping point south of Spokane Falls" and by taking the Whelan route the railroad would generate ill will in Pullman which would benefit the ORN. The *Herald* April 19 declared that Moscow and Whelan were for no good reason in opposition to the extension being built from Pullman. By April 27 tents and outfits for the engineers had been shipped to Whelan. It was also reported that Lewiston had definitely raised a $65,000 subsidy and secured the right of way from the west end of the reservation into Lewiston.[26]

The S&P Trustees April 28, 1890, authorized the construction of a line from a point between Brannan [Whelan] and Staley via Moscow, Bear Creek, and the Clearwater River to Lewiston, about 65 miles, and up the Snake River to a point opposite Asotin, about five miles, and up Tammany Creek about six miles. On May 27 the Trustees adopted a definite location from Lewiston south on the east bank of the Snake River to opposite Asotin and from Tammany Creek to Lake Waha. On May 15, 1890, Donald, Smith & Howell of Tacoma contracted to construct a single track railroad as the trustees had authorized except, "from a point at the mouth of Tammany Creek...to a point in Tammany Hollow known as the School-house." The contract was to be completed by December 1, 1890.[27]

In the meanwhile Van Arsdol's survey parties were busy, particularly on Bear Creek and from the mouth of the Potlatch River to Lewiston. Huson said that the station grounds in Lewiston were to be located so that no one could get between the S&P and the river. The Tammany people had raised a $12,000 subsidy and a guarantee of right of way from Lewiston. Van Arsdol determined that about a quarter of mile above the mouth of Lapwai Creek was "probably as favorable a place for crossing Clearwater as any and from there to Lewiston I think south side will give better alignment and lighter work than the North." Parties were asking from $200 to $300 an acre for right of way between Moscow and Cornwall; Van Arsdol wanted to know whether the land should be condemned so work could begin. The station grounds in Lewiston were selected as Huson advised, but some citizens thought the station grounds should be on the bench south of the city where the necessary land would be contributed. On the river bank, the owners were asking several times the property's former value, $10,000 for a small lot and $20,000 for a half block. The committee got the price down to $4,000 and $8,000, "which is still very high." By May 16 the committee had raised between $12,000 and $13,000, but estimated that they would need $20,000. The Lewiston people were not disposed to furnish right of way beyond the depot grounds, but the city would grant right of way south to the city limits. By May 25 clearing of right of way had begun and the location through the Nez Perce Reservation was completed.[28]

Congress approved Public Law No. 108, May 8, 1890, granting the S&P a 100-foot easement across Indian lands. The Indians were to consent and the secretary of interior was to approve the map and the compensation paid to the Nez Perce Indian Tribe and to individual Indians. On May 21 the Department of Interior gave permission to the S&P to survey on the Indian reservation "with the distinct understanding however, that no work in the construction of such road shall be begun or attempted upon said reservation until further orders from the Department." On June 2 Van Arsdol was instructed "not to allow contractors to take timber from the reservation, or to make any depredations thereon."[29]

On May 28 the Lewiston City Council granted the S&P the requested right of way. Earlier in the week UP President Charles Frances Adams and other officials were in Lewiston. Adams cautioned against giving away water frontage to other railroads. Adams thought it likely that the UP would build down the Snake River from Huntington. Kendrick wired Oakes June 3 that the cost of station grounds selected at Lewiston were more than the citizens of Lewiston could raise; an additional $30,000 would have to be paid by the NP. Oakes approved the money a day later. On the 6th Huson wrote Van Arsdol that in Moscow, except for UP property, he expected the station grounds to be contributed. Huson told Van Arsdol that he had "fully determined" to begin the line at Whelan, but he did not want to make it public until right of way between Whelan and Moscow was secured. Van Arsdol was to move his headquarters from Pullman to the Whelan depot. The next day Huson told Van Arsdol to secure the right of way from School-house to Lake Waha and to contract to have that right of way completed on or before December 31, 1891. Soon after its incorporation the NPI received all the papers, grades, and plats of the Idaho Transit. The first party of construction engineers for the Tammany line passed through Lewiston June 5. By the 7th Van Arsdol had secured the right of way from Lewiston to Tammany Creek except for two miles which would probably have to be condemned. By the 16th a continuous profile from the mouth of the Potlatch to Asotin had been made.[30]

On June 7 the Pullman *Herald* said that grading was being done between Moscow and Cornwall.[31] On the 9th grading began on the line surveyed by the IT. By the 11th all the right of way from Whelan to the state line had been secured except for three adjoining parties who would neither give nor sell at a reasonable price. Land was selling for about $20 per acre, for about 1.9 miles of right of way the owners wanted $2,400. Van Arsdol recommended that the land be condemned "as early as possible." By mid-June $10,000 of the Lewiston depot money had been transferred to Huson and ground would be bought as options expired. On June 21, 13 teams commenced to scrape on two big cuts at the mouth of Tammany.[32]

The Pullman Board of Trade wrote the Spokane Falls Board of Trade on June 16, 1890, asking that it support building the Lewiston extension from Pullman rather than Whalen.

> Whelan is five miles north of here, and is only a flag station. If the extension starts from there it leaves Pullman on a spur of a branch line, practically cut off from the through travel from Spokane, the effect of which would be injurious to our business interests and growth, and as the road reaches Moscow, the same as by the Whalen route, the only interest that Moscow can have in fighting us (which they are doing), is for the purpose of injuring Pullman, without adding one particle to their own advantage, only so far as they would reap the advantages of our misfortune.

The Spokane board endorsed Pullman's position in a letter to Oakes.[33]

On June 18 the line from Whelan to Moscow was nearly located and partly cross sectioned. About half of the right of way had been secured and 20 to 30 teams were grading. Four days later a survey party was sent to the Sunshine (north of S. Palouse) route to Moscow. Van Arsdol wrote that the Sunshine route, "Distance to build, grades and cost of work about same as Whelan line. Heaviest cuts will be lighter than the two heavy cuts on the Whelan line." Van Arsdol pointed out that there were conditional agreements for depot grounds and right of way in Moscow on the Whelan route and about $400 of grading had been done. "I think you may get grounds you desire in Moscow, on Sunshine route, if you demand them. At this point I have made no inquiries…Pullman people have taken agreements for half of right of way to Moscow on Sunshine route and propose to get right way to Moscow with little cost to the company." On the 20th Van Arsdol informed Huson that about $4,000 had been spent for right of way on the Whelan route with three pieces remaining for which the demand was over $3,000. A day later Van Arsdol wrote that the Pullman people had right of way agreements for the entire line to the Idaho boundary at a cost of about $2,800. Regarding the third alternative to Moscow, the South Palouse River, Huson responded, "The Sunshine route is much more favorable. I think before you receive this you will have instructions to adopt the Sunshine route."[34]

It was variously reported that on either June 23 or the 26th the construction crew was withdrawn from Whelan. On the 24th Huson for the S&P and A. T. Ferris, for the citizens of Pullman, entered into a contract:

> that in consideration of the Company extending its Lewiston line of road from a point near Pullman, up the Sunshine Valley to Moscow …[Ferris] hereby agrees for himself and the said citizens of Pullman that they will furnish for said Company free depot grounds at Pullman, as may be selected by said Company, and that depot grounds to the extent of fifteen (15) acres, if that amount shall be required, shall be furnished in the City of Moscow, free to said Company and reimbursement for amounts expended by the Company for work abandoned by the Company on the Whelan Route not to exceed $500 by [Ferris] and citizens of Pullman.[35]

The citizens of Pullman secured for $500 the depot grounds in Moscow without aid from Moscow. On June 30 Oakes wired Kendrick, "Miles C. Moore wires me mistake is being made in changing point of junction of Lewiston extension as it will lengthen line eight miles. To what does he refer[?]." Kendrick wired back the next day,

> It was originally intended to make Whelan point of departure for Potlatch Country. Citizens of Pullman about eight miles south of Whelan have made vigorous effort to have line start from their place. Length of new line to be

> constructed would be about the same in either case. The distance from Lewiston to Marshall Junction is six miles longer via Pullman than via Whelan I regarded it as a matter which should be decided by traffic dept. Hannaford was anxious to make Pullman the point. By so doing we get free right of way to Moscow also station ground, a saving of about ten thousand dollars. Think we are all right.[36]

Van Arsdol agreed June 17, 1890, to give the citizens of Tammany Hollow a year after the completion of the line to the School House to pay for right of way and released the citizens from paying damages to UP lands. The citizens on the 24th promised that once the new agreement was executed by the railway they would turn over the right of way money that had been raised by that time. The *Teller* reported July 3 that the grade through Tammany was being steadily built, but work apparently ended in early September. A new agreement with the Tammany subscribers was executed by January 3, 1891. In the meantime, the Lewiston and Southeastern Railway Company (LSE) was incorporated in Idaho, June 7, projecting a line from Lewiston up Tammany to Grangeville in the Camas Prairie, about 60 miles. The incorporators were local men, but it was surmised that the capital was from Portland. Most of the right of way was reported to have been secured and the line would be completed by January 1, 1891. It was reported on the 12th that the steamer *Spokane* was at Riparia being readied to carry UP machinery and supplies to Lewiston to begin work on the LSE. Three weeks later UP engineers were cross-sectioning the line.[37] Apparently nothing further came of this endeavor. The story of Tammany Creek continues in chapter XVIII.

On June 23, 1890, Huson instructed Van Arsdol to have the contractors clear the right of way down Bear Creek as quickly as possible, even if it was more costly. It was reported on the 26th that UP surveyors were running a line from either Farmington or Garfield to the Palouse and Potlatch rivers with the ultimate objective being the Grand Ronde River line in Oregon then being built by the UP. A week later it was reported that the UP was paralleling the S&P in the Potlatch country. Into late September there were reports of UP surveys in the area.[38]

The *Teller* reported July 3 that some $30,000 of NP money was bringing prosperity to Lewiston. The Northern Pacific Elevator Co. would seek sites at Sunshine, Moscow, Vollmer, Kendrick, Juliaetta, Asotin, and Tammany School House. The elevator at Juliaetta was to have a capacity of 500,000 bushels. If another elevator company wanted to put up buildings Huson wanted information on the kind of building, cost, capacity, and location for consideration by his office. In mid-July grading was slow because of insufficient men and teams. Contractors were paying $4 per day for a team with driver, $2 to $2.25 for laborers, and $35 per month plus board for drivers, which were in short supply. Contractors were trying to get more men, but many brought to the site left without going to work. Van Arsdol sent distances to Huson: from the junction near Pullman to Tammany school house 71.4 miles, to Lake Waha approximately 84.5 miles, west boundary of reservation to Lake Waha approximately 32 miles. According to Huson "under the laws of Idaho a chinaman can not own real estate." Therefore, to get title to the land for the Lewiston depot from the Chinese owner, they would have to work around the law. At the end of July Huson wrote, "[t]he excessive heat of the past few days has made the work of construction very trying, many have been obliged to quit, but the new supply coming in keep the force engaged on the increase constantly."[39]

On July 31 Van Arsdol wrote Huson that the Cornwall people "are somewhat out of humor" and will do nothing about the station grounds. Mr. Kaufman offered half interest in a 40-acre townsite a half mile west of Cornwall if the depot was located there. Van Arsdol thought it was a good site and asked if Huson wanted to act on it. Huson replied to accept Kaufman's proposal. Kaufman wanted to name the site "Joelville" in honor of his son. Huson preferred to call it Cornwall as to not to further antagonize its inhabitants, but he would consent to "Joel." Thus Cornwall disappeared. On August 2 Huson wanted to know when he could expect surveys on the reservation "so that the right-of-way can be taken up with the Government."[40]

By August 9 the entire line had been located and there were resident engineers on all divisions. The force then deployed would need to be trebled to complete the grading in December. Very little of the line between Vollmer and Tammany, outside of the reservation, was occupied by graders. Van Arsdol said he had repeatedly told the contractors of the necessity of increasing the work force. On the 18th track laying began at Pullman Jct. On the 28th Van Arsdol wrote Donald, Smith & Howell that men came into the Pullman office claiming that they were brought by the contractors from Spokane for track work, but were told by the foreman that they would not be hired. "Please state whether you intended increasing track force. Sufficient force should be put on at once to handle material as it arrives and at same time continue track-laying properly. The track that is already laid should be put up in shape at once, that is full tied, full spiked

The Cornwall trestle about a mile west of Howell. When built in 1891 it was 878′ long and 40′ high and cost $8,975 (UMT 128.372.521). About 1905 a concrete arch was built over the waterway, later filled in 1908. (MHS 134.F.6.7.B #1063). *Photograph PG90-BK4-140, Special Collections & Archives, University of Idaho Library.*

and full bolted, and thrown into reasonable line, as steel is being much damaged with track in present condition."[41]

On September 8, 52 men were brought to Pullman from Spokane, their fare and first meal were paid. In the morning only eight or nine showed up for work. The Pullman *Herald* was quoted as saying, "This wholesale importation of 'vags' and 'hobos' goes merrily on, and is becoming intolerable to those who desire order and decency in the city. Three of the last importation are now in the 'cooler,' one for indecent exposure and two for theft. These things are probably the price of prosperity, but are none the less disgusting." Huson was in Pullman on the 13th and said,

> The Lewiston extension cannot be finished before next spring. A little delay has been caused in trying to obtain a right of way across the Nez Perce reservation, but the bill has passed both houses of congress and has been approved by the president. The interior department is now negotiating with the Indians and a conclusion is expected any time. Track is laid almost to Moscow and will be extended as far as Kendrick in time to haul way this year's crop. Regular trains, however, will probably not be put on before January. Freights will make irregular trips and some kind of accommodations will be provided for passengers. The great scarcity of labor has retarded the grading and the same difficulty is met in tracklaying.[42]

On September 16 Oakes wired Kendrick: "Suspend all construction work you can every where or make it as slow as you can so that your demands for money can be reduced to lowest possible limit." Oakes wired Kendrick October 10: "What I desired above all things was to spread payments over long period I see you have practically bunched them in 3 months the very 3 months in which we need relief. Can you not do better." The financial problems continued, Kendrick wrote Oakes December 11 that contractors were having difficulties getting money from banks on the NP acceptances issued to them. Huson on September 27 worried that government inspectors would seize the ties that J. P. Stone was cutting. He instructed Van Arsdol to put on two trains to haul ties and if the ties could not be unloaded in the track the railroad would unload them at its expense.[43]

On October 11 the *Herald* reported that the grading of the depot grounds and side tracks at Moscow were about completed and the foundation of the depot was completed. The report on October 23 was that a thousand men were rapidly laying track from Moscow to Kendrick. The track laying machine was capable of two miles per day. By the end of the week of the 25th about 30 percent of the grading had been done between Vollmer and Kendrick. At that pace Kendrick would not be reached until about April 1. Two weeks later, Van Arsdol wrote the contractors that in order to complete grading to Kendrick by January 1 a force of four times larger was needed. It was "essential" that Kendrick be reached by that date. Several crews of Nez

The Moscow, Idaho, combination depot with Haynes' car in front, February 1892. Built in 1891 the depot was two story 24′ x 28′ and one story 24′ x 112′. The depot was converted to a freight house in in the late '30s and destroyed by fire in 1950. *Photograph: H-2691, Montana Historical Society, Haynes Foundation Collection.*

Perce Indians were working on the railroad; contractors reported that they were good workman. By the end of October the NP issued notification that it was prepared to receive freight at Moscow. November 7 it was reported that the NP was building a temporary depot at Moscow.[44]

Between October 21, 1890, and May 8, 1891, the S&P Trustees adopted definite amended locations from Pullman Junction to Lake Waha and opposite Asotin.[45]

The *Herald* said, "The large bridge between Cornwall and Vollmer will cause some little delay, it being a gigantic structure, and over half a million feet of lumber will be used in its construction." By the end of the week of November 15 grading was completed to Vollmer, between Vollmer and the reservation about 40 percent was done. Between the reservation and Lewiston, including Lewiston yard, at the rate grading was being done it would be completed by about December 15. By the week ending November 22 all the track forces had been sent to the Farmington branch. On December 8 Huson expressed concern that the track was being damaged because the length of time between being laid and surfaced. By December 20 the grading force between Vollmer and Kendrick had been increased and work was progressing more rapidly. In December laborers with checks on Spokane banks were unable to cash them because the railroad was behind in paying the monthly estimates and the contractors did not have the money to meet their payrolls.[46]

On January 12, 1891, Kendrick informed Oakes that they could not proceed further on the extension until there was a settlement with the Indians. The Interior Department informed the Indian Agent that he should convene the Indians and proceed to secure right of way. The Indian Agent said that it would take time to do that as the Indians were in winter quarters in remote parts of the reservation and could not be assembled until spring. In 30 days the track should be completed to Juliaetta and construction should stop at that point until the right of way question was settled. The Indian Agent wrote Van Arsdol February 16, "I do not know what is the cause of delay in conducting the negotiations with the Indians, and am unable at this time to give any idea as to the time it will yet require to conclude the matter, nor do I know of anything in the way of a suggestion that would expedite matters."[47]

By mid-February depots were open at Moscow, Vollmer, and Kendrick and in mid-March the Joel depot opened. The NP Elevator Co. February 24 expressed apprehension that their grain stored at Kendrick and Juliaetta was not protected from flooding. Van Arsdol responded that the road was not yet in condition to haul freight from Kendrick. The weather was such that little could be done, but the grain would be moved as soon as possible. On the 25th Huson wrote Van Arsdol to tell the contractors "to go ahead with the line [from the west boundary of the reservation] to Lewiston and the School house as fast as they may desire. Every effort should be put forth to secure right-of-way across the reservation." The *Teller* on February 26: "Chief Engineer Huson in a recent interview at Spokane said that the Lewiston branch would be completed at once and that arrangements were being made to extend the line from Lewiston to Camas Prairie. The route is already located...the contract for building the branch will undoubtedly be let this spring. No objective point has been decided upon. A line also will be extended from [Lewiston] into Asotin county."[48]

Van Arsdol reported the week ending March 7 that the track between Howell and Kendrick was laid in the snow and mud and particularly between Vollmer and Kendrick was badly out of surface and operated only when compelled to. The track force had been taken off because with frozen ground nothing could be done at a reasonable cost. Grain was being moved from Vollmer as fast as it could be loaded, but Kendrick would have to wait until the track was in better condition. The secretary of war on March 28 approved a bridge across the Clearwater River about 11 miles above Lewiston.[49]

Van Arsdol was informed by E. H. McHenry, the new principal assistant engineer, April 3, 1891, that no further work should be done south of Juliaetta until further notice. Van Arsdol responded that other than a little work on buildings nothing was being done and that he was reducing the force whenever practicable. On the 6th he reported that grading was being done from Juliaetta to the north boundary of the reservation. On the 10th he wrote that passengers and express were using a caboose without cushions or any other conveniences for passengers.[50]

On April 13 the Acting Commissioner of Indian Affairs wrote a lengthy letter to Indian Agent Warren D. Robbins instructing him about the right of way negotiations between the railroad and the Indians as provided for by the Act of Congress May 8, 1890. The definite location of the railroad and grounds for two stations had been approved by the Secretary of Interior on the 2nd. Robbins was to call together the Indians in council at the earliest practicable date and to submit the matter clearly and fully and have them pass on the question of whether they would give their consent. He was directed to make sure the Indians were fairly compensated for right of way and damages and "You will be present during the negotiations of the Company with such individual occupants, and see that such Indians are not over-reached by the Company in the transactions." Further "no work of construction can be commenced by the Company until the proceedings of the Indian Council and the settlements of the Company with the individual occupants shall have been approved by the Department." Agent Robbins had written the Commissioner in December that the location of the proposed line did as little damage to individual Indians and the Indian Agency as any survey that could be made. On April 24 permission for right of way across the reservation was received from the Attorney General. About May 1 Robbins and Van Arsdol met with the Indians and it was agreed the railroad would pay $20 of damages for every acre of tribal land the line passed though. Where the land had been allocated to individual Indians the damages had to be determined individually. For several days in June Van Arsdol and Robbins secured right of way agreements from individual Indians. On July 8 Van Arsdol sent McHenry a list of 24 individual claims, totaling $3,876, for reservation right of way. The Indians had to be paid before the Indian Commission would turn over the right of way. On September 16 Van Arsdol wrote McHenry that Robbins had been very helpful in securing the agreements and had saved the company a good deal of money. Van Arsdol inquired about compensating him for his work; Robbins did not wish to make a statement or bill. Van Arsdol wrote October 3 that he thought Robbins was entitled to 25 days' time amounting to $250 and that the interpreter about 10 days at $5.00 per day. McHenry responded that he was sending Robbins a Bank Exchange for $300. "Payment in this form will not give any information to the Bank through which the draft passes, in accordance with Mr. Robbins' request." The *Teller* reported on December 31, 1891, "The encouraging news is at last confirmed and it can now be asserted on full authority, that the right of way controversy, so long pending between the government, the N. P. railroad and the Nez Perce Indians, is definitely settled, and the [S&P] has now a clear right to enter upon the reservation and complete their lines into Lewiston." Even that turned out to be overly optimistic; final permission was not received until March 1893.[51]

In mid-April train service to Vollmer was resumed. It had been discontinued during the winter on account of heavy snow drifts and mud. On April 14, 1891, Van Arsdol wrote the contractor that a second engine had been obtained as requested, but the work force was insufficient to keep two construction trains running. The contractor was instructed to increase his work force to 110 to 120 men or the second engine would be returned. Principal Assistant Engineer McHenry wrote Van Arsdol April 22 that the money market in the east was such that the Company was unwilling to make expenditures beyond those necessary; it was unlikely that construction to Lewiston would be completed that year. Construction should be closed as soon as possible and only sufficient men should be kept for work to Juliaetta. The track should be laid "in perfect condition" to the north boundary of the reservation. It was unlikely that within a reasonable time the company would have right of way through the reservation. On the 28th Van Arsdol thought that track to Kendrick would be in condition to haul material by about May 6. The first passenger train was to run to Moscow on May 10.[52]

On May 14 Oakes wired Kendrick in cipher that expenditures were exceeding resources even on the basis earlier agreed to and they would have to be reduced. On the same day the *Teller* reported that surveyors had moved onto the reservation. Regular trains were running to Kendrick and a great deal of construction material had been forwarded to the front. Twelve miles remained to complete to Lewiston and NP officials announced that they would be selling tickets to Lewiston by July 1 and would run an excursion to the city on July 4.[53] The newspaper and the railroad were not on the same page.

Van Arsdol reported to McHenry that on May 15 the air failed on a gravel train pushing 16 loads down from Howell. The engineer reversed the engine pulling the draw bar next to the engine. The cars left the track in the Vollmer yard. No one was injured and there was no damage to the engine. Seven of the flat cars were stripped of their trucks and one had a broken sill. The estimated damage to the cars was $930 and both the main and passing tracks were torn up for about 500 feet. The accident was caused by the air pipe not being opened when the coupling was made. Two brakemen were discharged and the conductor was put on leave pending McHenry's decision. The hand brakes on the cars had been removed to enable the use of a plough. McHenry approved the discharge of the brakemen and determined the conductor should be off for 30 days. He thought that a hand brake on every other car would suffice even on a 2 percent grade. The engine should be below the train rather than above.[54]

While construction was underway freight traffic revenue from November to May was $68,281. Van Arsdol reported June 12 that all the grain at Joel and most at Vollmer had been moved. Grain was being moved from Kendrick as construction work allowed.[55]

McHenry told Van Arsdol June 2 to have the track work completed to the 40th mile and to wind up construction to turn over the road by July 1. He would try to get the reservation right of way settled so there would be no delay when work resumed. Rains delayed track work and completion to the mile 40 was predicted as no earlier than mid-July. Van Arsdol reported that as of June 25 $211,489 had been spent west of the reservation boundary on station grounds, right of way, grading, etc.[56]

Following a mass meeting in Lewiston, Kendrick was telegraphed June 24 advising him to come to Lewiston. "Our citizens are still alive to the fact that we must have the road completed this year and will leave nothing undone to accomplish this end." A year earlier the citizens had pledged to raise 10 percent of each person's 1889 assessment on condition that the S&P was completed to Lewiston by January 1, 1891. The pledge became void because of the delay in getting right of way across the reservation. A quarter of million dollars in property changed hands after the subsidy was agreed to. The bulk of the property went to outside investors. On June 28 Van Arsdol and McHenry said in Lewiston that if $75,000 were raised the road would be completed that year. An enthusiastic meeting was held on 29th. While they could not raise 10 percent, they would offer 8 percent of the 1890 assessment; "the citizens of Lewiston can do no more." McHenry wrote Van Arsdol on July 7 that it was beyond doubt that work would have to be stopped as soon as line to the reservation line was completed. "I have notified the Contractors accordingly." He had heard nothing from the citizens of Lewiston, but he had little hope that anything they might say would cause any change.[57]

On July 9 Kendrick reported to Oakes that McHenry was of the opinion that the subsidy papers for $75,000 from Lewiston were defective. The estimate to extend the track to Lewiston was $100,000, including a temporary bridge across the Clearwater River, which would serve as a false-work for a permanent bridge. The necessary structures at Lewiston and a permanent bridge would cost $75,000 more. Most of the bridge materials were on hand and 12 miles of grading across the Reservation remained to be done. Prolongation of the work would be damaging to the contractors. If a subsidy of $75,000 were paid the work should continue because of the business that would be derived and to avoid having to settle with the contractors. He thought the contractors would be willing to take 50 percent of their estimates and six months acceptances at 7 percent. If this were done the company would have to raise between then and November from $100,000 to $125,000. On the 10th McHenry wrote Van Arsdol that the most the citizens would be able to raise was $60,000 and Kendrick had decided under the circumstances to shut down the work soon as it was completed to the reservation. On the 13th Kendrick wrote Oakes that business on the extension was not handled until January 1891; nevertheless between 500 and 600 cars of wheat

An early photo of today's Troy, Idaho, carries a handwritten caption: "City of Vollmer on Spokane & P R Road, 14 miles East of Moscow, Looking up Main Street, 5 months old [1890-91]." Compare this image with the one of Colfax (p. 6), taken about seven years earlier. *BNSF Archives.*

and flax have been hauled and considerable merchandise to Moscow, Vollmer, and Kendrick. He believed that shutting down the work "will have the effect of securing to the Company a guaranteed cash bonus amounting to about $80,000, for the extension of the line to Lewiston during the season of 1892." On the 17th Oakes telegraphed Kendrick, that if the subsidy could be raised he should accept it and he would raise the balance.[58]

On July 24, 1891, Van Arsdol submitted a month by month, August 1891 to January 1892, estimate of $353,183 as the cost to complete the line from the north boundary of the Reservation to Lewiston. On the 28th Van Arsdol reported that most of the track would be surfaced from Pullman Junction to Juliaetta before the first, but in places the track would have to be brought up to grade because of settling under traffic. The remainder of the track work would not be completed earlier than August 15.[59]

Van Arsdol on August 1 wrote McHenry that the Lewiston committee was anxious to know if they raised $75,000 to $80,000 would the NP build to Lewiston. McHenry responded that he had not been advised by Kendrick as to what should be done about the proposition. The matter had been referred to Oakes. On August 16 Van Arsdol reported that he had met with the Lewiston committee on the 14th. They were anxious that the line be extended to Lewiston that season and if they had assurance that would be done they could raise $80,000 in two weeks. It was reported that the Lewiston citizens had raised $40,000 in cash and $40,000 in real estate, but the railroad declined, preferring $75,000 in cash.[60]

On October 3 Van Arsdol informed McHenry that the track work was nearly done, nearly all the buildings were done, and most of the fencing completed. Van Arsdol had written to the contractors about unfinished or improper work on a number of occasions. McHenry commented October 5, "It seems an almost endless job to get [Donald & Howell] to finish up their work."[61]

In March 1892 Oakes directed Kendrick to reduce fiscal year expenditure for filling in main line and branch bridges to less than $250,000. On the 13th Oakes, in response to a question in Spokane said, "We shall build no more branches this year." He specifically included extension to Lewiston. Asked how much it would cost to extend to Lewiston, he replied, $300,000. The reporter thought that was not very much considering the business. Oakes responded,

> That is not the point. We have decided to change our policy regarding the construction of branch lines. Heretofore we have been building them out of our earnings. A halt had to be called some time and we have decided on one now. Our main line will require the expenditure of vast sums of money to put it in shape to handle our business to the best advantage. We shall have to meet extraordinary competition and we must prepare ourselves for it.

The reporter asked him about the proposed branch from Palouse City to Colfax. Oakes responded that the best he could do was, "If they build and equip it for us we

The Vollmer, Idaho, combination depot, two story 24′ x 24′, one story 24′ x 31′ built in 1891. This Haynes photograph was taken February 1892. The second story was retired in 1960. In 1903 the station name was changed to Troy. The engine is NP No. 192, 4-4-0, Class C-13, built by Portland 1883 and retired in 1896. *Photograph: H-2689, Montana Historical Society, Haynes Foundation Collection.*

will operate it." The same day Oakes received a Lewiston delegation, headed by John P. Vollmer. According to the *Review*, they presented a petition signed by about 200 Spokane businessmen, but he gave them no encouragement. The Lewiston *Teller* had a different view: "The members of the committee are much encouraged by the interview and think that now there is hardly a doubt that the road will be completed in time to remove this year's crops." Private letters received in Lewiston later in the month were reported to have plainly stated that if the subsidy were raised the S&P would be completed that summer. The *Teller* said, "There is no longer any time to parley and debate chances of future greatness. This opportunity if offered should be grasped or the future is gloomy and uncertain." Oakes asked a delegation from Colfax what inducements they had to offer. They responded that they would give free right of way, terminal grounds, or a cash bonus. The *Review* was not persuaded by Oakes. According to the newspaper the real reason for not building branches was the NP's inability to sell bonds. On the other hand James J. Hill's Great Northern had been able to sell bonds for its construction. It was hoped that the NP would be able to compete with the GN, but unfortunately for the NP, the GN was the best managed transcontinental road in the United States. A meeting was held in Pullman, April 2 to form committees to induce the UP to build from Pullman to Palouse City via Viola and from Pullman to Lewiston.[62] The GN began daily service from St. Paul to Spokane in August 1892 and was on Puget Sound in January the following year.

On April 20, 1892, Kendrick called to Oakes' attention that the Congressional act of May 8, 1890, granted the right of way on condition that line was in "running order across said Reservation within two years from the passage of this act." Also the company secured pledges of a bonus and free right of way from citizens of Lewiston on condition of construction within a certain time. Grading had been done to both boundaries of the Reservation. The terms of the act "were scrupulously observed." The $5,485 owned to the Indians was paid. On January 29, 1892, the commissioner of Indian affairs notified Agent Robbins that the railroad was authorized to proceed with construction. Twenty-one months had been consumed in settling with the Indians and the construction force had been discharged. McHenry sought a two-year extension on construction. Attorneys advised McHenry that it was not practicable to get the extension from the present Congress. The NP general counsel informed Oakes April 22 that he had prepared a bill extending time for two years. He thought it would be difficult to obtain a longer extension. McHenry in an 1894 deposition stated that he was unable to secure consent from the Indians until after the financial situation had made it impossible to secure the funds for the remaining construction.[63]

The Juliaetta, Idaho, combination depot, two-story 24′ x 24′, one story 24′ x 36′, built in 1891. In 1943 the one-story freight room and the second story living room portion were removed, leaving a one story 24′ x 36′. The depot burned in 1978. *Photograph L86-970, Cheney Cowles Museum/Eastern Washington State Historical Society.*

An enthusiastic meeting was held in Lewiston December 8, 1892, to raise a subsidy to have the railroad built in the spring. It was understood that if the railroad was reimbursed the $75,000 that it had paid for right of way and depot grounds, the road would be built at once. Kendrick wrote Oakes April 20, 1893, that a committee of citizens in Lewiston had proposed to deliver notes for $75,000 and to secure from the city council right of way in consideration of daily trains to Lewiston on or before January 1, 1894. The cost of completing the road to Lewiston from the end of the track would be $519,350, of which $135,000 had already been expended. The remaining $384,350 consisted of steel rails, internal charges, material in the store department, and a cash outlay of $225,150. Kendrick wrote the citizens' committee May 12 that President Oakes "regrets to say that this is a matter which cannot be considered at the present time. You are of course aware of the extreme stringency of the money market, and that it is a most unfavorable time to inaugurate any enterprise requiring considerable expenditure." The Lewiston *Tribune* responded: "While exceedingly disappointing, this result is by no means discouraging and in fact it will simply stimulate and serve this large-hearted, energetic people to new endeavors and greater exertions, each one of which will leave its impress in some improvement some development some new accessions which make and build up cities."[64]

C. The Farmington Branch

In 1890 during construction of the Lewiston extension the NP built the S&P's Farmington branch. Farmington had a post office in 1879 and was incorporated in 1888 with a population of 1,200.[65] The reader may recall that Farmington was to be the destination of an OR&N branch in 1880, was specifically mentioned in the NP-OR&N traffic contract of October 20, 1880, and was the original intermediate objective of the S&P in 1885–86. The C&P to Farmington was opened September 1886. Despite the favorable early prospects and a subsidy by Farmington residents and local farmers, the branch was insignificant and should not have been built.

NP President Thomas Oakes recommended to NP Chairman Henry Villard, December 17, 1889, that branches to Farmington and Colfax should be built in retaliation to the OR&N building to Spokane. NP Division Engineer C. C. Van Arsdol informed NP Principal Assistant Engineer H. S. Huson, January 20, 1890, that a line from Belmont to Farmington would be roughly five miles and cost $2,500 per mile for grading and bridges. While in Farmington Van Arsdol visited T. R. Tannatt, former Oregon Improvement Official, who said that the people in Farmington were anxious for the NP to build and that the right of way and station grounds might be obtained without cost. Tannatt said that the Deep Creek country, six to ten miles southeast of Farmington, was well settled excellent wheat country with timber east of the valley and could be accessed by a low pass from Farmington.[66]

Tannatt wrote Oakes January 28 that the C&P was running, but Farmington had been six and eight days at a time without trains or mail. Farmington was harmed by its dependency on a single railroad and its elevator prices. He urged that a line from Belmont be built by spring or summer and that a few miles be graded southeast from Farmington. NP Chief Engineer J. W. Kendrick wrote Oakes that the line to Farmington would cost no more than $10,000 per mile, not including right of way and depot grounds promised by the citizens of Farmington. "It is very doubtful if it will be found desirable to build from Farmington to the Potlatch country, or in fact whether a practicable route exists below Farmington." The Farmington *Register* wondered in May whether right of way, depot grounds and $20,000 would induce the NP to build. In mid-May Kendrick asked Huson to look into building to Farmington. "We should expect gratuitous right of way and terminals as a matter of course. Think if they will also do the grading, the scheme can be put through, provided it is a good thing commercially."[67]

The Farmington *Record,* in late June 1890, was almost assured that the NP intended to build from there to Pullman or Moscow because it had asked the citizens to procure right of way five miles east from Farmington. Huson informed Van Arsdol June 30 that lines would be located between Belmont and Farmington and 10 to 15 miles beyond Farmington into the Dry Creek country and into the head waters of the Palouse River. Three days later Van Arsdol was told that Farmington citizens would raise $10,000, half to be paid the first of January and the other half a year later. Based on the location of July 14 the estimate to Farmington was $85,043 for 6.1 miles, plus one mile of siding, etc. Two weeks later Van Arsdol was told to get the right of way for less than the exorbitant prices owners were seeking. A locating engineer wrote Van Arsdol August 9 that a line to the crossing of Deep Creek, about a mile from the Palouse River, was located. Two miles of heavy work and little bridging would be required except one trestle 45 feet high and 600 feet long. A preliminary line was also run from Deep Creek east to Gold Creek.[68]

The Lewiston extension contract was modified to include the Farmington branch and awarded to Donald, Smith & Howell, the Lewiston contractors, on August 9, 1890. The line was to be completed in time for the year's crop to be moved. Farmington people had arranged the right of way and the subsidy would be turned over in a few days. Three days later Frank Howell said that from Farmington the branch would be extended farther into the Palouse wheat fields. On August 21 the NP board of directors approved construction of the branch. In late September Kendrick wired J. B. Williams, NP vice president and S&P president, for authority to construct from Belmont to Farmington and surveys 25 miles beyond Farmington. On October 6 the S&P trustees authorized the surveys and construction of a line from south of the Belmont depot to Farmington, 5.78 miles.[69]

Construction had begun about August 28 and 12 days later Van Arsdol reported that grading was going on and would be in Farmington in 30 days. On October 24 Huson wrote Van Arsdol: "Do not let the grass grow under your feet until this branch is completed. Push it through, even at the sacrifice of the Lewiston Extension. If necessary I wish the depot grounds condemned, if nobody else will put up the money...Proceed on this basis." The next day Van Arsdol reported, that with the existing forces, grading would not be completed until December 1. In late October the difficulties regarding right of way and depot grounds had been cleared away and the "chief engineer" gave his word that wheat would be hauled out by November 15. Van Arsdol informed Huson November 4 that the NP Elevator Company and

Galland Bros. of Farmington would both commence putting in platforms for handling grain and by the 28th the Galland Bros. grain platform began receiving grain; the platform was the foundation for a large warehouse. During the week ending November 29 all of Van Arsdol's track forces were working on the branch. Huson informed Van Arsdol that he had written the contractors that, "The line into Farmington must be put in shape at once...[and] if they do not do so at once the Division Superintendent will be requested to put the track in shape and bill us, then we will bill the contractors for the expense."[70]

The report to the ICC states that construction ended December 6, 1890. The branch of 6.09 miles was turned over to the operating department December 10, 1890. On May 31, 1894, the total expenditures for construction were calculated to be $66,692 for 6.1 miles of line ($10,933 per mile).[71]

On January 14, 1891, the S&P trustees approved the definite location of the Farmington branch. A statement the next day lists a third class combination depot, two stories, a section house which was a dwelling moved to the site, and a tool house. It was reported that the branch would "certainly" be extended in the spring.[72]

Van Arsdol wrote E. H. McHenry, NP principal assistant engineer, May 14, 1891, he had heard that the UP was surveying an extension south of Farmington into the Deep Creek country and that they had right of way agreements on a portion of the land to Jamestown [location not known] and an agreement for station grounds at Jamestown. Such a line would cut very heavily into the Farmington business. Two days later, McHenry wanted Van Arsdol to verify the rumor. He thought it doubtful that it was true because of the agreement with the UP not to extend without notification and the UP was "extremely hard up" and probably did not have the ability to complete the lines already under construction.[73]

In the summer of 1891 the Farmington Alliance Warehouse Co. was preparing to erect a large grain house and elevator at Farmington. Nearly all the farmers of the area had subscribed. The Hayfield Brothers would build a large warehouse on the NP at Farmington; they also had a warehouse on the UP.[74]

T. R. Tannatt wrote Oakes March 1, 1892, about Farmington lots owned by the NP. Paul Schulze, NP general land agent, wrote that he was unaware of such lots. McHenry reported that the company had an interest in 73 lots, for 16 the title was absolute and the remainder were undivided half interests. The cash subscription was for $8,243, half payable January 1, 1891, and half the following January 1. The Bank of Farmington forwarded to the company $1,000 and had approximately $600 more. In addition to the cash subscription the subscribers agreed to pay the cost of the right of way between Belmont and Farmington, $4,388, making a total subsidy of $12,630. Probably the right of way subscription could not be collected; the agreement with the citizens was very loose. The $8,243 might be collected after the next harvest. All the parties would be notified and given 45 days to pay in cash or notes. McHenry wrote, "I regard this, however, as more of a bluff than anything else, as it is somewhat doubtful as to whether we can obtain judgment under the agreement...I do not understand why the Citizens Committee were not required to purchase and pay for this right way, themselves. There was no reason for the Company loaning them the money, and standing the subsequent risk of loss in the collection. In all other cases our experience has been invariably the same, the Company has paid the full amount of right way, and then looked to the citizens for reimbursement without success." McHenry reported May 31 that a total of $5,111 in cash and notes had been collected and that a possible $2,000 might additionally be collected. He thought if $7,000 were collected, "we will have done unexpectedly well in this matter." Kendrick reported to Oakes in late November 1892 that about $7,500 of the $8,243 and nearly $1,100 of the right of way amount of $2,531 had been collected. Kendrick thought McHenry had done a good job in getting such a high percentage.[75]

During the NP receivership in 1896, Kendrick prepared a report on the S&P for the receivers. He had little to say about the Farmington branch but noted that at $12,000 per mile it would be the least expensive part of the S&P to duplicate. NP President Howard Elliott traveled on the P&L in July 1904, and found the Farmington branch to be "in sufficiently good condition to switch wheat and an occasion freight car back and forth."[76]

The Washington State Railroad Commission in September 1906 ordered the NP and OR&N to make connections at a number of places including Farmington. The commission repeated the order in May 1907. Failure to do so was a $250 per day fine per connection per railroad. The NP appeared willing to make the connections for one-half the cost. In June the OR&N objected to the Commission's orders, denying that Farmington was an important shipping point or entitled to better facilities than it then enjoyed. The OR&N appealed to the Washington State Supreme Court that the penalties were excessive, "thus making it necessary to comply with the orders of the commission rather than resort to the courts for a decision as to the validity and reasonableness of the orders." No evidence has been found that a connection was made at Farmington.[77]

For 15 years the usual warehouse charge was 50 cents a ton, but the warehouses added 25 cents about 1907. James Walters, "a veteran farmer," reported:

> We could stand it no longer, and we met and organized 'The Farmers' union.'...we now have 130 members and are handling our own grain.
>
> After we organized at Farmington we wired the general freight agent of the O. R. & N. to meet us...the agent came and we informed him that we had organized and that the farmers of Farmington would henceforth handle their own grain, and that he would oblige us if he would lease us the warehouses owned and controlled by the company. ...He informed us that he could not think of such a thing, as their houses were already leased. We then informed him that if we did not get the warehouse his company could not possibly hope to get any of the wheat hauling from Farmington. He then said he would wire us inside of two days from Portland, but he failed to do so.
>
> We then took the matter up with Northern Pacific company, and had satisfactory arrangements made in a very short time. We have purchased for $3750 the old Alliance warehouse on the Northern Pacific and have leased another house, and we are receiving grain so rapidly that we are now obliged to build a big platform.
>
> As soon as we had purchased the big warehouse we held a meeting and decided to order our twine and sacks, which we did at once, thereby saving the middleman's profit. We had just gotten our business well under way with the Northern Pacific when the O. R. & N. got wind of it and they swooped down on us and begged us to at least give them a part of the business. They said they were getting no grain, and that we were welcome to their warehouse free of charge if we would only divide up. We said: "No gentlemen: although some of the farmers in our organization may be socialists, and may be accused of wanting a division of property, yet we have not learned of any of them that are anxious to divide up with your company on this wheat hauling ... we went to you first and asked you to lease us your houses, but you simply ignored us, and now gentlemen, we can do nothing for you, and we want to inform you right now that your warehouses will remain idle this season, for you will not haul a sack of grain from Farmington this year."
>
> ...We shall ship not less than 400,000 bushels of grain from Farmington this year, and it will all go over the Northern Pacific.
>
> As soon as the busy season is over we shall organize the farmers union in every town and hamlet in the Inland Empire...in less than two years' time the farmers of the Inland Empire will own and control a system of warehouses, not only throughout the wheat-growing sections of the state, but on the Sound and at Portland as well.[78]

The Farmington branch was never an important freight or passenger contributor to the S&P/P&L. In 1961 it was the first abandonment of an S&P line. When 5.33 miles of the remaining 5.60 mainline miles were removed, 0.27 was retained to reach a 0.02 spur installed in 1954.

Appendix I: S&P Track Laying Record, Pullman Jct. to Juliaetta, 1890–91

Date	Distance from Pullman Jct.	Sources and Notes
Aug. 18, 1890	Track laying began.	(4) (5) At Pullman Jct., H.B. 1.56 miles from center of Pullman depot. All mileages below are from Pullman Jct. head block.
Aug. 21		(6) About a half mile of track laid.[79]
Aug. 23	Between MP 1 & 2.	(1) Before Bridge #4.
Sept. 6	Before MP 5.	(1) Beyond Bridge # 9. Center of siding at Sunshine, 3.76 miles.
Sept. 16	MP 5.	(2)
Sept. 20	MP 6.98, about 7.9	(2) Washington-Idaho Boundary, MP. (3) 7.9 miles laid and 3 miles surfaced.
Oct. 16	Before MP 10.	(1) Beyond unnumbered bridge 59'. Center of Moscow depot 8.83 miles.
Oct. 30	MP 11.98	(2) Five miles into Idaho.
Nov. 1	Before MP 14.	(1) Beyond unnumbered bridge 45.5'.
Nov. 8	MP 16.98	(2) Ten miles into Idaho. Center of Joel depot 15.26 miles.
Dec. 8	Before MP 19.	(1) Beyond Bridge #44, Middle Potlatch.
Jan. 6, 1891	Before MP 21.	(1) Between two unnumbered bridges 150', 100'. Center of Howell telegraph office 19.5 miles
Jan. 13	Before MP 22.	(1) Beyond unnumbered bridge 100+'. Center of Vollmer depot 22.41 miles.
Jan. 19	Before MP 25.	(1)
Feb. 1	Before MP 33.	(1) Center of Kendrick depot 33.93 miles.
Mar. 7	[MP 34]	(7) Van Arsdol: track between Howell and Kendrick laid in snow and mud, between Vollmer and Kendrick badly out of surface, operated only when compelled to.
June 25	Before MP 39.	(1) Before unnumbered bridge 75'. Center of Juliaetta depot 37.94 miles.
July 31	End of track MP 40.05	(1) North boundary of the Nez Perce Indian Reservation.
		(1) Surveyed to MP 52+, west boundary of the Nez Perce Indian Reservation.
		(1) Grading MP 52+ to MP 60, Lewiston, Aug. to Dec. 1890. MP 61 survey.
		(1) Grading MP 62 to MP 66 (MP 65 Tammany Creek), June to Sept. 1890.
		(1) Surveyed MP 67 to MP 71+ with some grading between MP 70 and 71, no date.

Sources: (1) Construction Profile, MHS, 134.L.18.8.F; (2) UMT 128/286/4 [Because of bonding Washington and Idaho mileage were accounted for separately]; (3) UMT 128/371/516; (4) SR 8/19/90, 3; (5) mileages from Pullman depot and from Pullman Jct. UMT 128/368/1; (6) SR 8/23/90, 8; (7) UMT 128/372/521.
Second hand steel rail was used on the Lewiston extension (UMT 128/372/521).

James J. Hill, the Great Northern, and the Palouse to 1894

During the time of this chapter Hill did not build nor acquire a railroad in the Palouse. Nevertheless there was a wide spread perception that he would and that if he did it would have a dramatic effect. This chapter will consider, as they pertain to the Palouse, the Great Northern (GN) building into Spokane, Hill's relations with the ORN and UP, his involvement with the Oregon & Washington Territory Railroad (OWT) and the Seattle, Lake Shore and Eastern Railway (SLSE). Recall from chapter VII that in 1886 Elijah Smith and Hill explored the possibility of connecting the GN and ORN at Missoula, with the GN then running to Spokane over the Washington & Idaho (WI).

A. The Great Northern and South of Spokane

Hill's St. Paul, Minneapolis, & Manitoba Railroad (Manitoba) was at Helena, Montana Territory, by the end of 1887. At the same time it was reported that the ORN was surveying from Grange City toward Wallula as part of a line over the Bitterroot Mountains. The ORN, it was suggested, wanted to establish priority over the Manitoba in the Clearwater Valley. In mid-March 1888, an ORN right-of-way agent was in Lewiston seeking right-of-way on the condition that the ORN would within two years build from Riparia to Lewiston. Many citizens signed petitions for bridges over the Snake and Clearwater Rivers, but most would not sell rights-of-way that would block other railroads for two years. In the same month, U.S. Senator Dolph introduced a bill to grant the ORN right-of-way though the Nez Perce Indian Reservation. The right-of-way was granted and surveying was taking place above Lewiston in July. It was the opinion of the *Gazette* that if the Manitoba passed through the Nez Perce country on the way to the Sound there would be a Palouse branch. Hill reorganized the Manitoba into the Great Northern Railway September 1889. In October Hill ordered surveys for an extension to the West Coast. In late December Hill wrote his chief engineer discussing reaching both Portland and Puget Sound via the Clearwater and Snake Rivers.[1]

In spring 1890 a GN route across the Cascades west of Wenatchee was located. But hopes in the Palouse did not die easily. The *Review* in mid-September said it had solved the mystery of a survey party in the Palouse that neither the NP nor UP claimed. It was sponsored by the GN. "When the Great Northern is completed to Spokane Falls it will be all ready to begin work on its line southward." The *Gazette* in early December was sure that "there is no longer any doubt that Jim Hill is fully determined to build his road directly through the great wheat belt of the Palouse."[2]

In May 1891, articles of incorporation for the Spokane & Southern Railroad were filed in Spokane. The trustees included F. Lewis Clark and A. A. Newbery of Spokane. Newbery and Clark had recently met with Canadian Pacific Manager Van Horne in Victoria and it was alleged that the railroad was the result of the conference. While no definite route had been decided upon it was understood the route would be up Hangman Creek south to Penawawa on the Snake River via Oakesdale and Colfax.[3] A Spokane Southern Railroad was incorporated in June for the same purpose by the same persons. In mid-September Hill said in Spokane that the wheat fields of eastern Washington "amazed" him. The New York *Times* in late October reported,

> The Spokane Southern articles of incorporation provide for the building of a road from Spokane to Snake river, which will make a loop for the Great Northern from Spokane via Seattle, Portland and Almonta [sic] back to Spokane. W.B. Loss, a contractor, is surveying a line from the Klickitat river cascades. Mr. Loss says the present outlay is made by an English syndicate intimately associated with "Jim" Hill, and if the ascent and descent...of Klickitat can be made with nothing more than a 2 per cent grade Mr. Hill will build a road to an eastern connection. The

> project, Loss says, is fraught with considerable uncertainty. Two corps of engineers have already succeeded in running lines to the summit, but lost them in trying to get down on the other side. President Hill is confident, however, that it can be done.[4]

A delegation from Colfax conferred with Hill in Spokane in February 1892 about a Palouse line. He told them that the proposition would be received within two or three years after the GN main line was built. Malone comments, "An arc through the productive terrain of southern Washington had never really been an option. This was NP territory, and by agreeing not to parallel its lines into the rich wheat region south of Spokane, Hill gathered valuable bargaining chips with the NP." On May 30, 1892, GN track was laid to a junction with the ORN at the eastern approach to the Spokane Union Depot. Daily passenger service from Spokane to the east began August 17, 1892. Track was completed to Everett on Puget Sound, January 6, 1893.[5]

It was reported in early April 1893 that the GN within 30 days would make a Palouse survey. According to the *Review,* right-of-way to Palouse City had been secured. The line would leave the main line in the vicinity of Medical Lake, run to the North Palouse River at Elberton, up the river to Palouse City then to Pullman, down Steptoe canyon to Lewiston, and thence to the Camas Prairie. The news of the proposed line generated considerable interest and other communities sought to have the line come their way. Communities not on the original line proposed that the branch leave the GN main line at Harrington, hence to Sprague to St. John to the Palouse River below Colfax, up river to Colfax and south to Union Flat, Lewiston, and the Camas Prairie. In early May 1894 Hill, in response to a request that he consider building from the Camas Prairie into southern Idaho, wrote that the GN had no desire to undertake new work, particularly into undeveloped country.[6]

B. Hill and the ORN

Henry Villard, seeking harmony, sounded Hill out about purchasing his Manitoba stock. Hill, "resenting the implications of such a possibility and even such an inquiry, gave a non-committal reply." According to Pyle, third parties deceived Villard into thinking that a decisive interview had been arranged, but no one but Villard appeared at the meeting. Villard's interpretation was that Hill backed out at the last minute. Hill sought to check any plans Villard had by increasing his and friends' holding in Villard's Oregon & Transcontinental (OT).[7]

At about the same time, September 1889, UP President Charles Francis Adams made a loose agreement with Hill which "he quipped, committed the UP 'to absolutely nothing except giving Hill power to fight the Northern Pacific at his own expense as much as he liked.'" Adams wrote "Hill's methods of discussion are simply bewildering." In October 1890 the UP's Oregon Short Line and Utah Northern Railway and the GN entered into an agreement for the construction of the Portland & Puget Sound Railway between Portland and Seattle. The UP had begun construction in 1889. The line was to be completed by December 31, 1891. The agreement included a traffic contract between the ORN and the GN providing for the two roads to connect at or near Spokane and that the ORN would haul interchanged traffic to and from Portland and points beyond. Adams preferred to build the line outright and rent trackage rights to the GN, but the financial situation of the UP was increasingly difficult. Adams wrote Grenville Dodge in May that he was concerned about financing the line and "I shall not recommend the building of this thing until I see the money provided." On November 26 Adams was forced to resign as president of the UP. The UP came under the control of Jay Gould, and the new president, Sidney Dillon, wrote ORN General Manager Holcomb regarding the Puget Sound extension, "Do not stop the work entirely or give publicity to the curtailment, but quietly see that it goes very slow." After spending a million and half dollars on the line, the UP suspended work in December 1890. Gould reconsidered the matter and sought to renew the contract, but Hill declined to listen to Gould and declined to have further dealings with him. The following August, Dillon and Hill agreed to abandon the Portland to the Sound project.[8]

In April 1890 the ORN shops at Wallula were being torn down to move to Tekoa. From September 1891 through May 1892 there were rumors that the GN would lease the ORN shops at Tekoa and run its trains to Portland over the ORN. But in June it was settled that the GN shops would be north of Spokane.[9]

As the financial condition of the UP worsened in 1892, Burlington President Charles Perkins tried to interest Hill in acquiring the OSL and ORN. After appearing to give encouragement, Hill decided against it and wrote Perkins: "The lines are located in a good country, some of it rich, and producing a large tonnage; but the capitalization of the company is far ahead of what it should be for what there is to show, and the selection of the route and grades is abominable. Practically it would have to be built over."[10] Beginning in November 1892, and well into 1894, there were many rumors and statements reported that the Burlington would or was already building west from southern Idaho or from Butte to Spokane or would use NP tracks from Billings to Spokane.[11]

After the ORN and OSL went into bankruptcy and were no longer controlled by the UP, the Burlington considered building to connect with the OSL and gaining control before the UP could regain control. In the latter part of 1894 Burlington interests bought a substantial interest in the ORN. In the fall of 1895 President Perkins again suggested to Hill that they jointly gain control of the ORN. After the OSL regained control of the ORN, Perkins tried unsuccessfully to persuade his board to acquire the OSL. Years later Hill told Perkins that he regretted not joining in the proposal. Edward Harriman reportedly never understood why the Burlington let the opportunity slip by. Meanwhile in October 1894 the Burlington completed a connection with the NP near Billings. In April of the same year the two roads had entered into a traffic agreement which was favorable to both railroads. In November 1895 the Burlington board decided to attempt to gain control of the bankrupted NP, but nothing came of it. The connection with the NP and the traffic agreement, in the long run, ended. The Burlington pushing westward but rumors and speculation continued for over a decade.[12]

C. Hill and the Oregon & Washington Territory Railroad

As described in chapter IV, the Oregon & Washington Territory Railroad (OWT) under George W. Hunt was viewed by the ORN/UP as an indirect NP invasion of ORN territory south of the Snake River. While NP Director C. B. Wright helped gain financing for the road, the evidence suggests that the company did not initially give significant aid to the line, but with an OWT connection at Hunt's Junction, just north of Wallula, the NP did gain access to traffic from south of the river. A report from Wallula in November 1889 claimed that the GN would cross the Columbia at Wallula and that Hill might take possession of the OWT. Hunt announced in early 1890 that the railroad would build to Portland and Gray's Harbor in order to guarantee his local backers favorable rates to tide water. He sought money in the east. The NP actively began to impede Hunt both financially and on the ground.[13]

On October 5, 1890, it was reported that OWT bonds were placed in London with the aid of the Burlington and that the latter would build west over the Bitterroot Mountains to Lewiston to connect with OWT, and also build a branch from some point between Lewiston and Riparia to Spokane. The *Statesman* reported on the 25th that a vice president of the Burlington said "there was not a word of truth in the whole story" about the Pacific extension and "We have given the Hunt road no assistance whatever in floating their bonds." On November 1 Burlington President Perkins was in Tacoma. The press said he did not contemplate any extensions to the west, at least not then.[14]

The Spokane *Review* reported that on October 7 Hill met in Portland for three hours with Portland banker William S. Ladd. Ladd was known to be a friend of Hunt and had underwritten $500,000 of the $2,000,000 Portland subsidy subscription for the OWT. This probably accounted for the fact that Ladd had not been elected ORN vice president in June. Hunt had been unable to place his bonds because of opposition from the UP and NP. The newspaper commented, "The conference between President Hill and Mr. Ladd is regarded by business men as being very significant—it has been whispered for two or three days that President Hill had agreed to place the Hunt bonds and come into Portland over the Hunt system. Another report had it that he had already placed the bonds. The conference adds color to the story." "A prominent man who had a talk" with Hill thought the GN would build from Spokane to Lewiston and connect with the OWT. On October 8 the *Review* dismissed the idea that the Burlington had any connection to Hunt. The editor went on,

> Hunt himself was a poor man, and could not have built a suburban street railway without the assistance of some powerful financier. Ladd is the man who has built the Hunt roads....For a long while it appeared as though the Portland banker was aiming a savage blow at his own town and therefore at his own interests, by helping to build a system in direct competition with the [ORN], and playing right into the hands of the Northern Pacific. As a matter of fact, Ladd foresaw the inevitable tendency of the times. He heard the cry of the people of Eastern Washington for railway competition, and he undertook this brilliant concept by which the people of the inland empire were induced to raise royal subsidies and insure the success of the enterprise.

> Now that the system has been perfected, Ladd and his associates are ready to cut loose from the Northern and to form an alliance with the Great Northern, by which the bulk of the traffic of Eastern Washington will be turned to Portland.
>
> ...Hill is surely going both to Puget sound and the Columbia river, and that means two new highways to the sea, and lower grain rates for producers of the interior.

When asked on the 9th whether he had decided to float the bonds of the OWT and build from Spokane to Lewiston, Hill responded, "That is a very big question, and one that I am not willing to answer." The *Spokesman* on the 10th dismissed the *Review* editorial of the 8th as fanciful. Hunt arrived in St. Paul on the 17th and stayed for several days. He said the report that the GN had secured control of the OWT was "without foundation and furthermore, the subject has never been mentioned to him by anyone connected with the Great Northern." In the meantime Hill on October 14 wrote regarding the Hunt lines, "If the portion to be completed is built with low grade and economy...the property would be an exceptionally good one. If [the situation were examined] with a competent engineer to approximate cost of such a line as situation calls for, I am satisfied parties going into it would make large profit. But the whole country and its business are on such a large pattern that nothing short of personal examination should be taken."[15]

Harvey P. Barbour urged NP President Oakes December 10, 1890, to act with dispatch in gaining control of the Hunt roads. Hill had told Ladd and others at Portland that he would take control of the Hunt roads if given a chance. Barbour continued, that unable to sell his bonds, Hunt had given up hope of retaining control of his roads,

> and intends to make any deal he can with Hill.... Hill assured Hunt last week that he would make Hunt a good offer and arrange the details of the deal. His statement that he would make a deal with the Northern Pacific...if he did not make a deal elsewhere is false, as he now says that he never at any time intended to make any such deal.... The Hill programme is for a syndicate composed of Hill, and other friends to get control of the Hunt road and probably later to turn it over to the Great Northern. There are some Englishmen in the syndicate.... Hill assured Hunt he would...arrange details, to-day (Wednesday) he and [others]...would make Hunt a good 'offer'...Hill believes the Northern Pacific is not in sufficient funds to deal with Hunt now and as a consequence of that opinion he may delay a little, and thereby enable the Northern Pacific to secure the road.[16]

On February 25 the NP filed suit against Hunt on a promissory note of $135,000. On the 27th Hunt agreed to deliver to NP Director C. B. Wright 51 percent of the capital stock of the OWT and thereafter other portions of the stock, most of the bonds of the OWT, and a large amount of equipment and material belonging to Hunt individually; if the line was deficit in condition, Hunt would bring it up to the reasonable satisfaction of the NP president and chief engineer. Hill remained interested in the Hunt lines, but perhaps ignorant of Wright's and NP's involvement. On the 28th Hill was sent a letter saying that the Hunt matter had been reduced to a contract. "The gist of it is Hunt sells out at $15,000 per mile in money $500,000 cash on April 17 and the balance deferred payments." Ladd in Portland said "Whether Hunt's reputed negotiations with Jim Hill have had anything to do with the precipitation of this matter I am ignorant." On March 6 Wright wrote Henry Villard, "I wish it to be understood that the N. P. Co. will not be under any obligation to take this enterprise if it does not choose to do so."[17]

According to a story from Portland, the Seattle *Telegraph* said March 5 the NP was forced to buy the OWT because Hill and the Burlington wanted it to reach Portland. Hill could not raise $3,000,000 cash because his construction was eating up the money and the deal was made too quickly for the Burlington. The NP had given Hunt an outlet for his traffic, but Hunt broke away and arranged with the UP to send his traffic to Portland, at the same time he was working with the GN. Hill made various promises and statements to Hunt, but he hedged himself with the argument that the OWT was too far out of the way. The NP checkmated Hunt's every move to float his bonds and as result Hunt was rendered practically bankrupted. "Had Hunt made the financial deal desired and had T. B. Wilcox, who went East in the interest of W. S. Ladd been successful in floating the bonds for him, he would have built the road perhaps without the assistance of any other corporation." The following day the *Union* reported that the *Oregonian* realized that "[n]o one doubts the intention of the Northern Pacific in building up Tacoma, nor can anyone, unless indifferent, fail to realize the manifest injury done this city" by the sale of the OWT to the NP. In a Spokane speech February 19, 1892, Hill gave a different, but not inconsistent, account of what happened: "we abandoned our first line by way of Great Falls, Helena, Butte City and Anaconda and through Lolo pass to the Clearwater, although we had held the securities of the Hunt road in our box for over a year, when we found [1889–90] we could cross the main range of the Rocky mountains on a 1 percent grade."[18]

The *Review* said of the sale, the NP wanted the road,

but was unwilling to pay "a fancy price for it." The NP's claims on Hunt "forced him to give it greater consideration than he would have done if he had been free from his financial troubles." By purchasing the line the NP will send "at least seven-tenths of the wheat of Eastern Washington" to Tacoma. "If Portland people had come to Hunt's assistance or had taken control of the road they… would have diverted nearly four-fifths of the grain from Walla Walla, the Pendleton district, and they would have gone up and tapped the Big Bend country."[19]

The stockholders of the OWT April 30, 1891, elected C. B. Wright Jr. to the board as well as vice president and general manager. Hunt remained president. The OWT would be transferred to C. B. Wright on May 1. The senior Wright stated that the OWT was an independent road, not owned by the NP "at the present time" and "although he was not in a position to talk about the extensions contemplated by Mr. Hunt he inferred that the ground would be looked over and in all probability the new roads would be built." It was reported in early June that J. M. Ashton of Tacoma negotiated the transfer of the Hunt lines to Wright. He said, "There is no doubt but that J. J. Hill…had designs upon this road. His claim against the Hunt system, however, was paid in full."[20]

On August 4, 1892, the Washington & Columbia River Railway (WCR) was incorporated by Wright to buy the OWT. The deed was executed October 1, 1892, and on the 5th Wright conveyed the OWT to the WCR for $1,250,000. On November 5, 1892, the formal transfer of the OWT to the WCR was made. The WCR was deeded to the NP June 18, 1907.[21]

D. Seattle, Lake Shore and Eastern Railway[22]

The NP favored Tacoma over Seattle. As a response the Seattle, Lake Shore and Eastern Railway (SLSE) was chartered April 15, 1885, to build a railroad from Seattle to Walla Walla with a branch to Spokane. Construction began in western Washington March 21, 1887. In mid-summer 1887, Vice President D. H. Gilman denied rumors that the SLSE was out of money and that C. B. Wright had made an offer for the railroad. In late September 1887 George W. Hunt was awarded a contract to build the SLSE east to the summit of Snoqualmie Pass. The contract was to be completed by October 1, 1888, and W. S. Ladd of Portland guaranteed Hunt's faithful performance. Gilman denied any formal agreement to connect with the Manitoba.[23]

In March 1888 Seattle newspapers reported that A. M. Cannon, recently resigned as S&P president, was associated with the SLSE. While he did not confirm the association, he did say that the people in Spokane were anxious for the road and if the road was not finished to Spokane by the end of 1889 it would not be their fault. On April 7, 1888, J. R. McDonald, SLSE president; Thomas Burke, attorney; and Paul F. Mohr, formerly S&P engineer in charge, now SLSE chief engineer, spoke at the Opera House in Spokane. The meeting was to consider the railroad's proposition that it would commence building westward from Spokane in 30 days, provided that $175,000 of stock was sold. By the middle of April the board of trade had raised sufficient money to subsidize 40 miles of railway to be in operation by December 1, 1888.[24]

The SLSE began construction at Spokane Falls May 3, 1888. A contract for 225 miles connecting the western and eastern Washington segments of the Lake Shore was let on the 21st. On September 15, 1888, two engines arrived at Spokane named "Paul F. Mohr" and "A. M. Cannon."[25] Construction reached Wheatdale, 44.34 miles, on December 3, and Davenport on October 17, 1889, after the residents of that town subsidized the five miles from Wheatdale. The bridge over the Spokane River west of Spokane was opened November 2. This together with the 60.17 miles opened July 3, 1888, west of the Cascades presented the possibility of a competitor to the NP and ORN in eastern Washington. The NP responded by beginning construction of the Central Washington Railroad west of Cheney on July 10, 1888. The chief threat to NP was that the SLSE would be controlled by either the UP or GN.[26]

In May 1888 the SLSE board adopted two maps, a definite location from Spokane to the western boundary of Idaho, 51 miles, and a preliminary location to the head waters of the Clearwater, 128 miles. "A prominent eastern capitalist, who is connected with and interested in the SLSE, was heard to say six months ago: 'It is no longer a question of connection with the Manitoba road; it is simply a question how big a slice we can get ourselves. I hope we will be able to get as far as the Clearwater in Idaho by the time Hill's road reaches that stream.'"[27]

SLSE Vice President Gilman told a Seattle reporter in December that the line would be built across the Cascades in 1889 and completed in 1890. There were reports after the first of the year that the SLSE would be extended to Cheney, Rosalia, and Colfax. In a book published by the SLSE in 1889, W. H. Ruffner recommended that the road build a branch through Sprague and Colfax to Lewiston; it "would cross some rich, unoccupied territory, and everywhere would compete for business on fair terms." It was claimed that Colfax had annually $225,000 in freight, and five firms claimed to handle annually 2,075,000 bushels, or 62,250 tons, of wheat.[28]

In October 1889 there were rumors that the Manitoba was buying SLSE stock and that Hill had a majority of the stock. It was reported in November that the GN intended to acquire the SLSE and they would meet in Spokane Falls via ORN from Missoula and that the GN would use SLSE terminal facilities in Seattle.[29]

In February 1890 SLSE bondholders applied for an injunction in Spokane Falls against the delivery of bonds and stock to the construction company, to appoint a receiver for both companies, and a decree that the construction contract was fraudulent. Thomas Burke, SLSE attorney, said, "The object is perfectly plain. It is a conspiracy concocted by the [NP] to do by illegitimate means which they have utterly failed for the past two years to accomplish by negotiations, namely, either to get control of the [SLSE] or wreck it, or both." The NP denied being involved in the suit. In the spring of 1890 the SLSE was offered to the UP for a rental of $2,300 per month, but its net earnings were scarcely a thousand dollars a month.[30]

GN Vice President William P. Clough looked over the SLSE in February 1890, but left without comment. In March the GN formed a west coast subsidiary, the Seattle & Montana. Two former officers of the SLSE were officers in the new company. The primary purpose of the company was to secure waterfront in Seattle. Hill wrote in early June that he doubted the SLSE people would be willing to sell for a price the GN would be willing to pay. Hill believed that most of the line would have to be rebuilt before the GN could use it. On the other hand it would be worthwhile to get the line out of the way and to have its terminals. "If anything should occur whereby the Lake Shore people would be willing to sell at fair price, I would always be glad to hear from them." In the summer of 1890 Stevens Pass was selected for the GN crossing of the Cascades.[31]

The NP executive committee, June 5, 1890, noted that the Oregon & Transcontinental had purchased a majority interest in the SLSE at the request and benefit of the NP. Under a contract of that date the SLSE would be turned over to the O&T July 25. The status of the SLSE was a matter of considerable speculation for several months. The *Review* commented that NP control was "detrimental to the best interests of the city, in that it lessens the chances of another competing line to the Sound." An official of the GN said, "We don't want the [SLSE], nor did we ever make any effort to secure it. We could have purchased it some time ago, but found upon examination that it was not what we wanted." Clough, interviewed in Seattle on June 25, did "not see the slightest prospect" of the GN purchasing the SLSE and there was no truth in the sale of the road to the NP. It was said that the GN wanted the SLSE, but financial difficulties stood in the way and the NP quietly bought a majority of the stock. NP President Oakes July 21 announced that the NP had purchased a little more than half of the capital stock of the SLSE. The property was leased to the NP for a guarantee of 6 percent on the outstanding bonds and sufficient additional bonds to complete the line to the international boundary. The annual rent was $80,000 per year. SLSE President A. S. Dunham told a Seattle reporter that the Spokane division would be operated by the NP on September 23, when it became the Spokane branch of the Idaho Division. It was reported that the west end of the SLSE would be turned over to the NP operating department on June 5, 1891, at Sumas.[32]

The transfer of the SLSE to the NP was completed March 14, 1892. The next day the NP began operating the SLSE under a traffic agreement. On June 27, 1893, a receiver was appointed for the SLSE. The western lines of the SLSE were reorganized in 1896 as the Seattle & International Railroad and the eastern as the Spokane & Seattle Railway. April 1, 1901, the lines were absorbed into the NP.[33]

A February 18, 1893, NP stockholders committee report on the acquisition of the SLSE said, "The acquisition of this property for the price paid and under the conditions existing at the time seems to have been an act of stupendous and incredible folly." The strategic advantages to be gained by the acquisition were not fulfilled; the GN reached Spokane and Seattle undeterred by the NP action. They asserted that the NP undertook a burden of about $7,500,000 which it could have acquired for less than $2,500,000. The response of the NP directors was that purchase of the SLSE ended plans of the UP, GN, and Canadian Pacific, and traffic from the SLSE was a net gain to the NP.[34]

NP Receiver Edwin H. McHenry sent General Manager John W. Kendrick's report on the SL&E to Bond Holder's Chairman Edward D. Adams on April 10, 1896. His report was not substantially different from the above report in its conclusions. He began his report, "You are already familiar with the general subject of the earlier financial transactions of this company. The record is a disgraceful one. Even before the acquisition of stock by the Northern Pacific, the enterprise appears to be been robbed by its promoters."[35]

Hill had an early interest in the territory south of Spokane, but in the time period of this chapter his main focus was on the completion of the GN to Puget Sound. As we shall see he developed a strong interest in gaining access to the Palouse and eastern Washington generally. He hoped to achieve that by use of the NP or ORN or both and thus avoid building lines.

E. Other Railroads and the Palouse

There were many reports of other possible railroads in the Palouse. In August 1889 it was said that the Southern Pacific had made a "preliminary survey" from Portland to Spokane and that the route was "feasible." The Chicago & Northwestern and the Illinois Central were also reported that year to be surveying in the Palouse and in the vicinity of Spokane. In April 1890 Paul F. Mohr spoke of "a new railroad scheme that will make Spokane Falls the northern terminus of one of the most gigantic systems of railroads this country has yet seen. He said: "The idea is to begin at Spokane Falls, run south… through the Genesee country of Idaho striking Salt Lake City…and go on to the City of Mexico." In November 1890 a dispatch from Garfield said that the Farmers' Alliance of Whitman County would construct a railroad from the Palouse country to Puget Sound. The articles of the Seattle, Boise City and Salt Lake Railroad Company were filed at Boise in December 1890. The line would run from Seattle to Spokane, to Lewiston via the Palouse, to Boise and Salt Lake City via the Seven Devils area. The *Gazette* said, "It is quite doubtful if an entirely new and independent line is projected. But in whose interests is this new road to be build? This is a question that the people of the Palouse would like to have answered."[36]

The Palouse Railroads during the Northern Pacific Receivership, 1893–96

A. The Northern Pacific Receivership and James J. Hill

In late September 1892 Oakes said that from a financial standpoint the NP had never been more prosperous. At the October 20 stockholders' meeting a special committee was appointed to investigate the affairs of the company. On February 18, 1893, the committee report by Henry Clews, Brayton Ives, and Jay Cooke Jr. contained "Such phrases as 'stupendous and incredible folly,' 'deplorable financial condition,' 'the present disjointed policy,' 'a menace to stockholders,' and 'reckless course' are used [to describe] existing conditions in Northern Pacific affairs." Among the matters criticized was a $725,000 loan from Villard to the NP at 8 percent when money was available at 5 percent or less.[1]

June 21, 1893, the NP directors accepted the resignation of Villard as director and chairman effective July 19. On August 15 Oakes and two others were appointed receivers of the NP. The petition for receivership alleged the company had no funds to meet payments due September to December.[2] The receivership was claimed to be necessary because of a sharp decline in earnings because of the national depression. A report to German investors in November 1893 also blamed Hill's "reckless rate war." Brayton Ives issued a statement that the NP was still under the control of Villard who had mismanaged the company and enriched himself. At the annual NP stockholders meeting October 19 an anti-Villard ticket gained control of the board electing five new members, including former NP President Robert Harris, who the next day was elected vice president. Ives was elected president. Separate local receivers were appointed for over 20 branch lines. Henry Stanton was appointed general receiver. On October 28 Edward D. Adams was elected chairman of the American Committee of Bond Holders.[3]

Villard claimed November 3 that he had no individual responsibility for the NP situation beyond being a member of the board of directors and that as a large investor he had lost millions of dollars. The NP board initiated a suit December 28 to remove the three receivers. The allegation in part was that Oakes, as NP president, had acted against the interests of the NP. The court dismissed the action October 1894; the court found no evidence that Oakes had personally benefited financially, but it did find that, unknown to Oakes, Villard had made unlawful gains of $363,602. On June 27, 1895, the court ordered the receivers to sue Henry Villard to recover about $550,000 and to begin suits against all NP officers who were believed to have obtained money from the company illegally. On September 8, 1894, it was announced that the receivers of 24 branch lines were to be terminated, a trustee was to manage the lines for a fixed sum and the NP receivers would operate the lines under a traffic agreement.[4]

Reflecting on the NP and UP bankruptcies at the end of 1893 the *Review* said,

> Events of the past four months have proved that President Hill of the Great Northern made no idle boast when he affirmed in the presence of a group of Spokane business men that it lay within his power, by inaugurating a rate war, to put his competitors in the hands of receivers.
>
> The story is readily told: mismanagement and downright dishonesty. In flush times these great railroad systems were strained to the danger point, and when hard times came along they yielded, just as the enfeebled constitution yields to the germs of disease. We are now to have an era of reconstruction that will prove of untold benefit to the sections served by these systems. The water is to be evaporated, and the roads are to be relieved of the requirement of paying profits on extravagantly built roadbeds. Henceforth the transcontinental railroad will earn a fair profit on what it is worth, not upon what it cost the stockholders. Industry and commerce refuse longer to pay for the consequences of individual folly.[5]

A plan of reorganization of the NP was worked out by the Adams committee, Hill, J. P. Morgan & Co., and

Deutsche Bank in May 1895. The "London Agreement" provided that the GN would receive half the NP stock in exchange for an unconditional guarantee of the principal and interest on new NP bonds. Hill when asked if he would aid in the NP reorganization, said, "I am not prepared to say what the Great Northern will do further than to state that you may depend on the Great Northern looking out, to the best of its ability, for its own interests. It will be most glad to co-operate with the bondholders of the Northern Pacific to...put that company on a sound basis." As to whether the GN had gained "absolute control of the Northern Pacific," Hill said "there is not a word of truth in it." Control of the NP was not a settled matter. A Chicago *Times-Herald* report said that "it is sufficient to say that Brayton Ives is utterly opposed to the deal.... Back of him is a much larger proportion of the securities than is back of the faction favoring the Hill deal." In early June, Hill asked whether he was to gain control of the NP, replied slowly, "It will be reorganized and placed on a sound basis. This is about all I know about it."[6]

E. V. Smalley, editor of the *Northwest Magazine* and author of the 1883 history of the NP, commented in early August 1895 that the statutes of Minnesota, North Dakota, Montana, and Washington would ultimately defeat the scheme to consolidate the NP and GN. "Some of these great New York bankers are discovering, for the first time in their lives probably, that the people's will, expressed in statute books, is more powerful than their money bags." Ultimately the agreement plan failed when the United States Supreme Court ruled March 30, 1896, against combining the two railroads, but by then there was a different plan for reorganization.[7]

J. P. Morgan and Deutsche Bank on March 16, 1896, adopted a reorganization plan. To protect Morgan and others the plan created a voting trust to hold the NP stock until November 1, 1901, or earlier if the members of the voting trust so decided. In the meantime stock holders would receive Trust Certificates for their stock. Prior to the reorganization taking effect, April 2, 1896, Morgan, Hill, and Deutsche Bank agreed to the "London Memorandum" which abrogated the "London Agreement" of 1895 and agreed that the NP should be reorganized under the March 16 plan independent of the GN or any other company. Furthermore, the GN would not compete with bondholders of NP branch lines for control of the branches. It was agreed that the GN and the reorganized NP "shall form a permanent alliance, defensive, and in case of need offensive, with a view of avoiding competition and aggressive policy and of generally protecting the common interests of both Companies." With respect to the ORN, the GN and NP agreed that so far as they could they would keep it as "an independent corporation keeping good and equitable relations" with the GN, NP, and other neighboring companies. The object was to prevent others from securing control of the ORN and to permit the UP, CB&Q, or any other company to use the ORN lines upon fair and equal terms. The Morgan Company and Deutsche bank agreed to vote their NP stock in favor of directors proposed by the GN in proportion to the NP stock holdings of GN parties. The reorganization "ushered in a period of uncertainty and frustration for Hill and his associates." Morgan and Deutsche Bank controlled the board, and the GN for a time had no representation. Morgan selected against Hill's wishes Edwin Winter and Charles Mellon as NP presidents. J. P. Morgan in April 1897 denied an alliance had been arranged between the NP and GN.[8]

By April 27, 1896, all the parties to the NP bankruptcy had agreed to a foreclosure sale of the railroad. Ives said the fixed charges had been reduced by a million dollars a year and thus fair to the stockholders. On May 12 the United States Circuit Court ordered the sale of the NP. The property of the Northern Pacific Railroad Co. was sold to the new Northern Pacific Railway Company (NP) for $12,500,000 at West Superior, Wisconsin, July 25, 1896. The new company began operation September 1. Ives left the NP presidency June 30 and on July 21 Edwin W. Winter became president. McHenry, a receiver at the time, returned as NP chief engineer.[9]

The annual meeting of the NP stockholders was October 6, 1896, and on the 26th the directors elected Edward D. Adams, chairman, and Edwin W. Winter, president. Brayton Ives remained on the board. Except for Ives and one other, the receivership board was replaced. Among the new board members was Charles Henry Coster, representing J. P. Morgan & Co.

B. The Spokane & Palouse Receivership

The S&P was operated by the NP under leases of May 1, 1886, and June 1, 1887, until August 15, 1893, for an annual rental equal to the funded-debt interest and sinking-fund contributions. There was no need for an S&P receivership; it was managed by the receivers at a reduced rate. December 15, 1893, the NP receivers instructed General Manager Kendrick to report on the desirability of taking S&P out of receivership. The NP assistant general auditor wrote Kendrick January 18, 1894, to say that if the S&P were given equally favorable terms as other branches, "there would be no difficulty about their earnings meeting operating expenses and fixed charges." On the 31st Kendrick wrote NP Receiver Oakes that the bonded indebtedness of the S&P was $2,984,000 of which $1,766,000 was publically held and those 6 percent bonds had a yearly payment of $105,960. The remainder of the bonds, $1,218,000, were owned by the NP at 5 percent. The NP owned all 10,000 shares of stock. Kendrick agreed that the S&P was economically viable if treated on "a fair and reasonable basis." Kendrick recommended termination of the S&P receivership. He noted, "My letter is based upon the fact that the Spokane & Palouse is so situated with reference to other roads—the Union Pacific and Great Northern—that it is not in any large sense dependent upon the Northern Pacific for traffic relations." In December 1893 an S&P first mortgage bondholders committee was formed "to protect and enforce the rights of all bondholders." The S&P receivers were discharged November 17, 1894, when the NP receivers retroactively leased the S&P from August 15, 1893. Because the Washington and Idaho portions of the railroad were separately bonded, they were legally distinct under the NP receivership, but the railroad was operated as a unit. The *Times* reported the receivers reached an agreement with the bondholders committee that both portions of the road would be leased to the NP receivers at a reduced interest charge of $167,000 for the first two years and $132,000 for the second two years. The bondholders committee announced June 2, 1896, that the bondholders could participate in the planned reorganization of the NP up to June 15. They would receive for each $1,000 bond, with all coupons attached, $525 in cash on January 1, 1897, $525 in new 3 percent general lien bonds, and $250 in new preferred stock trust certificates of the reorganized Northern Pacific Railroad. The NP receivers leased the S&P until August 31, 1896. The reorganized NP operated the S&P without a formal contract from September 1, 1896, to February 21, 1899, the date it was sold to the NP.[10]

In late 1894 the NP receivers received a detailed report from Chief Engineer McHenry (he was not yet an NP receiver) on completing the Lewiston extension. He estimated the cost for 20.6 miles of main track and 2.0 miles of siding etc. at $364,000. The grading from the west line of the reservation, 8.3 miles, was practically completed, leaving 12.3 miles through the reservation to grade. After rental of equipment, traffic charges, and truss-bridge iron on hand were removed, the cash outlay was estimated to be $267,500. If old rail from the main line were used the cash outlay would be $211,700. Van Arsdol had estimated that a $50,000 to $60,000 subsidy might be raised. The amount already expended on the Lewiston extension was $1,333,455. "The addition of the uncompleted mileage to Lewiston should operate to increase the traffic, and very greatly reduce the operating expense per ton mile. In other words, the expenditure of the comparatively small amount required to complete the line, will increase the value of the entire system to a degree out of all proportion to the amount expended." Kendrick agreed with McHenry, but added that Asotin, three miles above Lewiston, should be the objective if construction was resumed.[11]

In November 1895 the supervising Idaho judge, receivers, and NP officials were in Lewiston looking to extend the S&P. On the 29th one of the receivers wrote, "[T]here is no immediate probability of extending the Lewiston branch, although we hope at no distant date this matter can be taken up and pushed vigorously, as it has the unqualified support of all concerned.... As long as our affairs are in the present mixed up condition it is hopeless to expect any action in this direction, but I think the concerted action on the part of a unified receivership would possibly effect it." Receiver Oakes in early April 1896 said in Tacoma that the extension to Lewiston would not be built that year.[12]

The *Review*, from a study of the traffic and earnings of some NP branches in the state, concluded, "the main line has milked these roads and how false is the old and threadbare statement that it has lost money in their operation." Using numbers only slightly different than those found in the Kendrick-McHenry report, the newspaper concluded from July 1, 1893, to June 30, 1894, that while NP claimed that the S&P had an operating deficit of about $37,000, the NP mainline had a net surplus of almost $159,000 on business from the S&P. "The truth is the Spokane & Palouse road is a splendid property, and under capable management should have paid dividends upon its stock." It wondered whether the bondholders would have consented to a reduction in the interest on the bonds from 6 to 4 percent if they had taken the trouble to analyze the figures. The *Review* concluded that the Central Washington and Seattle, Lake Shore & Eastern branches were also profitable.[13]

C. The Kendrick-McHenry Report on the Spokane & Palouse[14]

On March 24, 1896, General Manager John Kendrick sent receivers Edwin H. McHenry and Frank G. Bigelow a report on the S&P. From Spangle to Genesee, Farmington, and Howell the line traverses "a very fine agricultural country, the greater part of which is under cultivation, principally devoted to wheat raising; in addition, stock is raised and fruit and vegetables." Later referring to these sections of line,

> [t]he line was very poorly located, both with respect to grades and curves. The greater part of the curvature is unnecessary and foolish. The route selected, cross cuts the drainage, instead of following the crest of prairie divide as it should have done. The natural rise and fall over this route being very great, it follows...that undesirable grades occur. The maximum grades opposing north bound traffic (the direction in which the wheat moves) are 1.2%, between Marshall and Genesee, and 1.5% between Pullman and Howell. The grades opposing south bound traffic are 1.7% and 1.75% respectively.

The section from Howell to Juliaetta was in a deep canyon and had "excessive" grades of 2.4 percent. Timber was present and the plateau on either side was under cultivation.

The track and road bed were generally in fair condition. An excessive number of pile bridges were built, but many had been replaced by fills and culverts. The track between Marshall and Genesee was laid with new 56-pound steel, except for 7.64 miles near Marshall, where second-hand 56-pound steel was used. The road bed between Pullman Junction and Juliaetta had second-hand 56-pound rail, and between Kendrick and Howell there was new 66-pound steel on the grade. There was a deficiency in ballast in many places, but was sufficient for the purposes. The bridges were in "fairly good condition," the buildings in reasonably good repair. The rails were in good condition and ties in average condition, requiring the usual annual renewal. There remained to be secured 105.32 acres of right-of-way at an estimated cost of $3,184.

The lines of the ORN are more advantageously located in that they follow the natural east and west drainage. The most serious consequence of bad location could be avoided by diverting traffic via the ORN to Connell if "a desirable traffic contract could be secured, or if the two companies were amalgamated, as they should be."

If the ORN or GN were to gain control of the line the freight and passenger business then interchanged would probably be lost. The interchange earnings for 1895 were $600,000. The report continued, "[t]here is no doubt that the Spokane & Palouse is a very valuable feeder to the Northern Pacific, and if it were not already built, I would strongly recommend the construction of a line serving that territory." Kendrick estimated that the cost to duplicate the line was $2,530,613 or about $16,750 per mile.[15] The remaining uncompleted 20.6 miles to Lewiston cost an estimated $150,000 bringing the total to $2,680,613. In his discussion of operation Kendrick said:

> The line is subject to strong competition by the [ORN] which crosses it at several important stations. Train service consists of a passenger train each way daily between Spokane and Juliaetta, and a local freight daily each way, except Sunday, between Spokane and Genesee, which is run as a mixed train between Pullman and Genesee, making connection at Pullman with the passenger train run between Spokane and Juliaetta. There is also a freight daily except Sunday between Juliaetta and Pullman. In addition to...its regular runs, this crew and engine are used during the busy season to handle grain between Juliaetta and Pullman, and also between Pullman and Genesee. It is necessary during the grain season to run extra trains, varying from two to six trains per day. During the season of heavy business, it is also customary to use helper engine between Belmont and Marshall Junction. All freight trains are handled by Mogul [2-6-0] engines.
>
> The line is exceedingly unfavorable for economical operation on account of heavy grades, the heavy engines used being unable to handle more than 14 fully loaded cars. These grades are particularly bad from the fact that they are so separated that helper engines cannot be used with advantage. One of the principal disadvantages in operating this branch is the unfortunate point of connection with main line at Marshall Junction, the bulk of the traffic for Puget Sound points, and the main line grade being heavy and adverse to the traffic between Marshall Junction and Cheney. Another noticeable disadvantage is the small volume of traffic out of Juliaetta and Kendrick, making it impossible to properly operate the mountain grade between Kendrick and Vollmer. This disadvantage would be largely removed by the extension of the line to Lewiston. The great part of the line is not subject to physical troubles, being comparatively free from snow. That portion of the line between Belmont and Marshall is subject to over-flow at points during the spring months, and between Kendrick and Vollmer to land slides during the same season. A lack of ballast is a serious obstacle to economical maintenance.

McHenry forwarded the report with a letter to Edward D. Adams, chairman of the reorganization committee. McHenry's cover letter begins with a brief history of the construction of the line.

> A. M. Cannon, at that time a capitalist of Spokane, now deceased, was President. The Chief Engineer of the Company began at the foot of the ladder, in the capacity of Chief Engineer, not having had any previous experience. He was appointed to the position, for the reason that he would not make a good General Counsel. This may appear a curious reason, but it is literally true, as his appointment to one of the two positions was request by Mr. Cannon, and unfortunately, his unfitness for the position of General Counsel having been ascertained by a lawyer, it was decided that he would naturally make a good engineer. The line is villainously located throughout, and its operation has entailed expenses otherwise unnecessary, amounting to hundreds of thousand[s] of dollars. The usual townsite scandal attended the construction. These remarks apply only to the portion originally construction between the main junction at Marshall, and the Genesee terminus. The Farmington branch, and the partially constructed extension to Lewiston, were built by the Construction Department of the Northern Pacific Railroad.

The business of the line was thought very valuable and should be retained by the company. "The necessity for completing the extension to Lewiston is imperative," and branches should be constructed to the Camas Prairie, on the Snake and Clearwater rivers above Lewiston, and on the Snake River below Lewiston. The competition of the ORN "is exceedingly burdensome, and its control or absorption by the Northern Pacific would avoid duplicate train mileage and station expenses...." With respect to operations,

> With the exception of a small amount of grain converted into flour at Spokane, the remainder goes to Portland, or Puget Sound points... under the present conditions, we are forced to haul the grain over very unfavorable grades around two side of a triangle, the apex of which is at Marshall Junction. The operation of the [ORN] is almost equally asinine, as their grain is hauled down to and across the [Snake River] which lies 2000' below the level of the plateau, and is subsequently transported to Portland, over a tortuous route crossing several high summits en route, in one case with 3.0% grades. The grain collected by both the [S&P] and the [ORN], could be delivered to the main line of the [NP] at Connell, in long trains over low grades with a probable saving of at least 66% of the present train mileage, now required by both companies....The [ORN] business could be again delivered to it at Wallula junction...the [NP] would follow the same route, instead of the present round about detour byway of Tacoma.

Little doubt was expressed that the ORN would build from the Columbia River up the Snake River to Lewiston. If the two companies remained independent, the NP should be the first to build from Pasco. "The prospective returns are ample to justify additional railroad construction, as soon as the companies are in a position to provide funds, and the future struggle for supremacy between the two systems will entail an expenditure of millions of dollars in duplicating each other['s] lines."

Improvements and betterments would require expenditure of $572,075, $42,000 for 70 miles of ballast and the remainder for permanent renewal of bridges. To renew bridges in the existing form would cost $121,827. "The bridges on the older portion of the line must be replaced as rapidly as possible."

This report was not free of bias. Clearly the S&P was expensive to operate because of curvature and grades. The causes of this were several: the beginning point and the objective(s), the importance of intermediate points, the topography between the points and the objective(s), and the skill of the locating engineers. The C&P was located in a more favorable entrance to the Palouse from the west. After the NP lost control of the C&P it shifted to entering the Palouse from the north and further east on the main line. This made a good deal of sense even given that the bulk of the Palouse traffic moved west rather than east. Spokane was an up and coming place in which at the time the NP had a monopoly. With its abundant water power Spokane gave promise as a milling center as well as a supply point for the Palouse. The topography west and south of Spokane presented challenges to railroad construction. The engineers did consider Cheney as the beginning point for the S&P. While Cheney was more favorably located for westward traffic, the engineers concluded connecting Cheney to the Palouse was no more favorable than from Spokane and Cheney. The original objective of the S&P was Farmington, but it quickly shifted to Genesee further south after engineers concluded that Farmington was not well situated for a north-south line to the Snake River. Kendrick implies that important intermediate points were established by the railroad, but this was generally not true. The line to Genesee was located in 1885–87; Spangle, Plaza, Rosalia, Palouse City, Pullman, Johnson, Colton, Uniontown, and Genesee all had their origins in the 1870s and Garfield before the railroad was planned. Oakesdale was platted in 1886. Belmont was created by the railroad, because it chose to end construction there in 1886. After 1886 its importance diminished. McHenry claims that there were the "usual townsite scandals." Perhaps he is correct, but no evidence has been found. Cannon and his associates did organize the Palouse Improvement Co. Such companies are suspect in these situations, but nothing has been found in the NP files nor in contemporary newspapers suggesting scandals. The controversy at Genesee

Washington State Agricultural College (now Washington State University), Pullman, sits on the hill in c. 1896. At the base of hill is the college's power plant with a freight [coal?] car in front. The power plant was served by both the NP and UP on a very short joint track. At the extreme right is a grain warehouse with the ORN spur and on the other side, between the warehouse and the pump house, is the S&P spur. *Photograph 01-014, Manuscript and Special Collections, Washington State University Library.*

has been discussed earlier, but Harris' investigation largely exonerated S&P officials. Interestingly nothing has been found in contemporary newspapers about that controversy (Genesee newspapers, if there are any, have been unavailable).

The topography of the Palouse is rolling hills cut by streams. Kendrick claims that a line from the west, such as the C&P, would follow the stream courses and therefore have a more favorable location. In general this is probably true, but in particular is not always so. The C&P westward grade out of Colfax is more severe than any S&P grade and the eastward grade was comparable to S&P grades. If the C&P had not already occupied Colfax, the S&P would have gone there. The Pleasant Valley line, which avoided Colfax, was built later by the ORN, and has several eastbound grades over 1 percent and several westbound grades of 1 percent. Kendrick said the S&P should have been built on prairie crests not identified. There are no crests that would solve the problems of a north-south line. Such a line cannot avoid the obstacles of Pine Creek, the Palouse River, and, as located through Pullman, the South Fork of the Palouse River. Both Kendrick and McHenry were NP chief engineers so their comments need to be taken seriously, but their comments do reveal ignorance or deliberate misrepresentation of the topography.

McHenry said that the S&P was "villainously located throughout." This comment follows his story of how the "Chief Engineer" of the S&P was selected. Paul F. Mohr was the "Engineer in Charge." But no instance has been found in which he is referred to as "Chief Engineer." It is clear that Cannon and Mohr were associates; in addition to the S&P, they were later associated with the SLSE and they and their wives traveled together. Nothing has been found to support McHenry's account of Mohr's appointment. The author has read a great deal of Mohr's correspondence and newspaper accounts of him. There is nothing suggesting that Mohr considered himself a lawyer. Mohr was born in the United States to German immigrants and claimed a formal engineering education in Germany. He worked as an engineer on other railroad projects not associated with the NP. He went over the ground where the S&P was to be located more than once and proposed alternative locations. NP Chief Engineer Adna Anderson approved his recommendations, treated him as an equal in correspondence, and defended him on occasion. C. B. Wright used him on surveys south of the Snake River. President Harris, a trained civil engineer, while not always happy with Mohr the person, did not in correspondence question his engineering. From this layman's perspective, his correspondence and other writings are those of a person with technical training. Mohr was not always a pleasant person and he appears to have annoyed Harris (a Spokane lot dispute is an example), but character flaws do not make one unqualified to be the "Engineer in Charge" of the S&P line to Genesee.

One last point on location: McHenry made a point of distinguishing the Lewiston extension from the line to Genesee as being done by the NP Construction Department and not the S&P. From Pullman Junction to Howell the profile of the line is hills and curves as is the earlier S&P line. Generally because of the topography this was unavoidable, but the clearest example of unnecessary grades is found on that extension. The C&P line between Pullman and Moscow is water level in the Paradise Creek valley. The valley is broad enough for two railroads, but the NP chose Sunshine Hill to Moscow. This line has grades up to 1.8 percent and generally more than 1.3 percent against the predominate traffic, and up to 1.75 percent in the other direction. The route did tap an area not served by the C&P, but it was not far removed from Paradise Creek or the S&P line south of Pullman. There is no location on the Marshall-Genesee line which so clearly shows a "villainous" location. Also the decision to begin the Lewiston extension at Pullman Junction rather than Whelan increased the distance and grades against the predominate traffic. In September 1901 NP Chief Engineer W. L. Darling went over the line and commented, "It seems quite impracticable to do anything in the way of radical improvements in grades. A matter to look into would be to use the ORN line from Pullman to Moscow...rather than try to improve our present line, which it is almost impracticable to do on account of the heavy hill...and the very bad alignment." The grades on the Pullman-Howell line were commented on by the division engineer in 1904 and 1905. (The three comments are reported in chapter XX.)[16]

Kendrick and McHenry, as well as Darling and others, argue that the rational treatment of westbound traffic from the Palouse is to send it to Connell. The argument is compelling from an economic perspective. But organizational dynamics and regional economic competition made it impossible. There were chances for such an arrangement, when the NP and ORN were both still involved in the C&P and the ORN had no physical connection to the C&P, when the NP and ORN were negotiating a lease, and when there was negotiations with the UP for a joint lease or an arbitration contract. Still later the NP surveyed from Pullman to Connell and inquired if the ORN would agree to leasing or giving trackage to Connell. The Clearwater agreements show what might have been achieved if economic factors had been strong enough. More on the Connell connection in chapter XVII.[17]

D. Spokane & Palouse Organization and Operation during the Receiverships

The gross earnings of the S&P for the year ending June 30, 1894, were $212,288 or $2,041 per mile. The NP wheat shipments from eastern Washington were 156,632 tons for the year; the S&P originated 75,165 tons.[18]

Flooding in spring and summer of 1894 disrupted railroad service all over the Pacific Northwest. On March 19 a northbound S&P train was detained by a slide between Vollmer and Moscow and a southbound train encountered so much water just south of Marshall that it extinguished the fire box fire. The ORN was blocked by a slide near Elberton. In June the water was over the piers of the ORN Snake River bridge at Riparia.[19]

Also in the spring and summer of 1894 there was railroad labor unrest on the GN, UP, ORN, and NP. At the end of June the NP Spokane railroad yards were closed by a strike and on July 6 the conditions at the yard were said to be a "riotous conflict." The *Herald* reported that on the 11th passenger trains on the S&P began running after a two week "vacation." On the 15th NP and ORN trains were again running.[20]

In June 1894 a Tacoma grain company purchased from receivers the N. P. Elevator Co. Included were warehouses on the S&P: Lewiston, Juliaetta, Kendrick, Vollmer, Joel, Moscow, and Sunshine in Idaho, plus Spangle, Plaza, Rosalia, Oakesdale, Kelly, Belmont, Garfield, Farmington, Palouse, Fallon, Whelan, Pullman, Staley, Johnson, Colton, Uniontown, and Leon in Washington. The only major shipping point missing is Genesee. The 1894 grain crop was "enormous." In mid-August the NP sent six hundred wheat cars into the Palouse. On the 19th Spokane handled 1,135 cars, the most ever moved on the division in one day. Nevertheless there was a shortage of cars on the NP and ORN which persisted into fall. Some of the problem was attributed to unloading cars; one Spokane flour mill was said to have a hundred cars to unload. A boycott against the ORN in Moscow was initiated when the ORN made the rate on hay $4.75 per ton, same as wheat; a rate of $4.00 a ton was sought. The farmers intended to patronize the NP which expressed a willingness to make the reduction. In March 1895 Palouse shippers of eggs, butter, and other dairy products were sending their shipments for Spokane and Coeur d'Alene mines by wagon to the ORN at Garfield. The S&P rate for butter from Spokane to Palouse was 25 cents per hundred, but from Palouse to Spokane it was 54 cents per hundred. It was reported in June 1895 that grain was moving east to Chicago which had a better price than at Pacific coast ports.[21]

A founder and the first president of the S&P, Anthony M. Cannon, died in New York City, April 6, 1895. Cannon was also a founder and former mayor of Spokane, and a leading banker, but was largely wiped out by the depression of 1893.[22]

A report in September 1895 said that in 1894 the ORN had given rebates on wheat shipments from Garfield and as a consequence it was receiving most of the wheat from Garfield; in the past the shipments had been more or less evenly divided between the ORN and S&P. The NP responded by increasing by a cent per bushel the amount paid by buyers on the S&P. The ORN matched the raise. A report in October said that ORN had about 75 percent of the Palouse wheat crop. Prior to the NP Elevator Co. receivership, the NP had a majority of the crop. The report said that Portland grain dealers had manipulated the cost of shipping from Puget Sound so that the advantage went to Portland in shipping to San Francisco. In mid-October the ORN warehouses in Garfield contained 300,000 bushels while the NP had 75,000, and in Pullman the ORN had 400,000 bushels and the NP 50,000. In late 1895 the Oakesdale flour mill closed because the price of wheat was too high and the price of flour was too low. It was thought that all the flour mills in the Palouse would shortly close.[23]

At noon, Monday, November 18, 1895, the cannon in front of the land office in Lewiston was fired. As the *Teller* put it, "This was the death knell of the great Nez Perce reservation." The next day the *Review* reported that the opening "was devoid of excitement, violence or suffering." Most of the land had been selected days before without legal challenge.[24]

It was reported from Moscow on December 24, 1895, that high winds and snow had packed the cuts with a wet, sticky snow that was impossible to penetrate. The S&P discontinued freight trains, but managed to go north with two engines and three coaches. The ORN train arrived an hour and half late, and the S&P southbound train was stalled in a cut about three miles from Moscow and arrived there 10 hours late. The train left for Kendrick, but about a half mile from the station both engines were derailed in a drift, one turning over on its side.[25]

On February 1, 1896, about 10:15 p.m., double-headed freight trains met at Oakesdale. A south-bound train of empties placed its cars on side tracks. The north-bound train of loads waited near the ORN crossing. It was given a signal to proceed, but "a drunken brakeman" neglected to close a side track switch and the train crashed into a string of empties. The momentum of the train caused cars next to the second engine to crash into it, tearing off the fireman's half of the cab. The fireman, shoveling coal, was knocked down and hot water and steam poured over him, seriously scalding him, but he survived. The first engine had minor damage, the second had major damage.[26]

Extreme heat and cold cause rails to expand and shrink, "crawl" as it is called. At the ORN Garfield crossing in the summer, the S&P cut off in bits as much as 10 feet of rail in the same place. "The rails apparently push down hill, for in the winter time when the cold weather contracts the rails it is necessary to replace the amount cut off during the summer and this splicing is done in this instance on the top of the grade more than a half mile from where it was cut off." Generally, the right hand rail crawls the fastest toward the direction you are facing; in the case of the north-south S&P, the east rails crawl fastest north and the west rails crawl fastest south.[27]

Railroads regularly offered excursion rates to various events on their lines. The Spokane Fruit Fair in early October 1896 attracted four extra trains on the S&P in addition to the regular passenger train. Each excursion train was six to ten cars and each began at a different point on the line. There were about 2,000 passengers. The ORN on the same day had an excursion train from Wallace. It was expected that ORN excursions from Moscow, Pullman, and Colfax would bring hundreds more.[28]

The price of wheat in October 1896 reached unusually high levels which caused an active market and large shipments at least into November. In late November 1896 a committee was appointed in Lewiston to confer with NP officials about getting an immediate extension. Giving the railroad a bonus was considered. At Oakesdale on the evening of December 26, 1896, two double-headed heavy S&P freights collided on a side track. The south bound train was waiting on a side track for the north bound when the latter, at about 12 miles an hour, ran through an improperly aligned turnout, pushing two cars into the south bound train. Cars were "piled up in a confused mass." A fireman received severe burns. Engines 504 and 343 were damaged.[29]

E. The Union Pacific, Oregon Railway & Navigation Co., and Oregon Short Line Receiverships[30]

The UP receivership began October 13, 1893. The UP had a floating debt exceeding $20 million dollars, over $12 million of this debt incurred in the purchase of a majority of ORN stock. The UP failed to pay the interest due on the ORN bonds in December 1893. Daggett wrote that, "The immediate problem was the floating debt, swollen to unwieldy proportions by the acquisition of branch lines, and in particular by the purchase of the [ORN]." The UP was virtually dismembered; from more than 8,000 miles the UP system was reduced to 2,000 miles during the receivership.

To avoid the likelihood that the UP receivers would use ORN profits for the benefit of the UP, the ORN bond holders petitioned in June 1894 for a separate receivership, which was granted July 3. Edwin McNeill, general manager of the Iowa Central Railroad, was appointed ORN receiver and general manager. Reportedly he refused an offer to be the GN general manager. It was thought that because Russell Sage, president of the Iowa Central, had a close relationship with the UP, McNeill was sent west to protect both Sage and UP interests. All UP equipment was ordered back to the UP, and ORN equipment was returned to it. McNeill spent nearly a half million dollars to put the ORN in much better physical shape than it had been. Traffic contracts with the GN and UP improved ORN earnings.

On August 11, 1894, O'Neill petitioned that the leases of the Oregon Railway Extensions Co. and Washington & Idaho Railroad be set aside and the ORN be released from the payment of rentals. The petition apparently named both ORE lines (one in Oregon and the Winona to Seltice in the Palouse) and the WI line from Tekoa to the Coeur d'Alene district, but not the WI Farmington to Rockford line which connected the ORN to Spokane.

The UP defaulted on the interest payments on the Oregon Short Line bonds and in early January 1895 the OSL bond holders applied for separate receivers, which were appointed in May and June. By this action the UP had no lines west of Ogden. The bankruptcy judge ruled that the OSL should not be managed in the interest of railroads antagonistic to the UP, "but for the benefit of the property as a whole." As Klein comments, with both the OSL and ORN gone "there was no automatic reason for the defectors to return once the Union Pacific" was reorganized. "Grave doubts existed as to whether Humpty Dumpty could ever be put back together again."

A reorganization plan for the ORN was made public August 23, 1895. The plan included a board of directors of 15 members, eight of whom were required by Oregon law to be residents of Oregon. The ORN was sold to the reorganization committee July 9, 1896, at Fairview, OR, for $9,437,250. The new company was incorporated July 16, 1896, in Oregon with a slightly different name: Oregon Railroad (instead of "Railway") & Navigation Co. (ORN). Eight of the directors were from Portland, six from New York, and Miles C. Moore, former Washington territorial governor, from Walla Walla. McNeill was a Portland director and was president and general manager. Alfred S. Heidelbach of New York was the chairman of the board. The charter of the reorganized company projected a line from Moscow toward Lewiston. The new ORN, as Asay writes, "started life as an independent and solvent common carrier, but occupied much the same precarious position as its predecessor during the period between Villard and Union Pacific regimes. The dilemma was essentially identical: should it remain an independent railroad or seek inclusion in a larger system?" The new company continued to favor both the GN and UP and operated passenger cars respectively between Portland and Spokane and Huntington. The WI and ORE were deeded to the new company August 17 and ceased to exist as separate companies. The new company began operation August 18. The Columbia and Palouse Railroad was operated without lease by the ORN, retaining a separate identity until purchased September 6, 1910.[31]

In early 1897 the Oregon Short Line and Utah Northern Railway was sold under foreclosure and reorganized as the Oregon Short Line Railroad Co. The UP receiver said in Omaha, December 5, 1896, "My judgment is that the owners of the Short Line property as reorganized will operate it as an independent property. Though probably in hostility to the interests of the Union Pacific, it will not materially affect the existing tariff relations. It will undoubtedly injuriously affect the Union Pacific if the Ogden and Denver gate is opened to all roads."[32]

F. The Great Northern Railway and the Oregon Railway & Navigation Co.

Beginning in July 1894 ORN receiver McNeill made traffic agreements with the GN for freight from Spokane to Portland, for passenger sleepers and coaches from Spokane to Portland via Pendleton, and opened several interior points, including Colfax, to the GN. There would be no change of cars between Portland and St. Paul or Duluth. Under the new arrangements points on the ORN would be treated as though they were on the main line of the GN. The agreement with the ORN was viewed "to be the consummation of a deep-laid plan formulated by Mr. Hill before he built the Great Northern. He is accredited with shrewdly bringing about the conditions that necessitated a separate receivership and the appointment of his confidential friend O'Neill as receiver.... While on the face of the court order all lines have equal privileges over the O. R. & N., the fact exists that none of them can obtain the benefits without President Hill's sanction." On August 11 a United States District Court in Portland ratified the GN-ORN traffic agreement. Other transcontinental railroads were concerned that O'Neill was determined to make the ORN a paying road and with the GN's agreement, the ORN would become a "scalping road." If so, it would seriously interfere with the rates of other roads. The *Wall Street Journal* reported in September 1894 that at a meeting of passenger agents in Chicago, the GN agent also represented the ORN.[33]

On April 3, 1895, it was reported that the GN was considering running through trains to Portland over the ORN. It had been recently announced that the GN would run through sleeper service over the ORN. There was speculation that the Spokane-Puget Sound line would become a branch because the GN switchback in the Cascades was inferior to the line to Portland. It was estimated that the UP had 85 percent of the business to Portland and Hill was seeking a share. In the spring of 1895 the ORN began extensive improvements in the Palouse, reducing tie spacing, replacing ties, and replacing iron rail with steel and dirt ballast with gravel. This was seen as making more than the necessary improvements. The possibility that the GN would use the ORN tracks to Portland was "quite generally credited as being the cause for fixing up so extensively." The *Review* predicted that the ORN would be absorbed by the Great Northern. "It is just the system Mr. Hill requires, as it would give him entrance to Portland, command of a large part of Oregon, and a distributing system covering a great part of the northwest. He must either buy or build. He can buy as cheaply as he could build, and thereby avoid competition." Not mentioned is the potential of opening all of eastern Washington to the GN.[34]

Hill was asked in Portland in early June whether he had any intention of securing control of the ORN. "I have never had the slightest idea of ever trying to secure control of the O. R. & N. Co." He went on, "As far as the good of the city of Portland is concerned it will be very much better for the O. R. & N. Co. to remain independent of all transcontinental railroads, and out of the possession of all. It is a splendid piece of property, and is admirably situated for all time to come." In January 1896 the ORN in Colfax advertised its through passenger service on the GN and UP to points in the midwest.[35]

In September 1896 ORN receiver McNeill said,

> The traffic contract with Great Northern for exchange of business at Spokane has proved generally satisfactory, but we stand ready to make any contract that we think will be advantageous. I cannot say positively whether we shall make a traffic deal with Northern Pacific. If we do business between us it will be exchanged at Wallula. Although no contract is at present in effect with Northern Pacific we are exchanging business with them to-day.[36]

The Completion of the Lewiston Extension and the Demise of the Spokane & Palouse, 1897–1900

A. Organization and Operation of the S&P

At the beginning of 1897 Whitman County had 638,690 of its 1,363,800 acres in cultivation, a higher proportion and a larger absolute number than another county in eastern Washington. Wheat was on 344,677 acres; oats 19,968; potatoes, 7,932; and corn, 2,210. The statistical report used to prepare the NP 1897 Annual Report showed that the S&P shipped in the year ending June 30, 3,472,300 bushels of wheat, more than any other branch or any main line division. The S&P and the WCR together shipped over 23 percent of the wheat on the NP. In addition the S&P shipped 172,400 bushels of coarse grain, mostly oats. The 1897 wheat crop was the largest on record and the price for wheat was higher than it had been for several years. A year before at Pullman the price was 48 to 50 cents a bushel, in 1897 it was 65 to 67.5 cents. NP President Edwin W. Winter said, in Spokane in late July, there would probably be some car shortage, but they would be able to haul all the wheat in their territory, but not all at once. A week later a "wealthy grain grower" said that the ORN would get 75 percent of the grain business. "The O. R. & N. officials have been indefatigable in getting the business, and they have things in such shape that they are going to get far more than their share in competing territory. I do not understand how it is that the Northern is so slow in this matter.... Last year it was the same." He pointed out that neither farmers nor grain buyers cared whether the grain went through Portland or Tacoma, they were interested in the best rate and treatment. The *Review* reported September 4 that there was no shortage of cars to haul the crop; there was at least four thousand cars available on the NP, GN, and ORN. The Washington wheat crop for 1897 was estimated at 35 million bushels. For the season July 1, 1897, to March 1, 1898, 13,178,600 bushels were shipped from Portland and 7,973,762 from Puget Sound. For the year ending June 30, 1898, the S&P shipped 5,557,600 bushels of wheat, 16.7 percent of the NP total wheat shipments. In other grains the S&P shipped 350,900 bushels, 10.4 percent of the NP total. The S&P had 53,891 passengers and revenues of $77,466 on passengers and baggage. The S&P carried 3.9 percent of the NP's passengers and had 2.2 percent of the revenue.[1]

The 1897 S&P assessment in Spokane County was 90 cents per main line foot, 40 cents for sidetracks, for a total of $121,766; the 1895–96 assessment had been $108,028. The ORN was assessed at one dollar per main line foot. All of the railroad assessments in the county were up substantially; the S&P assessment was sustained by the Board of Equalization. In Whitman County the S&P 1897 assessment was: main track, $5,500 a mile, $469,022; rolling stock, $952 per mile of main track, $81,153; side track at $2,200 per mile, $24,478; buildings, $12,150; a total of $586,803. The Board of Equalization subsequently reduced the assessment of main track mileage to $5,280. This change was requested by the NP; the ORN wanted the assessment reduced to $4,000. The total assessment for the ORN was $1,289,100. In mid-December the NP and Whitman County agreed on nearly $50,000 of back taxes. The railroad would pay by January 1 and when done the company would have all its taxes paid "which is the first time this has occurred in the history of the county."[2]

In late October 1897 a project to connect Genesee and Lewiston by electric railroad was reported. The president of the Spokane Electric Co. estimated that the line would cost about $10,000 a mile. The grades down Hatwai Gulch were 110 feet to the mile (2.1 percent); it was said to be possible to operate an electric railroad on a grade of 300 feet to the mile. The *Tribune* concluded, "If the scheme is properly pushed capital can be found to construct such a road."[3] Apparently capital was not found.

Thomas G. Thomson of Spokane wrote NP General Manager Kendrick February 1, 1898, about building a railroad from Lewiston into the Camas Prairie, unless the NP was opposed. NP President Charles S. Mellen (who had become president September 1) wrote Kendrick that he wished to discourage such a scheme. He was afraid that such a line would induce the ORN to connect with it and that it would then cost the NP considerably more than it was worth as a result of the competition; he wanted to let the matter slumber until Lewiston was reached and then if a further extension was desired the NP would build it. Chief Engineer McHenry responded to Thomson that the NP intended to fully investigate the country. The NP would not be unfriendly to an independent company, but because of blanket rates over a wide area without regard to the cost of construction and operating expenses, an independent line would likely be unprofitable.[4]

On February 14, 1898, the S&P stockholders agreed to convey the S&P to the NP and on March 22 the S&P Trustees voted to do so for one dollar. The resolution noted that the NP owned all the stock of the S&P and substantially all the bonds, and that the two railroads were neither parallel nor competing and formed a continuous main line. The Trustees also agreed that the railroad intended to build from the north boundary of the Indian Reservation to Lewiston, 20.5 miles. On April 11 the Trustees approved an amended map of the definite location across the Indian Reservation, 12.7 miles. McHenry was informed June 7, 1898, that the S&P had authorized branch lines up the Snake and Salmon Rivers.[5]

In early February 1898, as a result of a Chinook wind, the Potlatch Creeks flooded, the S&P bridge to the tramway warehouse at Juliaetta was destroyed along with about two hundred feet of track, and the contractor's camp was flooded. In March it was reported that the ORN's Snake River Valley would build to Lewiston and that CB&Q surveyors were below Kamiah working toward Lewiston. In June 1898 the NP made a reconnaissance from Spangle to Waverly, nine miles, for an extension to a proposed sugar beet factory. The line was not built. The ORN began laying track June 6 on a line from Fairfield on the Tekoa-Spokane line to Waverly. The branch was in service by mid-July. In August three grain warehouses were being erected on the S&P at McCoy. There were also four being erected on the ORN in Oakesdale and vicinity. The 1898 crop was expected to be smaller than the year before; it was anticipated that farmers would hold the crop from the market for better prices. By late September lumber was being secured for platforms for when the warehouses were full.[6]

Operation from the north line of the Indian Reservation to Lewiston, 21.11 miles, began October 1, 1898.[7] The 1898 NP Confidential Report concluded,

> The strategic importance of our position at Lewiston cannot be overestimated, as the [NP] can now feel that it holds the key to all of the valuable business, present or prospective, on the line or within the drainage of the Clearwater, Salmon and Snake, east and south of Lewiston. It is entirely optional with our Company as to whether it will retain its present advantages of position and priority, or will unnecessarily divide this business with the [ORN].
>
> Prior to the completion our line to Lewiston, the [ORN] boats were sometimes thirty days in arrears in the delivery of inbound freight, in striking contrast to the present conditions, when boats frequently arrive without any Lewiston freight.
>
> Our present excellent passenger service has also almost absorbed the passenger business, to the exclusion of the former uncertain boat service, with its midnight connections with trains at Riparia.

After two weeks of S&P mail service to Lewiston a dispute with the government on the terms of service caused the mail to be resumed on the stage route from Uniontown. By May 1899 there was Railroad Post Office car service from Spokane to Lewiston and Rural Route service from Belmont to Farmington and from Pullman Junction to Genesee on the NP.[8]

Following the completion of the Lewiston extension, the NP chartered the Clearwater Short Line (CSL) November 9, 1898. On the 19th the CSL began construction from the extension at Potlatch Junction (later Arrow) up the Clearwater River. The line was completed to Stites, 62.91 miles in May 1900. Also on 19th the CSL began construction from Lapwai Junction (subsequently Joseph and Spalding) up Lapwai Creek toward the Camas Prairie. The line was completed to Grangeville, 66.78 miles, in December 1908. Both of these lines were by 1928 part of the Camas Prairie Railroad, jointly owned and operated by the NP and UP.[9]

On December 12, 1898, a Lewiston bound freight was unable to hold the train on the grade above Kendrick due to frost on the tracks. Nine cars loaded with wood were derailed, six cars were totally wrecked.[10]

The *Review* said December 15 that "It is known that the Northern Pacific management has long been dissatisfied over the distribution of the grain shipment from the Inland Empire. The O. R. & N., though superior management, has captured the bulk of this immensely profitable tonnage. As a result, Portland's wheat exporting business has grown with immense strides in the past two years." Two days later the newspaper rejected Portland's claim that the reason for Portland's dominance was because shipping to Puget Sound was more expensive

This wreck in December 1899 at Kendrick, Idaho, is described on p. 168. Both of the wrecked engines returned to service and were not scrapped until the 1920s. *Photograph 78-917 (mislabeled), Manuscript and Special Collections, Washington State University Library.*

than to Portland. If Portland dominated grain shipments, it was because old time connections were not easily broken and because the ORN had a more extensive feeder system. In mid-December farmers were not selling wheat because of the low price. The warehouses in the Potlatch Valley held more grain than ever before. A large apple crop enabled farmers to hold out for better prices on wheat. By the end of December the price had risen and some wheat was being sold. It was estimated that 70 to 75 percent of the crop was still unsold, "a condition unprecedented in this country at this season of the year."[11]

The fill between two bents of the Cedar Creek trestle four miles south of Garfield washed out January 18, 1899. Passengers transferred at the trestle and freight trains were annulled. The trestle was about 700 feet long and 50 feet high at its highest. Trestle filling had begun in the fall and was nearly done when cold weather stopped operations. Thirty feet of a tunnel through the solid rock at the north end of the trestle remained to be dug. A thaw and rain caused the fill to become a dam which was over topped "with a roar which could be heard for miles." The bridge washed out again on the 20th. This time the damage was worse. Before only fill was washed out, now part of the bridge was gone and it "played havoc with the wagon bridge and demolished a blacksmith shop which stood below the trestle." Temporary repairs were made and trains were running as usual on the 24th. A May 1 report stated that refilling the bridge would begin the following week. The report on the 11th was that the filling was going slowly, but the tunnel had been completed. A new wagon road and bridge were also being built.[12]

On February 21, 1899, the entire property of the S&P was conveyed to the NP. This included all the lines constructed by the S&P (149.80 miles, consisting of Marshall to Belmont, 43.00 miles; Belmont to Genesee, 60.66; Belmont to Farmington, 6.09; and Pullman Junction to Juliaetta, 40.05 (2.5 miles beyond the Juliaetta depot); plus a partially graded road bed of 29.55 miles (upon which the NP constructed 21.09 miles [21.16 in report to ICC] of railroad to Lewiston). The deed for one dollar consideration was filed in Spokane February 28. With this action the S&P became the Palouse and Lewiston (P&L), Genesee and Farmington branches of the Idaho Division.[13]

It was reported April 12, 1899, that the two bridges along the Potlatch River below Juliaetta had washed out. The repair was expected to take several days. "The track is said to be in bad condition along the Potlatch and Clearwater, owing to high water and heavy rains." On the 13th about 9:30 a.m., 13 miles east of Moscow, the bank of a curved grade above Little Bear Creek gave way under the engine, tender, and four cars of the regular south bound freight. "As a result Engineer Matt Rowison and Fireman Fred Lemon are in eternity. The embankment was [undermined by] the stream, a hundred feet below. The cars are wrenched and splintered. At the bottom of the slide lies the dismantled locomotive, half imbedded in the yellow mud. The tender, minus trucks, lies bottom side up beyond the locomotive." On April 21 a trestle just east of Troy gave way beneath a freight train. High waters of spring thaws had loosened several piles and they sunk under the weight of the train. The train was not ditched.[14]

The *Review* noted that because of bad experiences with warehouse companies, "There is a noticeable tendency among farmers to build and control their own warehouses, and it begins to look as if the day is not far distant which farmers will handle their own grain in this way instead of patronizing the large warehouse firms and paying storage charges." A warehouse built by a stock company of farmers at Oakesdale was very successful. Similarly the Farmers' Warehouse Co. of Garfield had two houses there and one each in Elberton and Eden.[15]

In early October 1899 there was a shortage of grain cars in eastern Washington. The ORN was keeping up fairly well, but the NP was furnishing only about a fifth of the cars needed. "The worst effect of this car shortage is that the warehouses are being rapidly filled with wheat and when the rush really commences it will be almost impossible to handle all the grain." At the same time the Great Lakes were congested and freight that would normally go via the lakes was being hauled on an all rail route. In mid-October there were 490,000 bushels of grain stored in the vicinity of Pullman, 45,000 more than the year before. At Pullman the Tacoma Grain Company on the NP tracks had more grain in their warehouse than ever before. The *Railroad Gazette* was quoted November 1, "The reporters who have been so long talking about a 'car famine' are now telling about crowded elevators, and cars waiting to be unloaded. The need is not for more cars, but more facilities for getting the freight out of the cars."[16]

The 1898 wheat crop was the largest crop in regional history and while the price of wheat fell, there was sufficient volume to bring prosperity to the wheat growing areas. In 1899 prices fell further and shipping costs to Britain increased, but nevertheless 1899 joined the two preceding years in helping to increase land prices and bring general prosperity. For the year ending September 30, 1899, the revenue from traffic to and from south of Marshall Junction exceeded 1.3 million dollars.[17]

On December 15, 1899, a train of two engines, 19 cars of rails, and a caboose derailed at the east end of Kendrick yard. Engineers Arthur E. Bain and John A. Ogden, fireman Earl Bradshaw, and brakeman John B. Budge were dead at the scene. Fireman J. E. Peterman was taken to Spokane in grave condition and later died. Bain in engine No. 364 and Ogden in No. 700 began the descent from Vollmer (Troy) at about seven p.m. The rails were covered with snow and ice. Almost immediately there was a call for brakes and the cars were "double clubbed." There was hope that they could stop on level track six miles below Vollmer, but with the air brakes set and clubbed the rails were too slippery and the train sped on, "a streak of fire...illuminated the whole canyon." The train covered 12 miles in less than 10 minutes. Conductor W. E. Galbraith cut the caboose loose from the rest of the train and he and brakeman P. M. Baker were able to bring it to a stop. Brakeman Budge was seen running along the tops of the cars to the rear when about a mile from the wreck the last four cars broke loose of the train and jumped the tracks and carried him down the embankment. The enginemen stayed with the engines, apparently believing they had passed the worst of the curves and would be able to stop before Juliaetta. At the last curve above the Kendrick depot the rails could not hold them and "the engines and the [remaining 15] cars left the track on a right angle, plowing down into the river." All the cars were demolished. "The boilers of the engines are completely stripped of their wheels and cabs and are badly battered. One of the tenders is buried under a mass of rails, while the other is on the opposite side of the Potlatch some 75 feet from where the engines lay. Some idea of the speed at which they were running is shown by the fact that heavy rails were thrown 150 feet ahead of the wreck." The coroner's report was "unavoidable accident." Some railroad men believed that if the curve had been properly ballasted the track would have held. The December 12 flood had broken through the Kendrick curve. By the end of December both engines and the cars went to Spokane for repair. Both engines returned to service.[18]

In January it was reported that the noon NP train was stopping at Pullman for dinner instead of Moscow, "This change was made necessary on account of the condition of the streets in Moscow, it being practically impossible for the trainmen to get from the depot up town and back, there being no bottom to the mud."[19]

Sudden floods occurred throughout the Snake River country January 13, 1900, bringing extensive damage from

If the caption on this photograph is accurate, "Train wreck that caused 1900 flood in Kendrick. The wreck tore up dike track was built on which let high water through to flood town." This wreck is associated with the flood at Kendrick described below. *Photograph 10-9-4, Latah County Historical Society.*

Vollmer to Potlatch Junction. Three cars from a train sent from Kendrick to clear debris from bridges were washed away and a bridge above Juliaetta was taken out. "Railroad men are appalled at the damage done bridges, tracks and grades. For miles and miles along [Potlatch] river there is no vestige of tracks, ties or roadbed." The passenger train from Spokane could only get as far as Vollmer. Telegraph communications south of Vollmer were cut off. "The railroad track just above the mouth of the Potlatch is gone for three-quarters of a mile, and not even the semblance of a grade is left to show where the road ran. This is repeated up the entire line to Juliaetta." A truss bridge on the wye at the mouth of the Potlatch was gone and stranded in the river about 300 feet below the mouth. Above Kendrick six of the 12 miles were badly damaged with a big trestle gone, a mile of track missing, and the river running where the tracks had been. At Kendrick 40 tons of rails from the December wreck were left in the channel and collected drift, forming a dam that then went over the banks that had been undermined in clearing the wreck. On the 14th the NP began meeting the stage from Lewiston at Uniontown on the Genesee branch. By the 17th the trains were going as far as Vollmer. "In some places a new survey will be required, and the road will have to be built as though there had never been any before."[20]

By mid-January there was rumor that the NP would build to avoid the Kendrick hill by going from Cornwall down the Little Potlatch to Juliaetta. The distance from Cornwall to Juliaetta was six miles longer than from Howell to Juliaetta, thus the greater distance and lower elevation at the top would reduce the grade. Others thought the NP should build east from Genesee down Catholic Gulch striking the Clearwater just west of Potlatch Junction, thus avoiding the Potlatch River. Catholic Gulch faces south and was claimed to be free of water and timber. The Potlatch River was more likely to flood each year as the timber along it was cut. By the 19th some 50 men were at work near Kendrick repairing tracks. Another rumor was that the NP would abandon the line and run to Lewiston via Penawawa.

> [I]t does not appear that the repair work is carried on with a zeal which would be noticed if a permanent use of the road was intended. The Northern Pacific has met with heavy losses during the past few months on this line, the

> causes of which it will be impossible to ever remedy. . . . The Potlatch valley is very narrow, with only room for the river. In many places the grade necessarily interferes with the course of the river, and when a freshet comes the track is covered with water. There is nothing to hinder a repetition of the recent floods each spring. No amount of grade can withstand the force of so much water. [Much the same could be said about Bear Creek above Kendrick.]

A few days later a railroad man in Kendrick pointed out that the NP surveyed other routes including the Little Potlatch, which "is too narrow and precipitous, and besides would add nothing to the business of the road." The washout was not an annual occurrence; in the eight years the road had not suffered any great damage. The repair of the damage "is not of a temporary nature, and is being pushed with large crews with haste."[21]

On January 25, 1900, an assistant engineer was instructed to reconstruct the line north of Potlatch Junction to meet the superintendent's forces from the north. He was to commence as early as practicable. "Keep in mind the possibility of adjustment of the line where work can be saved thereby." Labor was being paid $1.50 to $1.75 per day. Construction trains on the Clearwater extension ran out of coal as a result of the destruction.[22]

On January 30, "Five hundred men are now engaged in repairing the road between Vollmer and Lewiston, and the work is being pushed along with all possible dispatch." On February 5 repair work continued, with a pile driver above Kendrick working on a four hundred foot bridge across Bear Creek. All the "white men" had been discharged and replaced by Italians. On February 13 the first train since January 13 arrived at Lewiston to be met by about five hundred people and a band. Heavy rains in late February again cut service to Lewiston. The newly repaired track was "injured," as were two bridges below Juliaetta. At Clyde's spur between Vollmer and Kendrick three long bridges were out of service and a passenger train was stranded at Juliaetta. Between Moscow and Lewiston the grade was very soft and the weight of trains was eroding fills. Almost every day a train derailed. When service to Lewiston was restored is not clear from the reports examined.[23]

General Manager Kendrick decided to relocate the line to the east side of the valley about five miles below Juliaetta at MP 120. In response to the decision McHenry wrote March 10 that the west side grade had washed out three times in the past year. "The cost of the proposed revision will be considerable as it requires the reconstruction of new line not only on the section opposite the channel change but also on the approaches for a considerable distance....In addition a new [county road] would have to be provided on the steep side hills on the slopes above the track." Two days later McHenry estimated the cost of restoring the line and channel improvements at MP 120 was $10,000. The proposed revision of the line would cost at least $20,000. "If the present location is retained, the line will be safe in all ordinary floods but it is quite possible that a similar extraordinary flood may again wash it out; on the other hand this contingency is equally probable on the new location." In late March the NP was working on the west side about a mile on either side of MP 120 on a new raised alignment. Permanent ballast consisting of clay and small rocks about the size of eggs were being used and once set it was like concrete.[24]

By June 1 trains were running on the relocated line below Juliaetta. But "a large force of men" were still at work between Vollmer and Juliaetta. In mid-June a large force was working below the mouth of the Middle Potlatch filling trestle and restoring the river to its original channel. A stone derrick was working seven miles above Kendrick. In the prior four weeks a hundred cars of cattle and about that many of sheep, hogs, and horses had passed through Kendrick. Business had increased such that it necessitated extra freight service and a pusher was kept at Kendrick. At the top of the grade at Howell a 56-foot turntable had been installed because engineers were opposed to running backward on the mountain grade.[25] The June 30, 1900, NP Annual Report noted:

> In January, 1900, an unprecedented flood, resulting from the rapid melting of the deep snow on the tributaries of Potlatch Creek, was experienced on the Palouse-Lewiston line. All of the pile bridges and much of the roadbed were swept away. They have since been reconstructed, truss bridges being provided to take the place of the former pile structures. No effort or expense has been spared to make the new line permanent.

In late May President Mellen's train passed from the ORN at Moscow to the NP via a temporary connection (temporary connections had been used at least twice before). On about June 7 the first car load of cherries for the season from the Snake River went east on the NP. This was two weeks prior to the year before.[26]

The assessed values in Whitman County in 1900 were $14,371,277, a gain of $1,693,114 over 1899. Railroad realty was $1,547,741 and farm, $7,888,095. The total valuation for Colfax was $586,195, Pullman $296,470, Palouse $1,956,700, and Oakesdale $123,625; all other towns were under a hundred thousand. The 1900 census found that Spokane County was the second largest county in the state with a population of 57,542, and Whitman was fourth with 25,360. The Whitman County wheat crop for 1900 was large and several hundred cars of fruit were shipped.[27]

B. Completion of the Lewiston Extension

The NP board of directors authorized the Lewiston extension construction December 10, 1897. Chief Engineer McHenry wrote Division Engineer C. S. Bihler that work on the extension should begin at once. The first thing to do was to finish securing right-of-way. The citizens should be assured that once the right-of-way was secured construction would begin. He preferred that Van Arsdol be put in charge of construction. Van Arsdol would be an aid in securing right-of-way particularly if his employment was contingent on it. McHenry called Bihler's attention to the survey which avoided the river bends along the Potlatch River; it would involve heavy rock work and was unnecessary. The basic message was keep the cost down. McHenry wrote John Vollmer that construction beyond Lewiston and any branches were not contemplated. Bihler confirmed on the 18th that the right of way had been secured and that Van Arsdol would be in charge. He was concerned about bridging the Clearwater before high water in June. He had the iron for five 150-foot Howe truss spans and most of the iron for the draw span including turn table and end lifts from "the old Tacoma draw." He might be able to put the false work in place before the advance of the track. On the 20th McHenry wrote Vollmer objecting to the 90 days allowed for deeds to be put in escrow. Construction would begin once 75 percent of the deeds had been placed in escrow. "Delays are dangerous, and I think it to the best interests of all concerned that this matter be expedited to the best ability of your committee." On the 24th it was reported that a bond had been signed between citizens of Lewiston and the NP; if the railroad was completed by December 1, 1898, the citizens would guarantee the right-of-way. The committee had raised $4,500 of the $5,000 needed for right-of-way purchases. On the 30th McHenry wrote Bihler that the bids should be in McHenry's office by January 10. "Mr. Mellen's previous experience with Engineers' estimates has been some what unfortunate, and he seems to be somewhat skeptical concerning the value of the estimates furnished him.... Accordingly I would like to have you give these construction matters your closest attention, in order to insure due economy and to avoid waste of money in any direction."[28]

On December 29 ORN President A. L. Mohler wrote A. S. Heidelbach, chairman of the ORN board of direc-

This is the original Clearwater River Howe Truss Bridge as it appeared in April 1914. The piers for the new bridge appear white in the image. The swing span 200′ long is second from the right; the remaining 5 spans are each 155′. *Photograph P1985-42.27, Photographer A. W. Stevens, Idaho State Historical Society.*

tors, about the "well defined rumors" that the NP would commence construction into Lewiston. "We hoped this extension would not be found necessary, and especially in view of some of the embarrassing features which we believe will develop and ultimately affect the revenues of both the Northern Pacific and this company." If the line was built the ORN would lose the Riparia to Lewiston boat traffic and it would be necessary to extend a line to Lewiston. But his main concern was grain rates to Tacoma, Seattle, and Portland. The ORN distances and grades to Portland were less than the NP and as a consequence the ORN earnings per ton mile were "much higher" than the NP's. By continuing in the business the NP implied that it could operate profitably at its rate per ton. Prominent members of the legislature had raised questions about the ORN rates and "when our rates are attacked by the Legislature it will be difficult for us to sustain a position for a higher rate per ton mile than our competitors in the same territory." Ultimately the rates to the three ports would be the same.[29]

In early January 1898 President Mellen ruled that repair of the unused line from Juliaetta to the reservation line would be charged to construction; it had suffered a "heavy washout" and ultimately $5,000 was added to the cost of construction south of Juliaetta. In addition, the grading done prior to the termination of construction seven years before had deteriorated. McHenry estimated February 15 that the cost of the extension of 21.14 miles, and two miles of siding, etc., would be $300,000. The contract would be made in the name of the S&P rather than the NP.[30]

In late January the NP bridge crew was putting a temporary bridge across Little Potlatch Creek so that supplies could be moved to where grading would begin. Once the water was low enough the creek would be turned and a permanent bridge installed. In early February the machinery for driving the Clearwater bridge was hauled to the river. Later in the month, track laying was suspended because the depth of the mud in the new grade. "Between two and three hundred men are at work, and the changes in the gangs, occasioned by men having become dissatisfied or 'their allotted time,' keep the tracks lined with men tramping both ways."[31]

A contractor said in late February: "We have now eight camps scattered along the line and 125 teams and 250 men at work throwing dirt on the grade. Material is now at the [Clearwater] bridge site for the pile driver and scow and as soon as the water recedes 400 piles and 350,000 feet of lumber will be boomed down the Potlatch and work will be immediately begun on the foundation for the piers. If the weather does not interfere we will be in Lewiston on schedule time." On March 7 the foreman in charge of construction said grading to the Clearwater River from Juliaetta would be completed by the 20th and trains would be running to the river April 1. Pile-driving on the bridge was being pushed and bridge timbers would be hauled to the site as soon as track was laid. The contractors had 300 men and 75 teams at work. On the same day McHenry wrote the contractor concerned about slow work and the need to increase the force. The contractor responded that the delay had been primarily caused by a five day washout at Ritzville delaying the arrival of equipment, and flooding on the Potlatch had stopped work and caused many of the teams to go home in disgust. To overcome labor shortages wages had been increased to $1.75 per day for men and $3.50 for teams. It had been raining and snowing since the morning before. The letter concluded, "Again assuring you that we will do all in our power to complete our contract on time." Van Arsdol told the *Teller* that men were at work every half mile and the gaps in grading were being rapidly filled. The river would be reached April 10 and then trusses being farmed at Juliaetta would be transported to the river. The piles for three of the eight piers had been driven securely into the river bed, then cribbed and filled with broken rock and riprapped to break the force of the current. It would take about two weeks to get the bridge up once the frame timbers reached the river.[32]

On May 25 McHenry wrote the contractors that while work on the Clearwater bridge had been delayed by high water more could have been done. "I am greatly disappointed to find, that notwithstanding the necessity for haste, that the work has been greatly handicapped and progress retarded by your failure to have an adequate number of scows on hand at the proper time.... The track reached the bridge about the first of the month, and I think the bridge should have been in now; whereas it appears from your message that you have not as yet erected a single span." He then reminded that "A contractors reputation is part of his capital." On the same day Bihler wrote McHenry telling him that all the piers were in except No. 4, which had been washed out. Pile drivers would be used at both ends of the bridge to put in the false work as soon as the river permitted. The river had been high almost the whole time since February. They should be able to cross the river on false work by the middle of June. Grading on the south side of the river should be completed by the time the track crossed the river.[33]

By June 17 only two miles of track had been surfaced. Grading was continuing along the south side of the Clearwater, "which includes some high precipices of rock, besides a tough dirt." By July 1 one span of the Clearwater bridge been laid and the piers were ready for

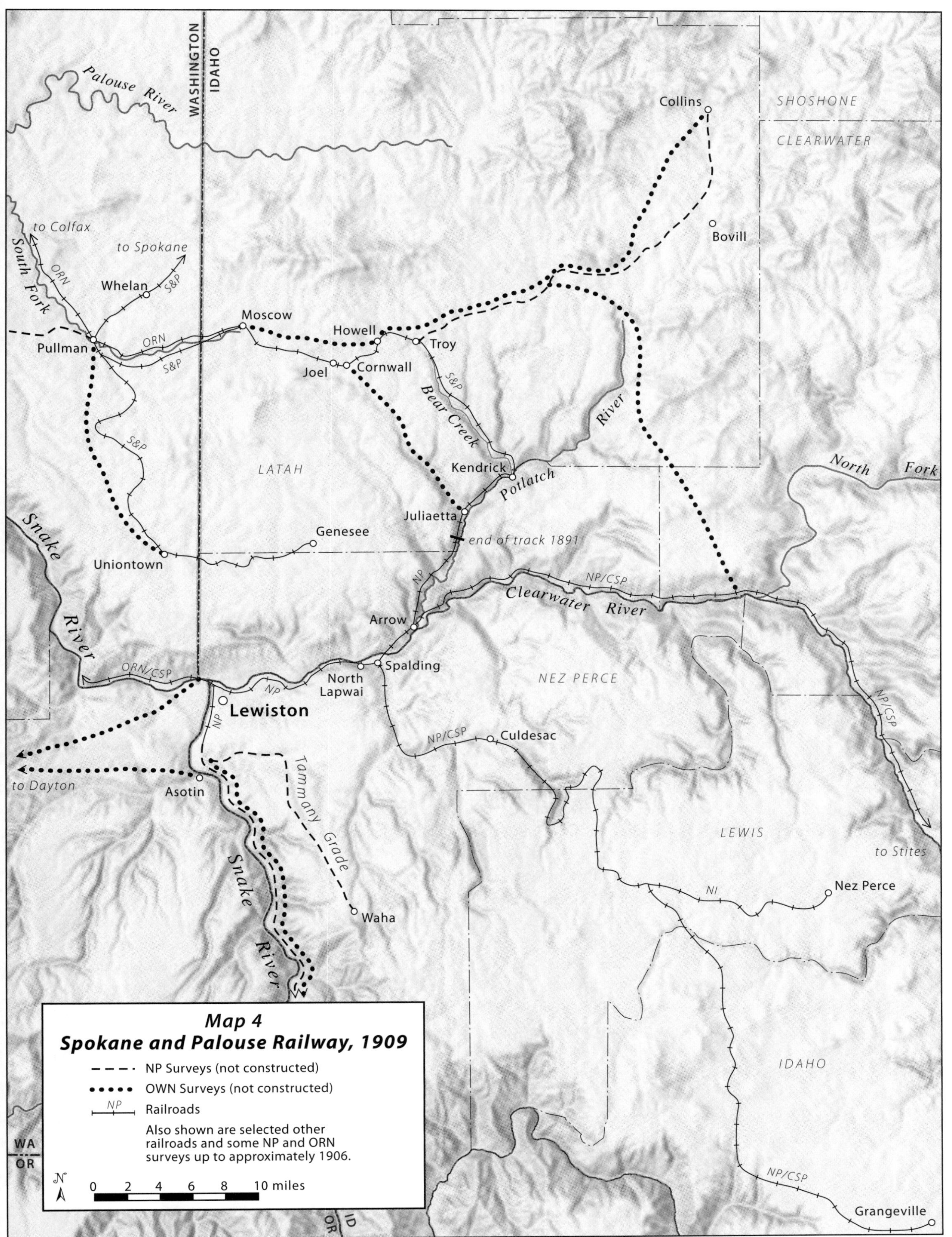

Primary source NP map 1906, MHS 132.1.4.4., traced by Philip Beach and drawn by Chelsea Feeney, www.cmcfeeney.com.

others. The 1898 NP Annual Report states that the first train crossed the Clearwater bridge July 18. Van Arsdol estimated that it would take about 10 days to have the track into Lewiston. In Lewiston work on the station and roundhouse would begin soon.[34]

On July 28 McHenry was still unhappy with the rate of progress; "in future work we will endeavor to make such arrangements as to prevent failures of this kind." He instructed Bihler to have the surfacing done closely behind the track laying, saying "we will have to pay enough to keep a full force." Bihler responded that he had been unable to get the contractor to expedite his work. Because of harvest there was great difficulty in getting workers and those available were unreliable and could not be held on the work. He was having the same difficulty with NP gangs. The track was in running order nearly to the Clearwater crossing. On August 3 General Traffic Manager J. M. Hannaford enquired whether the line would be ready to take carloads of green fruit and vegetables which were approaching harvest. McHenry responded that the tracks were within five miles of Lewiston and probably surfaced to North Lapwai. Construction trains in conjunction with the mixed train which left Pullman Junction at 6 p.m., arriving Juliaetta at 9:05 p.m. and leaving Juliaetta at 5:40 a.m., arriving Pullman Junction at 8:45 a.m., could accommodate the traffic. He would contact Bihler to run extra trains if necessary. The first carload of freight reached Lewiston the 11th. Construction continued to be delayed by a shortage of workers. There were less than 70 employed although several hundred had been brought from Spokane.[35]

According to the NP annual report track was laid into Lewiston August 23, 1898, and regular trains operated September 11. In early September the Lewiston depot and turntable were not completed. The Spokane Chamber of Commerce was planning a September 8 excursion to Lewiston. They would have to use sleeping cars because of a shortage of hotel rooms in Lewiston. The successful excursion included a visit to Vineland (later Clarkston) across the Snake River in Washington. The Lewiston *Tribune* reported that at 7:40 a.m., September 20, 1898, engineer Gus Bowman received the signal from conductor Bill Hale to open the throttle of engine 840 for the first regular passenger train to depart the Lewiston depot for Spokane. A large crowd was at the depot following three days of "the railroad festival." The train consisted of the engine, a combination mail and express car, and a first class coach. Bowman recalled arriving at Spokane at 2:05 p.m. McHenry wrote Bihler, October 1, saying he had set that date as the official date the line was turned over to the operating department. He was not informed that the extension was turned over to the operating department September 11 as no authority had been received from him. Operation prior to the 1st was to be charged to the construction department. Also on the 1st Kendrick issued a circular announcing that the extension, 23.22 miles from Juliaetta to Lewiston, had been completed and turned over that day to the operating department; it would be operated as a portion of the Idaho Division. The stations and mileage from Marshall Junction were Potlatch Junction, 122.52; North Lapwai, 128.02; Lewiston Depot, 137.51; and End of Track, 138.24.[36]

On September 12 McHenry wrote L. A. Porter of Lewiston that he had been informed that the ORN had purchased a river bank warehouse in Lewiston. The warehouse had been independent, and its purchase by the ORN would handicap the company. He asked Porter to make a confidential inquiry. He warned that if satisfactory arrangements were not possible in Lewiston the NP would divert as much wheat as possible to Lapwai and would be compelled to extend its line to Asotin. Porter responded on the 20th. His understanding was that the warehouse remained independent and the NP could extend a track to it. The warehouse had been offered to Van Arsdol three or four years earlier and a lease had been consummated. J. P. Vollmer, the NP's agent in Lewiston, held a quarter interest in the warehouse and had signed the lease to the ORN. Porter recommended that the NP extend its line to the Asotin ferry and acquire another piece of land in Lewiston for a warehouse and stockyard. McHenry sent Porter's letter on to Hannaford. Mellen had authorized the purchase of the land recommended by Porter and the city would give the NP frontage for a warehouse. "You will note how closely Mr. Vollmer protects our interests; his zeal in this matter is as great as it ever was. If he has sold his interest to the O. R. & N., without protecting Northern Pacific interests, or notifying you, I should consider it quite inexcusable." October 10 Hannaford wrote McHenry that Vollmer said that he had not signed the ORN lease and it was presented to him after a majority of the ownership of the warehouse had agreed to it. Hannaford was disposed to believe Vollmer, but "I have not felt at any time that Mr. Vollmer would do a great deal for this company unless there was a personal gain in it…but I have not in any instance found where he worked against us in any way, and would not want to think that he neglected our interests in this matter." McHenry responded on the 13th, "I am afraid that I am so prejudiced in the case of Mr. Vollmer, that I am unable to see any good in this gentleman, and fear that my case is incurable."[37]

Appendix: NP Track Laying Record, Juliaetta to Lewiston, 1898

Date	Approximate Distance from Marshall.	Sources and Notes
March 22	Beginning of track laying, north boundary of Nez Perce Indian Reservation, mile 117.5, to MP 119.	1899 Profile.
April	To Potlatch Junction, mile 123.4.	1899 Profile.
May	To MP 126, north end of Clearwater Bridge.	1899 Profile.
July	Track laid across Clearwater Bridge July 18 and by end of July to mile 131.5.	1899 Profile. First train crossed Clearwater Bridge July 18 (NP Annual Report, 1898; LT 7/22/98, 1, has the 20th).
August 19	Reached site of original Lewiston depot, mile 137.7.	1899 Profile.
September 12	Track laying resumed, reached mile 138.25.	1899 Profile.
December 5 & 6	Track laying resumed, reached end of track mile 138.4.	1899 Profile.

The Northern Pacific, James J. Hill, and E. H. Harriman and the Snake River Country, 1897–1901

This and the four following chapters continue the major railroads' attempts to regulate their competition in the Snake River country. This and the next chapter focus on the actions of the principal actors: NP President Charles Mellen, succeeded by Howard Elliott; GN President James J. Hill; UP President Edward H. Harriman; and ORN President A. L. Mohler. Their rivalry was national, beginning in eastern Washington. Chapters XVII and XVIII focus on the four railroads' actions on the ground. Chapter XIX examines new railroad ventures in the Palouse. One of these was a secret expansion of the UP and the other became a vehicle for the GN to enter the Palouse. In the 1890s Hill's involvement in the affairs of the NP became extensive and lasted the remainder of his life. This book focuses on his involvement in the Snake River country, a small part of the Hill/GN relationship with the NP.[1]

Both the NP and ORN emerged from receivership in 1896. The NP was controlled by a voting trust organized by J. P. Morgan & Co. While Hill and associates owned a great deal of NP stock, their influence was limited by the Morgan company. The OSL, which leased the ORN, remained in receivership, as did the UP. On February 15, 1897, the NP, GN, J. P. Morgan & Co., and Kuhn, Loeb & Co. agreed that the NP and GN would each acquire one-fourth of the preferred stock of the ORN. The remaining half would be held in trust by the finance companies for the reorganized UP/OSL. The contract stated the NP and GN desired that the ORN have a full and ample opportunity, without preference, to secure the freight and passenger business of the NP, GN, OSL, and UP on terms equitable to all five companies. The hope was that conflicts among the NP, GN, and ORN would be settled before the UP and OSL acquired the stock held for them. NP Chairman Edward D. Adams wrote NP President Edwin W. Winter that the agreement endeavored to protect the NP Portland business, to prevent encroachments by the Burlington, to prevent a UP-GN line between Seattle and Portland, and to guard against the Washington & Columbia River Railroad (WCR, former OWT) coming under the control of adverse interests.[2]

The OSL emerged from receivership in March independent of the UP. In June the OSL declared the Ogden gateway open to all. Formerly the UP had determined the rates and allotments and the OSL was not permitted to interchange business with other roads. The UP retaliated by sending freight via Southern Pacific to Portland rather than via OSL and ORN, and refused to agree to a division of rates made to the OSL and ORN by other railroads. By mid-October the difficulties between the UP and OSL were worked out and with the ORN a few days later.[3]

Charles E. Perkins, the Burlington president, wrote in 1897, "The key to the Pacific Railroad situation is the control of the Oregon Short Line. Anyone owning the majority of its stock can do more to keep the peace west of the Missouri River than all other influences put together." The ORN gave the OSL and GN access to Portland. The GN and the NP wanted control, or failing that they wanted a neutral ORN. The UP wanted a neutral ORN only if it did not control the OSL. It was announced that on April 18 the ORN would commence two transcontinental trains from Portland. One would connect with the UP and the other with the GN; before there was only a UP transcontinental train.[4]

By spring 1897 the NP operated with too much independence in Hill's view and he pushed for an NP "management 'cordial and sympathetic' to him personally—a new aggressive president, a strong general manager, and three directors of his nomination." In early April Hill backed Daniel S. Lamont to replace Edwin W. Winter as NP president. But Morgan wanted Lamont in New York to handle corporate and financial affairs. On April 29, 1897, Winter resigned as NP president effective on the appointment of a successor. Winter's authorized statement said "his resignation was tendered in view of the recent acquisition of a considerable minority interest in the property by parties of whose cooperation he is not assured, and that without such assurance he is unwilling to continue his administration." In another place Winter was quoted as saying,

> I have tendered my resignation because Mr. Hill and his

> associates have acquired an amount of the capital stock which combined with the friendly holdings in Europe, entitles him to have a strong voice in Northern Pacific affairs. My action was entirely voluntary, and I trust the best of personal feelings exists between Mr. Hill and myself. I admire his ability and have regarded him as a friend for almost as many years as I have been in the railway service, but he could not name a sum that would induce me to work under his direction.

J. P. Morgan & Co. issued a statement that they had assured Winter "that if he remained with the property he should continue to have our entire confidence and fullest support, but for the reason given by him and none other he has tendered his resignation." Some thought that Winter wanted to make more NP improvements and extensions than Hill would tolerate. The *Review* commented, "Although Mr. Hill continues to state that he 'does not own a share of Northern Pacific stock.' No one doubts now that he has achieved the end for which he has been striving for the past three years, and that the Great Northern and the Northern Pacific will henceforth be operated substantially as one great system."[5]

A. L. Mohler was appointed ORN vice president and manager May 17, 1897. Hill had lost confidence in Edwin McNeill. Mohler succeeded McNeill as president, September 3. McNeill had been both manager and president and was credited as an able railroad executive. Mohler had been with the GN and predecessor Manitoba from October 1882 to July 1894. His advent on the ORN was hailed as evidence of Great Northern control. Mohler said the independent policy of McNeill would be continued. With Mohler as ORN president, Alfred S. Heidelbach as chairman of the board and W. L. Bull as chairman of the executive committee, all friends, Hill had reason to believe agreement with the ORN was in sight.[6]

On July 27 Hill wrote a cordial letter to NP Chairman Adams, which in part said, "Our respective interests in the O. R. & N. are sufficiently large to warrant us in placing them in a position to transact their business on advantageous terms, to themselves as well as to both our Companies." As to the division of business between the NP and GN: "I am always willing that any business which both Companies can do, and which is fairly tributary to both, shall be equally divided, no matter where the business may be, and this rule certainly should hold good in all business to and from the O. R. & N."[7]

On August 5 the ORN and NP signed the "Portland Protocol" agreeing to avoid competitive building and to take no action without consultation which impaired the other's revenues. The NP had a right to complete its Lewiston extension (which was expressly agreed to by the ORN November 1) and neither was to acquire the WCR without consultation. The NP would seek to prevent the WCR from cutting or manipulating rates on business competitive with the ORN. The ORN would interchange eastbound business at Wallula rather than Spokane. The NP would abandon operation of the Farmington branch if it were practicable to do so. In northern Idaho the NP would abandon the narrow gauge line between Mission and Wallace and the ORN would abandon the washed out line between Wallace and Mullan. Before the end of the year both lines were abandoned. The ORN contended that it had a priority of right to occupy the country, but "the history of railroad development does not contain a precedent for any such argument."[8]

Mohler wrote Heidelbach that he approved of the "Portland Protocol." He preferred that the NP not build to Lewiston, but the NP had invested a great deal of money. He thought the NP would exercise power over the WCR, but the line properly belonged to the ORN. If there was harmony between the NP and ORN, the NP would not object to the ORN taking over the WCR, given its financial stake in the ORN. Mohler wrote Hill August 13 that the situation of the ORN was good and he was reducing the curvature on the line from Portland to The Dalles. He concluded in part, "[I] trust that my action so far has not been disappointing but is meeting with your full approval." Jacob H. Schiff of Kuhn, Loeb & Co., wrote Hill August 17 that he thought the NP should not have two members on the ORN board and that the GN should not be represented either directly or indirectly. Heidelbach and Bull had agreed to represent GN interests on the ORN board.[9]

On August 12, 1897, Charles S. Mellen, second vice president of the New Haven, and Morgan's choice, not Hill's, was elected president and director of the NP effective September 1. Lamont was elected vice president. Hill did not get his way regarding the general manager nor the three directors. Charles H. Coster of the Morgan company, and a NP board member, said the appointments were a decisive indication that the NP would "continue to be run as an absolutely independent property." Coster added that friendly relations between the NP and GN would continue but "each property must be allowed to stand on its own merits."[10]

In Spokane on September 16, Hill was asked "whether or not you and your associates exercise a controlling influence in the Northern Pacific affairs." Hill responded that he had been asked the same question a few weeks before. "I can't see why I should be bothered with it again. I am not an officer of the Northern Pacific, never have been and do not expect to be. I have all I can do to take of the Great Northern interests in my charge." A few days later Mellen was in Spokane. The reporter got less information from Mellen than Hill; the headline for the interview read: "Not Like Mr. Hill; President Mellen Does Not Joke Like the Other One."[11]

The ORN traffic manager wrote Mohler October 1 that the NP was loading wheat on the main track of the Farmington branch, avoiding warehouse charges and saving the owners of the grain as much as three cents a sack. "From a traffic standpoint the practice is irregular and unusual, and is unquestionably a violation of spirit of the President's protocol." If this were to spread it would "prove disastrous to investments already made in warehouses at regular stations," Mohler wrote Mellen, who responded that the August agreement contemplated the abandonment of the Farmington branch. "Surely you cannot object to the use of this line as a side track if we should abandon it as a main line and I do not see wherein there should be any difference to you." Mohler responded that the purpose of the agreement was to conserve revenue and not give legislatures an opportunity to intervene. The NP was informed on the 20th that the ORN was paying ferry charges on wheat from the Washington side of the Columbia River to the Oregon side. Mellen requested Mohler in accordance with the August 5 agreement to "cease your efforts to divert our local trade from its legitimate routes to destinations by our own lines." He went on to say, "We construe the contract... as requiring you 'to avoid taking any action against the other which will impair the revenues of either of the companies.'" Mohler responded suggesting the Mellen did not understand the contract; the provision of the contract pertained to only new business and "this company does not consider its present action any violation of the agreement, as the practice has been in vogue for years." Mellen responded, "After being so positively assured we do not know what we are talking about, we appreciate the uselessness of further pursuing this subject."[12]

On July 1, 1897, the Union Pacific Railroad Company (UP) was incorporated in anticipation of the foreclosure sale of the Union Pacific Railway. The new company purchased the latter in November and took possession February 1, 1898. Beginning in October 1897 the UP reorganization committee began buying OSL stock and by December had over a third of the capital stock of the reorganized OSL. Coster wired Mellen January 28, 1898, that Schiff of Kuhn, Loeb & Co. would, under the contract, deliver ORN preferred held by the GN and NP to the UP at cost. Mellen responded that if the NP got trackage rights between Wallula and Portland, and La Crosse and Connell, with the right to build from Pullman to La Crosse, keeping far enough south of the ORN to avoid competition and parallel lines would be exchanged, he would recommend Schiff's desires with respect to the stock. In April 1898 three UP representatives replaced Morgan representatives on the OSL board. The OSL owned a majority of the ORN common stock, but the UP, NP, and GN jointly owned a controlling interest in the preferred stock. Edward Henry Harriman was elected December 6, 1897, to the first board of directors of the reorganized UP and on May 23, 1898, elected chairman of the UP executive committee. Harriman convinced the UP Board to approve an extensive improvement program which included the ORN, once the UP achieved control. In October 1898 the UP gained control of the OSL board of directors and Harriman was elected to that board.[13]

The ORN announced in early February 1898 that because the NP was resuming construction to Lewiston it would build to Lewiston on the north bank of the Snake River. On the 19th NP Chief Engineer Edwin H. McHenry wrote Mellen that he learned that the ORN was "looking up their old location for a projected extension between Pullman and Genesee.... We derive a large amount of profitable business from this section, and it is easily accessible to the O. R. & N. by the construction of a low cost line."[14]

Through the Northwestern Improvement Co., the NP on February 17, 1898, purchased from C. B. Wright the stock and bonds of the Washington & Columbia River Railway (WCR, formerly Oregon & Washington Territory Railroad). Wright in a report from Philadelphia on the 21st said "the Northern Pacific has absolute control of the road." The NP June 30, 1898, annual report said the WCR, 162.73 miles, in Washington and Oregon had been purchased for $592,316. The purchase included $3,000,000 in stock and $2,245,000 par value bonds. While WCR continued to operate independently, it was quickly integrated with the NP with formal control occurring in 1907.[15]

On the same day as the purchase of the WCR, Mellen wrote board chairman Adams that the WCR should belong to the ORN and that the ORN should have all the lines south and west of the Snake River, and the NP the lines north and east. The NP and GN should have trackage over the ORN from Wallula to Portland, and the GN over the NP from Spokane to Wallula. The NP and the UP should jointly lease the ORN with the latter operating the ORN lines to Portland and south of the Snake River. He thought all of this should be done before the UP regained control of the OSL and thus the

ORN. If necessary the UP could have a traffic contract for reaching Puget Sound. The next day Mellen wrote Hill asking, "Can we not work together in this matter, making our preferred stock a much better investment than at present and getting rid of the Union Pacific as a disturbing element in Spokane and in the Coeur d'Alene and Palouse Countries?" On the 18th Bull wrote Hill that Mellen's letter to Adams had been read at the ORN executive committee the day before. He concluded, "Perhaps under these conditions the arrangement suggested by Mr. Mellen is as favorable as any for which we could hope."[16] Aside from the issues of whether the companies involved would agree to the proposal and whether it would be found legal, this was probably the simplest proposal in the long line of proposals for governance of competition among the railroads in the Snake River Country.

Mellen wrote Mohler March 17, 1898, asking whether the ORN would "consider the sale to us of your line from Connell to La Crosse, or a lease of the same for a term of years?" This letter is examined in chapter XVII on the Columbia & Palouse Railroad and the La Crosse Gateway. Two days later Mellen wrote Mohler, "Please do not forget you are going to make me a trackage proposition, for our handling our trains by our own power between Wallula and the Terminal Company's lines in Portland." Regarding the latter, Mohler responded, "Unless something develops different from what occurs to me now, for the best interests of all concerned I am inclined to recommend such an arrangement as you propose."[17] Nothing came of either request.

Beginning in 1898 both the NP and the ORN began chartering competitive railroads. The first of these, March 3, 1898, was the ORN's Snake River Valley Railroad Company (SRV), a joint venture with the GN, with a supplement December 27, projected nine lines in the Snake River country. Six were in the Palouse region. Surveying and some right-of-way was secured, but only the line between Wallula and Lewiston was ultimately built.[18]

In March 1898 the NP had reports of ORN extensive surveying in the Palouse, Camas Prairie, and Potlatch. Mellen wrote Coster that he had received a report that the SRV was surveying "right through our station grounds in Lewiston." The stated object of the SRV was from Umatilla via Snake River to Lewiston and Huntington, but "the real object is simply the construction of a line from Riparia to Lewiston to tap country at present served by our line." The same day Coster wrote Bull, chairman of the ORN's executive committee, of reports the ORN had surveying parties on the Snake River between Riparia and Lewiston, violating the Portland protocol. Coster reminded Bull he had said he had no knowledge whatever of any authority given Mohler to make such surveys. He referred to a message from Mohler on the 19th that the surveys were "confined solely to legal and statute requirements." Coster contended that the rights under the surveys had expired at least five years earlier. Mellen offered to share the purchase of the WCR with the ORN, "that is certainly ignored in the present action of President Mohler." Coster concluded, "From my standpoint as a [ORN] Director...in view of the statements above reported to me I can only consider this action as an aggression against the Northern Pacific." Bull wrote Adams on the 28th that Mohler was greatly disturbed by the NP's purchase of the WCR which was a violation of the Portland agreement. Mohler acted to protect the existing rights of the ORN.[19]

Hill wrote Adams March 28 and Bull April 4 essentially the same letter. Using the latter letter as the example, Hill wrote that Adams "apparently overlooks the fact that the Northern Pacific cannot legally acquire the parallel or competing lines of the Navigation Company North of the Snake River; and...such move would be strongly resented by the people of Portland and of the State of Oregon." No additional construction was necessary, the ORN "can be best used as an independent railway serving all the interests desiring to use its lines which may connect with it either at the Huntington gateway or by the Spokane gateway. The Great Northern must have access to the Palouse country and the Walla Walla country, either by the lines of the Navigation Company or of the Northern Pacific Company, on fair and equal terms, or it would be compelled to build a line of its own into that country." The present arrangement between the GN and ORN made construction unnecessary. It was not reasonable to require the NP to share the business of its Palouse lines given that the GN had no investment in the NP lines (how this observation fits with Hill's threats is unclear). He also did not think that even if the UP achieved control of the ORN that it would serve their interest to break the arrangement with the GN. The UP, NP, and ORN were overcapitalized "to a degree that is exceedingly top-heavy, cannot afford in my opinion to drive the Great Northern into a position where it would be compelled to build any lines South of Spokane Falls. A comparatively small investment, not to exceed $6,000,000, at the outside, would give the Great Northern an independent connection from its present line West of Spokane Falls into Portland, and a line into the Palouse and Walla Walla country."[20] This is representative of Hill's often repeated position: the GN has a right to have access to the territory south of Spokane, on "fair and equitable terms" and "fair and equal conditions," on railroad lines that the GN had no investment in.

Engine NP No. 673 is probably about to leave Lewiston's first depot with train No. 10 for Spokane. The engine was originally built in 1889 for the Oregon & Washington Territory Railroad, as their No. 6. *Photograph 032521, Bancroft Library, University of California, Berkeley.*

Adams wrote Hill, March 31, that Mohler's response to Mellen's February 17 letter with respect to the WCR was "that he did not consider it a desirable line for the Navigation Company to own" and he had been advised by counsel that the ORN could not safely operate the WCR "under the statutes of Washington and the general laws." Mohler recommended to his executive committee that the NP be granted trackage from Wallula to Portland, but the committee declined to take up any of Mellen's suggestions. Adams wrote, "I am anxious to do all possible to ensure the maintenance of close and harmonious relations between the two companies, as contemplated under the Portland protocol of last August. For the purpose of cultivating such conditions I have arranged for Mr. Mellen to accompany me with Mr. Mohler over the Navigation system in May."[21]

On May 16 Adams wrote Mellen that Bull had repeatedly assured him that Mohler had not requested nor been given any authority by the UP executive committee for construction. The same day McHenry telegraphed Mellen, "O. R. & N. Clearwater survey east of Potlatch river is distinctly aggressive. If authorized will organize additional party and locate lines to Colfax and La Crosse; also from Clyde [on the WCR's Pleasant View line in Walla Walla County] east to Pomeroy and beyond." Mellen telegraphed Adams, "Have authorized few surveys in O. R. & N. territory for information purposes myself. Seems to me desirable both parties should be posted as to best places to build in each other's territory. Information should not be one-sided."[22]

Mellen June 10 wrote Bull thanking him for letting him read Mohler's and Hill's letters because they revealed serious misunderstandings of Mellen's actions. Mellen said of Hill,

> I supposed I was acting in full accord with him and his approval. It was never my thought that we should acquire any portion of the O. R. & N. system, and as a result exclude Mr. Hill from doing business with the same. On the contrary it was my intention, had we made the territorial division north of the Snake River, to have admitted the Great Northern System to a traffic arrangement with all of our territory south of Spokane, including not only the lines we should acquire from the O. R. & N. but also the balance of the Northern Pacific System's lines in that territory.
>
> ...I regret that Mr. Mohler has appeared to understand

> the action of the Northern Pacific as inimical to him or his company's interests, and have sent his surveying parties out to cause us the trouble they have in connection with our Lewiston Extension and in other portions of our territory; and further that I have felt obliged as a result of his action to send our own surveyors out to run lines that are in the nature of reprisals.
>
> I shall be only too glad to give an order to stop the whole business and agree with you regarding all construction in territory whether the interests of your company is in any degree affected, and will make that agreement in writing that there may be no misunderstanding if it is your desire.[23]

Mellen telegraphed Coster June 29 from Portland that UP President Horace G. Burt and Harriman had requested an appointment the next day. Mellen repeated what he wrote Coster the preceding January in regard to the ORN stock, that if his position then was met, "I should be in favor of conceding Mr. Schiff's desires regarding price Navigation stock. Situation is one that must be dealt with comprehensively and I have no faith to believe it can be adjusted with present officials O. R. & N. but believe it could be with present officials U. P. Am surprised at Hill's disposition to concede what Schiff asks for he stated to me most positively he would not turn in his stock at such price; indeed has said he did not propose let his half go at all." Coster responded July 1: "Have seen Schiff. Strictly confidential. He says whatever agreed upon by you, Burt and Hill, can be carried out. Cannot you three make a definite agreement covering all points involved?" Mellen responded: "Had long interview with Burt and Harriman yesterday. Have greatest confidence to believe can agree with them on all points.... Have no idea I shall be able agree with Hill but will make attempt and do my best.... I believe they were both agreeably impressed with our fairness, and I would like you to see Mr. Harriman...and see whether or not I deceive myself in this regard." Mellen was impressed by the prospect that the UP would take over direct management of the OSL and ORN, "for this will eliminate Mr. Mohler and his satellites, who are nothing but creatures of Mr. Hill. It will also eliminate Mr. Hill from further connection with that property, and with fair-minded, unprejudiced men to deal with we should secure what is equitable for us in that territory and be willing to give the Union Pacific all it requires." Mellen warned Coster not to agree to "the disposition of any portion of our Navigation stock as is desired by Mr. Schiff. The end sought...is to perpetuate the independent management of the Navigation Company under Mr. Mohler and make the whole property, with a small investment of capital, subservient absolutely to the Great Northern Railway and Mr. Hill, as is the situation at the present time." Hill plainly saw that he would lose control of the ORN if Harriman and Burt had their way. If Schiff were to succeed he would be pulling Hill's chestnuts out the fire and "perpetuating a condition of affairs well-nigh intolerable, for we have no influence whatever in the management of the Navigation property, and I do not well see how it could be operated more to our detriment than has been the case since I have been connected with the Northern Pacific... I want to see the Union Pacific control the property."[24]

At the end of June Bull and Mellen agreed to discontinue surveys to reduce friction. On July 1 Bull wrote Hill that NP surveyors were not very prompt about withdrawing and were in territory not naturally connected to the NP and hitherto exclusively belonging to the ORN. "So far as we can judge it is intended for use in an argument with us regarding trackage rights over our line between Pullman and Connell." On the 2nd Hill wrote Bull that he had talked to Coster the day before about Mellen's failure to take his engineers out of the field. Coster suggested that there be a meeting of the parties, "hope we will be able to secure reasonable and fair conditions for all concerned, and that the Navigation Co. will be placed in a position where it will have no doubt or anxiety as to the protection of its territory, and all the other parties will be protected in their respective interests." In mid-June Mellen had given McHenry verbal orders to cease NP surveys. McHenry responded August 15, "The whole matter may be summed up by saying that our parties were not started in the field until long after the advent of the O. R. & N. parties and the surveys were abandoned as it was practicable to get orders to them. No other parties have been sent out, nor surveys made in that region."[25]

Hill in a letter to NP Vice President Lamont July 17, 1898, after a long list of complaints about Mellen, concluded: "All these things force me to the conclusion that Mellen, whatever ability or experience he has as a railroad traffic man and accountant, has no business judgment more than a child. He appears to have lost his head completely, and is unfit to occupy the position he does at the head of a corporation representing so large a capital." Mohler and Mellen had conferred in Hill's office where he urged them to use the existing lines for business rather than duplicate mileage in a country that was over built. Both lines were capitalized in excess of what the courts were likely to allow them to earn money on.

> Today the Northern Pacific is being attacked at Spokane and almost every town in eastern Washington to largely reduce its rates...and in the face of this, its president has had several parties out running lines for new construction

> and in his trips at least gives the impression that the company is ambitious to take into its system lines that have no value and from their inception were uncalled for.... If in place of showing such an anxiety to build railways, a policy was adopted and strictly adhered to by which the public would understand once and for all that railways could not be built and maintained unless they paid at least a reasonable return on the money invested...I would abandon a few of the lines that never have been of value to the company and never will be...it would go farther than anything else to change the tone and attitude of the public towards the railway companies.[26]

On July 22 Harriman wrote Burt that, "The most important matter we now have before us is the closing of the purchase of the [ORN] Preferred Stock for this company, and obtaining absolute control of that property." But some way had to be found to assure the GN and NP access to Portland over the ORN. "My opinion is that any pure and simple trackage arrangement will prove unsatisfactory in the future."[27]

In the NP files is a "Memorandum For Proposed Agreement" between ORN and NP dated August 6, 1898. There is also September and October proposals plus an undated proposal. The August proposal gave the NP trackage from Wallula to Portland and Pullman to La Crosse. The ORN would sell to the NP the lines between Pullman and Moscow and between La Crosse and Connell. The ORN would have trackage from La Crosse to Wallula. The NP would sell the WCR to the ORN. Trackage did not include local business. It also provided that "no new lines to be built by either road in the territory of the other, without conference and agreement first." The September proposal is similar. The October proposal's most radical change was that the NP would sell the WCR's 161 miles to the UP for the same number of miles north of the Snake River, excluding the lines in the Coeur d'Alene country. The NP did not want trackage from Wallula to Portland unless it included local business. The four memoranda show attempts by Mellen (and Harriman?) to find an agreement which would not be harmful to either the NP or the ORN. Because of the interlacing of actual and potential lines and Hill's demands, agreement would have been difficult even if the parties trusted each other. Eventually agreement would be reached, but not along the lines suggested here.[28]

Coster wrote Mellen, September 26, that in view of the ORN's aggressive attitude he and Adams thought it desirable that the NP physically occupy Lolo Pass "with the least possible delay.... I urge that we do not allow our Great Northern-Union Pacific-Short Line-Navigation friends to get ahead of us in this matter." Three days later Mellen responded that the NP could effectively occupy Lolo Pass with a relatively low cost line of 75 miles east from Lewiston which "would be unquestionably of large profit....Our situation in Eastern Washington and Idaho is a very precarious one, owing to the length of our line to the Coast. We need a short cut across from Pullman." Hill ordered a reduction in the GN wheat rates, which would cause a reduction the whole length of the Washington Central and if carried to Spokane would affect the ORN and the S&P. "This will cause a loss to our line of not less than $100,000 per annum, and as Mr. Hill handles comparatively none of this business, it will affect him but little if any." Mellen had heard that Hill would pursue this policy until the NP was tractable, and bring the common stock down to where he could buy control. "[W]e cannot successfully cope with this policy, unless permitted to construct some cut-offs and extensions remedying original defects....We must force our way out regardless of what others do. Our business is much too valuable to surrender it.... We have nothing to fear from extensions of the O. R. & N. We can afford to ignore that Company if we are permitted to help ourselves."[29]

Beginning in late September letters were exchanged between Hill and J. P. Morgan Co. Hill complained about the NP's independence from Hill's influence: ending of the voting trust was too slow, the NP should not have acquired the WCR, and the NP was invading ORN territory. Coster responded that Hill was wrong in some of his facts: Hill exaggerated the actions of the NP, and the NP had justifiable complaints against the GN, and Hill and others signed an April 2, 1896, London agreement that the NP "shall be reorganized independently of the [GN] or any other company of interest." The Morgan company hoped that the NP and GN would work in harmony, but the former was not to be controlled by the latter. Hill wrote his associate Lord Mount Stephen that the year's success of the NP had inclined Morgan to continue the voting trust. Hill would insist that he be given three more members on the NP board of directors (two were subsequently added). "The Northern Pacific is getting into rather unsatisfactory shape in the West.... The greatest weakness of the Northern Pacific is the want of judgment and ability in directing its policy, there is great danger of [Mellen]...starting a fire that he cannot quench." The GN would not suffer as the NP would from lower rates. "If we should be unfortunately forced into fight with the Northern Pacific, there would be no doubt as to the outcome; and the Great Northern will not at any time reduce its dividends or be found with less than a good round surplus."[30]

On October 3, 1898, Hill, Harriman, Mellen, Coster, and others met in New York City (Mohler was not present). Coster reminded the others that the February 1897 contract defined the ORN as a neutral company, open to all and exclusive to no one. Hill said that political hostility in Washington State made it folly to build any more lines and that the GN wanted only "equal relations and equal terms with the Huntington gateway." Coster said that the NP wanted "permanent harmony in that territory," which would be achieved by a division of territory with the NP north of the Snake and ORN south. Harriman asked if the division meant with respect to traffic going east or west. Coster responded, "Both; east and west." Why, asked Harriman, when the ORN was "the shorter and more natural line." Harriman said he saw the February 1897 contract as joint ownership of the ORN by the OSL, GN, and NP. Coster responded that the assumption was that the ORN would be an independent company. The GN-NP purchase of ORN stock was to delay OSL and UP control of the ORN to allow sufficient time to work out a harmonious arrangement. Harriman said, the ORN "should be placed in a position where all three companies should have equal rights.... I do not want to divide territory. That did not seem to be in contemplation when any of the agreements were made." Coster responded, "Then I do feel very apprehensive." Harriman thought harmony was possible and essential, but it was "inadvisable for political reasons to agree upon absolute territorial lines." But he had no plan.[31]

A month later, November 14, President Mellen reported to the NP executive committee on the October 3 meeting. Mellen said it was informally agreed that: (1) the NP would build from Missoula to Lewiston and the ORN would build from Lewiston to Wallula, with the NP having the right to connect to it from Ainsworth; (2) the NP to have trackage rights over the line from Lewiston to Wallula, with the right to do business thereon to and from all NP points; and all business on the line exchanged between the NP and ORN to be done at Lewiston; and (3) it is understood the NP would have a suitable trackage contract, with right to do local business, between Pullman and Garfield and Connell. At the meeting Mellen, Mohler, Harriman, and Coster were informally appointed as a committee to carry out the above. As the meeting was breaking up the following dictated clause was added: "It is understood that the Northern Pacific shall have no right to build west from Lewiston and that the Navigation Company shall have no right to build on the line from Lewiston to Missoula or north thereof." On October 4 the NP notified the ORN that it waived any

Four NP engines at Kendrick after the 1897 renumbering. From the left the first engine may be a 2-8-0, the next No. 700 a 4-4-0, one of the two engines in the 1899 wreck at Kendrick, the next may be 4-6-0 and the engine partially behind the water tank also probably a 4-6-0 on the passenger train. At Kendrick helper engines were turned for the trip up the 2.2 and 2.4 percent grades to Howell. *Photograph 78-910, Manuscript and Special Collections, Washington State University Library.*

right to do local business between Pullman and Garfield and Connell. The Mellen, Mohler, Harriman, Coster committee met October 25. The ORN wanted to be able to build in the Clearwater Valley parallel to the NP line. The NP objected. The point of the meeting on the 3rd was to prevent construction of parallel and competing lines. The ORN was unwilling to accept the position it could not build in the Clearwater Valley. There was consideration of the right of the NP to build west of Lewiston and what trackage rights it would have on ORN lines west of Lewiston. The ORN opposed the NP connecting with the ORN west of Lewiston with lines from Pullman and Pleasant View. As of November 14, Mellen wrote the ORN had made no further suggestions, but it was understood that it would. The NP would "try to adjust differences and discourage purely retaliatory measures."[32]

In the meantime, GN's ORN director Bull wrote Mellen, October 28, objecting to NP surveys west of Lewiston as a "contravention" of the agreements made October 3. Hill wrote Bull October 31, that Mellen was holding Mohler in New York while putting men in possession of the important points between Summit and Pasco. Mohler should go west and place the line west of Lewiston under construction. "Morgan's people do not want any trouble for Northern Pacific this time. If they are unwilling to recognize agreement October third, they will recognize a sharp attack on their traffic in the Palouse district.... I feel certain that Mr. Mellen's main object is not for the purpose of shortening their line, but rather for the purpose of making the excuse for shortening the line a basis for securing territory not now belonging to the Northern Pacific and which naturally belongs to the Navigation Company.... His policy seems to be first to get possession and settle conditions afterwards." Hill saw two ways of combating the NP: by occupying valuable territory or "by a sharp reduction of rates." The first would be very expensive and unnecessary. A reduction in rates would be costly in the short-run, but not permanent. Hill said he was able to stop extension of the Washington Central by reducing rates and threatening to reduce them further. "The Navigation Company...cannot afford to accept the claim of the Northern Pacific for permission to occupy that territory farther than was discussed at the meeting of October third, and I think the cheapest and easiest way to prevent it will be to let them understand that it will cost them more money than they will ever get out of it." The cost to the ORN could be limited to from three to five hundred thousand and the people in Portland would co-operate. Hill had earlier taken the view that the NP had a right on the Clearwater east of Lewiston. Mellen responded to Bull November 7, "This Company is doing no work, surveying or otherwise, west of Lewiston." On the 14th Mellen thought a fuller statement needed to be made to Bull.

> The memorandum of agreement reached at the meeting of October 3d had no reference to surveys of any character, and was reached after such notice of the intended surveys had been given. Furthermore, as I understand the situation, the Oregon Railroad and Navigation Company, on investigation, is not satisfied with that memorandum and nothing is being done to carry it into effect.
>
> This Company does not regard any action taken east of Lewiston as in any way affecting the interests of the Oregon Railroad and Navigation Company, and it regards my letter of notification to Mr. Mohler that we were proposing to survey a line between Missoula and Pasco as a full compliance with equities and courtesies of the situation.

Bull responded the same day, "Your view of the significance of the memorandum of agreement adopted at the October 3 meeting differs so radically from my own that I do not think it advisable to discuss the question until [a meeting] has been held."[33]

McHenry wrote Division Engineer C. S. Bihler, November 1, 1898, "It appears, for some reasons with which I am not yet acquainted, that the necessity for haste in locating and commencing the construction upon the line east of Lewiston is quite imperative...which will probably be authorized before you receive this letter." Three days later McHenry wrote, "We have a decided advantage over the O.R. & N. in the matter of completion of surveys and filing the maps, and do not wish to lose it, and I trust that you will do everything your [sic] able to assure this."[34]

On November 2 the ORN, with both Harriman's and Hill's blessings, chartered the Clearwater Valley Railroad (CWV), which projected two lines competitive to existing or proposed NP lines; all were surveyed, but not built. Seven days later the NP chartered the Clearwater Short Line Railway (CSL), which projected two lines; one was completed from North Lapwai to Grangeville on the Camas Prairie and the other up the Clearwater to the Idaho-Montana state boundary was partially built to Stites. On December 5 and 13 three additional lines were projected by the CSL. All of these lines were competitive to either ORN lines or projections by the SRV and CWV. A December 8 WCR supplementary charter projected seven lines south of the Snake River challenging the ORN. The following February an NP official commented that the ORN "has now projected sufficient mileage to keep them building for next five years and to keep them in bankruptcy for next fifty years."[35]

In the meantime, Harriman and Coster met November 1. Coster wrote Harriman the next day, "The suggestions you made are such a radical departure from what has heretofore been discussed that I confess I do not quite know where they would land the Northern Pacific." Coster enclosed a memorandum based on their conversation: the ORN would give the NP trackage from Wallace via Oakesdale to La Crosse; the ORN would lease to the NP for its sole use the line from La Crosse to Connell; the NP would build in the Clearwater drainage and give to the ORN trackage; the ORN would build from Riparia to Lewiston and give the NP trackage (all trackage included the right to do local business); at some convenient point south of the Snake River, allow the NP a connection to Pleasant View; and the NP would not build any branch west of its line from Genesee to Rosalia, nor west of Lewiston. Harriman responded the same day that he thought in meantime the status quo should be preserved and the NP should withdraw its Clearwater surveyors. On the 4th Harriman thought it best to make arrangements on existing lines and postpone the building of any new lines. Coster responded that it was his opinion that the NP "is justified in surveying and building its line between Lewiston and Missoula via the Clearwater basin whenever it chooses." He noted that between Bull's letter of the 28th asking the NP to stop west of Lewiston and Harriman's request about east of Lewiston, left the NP without much freedom of action. On November 7 Mellen instructed McHenry not to do any work west of Lewiston, to concentrate on east of Lewiston and when surveys there were completed to run a line up the Potlatch from Kendrick. McHenry responded the same day that from talking with an ORN official he "distinctly gathered the impression that the utmost they hoped for was to be allowed to build the line between Riparia and Lewiston, granting operating rights over same to the N. P. Ry. Co. and failing in that would be satisfied with a joint ownership in such a line. It would of course be preferable in every way if this proposition could be reversed and the O. R. & N. allowed trackage to Lewiston....Even at worst a sharp and decisive war with the O. R. & N. Co. would be a cheap price to pay for the possession of the region east of Lewiston, and with our present position of advantage, I would not fear for the result."[36]

Coster and Harriman met and exchanged additional correspondence, but Coster was not happy with the results and wrote Harriman November 11 concluding,

> Let me say, too, that during the last seven or eight weeks, actuated by a sincere desire to promote peace and harmony, I have devoted an amount of time to this subject and to efforts towards its solution which has seriously embarrassed me in attending to other necessary business. I do not feel, therefore, like devoting much more time to it until somebody speaking for the O. R. & N. will be prepared to take the business up in a clearly-defined way and to make some clearly-defined proposition, thus avoiding further unproductive consumption of my time. Whenever this condition can be reached you will find me more than ready to co-operate in every way in any effort to solve pending questions under conditions as they then exist.[37]

In mid-November the NP board of directors authorized the president to build, at his discretion, extensions up to 75 miles in length, into the Clearwater and Nez Perces country, and to make surveys and acquire rights of way, "preparatory to further construction along the Clearwater River and its tributaries as he may deem proper for the protection of this Company's interest." The resolution made clear the authorization was to be part of a line from Missoula to Pasco, based on the NP's "inherent and equitable right to build the proposed line...and such construction east from its present line would not invade territory properly belonging to any other Company, and that the time has come when...such construction should be begun." The question of establishing the line from Lewiston to Pasco should be taken up with the ORN "in the most friendly spirit whenever the question arises."[38]

On November 19 a *Review* headline announced, "Big Railroad Fight is On; Northern Pacific cuts loose from the Great Northern and O. R. & N. and Will Push Extensions into Idaho and Oregon." At the same time the ORN had let a contract for building from Wallula to Lewiston. The ORN was not convinced that the NP intended to build the eastern portion of its projected Missoula to Pasco line and thus it would become a feeder in ORN territory rather than a shortening of the NP main line. The "uncalled for" invasion of ORN territory by the NP would likely involve the GN and UP defending "the interests of the O. R. & N. in its efforts to maintain its integrity and independence."[39]

Harriman wrote Coster November 21 that the ORN Executive Committee had appointed a committee "with power to act for the O. R. & N. Co. and to continue the negotiations." About the same time the NP executive committee appointed a committee to take up unsettled matters between the NP and ORN with respect to the NP's desire to shorten its line between Lewiston and Ainsworth and to avoid duplication of lines. McHenry wrote Mellen regarding the NP sale to the CWV of right-of-way between Wallula and Riparia, "I cannot understand...why we should not embarrass and hinder the O. R. & N. construction at all points both east and west of Lewiston, pending the completion of a mutually satisfactory agreement."[40]

Mellen said in St. Paul November 21 that the NP

would like to reach an agreement to use ORN's line west of Lewiston. There had been several conferences with the ORN "but no final conclusion was reached. We still hope to reach a settlement of the matter. The stories about a serious rupture are incorrect. We are no further removed from a settlement today than we were two weeks ago and there is good reason to suppose that an amicable settlement can be reached." The reported added, "the great activity of the O. R. & N. and N. P. construction corps in the Inland Empire continues and the impression is growing that it is a to be a real fight. This impression is confirmed by the secretive manner in which each road is going ahead and the pains each is taking to find out what the other is doing." Two days later Mellen admitted that there was disagreement between the NP and ORN over the latter's determination to build east of Lewiston.[41]

Serious negotiations ensued between the two committees and a memorandum was revised several times. On November 26 Coster defended provisions of the memorandum (probably of the 25th): "I think that matters are rapidly drifting towards a settlement on the basis indicated in the enclosed memo." Coster summarized from the NP perspective some provisions in question:

> (1) that it does not oblige us to build our line across the mountains until we want to; (2) meanwhile it gives us an outlet from the Palouse and Clearwater country via Pullman, Garfield, La Cross and Connell; (3) it gives us an absolute lease of the portion of this outlet between La Crosse and Connell. To be sure it lets the O. R. & N. into the Nez Perces country at once, but it is really impossible to negotiate on any other basis. I have fought hard for the Northern Pacific, but at the same time I must say that if I were on the Navigation side, I could make out a pretty good case for that Company. I appreciate of course that if it got to an open rupture with the O. R. & N., it probably would not take very long to bring them to terms but on the other hand I do feel that, looking at the entire situation, we accomplish a great deal in fixing Lewiston as the eastern limit to which the O. R. & N. can build and in having the right to the Northern Pacific to build in any of the country east thereof.

Coster warned that failure of the NP and ORN to agree could lead to the GN building into the Palouse "and this circumstance should not be lost sight of." Mellen was not satisfied and wondered, if the NP decided not to build from Missoula to Lewiston would the NP be able to use the line from Wallula to Lewiston. Without extending to the Clearwater country and without the right to do local business he did not think the NP could afford to pay an adequate rent on trackage over the ORN from Pullman and Garfield to La Crosse. "To rent one hundred miles (which is the approximate distance between Pullman and Connell) without any business; that is to practically pay all the expenses of a line without getting any income, is a greater burden than to haul the business by our existing line via Marshall." Mellen objected to giving the ORN trackage within the Nez Perce Reservation, and had other objections. Mellen enclosed a memorandum of his own (what follows is probably from that memorandum, but that is not certain). It allowed the ORN to construct a line from Lewiston to Wallula with the NP to have trackage; that the NP had a right to occupy all territory east of a line from Lewiston to Rosalia and the ORN to occupy all territory west of that line; the NP would give the ORN trackage with local rights on the line from Moscow to Lewiston and "upon such other lines as it may construct from time to time within the limits of the Nez Perces Reservation"; the ORN would lease to the NP the line from La Crosse to Connell and give the NP trackage with local rights between Pullman and La Crosse. Once the Lewiston-Missoula line of the NP and the Lewiston-Wallula line of the ORN were built, Lewiston would be the gateway for the exchange of traffic between the NP and ORN upon the equivalent division to those at the Huntington and Spokane gateways. Nothing in the memorandum was to be construed as restricting the ORN or the WCR "in the construction of necessary lines for the development of the territory served by each." Regarding his memorandum Mellen wrote, "I have conceded everything, it seems to me, that I can afford to, in the interest of peace. Not because I believe peace is the best thing for us, but because I believe you and your associates desire it, and I, in turn, desire to conform to your wishes. We can get along with this, and it is less objectionable than the memorandum you enclose. It should be satisfactory to the O. R. & N. if it is at all disposed to deal fairly with us, which I fear is not the case." He thought Coster's and his memorandums were, "simply postponing trouble. It is, perhaps, relieving the financial interests in New York of some present embarrassments, but it is producing a never-ending one for the management in the west.... If the interests controlling our property could be patient yet a little while, I believe the situation would resolve itself into one much more for our interests than any compromise that can be effected. There is no part of our territory wherein we are so strong; there is none where in our competitors are so weak... To sum-up the situation,...it appears to me we are taking a half interest in an unproductive line [Wallula to Lewiston],—of low grade, to be sure, and to be more economically operated than any other accessible to us out of [Clearwater]...country,—and giving in exchange a half interest in extremely productive lines that will cost less to build, maintain, and operate; and unless we are sure we are going to shorten our line by building through to Missoula... the balance of advantages seems to me to be conclusively with the O. R. & N. Company." So far as the GN threat in the Palouse, Hill "would be there today but for his fear of reprisals in the Red River valley [Minnesota and North Dakota], and he will go there whenever he feels we are either sufficiently well frightened not to attack him in return, or sufficiently well tied up that we cannot make reprisals." Mellen suggested that the NP and ORN compromise by both abandoning all construction and surveys—he preferred this to either memorandum. Such an "action will be commented on as a surrender to the O. R. & N. but the dollars will be with us, and I shall be comforted by the hope that after another year's work with the Company, I shall have acquired the confidence of you all to that extent you will be willing to back me for a fight, if necessary, to preserve rights which it is admitted we have but which our surroundings at present time seem to make it impolitic to enforce." The ORN's construction and surveys "indicate that they have no well defined plan...and I believe all of the work done thus far by the O. R. & N. is to affect you people in New York and force a compromise detrimental to the interests of this Company." Mellen asked Coster to slow negotiations so the NP would have time to file additional charters.[42]

On December 7 Mellen wrote Coster the only ORN construction was between Wallula and Riparia, but it was not very vigorous. They decided it was too expensive to build Riparia to Lewiston. "They still have parties in the Clearwater country surveying, apparently looking for something they want to find, but do not know just exactly what, or where." In the meantime NP surveys and construction in the Clearwater were proceeding satisfactorily. Mellen had not authorized any surveys west of Lewiston. "I could not ask the situation with the O. R. & N. to have developed more to our advantage than appears to be the case up to the present moment. They have frittered away their time, have accomplished absolutely nothing, while we have progressed tremendously in the direction of securing the Clearwater country to ourselves."[43]

The *Review* interpreted the CSL charters and the NP's actions in the Lewiston and Dayton areas as evidence that the NP was prepared to counter any move the ORN made. "J. Pierpont Morgan and President Mellen... are making the greatest railroad fight ever known in the northwest to compel the [ORN] to come to their terms regarding the division of Idaho territory." A day later the thought was that the NP action was a bluff to get the ORN to stop interfering in the Clearwater basin.[44]

In a statement December 14, Mellen explained, "The only construction which the Northern Pacific has in progress is about 75 miles in the Clearwater country, in Idaho. The NP is the only line in that country or within 50 miles of it. A question has arisen between the Northern Pacific and the [ORN] as to whether the latter should not also be allowed to occupy that country without being considered as invading territory of the Northern Pacific." Two days later the *Review* had a different view:

> President Mellen denying that the Northern is engaged in a fight sounds singularly absurd here, where that company and its branches have just filed at Olympia the locations of 11 lines paralleling or otherwise cutting in to the territory of the O. R. & N. His declaration that the Northern is the only line in the Clearwater country, is technically correct, but it is well know that in building to Lewiston the Northern cut off a large portion of the trade previously held by the O. R. & N. in that territory, the O. R. & N. having maintained—and it still maintains—a steamer line from its railway at Riparia to Lewiston. His shifting the responsibility for starting the invasion of territory to the shoulders of the O. R. & N. is for New York ears.
>
> The impression is growing that there is a division in the management of the Northern Pacific railway. In the general offices at St. Paul and among the high officials in this state there is an evident strong sentiment against the O. R. & N. and a disposition to make the fight a hot one. In New York, however, where Dan Lamont, the vice-present holds forth and where the financial operations of the road are conducted, every one seems most friendly to the O. R. & N. and to deprecate any talk of a fight. Mr. Mellen in New York talks in a different strain from that in which he talks in St. Paul. His New York utterances more nearly resemble those of President Hill....
>
> Possibly President Mellen, who is considered to be one of the advocates of war, has been summoned to New York and told to change his ideas and to act on some sort of a peace commission.[45]

The editor of the *Oregonian* traveled with Mohler to Lewiston, and returning to Portland wrote an editorial which was quoted at length in the *Review*. The Spokane paper thought that it was a fair assumption that the editorial reflected the views of Mohler. The ORN with its water level line to tidewater, had an "incomparable advantage" and "it is the duty" of the ORN "to maintain this position; to strengthen it by extension of its lines to all available and productive territory within the great valley of the Columbia.... Omission to do the right and necessary things, and to do them now, will meet the penalty hereafter in the deterioration of the property, in the loss of its traffic and prestige, in transfer to aggressive neighbors of territory belonging by natural topography to itself. In other words the O. R. & N. ought to push now, and to push vigorously, extensions into territory naturally tributary to its lines." The Clearwater country was specifically pointed to as a place the ORN should occupy which "would strengthen its position beyond all power of calculation; it would give great additional support to Portland, with whose interests those of the O. R. & N. are indissolubly bound up; and by this aid to Portland it would enable Portland to extend increasing help and support to the O. R. & N. system." On December 13 the ORN's SRV filed intentions to build nine additional lines. The *Review* commented that the ORN had met bluff with bluff and that "twenty new lines in the Inland Empire are a few too many for the most sanguine to anticipate." The *Review* gave its response to the *Oregonian* on the 28th. The ORN "wants their neighbors to grow the cow and produce the milk and permit them to slip in at a late hour and skim off the cream.... For 10 years it made no move toward the Lewiston gateway. It gave the people there an indifferent service by steamers from Riparia, and was deaf to all appeals for railway connection. Then when the Northern Pacific plucked up enterprise and extended its Spokane & Palouse branch to Lewiston, and perfected its plans to build on into the Clearwater country, the Oregon road began to buster because 'its field was invaded.'" The NP "would be weak and short-sighted to permit the O. R. & N. to bluff and bulldoze it out of its rights."[46]

Meanwhile McHenry wrote Bihler December 20, 1898, that he had received additional instructions from Mellen authorizing surveys and locations for eight lines in eastern Washington and Idaho. All the lines would be offensive to the ORN/UP.[47]

On the 26th Mellon stated that the controversy over the Clearwater was "likely to be amicably settled early next month when negotiation are to be resumed." He went on to say, "There are contracts which have been in existence since 1880, signed by the presidents of the two companies and ratified by both boards of directors, specifically assigning the Clearwater and much other territory in that region to the Northern Pacific. The Northern Pacific is not building in any direction where any other railroad company has a right, morally or equitably, to object...." An official of the ORN said December 29, "If the Northern wants to dispute with us the possession of the Clearwater basin we will doubtless dispute with them the possession of the Big Bend country."[48]

An NP History Lesson for the ORN

The NP negotiating committee on December 29, 1898, wrote to the ORN committee that they had "strenuously asserted" the ORN would not have built "Portland to Wallula had it not expected to build extensions there from to drain the Palouse country, the Nez Perces country and the Clearwater country and...the Northern Pacific has no equitable rights in the territory mentioned." It was also asserted that the NP "line in the Palouse country from Marshall to Lewiston is an 'intruder,' and that it ought to be turned over to the Navigation Company in order that the Navigation Company should have complete and undisturbed possession the Palouse country and also of the Nez Perces and Clearwater country." The NP committee claimed that it had only recently become aware of the October 20, 1880, and August 17, 1882, agreements [see chapters I and II]. Under the 1880 agreement the ORN would build Portland to Wallula so that Wallula would become the point of interchange between the two railroads; that the ORN conceded to the NP all the territory north of the Snake River except for the Texas Ferry (Riparia) to Colfax and Farmington line; that the NP was given "an express right to build a line on the north bank of the Columbia Parallel to and in competition with the very *main line* of the O. R. & N. for its entire length"; that Colfax was recognized as a competitive point; that the agreement recognized that the NP intended to build branches "*into and beyond* the Palouse country"; that the Nez Perce Reservation was at the time closed, thus the Clearwater was only accessible from the west through the Palouse Country; that no part of either the Clearwater or Nez Perce countries are south of the Snake River; and that the ORN was allowed to operate boats on the Columbia and Snake rivers, "but that right was not extended to the Clearwater." In the 1882 agreement the ORN agreed to abandon construction of the one line allowed the ORN in the 1880 agreement, "but this agreement was not carried out by the O. R. & N. Co. On the contrary, the O. R. & N. Co. proceeded to build that line and also, in 1884 and subsequently, to acquire other lines in the Palouse country, and such action appears to have constituted the first source of the continuous trouble between the O. R. & N. and N. P.... Among the very lines which it so acquired was one which the Oregon & Transcontinental Company built for the Northern Pacific, being the Northern Pacific's intended line to Colfax, provided for in the contract of 1880. The O. R. & N. Co. thus kept the N. P. out of Colfax. The O. R. & N. Co. now claims that the N. P. should never go into Colfax, the equitable right of the O. R. & N. Co. to Colfax and the rest of the Palouse country, based on *prior occupation,* being superior in its opinion to those of the Northern Pacific!"[49]

On December 30 Mohler wrote Hill that the ORN had acquired most of the right-of-way in Nez Perce Territory. "I am now waiting for Mellen to show his hand elsewhere, which he has not been doing. We are ready to strike at moments notice, and I feel exceedingly comfortable over the situation for he cannot make a move which we cannot more than duplicate. I am being well supported by our people in New York." In an interview in Lewiston on the same day Mellen "made light of the fight between the O. R. & N. and his company, and suggested as a possibility a joint building by the two companies of the line down the Snake from Lewiston." He said the fight between the two companies "was by the newspapers, and between local officials; that the heads of the companies were on good terms."[50] It is not unreasonable to assume that Mellen, as well as Harriman, viewed Mohler, in Portland, as a local official.

Mellen wrote Mohler January 9, 1899, in response to correspondence in December (which has not been found):

> You are in error in assuming...that this Company contemplates doing anything by way of 'reprisals.' My letter was solely to call your attention to the fact that if your Company should build lines depriving this Company of business which it now enjoys, this Company would necessarily have to build lines to recover the business so lost, or other equivalent business.
>
> You are in error, also, in assuming that the Northern Pacific acquired the Hunt System 'contrary to the written agreement' or that its construction in the Nez Perces territory is an invasion.
>
> I lament to observe from your letter a disposition to reach conclusions unfavorable to the Northern Pacific, without presentation of facts. This Company has sought throughout all the recent discussion affecting your company, to approach the matters involved in a very different spirit.
>
> I heartily join however, in the view expressed towards the end of your letter, that 'ruinous extensions and contentions at this particular time, are unfortunate, unwise, and, in our judgment, unnecessary.'[51]

A little later an ORN official was quoted as saying, "Railroad building in the Inland Empire and in the northwest generally will not be so rapid or feverish as some people seem to think.... What is now being done is being done cautiously and conservatively.... They are spying out routes and locations of possible lines, but to think that they are going to throw millions into construction all at once is nonsense. They know what they are doing and are proceeding with care." On January 19 in St. Paul Mellen said, "I saw the report that the differences between the roads had been settled, but I know of no foundation for it.... There is still a difference of opinion regarding territory, but it is not irreconcilable. I have always thought this matter could be fixed up, and still think so." The *Tribune* commented on January 20, "The statement of President Mellen...that the reports of the settlement of the Clearwater controversy are unfounded may be significant in view of the new engineering operations down the Snake. Heretofore the presidents of the two systems have either denied there was any controversy or have claimed the controversy was likely to be settled. The apparent anxiety of President Mellen now to insist that there is a controversy and that it has not been settled looks like the Northern is in a fighting mood and that it is getting ready for the conflict in the most advantageous positions." The *Review* added "when a railroad president says his is not at peace with another road he is much more likely to be believed than when he says he is."[52]

The OSL stockholders in January 1899 agreed to exchange their stock for UP common stock, which was completed by early March. Given the price of UP stock, the UP acquired the OSL for $11.5 million or $7,567 per mile. The three transcontinental railroads and the OSL each had a quarter of the ORN preferred stock under the Morgan 1897 arrangement. The jointly owned preferred stock had the power to elect two-thirds of the ORN board for ten years or until the company paid a 4 percent dividend for five consecutive years. As Klein says, "Navigation occupied the bizarre position of an independent line under the joint rule of three competing systems." In early March Hill was quoted in St. Paul:

> As long as the Great Northern and the O. R. & N. remain on friendly terms the Great Northern will not build to Portland. We operate over the O. R. & N. tracks and the O. R. & N. enjoys the right of transportation over ours; and though even the Union Pacific may eventually own the O. R. & N., it is doubtful if it would want the Great Northern to build a competing line into its territory. For that reason, among others, I think the present relations between the two companies will be maintained.[53]

On January 18 Coster wrote Mellen that Hill was "somewhat inclined to favor" acquisition of the ORN in the common interest of the NP, GN, and UP. "I told him that if the scheme can be worked out satisfactorily so that each Company gets its needs, I should be inclined to view the project with favor." Mellen responded that the NP owned a quarter of the ORN preferred stock, "yet you know that if the property was owned by either the Great Northern or Union Pacific solely it could not be handled more to our detriment than it is at the present time....As matters now stand I should be heartily in favor of disposing of the interest we now have in the preferred stock of the O. R. & N." Mellen proposed that all the capital stock of the ORN be held one-third each by the NP, GN, and UP, and that all 1,124 miles of the ORN (including Wallula to Grange City under construction) be leased. The 234 miles west of Umatilla would be leased jointly to the three companies. The UP would lease 285 miles southeast of Umatilla. The GN would lease 353 miles from Spokane to Wallula via both Walla Walla and Snake River routes and the branches between Walla Walla and the Snake River. The NP would lease 175 miles east of Tekoa plus La Crosse to Connell and Moscow to Colfax. The NP and GN would jointly lease 77 miles from Tekoa to Oakesdale, Colfax to La Crosse, and Umatilla to Wallula. On the 26th Coster responded that he did not think the UP would agree because it would be shut out of the Walla Walla and Palouse countries, but Hill ought to agree because it gave that country to the GN.[54]

On March 16, 1899, McHenry sent Mellen a report and maps of NP surveys on the north bank of the Columbia River from 1873 to 1882. On the 18th McHenry wrote, "The notes of surveys by G. W. Hunt would doubtless prove cheap at the sum of $2,000 if construction proceeds, as the sum would represent very little more than the cost of one party for thirty days, but if it is simply desired to make a hasty survey to file a map to obtain priority of location, our own map of 1882 would answer all purposes." On the 20th Mellen concluded, "I am well satisfied that, eventually, we are going to agree with the O. R. & N. and secure trackage from Wallula into Portland, which will be much better than to build a line on the north, unless it should be found upon investigation there is a local business to be obtained by a line on the north bank which will prove an important factor in the earnings of such a line."[55]

On April 4 McHenry informed Mellen that four small ORN crews were grading between Riparia and Lewiston. ORN surveying was taking place near Pullman, Moscow, and Genesee, the upper Clearwater and from the Clearwater to the Camas Prairie, and on north bank of the Snake River down from Lewiston. They had made right-of-way purchases paralleling the S&P east of Moscow. It looked like the ORN intended to build that line, and had contracts on right-of-way to July 1 on Union Flat. They had also obtained contracts for right-of-way on the south bank of the Snake "evidently done for the purpose of blocking us." McHenry was informed April 6 that except for on Union Flat and near Moscow, the ORN had withdrawn their survey parties. The NP made extensive surveys in 1898 and 1899 east and north of the Snake River.[56]

In letters to Morgan & Co., in March and April 1899 Hill pushed for joint ownership of the ORN. Once there was a "fair and equitable" basis of ownership, "the whole question seems to be solved." Coster wrote Hill that the suggestion a new company acquire the ORN by lease might be feasible. Coster thought such a plan might work if NP had either trackage over ORN lines west of Lewiston and Pullman to its mainline, or was allowed to build such lines and the ORN would not build east of Lewiston nor elsewhere in NP, GN, or UP territory. He urged both Hill and Mellen to confer.[57]

An unnamed NP high official said in New York April 14,

> I believe we may eventually settle that Clearwater affair, but if it is not settled by the time our line is completed east of Lewiston we will certainly build west of Lewiston.... Northern Pacific relations with the Great Northern seem pleasant just now.... The O. R. & N. through the Clearwater company has filed supplementary articles of incorporation...announcing its intention of constructing lines which would take 25 years to build. The effort is to handicap us in case we try to build west of Lewiston.... By a contract far back in the '80s the territory was divided and marked off on a map which still exists. We have faithfully adhered to the terms of our part of the contract and it's foolish for any one to say we are trespassing on their boat traffic on the Clearwater or Snake rivers by the present undertaking.

Three days later the *Review* said the general suspicion was the "high official" was Mellen. The statement that the contract of 18 years before was being faithfully adhered to "in all fairness...is to say the least, not a little doubtful." Until the NP built to Lewiston the products of the Lewiston and Clearwater region had gone out by ORN boat and the building of the new NP steamer *Hannaford* was viewed by the ORN as violations of that contract.[58]

Hill, Mohler, and Mellen met in New York, but on April 21, 1899, it was reported that the NP and ORN had agreed to disagree and that Mellen and Mohler returned west and Hill left for Europe. The Clearwater basin was happy with the result. The fear was that they would agree and the ORN would not build up the Clearwater and the NP would not build down the Snake nor to the Camas Prairie. Now there was a prospect for extensive building into the Prairie and on the Snake River. Mohler interviewed in Spokane indicated he was pleased with the outcome of his conference with Mellen. Asked about a survey from Moscow to the Clearwater, "'Yes, I think we shall have to build something,' said the president with a smile. 'We are certainly going to do some building, but I cannot say exactly what it will be. Don't understand that I mean we will certainly build any particular line, but some line.'" ORN Chief Engineer Kennedy with a full corps of surveyors left Portland for Lewiston shortly after Mohler arrived in Portland.[59]

On April 21 Harriman wrote Mellen that he accepted the suggestion that the line from Lewiston to Wallula be jointly owned if it also covered from Lewiston east and that construction of the latter be suspended until matters were finally determined. Mellen responded on the 25th that it was impossible for him to stop construction east of Lewiston "as I have before explained to you, and we are so far apart regarding the rights of our respective companies there it seems useless to discuss this matter further." Mellen proposed that the NP build from Lewiston to Riparia and sell an undivided half interest to the UP or lease with local rights, and that the ORN do likewise for the NP the line from Wallula to Riparia. Once the UP was at Lewiston by such an arrangement the issue of east of Lewiston could be taken up. Harriman responded May 1 that the position of the NP regarding the Clearwater-Nez Perce territory "is so shifting that it seems to me it would be impossible for us to arrive at any satisfactory agreement at this time." Harriman said "undoubtedly...the best method for accomplishing what we all desire" was to postpone construction east of Lewiston to the following year. Mellen responded that the NP position on the Clearwater and Nez Perce country "*has* been consistent from first to last.... We claim the right to develop that country at our will. We do not admit your right to question us in our action there until you reach a point where you are within reasonable distance of the country in question." Mellen would regret if there was any unnecessary construction, but if the territory of the WCR or NP were attacked "you must be prepared for reprisals, for they will surely be made." Harriman wrote May 9 that the ORN looked upon NP construction in the Clearwater "as being unfriendly and unwarranted." The NP route into the Clearwater was "unnatural and circuitous" compared to the ORN route which was "direct and economical." To avoid unnecessary duplication of line, Harriman suggested a joint interest from Dayton to Covello,

> on an understanding that no further construction shall be engaged in by your Company other than that already under contract and which you have explained to me, (90 miles in all; 12 miles up [Lapwai] Canyon and 78 miles [into the Camas Prairie]) and no further construction shall be engaged in by the O. R. & N. Co. except that now under contract between Wallula and Grange City until formal notice of ninety days on the part of either.... Nothing herein contained to be construed as in any way abating the claim of the O. R. & N. to its occupancy of the Nez Perces territory with lines of its own or jointly with Northern Pacific Co. Further provided that agreement is reached whereby the O. R. & N. is to have equal rights on the line build in Nez Perces when the O. R. & N. shall have built to Lewiston; the O. R. & N. giving traffic or trackage contract to Northern Pacific from Lewiston to Wallula with full local rights.[60]

On May 16, 1899, the NP executive committee authorized construction from Pullman and Lewiston to Pleasant View. Prior to leaving May 31 for his scientific expedition to Alaska Harriman took an excursion from Pendleton through the Palouse and took a NP special to Lewiston where Mohler met him for a cruise down the Snake River to see the battleground.[61]

On June 15 Mohler and Hill had "a long consultation" in Mohler's private car in Spokane. Mohler responded to an interviewer, "I am a subscriber of the *Spokesman Review* and read its railroad news diligently so as to keep posted on what my company is doing." Hill closed by saying, "I am sorry, but really there is no news to tell you—we have nothing for publication." Mohler said in Lewiston that the ORN lines through Lewiston and to the Camas Prairie, "will be a most excellent piece of work and will be cast [?] on high class lines throughout. Our gradients and curvatures are superior to any other, we will be in the heart of the best country and the right-of-way has practically all been bought and paid for from Riparia to Mt. Idaho [south end of the prairie]. I say this with reference to the Northern Pacific's claim that we had gone out of business in the Clearwater country.... Our plans in the Clearwater country have not changed a particle, our activity has not been relaxed at any point and will not be relaxed in any respect."[62]

On June 18 Mellen inquired with Mohler whether the ORN would grant the NP trackage west of Lewiston or whether the NP must consider building its own line west of Lewiston, over which the NP would offer the ORN trackage. Mohler replied July 3 that the ORN intended to build between Riparia and Lewiston "promptly, and will be glad to consider any proposals for traffic use and will give the same careful attention." Mellen responded on the 17th seeking clarification of Mohler's use of "traffic" instead of trackage with full local rights which the NP required. Until there was an understanding between the companies, the NP would consider work on the Riparia-Lewiston line to "necessitate measures on its part which it would much prefer to avoid." The NP had informed W. L. Bull, ORN chairman, in March that either a line from Riparia to Lewiston or from Moscow to Lewiston by the ORN concerned the NP because the former would parallel a line the NP must have, either by ownership or trackage, as part of its Missoula-Wallula cut-off and the latter would reduce the value of the Marshall-Clearwater line. Furthermore, the ORN had no rights from either line in the direction of the Nez Perce and Clearwater country.[63]

The June 30, 1899, NP confidential report justified Clearwater Short Line activity and construction:

> The necessity for further construction in the Clearwater region arose from the aggressive action of the [ORN], which to the best of my [McHenry's] knowledge and belief was unprovoked by the [NP]. Examinations by the [ORN] for projected extensions in the vicinity of Pullman and Genesee were made in February, 1898, and on March 14th three field parties appeared at work at Riparia and Almota and near Lewiston. Surveys were made for a terminal in Lewiston and in April [ORN] Engineers were reported on the Snake River. In May, cross-section parties were at work between Riparia and Wallula Junction. When the hostile intentions of the [ORN] became fully apparent...several parties were organized during the month of May and directed to make examinations for routes on the Snake River between Lewiston and the Salmon River, up the Clearwater east of Potlatch and from Pullman to Connell via La Crosse. Subsequently on the appeal of Mr. A. L. Mohler, President of the O. R. & N. Co., our work was stopped and all field parties of both Companies were disbanded. It was supposed that this was the end of the matter, but in October or November, 1898, without prior notice to this Company, the [ORN] resumed its explorations and surveys on an extensive scale and at the time let the contract for the construction of the line from Riparia to Wallula, and incorporations and routes were filed between many points too numerous to mention. Defensive measures were promptly undertaken by this Company.

A "high" ORN official interviewed in New York, July 1, 1899, stated that the NP did not object to the Wallula-Riparia construction by the ORN, "rather favoring construction." The NP did object to the continuation of the line to Lewiston, which was then served by ORN steam boats. The ORN did not object to the NP's Lewiston extension, but did object to the NP building east of Lewiston "because the Northern Pacific has made no arrangements with it for hauling traffic from this rich country."

> For the present there can be no open collision because the Northern Pacific has its lines east of Lewiston to complete and O. R. & N. has its Riparia-Lewiston line to build. When these are constructed, unless by that time a traffic arrangement has been agreed upon, the fight between the two companies will begin in earnest, and a fight of no mean proportions it will be.
>
> [The ORN]...has offered the Northern Pacific a short route via Connell, but the Northern Pacific wants more liberal considerations than the O. R. & N. deems reasonable or than are usually recognized.[64]

On July 12 Mellen telegraphed Daniel Lamont that the ORN had let a contract for the Riparia-Lewiston line. "If report true action by our people cannot be delayed with safety. It is impossible to consider O. R. & N. going to Lewiston and stopping there." In a telegram two days later to Coster, Mellen believed that,

> vigorous prompt action our part will compel abandonment their present plans and make negotiations you are bound to have in New York much more favorable to our interests. Be assured I shall take no action that will embarrass situation though firmly convinced promptness our part in way construction will compel, O. R. & N. to same course it took in matter extension Dayton east. Our surveyors are done Pullman Lewiston and Pleasant View; right of way secured and contractors asked for proposals. Beyond this nothing will be done until advices received from New York.

Lamont responded July 18 that the NP executive committee temporarily postponed a reaffirmation of the May 16 authorization for construction of Pullman, Lewiston and Pleasant View lines "unless the O. R. & N. prior to August 1 shall either definitely accept the terms of settlement proposed or discontinue such construction [of the Riparia-Lewiston line]." A resolution passed on the 19th authorized construction of the lines "or such parts thereof as he may deem proper." The deadline for the ORN was extended to August 5. On the same day Coster wrote Mellen to be in preparation on the 5th if the ORN did not respond. He thought the Pullman-Pleasant View line should be begun first and that a line to Colfax would be too aggressive. "I think that, taken altogether, the Navigation people have made a big mistake and that they will be very sorry before they get through."[65]

It appeared to outsiders that the Hill-Morgan conflict over the NP was leading to a major fallout, but the situation appeared to change with the surprise announcement July 14, 1899, that John S. Kennedy, a long time Hill associate, would be elected to the NP board of directors. On the same day as the result of an agreement reached by J. P. Morgan & Co. and Harriman, the ORN directors voted to dissolve the voting trust, which meant that control passed from the preferred stock holders (NP, GN, and UP) to the common stockholders, the principal one being the UP controlled OSL. The *Review* pointed out that if the NP and ORN had been unable to earlier settle their differences in the Clearwater "they certainly have no decent chance of doing so now. Nothing in the nature of a settlement is in sight nor expected." As to the GN the newspaper said "the situation will be unchanged as Hill has been in sympathy with Mohler's actions in the Clearwater matter. Mohler can now proceed unhampered and that is what he will do."[66]

An agreement by the Morgan Co. and Harriman was not an agreement between parties sympathetic to Hill. Mohler's loyalty was tested. Symbolically, GN sleepers between Portland and Spokane were taken off. In early July Hill learned that the OSL was rearranging rates and diverting traffic from Spokane and the GN to Huntington. Hill threatened to build from Puget Sound to Portland if the UP did not give the GN favorable traffic arrangements over the ORN from Spokane to Portland. On August 1, 1899, Hill wrote Mohler that the GN traffic department was convinced that the ORN was,

> No longer neutral as between the Short Line and ourselves, and that we are not getting our proportion of the traffic. I am very sorry this has occurred, and unless it is remedied and at once I will take it up elsewhere in such manner as will certainly secure us the proportion we are entitled to receive. We want fair and equal treatment and have never asked for more and will accept no less.... Our Company has gone too far in building towards the Pacific Coast to be unfairly treated, or crowded out any section of business where it is worth our while to extend our line.

Hill sent a similar letter to Bull. Hill planned to "take up the whole question with the Union Pacific, who really are in control. Our position has always been to build up the Navigation Company, and the only condition we have made was that our privileges and facilities should be the same through the Spokane gateway as were enjoyed by the lines coming through the Huntington gateway."[67]

On July 29 Mellen wrote a lengthy letter to Coster summarizing his position. The NP never objected to the ORN building Wallula to Grange City. The NP would agree to the Riparia to Lewiston line if a settlement could be made with the ORN about trackage, with local rights, between Lewiston and Wallula. Harriman had refused to consider the question of local rights and was only willing to give the NP the same rights as the NP would grant the ORN east of Lewiston; this the NP had not been willing to consider. The only justification for building from Riparia to Lewiston, Mellen said, was the business east of Lewiston, which would constitute an invasion of NP territory. Thus the ORN should be stopped at Riparia, not Lewiston. If they built to Lewiston they would use the lack of local business as a justification for extending eastward. The NP should build Lewiston to Riparia and offer the ORN trackage, but there would be nothing in it for them. The line from Pullman to Penawawa and Pleasant View was thought as important as the Lewiston to Riparia in eliminating the NP's roundabout route from the Palouse. Faced with the possibility of the Penawawa line the ORN might be willing to grant trackage with local rights from Pullman to Connell. If the ORN would not agree, it was more vulnerable to losses than the NP. A line from Oakesdale to Colfax and another east of Dayton would cost the ORN more traffic than the NP would lose if the ORN built east of Lewiston. The joint use of ORN trackage would probably cause more problems than it would be worth. With an increase in business from the Walla Walla, Palouse, and Clearwater countries,

An NP 4-6-0 entering Troy, Idaho, probably from Spokane. *Latah County Historical Society.*

the feasibility of building a north bank line from Wallula to Portland would increase; such a line would be a great threat to the ORN. To stop the threat, the NP might obtain trackage on the ORN from Wallula to Portland. "One of the great difficulties we have been contending with in this contest has been the persistent statement by Mr. Hill to the O. R. & N. people that we would not construct; that our action was all a bluff; and that if worse came to worst, he could prevent us from doing anything; and if necessary to do this threaten us with construction by the Great Northern, which would surely bring us to terms." At the end of July Mellen stated on the NP-ORN division of territories:

> There has been and must necessarily be more or less competition between the two roads, and some friction has resulted, but the published reports have been much exaggerated. The door has always been open for the adjustment of these difficulties, and I see no reason why they should not be amicably settled. Neither company has up to the present time built into the other's territory and it is not likely that they will as the people who are furnishing the money to build railroads also see to it that it is not wasted and that no construction is done till they are sure of their territory. Neither side has as yet spent any money in this controversy, which has principally been caused by the jealousy of local officers.
>
> ...I don't see that [the recent changes in ORN management] can hurt us in any way, for I don't believe the O. R. & N. could possibly be operated more to the detriment of the Northern Pacific than it has been in the past. It will now all depends, of course, on the Union Pacific as to what changes will be made in the operation of the O. R. & N.[68]

On August 2, 1899, Harriman, Mohler, and Mellen met in Portland, and after a long conversation left on a five-car train. The next day they made an inspection of the Camas Prairie. In telegrams to Coster, Mellen said he believed it wise to accept Harriman's May 2 suggestion that if the NP limited construction in the Clearwater, he would discontinue construction from Riparia to Lewiston for six months. On August 7 the NP and UP/ORN put a six-month truce into effect. The truce together with the Morgan-Harriman agreement, July 14, represent the turning point in the Clearwater conflict in slowing competitive construction and directly leading to the settlement of the conflict ten years later. Hill's disruptive behavior continued, as well as the influence of the ORN's Oregon directors, but the die had been cast. On the same day Harriman wrote Mohler that he wanted improvements made on existing lines. Mohler was instructed to give "special attention to the improvements already begun on the Columbia River Line.... The money thus expended will produce better results than if expended in new and additional lines, and will materially strengthen our position." Mohler was to push improvements disregarding the source of the money. On the 31st Harriman wrote Mohler, "My desire is that there shall not be the least shadow of suspicion as to our living up in every way to the spirit, as well as the letter, of the agreement between Mr. Mellen and myself." Mellen had announced at St. Paul, August 10, "The Clearwater country controversy was settled by a temporary agreement between the [NP and ORN], that neither road would push its lines into disputed territory for the present, and in the meantime a permanent arrangement will be sought on both sides." Bull wrote Hill the 15th that Mellen was "flirting" with Harriman and had told Harriman that Hill was bluffing about building into the Palouse and could be brought up short if the NP threatened to build in the Red River Valley. Mellen at the NP's annual meeting in New York August 17 said,

> We have done more than agree on a truce for months. We have even begun to reach a basis of settlement... there will be no fight in the Clearwater country. I always insisted there would be none. We would have had far less trouble had the newspapers not made so much of the trouble, which was bad enough as it was. There are many details to be worked out and it may be some time before final settlement is accomplished.
>
> ...The recent acquisition of the [ORN] by the Union Pacific has facilitated a settlement a good deal because the Union Pacific being a very large corporation with many diversified interests has more at stake in bringing about a settlement.

He went on to say that there was now no need for the NP to build from Lewiston to Portland. The contractor on the Riparia to Lewiston line said that construction might stop after the ORN's September 7 meeting, but in the meantime he was ordered to get as much work done as possible. He thought the halt in construction would last only six months. The *Oregonian* said shortly after the agreement, "construction on both sides is for the present suspended. But it will be resumed within a short time, either through rivalry or through agreement.... The railroad problems of the northwest are simply in abeyance for the present, but the inaction will not last long. Agreement is possible, in order to avoid the duplication of lines; and yet the nature of the rivalry is such that no basis on which agreement may be reach is apparent."[69]

An important part of the August agreement was that the NP would sell its ORN preferred stock to "friends" of the UP. The NP sold its ORN preferred stock at $70 per share for $1,673,735. The sale of the stock was reported from New York August 26, 1899. On September 7 the NP directors on the ORN Board were replaced. Subsequently, the UP in an exchange of stock acquired the ORN at a cost of $24.3 million, including the NP's ORN preferred stock, or $22,788 per mile.[70]

On August 30 under the headline "Hill Bottled Up While Mellen is Calmly Sitting on the Cork," the *Review* provided its readers with insights from their reporter in St. Paul. Over a year ago Hill "declared war" on Mellen and Morgan, but has since been "completely thwarted." "'We have got Mellen bottled up,' boasted Mr. Hill less than two months ago, but it now appears that Mr. Hill is inside the bottle and Mr. Mellen is sitting on the cork." Hill's attempt to gain control of the NP ended when a new Minnesota law prohibited a railway charted in the state from buying a parallel railroad. Hill succeeded in getting Mohler appointed president of the ORN "on condition that in the management of the property he would implicitly obey every order of Mr. Hill, thus making Mr. Hill the actual head of the [ORN]." After Winter resigned as NP president, Morgan appointed, over Hill's opposition, Mellen as president. Mr. Hill evidently thought that Mr. Mellen understood that the NP and GN were to work together. There was an employee who was very successful in getting business for the NP which otherwise might have gone to the GN. Hill "demanded" that Mellen fire the employee. Mellen investigated and discovered that the employee was very valuable to the NP. Mellen paid no attention to the demand. Hill was furious and openly declared that he would get rid of Mr. Mellen, but Morgan did not cooperate with Hill's wishes. To add to Hill's annoyance the NP was prospering under Mellen and had enough surplus to pay a dividend. Hill opposed the dividend because he wanted the GN to appear as the more prosperous of the two and he "did not want the Northern Pacific to shine equally as bright in Wall Street." Morgan thought that the NP earned the dividend and it should be paid; a dividend of 1 percent was paid. Hill was alarmed by the NP intention to build from Missoula to Pasco which would strengthen its competition against the GN. "Mr. Hill accepted this as a declaration of war which he must meet. The battlefield was then transferred from Wall street to Washington." Hill then summoned Mohler to St. Paul and when the latter returned to Portland he announced that the ORN would parallel the NP's proposed line. So began the fight in which the ORN and NP sought to parallel each other's proposed lines. "All attempts to disguise the real feelings of the officials concerned in the matter has been cast aside, and there has been no attempt to conceal the hostility of Mr. Hill and Mr. Mohler toward Mr. Mellen." In the meantime the NP prevented the GN from reaching either Tacoma or Portland. Mellen had offered the UP the use of NP tracks from Portland to Tacoma in exchange for use of ORN tracks west of Lewiston. Pending such an arrangement the six month truce had been declared and it was suggested that if the UP refused Mellen's offer, the NP was prepared to build from Lewiston to Portland. At the same time the NP was threatening to increase its presence in the Red River Country in Minnesota and North Dakota. "With the Northern Pacific holding the key to the situation in Washington and North Dakota, it is not hard to identify the man in the bottle." In early June the next year the newspaper thought Mellen continued to best Hill, but the metaphors were then boxing and diplomacy.[71] Not mentioned is Mellen's sometime ally Harriman, and Harriman's probable restraint on Mohler.

On September 12, 1899, Hill sent Joseph H. Schiff, a close ally of Harriman and Hill's friend, a letter to pass on to Harriman. The sale of the NP's ORN holdings had left the situation of the GN's relationship with the ORN in too great an uncertainty to be allowed to continue for any length of time. "I have always considered it to be for the best interests for all concerned...a plan providing practically for the joint ownership of the Navigation Company in such manner as to secure to it the support and benefit of all the traffic of the other three companies." All three of the transcontinental lines should have equal access to Portland "as would accrue under separate lines owned by each." There should be an equal division of the business through the Huntington and Spokane gateways and the Portland and Puget Sound business would be included in the general arrangement. Hill claimed that he could build to Portland and into the most productive sections of the ORN for $7 million on which the annual charge would be less than guaranteeing the stocks and bonds of the ORN. He hoped that Harriman would look favorably on such an arrangement. He pointed out that the NP had to be included in such an arrangement because if it were left out it would be able to divide the business because its investment was less than the ORN and the latter would be unable to meet it. Harriman did not respond. Hidy & Hidy concluded,

> Hill was out maneuvered but admitted it reluctantly. At the moment he was unwilling to divert funds from significant projects to a probably marginal line to the Palouse south of Spokane, or to a more expensive one from Spokane to Portland along the north bank of the Columbia River, as suggested by NP officials. GN sold its ORN shares to UP in October 1899. The pain of the defeat may

A view of Kendrick, Idaho, from the northeast. The 56′ turntable, built 1891 and removed 1907, projects toward the Potlatch River, flowing right to left. Just beyond it is the coaling platform, built 1890, removed 1926. On the other side of the tracks there appears to be three grain warehouses. To the right is combination depot, two-story 24′ x 24′, one story 24′ x 33′, built 1891, and the water tank, built 1890. A two stall engine house was built in 1890 and removed sometime prior to this photograph. *Photograph PG 90-BK4-100 Clifford M. Ott Collection, Special Collections & Archives, University of Idaho Library.*

have been somewhat dulled by the profit of $689,076 on the $1,108,491 transaction that covered only 30 months.

If Harriman could not be brought to terms, Hill concluded that GN must be drawn closer to the NP. But as Pyle notes, "the management of the Northern Pacific was not altogether tractable. It was a big corporation, with big men besides Mr. Hill behind it."[72]

On September 18 Bihler reported that from Riparia to Lewiston the ORN had done work in patches with about 18 miles having some grading. Most of the heavy rock work was done. Bihler reported October 3 that ORN surveyors were active on the Camas Prairie; he thought the motive was to cause the NP difficulties in securing right-of-way and he had initiated closing up right-of-way contracts as rapidly as possible. Mohler interviewed in Spokane October 6 said, "We are building the line from Wallula to Grange City. Nothing is being done in the Clearwater or between Riparia and Lewiston. This covered by the six-month truce."[73]

Mohler telegraphed Harriman on October 6 and reported that NP employees were again at work from Pullman to Penawawa setting grade stakes, and considerable right-of-way had been acquired by cash purchases at high prices. Mellen wrote Harriman three days later that the NP was not working on the Pullman-Penawawa line and had not "for a long time back." The right-of-way agreements had "been hanging for several months." He concluded, "There has been nothing done by this Company that in any way infringes upon the terms of our agreement, nor will there be. Even if all the statements contained in Mr. Mohler's telegram were true, I do not see wherein our agreement is violated." A dispatch from St. Paul October 9 said that Mohler and Hill had met in St. Paul the past week and "declared that a state of war exists in the Clearwater country."[74]

The NP expressed an interest in expanding the Washington Central, located north of the GN mainline. Hill threatened to enter the Palouse in response. Coster wrote Hill in October saying that he hoped that a satisfactory arrangement could be made. "I cannot see how, under any circumstances short of a desire openly to attack the Northern Pacific, the Great Northern could 'build any line into the Palouse or Snake River country against the Northern Pacific.'" Hill responded, "The Great Northern does not desire to build any additional mileage in the West which can be avoided...the Great Northern has built a line to the Pacific Coast for the purpose of doing a full share of that Western business.... We do not mean to over-reach any one; and on the other hand, we do not mean that the Great Northern shall be crowded out of any section of country from which it might expect a reasonable share of traffic." The NP placed into operation all of the Washington Central, Cheney to Coulee City, Washington, almost 110 miles, on November 1, 1890, almost two years prior to the GN reaching Spokane Falls and prior to the GN locating a line west of Spokane. Thus Hill proclaimed the GN was entitled to a share of the traffic south of Spokane where the GN had no presence, and the NP should share traffic where it had a prior presence.[75]

On November 6, 1899, Jacob H. Schiff assured Coster that the UP interests, including Harriman, wanted to arrive at a permanent understanding with the GN and NP in Washington and Oregon and "I cannot see that there should be any difficulty to find a basis just and reasonable to all interests concerned...and I therefore hope, if [Mellen] and Hill will take up the matter in the proper spirit, that a solution can be reached." Coster enclosed Schiff's letter, writing to Mellen, "Glad as I should be to see an arrangement worked out, I confess that I am somewhat in doubt as to whether anything will be done." He had recommended to Hill the plan Mellen had outlined a year earlier to parcel out the ORN lines rather than share them. Mellen responded that he understood Hill as wanting to throw the ORN lines and the S&P "into one pot, they both being leased to an operating company." Mellen thought this "makes the thing palatable to Mr. Harriman and of course Mr. Hill, being practically excluded from all of the territory...stands to gain enormously by a division of the business into three parts.... There is little likelihood of my agreeing to any such scheme...unless there are reasons for making a serious sacrifice, of which I am not at this time advised."[76]

On November 15 two CSL lines, extended from the S&P, were opened to traffic; from Spalding up Lapwai Creek to Culdesac, 11.95 miles, and from Potlatch Junction (later Arrow, at the mouth of the Potlatch) up the Clearwater River to Weippe, 38.76 miles. In Portland November 17 the ORN chartered the Washington Railroad Co. which projected four branch lines south of the Snake River. One of these was from Pomeroy to Vineland [Clarkston]. In December McHenry sent Mellen a list of 24 routes the ORN had filed under various articles of incorporation. "It is quite certain that if all the projected lines are constructed, the object of such construction will be defeated, as there will be no land left upon which to grow wheat." He concluded, "Reading between the lines, this action on the part of the O. R. & N. Company appears to me to be an elaborate bluff, preliminary to a settlement with the Northern Pacific Railway Company." In late December the *Review* said that the signs were that construction would begin immediately after the ORN-NP truce ended February 4. The ORN had been aggressively acquiring right-of-way and station grounds in the disputed area.[77]

Coster wrote Mellen December 21 that Hill proposed that the Washington Central be transferred to the GN and recognize everything north of the GN main line west of Spokane as GN territory; everything north of the Snake River as NP territory; and everything south of the Snake River as UP territory. The line from Wallula to Portland would be used by all three companies and the GN would build south from its main line to the NP west of Ritzville, and would have trackage from there to Wallula. Coster was impressed by the plan. Hill's desire was that the GN and NP present a united front to the UP and in the meantime the UP should not learn of the plan. On the 26th Mellen responded that a territorial division was the only practicable scheme for a permanent peace. On transferring the Washington Central, he said the territorial division with the GN should not run west of the crest of the Cascades. On the division at the Snake River, Mellen said that he had always considered NP control of the WCR to be temporary. Mellen concluded, "I appreciate the necessity for an agreement first between the Great Northern and Northern Pacific. I believe Mr. Hill will have great difficulty in securing the assent of the Union Pacific to such an arrangement but I do believe if the Great Northern and Northern Pacific are united in the scheme, it stands some change of success....I am heartily in favor of giving him every opportunity to do what he can and am disposed to strengthen his hand in every way to that end." The *Review*, December 24, 1899, under the heading "Hill and Mellen Friendly":

> During the past three months evidence has been accumulating tending to show an increase of harmony between the Great Northern and Northern Pacific interests, and officials who have authority to speak, say that the coming year promises to be entirely free from friction between these two roads, either in acquiring new territory in the far west or in maintaining freight and passenger rates, says the Pioneer Press. This situation is said not to be due so much to financial interests in the properties as from a desire to make the roads develop all the revenue that they can earn and avoid the expensive luxuries attendant upon prolonged legal contests and a demoralization of rates.

Mellen interviewed in New York January 10 said the situation on the Clearwater truce was unchanged. He added that the Lewiston to Missoula line would be very expensive and would not be built until traffic was sufficient to justify it. The next day Mellen was quoted as saying that reports that hostilities would begin on February 5 were "without foundation as far as we are concerned."[78]

Harriman and Mellen on January 12, 1900, reached an agreement that with three exceptions neither the NP nor UP would, prior to October 1, 1900, survey, acquire right-of-way, or construct any line whatsoever between the Montana-Idaho boundary on the east and the NP mainline extended to Pendleton on the west. The NP would be allowed to complete a line in the Coeur d'Alene district and along the Clearwater River to the mouth of Cotton Wood Creek (Stites). The ORN was allowed to complete its line from Wallula to Grange City—which was opened to traffic December 1, 1899. If third parties were to "undertake in any way to interfere with the status quo" the two parties would confer and each would inform the other of any actions taken. (On October 2, 1900 the two parties extended the agreement until April 1, 1901, with the exception that the ORN could construct a line in the Coeur d'Alene district. On April 1, 1901, the two parties agreed to extend the January 12 agreement indefinitely subject to a 30 days notification by either party.)[79]

As a result of the January 12 agreement, McHenry informed Mellen on the 18th that "all surveys and right-of-way negotiations will be immediately discontinued in Washington and Idaho south of main line." Where right-of-way contracts were secured, the payments would be made and the deeds secured. All right-of-way agents in the region had been withdrawn and the engineer's office at Lewiston discontinued. On the same day McHenry instructed Bihler, "the spirit and intent of our agreement must be strictly carried out. My instructions do not apparently include the survey between Missoula and the Lo Lo Pass and this can be continued until further orders." In response to complaints from the UP, McHenry assured Mellen the 26th that all NP parties had been withdrawn as soon as they could be reached and "there is now absolutely no work in progress, other than on the construction of the Clearwater line to the mouth of Cottonwood Creek and on the Sunset line near Wallace." McHenry concluded, "Mr. Mohler's action is [inexplicable?] and very irritating as usual. He appears to seek every opportunity and pretext for imputing bad faith to this Company, and has done this in many cases, where our actions were palpably in accordance with the spirit and intent of the previous agreement with the O. R. & N. Co. Unless it is Mr. Mohler's desire to create and foment trouble between the two Companies, I cannot account for his action." Mohler reported to Harriman "all surveying, locating and negotiating parties are withdrawn absolutely from the field." Van Arsdol wrote Bihler February 10 that there were no signs of ORN preparations for work anywhere between Lewiston and Riparia. Three months later, the NP right-of-way agent at Lewiston informed Bihler that contrary to newspaper reports the ORN had not filed any maps in the Camas Prairie. In a letter on the 23rd NP Third Vice President J. M. Hannaford said that he had been advised that Mellen and Mohler had agreed that neither company would construct any more grain warehouses at their expense in competitive territory in eastern Washington, Oregon, and Idaho.[80]

Under the headline "War is at an End" the *Review* said January 20, 1900, "The termination of the Clearwater difficulty marks the end of one of the most bitter railroad wars ever waged. Every phase of railroad politics, diplomacy and force was brought into play by the lines interested, and the result is a clear-cut triumph for Mellen." The UP was still considering the proposal of trackage to Tacoma in exchange for trackage down the Columbia to Portland or the NP building from Lewiston to Portland. The next day the newspaper commented,

> The effect of the settlement on O. R. & N. plans remains to be seen. In making the compromise, or surrender, whichever it may be termed, it is evident that the interests of the O. R. & N. have been sacrificed for the benefit of the Union Pacific and Northern Pacific interests. The O. R. & N. loses the opportunity of securing valuable feeders, while the Union Pacific gets entrance to Tacoma and Seattle over the Northern Pacific tracks from Portland. If this to be taken as an earnest of the manner in which the Union Pacific is to handle the O. R. & N., of which it recently secured control, it is decidedly bad news for the Inland Empire. That is exactly the manner in which the Union Pacific formerly handled the road. Then the Portland line was used solely as a feeder for the big system, and local business was at all times sacrificed for through business. Under the regime of President Mohler the O. R. & N. has been operated in a decidedly different manner, and where before it was a losing proposition it became a big revenue producer. Local business was given every encouragement; feeders were built out in advance of traffic and efforts were made to build up the country, rather than to drain it of its wealth. Time will show whether the old policy is to be renewed or whether the more progressive Mohler policy is to be continued.

The newspaper wondered about the ORN's close traffic relations with the GN and Mohler-Hill "best of friends." "If Mohler leaves the O. R. & N., as it is predicted he will do. Hill's influence over that road will have departed. Present traffic arrangements may be broken off, and it will be then not improbable that Hill will build branches, and go for a share of the business of the Palouse country."[81]

Minneapolis *Journal* commented in early 1900,

> [W]hen President Mellen was looking about for some feature that would encourage an arbitration of the difficulty he sought E. H. Harriman.... Mr. Harriman never approved of the policy of the [ORN] that sought to invade the Clearwater country and obtain territory by conquest. In Mr. Harriman's opinion the Oregon road was going out of its way to continue a quarrel. But the man with the hoe was James J. Hill, and both Mellen and Harriman knew this fact only too well. As soon as Hill was left out of the calculation a settlement was speedily brought about. It was Harriman who proposed that the Oregon road abandon the Clearwater country. But he also decided that the Northern Pacific should pay its competitor for all the expenses incurred in making surveys and buying a right of way. This bill of expense was only a trifling sum of $50,000, and by its payment the Northern Pacific succeeds to the complete title to a right way through the very center of Camas prairie, which will become more valuable every day. Thus did President Mellen make a concession that redounds to the everlasting benefit of the Northern Pacific.[82]

A telegram from Portland in early February said that the reports that the Clearwater war was over to the disadvantage of the ORN were "unqualifiedly false." The ORN continued to spend thousands on surveys and right-of-way in the Clearwater country.

> Mohler took his road when it was a wreck and has brought it up to be one of the best paying lines in the country. Naturally his wishes and his suggestions would and will have weight with the stockholders. He is not avoiding an open battle with Mellen, and if he is given a free hand, as he probably will be, there can be but one, end—the downfall of Mellen—and that is the predicted end of the Clearwater railroad war. This big railroad battle is not ended, as a few days will prove, for on February 6 the six months' truce expires.

The next day reports from New York were that the truce had been renewed for six months and that the UP directors on the 5th had performed "the last sad rite over the corpse" of the Clearwater controversy.[83]

While Mellen and Harriman worked out their differences, Hill and the GN were not to be voluntarily left out of the Palouse. Mellen wrote Hill, February 8, 1900, concerning a memorandum that Hill had given him on a "Plan for joint operation of O. R. & N. by Union Pacific, Northern Pacific, and Great Northern railways." The plan was for leases of the ORN by the UP, NP, and GN similar to the leases in a memorandum Mellen sent Coster in January 1899. Mellen had concerns and wanted more information, but he concluded he would try to cooperate to make the plan a success; only a territorial division would provide a permanent arrangement in the Northwest.[84]

Mellen wrote Coster March 9 that the day before Hill was confident that everything would be arranged with the ORN, but in Mellen's view it was not possible to have an agreement on the terms of Hill's proposal and that even a slight modification was likely to make the arrangement more undesirable for one of the parties.

> I have encouraged him in every way I could. He seems quite friendly, more so than at any time since my connection with this Company, and is extremely complimentary and nice. Whether it is the results of the re-action from his recent experience with you, or his desire to have me assist him with Mr. Harriman, or what, the Lord only knows, and I suppose I shall always remain in ignorance. I am very glad of the change although I know it will be only temporary and the re-action will probably carry him as far in the opposite direction as he has been at various times before during my administration.[85]

The NP board of directors on March 20, 1900, passed a resolution memorializing the death of Charles Coster stating that they had suffered a great and irreparable loss and it was impossible to overestimate the value of his service to the NP. Hill had been impressed with Coster's good intentions and integrity, but thought him unyielding on many occasions. Another Morgan partner, E. Robert Bacon, replaced Coster on the NP board. Hill began to have more success in influencing the Morgan company.[86]

On March 31, 1900, Hill wrote NP Vice President Lamont that he had no response from Harriman regarding ORN matters. NP Chairman Edward Adams, writing Mellen concerning the Washington Central, April 3, concluded, "It would not be surprising if Mr. Hill should at this time endeavor to improve what he may consider his opportunity, since the death of Mr. Coster, to seek some advantage over the Northern Pacific that I do not believe he would have attempted when his acts were subject to the scrutiny of such a master mind." Mellen responded on the 20th, since Coster died he had only Adams to whom he could speak his mind. Hill had attacked the NP "in every way he desires...with his officials on guard without, and directors in his interest on guard within, it is a little short of miraculous we have been able to do so well." Mellen wished that Adam's banker friends would have "a little more independence of Mr. Hill; a little more knowledge of the conditions surrounding this property.... Mr. Hill is...making up his own figures" and his "whole end and aim is to acquire this valuable property to bolster up and sustain one not nearly so valuable, to add our blood to strengthen his wind.... I should be strongly tempted to encourage Mr. Harriman to make me the offer he has several times said only awaits my suggestion, that the same will be favorably considered."[87]

On July 21 Lamont wrote Hill that Morgan was "disposed to meet your views about matters in the West" and was anxious for an early settlement of matters with Harriman in order to reassure foreign security owners. "Mr. Harriman is disposed to delay the matter and will not of himself promote any early agreement."[88]

In early August 1900 Mellen in Spokane said that the NP did not intend to make any extensions in the Clearwater country and would not build down the Snake River from Lewiston. There was nothing to prevent the ORN from building to Lewiston, but "we would certainly resent their doing so.... By the present arrangement nearly all of the business comes from Spokane, but in the event that the O. R. & N. enters the territory by rail much of it will be diverted and Spokane business men would be the losers." The NP surveys in Montana and eastern Washington were for informational purposes and not because of contemplated immediate construction.[89]

In early November 1900 Mellen said that he had conferred with Hill and "we found that our ideas were much more similar than we had supposed. I may say that the relations between the two roads are as harmonious as those of any two competing roads in the country. At the same time a break might come any day, although the sky at present is quite clear." A report from New York on the 10th said Mellen viewed agreement with Hill as "far from being a cast-iron affair, but on the contrary is largely tentative and as yet quite incomplete." Another report the same day said that the GN was about to conclude a traffic agreement with the UP which had the exchange of business "on a more extensive scale." On the 15th Hill denied that there was any such agreement.[90]

It was announced November 12 that the NP voting trust of December 1, 1896, would be dissolved January 1, 1901 (rather than November 1, 1901, the original date). The voting trustees would distribute the shares of stock they held in exchange for the outstanding trust certificates. Stories prior to the 12th said Hill and associates had been buying NP securities and had obtained control of the NP in cooperation with J. P. Morgan. Mellen said, "If there is any truth in that story I am wholly ignorant of it." On the 21st Mellen said that rumors of a GN takeover had cost the NP a half million dollars because some of the NP's largest shippers were holding back to see what would happen. "Many of our best men have become frightened by the persistent report that President Hill...has secured control of the stock of the Northern Pacific...." Two days later the *Review* assessed the situation: "President Mellen may be literally correct when he declares that President Hill does not 'control' the Northern Pacific, but he can not convince the public that there is no foundation of fact in the news that the two companies have been brought under a close joint ownership. In all probability, the two roads will always be operated as separate systems and within certain bounds we may expect considerable competition for traffic. But there will be no rate cutting. There will be no building of rival branch lines."[91]

Henry Villard died November 13, 1900, at home at Dobbs Ferry, New York. Villard's direct NP influence ended in 1893. The *Review* noted that 18 years earlier the death of Villard would have thrown Wall Street and been a "sensation" on the Pacific Coast, but no longer; articles on his death were on pages six and nine. On the same day the Montana copper magnate Marcus Daly died, and the newspaper had stories on pages one, three, and seven.[92]

A report from New York December 22 said that the three principal GN stockholders, James J. Hill, John S. Kennedy, and Lord Strathcona were the three largest holders of NP stock. Strathcona was also on the executive committee of the Canadian Pacific. When Mohler was asked in Portland January 4 about railroad consolidations he responded, "All the information I have on these subjects had come to me thorough the newspapers. I have not been consulted in regard to them and know nothing further than you do."[93]

In a January 24, 1901, letter to Hill, Harriman, reflecting on their conversations, proposed a close traffic alliance between the three companies rather than trackage. The alliance would involve the leasing of lines, assigned territories, and divisions of traffic. Hill responded on the 29th that a close traffic alliance had "a pleasant and assuring sound," but it would be illegal and was more apt to lead to trouble than to avoid it. "I see no permanent relief to the situation except through control of the lines in competing territory, giving to each Company the benefit of natural or permanent reasons for such a division.... I am at last forced to the conclusion that no lasting settlement will be made except on some such basis as I have outlined in the enclosed memorandum." The memorandum was apparently the one that Mellen referred to in his letter to Hill February 8, 1900, above. Hill wrote NP Director Bacon, the Morgan representative, February 7, 1901, that he was getting the actual earnings of the ORN from Jacob H. Schiff, a Harriman banker.

> I do not think Mr. Harriman is inclined to give up the lines North of Snake River if he can avoid it. At the same

time, Mr. Schiff has always shown a disposition to arrive at an amicable and fair settlement. Mr. Harriman used the argument with him that our proposed joint guarantee, amounting to about $1,200,000 for half the mileage of the Navigation Company, is not enough, inasmuch as that Company's net income is over Three million dollars annually.... With the actual figures of the earnings of the lines North of Snake River, we can make an offer, based on the earning value, which will remove any strength there may be in Mr. Harriman's position. Mr. Schiff's last words to me were that an offer based on the earning capacity of the lines should form a fair basis of agreement.... If no agreement is arrived at, it will probably lead to the building of several lines of unnecessary railway.[94]

On March 6, 1901, the report from New York was that Hill and friends were seeking to gain control of the Burlington for the GN and NP. It was said that both the NP and UP had sufficient stock to have representation on the Burlington board. Also in March, following the failure of a deal to bring the Milwaukee Road under the control of the NP-GN, the road definitely decided to build west of the Missouri River, projecting a line from Evarts, South Dakota, to Helena, Montana.[95] Thus in March 1901 the struggle for control of the Burlington and the westward extension of the Milwaukee were set in motion while the situation in the Pacific Northwest remained unsettled.

XVI

Conflict and Agreement, 1901–1910

As related in the previous chapter, Mellen and Harriman reached a temporary agreement, renewed several times, on construction in the Snake/Clearwater country. The agreement did not satisfy Portland nor Hill. This chapter brings the actions of the principal actors up to 1910, by which time these matters were largely settled. Events on the ground are related in the following two chapters.

In early 1901 the conflict between Hill and Harriman turned national. National events provide context for the regional conflict. There are many accounts of the broader conflict, some of which are in the note to this paragraph. Klein summarized the situation: "Harriman had triggered…[the] events by seizing the Navigation line while negotiating peace in the Northwest. Hill retaliated by grabbing the Burlington, then refusing to share it just as Harriman had declined to share Navigation." Harriman then sought control of the NP to influence its half interest in the Burlington. Hill, obsessed with controlling his property, soon had $13 million of his own money invested in the NP. The price of NP stock rose to very high levels and more stock was promised than existed. The result was that Hill and J. Pierpont Morgan controlled the company by holding a majority of the NP common stock, but Harriman and associates had a majority of the NP preferred stock. In an attempt to bring stability to the situation on May 31, 1901, the Metropolitan Club (or Arbitration) Agreement was signed by Schiff, Harriman, Bacon, and Hill. The agreement authorized J. P. Morgan to name the new NP board. At Harriman's insistence the agreement also provided that a plan for establishing and maintaining uniform methods of management and accounting for the UP, SP, NP, GN, and Burlington would be formulated by representatives of the UP, SP, NP, and GN, and any disagreement would be referred to a third party. On November 12 a holding company, the Northern Securities Company, was established. Hill controlled the company, but Harriman had a large investment as a result of trading his NP stock for stock in the holding company. On March 14, 1904, the United States Supreme Court declared that the Northern Securities Company an illegal restraint on trade. Hill formulated a plan for the assets of the company, Harriman objected, but Hill was upheld in court in 1905. Klein captured the situation: "Seven years of struggle and negotiation had brought all sides back to square one in the Northwest, the only difference being a heightened level of bitterness and distrust."[1]

In the meantime as a result of the May 31 agreement there was an overhaul of the NP board of directors, with Hill, Harriman, and W. Rockefeller among others joining the board. Kendrick was replaced as NP general manager by W. G. Pearce. According to Martin, Hill insisted that Mellen be replaced as soon as Morgan could find a place for him. Mellen "was quickly isolated and forbidden to make any important decisions." Maybe not important decisions, but he nevertheless made decisions that irritated Hill. It was thought in June that Hill's friend, ORN President Mohler, would replace Mellen as president of the NP. Late in December Mellen found it necessary to issue a statement he had not resigned nor was he contemplating resignation. He said the railroad had operated independently and the same parties had owned stock for several years.[2]

In mid-July it was announced that NP Chief Engineer Edwin H. McHenry would resign effective September 1, 1901. When asked about his resignation, McHenry was quoted as saying, "I have not resigned because I need rest or am in ill health. Neither have I resigned to take a better position nor because I was asked to resign. I resigned because—well, because in trying to figure out the problem of grade reduction, I found a "hill" which could not be overcome." When McHenry was an NP receiver a story was that Hill demanded changes be made in accordance with GN plans, to which McHenry responded that the NP was running along lines favored by McHenry and his associates and not according to Hill's wishes. Both Mellen and McHenry favored aggressive expansion of the NP. One example of this was the Lind-Ellensburg cutoff, whose construction ceased at about this time. This was probably a "'hill' which could not be overcome."[3] McHenry was replaced by W. L. Darling.

Mellen, in Lewiston in August 1901, said that either the NP or the ORN would in the near future build from Riparia to Lewiston "intimating that the trackage would

NP engine No. 375 has train No. 10 to Spokane on the first crossing of Bear Creek just short of entering Vollmer, Idaho [later Troy] in 1902. The engine is a 4-6-0, Class E-2, built by Baldwin 1888. The last couple of cars are passing over the switch to the Vollmer Log Spur. *Photograph 80-4-89B (Banks Photo, Frank Hawkins Collection) Nez Perce County Historical Society, Lewiston, Idaho.*

be used by the two companies jointly." The CSL would soon build into the Camas Prairie, but in regards to the line to Missoula he did not give any encouragement. A contractor said he would commence construction of the ORN line from Riparia to Lewiston March 1, 1902, and that it would be completed in six to eight months.[4]

On May 9, 1902, Mellen returned to the NP general counsel a fourth draft of a contract between the NP and UP. The draft was a UP revision of a March 7 draft drawn up by the NP general counsel. Mellen strongly objected to a provision leasing to a new company the NP line from Potlatch Junction to Lewiston. It "should not, in my judgment, be parted with under any circumstances" and was inconsistent with the memorandum initialed by Harriman and Hill. He also objected to requiring the new company to lease the ORN bridge at Riparia, whose use would require an additional bridge at Lewiston. A line on the south bank of the Snake River could cross at Lewiston without assuming a rental on the bridge at Riparia which would be "wholly for the benefit of the O. R. & N. Company." He did not think Hill would agree to the bridge lease. Furthermore, the ORN should not be allowed to build a line from Huntington to Lewiston; if built it should be done by the new company. Other things in the draft were not discussed in New York including diverting NP business to the new company. Mellen and Harriman, meeting in Portland in May, agreed that the chief engineers of the two companies were to compare the north and south bank lines. In a speech in Portland May 19, 1902, Harriman announced that the Lewiston-Riparia railroad would be used jointly by the ORN and NP. When asked which railroad would build the line, Harriman responded: "That is a mere matter of detail that will be worked out in its time. The important thing is that the road will be built and operated in the common interest of the producers and business men as well as the railroads serving this important cause. The new road will be built just as soon as the men and materials can be assembled for it.... We are so adjusting affairs as to give the best service possible at the least cost price with justice to all." The report May 27 was that construction would begin no later than June 15. Hill was sent a fifth revision on June 2 plus earlier drafts and Mellen's May 9 letter. The new revision was claimed to be materially the same as the first draft agreed to by GN Vice President William P. Clough.[5]

On May 25 Darling sent Mellen a cost comparison of the Riparia-Lewiston lines. He concluded that the south bank line would cost $220,000 less than the north bank line. The ORN had expended $350,000 for the Riparia bridge and $146,000 for right of way and grading. If the decision was to use the north bank the NP should not be charged the cost or operation of the draw span at Riparia.[6]

On June 16 Mellen wrote Clough that he had just received a telegram from Harriman: "Agreeably with arrangement made when we met at Portland, I have authorized contract for the construction on north bank of Snake River from Lewiston to Riparia." Mellen immediately wired Harriman, "I certainly never have agreed to anything that can be construed as authorizing construction on north bank of Snake River between Lewiston and Riparia. I am agreeable to joint construction between those points, as stated to you in Portland, and will recommend this to our Committee, but am not prepared to recommend north bank, as our engineer reports it most expensive and least desirable." Mellen wrote Clough that he was willing to consider the relative merits of the two locations, "but I have not agreed with Mr. Harriman to do more, and just what he is at by taking upon himself the authority to do what his telegram indicates is something I am unable to explain or understand." Clough wrote Hill on the 18th that he had talked to Harriman earlier and that Harriman had revealed his telegram to Mellen. Clough said he expressed surprise because he thought the matter was settled that the line would be done jointly. Harriman "intimated that the conclusion of the business had been delayed too long and that the only way to get the work started was to start it. He also said that as the contract is proposed the NP would have two entrances into Lewiston, while the UP have but one. What he meant was the NP would continue to operate into and out of that place from Spokane by its own trains and at the same time share in the business of the lease company into and out of Lewiston. But this has been a feature of all drafts of the contract from the beginning. It necessarily results from the NP continuing to operate the line from Potlatch Junction into Lewiston." In a second letter to Hill, Clough wrote that Harriman was making "'a bluff' to cover up something else he is after." On the same day Hill telegraphed Harriman that Mellen and the NP engineers "know more about the country than Mr. Harriman or myself and am satisfied if matter is to be settled now it should be a southern line."[7]

On July 2 Harriman wrote Mohler that he had discussed with Mellen "which was the best side of the river as to strategic advantages." He asked Mohler what he thought of making the connection between the NP and the new line at Potlatch Junction rather than Lewiston. Mellen told Harriman that the NP had no preference for either line except for economy. Harriman asked Mohler to send ORN Chief Engineer W. H. Kennedy to St. Paul to meet with Darling.[8]

Kennedy and Darling on July 11 sent a joint letter to Mellen and Harriman and separate letters to their superiors, Mellen, Harriman, and Mohler. Both lines could be built to essentially the same standards and the comparison was made on that basis. A north bank line required two bridges, the Riparia bridge and a new bridge at Lewiston over the Clearwater River. A south bank line would require only a new Snake River bridge at Lewiston. A north bank line, including the Clearwater bridge, but excluding the Riparia bridge, would be $179,520 less than a south bank line. If the cost of the Riparia bridge were included, the north bank line would be $179,804 more than the south bank line, including the Snake River bridge at Lewiston. "For purpose of operation and maintenance the value of the two lines if constructed would be identical." The engineers recommended constructing the north bank line provided that the ORN be credited with $529,163 for the Riparia bridge and expenditures on the north bank line and credit the new company with the $179,804 which the south bank line would have saved over the north bank plus credit the NP with $20,381 spent on the south bank. In his letter to Mellen, Darling commented, "The location through the town of Lewiston, whether the line on the north or south bank is used, is very perplexing. The tracks and terminals constructed by the Northern Pacific are about five feet below high water. As [either] bridge is directly west of the depot and must necessarily be considerably above high water, the tracks and terminal in Lewiston will have to be raised up to the grade of the bridge or have to be moved to avoid excessive cost of grading." The cost of crossing the Clearwater and raising or moving the tracks and terminals would pay for construction of a line along the north bank of the Clearwater from Lewiston to the NP's crossing between Lewiston and Potlatch.[9]

Following a meeting with Harriman and Mellen in New York July 15 Kennedy wrote that Mellen "strenuously urged that the line instead of crossing the Clearwater River into the town of Lewiston should be built up on the north bank of the Clearwater to a connection with the N.P. near Potlatch Junction. I combated this as strongly as I know how, explaining how vital it might be in the future for our road to be extended on up Snake River to a connection with the Short Line at Huntington. The conference adjourned without anything being decided."[10]

On July 21 it was reported that ORN engineers were cross sectioning the Riparia-Lewiston line and for a month they had been surveying for a bridge across the Clearwater at Lewiston. Japanese graders reached Riparia by July 24. Mohler said in Spokane that the line would be jointly used by the ORN and NP, but nothing had been decided with respect to an independent company. On August 5 Mellen wired Kennedy that "We object most decidedly to construction of this line by O. R. & N. or by any other company in which we have no interest." On the 20th Mellen wired Harriman that a company should be formed to build the line and if Kennedy severed his connection with the ORN there would be no objection to him being president of the new company and awarding a contract if the UP accepted the joint recommendations of Kennedy and Darling. Clough wrote Mellen August 27, "There is good reason for believing that H. has arranged for work to go ahead on a line he will control up the river to Lewiston. The trouble is said to be that Stubbs [UP traffic director], Campbell [traveling freight agent?], and Mohler strongly oppose a joint line, except on condition of the N. P. getting out of Lewiston and that he is averse to turning down his staff." Two days later Clough wrote Hill that Harriman would soon let the contracts for building the Riparia-Lewiston line. "He said he had already waited four years; that no progress toward a fair adjustment of the mutual interests in the valley had been made.... He is anxious to reserve the Columbia Valley to himself; and fears the purpose of the Northern Pacific to be to get down the north bank. It has occurred to me that possible his real plan is to keep the Snake River Valley for the Milwaukee, when that road pushes toward the coast. It may be his associates, who have large interests in Milwaukee, insisted on him doing so." He went on to say that Harriman did not believe that the NP would build over the Bitterroots because of the difficulty of the mountain passes and barrenness of the country traversed.[11]

In late September 1902 construction of the Riparia-Lewiston line was delayed by low water in the Snake River. An ORN director said the line would be built in the winter jointly by the ORN and NP or by the ORN alone, but there was a difference of opinion between the two companies which was unlikely to be immediately, if at all, settled. At the same time the ORN was completing soundings for a Clearwater bridge at Lewiston.[12]

The negotiation of the traffic agreement to be made as a result of the Metropolitan Agreement was assigned to UP Traffic Director J. C. Stubbs and Hill's representative, Burlington First Vice President D. Miller. Miller wrote Hill September 14, 1902, "I have been very much disappointed to find how far apart the views of Mr. Stubbs and myself are as to what would be fair in this matter, and I have very little hopes of reaching an agreement with him without the assistance of yourself and Mr. Harriman." Hill responded on the 16th,

> [Stubbs] is evidently under the impression that Mr. Harriman and myself have made some other agreement or had some other or further understanding than that of the Metropolitan Club at which both you and himself were present, and know all that was said or done. There is nothing further to say or do, except to carry out the intention arrived at during that meeting.
>
> ...In others words, the whole subject will be disposed of, and on the lines as understood, or the whole will [be] abandoned.
>
> There has been occasionally some apprehension that some of Mr. Harriman's people do not desire to carry the understanding into effect. While we are ready to carry out our part freely and fully, we will not be either disappointed or inconsolable should they change their minds.

On September 30 Clough wrote Hill that negotiations with the Harriman interests had gone on day and night and on Sunday with little result. The other side constantly tried to enlarge the basic memorandum to their advantage. "Three or four times Mr. H. has pronounced himself satisfied and agreed only to have his representative appear the next morning and demand things that could not be conceded. I do not think Mellen has helped much to accomplish results because he honestly disbelieves in the Metropolitan Club memorandum and would like to see it kicked over and a ring formed for a fight over the whole Washington and Oregon situation. He thinks Northern Pacific would fair better in the end." In his proposals he has "advocated trackage for N.P. from Wallula to Portland and for O.R.N., Portland to Tacoma and Seattle, with an equal right of the two companies to pick up and lay down business at all intermediate points; so that U.P. would be into all Western Washington on practically an equal basis, for O. R. & N. would necessary be in a position to extend branches at pleasure.... He ignored the fact that N.P. must soon have a line of its own down the north bank [Columbia River] and that after taking trackage on the south bank it would be next to impossible to withhold from the O. R. N. reciprocal rights on the much more productive and valuable north bank." On the same day as Clough's message, Hill wired Mellen and Miller. He told Mellen, "Think you had better tell them that unless they are willing to accept substantially what was understood...the whole matter will be dropped until they are ready." He told Miller, "I think your time is wasted in pursuing matter any farther. Give them ultimatum and be done with it."[13]

Stubbs wrote Miller October 20, 1902, that he understood that there was agreement with Miller and Mellen on several points of negotiation: a joint line from Lewiston to Wallula on which the NP would have trackage if it built over the Bitterroot Mountains and the ORN would have trackage whether or not it built from Huntington to Lewiston; NP trackage rights between Potlatch Junction and Lewiston; ORN right to rebuild its road to Connell and use of NP tracks Connell to Wallula; authorization for NP to extend its line to Grange City; and neither the ORN nor Southern Pacific would construct north of the Columbia River and neither NP nor W&CR would construct south of the River.[14]

In an interview in Portland November 18, 1902, Mellen said, "I do not know what the O. R. & N. is doing or is going to do in the Clearwater country. The Northern Pacific is not doing anything. I can't say whether anything is contemplated. I don't know anything about the proposed cutoff through the Clearwater country to connect with the Butte line. The cutoff from Ellensburg to Lind has been surveyed, but nothing further has been done that I am aware of." When asked if there was any truth in the rumor that the Northern Pacific was to be given trackage rights over the ORN lines from eastern Washington into Portland, he said: "I know nothing that I care to tell the newspapers about it." Mohler wrote Harriman December 30, 1902, of the considerable public discussion and feeling over the lack of construction on the line from Riparia to Lewiston. There was also a growing desire in Oregon and Washington to increase taxes on corporations and a belief that the UP-ORN merger was preventing the development of the Western States by new railroad construction.[15]

Failing to have reached agreement in the Lewiston area, both the NP and ORN became active in surveying and the NP acquiring right of way on the north bank of the Columbia River between Kennewick and Vancouver, WA. In early 1903 Mellen failed to convince his directors on proceeding with a north bank line, abating conflict in that arena for a time.

In January and February 1903 the net earnings of the Chicago, Milwaukee & St. Paul Railway Company (Milwaukee) declined. This was attributed to the diversion to the GN-NP owned Burlington of eastbound traffic which had formerly gone to the Milwaukee and the Chicago & Northwestern. In October the Milwaukee issued $25,000,000 in new stock. On November 28, 1905, the Milwaukee directors formally authorized construction of a line extending from South Dakota to the Pacific Coast. Track laying on the extension was completed May

NP engine no. 698, 4-4-0, Class C-3, built by Baldwin 1882, the location identified as Juliaetta. If correct the canyon is likely the Middle Potlatch Creek. The underlying basalt of the region is clearly shown. *Photograph N6603 (F Jukes Photo, Abdill Collection) Douglas County (Oregon) Museum.*

14, 1909. MILW activity in the Palouse is discussed in chapter XIX.[16]

Mellen sent Harriman, March 6, 1903, a draft traffic contract which the NP was prepared to execute once Harriman approved it. The proposed agreement covered NP, ORN, and SP freight and passenger traffic between Portland and Wallula, and between Portland and Olympia, Tacoma, and Seattle. On the same day Mellen sent Harriman a fourth draft agreement on a new joint company to construct a "railway extending from Wallula along the Snake and Clearwater Rivers, easterly into the state of Idaho." Under the agreement the CSL would sell to the new company the Potlatch Junction-Stites line and the Lapwai branch and its location, right of way, and real property which had been intended for building a line from Lewiston to Riparia. The NP line from Potlatch Junction to Lewiston would be leased to the new company. The SRV would sell to the new company the Wallula-Grange City line and the location, right of way, and property intended for building from Riparia to Lewiston. The ORN line from Grange City to a point of connection at Riparia would be leased to the new company. The new company would build a line from Riparia to Lewiston. The territory of the new company would be "between Wallula on the west and the Montana-Idaho state line on the east, lying within the drainage of the Clearwater and Snake rivers and north of a due east and west line passing through Portland, Oregon." The new company could build future extensions and branches within this territory only as jointly requested by the NP and UP. Either company could build for itself any line requested, but not agreed to by the other company.[17]

A June 27, 1903, letter from Spokane informed the NP that several lumber companies were backing the construction of an electric line from Spokane to Coeur d'Alene City. Mellen wrote Clough July 10 that the line would not be built without the support of the UP and concluded, "I regard the action thus far taken as unfriendly, and not at all in accord with what we have the right to expect under the general understanding of peace and good-will with Mr. Harriman." Hannaford wrote Mellen on the 16th that he had been in Spokane and was told a large portion of the line had been graded and he personally inspected what he considered to be a permanent connection between the ORN and the proposed electric. Further investigation by the NP's agent in Spokane strengthened Hannaford's belief on the 31st.[18]

In retaliation for a reduction by the NP and GN on canned corn from the east to Spokane, Harriman reduced the rates on California canned corn from Portland to north of the Snake River. The NP-GN rate reduction shut Portland jobbers out of the Palouse; the Harriman rate turned the Palouse over to the Portland jobbers and cut the Spokane jobbers out. The NP immediately met the UP cut. In mid-July NP Vice President Hannaford promised to protect Spokane.[19]

In August 1903 the ORN chartered the Oregon, Washington & Idaho Railroad Co. (OWI) to construct from Riparia to Lewiston.[20]

Clough told Hill in mid-September 1903 that Mellen said he was a candidate for president of the New York, New Haven & Hartford, but was uncertain that he would get the position because of the opposition of Rockefeller. "If he does not go to the New Haven road, he will stick to Northern Pacific, as long as he can, and try to make himself acceptable." Mellen wrote E. D. Adams of his pending departure from the NP and said, "It will be a matter of great regret that the great work of double tracking, and construction along the north bank of the Columbia River, will devolve upon someone else."[21] Charles S. Mellen resigned as NP president October 23, 1903, to become president of the New Haven. The same day he was succeeded by Howard E. Elliott. Elliott was able to get along with Hill, but "It is not recorded that Elliott ever had any deep affection for Hill." According to the *Times,* in early December, the change resulted in ending the fight between the NP and Harriman over lines in Idaho. "President Mellen was very jealous of Harriman's proposed encroachment in Idaho, but the difficulty has been settled in New York, since Mellen's retirement." A dispatch from New York, December 21, 1903, said that Hill and Harriman had reached an agreement that the NP would use the ORN down the Snake River from Lewiston and the ORN would use the NP line to Seattle.[22] Nonetheless, negotiations collapsed by the end of February 1904. On March 14, 1904, the U.S. Supreme Court dissolved the Northern Securities Co. and attention was directed toward terminating the company.

On April 1, 1904, ORN President A. L. Mohler was transferred to the UP as vice president and general manager. Julius Kruttschnitt became director of maintenance and operation of the UP and SP; second to only Harriman, the title was meaningless. On July 1, J. P. O'Brien became general superintendent of the ORN. The ORN stockholders elected Harriman president September 4, 1906.[23]

From a trip down the Snake River in July 1904 NP President Elliott concluded that building on the south bank would be preferred. The captain of the steamer said 70 percent of the business was on the south side. NP Chief Engineer Pearson wrote Elliott, July 8, that a few years earlier when the NP and ORN were active in the Clearwater country, the ORN had a detective named Riley who watched the NP movements and followed the Mellen party when he visited the country. "The party giving me this information remarked that if the O. R. & N. should still continue an interest in that country that when they heard of presence of any N. P. Officers there Riley would probably appear. Cipher message from Lewiston yesterday advises that Riley is now on the ground."[24]

In January 1905 Miller summarized for J. J. Hill why no agreement was reached on the traffic contract contemplated by the Metropolitan Club agreement which provided "two essential arrangements": a traffic agreement on business between Wallula and Portland and between Portland and Seattle and Tacoma; and a joint line east of Wallula along the Snake River to Lewiston and beyond.

> Mr. Stubbs and myself were present at the Metropolitan Club conference and we were directed to formulate contracts to carry out the conditions arranged for at that conference. We completed a formal contract covering the traffic arrangement...in October 1902, which I understood was satisfactory to the O. R. & N. interests, until February, 1904, when they repudiated the arrangement, claiming that the compensation agreed upon for the service between Wallula and Portland was unsatisfactory, although such compensation was in excess of the customary allowance for similar service, and requested that additional privilege of handling business to and from the Grays Harbor territory.
>
> An agreement was reached as to the proposed joint line east of Wallula...except that the O. R. & N. demanded that the joint line should concede them the right to run their own trains between Wallula and Riparia, thus depriving that part of the joint line of revenue on any traffic excepting that destined to or originating on the joint line east of Riparia. They also demanded that any line constructed west of Vancouver along the north bank of the Columbia River should be joint. Both of these demands were additional privileges not contemplated by the Metropolitan Club Memorandum and were declined by the Northern Pacific at the conference in February, 1904, and I am not aware that there have been any conferences on the subject since that time.[25]

On January 25, 1905, the NP authorized a CSL line from Lewiston to Pasco. NP President Elliott, in an internal memorandum March 1, 1905, wrote:

> If we are going to part company with the Union Pacific entirely it is likely that we shall want a line from Lewiston down the Snake River to Riparia.... At Riparia we would either have to trade with the O. R. & N. for the use of their water grade line down the Snake or build up to Pleasant View...making the cost of a connection from Lewiston to Pleasant View, 93 ½ miles $2,582,000. The line between Pleasant view and Grange City would have a grade of 1.32 west bound along the Snake River and an adverse grade of .3 east bound.

In the memorandum he also took up the issue of building from Pasco to Vancouver on the north bank. He considered agreements with the UP from 1897 to the Metropolitan Club Agreement of 1901. He did not believe there was any legal obligation restricting the NP from building north of the Columbia River, including in the Walla Walla, Clearwater, and Palouse countries as well as to Vancouver; all of this amounted to an estimated $25,200,000 program. A plan for surveys in the Camas Prairie, up the Palouse River, Lewiston to Riparia, and in the Walla Walla country was issued two weeks later. A memorandum of April 13 outlined a general strategy and concluded that the NP should give the 30-day notice cancelling the truce of 1900.[26]

On May 13, 1905, a New York report said that Harriman had been constrained by his bankers from invading Hill territory. On the 23rd Elliott wrote Harriman, "The Northern Pacific Company, believing that it is desirable to have a railroad built as soon as possible between Lewiston and Riparia, accepts your proposition for a joint and equal ownership in such road, and is ready to proceed at once to do its part in building and paying for the road." The same day Harriman responded "we shall proceed to finish the railroad at the earliest possible day." A contract to build from Riparia to Grangeville in the Camas Prairie was signed on the 25th between the NP and UP. The UP would build on the north bank of the Snake River from Riparia to Lewiston and when constructed transfer to the NP, "a joint and equal one half ownership" upon payment by the NP of one-half of the cost. The UP would cause the ORN to grant the NP joint use of the line for a monthly rental. Similarly the NP would construct an agreed upon line to Grangeville or Mt. Idaho and grant the UP half ownership and trackage from Potlatch Junction to Grangeville or from wherever such line joined the NP. Lewiston to Potlatch Junction would be owned by the CSL and its use leased to the UP. The contract also provided for the joint use of the bridge at Riparia with each railroad owning an undivided one-half interest. The *Review* saw the contract as "shutting out competition from proposed electric lines." It was reported August 2, 1905, that work on the Riparia-Lewiston line had begun. A resident opposite Riparia said that "a large force of men and teams and railroad building machinery had arrived at Riparia to begin work."[27] Elliott, not committed as was Mellen to an NP monopoly on the Clearwater and Camas Prairie, provided a substantive reason for continuing the NP/UP truce. But it would be four years before a final settlement.

The consist of the train suggests that it is train No. 10 to Spokane. The train is on the west side of the Palouse River between the first and second crossings. *Bob West Collection.*

In late 1904 the GN and NP acquired right of way and terminal sites in Portland and Vancouver, Washington. In July 1905 the GN and NP authorized a line on the north bank of the Columbia River from Pasco to Portland, later changed to Spokane to Portland. In August the ORN secretly incorporated the Wallula Pacific Railway (WPR) to build on the north bank of the Columbia River. On August 22 the Portland and Seattle Railway Company (P&S) was incorporated by the GN and NP (renamed Spokane, Portland and Seattle Railway Company (SPS) in 1908). It was reported September 10 that the NP had acquired nearly all the right of way along the north bank of the Columbia and that the sites for the Columbia and Willamette River bridges had been selected and work had begun at Cape Horn and Kennewick. The WPR began grading on P&S right of way; with time some small sections of track were laid and some work was done on a Cape Horn tunnel. It was reported in 1910 that approximately $200,000 was expended by the WPR and Columbia Valley Railroad Company in an unsuccessful effort to thwart the NP-GN on the north bank.[28]

On September 24, 1905, it was officially announced that the Culdesac branch, from Lapwai Junction, would be used by the NP for the route to Grangeville. On October 21 NP and ORN engineers agreed that the Culdesac branch was the best route.[29]

On September 28, 1905, the North Coast Railway Co. (NC) was chartered. The principal backer of the line was Robert E. Strahorn. The first activity of the NC was in the Yakima area, where the NP had a monopoly. In January 1906 Strahorn and Harriman reached a secret agreement which gave Strahorn the resources to pursue railroad surveys and development in much of eastern Washington. The company was re-chartered as the North Coast Railroad Co. (NC) April 14, 1906. While the new company's presence was extensive, its main foci were from North Yakima, crossing the Columbia River at Kennewick, to Wallula and from Spokane south to the Snake River. The source of Strahorn's money did not become public until November 23, 1910, when the NC was specifically claimed as property in the UP-chartered Oregon-Washington Railroad & Navigation Company (OWRN). The NC surveyed and partially constructed a line in the Palouse from Spokane to Lewiston. An account of this activity is found in chapter XIX.[30]

Elliott said October 25 that there was harmony between Hill and Harriman. "I think there is altogether too much inclination to create a situation that does not exist. There is no friction anywhere." But the *Wall Street Journal* on the same day pointed out that while Hill and Harriman may reach agreement on "small details, like the Clearwater extension," upon the larger questions of the Burlington building to Salt Lake City to connect with the Western Pacific to San Francisco, the NP reinforcing itself in Portland, and the UP building to Seattle there was no agreement between the two and none was expected. Hill said November 1 that there was no quarrel with Harriman and that there was no cause for any. Six days later Elliott wrote Harriman that given the changed circumstances since the truce agreement of January 12, 1900, the NP wished to exercise its option of a 30-day notification of withdrawal. He concluded, "In making this statement, however, I wish to say that our interests will be glad to confer with those represented by you upon any and all matters of common concern, and hope you will feel the same way." The understanding of the UP was that the withdrawal had no effect on the agreements for occupation of the country between Grangeville and Riparia.[31]

On January 2, 1906, the *Review* headlined that Hill and Harriman were ready to fight and were engaged in a series of tit for tat on Wall Street and on the ground. The NC was UP's secret response to the P&S. The Portland *Journal* reported on the 4th that a large party of NP surveyors were to begin work on a line from Ainsworth to Riparia. The conclusion drawn was that negotiations with the ORN regarding the NP purchasing an interest in the ORN's Wallula to Riparia line had failed. Whether this meant that negotiations in general had failed was a mystery. On February 14 the NP executive committee gave authority to construct a line between Riparia and the main line at or near Wallula. J. N. Hill, NP vice president, favored this line for traffic reasons, and urged action because the prospect of the Milwaukee building over Lolo Pass would complicate the situation with the UP.[32] In the spring of 1906 the P&S began work on a branch from its Pasco-Spokane main-line to Riparia (see chapter XVIII).

Elliott wrote NP Vice President J. N. Hill, October 10, 1906 that he was having surveys on the south bank of the Snake River re-run from Clarkston to Riparia. His reasons:

> The Union Pacific are evidently considering seriously the question of building from Huntington down the Snake River to Lewiston, and probably from Union down the Grande Ronde River to a connection with this Snake River line.
>
> They also seem to be considering getting a line from Lewiston up the Clearwater east, as they have two parties east of Potlatch Junction. Just what their idea is of going east up the Clearwater neither Mr. Darling nor I can figure out, unless they are going to try to get across into Butte later on.
>
> It has occurred to me, however, that the Union Pacific might be looking at this situation as follows: That they would build down the Snake River to Lewiston, then up the Clearwater, stand behind the Lewiston & Southwestern and get into the Camas Prairies via Lewiston, and also get into the Camas Prairies from some point on the Clearwater line east of Potlatch Junction, try to hold the south bank of the Snake, and then attempt to break their contract with our Company, under which we are now building the Camas Prairie line for joint account, and they are building the Snake River line for joint account. If they should attempt to break that contract, they could offer their line down the Snake to the Chicago & North Western, and might try to shut us out between Lewiston and Riparia.
>
> If we have a definitely located line from Clarkston down to Riparia, with some right of way we should be in position to check-mate any such move as that, and we can at almost any time take up with the town of Lewiston the question of a bridge and terminal scheme there that would give us our own line from Lewiston to Riparia, where we could build a bridge to connection with our line Texas Ferry to Pasco.[33]

In the meantime the ORN was making progress in constructing Riparia to Lewiston (see chapter XVIII).

In early spring 1907, Hill agreed to sell a strip of terminal property in Seattle to the UP. The *Wall Street Journal* did not view this as a settlement between Hill and Harriman; Harriman had to pay 10 times what the GN had paid several years earlier for 140 acres of Seattle terminal property. On April 2 Louis W. Hill succeeded James J. Hill as president of the GN. The father remained chairman of the board. On October 18 J. J. Hill's son-in-law George T. Slade, formerly GN superintendent, became NP general manager in charge of eastern divisions. Vice President C. M. Levy remained in general charge of the NP. Levy wrote that the ORN was likely to insist on a separate operating organization for the Riparia to Grangeville line. If so, Lewiston would be the natural headquarters and the station ought to have a second story to accommodate offices. Nothing would be done about building the station that year, but agreement should be reached with the ORN so work could be started the next spring.[34]

Internally Elliott wrote in September 1907, "we are not able to handle the business offered the present railroad, and it seems useless to be building additional branch lines until we get our main line in better shape for handling the present volume of business." He went on to say "general railroad construction must wait until the public are more willing to let the owners of property manage their own affairs and are less ready to reduce rates and encourage all sorts of laws for increases in expenses."[35]

The ORN September 9, 1907, chartered the Bitter Root Railroad Company (BR) to build from Lapwai Junction east across the Bitterroot Mountains to Butte. There was skepticism that the Snake north bank line would ever be jointly operated and the NP would be forced to build a south bank line. In the meantime, the ORN would connect its north bank line with the BR and would build from Huntington to Lewiston, and Hill would counter by building from the Camas Prairie to the Pacific & Idaho Northern at Council, Idaho, for a connection to Boise. In October BR surveyors were reported to be in the Bitterroot Mountains. It was reported that the BR would be operated by electricity; men engaged in find-

The caption on the photograph says "First OR&N [ORN] train Portland to Lewiston May 2. 1908." The ORN Clearwater Bridge at Lewiston was completed the month before, but still has false work under the last two spans. The line was officially opened in July. *Photograph 77-95 0128, Corps of Army Engineers, "Historic Lewiston Photos" folder, National Archives & Records Administration, Pacific Alaska Region (Seattle).*

ing water power sites had arrived in Kooskia early in the season pretending to be placer miners. They had located eight potential sites. Later it was thought by some that the BR would be jointly built by the ORN and Milwaukee.[36]

In April 1908 rumors in Lewiston said that Hill and Harriman were having difficulty reaching agreement on the operation of the Riparia-Lewiston line. It was "almost absolutely certain Harriman would never relinquish the Riparia line because he would have no outlet for his Huntington line and the proposed Bitter Root line." A train of 11 heavy Pullmans and "the two best diners owned by the Southern Pacific system" carried a delegation from Portland to Lewiston, arriving May 2, 1908. A fruit grower on the Snake River said in early June that the bridge was in and trains had been run over the line, but he did not think it would be available for moving fruit and probably not the wheat crop. Aside from the Portland excursion only construction trains had been run over the line. He believed that Harriman would not open the line until there was agreement with Hill on joint operation. The Lewiston Commercial Club asked the Portland Chamber of Commerce to join in a protest to the Washington State Railroad Commission about the failure of the ORN to open the line.[37]

On July 7, 1908, the ORN's line from Riparia to Lewiston, 71.46 miles, all on the north bank of the Snake River except for a fraction of a mile, from the Snake River-Clearwater River junction to crossing the Clearwater River to connect with the NP in Lewiston, was opened to traffic. There was little traffic because the operating agreement had not been implemented. The ORN did not allow the NP to make a connection at Riparia and the NP was said to be holding off agreement until after the wheat crop was moved. The ORN countered by surveying up Tammany Gulch onto the Camas Prairie. Citizens of Lewiston were hoping that there would be a rupture of the joint use agreement so that they would have two railroads rather than one. In October the ORN was constructing docks two miles downriver from Lewiston. This would allow them to receive grain from above Lewiston—further evidence that the agreement would be abrogated. In mid-November it was reported that the spur and docks were for supplying the road building from Huntington. Through rail mail service from Portland to Lewiston was inaugurated October 12, 1908.[38]

Track laying reached Grangeville October 30, 1908. The roadbed from Culdesac to Grangeville was in bad shape, sunk into the mud, due to the demands of traffic.

Operation began—Lapwai Junction to Grangeville, 66.77 miles—December 22, 1908. This completed the agreed to joint line from Riparia to Grangeville. Officials of the ORN and NP inspected the line February 17, 1909. ORN General Manager J. P. O'Brien was expected to be president of the new line and NP Second Vice President C. M. Levy, vice president. Louis Hill and Harriman were together in California for several days in March. Harriman said difficulties "were as good as settled." Hill said, "There has been no real fight between the Hill and Harriman forces within the last nine years." NP President Elliott was quoted as saying March 30, "While we have many surveys in Washington at present we have no new lines under contemplation."[39]

On April 26, 1909, the ORN chartered the Montana, Idaho & Pacific Railroad Co. (MIP). The railroad was projected from Lapwai Junction to Missoula, Montana, about 220 miles and on to Deer Lodge and Butte. In early August 1909 NP surveyors were about five miles ahead of the ORN east of Lolo Pass, but about three miles behind the ORN on the west side. Both were bringing in supplies for the winter. In July 1910 plats were filed by the MIP from Lapwai Junction to Lolo Pass. Snake River Junction (on the SPS) to Riparia, 41.03 miles, began operation May 3, 1909. The NP purchased the line June 30 from the SPS, the cost was recorded as an expenditure of the CSL. It was officially announced May 25, 1909, that the GN and UP would use the NP's line from South Tacoma to over the Columbia River bridge at Vancouver and that the line would be double tracked. In early September the UP and NP had a 99-year agreement for the UP to use NP line from Portland to Tacoma. The UP began using the NP to Seattle January 1, 1910.[40]

"In view of the great activity of the Union Pacific in the Clearwater Country," Elliott in late April 1909 requested Chief Engineer Darling to have information ready on a south bank road from Lewiston. Darling was informed that, except for two and half miles in Clarkston and some other portions, most of the right-of-way had been forfeited. By mid-May maps had been made of a line from Lewiston to Riparia, 70.96 miles, crossing from the south bank to north bank at Riparia to connect with the recently constructed line to Snake River Junction and Pasco. In late August it was reported that the UP refused to agree to joint operation of the Lewiston-Riparia line and as a result the NP would build along the south bank

Troy, Idaho, from the southwest in 1907. From the right are three grain warehouses, then the depot and the water tank. Troy was an important lumber center, but that is not evident in this image. *Photograph 15-1-2 (from Nellie [Wellie?] Olson Johanson), Latah County Historical Society.*

of the Snake River to a connection with the Pasco-Riparia line.[41] But this was the last shot in the Clearwater War.

On September 1, 1909, the OWI, NP, and CSL contracted for the joint use of the lines, Riparia to Lewiston (OWI, 71.46 miles), Lewiston to Joseph [formerly Lapwai Junction] (NP, 12.87 miles), and Joseph to Grangeville (CSL, 66.78 miles). The companies agreed to grant "equal joint possession and use of one another's lines between Lewiston Junction [Riparia] and Grangeville for 999 years from December 3, 1909." Harriman lived barely long enough to see the agreement. He died at his home in Arden, New York on September 9, 1909. On November 4, 1909, the Camas Prairie Railroad Co. (CSP) was incorporated to carry out the September 1 contract. The incorporators were two officials each from the NP and ORN. Two additional contracts were made November 11, 1909, to implement the terms of incorporation. The CSP began operating December 3 as strictly an operating company; all physical assets remained the property of the contracting companies. The earnings on through business were retained by the owning company handling the same; the earnings on local business were applied to the maintenance and operation of the joint lines. On December 23, 1910, the OWI deeded its property to the Oregon-Washington Railroad & Navigation Co. and on June 23, 1914, the CSL deeded its property to the NP.[42]

In an NP memorandum written in 1927 recounting the NP-UP negotiations in the Lewiston area, the unknown author writes: While from time to time there were charges made by both the NP and ORN that the other was violating the agreements of August 5, 1897 and January 12, 1900, "generally speaking those agreements have always been lived up to." The NP did purchase the W&CR in a manner the ORN claimed was a violation of the August 5, 1897 agreement; "the Northern Pacific was willing to sell a one-half interest to the O. R. & N. Company." The violations complained of were mainly surveys, but "little new construction was done by either company that did not have the sanction of the other." Territorial division did not materialize. The only lines constructed in the Clearwater territory since the 1900 agreement were specifically sanctioned under the terms of the agreement. The largest construction was ORN from Riparia to Lewiston and NP from Lewiston to Grangeville. "These two lines were specifically covered by an agreement entered into by Mr. Elliott and Mr. Harriman on May 25, 1905, under which it was stipulated that those two lines should be constructed for the joint and equal benefit of both parties. In addition to this, the Northern Pacific has, under an agreement with the Union Pacific, recently constructed a new line between Orofino and Headquarters for the equal use and benefit of both lines." The NP had been approached for extensions in the Clearwater territory and offers to sell small lines. Generally these were discussed with the UP, but no investments were made because it was not likely to increase revenues because the Lewiston rate would probably be applied. On May 2, 1912, NP President Elliott wrote OWRN President Farrell that he hoped the same verbal understandings he had with Kruttschnitt that neither company would promote construction in Lewiston or Camas Prairie without consulting the other would continue. Elliott believed the returns had not been such as to justify the creation of additional railroad facilities. On May 10 Farrell responded that the earlier understandings would be respected although Farrell felt that there was doubt as to their legality. He also questioned the wisdom of exchanging letters on the subject. The memorandum concluded, "The files I have examined clearly indicate that the Northern Pacific and Union Pacific have agreed that the Clearwater territory should be considered joint territory and that if either company constructed or acquired additional mileage the other should have an opportunity to use that mileage if it desired to do so."[43]

The Columbia & Palouse Railroad and the La Crosse Gateway, 1887–1980

This chapter continues the story of the C&P begun in chapter II. The two previous chapters examined the interactions of the principals from roughly 1897 to 1910 with regard to the territory on the margins of and north of the Snake River. This and the next two chapters examine railroad actions on the ground in the same time period. As developed in chapters II, IV, and appendix 2, the ORN purchased the C&P in early 1884, and the Oregon Short Line Railway Co. (OSL), on behalf of the UP, leased the ORN April 25, 1887, retroactive to January 1, 1887; an additional retroactive lease to that date gave the C&P to the ORN.[1]

The Palouse *Gazette,* June 24, 1887, carried a letter from traveler, L. F. B.:

> It takes seven hours to run from Palouse junction to Colfax—80 miles. People who come in here over that road to 'grow up with the country' usually find themselves done growing when they get here.... There is an immense agricultural country surrounding it, and the city can afford to be walled in by high hills so long as they are covered with fields of waiving grain.... There are numerous small towns throughout the great Palouse country, but Colfax seems to be well qualified to maintain its position as the leading center.[2]

On June 14, 1887, Thomas J. Potter, UP vice president and joint manager of the UP and ORN, sent ORN President Elijah Smith a "Memoranda for New Lines." The first of 13 recommendations was: If there was no agreement with the NP for train mileage from Palouse Junction to Wallula, the line from Texas Ferry to the 53rd mile of the C&P should be completed, a distance of about 25 miles, costing with inclines at Texas Ferry about $350,000. On July 26 the ORN executive committee adopted the 13 recommendations.[3] The Second Supplemental Articles of the C&P, August 17, 1887, proposed three new lines: Pullman to Genesee, about 35 miles; the Texas Ferry line; and from Moscow southeasterly and along Potlatch Creek to the Clearwater River, about 40 miles (for this line see chapter X). Only the Texas Ferry line was constructed.[4]

The traffic contract negotiations with the NP related in chapter II continued. NP President Harris responded to Oakes, July 29, 1887, "In view of the action of the O. R. & N. in utterly ignoring their contract with this Company in the matter of promoting Roads North of the Snake River, would it not be very unwise for us to furnish them trackage between Palouse Junction and Wallula Junction on any terms? It seems to me so. Whilst the [Oregon & Transcontinental] are doing their utmost to delay and obstruct the extension of the Spokane and Palouse, I think we should go slow in giving the O. R. & N. additional facilities. Don't you think so?" But Harris came to accept Oakes' view that trackage arrangements with the ORN should be made "with the distinct understanding that it should not include business North of Farmington."[5]

On May 30, 1888, the ORN resumed construction of the South Riparia (Texas Ferry) to C&P line. Oakes wrote Harris on July 17 that he did not believe that Potter was sincere in his suggestion of 60 cents per mile for trackage. "What his company seeks is an excuse for ironing the old grade and putting in a bridge across Snake River at Texas Ferry. This done, an extension from Palouse Junction into our territory would follow." Potter had not responded to Oakes letters on the subject.[6] South Riparia to La Crosse Junction, on the C&P, was opened to traffic on August 28, 1888 (see chapter VII). That year Palouse Junction was renamed Connell honoring a former NP station agent, and ceased to be an important interchange point.[7]

On November 16, 1888, the brakes of an eastbound freight train failed descending into Colfax, striking the rear of a passenger train. The engine telescoped the baggage car two thirds of its length and threw the coach into the ditch. Few people were on the passenger train, but there were serious injuries and the fireman of the freight ultimately died. In October 1891 a runaway went through Colfax before it was able to stop.[8] Uncontrolled trains on the grade into Colfax from the west were reported over the years.

Receivers of the Union Pacific System began operating the C&P October 13, 1893. Operation was turned over to the ORN receiver July 4, 1894. Beginning March 27, 1895, the Washtucna to Connell portion of the line,

29.73 miles, was not operated. The Oregon Railroad & Navigation Co. (also ORN) acquired the Oregon Railway & Navigation Co. August 17, 1896, and without a formal lease, operated the C&P from the next day to September 6, 1910, when it was purchased by the ORN.[9]

In the March 24, 1896, report on the S&P NP General Manager John Kendrick noted that the principal disadvantage in operating the S&P was the long haul to connect with main line at Marshall. This disadvantage could be overcome by diverting traffic via the ORN [C&P] to Connell.[10]

Kendrick wrote President Mellen in October 1897 that the ORN recently examined the C&P from La Crosse to Connell to determine the cost to reestablish operation. Mellen in late January 1898 indicated a willingness to make concessions to the UP, if the UP would among other things "give us trackage rights between La Crosse and Connell." Mellen wrote ORN President Mohler on March 17 asking whether the ORN would "consider the sale to us of your line from Connell to La Crosse, or a lease of the same for a term of years? ...If we should buy your line to La Crosse we should either want to make an arrangement in the way of trackage by which we could reach Pullman, via your existing line, or to build from La Crosse, keeping as far away from you as we could, for our desire is not to damage your property but simply to help our own unfortunate situation in this country, connecting with our existing lines at or near Pullman." Mellen repeated the offer in late June. At the time he was optimistic that Edward Harriman would agree to such an arrangement if the UP took direct management of the OSL and ORN.[11]

Sometime in early May 1898, NP Chief Engineer McHenry asked Mellen for authority to locate a line from Colfax to La Crosse in response to ORN "aggressive" surveying in the Potlatch country. Mellen authorized a survey and location from Pullman via La Crosse and Washtucna to the NP at Connell, about 90 miles and a branch to Colfax, about 10 miles (in June the S&P filed supplemental articles with the same descriptions). In McHenry's instructions to Assistant Engineer Bihler, from Pullman west it might be necessary to have a short pusher grade, but the remainder of the line should not exceed 0.4 percent. In May NP surveyors ran two surveys down Union Flat toward Connell. The *Herald* was sure the line would be built because it would save 100 miles and eliminate "some of the hardest grades in the road." When the Lewiston extension was completed work would commence on the line to Connell. The *Gazette* commented, "The new line will catch nearly all of the immense crops that now go to Almota and other points, making a great saving to the grower." The *Review* reported that surveys were being made from Pullman and Staley into Union Flat. In June Mellen visited Pullman. It was thought significant that the surveys stopped at La Crosse.[12]

At the end of June 1898 NP and ORN agreed to discontinue surveys to reduce friction; NP surveyors completed a preliminary line to La Crosse and then stopped work. On September 29 Charles H. Coster, J. P. Morgan agent, wrote Mellen to say that he believed it would be very difficult, if not impossible, to get agreement to construct a line from La Crosse to Pullman. "I therefore told Mr. Bull [ORN executive committee chairman] that I should be glad to know the basis on which the O. R. & N. would lease to the Northern Pacific the joint use, including the right to do local business, of its lines from Connell to Pullman and from Colfax to Garfield.... I told him I did not know whether you would be satisfied with this roundabout line, but that if his people would make a reasonable proposition I would urge you to do your utmost to make it meet the exigencies of the case. We will see what comes of it."[13]

The end of September Bihler sent McHenry maps, profile, and an estimate of cost of the preliminary line from Pullman to La Crosse. The line left the South Fork of the Palouse River at Pullman, up Dry Creek to the divide between it and the Union Flat drainage, 275 feet above Pullman, then followed Wilbur Gulch to Union Flat Creek and then down Union Flat to about two miles north of La Crosse. Except for the grade out of Pullman the maximum grade westward was 0.4 percent. The eastward grade was a maximum of 0.9 percent except for a two-mile fall of 270 feet in Wilbur Gulch. In that case a loop of about five miles was developed. If a 1.2 percent compensated grade were used the distance would be about two miles less. Because of the need to conform to the street grade, the line out of Pullman was 1.8 percent. If the line started about two miles south on the Genesee branch the line could be a 1.2 percent compensated grade. The distance would be about the same, but would entail heavier work. Because of the hurried withdrawal of the survey parties it was not possible to make an estimate on the latter line nor the approach to La Crosse. The estimated construction cost for 50.7 miles of main track and 4.3 of sidings, was $646,000 or $11,745 per mile. McHenry reported to Mellen, October 5, 1898, that he thought Bihler's revenue estimate was too low, he would double it to $256,000. He estimated the operating costs, interest, and the expenses on interchange business to be $152,000, "leaving an apparent net profit of $104,000, equivalent to about 16 percent on the investment." If a connection to Connell could be secured "the profits would be considerably increased." The next day McHenry wrote Bihler. "The 1.8 percent grade out of Pullman is quite obnoxious, but we may find it preferable to the alternate longer route." Much of the letter was a critique of Bihler's estimate of revenues. Bihler responded that his estimate did not include the first 10 miles out of Pullman nor grain from west of La Crosse.[14]

The Clearwater Short Line (CSL) Charter, December 5, 1898, projected a line from near the junction of Potlatch Creek and the Clearwater River northwesterly to Pullman and west from Pullman through Washtucna to the NP main line at or near Connell and a branch through Colfax to Oakesdale, approximately 140 miles total. McHenry thought that if the NP constructed to La Crosse it was unlikely that west of La Crosse would need to be duplicated. A satisfactory arrangement would be to use the ORN to Connell or preferably the line between La Crosse and Riparia if the Riparia-Wallula line were constructed.[15]

The December 27, 1898, supplementary charter for the ORN's Snake River Valley (SRV) projected a line from the C&P between Winona and La Crosse up Union Flat to its head, which would be Uniontown or beyond, and another either from near Elberton or Garfield on the C&P to the head waters of the Palouse River in Washington State (which would be south of Pullman). Both the Union Flat line and the Palouse River line would parallel portions of the S&P. The NP filed a right-of-way certificate January 1899 for a line from Pullman to Connell with a branch to Colfax and Oakesdale. In the meantime, NP surveyors were in south Colfax surveying on land recently purchased by the SRV. On April 3 Van Arsdol reported that an ORN party was on Union Flat working toward La Crosse. Reported April 5 was that the CSL was buying right-of-way from Pullman to Connell.[16]

The ORN Colfax depot, including freight, baggage, waiting and ticket rooms, burned January 7, 1899. The loss was about $4,000. ORN President Mohler said in Colfax on the 11th that Colfax would have two new depots, for passengers and for freight. By late January a temporary depot was completed. Mohler said February 1 that negotiations for a new depot site in Colfax were permanently broken off because of excessive land prices. A few days later the ORN land agent "reluctantly admitted" that property had been bought near the old depot. Whether the land was for a new depot or for a wye was unknown. Ten days later it was reported a wye had been staked out. Where the new depot would be built "is as much of a mystery as ever." Construction of a new 25'x96' depot on the main track began May 5. On June 16 the new depot was nearing completion and was being painted railroad red. In mid-August the new depot was unoccupied because it was alleged that the "building was erected without consulting the operating department, which can not use it at its present location" because there was no room for a side track for connections with the Moscow train. In September surveyors were locating a side track on the north side of the new depot and locating a new freight house. By October 19 orders were received to occupy the new depot and be ready to receive train No. 4 when it arrived in Colfax at 4 a.m. on the 20th. The old freight house was being rebuilt in December 1900. It wasn't until March 1906 that construction began on a new freight house.[17]

An ORN high official was reported to have said in New York City July 1, 1899, that the ORN offered the NP a route to Connell, but it wanted more liberal traffic considerations than the ORN deemed reasonable. On July 29 Mellen wrote Coster that, faced with the possibility of a line from Pullman via Penawawa to connect with the Washington & Columbia River south of the Snake River, the ORN might be willing to grant trackage with local rights from Pullman to Connell. The Pullman *Herald* commented September 23, 1899:

> It is evident that the Northern Pacific must ultimately build the line of road from Pullman to Connell, thus cutting off over 100 miles of haul from the Palouse country to tide water, and eliminating some of the steepest grades on the line. This branch will prove an immense profit to the railroad, and as it is profit the company is looking for, the cut-off will certainly be constructed. The company has already expended large sums on the surveys, and interest in the work has lately been renewed by the activity of the company's agents in the purchase of right way.

The *Herald* quoted a Tacoma *Ledger* story that a "prominent railroad official" said the cutoff to Connell in conjunction with the CSL line to Missoula would handle all the grain from the Palouse, Idaho, and Montana.[18]

It was reported that with the ORN line from Wallula to Riparia nearing completion, the railroad had by September 28, 1899, "completed all arrangements preparatory to the removal of the shops to" Winona on the C&P. A site of 32 acres had been secured. The shops at Tekoa and Starbucks would be consolidated at Winona and it would become the division point. The shops would employ about 100 men and the train crews of both divisions would have their layover there. The dispatcher and an assistant superintendent would also be located there. "It is now definitely understood that these changes will be made before the end of the year. It is safe to predict that in a short period of three months Winona will grow from a village of 50 persons to a town of 1200 inhabitants." A number of businessmen from the area were securing options on desirable sites. In late November the division superintendent and dispatchers at Starbuck received orders to move their offices to Winona December 1. ORN employees at Starbuck were very unhappy with the move, especially those who owned homes. "Almost to a man they declare they will never build a house in Winona, as they do [not] think that it is any more liable to be a permanent location than this place or Wallula, where they build homes when the shops and division were there." By December 11 there was uncertainty about the move; the superintendent and dispatchers had not moved and very little money had actually been spent on land by the railroad. A contract with the railroad called for the construction of a 24-stall brick roundhouse, a large machine shop, side tracks, and full equipment for division headquarters. By spring people in Winona were discouraged about the prospects, but were relieved on May 24 when surveyors arrived, spent a few hours at the shop site, and then departed.[19]

In late March 1900 the ORN began filling large trestles between Colfax and Crest. "The fact that work has been started on this makes it appear about certain that the Snake river cut-off [down Penawawa canyon] will not be built and the 'hill' which has been a bugbear since the road was built is to be improved and used permanently." Two months later, two of three bridges had been filled and the longest one, 65 feet high and 544 feet long, was nearly filled. Approaches to new steel bridges over the Palouse River at Elberton and Colfax were filled and when work was completed on Crest hill the work train would be taken to the Moscow branch to fill a trestle which had earlier replaced a Howe truss. Early in 1902 the ORN made extensive improvements, including steel bridges, between Colfax and Spokane.[20]

In May 1900, the *Gazette* reported that "from a source which gives it some authenticity and dignifies it with something more than common railroad rumor," the ORN would reconstruct the line from La Crosse to Connell in response to a fear that the NP would parallel the line and build from La Crosse up Union Flat to Pullman. "At present none of this line is in use except from La Crosse to Washtucna, with three trains a week. Beyond Washtucna to Connell the road is a wreck, many of the rails having been removed. The bridges and culverts have fallen in decay and nothing but the roadbed and right-of-way remains." The newspaper concluded: "Pioneer travelers still tell many good stories of the miserable service of the creeping train across the deserts and sand dunes until the soil capped hills of the Palouse country were reached, at 7 cents a mile, and of torturing discomforts of the weary layovers on the desert at Palouse Junction, where the hotel accommodations broke down the strongest constitutions and drove unfortunates to bedbug murder."[21]

Almost a year later it was reported that rebuilding the C&P from Washtucna west to Kahlotus would begin May 1. There had been substantial growth west of Washtucna and the road had been petitioned by local settlers. Settlers had used the ties for fire wood, but the roadbed was in fair condition. The year before the La Crosse-Washtucna branch handled about 620,000 bushels of wheat. Rebuilding to Kahlotus began June 1, 1901, and by the 15th four miles had been relayed. It was reported July 18 that the ORN had completed the extension to Kahlotus and it would be extended two miles to Harter's ranch where a new town, Hartersville, would be built. Washtucna to Kahlotus, 14.2 miles, which had not been operated since March 1895 was reopened September 1, 1901, and regular train service began November 3. In mid-February 1902 train service between Kahlotus and Washtucna was reduced to one round trip per week, on Tuesday.[22]

Early in March 1903 the ORN trains from Pendleton had been late most days because of the number of immigrants. Passengers from Moscow and Pullman had to wait at Colfax two to six hours for the Spokane train. "Local travel is demoralized and patrons of the road are preparing to enter a vigorous protest against the unsatisfactory service." As a result the NP was getting nearly all the passengers from the two towns.[23]

An ORN official predicted in mid-July 1904 that trains would be operating into Connell within the next four weeks. The Pacific Coast Elevator Co. planned to build wheat warehouses at Sulphur Springs and Connell. "Extend the road to Connell will not be a difficult matter, as the road bed is still in a good condition." But the same official a few days later said that the road bed had deteriorated considerably and the nearby farmers had taken the ties for firewood and only the rails remained. Six of 16 miles had been repaired by the 30th.[24]

As early as 1892 the Palouse River, west of Hooper on the C&P, was viewed as a source for both public and private irrigation projects. Around 1893 flumes were constructed along the hillsides between Washtucna and Hooper. In May, 1904, a United States Geological Survey engineer posted several notices in eastern Washington announcing an irrigation project using the Palouse River augmented by water diverted from Hangman Creek and a Rock Lake dam to irrigate about 250,000 acres in Whitman, Adams, and Franklin Counties.[25]

In mid-August 1904 the chief engineer of the United States Reclamation Service met with ORN General Manager E. E. Calvin to arrange a settlement regarding the rebuilding of the C&P through Washtucna Coulee, the reservoir site for the Palouse River irrigation project. The *Review* said, if the railroad gets out of the way there would be in three or four years water in abundance. "Should the government decline to spend nearly $2,000,000 in diverting water for the reclamation of nearly 100,000 acres of arid lands in Adams and Franklin counties...the O. R. & N. Co. will be to blame." The *Herald* reported that F. H. Newell, head of the Reclamation Bureau, said, "the railroad company now holds the key to the situation. Unless the company will change the location of its track from the bottom of the coulee to the adjoining hills...the work will be blocked." The government engineer said, "I was surprised...to learn that the company was putting a track along the old roadbed. We have laid the matter before the company and asked it what plan it suggests. I saw Manager E. E. Calvin of the road in Portland, but he was very indefinite and said he would let me know." From an editorial in the *Review*:

> The railroad's course has every appearance of bad judgment. Defenders of the doctrine of leaving the railroads unrestrained by the state have argued that state control was not needed, as the railroad companies would always be restrained by their own "enlightened self interest." That is, they would do nothing which would injure the people or the country, because their officers would always know that injury to the country would be injury to their company.
>
> But here is the O. R. & N. company blocking the greatest government enterprise ever undertaken in the state—an enterprise that bids fair to add 100,000 population to eastern Washington. In the face of shortsightedness, what are we to think of the fine doctrine of "enlightened self interest?"

Calvin responded in a lengthy statement August 26, that the ORN had operated the line in question for ten years and then discontinued operation, "during the entire period mentioned it has paid taxes on the line between Washtucna and Connell at the same rate per mile as it paid on other portions of the branch in the same county." The ORN "never had any intention of abandoning any portion of the lines and always intended to use the same whenever traffic demanded such use." Crop conditions in 1903 did not justify rehabilitation, but those in 1904 did. The railroad wanted to complete the work for the movement of the 1904 crop. To build the line on the north hill side would require a large expenditure of money for right-of-way and roadbed in comparison to the amount necessary for relaying the track. "Furthermore, none of the land to be reclaimed is tributary to the lines of the navigation company, and yet without any suggested compensation or recompense, despite the evident intent of the national irrigation act that the lands benefitted should bear the cost of the improvement, the navigation company is apparently expected to abandon 16 miles of its present railroad, construction of 16 miles of new railroad, and subject itself and the settlers on the south side of the coulee to continuing losses and injury." At the same time the feasibility of the project had not been established by the government. The government engineer wrote Calvin, "In going over the ground and discussing the preliminary estimates it appears that the project, while favorable in many respects, is on debatable ground of feasibility and unless you assist liberally it will not be favorably considered." Calvin responded, "I see no reason why persons having private interests within the limits of these irrigation schemes should sacrifice their property without compensation in order to avoid being regarded as obstructionists."[26]

On July 25, 1904, NP President Howard Elliott telegraphed UP Director of Maintenance and Operation, J. Kruttschnitt, that he understood the line to Connell would be restored. "Do you not think we should have joint conference before you go into our local territory?" The next day Elliott wrote Kruttschnitt, that he thought the road was unnecessary given the new ORN line from Riparia to Wallula. Furthermore, building the line would defeat a large irrigation project which would benefit the UP because of its ownership of NP stock. Elliott wrote NP Vice President Lamont on the same day, "It strikes me that spending money on this line is a waste of capital. The Union Pacific can do nothing but take away some of our purely local business, which is improving in that vicinity, and I do not call the proposed action in harmony with the idea that we were to work harmoniously in the Snake and Palouse River country." By mid-August Elliott had no response from Kruttschnitt; he again wrote saying that he considered rebuilding the line a violation of the agreement of January 12, 1900, signed by Harriman and Mellen, which had no provision for rebuilding. Elliott was informed that the ORN laid steel into Connell on August 13, 1904 (and began running a regular train on the 20th). The NP supplied water at Connell. The ORN would put in their own depot, no joint agency. Their reoccupying the wye required the NP to relay at least 2,000 feet of warehouse track and the ORN would put in a warehouse track one and half miles south of Connell to hold the grain that would otherwise come to Connell. The crop tributary to Connell that year was 500,000 bushels. The people in the area were "bitter" about the UP interfering with the Palouse irrigation project. Elliott wrote Lamont that to protect NP interests, the company consider withdrawing from the January 1900 agreement, which had been extended on April 1, 1901. Elliott suggested several lines to consider building after such a withdrawal. Kruttschnitt replied August 17 claiming the telegram of July 25 was not received and he did not see the letter of the 26th until August 10 because of travel.

> In reply, we represent that the repair of this line was considered in March, 1903, before we knew anything of the Government's intentions, and the failure of crops was the only reason why the work was not then done; that the heavy crops of this year which the farmers wished to have moved, justified the overhauling of a piece of track which was never abandoned and never taken up. It has always appeared on our time-cards, appears on our annual report map of 1903, and your own, and is a part of our system of as much permanence and importance as any other part.
>
> Originally want of traffic made us discontinue train service from Washtucna to Connell, 29.6 miles. In the fall of 1901, long before the Government's intentions of examining this valley as a reservoir site were known, the line from Washtucna to Kahlotus, 14.2 miles, was overhauled and repaired by doing exactly the same kind of work on it that we are now doing from Kahlotus to Connell, 15.4 miles. Mr. Mellen and the Northern Pacific officers knew of this but made no objection or protest....
>
> We desire to co-operate with you fully and freely, and to deal with you with the utmost frankness, on the lines of our conference in Chicago. We regret you look on our action in repairing our line as you do, but sincerely hope that on reviewing this matter with additional light thrown on it you will agree with us that we have given you no valid cause of protest or complaint.

Elliott responded two days later that he still believed that it was "an unnecessary piece of railroad work" and defeating the irrigation project was "unfortunate."[27]

In the meantime government and railroad engineers went over the territory. The government estimated that the ORN would lose about a quarter of the business south of the reservoir, but gain some from the NP on the north side. In early October Calvin gave the ORN response to the government,

> we have decided that if the people who have settled the country south of the line between Kahlotus and Connell are properly protected, we will assume some loss for the benefit of the country that is to be irrigated.
>
> If the reclamation fund will build us a new line on the north side of the coulee or reimburse us for such expense (which is roughly estimated at $300,000) and establish and maintain permanently free ferries at the two points between Kahlotus and Connell where we now have sidings located—one being about one mile west of Sulphur Lake and the other about half way between there and Kahlotus—we will give up our rights in the coulee and allow it to be used for reservoir purposes.
>
> You understand, of course, that this would give us a much more expensive road to maintain than the present one, and we would reserve the right to make the location of the new line ourselves in order to cut out the high trestles which are necessary by the line located some time ago. In this however, we would be entirely fair, and would expect the cooperation of yourself and such engineers as you might designate. It is to be understood, also, that our entrance into Connell on the new line must be such as to enable us to use our present trackage at that place and our present main line connection with it.[28]

Later in October three government engineers, after spending five days investigating, concluded that the irrigation project was feasible for $3,500,000. Water would be diverted from the Palouse River at a point near Hooper and flow by canal to Washtucna Coulee. The western half of the coulee, about 17 miles, from Kahlotus to nearly Connell would be a storage reservoir. The Palouse project was given preliminary approval in mid-November 1904. The U.S. Geological Survey said on February 12, 1905, that construction depended "upon the satisfactory adjudication of the pending negotiations which will determine the financial feasibility of the project." NP President Elliott in a memorandum, March 1, 1905, expressed concern that the ORN would be offered considerable money to relocate its line to higher ground on the north side of the coulee and then build north into Adams County and threaten the NP at Providence, Lind, and Ritzville. "I have given orders, therefore, to have an examination made of the possibilities of extending a line from one of these stations over into that country so as to protect us." The NP ascertained in April that nearly all of the country north of the Washtucna Coulee was under cultivation.[29]

In March 1905 ORN surveyors were in Washtucna Coulee to make a detailed estimate of the cost of moving the track out of the coulee and on to one side or other of the coulee. A statement by the ORN said that it did "not want to be understood as an obstructionist it is willing to do anything it can for the general good and is willing to submit to a change of line if the government will make good on the cost." According to the *Gazette*, "The reclamation services has used the argument that the O. R. & N. should make the changes at its own expense, because the service was proposed to irrigate [elsewhere] 450,000 acres tributary to the Harriman system." In early April the project was assured: $3,000,000 was available and problems associated with condemning land had been settled. About 100,000 acres north and east of Pasco would be irrigated.[30]

The Reclamation Service assistant chief engineer said April 21, 1905, "The estimated expense of the Palouse irrigation project is so great that it is doubtful if it is carried out now." Porous ground portions of the reservoir and canals would have to be concrete lined. The government offered the ORN $100,000 to move its railroad. The project would cost $35 per acre not including the costs of moving the railroad. "Officials of the interior department say that failure on the part of railroad company to pay a great part of the cost of removing the tracks would mean the abandonment of the project." An engineer in early May said in Connell that the Palouse project was feasible and it had not been abandoned. The physical obstacles were not serious, but they would be expensive to overcome. "The obstacle caused by the O. R. & N. attitude concerning the Washtucna coulee was of much greater moment." In November the project was granted $2,800,000, but was postponed. A consulting engineer examined the project in spring 1906. He reported that the original estimates of over $6,000,000 would not produce a successful work. He examined cost reductions, but the results would be risky and dangerous.[31]

The public Palouse irrigation project was dead. Did the ORN kill it? Gill takes the view that service was restored to Connell because of the general development of the country and "it was expected that a large reservoir would be built in the vicinity of Connell, which would make possible great agricultural development." Lewty's view is different: "This surprising resurrection was part of the power play between the railroad giants. By reopening the railway, Harriman blocked plans...for the Palouse irrigation scheme and thus prevented Hill's Northern Pacific Railway from selling large tracts of otherwise worthless land."[32] The UP may have been ambivalent about the project and thus both views may have some truth. The newspaper accounts placed much of the blame on the failure of the ORN to cooperate in moving their tracks. The ORN's cost estimate of $300,000 for building 16 miles of track was not unreasonable. In the author's opinion, the ORN was a minor factor; more important was the high cost per acre and that there was a more attractive alternative irrigation project in Washington State in the Yakima Valley, which was approved and carried out.

In January 1906 snow on the mainline caused the NP to use the ORN south of Spokane. On the 26th the North Coast Limited was stuck twice on the hill between Colfax and Crest. It required three engines to get the train up the 3 percent grade. ORN trains were frequently delayed by NP trains. On the 27th the North Coast Limited apparently broke a rail on the grade and an east bound ORN passenger train was flagged down as a result of boys notifying the section crew in Colfax.[33]

In early 1906 the ORN's SRV filed articles including C&P revisions between Colfax and Winona that more closely followed the Palouse River, avoiding the heavy grades west of Colfax; Endicott, Diamond, and Mockonemo would no longer be on the main line. It was reported January 18 that surveyors were working between Colfax and Winona.[34] The revisions were not built.

In April 1906 NP Chief Engineer W. L. Darling wrote Elliott that the Pullman to Penawawa line would not be in line with developments in the area, "but instead a line should sometime be constructed from Pullman west to connect with the Portland & Seattle at mouth of Union Flat Creek." Elliott responded that, "It seems to me that one of these days it may pay us to get a line from Pullman west to connect with our new Snake River line."[35]

The Washington State Railroad Commission, September 18, 1906, ordered physical connections at several locations, including the NP and ORN at Connell. The NP expressed a willingness to pay half of the cost, but the ORN declined. For several years the ORN fought all such orders in the Palouse (see chapter XX). On October 18, 1908, a train bearing ORN officials arrived in Connell over the C&P, but the train left over the NP. The *Review* commented: "The tracks were connected for the purpose of allowing the train to pass from one road to the other, and then as soon as the train had passed to the Northern Pacific tracks the connection was again broken. This incident is interesting to shippers, as it suggests the question. Why, if to accommodate, officials, a connection can be established between the roads at this point, can not the connection be made permanent, so as to accommodate shippers?" There are at least two plausible interrelated answers to the *Review's* question: ORN traffic to Puget Sound would have a shorter route if it traveled via Connell, and a connection at Connell would likely increase the pressure for joint rates, which the ORN opposed. The Commission's *Tenth Annual Report,* 1920, noted that the Town of Connell petitioned to compel the connection. The decision was under advisement. It was continued in the *Eleventh Annual Report* and dismissed without prejudice in the *Twelfth.* At that point the trail is lost. The 1925 and 1931 interchange tables prepared by H. H. Copeland & Son do not show Connell as an interchange point between the NP and OWRN (UP). In January 1949 the NP did not include Connell as an interchange point. In 1954 the UP listed Connell as an interchange point with the NP.[36]

A report February 21, 1907, said, "There is not a safe bridge left on the branch. The whole Oregon Railroad & Navigation line is a wreck from La Crosse to Connell. Miles of track have been swept away below Kahlotus. In the washout west of Hopper one can put a house under the track. Near Washtucna station the channel is 60 feet wide and 15 feet deep, carrying away tracks." A report in mid-March said that the ORN would relocate several miles of the line from Kahlotus to Connell that was subject to washouts any time of the year.[37]

There was a general shortage of cars to move the 1906 crop. A Wednesday May 1, 1907, report indicated that the shortage remained on the C&P. According to the *Review,* warehouse men at Washtucna had "a theory that the railroad furnishes just enough cars to quiet the clamor and then when the act is mentioned in the news dispatches the company takes its cars to main line points or those which are situated on competing lines." The ORN on the preceding Saturday left enough cars at Washtucna for 10,000 bushels. By Sunday two cars were loaded but two trains on Sunday did not pick them up. Three hundred cars of grain remained in the warehouses at Washtucna, 80 at McAdams, 40 at Estes, and 40 at Sulphur, and the Pampa warehouse was "jam full." "The locomotive power on the Palouse branch is sufficient to haul from seven to nine cars in a train in addition to the regular freight. Only north bound trains [trains from Connell] haul wheat." At nine cars a day it would take about 55 days to clear all the warehouses. A report the following Tuesday said that 25 cars were moved Sunday from the above stations. The report also said that a principal reason for the slow movement was,

> because the track and roadbed are so unsafe that the use of heavier engines is impossible. Repair crews, making slow progress, have laid heavier steel between La Crosse and a point four miles north of Washtucna, but the roadbed on which the new rails are laid is by no means in a state of perfection and old ties are still in use. The Palouse branch has never received a general overhauling since the line was built.
>
> It was only last week that the section crew at Washtucna removed a rail a few hundred yards below the station which was so badly mashed that the flanges of the car wheels had made their impression on the spikes on the inside of the track. An inspection made by *The Spokesman-Review* representative showed that the rails in numerous places in the vicinity were mashed and splintered, especially at the joints. Trainmen make it a point not to run over the branch at night, if night trips can possibly be avoided. The results of the flood last winter which put the line completely out of business for weeks at a time, are still visible.

The report May 24 was that extra trains were being run every day and wheat in large quantities was being shipped. On May 31 it was noted that most of the cars being used for wheat were NP rather than ORN.[38]

The Pullman, La Crosse & Columbia River Railroad (PLCR) was chartered in spring 1907 as an electric railroad from Pullman to La Crosse to connect with the ORN and to Hooper to connect with the Portland & Seattle (P&S). The power would come from Palouse Falls near Washtucna. Right of away agreements were being made by some company for a projected line from near La Crosse to Pullman in early April. Darling wrote Elliott, "It looks very much like an O. R. & N. proposition, and in a country that would be of considerable importance to the Northern Pacific or Portland & Seattle to acquire." PLCR Manager J. O. Staats of La Crosse was in Pullman in May to confer with members of the Pullman commercial club. He said that 20 miles of right-of-way had been acquired. In July a surveying crew, believed in Pullman to be NP, came from the P&S through La Crosse into Union Flat, "farmers along the way say it is impossible to get any information from them." There was a report from Washtucna that the promoters of the PLCR were empowered to buy right-of-way for the NP from Pullman to the Portland & Seattle at Washtucna. Staats wrote Elliott, August 20, that a survey from Pullman to Hooper averaged 10 miles from the ORN and from the Snake River. The farmers were enthusiastic and would take out stock. The estimated construction cost would be $750,000, with $500,000 in bonds. He sought a guarantee on the bonds and a traffic agreement making through rates to Portland and Puget Sound. They would be pleased to handle NP through business from Pullman, with all business to be turned over to the P&S at Hooper. Elliott responded that given financial conditions and the attitudes of legislatures, federal and state, the NP could not guarantee the bonds or make a traffic contract. In September the NP was informed that 25 miles of right-of-way had been "signed up." In November Elliott said that he did not want to furnish rail for the project. Dr. H. M. Greene, president of the PLCR, said in November that the railroad would have at least 25 miles built by the following September. They had on hand $35,000 for construction and grading would begin shortly. Many farmers had already made application for sections of the grade and the construction work would be done in that manner.[39] No railroad was built.

The Moscow, Idaho S&P/NP depot in c.1909. The ORN depot is on the right. Photograph L86-474 *(Edward W. Nolan Collection) Cheney Cowles Museum/Eastern Washington State Historical Society.*

Winona suffered serious damage August 3, 1907, when sparks apparently set the depot on fire, which then led to an explosion of gasoline and dynamite in the section house. In mid-September Washtucna grain buyers were not taking wheat because of an inability to arrange for cars from the ORN. The year before grain rotted on the ground and the buyers had to take the losses. At the same time used rail from the Winona-Endicott line was being laid from La Crosse to Washtucna. In June 1908 ties were being unloaded between La Crosse and Washtucna.[40]

In response to the building of the SPS, the ORN began in 1908 putting in new ties and 75-pound steel on the Pleasant Valley line to shorten the running time and distance between Spokane and Portland. This route avoided the Colfax grade. To counter the 14.5 hours SPS-NP passenger train running time from Portland to Spokane the ORN reduced its time to 14 hours. The first train under the new schedule reached Spokane December 7, 1908. The ORN had spent more than $1 million upgrading the entire line. Much work was done in the vicinity of Troutdale, Oregon.[41] On May 3, 1909, the SPS began service from Portland to Spokane and the NP began operating the Snake River Junction to Riparia line (see chapter XVIII), giving the P&L a western exit, thus making a La Crosse gateway less valuable to the NP. But interest in a Pullman-Connell line persisted for some time.

Because of flooding, the first train since January 18, 1909, reached Washtucna February 6 and returned to La Crosse. Another train reached Washtucna in the evening and went as far as Kahlotus. Work would start the 15th at Sulphur Lake where the line would be entirely changed and regraded. A westbound train was able to reach Connell on March 7.[42]

In Colfax, the Spokane & Inland Empire (SIE) (see chapter XIX) in early July 1909 was installing an interlocking plant where its line crossed the C&P at the north end of Colfax. Levers from a tower would cause semaphores to tell trains whether it was safe to cross the tracks of the other railroad without stopping. The interlocking was first used May 7, 1911. The interlocking system had been put in the year before, but it was damaged by the flood of March 1, 1910. The tower was occupied by three men on eight hour shifts. As a train approached it whistled and the tower man either gave it a clear signal or not. "The men in charge are accommodating, it being no trouble to explain, as well as to show, the workings of the mechanical wonder." In 1928 an automatic interlocking and an electric gate machine were installed and the tower removed.[43] So far as known this was the only interlocking plant in the Palouse country.

In late October 1909 at La Crosse, the Pacific Elevator Co received 250,000 bushels, Kerr-Gifford Co., 100,000, and Interior Warehouse Co., 100,000. At Pampa four miles west 300,000 bushels were received. "As an old timer expressed it, 'It is less than 10 years since we considered the bunch grass lands hereabouts fit only for cattle and sheep, little dreaming that it would ever become a great farming and fruit raising section.'"[44]

It was reported from both Hooper and Pullman in early December 1909 that surveyors of the SPS were locating a route between the two points and that right-of-way was being bought from Hooper via La Crosse to Pullman. The year before NP officials promised that the road would be built when the SPS was completed. Also a party of surveyors who claimed to be Washington State College students, but looked like veterans, were in the Colfax area in early December. Whether they were SPS or Milwaukee was uncertain.[45]

On December 16, 1909, the ORN filed a charter for the Union Flat Railroad (UF). A 48-mile line was projected from La Crosse to Uniontown. A party of ORN surveyors arrived in La Crosse. The reason given for the sudden activity was to beat the SIE to the Snake River. By early January definite locations were made by the ORN from approximately one mile south of La Crosse to Wilcox in Union Flat, 14.8 miles.[46]

In the meantime, December 21, SIE surveyors arrived at Wilcox to survey from Colfax down Union Flat, possibly via Dusty, to the SPS near Hooper. Another route thought to interest the SIE was the NP right-of-way to Penawawa, then crossing the Snake River and into the country back of Asotin with a possible extension to Walla Walla. On the 23rd the NP Lewiston agent reported ORN and SIE survey parties on Union Flat Creek. The agent noted about a third of the grain handled at Johnson and Colton came from the territory and practically all the grain raised east of Wilcox was hauled down to the Snake River at Penawawa, Wawawai, and Almota to the new Camas Prairie Railroad. If the ORN built a line it would take at least 50 percent of the Snake River tonnage. The NP could build a spur from Colton more cheaply than either the ORN or SIE could build into the territory. On December 31 the NP chief engineer sent the SIE chief engineer maps and profiles, Pullman to Snake River via Penawawa and to La Crosse. In January the SIE engineer responded that he expected to have surveys completed with maps, profiles, and estimates as far as La Crosse on the line from near Pullman to the SPS west of Hooper, by the 20th of the month and the remainder by the end of the month.[47]

On the margin of a newspaper clipping about activities on Union Flat, NP Vice President Hannaford wrote Elliott, "If the Un Pac [Union Pacific] will withdraw force and abandon work we can leave this line to future conditions." On December 31 Elliott wrote J. J. Hill, "As stated to you the other day, it seems to me a railroad is really not needed there, and I hope the result of the activity of the Inland may bring about a condition, when neither the Inland nor the Union Pacific will build." Elliott conferred with the UP President R. S. Lovett who agreed to withdraw if the SIE would. On January 11, 1910, the same day he was informed by Elliott of the UP position, J. J. Hill telegraphed in cipher to SIE President Jay Graves: "Union Pacific have agreed to withdraw surveyors from Union Flat country at once provided Inland Empire does the same. Will you please have your party withdrawn?" On January 13 the SIE surveyors were recalled. The ORN surveyors also withdrew. Milwaukee surveyors were reported on the 14th to be camped in Four Mile Valley about eight miles from Colfax. They were said to be following an old survey from Colfax onto Union Flat.[48]

Service from La Crosse to Connell was out in late January 1910 because of flooding. On February 28 Colfax was flooded. The first train from Spokane did not reach it until March 3. The SIE depot was demolished, its South Palouse bridge was undermined, the Palouse River bridge north of town was carried away, and the bridges on either side of the tunnel north of Colfax were gone. The ORN bridge was wrecked. The March 1 flood carried away the ORN track in many places between Colfax and Pullman and nearly every bridge was damaged and 10 bridges were destroyed, three in Pullman and seven between Pullman and Colfax. All the bridges below Colfax on the Palouse River were damaged. "The big new steel bridge at Winona, which was supposed to be so high that no flood would ever injure it, was washed away and carried down the stream several hundred yards." By March 18 Spokane-Portland trains were running, but it was two months before trains would run normally on all lines. The ORN Colfax-Moscow line resumed service on March 30. The SIE on the 18th was closed between Steptoe and Colfax—"there is not 200 yards of the track in any place in the first three miles out of Colfax, over which a hand car could be run." The passenger train from Moscow to Colfax was delayed May 26 at the first bridge from Riverside. If the section foreman had not discovered the weakened condition of the bridge a "disastrous wreck" could have occurred. New Colfax depots for both the OWRN and SIE were discussed in the early fall of 1911. A request for bids on the SIE depot were made in late October.[49]

SIE President Graves wrote Elliott June 1, 1910:

> I should be pleased to have you instruct us concerning the Colfax to Pullman line and the securing of right-of-way and surveying of the Hooper line as suggested, at your earliest convenience, believing that while it will not be necessary to build that line from the junction to Hooper this year, it should be surveyed to hold the territory, that is, provided we build the line from Colfax to Pullman as we have recommended. If you will take this up with Mr. Hill at your earliest convenience and reach a conclusion, I will be obliged.

Elliott and J. J Hill wrote Graves December 8, 1910, that building from Colfax to Pullman and electrifying the NP to Moscow and to Genesee ought to be postponed "until we know something more about the course of general business in the United States."[50]

On July 27, 1910, the C&P directors authorized conveyance of all C&P property to the ORN. On September 6 the C&P was sold to the ORN which in turn was sold to the UP's Oregon-Washington Railroad & Navigation Co. (OWRN) December 23.[51]

The Pullman city attorney on December 24, 1910, wrote W. Connolly, ORN superintendent of construction at Spokane, about three trestles that the railroad built to replace bridges washed out in March. At the time city officials protested "these trestles would in times of ordinary high water cause ice jams and completely dam up the river, making the danger of damage to property in Pullman even greater than it had been before." The railroad had assured that the trestles were temporary, so they were permitted. "Now the heavy rains and snowfalls are coming on again and the O. R. & N. Co. has done nothing to remove these causes of dangerous floods. The only remedy we can see is for the company to remove these trestles and replace them with span bridges where they cross the main channel of the river." Connolly was in Pullman in early January; he could not promise new bridges, but he thought the railroad would agree.[52] Span bridges were subsequently built.

NP Fourth Vice President H. C. Nutt wrote Elliott April 18, 1911, that he had been approached about whether the NP cared to consider taking an interest in a line from Pullman to La Crosse. Nutt did not believe there was any need for such a railroad. Elliott agreed and did not think the UP or the Milwaukee would take up the matter, but he asked Nutt to keep watch for surveyors or other work. Elliott also wrote J. N. Hill asking him to discuss it with UP President Lovett. Hill wrote back that he had had a satisfactory discussion with Lovett. An NP agent wrote the General Western Freight agent November 16, 1912, that on December 5 farmers on Union Flat would have a meeting in Colfax to take some action toward either building themselves or getting someone else to build from either Colfax or Pullman. The OWRN had given poor service and the farmers would much prefer the NP or SIE—if that were done the OWRN would not get 5 percent of the business. At non-competitive points the farmers had less than fifty cars for the season. "As a matter of comparison we have shipped 265 cars out of Genesee, 165 out of Uniontown and about 90 out of Colton. The farmers in the Union Flat district as a rule are very well fixed and are perfectly able to build eight or ten miles of railroad should they decide to do so." Elliott wrote December 3 "There is no reason for building the proposed Pullman line, and we should not encourage it." On December 24 Elliott wrote SPS President J. H. Young that "The finances of the S.P.&S. and of the Inland are

Connell, Washington, flooded in 1910. To the left is the NP water tank and depot. In the right-center, with the station board under the eves, is the UP depot. The C&P built east to Colfax from an NP connection here, but in this photograph (almost thirty years later) there was no connection between the NP and UP. *Manuscript and Special Collections, Washington State University Library, Historic Photographs Subject File, Box 7 folder 50.*

certainly not such as to justify any railroad extensions." On the same day Elliott wrote his assistant Geo. T. Reid:

> This is something that has been discussed for the last five or six years. When Mr. Graves was in charge of the Spokane & Inland Railroad he was very anxious to build a line in there, but we could not see why any money should be put up for that purpose, especially as the Inland road was barely earning its interest.
>
> Judge Lovett, Mr. Kruttschnitt and I had several talks about the matter, because we felt that probably each company would be urged to build a road, and it seemed an unnecessary waste of capital, considering the fact that there was a road on the north and a road on the south, and that the only thing the new road would do would be to shorten the wagon haul slightly.
>
> While there was no understanding between the two companies about building, both thought that the money could be spent to better advantage in improving existing railroads, rather than by burdening the country with an additional transportation line in a section where there are if anything too many roads now for the volume of business.

A rumor circulated in late 1916 that farmers in Union Flat were attempting to get the Milwaukee to build into the flat west of Colfax. The NP investigated the matter and concluded, "that it was nothing but a newspaper story...none of the farmers seemed to know anything about it except what they had read in the papers."[53]

Despite serious washouts, the UP having reopened the line to Connell was compelled by the government to keep it open. The west end of the C&P became the OWRN Connell branch which extended from MP 0, at MP 305.04, La Crosse, on the UP Ayers to Spokane main line, to the end of track at Connell, MP 53.06. The section included the wye and house track of the Connell branch at La Crosse plus other side tracks totaling 3.52 miles. Hooper Junction to Connell, 37.25 miles, was abandoned August 8, 1979, and 0.28 miles in Connell was abandoned October 19, 1982. Hooper Junction to La Crosse was retained to connect the UP mainline to Spokane with the line to Colfax.[54]

Prior to its abandonment the UP approached the Burlington Northern (BN) with an offer to sell the line from Washtucna to Connell. With upgrading, the C&P line would connect the former NP and SPS Pasco-Spokane mainlines into a single line south of Connell, thus avoiding the adverse grades on the NP north of Connell and the SPS line in the Snake River Canyon. In 1982 the BN decided not to purchase the line because the BN senior management had lost confidence in the railroad business. After the SPS was abandoned in 1989 the BN contacted the UP about purchasing the right-of-way, but much of the right-of-way was in other hands.[55]

Additional information on C&P finances, physical plant, stations and spurs, and selected scheduled passenger and freight service are found in appendix II.

Projections, Surveys, and Construction, 1886–1913

While the principals were involved in negotiations, NP and ORN engineers were engaged in laying out new lines and resurrecting old. This chapter concerns NP and ORN surveys from Colfax down Penawawa Creek to the Snake River and in the Snake River Valley west of Lewiston, and surveys eastward into the Potlatch Country by both the NP and ORN and toward the Camas Prairie.

A. Proposed Penawawa Extensions

Penawawa Creek is approximately 16 miles west of Pullman and is the closest feasible railroad access to the Snake River from Pullman and Colfax. The mouth of Penawawa Creek is approximately 24 miles east of Riparia. The Pullman to La Crosse surveys from Pullman to Union Flat overlapped and in some cases were partially the same as the Penawawa surveys.

In early March 1898 NP Chief Engineer McHenry wrote President Charles Mellen of rumors of an ORN extension down Penawawa Creek. The NP had "at different times, seriously considered this construction. The county is thoroughly well cultivated, and would doubtless give the same earnings as a similar line in the country around about Dayton and Pendleton." Mellen asked McHenry for a survey and a recommendation. In same month the ORN filed a charter for the Snake River Valley Railroad Co. (SRV), which included a proposed line from Colfax via Spring Creek and Penawawa Creek to the Snake River and on the ORN between Winona & La Crosse up Union Flat to the head of Union Flat (Uniontown or beyond and could connect with the Penawawa route).[1]

In September 1898 the *Gazette* reported surveyors at the south end of Colfax and up Spring Creek. "This party it is reasonably certain is in the employ of the O. R. & N. Company, and the theory that Mr. Lewis has been buying South Colfax property for the a terminal of a Northern Pacific branch seems exploded." The alleged purpose of the line was to avoid the existing westbound grade out of Colfax. "Mr. Lewis has for several years been connected with the Northern Pacific railway but what his connection may be with the company now is not known." A few days later the *Review* said there were two survey parties in Colfax, one in the south end and the other in the north end near the ORN yards. Neither would reveal who they represented. A month later surveyors were up Spring Flat seven miles further south, too far for an ORN cutoff of the westbound grade. Asked the direction they were going, a surveyor replied, "Since getting out among these hills I have become completely turned around." Several years earlier the surveyor had been employed by the NP. A report from Colfax on December 8 said, "The surveyors are as 'closed-mouthed' as ever and are pushing steadily along down Penawawa creek." Late in December the surveyors were identified as ORN. By the end of the year the *Gazette* had ascertained the deeds secured by Lewis in south Colfax were made to the SRV.[2]

On November 9, 1898, the NP chartered the Clearwater Short Line Railway Co. (CSL) which became the principal NP subsidiary involved in projected and constructed extensions. McHenry wrote Assistant Engineer C. S. Bihler December 15 that if construction of the Oakesdale-Colfax line was decided, he hoped a better line could be found than that of C. C. Van Arsdol in 1890; his profile showed three summits and grades as high as 1.7 percent.[3]

Bihler instructed Van Arsdol, January 10, 1899, to "quickly as possible...retrace the old survey from Colfax, via Spring Creek, Union Flat and down Penawawa Creek. Do no more work in retracing this line than is necessary for refiling of our maps." By early February NP grades on the Penawawa were to be reduced to 2.2 percent and a better connection made from Pullman to the Colfax line by a reconnaissance on the north side of the South Fork of the Palouse River to a point where an overhead crossing of the ORN and the river could be made. In mid-January McHenry wrote Mellen that the ORN was grading on the north bank of the Snake River at Almota and Penawawa. This indicated to McHenry that the ORN feared the NP would attempt to occupy the north bank and the grading at Penawawa was to hinder the NP. ORN President Mohler in early February said in Colfax, "I can tell you nothing about new lines. You can probably tell me more than I know." Van Arsdol in mid-February was instructed to look for a suitable crossing of the Snake River below the mouth of Penawawa Creek.[4]

In mid-February both the NP and ORN were surveying in Union Flat. The ORN line ran from Colfax to Union Flat to the South Fork of Penawawa Creek, down to the Snake River and down the Snake to Riparia. The NP survey south of Colfax paralleled the ORN survey along Spring Creek but went a mile further south before turning to Union Flat and the North Fork of Penawawa to the South Fork and then paralleled the ORN to the Snake River.[5]

In February and March 1899 there were numerous newspaper reports of NP and ORN Penawawa surveying. Both railroads were guarding their camps "with regular military severity and all their actions and intentions are kept a profound secret." On February 20 Van Arsdol wrote Bihler that the line in Penawawa Canyon had been retraced and the ORN had quickly followed. About a mile and half of right-of-way in the canyon had been secured. The ORN having fallen behind were setting stakes by moon-light across the NP line at the mouth of Penawawa where the NP had already secured right-of-way. The ORN was surveying in Union Flat and one party was following the NP's 1890 survey up Union Flat, and were within nine miles of Colton and had secured some right-of-way in the direction of Colton. The ORN was acquiring right-of-way in Spring Creek and claimed that it had acquired all the available right-of-way down Penawawa Creek, but the NP had deeds made out to the CSL in the Penawawa Canyon. In the meantime, the survey parties of the two railroads were ignoring each other even though at times they were working side by side. An ORN official said that the NP action was a bluff: "the farmers had been hoodwinked and the railroad company having nothing to lose can and will throw up the contract when its scheme fails to work." W. J. Hamilton, Colfax druggist and rancher, said that both roads had made surveys through his 1200 acre ranch and "when the O. R. & N. purchased right-of-way through the land of one of his neighbors on Union flat for a consideration of $30… the right-of-way agent said to the farmer: 'We may want the land in one year; maybe in five years, and maybe we won't want it at all.' [Hamilton]…thinks both roads are bluffing and declares that little money has been paid by either road for right-of-way, what purchases have been made being for considerations ranging from $1 to $50 and these, he says, are in scattered localities and in many places in utterly impracticable routes." The NP right-of-way agent confirmed reports that the NP had purchased right-of-way through an orchard on Penawawa Creek for about $1,000 rather than the rumored $5,000. On March 16 McHenry told Bihler to acquire right-of-way as rapidly as located. By mid-March the NP made a preliminary location from Pullman west on a 0.75 percent grade to above Colfax. The ORN party on Union Flat continued to Uniontown. The *Review* reported March 17 that both roads claimed to have secured right-of-way down Penawawa and the other was bluffing. It appeared that the ORN was securing right-of-way for both a Colfax to Penawawa line and a line from a point between Winona and La Crosse to the head of Union Flat.[6]

On March 24 Mellen wrote McHenry,

> It is of the highest importance that you keep me posted regarding the movements of the O. R. & N. east of Riparia, between that point and Lewiston and also Pullman for the reason that the disposition of our people is to authorize the construction on our part from Pullman to Penawawa and Lewiston to Pleasant View if the O. R. & N. make any serious attempt to construct its lines east of Riparia without an agreement with us for the use of such lines under a trackage contract.[7]

On March 22 the ORN filed suit against Hamilton to condemn right-of-way on Union Flat because the SRV needed the land "for the construction of a line of road leaving the main line of the O. R. & N. at some point between Winona and La Crosse, and running then up Union flat to the head of Union flat." It was generally believed in Colfax that the NP desired to build from Pullman to Connell; the Penawawa line was a bluff to cut off the ORN. The ORN on the other hand desired to build up Penawawa Creek to Colfax, but was also trying to block the proposed NP La Crosse cut-off which would pass through some of its territory. No money had been paid by the ORN for the contracts down Penawawa Creek, "the land owners merely agreeing 'when the railroad shall have been built' to make a deed to the company for the land." The ORN filed several deeds for right-of-way at Colfax for considerations ranging from one dollar to $180 each.[8]

On May 5 Mellen expressed annoyance that the right-of-way from Pullman to Penawawa and on to Pleasant View had not yet been acquired. On June 1 Van Arsdol sent Bihler maps, profiles, and estimates of the location from Pullman to Union Flat and from Union Flat to the mouth of Penawawa Creek to a connection with the location from Lewiston to Riparia. The grades were 0.75 percent westbound and 2.2 percent eastbound. McHenry reported to Mellen December 16, 1899, that 26.36 miles of right-of-way had been secured between Pullman and the Snake River on the Penawawa route, leaving 10.24 miles to complete. Negotiations for the right-of-way were "substantially completed for a large percentage of the remainder and the right-of-way on the Penawawa line is in fact nearly all secured."[9]

On June 12 McHenry sent Mellen an estimate of $1,072,014, $29,290 per mile, Pullman to Penawawa (36.6 miles), including a Riparia bridge. An estimate sheet dated April 1899 for 12.3 miles of main track and 1.7 miles of siding, etc., from Spring Flat to Colfax was $207,460, $16,860 per mile. The June 30 Confidential Report said that Pullman to Penawawa "is a line of great promise and will afford large revenues to the Company, if constructed." Through December 1903 little more was spent on either of these extensions.[10]

NP President Howard Elliott's visit in July 1904 to the Pullman area renewed hope that the Penawawa line would soon be built. The route from Pullman was described as crossing the ORN about a mile north of Pullman, skirting the brow of the hill gradually raising until it was out the canyon then southwest across the head of Spring Flat to Union Flat, down the flat to a point opposite Little Penawawa creek, down that creek to the Snake River. In April 1906 the president of the Pullman Club said that he had been assured the NP would build "in the near future" from Pullman to the Snake River and Pullman would have car shops and a roundhouse. Two days later, NP Chief Engineer Darling wrote Elliott that the Pullman to Penawawa was not in line with developments in the area. Elliott in response agreed with him. In January 1907 Elliott wrote a correspondent that the line from Pullman to the Snake River via Penawawa "would cost $35,000 a mile and would be a heavy grade line. My judgment is that we do not want to undertake the building of a line of this character at the present time." In 1911 the NP valuated the 236.39 acres it owned for right-of-way and station grounds on Pullman to Penawawa at $150 per acre for a total of $35,459.[11]

B. Snake River Extensions[12]

The Lewiston *Teller* reported in April 1887 that C. C. Van Arsdol was surveying a line for the UP down the north bank of the Snake River from Lewiston.[13] The surveys continued into September. On October 11 the ORN filed supplemental articles which included from Wallula, following the Columbia and Snake Rivers, to Lewiston, up the Clearwater River through the Bitterroot Mountains to Butte, about 450 miles. The Walla Walla *Union* November 8 said that there was little doubt that the money just obtained in Europe would be used to build this and other branches authorized by the stockholders June 20; "the public cannot fail to note the absence of any extension that may be regarded as an invasion to the territory recently set off by agreement to the Northern Pacific. There is no reaching out for any business north of Snake River." The *Gazette* reported in December the ORN reported that it took possession of right-of-way along the Snake River below Lewiston. "It is thought this move was made by the ORN to shut out the Manitoba, which is coming across the continent with marvelous speed, without either land grant or subsidy to aid it."[14]

In February 1888 the ORN's estimated cost of building from Riparia to the junction of the Snake and Clearwater at Lewiston, 71.5 miles, was $1,684,569. The ORN board of directors in March adopted a map from the west boundary of the Nez Perce Indian Reservation to Riparia, 77.7 miles. ORN Manager W. H. Holcomb urged against the Riparia-Lewiston line in the short-run. The ORN boats on the Snake were adequate to move the traffic and were cheaper than building a railroad and there was no other place to use them. In the longer term a line from Riparia to the Clearwater River was desirable. Nevertheless 11 months later, "It is reported that the ORN will shortly proceed to make permanent location of a route from Riparia to Lewiston, with the idea of extending the same to Camas prairie."[15] An amended charter of the Oregon Railway Extensions Co., February 6, 1891, projected several lines including from Wallula east to Lewiston and thence over the Bitterroot Mountains to Butte, Montana. The receiverships of the ORN, UP, and NP in 1893 suspended consideration of additional construction.

The ORN, under the joint control of the bondholders and the GN (see chapter XVI), chartered the Snake River Valley Railroad (SRV) March 3, 1898, to project a line from Umatilla, Oregon, to Lewiston and then to Huntington, Oregon. On the 14th McHenry informed Mellen of ORN surveys on the Snake River above and below Lewiston. ORN President Mohler wrote A. S. Heidelbach, chairman of the UP board on the 21st: "From Riparia to Wallula the location is an absolute necessity as we obtain substantially a 3/10 grade as against our present 3 percent, [the Alto line to Walla Walla] and make a line sixteen miles shorter.... It is not intended at this time that we will commence any construction." On the same day he wrote a second letter to Heidelbach saying they had learned that Burlington surveyors were east of Lewiston. "The occupation of the Snake River Valley by our company I consider timely and necessary for its ultimate protection. By the location of the line from Wallula to Lewiston we have secured our rights for five years."[16]

By mid-April 1898 the ORN was cross sectioning between Riparia and Wallula. On the 12th McHenry did not think that the ORN between Riparia and Wallula would cost the NP any traffic; the ORN would be better off arranging with the NP to take traffic from Connell to Wallula. Unless the line was part of a through route, its construction "would be, in my opinion, a very foolish procedure, as it would entail heavy operating and interest charges, without adequate compensating advantages. I feel very much surprised that Mr. Mohler would undertake so large and important an enterprise, without the authority of his board of Directors." Bihler reported that the ORN had surveyed on both sides of the Snake River from Lewiston up river to the Grand Ronde River. The ORN also had a locating party on the Clearwater above the Potlatch River. The S&P directors May 23 voted to build a branch from Lewiston up the Snake River to the mouth of the Salmon River and up it to its junction with the Little Salmon River. Surveys were made, but McHenry in his report to Mellen he said local traffic would amount to almost nothing and "Until the future development of the country creates the necessity for such route, it is not advisable to consider construction in this direction."[17]

McHenry sent Mellen on July 18, 1898, a discouraging report on an extension from Pleasant View, on the Washington & Columbia River Railway (WCR, originally G. W. Hunt's Oregon & Washington Territory Railroad), to Riparia. It would cost no less than $35,000 per mile. "I would recommend against such construction." The next day Mellen wrote back that he had no intention of building the line.[18]

McHenry informed Mellen September 19 that E. F. Libby, president of the Lewiston Water & Power Co., said that the company would build a steel bridge across the Snake River above the junction with the Clearwater River. Libby was confident that his company would be willing to consider a joint wagon and railroad bridge. McHenry responded with details of constructing and financing a bridge that included an electric railroad. On October 25 Mellen wrote Charles Francis Adams, former UP president, who was a stockholder in the Lewiston company and had other investments in the area, if "we should deem it advisable to construct a bridge across the Snake at Lewiston, we shall not be disposed to make it available for other than railroad purposes and shall in no way be a competitor with your project." In early December the power company's Lewiston-Vineland bridge, 1,650 feet long including approaches, was under construction. It would be 50 feet above high water and include a street railway.[19]

In November and December 1898 a CSL filing projected a line east from near the mouth of the Clearwater River to the Bitterroot Range near Lolo Pass, on to the vicinity of Missoula, and west along the south side of the Snake River to near the junction with the Columbia River. In the meantime, ORN Clearwater surveyors were thought to be working toward the Camas Prairie.[20]

It was reported from Portland November 20 that the ORN had awarded a contract for 140 miles of line from Wallula to Lewiston. Portland interests were "delighted" by the construction. Officially the SRV began construction, Wallula to Grange City Junction (65.85 miles) in December 1898 but was reported to have begun work in late November working west from Riparia toward Wallula. By January 14 over a thousand men were at work. A December 9 report said that the ORN had broken ground on a bridge site opposite Spalding, near the S&P crossing of the Clearwater River.[21]

Early December 1898 Mellen authorized a survey on the south bank of the Snake River west from Lewiston to approximately the mouth of Alpowa Creek, the "object of such a survey is to get prior rights of location, in advance of possible locations by the O. R. & N. Company." The same month the NP deeded to the CSL, for $2,943, all of its right-of-way interests within the NP's 40-mile limit land grant in Walla Walla and Columbia counties. On December 28 the SRV sued the NP alleging that the sale was to prevent the SRV from condemning land for right-of-way and was not executed in good faith with the intention of constructing a railroad and that neither the NP nor CSL had located a line across the lands. The SRV offered to buy the land, but the NP refused to sell except if the SRV was located to the satisfaction of the NP. On January 10 Bihler instructed Van Arsdol to begin surveying on the south side of the Snake River between Lewiston and Riparia before the 24th, the day the ORN condemnation proceedings for right-of-way below Riparia was scheduled to begin.[22]

In January 1899, it was reported the ORN intended to build a railroad bridge, with provision for wagons and streetcars, across the Snake River above the Clearwater River. Shortly afterward, the ORN began condemnation on property opposite Lewiston. A late January report was that the NP was surveying a bridge site on the Snake River also just above the Clearwater. In late January ORN Chief Engineer Kennedy said, "it will take about four months to build the Riparia-Lewiston division. I do not think the company will wait to finish the Wallula Riparia division before actively engaging in the Lewiston division."[23]

McHenry in Lewiston in early February 1899 said he was "not at liberty to say" when construction would begin on the south bank of the Snake. Bihler instructed Van Arsdol February 18 to quickly make a survey from below Grange City up the Snake River. He was also to look for a suitable crossing of the Snake River below the mouth of Penawawa Creek. On March 18 Bihler was told to locate a line from the end of the track at Pleasant View to Riparia via Grange City. Van Arsdol wrote Bihler he had gone over the ground and found the terrain "rather peculiar" and did not think it possible to get a continuous descending grade from Pleasant View to the river. In mid-April Van Arsdol sent Bihler maps and profiles from Lewiston to Riparia, 75.39 miles. Mellen was annoyed May 4 that the Lewiston to Pleasant View right-of-way had not been acquired. Van Arsdol wrote that a grade of about 1.33 percent could be obtained from Pleasant View to a connection with the ORN at the mouth of the Tucannon River. The line would go up the Tucannon and then turn with a bridge 40 feet high and 400 to 500 feet long over the ORN and the river. The only other heavy bridge would be over Field's Gulch at 60 feet high and 500 to 600 feet long. On July 13 Bihler wrote McHenry that a line from the mouth of Tucannon to Pleasant View would be too steep to permit trains rated for the grades between Lewiston and Riparia to be taken up to Pleasant View with one helper, even of the heaviest class. The operation would require turning the power at Riparia or the mouth of the Tucannon and taking the train up the hill with two heavy engines."[24]

By mid-March 1899 the SRV was moving rapidly on the Wallula to Riparia line with 1,600 men and about 500 teams; it was expected the work force would reach nearly 2,000 in a week. "All the laborers here [Starbuck] that could be induced to go to work are now employed and the hobo element, which assumed huge proportions last week, vanished with the demand for laborers. Where they escaped to is a mystery that few are particular about. They are gone and with their departure a peaceful feeling settled over the community from which our citizens would not care to be again awakened." NP reports in March said the ORN between Riparia and Lewiston had four small grading camps working on rock work in the roughest points where the rock ledges projected down to the river.[25]

The ORN's Clearwater Valley Railroad supplemental charter of March 13, 1899, projected a line from the mouth of the Clearwater River up the Snake River to Huntington, Oregon. No construction occurred, but right-of-way was acquired from Clarkston up the Snake River. The right-of-way was sold to the ORN's Northwestern Railroad Company November 21, 1910. The supplemental charter of the SRV, December 6, 1899, included a projection up the Salmon River to the Lemhi River and then over the Bitterroot Mountains in the vicinity of Bannock Pass.

McHenry thought the objective of the ORN between Riparia and Lewiston was to interfere with the NP, particularly the Penawawa branch. McHenry reported to Mellen on May 12, 1899, that ORN activity between Lewiston and Riparia was as it had been for months past, four camps averaging 12 to 17 men. He commented, "there is no truth in the recent newspaper reports that the O. R. & N. had put on a large force and commenced work on the line above Riparia." Van Arsdol wrote that the ORN between Riparia and Lewiston had done a few hundred feet of grading and had expended about 3,000 days of work on rock removal. Later Mellen was informed that the ORN was locating a route between Elgin, Oregon, and Lewiston via the Grande Ronde River. McHenry wrote, "it does not appear that the O. R. & N. has yet been able to settle upon a definite plan." In the latter part of May the *Review* reported that the ORN was actively securing right-of-way between Riparia and Lewiston and that seven ORN railroad grading outfits had arrived at Lewiston.[26]

President Libby assured the NP that he would not grant right-of-way to either the NP or ORN until satisfied they would not interfere with each other. On June 6, 1899, Van Arsdol sent Bihler a map of Vineland [which would become Clarkston on January 1, 1900] showing the lands of the Lewiston company, the ORN river crossing, right-of-way and station grounds, and the CSL locations. The ORN would bridge the Snake River below Vineland and its line on the south side of the river would cross the NP location twice and parallel the NP through Vineland and cross the approach to the NP bridge between Lewiston and Vineland; the presumed object of the latter was to block the NP by establishing grades to which the NP could not conform because of the proposed bridge crossing.[27] The Lewiston company asked $8,300 for the right-of-way, station grounds, and warehouse land, 24.63 acres. Libby said the ORN would be paying a proportional $15,000. Van Arsdol noted, "It looks to me like a very high figure, considering the real selling value of the land." Libby said he would allow the ORN to cross the CSL to access warehouses and landings on the river and would protect the CSL in crossing the ORN. Libby said the ORN was pressing him to complete the right-of-way arrangements. On the 29th Van Arsdol informed Bihler that he had made an agreement with the Lewiston company for a right-of-way 60 feet wide, approximately 20 acres, for $3,875. The deed omitted station grounds of 100 feet wide and 2,000 feet in length. In early July newspapers reported that both the ORN and NP had bought depot sites in Vineland for about $1,000 an acre. The NP's three-acre site was at the end of the proposed Snake River bridge from Lewiston. The ORN seven-acre site was on both sides of the wagon bridge terminus and would connect the ORN Snake River bridge with its proposed Grand Ronde River line.[28]

Beginning July 9, 1899, there were several newspaper reports of ORN work on the Riparia to Lewiston line. Contracts had been let from Riparia to Mt. Idaho in the Camas Prairie. Cross-sectioning was being done on either side of Almota. Steamers were unloading workers, teams, and grading machinery at Almota. About 500 laborers were on the ground and when grading was completed on the Wallula-Riparia line it was expected that 2,000 would be at work. Toward the end of July construction activity slowed because of a labor shortage. The contractors were offering $2.00 a day and farmers $1.75 including board. "The heat has been intense and workmen seem to prefer drinking buttermilk with the farmers rather than shoveling dust and sand for contractors." On August 7 the first Mellen-Harriman truce was agreed to (see chapter XV). According to Gill, work was suspended August 10 on the SRV's line from Riparia to Lewiston. But a newspaper report on September 9 said that construction was ongoing—on the 30th the newspaper said the work had been suspended. An NP report said that from Riparia to Lewiston about 18 miles of grading was partially done, mostly in areas of light scraper work. The *Herald* on the 30th quoted the engineer who closed the construction because of the truce, "The road from Riparia to Lewiston is easy to build. There has been much of the rock work done, and if the company decides to take up the construction again and concludes to push it, the line can easily be finished in 90 days.... It will not cost over $10,000 a mile to grade and timber the road ready for the rails."[29]

In the meantime work continued on the SRV's Wallula to Grange City line. By early August, 30 miles of track had been laid at the west end of the line when the track crew was moved to the east end. It was expected that 30 miles would be laid in about three weeks and then the crew would be moved to the west end to resume work. In late September 700 men and 50 teams were at work, all the grading was done, and crews were at work on tunnels, track laying, and ballasting. The line would reduce the distance between Wallula and Grange City by 21.5 miles, was all at water level, and it was estimated that a locomotive could haul 40 loaded cars from Riparia to Portland, in contrast with the existing line in which four engines were needed to haul 26 loaded cars from Starbuck south over Alto hill, 13 miles, on a grade of 3.3 percent. The 65.85 miles between Wallula and Grange City Junction, where connection was made to Riparia, was opened to traffic December 1, 1899.[30]

Bihler sent the table below to McHenry, December 9, 1899, showing the secured right-of-way on the NP's lines from Lewiston to Pleasant View and from Pullman to the mouth of Penawawa Creek. The location between Riparia and Grange City was almost entirely on ORN right-of-way. An offer to the ORN to straighten their line at the NP's expense received no response. Between Pleasant View and Grange City little had been secured because a relocation would reduce curvature and save two miles. The time afforded by the truce with the O. R. & N. Co. was used to make settlements on right-of-way.[31]

	Miles	**Right-of-way**	
		Secured	**Unsecured**
Lewiston to [S.] Riparia	70.50	42.75	27.75
[S.] Riparia to Grange City	4.90		4.90
Pleasant View Branch	18.30	2.50	15.80
Total	93.70	45.25	48.45
Pullman to Union Flat	12.00	9.58	2.42
Union Flat to Penawawa	24.60	16.78	7.82
Total	36.60	26.36	10.24
Grand Total	130.30	71.61	58.69

In late December the Lewiston *Tribune* was of the opinion that when the NP-ORN truce expired on February 4 construction would commence. ORN right-of-way agents were still busy acquiring property along the Clearwater. It was predicted that the Pacific and Idaho Northern Railway would build north to Lewiston and thus drain traffic from central Idaho to the Northern Pacific. On the other hand, the *Herald* reported that the ORN had paid $15,000 for Vineland right-of-way, its depot being just at the end of the Lewiston bridge. The purchase seemed to confirm the report that the ORN would build up the west bank of the Snake River to meet the Pacific and Idaho Northern and probably make a junction with the NP in Clarkston.[32]

By early March the location for the Pleasant View extension had been revised, but McHenry found the revision disappointing, particularly the large trestle across Field's gulch. He concluded that nothing more would be done at present, but if construction was authorized investigation would be undertaken to see if the height of the trestle could be reduced. The Field's gulch trestle was 800 feet long with an extreme height of 90 feet for approximately 150 feet. Mellen wrote on the bottom of the letter: "I…think you should put in a permanent structure in place of the trestle 3/12/1900." Bihler wrote McHenry that in addition to the revision there was a preliminary line at a lower crossing of Field Gulch. Correspondence continued for another six days on lowering the crossing.[33]

McHenry sent Mellen, June 12, 1900, estimates and expenditures for eight projected lines in eastern Washington and north central Idaho. The lines totaled 266 miles with an estimated cost (including Snake River bridges at Riparia and Lewiston) of $6,102,592, $22,929 per mile. The total expended as of April 30, 1900, was $124,880 including $54,097 for right-of-way. The 75 miles from Lewiston to Grange City was estimated to cost $2,121,350 ($28,172 per mile), and the 18 miles from Grange City to Pleasant View was estimated to cost $461,720 ($25,299 per mile). The June 30, 1900, NP confidential report said that the line from Lewiston to Riparia [Grange City] was ready to be put under contract at any time. McHenry wrote that the "great strategic and commercial advantages to accrue to this company by the early construction of the projected extensions from Lewiston to Riparia and Pleasant View…justify a recommendation to construct such lines during the ensuing winter."[34] For the next five years little was expended by either railroad between Lewiston and Riparia. Most NP construction was east of Potlatch Junction on the Clearwater River line.

NP Chief Engineer Edward J. Pearson, July 9, 1904, sent NP President Howard Elliott an extensive evaluation of the proposed line from Lewiston to Pleasant View. He concluded that the route would not result in much increase in traffic and would cost annually nearly $185,000 in interest and maintenance which would require, at 60 cents per train mile, $316,510 additional train miles, revenue to cover the annual cost, "which is very much in excess of what will be required to handle traffic from the Lewiston and Clearwater district via the Marshall route." He concluded, "Some time in the future it is believed the through traffic in addition to the local will justify a line across the Bitter Roots and down the Clearwater and Snake Rivers to the Coast. This, however, is at present remote, and it is believed so far as this valley line is concerned that all that is justified at this time is such action as may be deemed advisable for the protection of the route for the future." Pearson noted that most of the local traffic from Clarkston to Riparia was on the south side of the Snake River. Elliott visited Lewiston, the Clearwater, and Camas Prairie in mid-July 1904. Elliott said, "Our road can not go ahead with any more line building until our legal difficulties arising from the Northern Securities case are settled."[35]

In September 1905 the ORN started borings for a thousand-foot bridge across the Clearwater River at Lewiston. In February 1906 the SRV's Riparia to Lewiston line was deeded to the Oregon, Washington, and Idaho Railroad Co. (OWI). In early June 1906 the superintendent of the contractors said the first train would reach Lewiston as early as November 1. Fifty miles had been graded and was ready for track laying. Six hundred men, with another thousand coming, and four steam shovels were working on the remaining 20 miles. He expected track to be laid half way to Lewiston by August 1. In the summer construction was delayed by heat, dust storms, shortage of labor, and low waters in the river. The steel for the bridge at Lewiston was delayed at Riparia in part because of low water. In mid-December 1906 there were nearly 650,000 sacks of grain in warehouses between Lewiston and Riparia. The Snake River boats were too busy hauling material for the ORN to haul away grain.[36]

By mid-October 1906 the press reported NP surveyors on the south bank of the Snake River and the ORN surveying up the Clearwater and eyeing taking over the Milwaukee survey over Lolo Pass. By the end of October all but nine miles of the 73 of the north bank line from Riparia to Lewiston had been graded and 22 miles of track had been laid. By the end of 1906 the line was completed from Riparia to Almota and most of the remainder was graded. The following January the ORN surveyors were using the Milwaukee field notes.[37]

The June 29, 1907, report on the ORN's Riparia-Lewiston line was that rail was being laid one mile per day. Work on the center pier of the Clearwater bridge would begin when the water receded in August. The ballast was not fully in place, but the railroad was accepting small shipments. In early October the ORN laid track to the north abutment of the Clearwater bridge. Construction was idled by a "flurry" in the money market in November; it was expected to resume after winter. The December 8 report on the Clearwater bridge said, "One pier alone is built, the staging and false work for the others are completed and these remain as they were when the crew so hurriedly abandoned the work on orders coming direct from Harriman." A report from Lewiston March 30, 1908, was that work on the last steel span of the Clearwater bridge would begin that day.[38] As noted

Riparia, Washington, after June 1908. The ORN train on the left is bound for Spokane. The ORN train to Lewiston is in the center, above and to the left of the train is the ORN depot. *Whitman College and Northwest Archives.*

in chapter XVI, Riparia to Lewiston, 71.46 miles, was opened July 7, 1908. In May 1909 the Idaho Brick Co. wanted the new OWI bridge opened for a shipment of bricks, but it was discovered that the bridge could not be opened because the rails on the bridge were continuous, violating the franchise requirement that the bridge not interfere with navigation.[39]

The Portland & Seattle Railway (P&S) was chartered jointly by the NP and GN August 23, 1905, to build on the north bank of the Columbia River from Vancouver, Washington, to Kennewick. It was soon decided to extend the line to Spokane. On February 13, 1906, the P&S board authorized construction of a branch from its proposed Pasco-Spokane mainline to Riparia. It was originally thought the line would leave the P&S at the mouth of the Palouse River, about eight miles west of Riparia, but to maintain a 0.4 percent grade the junction was moved to Snake River Junction, about 27 miles east of Pasco. In mid-April the P&S let a contract for 42 miles of substructure between Pasco and Riparia. It would require more than a year to build four tunnels and to handle 1,600,000 yards of dirt and 1,500,000 yards of rock. In April the P&S, in locating a Riparia connection with the Riparia-Lewiston line, came into conflict with the ORN. The P&S sought to condemn the property in June 1906 but the court found that the P&S failed to show necessity for the property in that the P&S had two other feasible routes. The P&S became the Spokane, Portland & Seattle Railway (SPS) February 1, 1908. The NP began operating Snake River Junction to Riparia, 40.98 miles, on May 3, 1909, the same day SPS service from Portland to Spokane began. The Snake River Junction line, determined to be of no use to the GN, was sold to the CSL June 21, 1909. In September 1909 the NP received permission to use the SPS line from Ainsworth Junction to Snake River Junction, 23.2 miles, for a trackage charge of 2.5 cents per car mile with a minimum of a dollar per train mile. The Camas Prairie Railroad (CSP) charged the NP and OWRN for expenses on the Lewiston-Riparia line based on their share of the train and car mileage. Each railroad was also charged an annual rent equal to one-half of 4.5 percent of the actual cost of the property and improvements. The NP's fixed monthly charge in 1920 was $6,446. Despite the easier grades and shorter distance for westbound traffic, the NP preferred to use its line to Marshall so that it would not have to share revenue with both the SPS and CSP (and UP). When the line was abandoned in the 1960s the original 85-pound rail laid in 1908 was intact.[40] Whether the construction of the north bank Snake River line was the best alternative for the NP and ORN is debatable: joint construction of a south bank road from Lewiston to Grange City and trackage on the ORN from Grange City to a connection with the NP's Snake River bridge at Ainsworth would have given the NP a water level route from Lewiston to Pasco and eliminated the need for the Riparia to Snake

River Junction line and the need for the ORN's Riparia to Lewiston line, including the Clearwater bridge.

The *Review* reported December 15, 1910, that the OWRN closed a deal with the Lewiston-Clarkston Improvement Co. for terminal grounds in Clarkston for $100,000. The right-of-way was along the Snake River and provided for a Snake River bridge between Lewiston and Clarkston above the Clearwater River. President Libby of the Improvement Co. denied that negotiations had taken place, but employees said the deal had been closed. In 1910 the NP built a combination depot in Clarkston; the estimated cost of reproduction in the engineering report of June 17, 1917, was $2,186. Correspondence in 1937 said, "I think the real reason for its construction in the first place was to satisfy the demand of Mr. Clark for whom the siding is named and who at one time had large interests in that neighborhood." The depot was apparently sold in 1937 for $200. No evidence has been found that the NP laid any track in Clarkston. In 1911 the NP valuated the 399.09 acres it owned for right-of-way and station grounds on the south bank of the Snake River, Lewiston to Riparia, at $100 per acre, $39,909 total.[41]

NP President Charles Donnelly recommended to NP Chairman Howard Elliott, December 15, 1925, that the railroad return to the U.S. Government the NP's rights for the line from Lewiston to Riparia. "We have considered that project abandoned for many years...since we entered into the contract with the Union Pacific to use that company's line for a period of 999 years."[42]

C. Proposed Tammany Creek Extensions

After the line to Lewiston was completed in 1898, the NP surveyed several routes on to the Camas Prairie plateau. The first, and ultimately the only, approach to be constructed was from Spalding to Culdesac. The Lapwai branch, 11.95 miles, opened to traffic November 15, 1899, and opened to Grangeville December 22, 1908. Another possible route was Tammany Creek south of Lewiston which was actively considered during construction toward Lewiston in the early 1890s (see chapters X & XI). The ORN maps of 1899 and 1903 show a projected line from Lewiston via Tammany to Waha.[43]

C. C. Van Arsdol wrote NP Chief Engineer W. L. Darling in October 1902 that he had examined a route via Tammany Creek to the head of Mission Creek. The 20-mile route presented difficulties and would average between $30,000 and $40,000 per mile. Van Arsdol in January 1903 made a detailed report on several alternatives to Tammany Creek. Also he found a more favorable Tammany route which was four miles longer. That line was compared with three other possible lines to Grangeville. The Tammany line was the longest, 98 miles, and the most expensive, $1,614,000. The other three were from 63 miles to 89 miles in length, and all less than $1,400,000. In comparisons apparently done in mid-1905, Tammany, with the greatest cost and the most elevation gain and loss, was viewed as the least desirable.[44]

Z. A. Johnson of Nez Perce announced plans in April 1903 to establish electric lines from Lolo Creek to his mills at Nez Perce and to build electric railroad lines to Culdesac and the following year to Lewiston. Johnson's plans resulted in the incorporation of the Lewiston and Southeastern Electric Railway Company (LSE)[45] in October to build an electric or steam railroad from Lewiston to Grangeville via Lake Waha with a branch through Ilo (near Craigmont) to Nez Perce. A report from Lewiston in May 1905 said the LSE had put 55 men with teams and scrappers to work at the mouth of Tammany Creek. A spokesman for the railroad declared they were ready to eject NP surveyors from the right-of-way. The NP put in surveyors and the two groups pulled up each other's stakes. C. M. Levy, assistant to NP President Elliott, said the NP would build to Grangeville once the route was selected. If the Lewiston route was selected the NP would parallel the LSE on an old NP survey. NP surveyors were shortly withdrawn. The *Herald* commented, "The fact that the hand of the Oregon Railway & Navigation company has not appeared in these recent developments, lends color to the report that that system has come to some agreement with the Northern Pacific relative to the Clearwater country and operations therein."[46]

In 1904–05 the NP considered its right-of-way up Tammany Creek, concluding "we have very little to sell at this late date." In 1904–06, Darling and President Howard Elliott corresponded about LSE locations. Darling wrote, "If the project is in the interest of a competing railway company it is being thoroughly concealed even to the extent of poor work as to the line surveyed...[and] the line will be located in such a manner that it will not be practicable for use as a steam road in the handling of heavy tonnage." Elliott wrote Darling that it was rumored that the UP was secretly backing the LSE and "The line was offered to us about a year ago, but we thought it was not worth taking up."[47]

In March 1906 a contract for the first five miles of the LSE was awarded and work was to begin a few days later a quarter of a mile inside the Lewiston southern town limits. A mile and a half of the old NP grade would be used. "The Northern Pacific has abandoned the right-of-way for 15 years, and has no just claim."[48] Not much was actually done on the ground; well into 1907 financing was the chief topic of discussion in the press.

In July 1906 Darling informed Elliott that the location of the LSE between Ilo and Nez Perce was practically the old NP location made in 1889 for which the NP had title to all right-of-way—the 1889 date is interesting in that it is the only reference found to an NP (probably S&P or IT) survey on the Camas Prairie plateau that early. This may be the surveyed line mentioned by Chief Engineer Huson in Spokane February 1891 (see chapter X). The 1916 Valuation Report says the CSL owned right-of-way, purchased in 1899 and 1900, from Cold Springs Creek to Nez Perce (10.0 miles).[49]

The LSE received a proposal from Jay Graves of the Spokane & Inland in February 1908 to build the road to Nez Perce and Grangeville. Graves visited Lewiston and went over the line, but in July Graves declined to be involved with LSE (see chapter XIX).[50]

Z. A. Johnson in July 1908 said that the NP told him to go ahead and construct the line between Vollmer and Nez Perce and "they would not attempt to harass him in any way but, on the contrary, they offered him exceptional traffic concessions." In mid-July the NP warned that its right-of-way from Vollmer to Nez Perce should not be infringed on. A few days later the report was that the NP would refuse to make connection with the road. In late August it was reported that the NP had dropped its opposition. In September 1908 the Nez Perce & Idaho Railroad Company (NI) was incorporated by Johnson to construct from Nez Perce to Lewiston, 75 miles. The NI surveyed from Vollmer west to Forest, to serve a large sawmill to be built there; from there it would use the survey of the LSE to Lewiston. Using five miles of grade completed by LSE and 10 miles of right-of-way from Cold Springs Creek to Nez Perce sold by the CSL to Johnson, June 30, 1909, the NI line was completed from Vollmer (Craigmont) on CSP to Nez Perce on June 6, 1910; freight service began three days later and passenger service on the 24th. The line survived in a precarious state, under different company names, for many years.[51]

The NP and UP were concerned that another railroad, possibly the Milwaukee, would build into the Camas Prairie and compete with the CSP. One possibility was that the NI would build into Lewiston and be sold to a rival company. On the other hand, Johnson was popular in the area and CSP officials wanted to stay on good terms with the public. Johnson sought and received a lease of CSP rails which allowed him to build from Lewiston to Waha and from there to connect with the NI at Vollmer. He had limited resources and was burdened

Lewiston & Southeastern engine No. 1, 4-4-0, helping lay track in Tammany Gulch c. 1914. *Photograph MG 183-21-3, Special Collections & Archives, University of Idaho Library.*

with a lease which was "as binding as possible" and he would have to build over several miles of barren country before he could generate any traffic. By 1914, Johnson was able to construct about 12 miles on the LSE grade up Tammany Creek where it stopped in the middle of a field. He sought to have the CSP take bonds as payment for the lease of 12 miles of rails, but the CSP refused. According to an unidentified NP officer Johnson offered in late February 1914 to sell to the NP his completed line from Nez Perce to Vollmer and a line from Lewiston to Waha that he would build. The officer wrote, "I think this is a most excellent joke" and "ridiculous." "Johnson must figure that he is entitled to a profit on his two properties of about $250,000." Plagued by financial difficulties the line was re-incorporated as the Lewiston, Nez Perce & Eastern Railway (LNPE), in March 1915. In 1917 Johnson sold the NI so he could concentrate on the Tammany line. He paid a third of the amount owed to the CSP and asked for an extension on the remainder to 1918. In 1919 he was able to get enough money from lumber interests to become current on his CSP debt. Johnson asked for credit for another 11 miles of rail, but this would not be enough to reach timber that would generate some traffic. The CSP refused and Johnson had nowhere to turn, the Milwaukee being too deep into its own problems. The CSP threatened to remove his track and when Johnson's appeals to the state and federal governments were not successful, the CSP began removal, which was completed September 1922. The LNPE went out of business in 1928.[52]

D. Lewiston Orchards Extensions[53]

From fall 1912 into the following spring consideration was given to building a line from the CSP's Lewiston Terminal to Lewiston Orchards, on a bench 700 feet above. The NP surveyed several different approaches to the bench, including Tammany Creek. Estimated costs of two lines from main track through the orchard district were calculated: "low" line, $273,896 (10.58 miles); "high" line, $228,277 (10.09 miles). Both lines had slightly over a 3.0 percent grade. The "high" line became the preferred route. By August 14, 1913, $3,693 had been spent on surveys. It was estimated that the peach crop on the extension would generate 206 cars annually for the next five years and the apple crop would generate 226 cars in 1913, increasing to 1,262 cars in 1917.

By this time Z. A. Johnson had completed his Nez Perce & Idaho line with a net income of $19,763 for the

Lewiston, Nez Perce & Eastern, a 4-4-0, probably the same engine as in the preceding photograph. Beyond the engine are box cars at the Lewiston Grain Growers warehouse on the NP line on the east bank of the Snake River at Lewiston, c. 1915. *Photograph DHR L,NP&E-1 (Ivan English copy negative) Oregon Historical Society.*

year ending May 31, 1912. Johnson announced in August that he would under certain conditions extend his line to Lewiston via Waha Lake and Lewiston Orchards. An NP official wrote, "Johnson by reason of having successfully accomplished the seemingly impossible has made for himself a very good reputation and secured the confidence not only of the farmers but of nearly all the business men as well." The line could compete with the NP and OWRN by connections with boats or with the Milwaukee or SIE. The NP calculated that if Johnson were successful the CSP would lose about $123,000 per year from reduced rates in addition to the traffic actually diverted.

In a March 1913 letter to NP President Elliott the NP general manager concluded, "It is my opinion that there is no financial justification for the construction of a line to serve the orchard district, and much less for the proposed extension from the orchard district to Waha." Six days later Elliott wrote E. C. Blanchard, CSP president, there would be no construction to the orchard district that year. A few days later NP Vice President W. P. Clough wrote Elliott that it was likely that the financial limit of apple production in the northwest had been reached for some time and that much of the irrigated lands in the district would have to be planted in other crops.

E. The Potlatch Country and the Moscow & Eastern Railroad[54]

The extensive stands of white pine east of Moscow on the upper reaches of the Potlatch River attracted considerable attention. After extensive surveying which resulted in no construction, the country did get a railroad in the first decade of the twentieth century in the form of the Washington Idaho & Montana (WIM) (see chapter XX).

In late May 1887 the *Gazette* reported that ORN surveyors were eight miles east of Moscow and by September they had run a line from the Potlatch country toward the Clearwater River, but were not permitted to cross the Nez Perce Reservation. In spring–summer 1890 the ORN surveyed from Elberton via Palouse City and the upper Palouse River to the Potlatch country. The Palouse *News* expressed concern in July that the survey was two miles north of Palouse City. "If they should build there it would be a serious loss to Palouse City."[55]

In the spring of 1895 it was reported that Senator R. S. Browne, president of the Moscow National Bank, would go to Europe to secure financing for a railroad into the white pine belt and that parties in the lumber business in Michigan had visited the area. The July 16, 1896, charter of the reorganized ORN projected a line from Moscow toward Lewiston. In January 1897, ORN officials were in Garfield discussing a line from Garfield to Bear Creek in the Potlatch country.[56] The ORN's charter of March 3, 1898, for the SRV included a line from Elberton or Garfield to the head waters of the Palouse River, which would place the SRV over a divide from the white pine belt.

In early March 1897 Charles Odell Brown, after three years examining the white pine belt, reported an estimate of 480,000,000 feet of white pine and 43,000,000 feet of other timber in trees of at least 20 inches in diameter at the stump. The charter for the Moscow and Eastern Railroad Company (M&E) was filed on April 1, 1897, to build a railroad from Moscow east to the head of Big Creek, about 35 miles. The seven incorporators were all from Moscow. Brown was named general manager. In early May it was reported that the ORN would furnish a survey party. Officials of the road thought at least 24 miles would be completed that season.[57]

On May 5 McHenry wrote Mellen that he had met with M&E officials. He thought the potential traffic was sufficient to justify construction. "If the road were managed by interests hostile to the [NP], it would...intercept a considerable volume of wheat which now reaches our line in the canyon in the vicinity of Vollmer." McHenry's impression was that the ORN had made no offers to aid construction. He suggested that Mellen give them as much encouragement as deemed proper in order to keep them out of the hands of the ORN. Their need for rails would be a powerful lever to secure a favorable contract. McHenry wrote Mellen in mid-May that ORN officials were taking a great interest in the M&E. The suggestion to connect with the NP at Howell had been received favorably, which would save considerable intermediate local traffic. The ORN survey from Moscow to Howell paralleled the S&P, then via Bear Creek to a point 36.4 miles from Moscow and from there five extensions were made, the longest being a line extending from the forks of the Potlatch River up the East Fork, 20.2 miles, into the Elk Creek Basin.[58]

The SRV supplementary of December 27, 1898, projected a line from Moscow to Collins in the Potlatch country with a branch southeasterly to a point on the Clearwater River. In late January 1899 the NP Moscow agent reported that a party of 11 engineers were camped about seven miles east of Moscow. The party was thought to be ORN, but the chief of the party would only say, "We are going to build a railroad." It was confirmed a few days later that the survey objective was Collins. In early

February the Moscow agent reported that he understood that ORN President Mohler had been in Moscow in disguise the week before and had conferred with M&E officials. On February 18 McHenry informed Mellen that Brown wanted trackage arrangements between Moscow and Howell and to purchase rails. Brown was confident that he could raise capital from eastern lumber men once he had favorable trackage rates. McHenry examined the preliminary maps and surveys and his "opinion of the route is very unfavorable, as it is located across deep drainage lines, making heavy work and extremely unfavorable grades.... The line is not one that we would care to own...I would recommend that reasonable degree of consideration be accorded this project, but see no reason to recommend unduly favorable terms." McHenry did not think the project could be carried out because they expected to spend less than half of what it would cost to build the surveyed route. M&E officials had gone to Portland and received an intangible assurance of assistance, particularly with respect to rails from the ORN. The ORN was at a disadvantage by not being able to furnish trackage east of Moscow.[59]

On March 4 Van Arsdol reported that an ORN locating party had run a line down the North Potlatch from Cornwall about seven or eight miles and from there up the south branch about five miles nearly to the benchlands in the direction of Genesee and Moscow. If the ORN built east from Moscow it would cross the NP tracks. The NP had an engine in Moscow steamed up 24 hours a day to prevent the crossing and it was reported the NP would also prevent a crossing at Joel. McHenry doubted the wisdom of keeping an engine at Moscow to stop the ORN from crossing; inevitably they would gain the right to do so despite any NP effort to prevent them. Mellen criticized the action as "child's play" and Kendrick in investigating the matter wrote, "we have gone to considerable expense and made ourselves ridiculous, all for no purpose." McHenry wrote Mellen, "Mr. Mohler has changed his plans and now expects to reach the Upper Clearwater via Moscow." On March 10 a report said surveyors were running a line into Genesee and the residents were jubilant. In mid-March the ORN had several surveyors in Moscow "for the purpose of marking out the depot grounds and establishing their boundaries." The general belief was that work would begin on the Clearwater extension within the next month or so. The ORN would cross the NP main line at the east end of the Moscow yards and parallel the NP to near Joel then south down the Potlatch to the Clearwater and thence up the Clearwater to the mouth of Big Canyon and on to the Camas Prairie to Grangeville via Cottonwood. On March 24 the NP agent reported that the NP attorney in Moscow now worked for the ORN. A note attached to the letter indicated that the NP was still keeping an engine in Moscow to block the ORN.[60]

Bihler reported to McHenry on April 5 that the ORN had not made surveys down the Little Potlatch. Their movements lead Bihler to believe "that they intend to... get to Genesee, rather than to reach the Clearwater." On May 9 Van Arsdol confirmed Bihler's belief about Genesee, but the ORN also made a survey down the Middle Potlatch to a point just above Juliaetta.[61]

A report from Moscow on May 5, 1899 said, "It is now confidently asserted that the Moscow & Eastern railway to extend from Moscow to Collins...will be built this year and that the mammoth lumber mills will be located at or near Moscow." A letter from Brown gave assurances that the ORN would guarantee the interest on the bonds and float same for construction of the road. McHenry wrote Brown,

> I am indirectly informed that your Road has entered into close relations with the O. R. & N. Company. I trust that the report is without foundation, as I feel quite sure that it will not be to the best interest of yourself or any of the parties interested with you.... I am personally quite confident that our Company never will permit the occupation of this region by a rival Company without using every means within its power to offset same and I feel confident that if the final choice lies between the N. P. and the O. R. & N. Companies, that there is but little doubt, as to which one would be most valuable to you, from a business standpoint.

Brown assured McHenry of the road's independence. The funds for the road would come from an unnamed lumber company and they had instructed Brown to survey west to Moscow from Bear Creek and another south down Bear Creek to Kendrick. The decision on which to build would be determined by advantages and cost.[62]

On June 12, 1899, McHenry wrote Bihler that construction of 25 miles, more or less, up the main Potlatch from Kendrick would probably be authorized and a survey should be made "having in view the best access to the large bodies of white pine timber and also with respect to a connection from the north." A connection from Farmington should be compared to one from Palouse City. "[I]t should be done as unobtrusively as possible." Beginning in early July the NP had surveyors working up the Potlatch River from Kendrick. In the meantime, M&E surveyors had established a camp at Joel. Nearly a month later they were cross sectioning and camped six miles beyond Vollmer.[63]

On July 15 the M&E's name was changed from "Railroad" to "Railway" for the purpose of building a railroad east from Moscow to Elk Creek and also a line from Bear Creek, near Deary, down the creek to the NP, near Kendrick, about 70 miles. Three of the earlier incorporators had dropped out and one was added, all still from Moscow.

Wisconsin Governor Edward Scofield arrived in Moscow July 23 to investigate the country and route of the M&E. A few days later a timber man from Michigan said the NP decided to build the Potlatch branch three months earlier "and assured his company to that effect, so that immediately they sent the surveyors and estimators into the white pine." Scofield in Spokane in early August said he would not invest in the white pine belt: to be profitable a great deal of timber would have to be acquired; the state required that the timber be taken out in 20 years and his experience with such contracts was not good; and the cost of building the line east from Moscow was grossly underestimated—it could not be done for less than $500,000 to $600,000. He was not sure who was behind the M&E, but thought it was the ORN.[64]

McHenry wrote Mellen August 28, 1899:

> Mr. George Creighton [M&E President and Moscow dry goods merchant] called on me.... It is quite apparent that our surveys east of Moscow are causing him much concern. As a result of my interview, I am left with a very decided impression that the negotiations between these people and the O. R. & N. had progress to a point that threatened our interest. Our latest agreement with Mr. Harriman has unexpectedly deprived them of this support and they are now again looking to the Northern Pacific for assistance. Mr. Creighton did not present any arguments that would appeal to you in favor of his plan to make Moscow the saw mill point on the track. The longer he talked, the more apparent it became to me that it is greatly to our interest to have the timber sawed elsewhere at some non-competitive point on our line. It is true that the lumber for the Palouse Points would have to be drawn up grade, but it has now become apparent that the best point of departure will be from Vollmer instead of Kendrick and the length of the adverse grade will accordingly be very much reduced.
>
> I do not believe that the charter of the Moscow & Eastern Ry. has any value whatever to this Company, unless it could be acquired wholly without conditions and was purchased for the purpose of preventing possible construction. The location is exceedingly undesirable from every standpoint and the amount of adverse grades . . . . would be considerably in excess of that between Vollmer and Moscow. A further argument in favor of the proposed connection at Vollmer is the existence of the mills, already in operation at this point.
>
> It was apparent throughout the conversation that...this line would virtually operate as an extension of the O. R. & N. into the region east of Moscow, which would not only be competitive with us for the timber, but would also cut off from our existing line a large amount of grain and incidental traffic, which now tributary to it.[65]

McHenry September 4, 1899, sent Mellen information on a reconnaissance "for a route from the Palouse and Lewiston line to the white pine timber lands at the head of the Potlatch River and its tributaries." Four routes were considered, three from Kendrick and one from Vollmer. The preferred route diverged from the Palouse branch a mile and half above Vollmer and ran over 35 miles to a terminal on the West Fork. "This line is not very far from the located route of the Moscow & Eastern Ry. And all things considered seems the best that can be found, particularly as it avoids the duplication of the long descent to Kendrick and traverses a country ultimately adapted to agriculture." The exploration demonstrated that impracticability of connecting the white pine lines to the Farmington branch because of the high divide to the Palouse River. "The intermediate territory will be best and most cheaply served by a line from Palouse City up the Palouse River." On the 19th the NP executive committee rescinded a June 9 resolution authorizing construction from Kendrick up the Potlatch River, 25 miles, and instead authorized the president to construct a line from Vollmer to the white pine belt, 35.5 miles. That day McHenry wrote Mellen that the amount of merchantable saw timber in the Potlatch and Elk Creek districts was less than earlier estimated, but "it will be sufficiently profitable to justify the proposed construction." On November 15 Bihler was sent a map and profile of the first 10 miles of the Potlatch branch, beginning a short distance below Howell, shortly changed, to achieve less gradient from Howell to Collins post office, 29.91 miles. Bihler wrote McHenry on the 29th that the M&E was buying right-of-way that closely paralleled the NP line for some distance and crossed it several times in the vicinity of Howell.[66]

On March 27, 1900, McHenry wrote Mellen, "I have little doubt that the promoters of the Moscow & Eastern Railway have found it very difficult to raise money for their project with prospect of parallel construction by the N. P. Railway to confront and they are doubtless fishing for some assurance that the N. P. branch will not be built and at the same time hoping to find it possible to effect some arrangement to construct their road with the assistance of our Company." Mellen responded April 17 wondering about acquiring all the securities of the M&E.

Would McHenry recommend its acquisition? The next day McHenry responded that the M&E had nothing to sell "except its undesirable survey" and its charter. He would not recommend its acquisition. "It would seem to be very much better, more satisfactory and cheaper in every way to retain any construction in this direction entirely within our own Company, if it is to be built at all, as our past experience proves that lines built under such auspices...are very unsatisfactory." McHenry sent Mellen construction estimates June 12, the Potlatch branch, 30 miles, was $510,000, $17,000 per mile. Expenditures on the line to April 30 were $7,423, all for engineering.[67]

In late May 1900 a Wisconsin lumbermen visited Brown and inspected timber in the vicinity of Collins. They proposed that Brown work for them and when the deal was confirmed in mid-June Brown learned that he was the local agent, at $150 a month, of Frederick Weyerhaeuser who had recently acquired nearly a million acres in the west. Within a few months 50,000 acres in the white pine belt was acquired.[68]

In April 1901 it was reported that the M&E had secured some right-of-way from Moscow to Collins, 42 miles. In late 1901 and into early 1903 there was an active market selling white pine lands. It was reported in mid-July 1902 that it was "practically certain" that Weyerhaeuser would build a 250,000 feet per day mill at Lewiston. Weyerhaeuser had about 90,000 acres of white pine. In early 1903 the Lewiston Commercial Club and the city council favored state legislation which would allow Weyerhaeuser's Clearwater Timber Co. to construct booms, cribs, and other appliances on the Clearwater River for logging and lumbering purposes. Some land owners on the upper Clearwater opposed the legislation because it would give the Weyerhaeuser Co. a monopoly on Clearwater timber and therefore reduce the value of their land. In early March the bill was defeated in the Idaho legislature.[69]

In July 1903 the M&E reportedly had secured most of the right-of-way from Moscow to Elk Creek, 60 miles. In October M&E and ORN had secured right-of-way from Moscow to Howell. In July 1904 M&E directors decided to perfect title at once for the right-of-way from Moscow to the Potlatch River. A month later plans were being made to construct the next year from Moscow to Potlatch, Idaho, on the Palouse River, 42 miles.[70]

On March 10, 1905, the Washington, Idaho & Montana Railway (WIM) was chartered in Maine by the Weyerhaeuser interests. The purpose was to construct a railroad east from Palouse, Washington, into the white pine belt. Construction began in May and by mid-November it was opened to Potlatch, Idaho, and in October 1907 it was completed to Bovill. This ended M&E prospects and serious consideration by the NP and ORN to extend into the white pine belt, but the Milwaukee and the Spokane & Inland Empire were attracted to the area (see chapter XIX for accounts of the WIM, Milwaukee and SIE).[71]

New Railroads in the Palouse, 1901–1910

In this chapter we examine five companies new to the Palouse. Three were built and operated lines: the Spokane & Inland Empire (SIE), the Washington, Idaho and Montana (WIM), and the Milwaukee. The fourth line was bought by the mysterious North Coast Railroad (NC), the fifth line, which had no completed construction in 1910. Interurban fever reached the Palouse, but except for the Inland Empire none were built.

A. The Spokane & Inland Empire Railroad Company[1]

The Spokane & Inland Empire Railroad, chartered November 9, 1906, was by early 1908 an amalgamation of Spokane street lines and interurban lines controlled by Jay P. Graves. The first interurban line began operating from Spokane to Coeur d'Alene in December 1903, and subsequent lines were constructed from Spokane to Colfax and Moscow. The latter lines are the subject here. Prior to being the SIE these latter lines were the Spokane & Inland Railway and the Inland Empire Railway. Up to its bankruptcy in 1919, except for quotations with other names, "SIE" will refer to the Palouse interurban lines projected and constructed by Jay P. Graves.

In mid-December 1903 organizers of the Palouse and Spokane Electric Railroad (PSE) sought a franchise in Whitman County for an electric railroad from Rosalia to Penawawa via Thornton and Colfax with branches to St. John and Oakesdale and to Spokane via Waverly.[2] About the same time the Spokane utility, Washington Water Power Co., organized the Spokane and Southern Traction (SST) with a projected route from Spokane via Moran Prairie to Pine City and Colfax. In early January it was reported that Jay P. Graves was considering whether to extend his street car line to Moran Prairie in conjunction with SST.[3]

In August 1904 Graves inspected the PSE survey from Colfax to Waverly. In September Graves sent a circular letter to a thousand Palouse farmers inquiring how much business an electric railroad could expect from them. In November the capital stock of the SST was increased and it was seeking subscriptions from residents along the proposed route. Work necessary for grading had been done for 11 miles and two other routes were being preliminarily surveyed. By late February 1905 the SST had surveyed a route from Spokane to Oakesdale shorter than any other railroad. In March there were rumors that Graves and the SST would compromise, but both sides denied it.[4]

Louis W. Hill wrote a GN official in December 1904 with respect to Graves' claim of support from J. J. Hill and himself: "Graves has no reason to represent Great Northern favorable nor are we encouraging construction.... I do not believe scheme practical not enough population for electric line and not enough tonnage for steam line." Graves' risk is no affair of the GN, "if he wants to take chance and should understand we are not encouraging it."[5]

A committee of businessmen in Colfax, Pullman, and Moscow was formed in January 1905 to press for an electric railroad from Spokane. A map in the Pullman *Herald* showed a line reaching Colfax via Rosalia and Pine City, up Spring Creek to Pullman, up Union Flat to Colton, and descending to the Snake River via Steptoe Canyon to Lewiston, with a branch from Pullman to Moscow. Compared to the NP it claimed to reduce the distance between Pullman and Lewiston from 65 miles to 35 miles. A meeting in Colfax on the 21st was attended by Graves. Additional meetings and fund raising followed. In mid-March Graves made a contract for 22 miles south from Spokane. In late March a Colfax resident active in the joint committee said, "there is no use to disguise the fact that an easier line has been found for the main line to Palouse, than to Colfax. Meanwhile I have obtained from Mr. Graves and associates a definite statement that if Colfax will do something toward off setting this natural advantage in favor of Palouse, the main line will come to this place." Fifty thousand dollars were needed. After difficulty finding a satisfactory route down to the Palouse River, SIE engineers reached Colfax April 5. There was concern that the line would stop at Colfax, but the ORN right-of-way up Spring Creek was said to be available if the ORN did not occupy it. It was up to farmers to raise $1 per acre in a three-mile strip on each side of the line. Some farmers were unhappy that not all farmers were willing to provide free right-of-way.[6]

NP Vice President J. N. Hill wrote Vice President D. S. Lamont, April 26, 1905, that Graves admitted he had told people that he and his father "were friendly to helping in this Palouse project. I frankly told him that, if he gave such impressions, it would force me to discredit him as he knew he misstated my views and position in the matter. The fact of the whole matter is he is desperate, as he sees a poor chance of financing this scheme with the opposition he is now meeting,...he sees his possible profits fading away."[7]

A letter from NP Vice President J. M. Hannaford to President Howard Elliott, June 23, 1905, reported conversations with "an expert" hired by potential SIE bond purchasers. The sale of the bonds seemed assured at $20,000 per mile (possibly $25,000), the exact terms not established. Hill was shown maps and Graves told him of his plans, but he "did not speak as though he had any assurance of assistance from Mr. Hill." In August Graves offered to sell at $75 per share 35 percent of the capital stock of the SIE to a Burlington official.[8]

In late September the SIE was located into Colfax and had bought terminal and yard sites for more than the $50,000 raised by Colfax. By mid-October the SIE had right-of-way south through Colfax in the bed of the South Palouse River allowing the railroad to build toward Pullman without interfering with the ORN nor crossing streets. By the end of 1905 the line had built 6.56 miles from Spokane on to the Moran Prairie.[9]

Elliott wrote NP Third Vice President C. M. Levy on October 28, 1905, that Grave's scheme for Spokane south was better than the SCRRN (Spokane & Columbia River Railroad & Navigation Co.) (see sections below), but "Good as that is, there is some talk in Chicago that, before they get through with it, they will have to go into the hands of a receiver." ORN Superintendent J. P. O'Brien wrote UP Vice President J. Kruttschnitt, November 5, 1905: "It is stated that Mr. Graves is very friendly with Mr. Hill. Have agreed with Mr. Levy that no connections will be made with the electric line without conferring with each other, and if the line is being built or will be controlled by the Northern lines, I am satisfied that it will be by the Great Northern."[10]

SIE surveyors reached Moscow from Palouse in early December. It was still undecided as to whether the route would be from Palouse or Colfax. By early January 1906 the SIE had definite locations in Palouse which closely matched what was subsequently built. In mid-January the contract for grading and tunnels at Palouse and north of Colfax had been let. Graves said that extensions to the Snake and Columbia Rivers would be decided later. Work on the tunnel north of Colfax began March 8.[11]

Louis Hill wrote his father James on January 31 that Graves had approached him about investing in the SIE: "I think he is very anxious at present to trade." Graves asked to recommend to his father that investing would "be a good thing." Graves proposed that their investment be through him rather than independent of him.

> Naturally this did not appeal to me. I told him I certainly would not recommend anyone to go into it as investment, unless they secured control independently of his friends' holdings as his people might sell out at any time and the control might go elsewhere, but that we might possibly be able to find parties who would acquire control and turn the management over to him as none of our people would care to undertake the management or direction electric lines: This appealed to him as there are two things he wishes, First, To retain the management. Second, to unload some stock and get a strong crowd interested with him.
>
> ...My impression from him is that it would take about two million dollars to buy the absolute controlling interest (51%) in this property. With this holding the property could then be left in the management of Graves as long as advisable and it would not be necessary to have it known who had acquired the 51%.

On March 2 Louis wrote, "Personally I should rather keep my money in hand rather than invest in any of Grave's electric schemes." On April 5 J. N. Hill wrote Louis Hill that he had talked to Graves about taking an interest in SIE. "I must say that at present I cannot see any reason why we should do so.... I believe that his concern will go broke, and that the Northern Pacific will very greatly increase its business in the territory about to be occupied by Mr. Graves, which increased business will be taken away from his railroad." Graves, who knew J. J. Hill from their involvement in mining in southern British Columbia, went to see Hill in St. Paul in April. Graves contacted Hill again in October and Hill eventually bought 21,000 shares.[12] Beginning in May 1906 the NP, under the direction of J. J. Hill, bought common and preferred stock in the SIE. By February 1907, according to Carter, J. J. Hill "owned a large block of SIE stock."[13]

In January 1906 the NP had sought to block the SIE in Oakesdale, but the town refused to grant a franchise and obstructed NP construction. An ORN survey from Colfax to Winona ran nearly all the way on SIE right-of-way, causing unease. The general manager of the SIE said in late March that the route to Moscow, whether from Palouse or Colfax, had not been decided upon nor had an extension to Lewiston. "All our energies are directed in getting to Colfax and to Palouse this season." Representatives of the SIE met with a committee of the Pullman Club April 5, 1906, "and as a result of the conference the line will undoubtedly be built into Pullman by Jan. 1st,...the town will be called upon to secure ample terminal and depot grounds and right-of-way through the city and right-of-way will have to be provided between Pullman and Colfax." By mid-April right-of-way from Palouse to Moscow had been secured and the Genesee Chamber of Commerce promised right-of-way to Genesee would be provided free of charge. The SIE met resistance in acquiring right-of-way from Colfax to Pullman, so consideration was given to building to Pullman from Moscow. Between February and September 1906, there was extensive correspondence between the NP and SIE about crossings at Rosalia, Oakesdale, and Garfield. The NP favored grade separations at all three locations, but SIE sought at-grade crossings.[14]

In July SIE surveyors were working to Pullman from Colfax. The right-of-way had been secured from Spring Valley to both Colfax and Moscow, and only the lack of labor and material could slow the rapid progress being made. On September 1 the NP told SIE contractors to cease pile driver work at the crossing north of Rosalia. The contractors did not comply. The newspaper noted that retarding the SIE would allow the NP to get that year's grain. In mid-October the SIE was grading at Garfield and both the NP and ORN employed guards to prevent the line from crossing their tracks. By October 22 the SIE had completed a preliminary survey from Colfax to Pullman.[15]

The NP agent at Moscow wrote in August 1906 that the SIE chief engineer stated in Moscow he was endeavoring to locate a line from Moscow to Lewiston and that they wished to tap the timber district east of Moscow and follow Elk Creek to the Clearwater North Fork to Lewiston. Early in September a preliminary survey was completed from Moscow down the middle fork of the Little Potlatch on a 2 percent grade. In the locating engineer's opinion it would be at least two years before the road could build to Lewiston. Elliott wrote J. N. Hill September 14 that if the SIE built into the Potlatch they would hand grain and lumber to the Milwaukee and Canadian Pacific, thus putting both into the Palouse-Lewiston country. Perhaps the NP should use its old survey to build into the area, but the NP had all the construction it could handle so it might be better to make some arrangement to control the SIE. "The matter, however, is of great importance." The NP agent at Moscow wrote September 21 that the ORN issued instructions to give assistance to the SIE in any way possible. He was informed the ORN line from Colfax to Moscow would be electrified and extended into the White Pine country and operated by the SIE to bring traffic to the ORN. The SIE was having difficulty finding a suitable route to Pullman from Colfax. In November Graves sought to buy the NP location and right-of-way from Colfax to Pullman. NP Chief Engineer Darling wrote Elliott that "I know of no objection to selling the right-of-way to some company that is friendly to the Northern Pacific interests." It was sold for $3,391.[16]

D. Miller, Burlington first vice president, wrote J. J. Hill August 25, 1906, advising against joint rates that Graves sought with the NP and GN. The northern roads had for some time insisted that interchange business be made on the sum of locals for several reasons: First, it was not advisable to establish a precedent of joint rates with electric lines. Second, while it would be advantageous for the GN to make joint rates because it had no line in the Palouse, but it would divert business from the NP. Third, a joint rate agreement "would place them in a position to raise all the capital they may desire to build branch lines and extensions into much of our most valuable territory." Nevertheless, the GN entered into traffic agreements with the SIE in October 1907, and joint rates the following February.[17]

In a solicitation to sell SIE bonds, reference was made in November 1906 to the white pine belt and an accompanying map showed proposed extensions from Palouse to Lewiston via Moscow, and Colfax to Moscow via Pullman. It was thought by some in Lewiston and Clarkston in December 1906 that the SIE was backed by Hill and that he would eventually lose control of the NP and thereupon the GN would enter Lewiston over the SIE which would affiliate with the Lewiston & Southeastern thereby giving the GN a line to Grangeville. In response to SIE service to Waverly, the ORN lowered its rate on wheat from there to Spokane by more than half. The SIE failed to reach Pullman by January 1 and thereby forfeited the Pullman bonds. The SIE paid a $1.25 per share dividend on preferred stock, January 20, 1907. Freight and passenger service to Rosalia began in February.[18]

Graves told the Spokane Chamber of Commerce in January 1907, "we have completed our surveys to Moscow and Lewiston and preliminary surveys have been run on southward to Dayton, Walla Walla and Lewiston. We are seeking a route by which we may get out of Spokane down the river and we have looked over the Big bend country, which looks mighty good to us."

A composite photograph of Palouse, Washington, from the west, c. 1908, the year the Spokane & Inland Empire was completed to Moscow and on the facing page prior to November 1905, when the Washington, Idaho & Montana was completed from here to Potlatch, Idaho. Both images show a log drive down the Palouse River to either or both the mills at Palouse and Colfax. In the facing page image are a string of grain warehouses on the south side of the S&P/NP tracks and a lone warehouse on the north side, between the lone warehouse and the left end of the string, the roof of the depot appears and beyond is the water tank. In the image above is the third crossing of the river via a Howe Truss bridge. Beyond the bridge is the right-of-way of the WIM and in the distance is the SIE trestle crossing the WIM and the river. *Left image: Photograph 1987-01-153, Whitman County Historical Society. Right image: Mike McMackin Collection.*

The same month a NP memorandum notes that Graves had taken "over the franchises, power sites and terminal grounds at Clarkston, belonging to the Charles Francis Adams people." The Graves railroads were "getting to be of such a size as to be a menace to the interests of the Northern Pacific.... It seems desirable to have some indirect control this entire enterprise, and then let it be managed by outside parties. If the Northern appears in the management of it, the public will not be satisfied, and others are likely to invade that field." On the 29th Elliott warned that the LSE could be used by Graves to become part of a line from Spokane to southern Idaho. A report from the Lewiston NP agent in mid-May 1907:

> Representatives of the Spokane Inland and the Walla Walla Traction Co., have been in Lewiston and Clarkston within the past few days. I have it from pretty good authority that the Spokane Inland is figuring on building from Moscow to Genesee and from Genesee to Clarkston, building down the Steptoe grade, coming out on Snake River at a point near Alpowa, some ten miles below Clarkston, at which point they are to make connections with the Walla Walla Traction Co. Who are to build from Walla Walla to Lewiston via Dayton and Pomeroy. I am also advised that the Spokane Inland is still negotiating and expect to close a deal with the Lewiston-Clarkston Co. for their electrical plants at Clarkston, Asotin and Grande Ronde. They will also take over the electric lighting system of Clarkston, Lewiston, Uniontown, Genesee, Pullman and Moscow. I find that [SIE] are handling fully 50% of the Spokane passenger business from Oakesdale and Rosalia. They are also handling 35% to 40% of the freight received from Spokane, and practically all of the forwarded business from the above stations, account of applying Spokane rates in both directions.[19]

The line to Colfax was completed July 6, 1907. By August 9 the SIE had three daily round trips between Colfax and Spokane, the same number as the ORN. By early October it was said that 27 grain warehouses were

on the SIE between Colfax and Spokane. Farmers in the St. John area were willing to provide right-of-way for the SIE to build from Colfax. A committee of five Spangle citizens met with SIE officials to request that it build from Steptoe to Spangle and from there follow Hangman Creek to Spokane.[20]

Graves wrote Elliott February 6, 1908, inquiring whether he should be involved in building the Lewiston & Southeastern through the Camas Prairie. "The gentlemen have been to me repeatedly with this project, and they have now presented it to me in a tangible form, offering to let me take it over without any promotion fees if I will promise ultimately to build the line.... I had practically made up my mind to wait at Moscow with the present terminal for the time being, and let development tell whether further extensions should be made or not. I should like to have an expression from you on this subject so that I might discuss it with these gentlemen." Three days later a report said that Pullman cheered the "semi-official" announcement that the SIE would build from Colfax through Pullman down Steptoe canyon to the Snake River. The directors of the LSE received a proposal from Graves February 10, 1908, to build it to Nez Perce and Grangeville. On February 13 the Clarkston *Republic* declared that the Steptoe canyon was the only practical route to the Snake River. At the annual LSE stockholders meeting, President Thompson was authorized by Graves to state: "I want to get into that country. I will build the line if I can get the money and I think I can get the money. This is what you can tell the people." Elliott responded to Graves' letter of the 6th, because the line to Grangeville was a joint line with the UP he should not expect to interchange traffic with the NP and would have to take it to Spokane for the GN. The surveyed route of the LSE "would be a very difficult line for the movement of freight business." Elliott said he doubted the wisdom of another line to Grangeville and "it would be too heavy a load for you to undertake in a country that is not very thickly settled.... My feeling is that it would be safer for you to stop at Moscow for a year or two, until you can find out how the country grows." Graves spent June 25, 1908, in Lewiston examining the maps and charts of the LSE. "Thoroughly pleased with a cursory inspection Mr. Graves called attention to the difficulty in bringing the Inland into Lewiston." He made three surveys: through Steptoe canyon, through Hatwai canyon, and through Little Potlatch canyon. In July Graves and an engineer went by automobile from Colfax to Lewiston over the proposed route of the railroad. On the 15th it was said the negotiations were broken off with the ORN over purchase of the Moscow branch and that the SIE would build from Colfax via Pullman and Colton to Lewiston. Graves wrote Elliott July 25 "that for the time being at least" he would not be building to Lewiston nor be involved in the LSE. "This is a difficult country to build into, and will mean a good deal of money expended in getting a suitable line to take care of the business." Graves wrote D. Miller, of the Burlington August 17, "We have given a great deal of thought to the extension of our railway into Lewiston, but no conclusions have as yet been reached concerning it, and it is not my intention to immediately take up that question.

We shall probably wait one or two years, or such matter, for development of business and experience in operation electrically before going farther then Moscow." In September the SIE sought condemnation of ORN property in south Colfax. This was taken as indication that the SIE would build to Pullman.[21]

With initiation of two round trip passenger services to Moscow September 15, 1908, all major construction on the SIE was completed. The line, 131.15 miles, ran from Spokane to Spring Valley, 39.53 miles, where the line divided to Colfax, 36.22 miles and to Moscow, 55.4 miles. South of Spring Valley all significant points were also served by either the NP or ORN or both.

A report in January 1909 said that the SIE had purchased the ORN's SRV right-of-way south out of Colfax into Union Flat and to the Snake River via Penawawa. In early April buildings on the SRV right-of-way were being torn down or removed. The *Herald* wrote, "That the railroad will be built to Pullman will admit of no doubt." It was assumed in April that the engineers taking measurements on the Lewiston-Clarkston bridge were SIE determining what was needed to run interurban cars across the bridge. The view was that the SIE would acquire the bridge by buying the Lewiston-Clarkston company and its other properties. Farmers in the Dusty area proposed the SIE build a line from Colfax to Central Ferry, about 40 miles. The farmer committee was willing to subsidize the line to about $25,000.[22]

In late 1909 SIE surveyors were busy between La Crosse and Union Flat until they were recalled in January 1910 (see chapter XVII). In early February 1910 the SIE secured a franchise in Moscow to extend its line to Sixth and Main where it was speculated that the NP and SIE would have a union station. A NP-SIE union station never occurred (the NP and OWRN/UP did later build a union station in Moscow). There was a report that the SIE would run its electric trains to Lewiston over the NP.[23]

J. J. Hill wrote Graves January 19, 1909, encouraging him to acquire additional stock to secure control of the SIE. Some of Hill's stock was held by the GN's Lake Superior Co. By April 26, 1909, the NP's Northwestern Improvement Co. purchased 42,883 shares of SIE common stock and 21,667 shares of preferred stock at a cost of $4,295,800. Hill also made short-term loans to the SIE which by April 1909 exceeded $1 million. Grande concluded that, "After a wreck at Gibbs [on the Spokane-Coeur d'Alene line], Idaho, July 31, 1909, Graves realized that the line would never be a financial success and tried to sell the line." By September 1909 Hill gained control of the SIE through stock purchases which were divided between the GN and NP. On September 26, 1909, J. J. Hill wired L. W. Hill asking whether Hill, Northwestern Improvement Co., and Graves should sell their 60 percent of the stock to the Milwaukee. J. J. Hill's final sentence was "however, do not see any reason for disposing of interest." Graves was discussing a traffic contract with the Milwaukee. Elliott wired Graves the next day saying, "My feeling is we ought not sell but will give consideration to your views and recommendations. Believe unwise give other people any encouragement as to sale while you are discussing traffic contract." Elliott on September 29 sent a message to L. W. Hill. "Inclined believe we would be better off without third partner and that it would pay us take over his share and be in absolute control.... Doctor says he must retire or die." Hill divided the common (voting) stock in the SIE: GN $3,465,300 and NP $3,465,200 ($10,000,000 issued) and preferred stock GN $1,083,400 and NP $1,083,300 ($6,409,100 issued). The general view was that Hill bought it to keep it out of the hands of the Milwaukee. Carter believed that an equally plausible reason was to save the road from bankruptcy. Fahey did not believe Graves could afford, because of other business interests, to double-cross Hill by selling to the Milwaukee. Given Hill's efforts related in this work, keeping the SIE out of competitive control served Hill's long desire to gain the GN an entrance into the Palouse.

The editor of the *Review* October 31, 1909, believing that the NP's Northwest Improvement Co. had bought a majority of the SIE common stock in order to prevent the Milwaukee from buying it, regretted Graves' withdrawal. "With Mr. Graves directing the fortunes of the road the extension of the system and the development of the country tributary to Spokane were inseparable." Within the Hill system the line would be of secondary interest and there would be no water power in the vicinity of Spokane not owned by Hill or Washington Water Power Co. "[I]t can hardly be expected that any one will care to enter the field with another electric line to take up the development work where Mr. Graves lays it down."[24]

In mid-January 1910 rumors were that Graves would resign as president and his son as general manager and that the SIE would be a division of either the GN or NP.[25] Elliott and J. J Hill on December 8, 1910, wrote Graves, who was still president of the SIE, that building from Colfax to Pullman and electrifying the NP to Moscow and Genesee ought to be postponed "until we know something more about the course of general business in the United States." They also wanted Graves to reduce expenditures to pay interest on the bonds and floating debt as well as make improvements. The SIE joint tariffs should be arranged for equal participation by the NP and GN.[26]

Graves remained president until June 15, 1911, when C. R. Gray, SPS president, became president of the SIE (SPS presidents remained SIE presidents until 1919). Just prior to Gray becoming president, Elliott wanted him to move away from Graves' policy of making tariffs "for the purpose of trying to make a temporary showing for the Inland, which tariffs at time may be hurtful to the Northern Pacific and Great Northern.... It is going to be necessary for the Inland at times to sacrifice some short haul business in order to protect the long haul business of the Northern Pacific and Great Northern, and too little attention has been paid to this by the Graves management." Following discussions with J. J. Hill, Elliott cautioned Gray,

> My suggestion is that you consider pretty carefully the local situation at Spokane in making up your Board and in making changes in your officers. Mr. J. P. Graves has a great many friends and admirers in Spokane who think the creation of the Spokane Inland Empire by him has meant a great deal to the building up of Spokane, and in this I think they are right, because it has brought the surrounding country closer to Spokane, and helped to develop it....
>
> Spokane is in some ways a very sensitive town, and it would be very easy to set them against us if they think we are taking away too much of the local management of the Inland Road, hence my suggestion that you consider continuing Mr. Graves on the Board, and Mr. Payne as representative in a commercial way.

Gray wrote Elliott June 17 regarding SIE records, "It looks to me as if the compilation of statistics has been turned over to some person with instruction to prepare them with a certain purpose in view, that purpose being to deceive."

In response to perceived threats from the Harriman lines in eastern Washington, J. J. Hill said in Spokane June 5, 1912, "We were the pioneers and we don't expect to lose our heritage." He said that terminal properties had been secured in Lewiston for the SIE and that it would be pushed from Genesee to Lewiston. The *Tribune* a day earlier had reported from Spokane, "Plans announced... by the Spokane & Inland...contemplate rushing an extension from Colfax, Wash., to Pullman, Wash., electrifying the Northern Pacific from Pullman to Genesee, Idaho, and the construction of a line from Genesee to Lewiston, Idaho." This was seen as a response to the UP activity in Union Flat. In early June the *Tribune* carried a number of stories about this development.

The company went into deficit in 1911. Hill interests continued to loan the company money and by 1918 the amount owed the GN and the Northwest Improvement Co. reached $6,211,242 and the annual interest on that exceeded the interest on the bonds; the total debt was $10,625,742. The total deficit for the three years 1916–1918 was $1,446,608 and the scrap value November 1918 was estimated at $5,949,724. On November 1, 1918, the SIE failed to pay the interest due on bonds. J. M. Hannaford, having become NP president, January 1, 1918, wrote former president Elliott, November 29, 1918, that he had tried to get the executive committee to put into the hands of a committee "the complicated financial situation that was worked up by Mr. Graves and the late Mr. Hill." He went on, "The Northern Pacific has its own lines into the very best of this territory and I do not think should have become a partner in this unloading by Mr. Graves and his associates." A receiver was appointed January 10, 1919. The receiver's sale was held in Spokane November 1, 1919. The GN representatives ceased bidding at $3.5 million; the bondholders bought the SIE using $3.6 million in mortgage bonds. The *Review* reported that the NP and GN each lost $6 million in stock purchases and loans.[27]

On January 6, 1920, the Inland Empire Railroad Co. acquired the SIE Palouse lines and the Spokane & Eastern Railway & Power Co. acquired the remainder of the property. On November 26, 1926, the two companies and the GN agreed the GN would acquire both for $1,250,000. On April 21, 1927, the GN's Spokane, Coeur d'Alene & Palouse Railway acquired the interurban lines. The operating deficits, largely from the Palouse line, began in the late twenties and by 1941 the revenues were $330,000 and operating expenses were $600,000. In 1939 passenger service on the Palouse line ended and in 1941 all freight service was dieselized. The GN began direct operation July 1, 1943. Hill's desire that the GN have a line into the Palouse came to fruition. On March 3, 1970, the GN lines were merged into the Burlington Northern Railroad. By the end of 1989 all of the route miles of the SIE's Palouse lines had been abandoned. So ended James J. Hill's Palouse folly.

The Palouse River Lumber Co. mill at Palouse, c. 1900. The mill and other property of the company were purchased in 1903 by Weyerhaeuser's Potlatch Lumber Co. On the right an NP freight train is at the second crossing of the Palouse River on a Howe Truss bridge. Below the bridge there appears to be a log drive. *Bob West Collection.*

B. The Washington, Idaho & Montana Railway Company (WIM)[28]

In early 1903 the Potlatch Lumber Co., a consolidation of Frederick Weyerhaeuser interests in Idaho and the upper midwest, purchased the Palouse River Lumber Co. mill and timber lands for $300,000. The Palouse mill's capacity was to be raised from 60,000 feet to 100,000 feet per day. By early May the new company had eight million feet of timber in the river and planned on another seven million to come down in the fall freshets. The ORN was willing to build to a new saw mill, but did not address transportation of logs to the mill. The NP had initially some interest in building into the white pine belt, but by the end of November 1903 the NP declined to build. By the end of November the Potlatch Lumber Co. was surveying possible rail connections with the NP and ORN at Garfield and Farmington as well as extensive surveys east of Palouse.[29]

GN Vice President L. W. Hill was informed in February 1905 that the Potlatch Lumber interests were desirous that Graves build the SIE to Moscow to connect with a line to the white pine belt. Graves was guaranteed half of their total output, about 5,000 cars. Burlington Vice President Miller wrote Elliott that he had been advised that Weyerhaeuser requested the ORN to build from Elberton to Palouse. The NP charge of $5.00 per car for switching lumber from Palouse to Garfield for the ORN was unsatisfactory to Weyerhaeuser. The UP suggested that the NP and ORN jointly build the line desired by Weyerhaeuser and that the NP give ORN trackage from Garfield to Palouse. Elliott, in a memorandum dated March 1, 1905, wrote "we should own and control the proposed Weyerhaeuser line from Palouse some sixty miles east.… If we are to act independently [from the UP] we should try to arrange with Mr. Weyerhaeuser to let us build and own the railroad." He seems "to prefer to build and own it himself, but states that we shall have the first opportunity to acquire it. I believe, however, that we could show to him that it is better for us to provide the railroad facilities in that country and for him to do the lumber business." On the same day Elliott wrote UP's Kruttschnitt that the rate to Garfield was satisfactory with Weyerhaeuser, therefore the Elberton to Palouse line was unnecessary. Elliott wrote NP Vice President Lamont that initially Weyerhaeuser did not want to be dependent on the NP, but Elliott's promise to take their line at cost, that the NP would make the same rates from wherever their mill was located as from Palouse, and a lower rate to Garfield changed his mind. On March 7 Elliott wrote Miller, "I am trying to hold off any railroad building in that section of the country until our general matters are a little more definitely settled, with the hope that any railroad necessary to serve the Weyerhaeuser people can be provided by the Northern Pacific exclusively." In a memorandum on the 15th Elliott wrote, "Surveying party will be organized at once to survey from Palouse east into the Weyerhaeuser timber track…arrangements to be made for actual work as soon as any right-of-way is obtained."[30] But it was too late. On March 10, 1905, the Washington, Idaho & Montana Railway (WIM) was incorporated by Weyerhaeuser in Maine. On April 26 the WIM directors agreed to extend from Palouse up the Palouse River to Bovill, Idaho, about 42 miles. The new mill was to be built at Potlatch, Idaho.

Concern was expressed within the GN that it was being left out of the Weyerhaeuser business. Miller tried on April 7 to clarify the situation. "Mr. Weyerhaeuser's interests in the Great Northern and Northern Pacific are very large and on that account he certainly cannot afford to take any position in the matter of his Palouse line that is not thoroughly friendly to the Northern Pacific and Great Northern interests. He will certainly want a division of the rate, which should be granted only in consideration of an option on the line."[31]

On May 5 Weyerhaeuser contracted for WIM construction east from Palouse 44 miles. Construction began on the 17th. Weyerhaeuser wrote J. J. Hill May 8 that he was anxious to have the line built because only 16 years remained to remove the timber on some of their land. The state no longer allowed floating logs to Palouse and Colfax and the company had nearly 70 miles of rail they could use on the line. "I can see no reason why, after the

In the Bear Creek canyon is the Bovard, Idaho, saw mill with two flat cars of lumber on the spur and laundry hanging at the house. By at least 1903 there was an "Adams" spur at about this location. It became "Bovard" in 1910. The spur was still listed when the Burlington Northern merger occurred in 1970. *Photograph 25-3-275 (from C. Cox), Latah County Historical Society.*

road is built, we cannot make satisfactory arrangements and turn it over to our friends." June 9 after conferring with Hill, Miller wrote Elliott: "I understand Mr. Hill to advise that no obstacle be placed in their way, and that Mr. Weyerhaeuser be advised that the Northern Pacific hopes that he can arrange, when the line is completed, to sell it to the Northern Pacific on a reasonable basis.... Mr. Hill, however, is very positive that no rate division should be made with the proposed line." Thomas Burg summarized the nature of these negotiations:

> The exchange is a glimpse of two heavyweights standing toe to toe slugging it out. Each took an extreme position: Weyerhaeuser wanting the NP to build his railroad and give him special rates, and Hannaford and Elliott considering the NP entitled to its territory and not wanting to commit without a proprietary interest in the traffic. Because Potlatch built the WIM itself, a strained relationship—sometimes helpful and friendly and sometimes obstinate and uncooperative—existed between the WIM and the Northern Pacific for many years. It was costly to both railroads.[32]

The UP sought equal rights with the NP for the ORN between Palouse and Garfield. Elliott wrote Kruttschnitt October 8, 1905, "Some time ago, arrangements were made between the traffic departments of the Northern Pacific, O. R. & N., and the Washington, Idaho & Montana roads, whereby loaded and empty cars are handled at a low price between Palouse and Garfield for interchange with your Company. We feel that we do not care to rent our track on the basis suggested by you." Almost a year later the UP again sought trackage rights for the ORN from Garfield to Palouse. Hannaford advised Elliott to decline the request and retain the handling of ORN loads at $5.00 per car. "The Weyerhaeuser lumber interests are going to be very large, and better for us to keep this arrangement in our own hands if we can." Elliott asked Hannaford to inquire whether the WIM was satisfied with the arrangements. The reply from the WIM was that "everything has been, and is, perfectly satisfactory."[33]

On November 12, 1905, traffic between Palouse and Potlatch began. In early June 1906 the WIM was operating about 16 miles of track and the offices of both the Potlatch Lumber Co. and the WIM moved from Palouse to Potlatch. By mid-September, 1906, the mill at Potlatch was ready to begin production. The mill was said to be the largest in the world. By mid-October, 1907, the WIM began regular service from Palouse to the end of the line at Bovill, 47 miles.[34]

The NP Chief Engineer inspected the WIM and reported April 1908 that he was impressed with the physical condition of the line and estimated the cost of the road, less equipment, to be $1,554,300. The report concluded, "I believe the line would be valuable to the Northern Pacific if it could be purchased anywhere near its cost of reproduction." Vice President Hannaford wrote Elliott, August 4, 1908, that the Weyerhaeuser interests had demanded that the Spokane rates on lumber from Palouse be applied to Potlatch. The SIE had done so. Hannaford discussed the matter with L. W. Hill, who said that there was nothing left for the NP to do but buy the road, if it could be done, but Hill was worried that such a purchase might shut out the GN from business which they had through the SIE. Elliott offered $2.5 million in cash for the WIM; the NP would build certain extensions to the road and give the same rates at Palouse and Potlatch as at Spokane, offer joint rates to the UP at Garfield, and to the Milwaukee at Rosalia. Weyerhaeuser declined Elliott's offer saying there was an oral agreement with the Milwaukee not to sell for ten years and nothing would be done until the WIM was connected to the Milwaukee. On December 28 the Milwaukee agreed to build to the WIM at Bovill and give through rates. In mid-January 1910 the Milwaukee began accepting freight at Bovill. In May the Milwaukee made a grain rate from Palouse to the coast which was the same as the NP and SIE. The WIM was building grain warehouses at Palouse and four miles east for shipments to the Milwaukee at Bovill. In June the Palouse local of the Farmers' Educational and Cooperative Union leased a large warehouse (40 feet x 180 feet) along the WIM. The Union operated two other warehouses along the line the year before.[35]

Hannaford wrote Elliott early April 1911 that the WIM had "tied up with the Milwaukee & Puget Sound in such a way that I question very much whether we, or the Great Northern, for that matter, would ever be used except as a matter of convenience. The Soo stands very well with the Potlatch interests." Burg wrote that the "NP had itself somewhat to blame, for being so tardy/nonproductive in production of empty cars. Milwaukee agreed to provide and the Potlatch mill needed plenty." The Soo reference is the shipping route from Potlatch to Bovill, Milwaukee to Spokane, Spokane International from Spokane to Eastport, Idaho, Canadian Pacific from Eastport to Portal, North Dakota, Soo from Portal to Minneapolis-St. Paul.[36]

C. The Chicago, Milwaukee & St. Paul Railway Company in the Palouse

The Milwaukee at the turn of the century was a prosperous midwest granger railroad. It had an important transcontinental interchange with the NP and GN at Minneapolis-St. Paul. When J. J. Hill gained control of the Burlington, much of that traffic was diverted to the Burlington. The formal response of the directors of the Milwaukee came November 28, 1905, in authorizing an extension from Evarts, South Dakota, to the Pacific Coast. A month and half earlier the Milwaukee incorporated in Washington State the Pacific Railway Co. whose name was changed in January to the Chicago, Milwaukee & St. Paul Railway Co. of Washington. Later in the month a railroad of a similar name was incorporated in Idaho. A month later a contract was let for construction across Washington. W. L. Darling, formerly of the NP, was the chief engineer of the project.[37]

At least as far back as 1903 there was considerable speculation about the route the Milwaukee would take across Washington State. The railroad fueled the speculation with extensive surveys from the Bitterroot Mountains to the Cascades and from the Snake River and Wallula to Hangman Creek. While surveying had been conducted for several months a route across the state had not been decided upon at the time of the decision to build. Milwaukee President A. J. Earling visited Spokane in late January 1906 and said, "From Butte through to the Idaho-Washington line we are still undecided. We know that we can go from Lolo Pass to Lewiston, Idaho and we now have surveying parties in the field whose reports will determine whether we can come by way of Spokane or the Palouse country." On March 16 maps were filed for a route across Snoqualmie Pass in the Cascade Mountains. U.S. Senator W. B. Heyburn sent a dispatch to Lewiston March 20: "Have introduced a bill at the request of the attorney of the Chicago, Milwaukee & St. Paul railroad authorizing the construction of a bridge across the Snake river at or near Lewiston, which leaves no doubt that your city will be on the line of the proposed road." In March and April the Milwaukee took options on property on the east and north sides of Rock Lake in the Palouse (the Milwaukee subsequently built on the east side of Rock Lake).[38]

In August 1906 contracts were let for construction from the Bitterroot Mountains down the St. Joe River to the Columbia River; the line was to be completed January 1908. But reports of surveys continued. The construction train from Lind reached Rosalia October 10, 1908. By that time the Milwaukee was operating from Lind to Othello. Connection to the tracks at St. Joe, Idaho, was expected within 30 days, but the route from Rosalia to Lind was not yet determined.[39]

Rosalia from the southwest, c. 1908, showing the Milwaukee Railroad at the bottom left and to the right the Spokane and Inland Empire with a single car interurban train to Colfax. In the middle distance is the NP with grain warehouses nearer than the depot and water tank. In the distance on the left is a long SIE trestle that was later filled except for the crossings of the NP and the road to Spokane. *From John A. Phillips III, Credited to the NPTellTale Collection.*

The Milwaukee's main line across Washington was completed May 14, 1909, local freight and passenger service began June 14, and through freight service from Chicago to Puget Sound August 1. The Milwaukee built a connection with the SIE at Rosalia. A surveying party was sent to Rosalia to locate a route parallel to NP to Spokane. A Milwaukee estimating engineer was in Colfax in late September 1909 and was to be there for the next two months. Five different routes into Colfax were examined. Offers were made for property, including trying to get the owners of Whitman Electric Railway & Power Co., which owned right-of-way in south Colfax, to put a price on the stock. The line into Colfax, if built, might be "the Spokane loop," a branch about 110 miles long from Spokane to Colfax, Pullman, and Moscow and west to the mainline at a point not yet determined. The route to Pullman might involve a tunnel of one to one and half miles through the hill south of Colfax. A month later the possible loop had been extended to the Walla Walla and Touchet valleys. In January 1910 Milwaukee surveyors were camped near Four Mile Creek about eight miles south of Colfax. It was rumored that the Milwaukee would connect with the WIM east of Palouse, pass over the NP and SIE around the east end of Kamiak Butte down Four Mile Creek to cross the South Palouse at Shawnee, traverse Union Flat to Winona and from there to the main line at Rock Lake. The Deary *Enterprise* predicted in early February that from Bovill the Milwaukee would go to Moscow along the M&E survey then to Pullman and Union Flat and west to the Milwaukee main line, about 75 miles. In May 1910, it was said that the Milwaukee and ORN agreed to meet at Orofino.[40] In late 1909 Milwaukee surveyors were busy between La Crosse and Union Flat (see chapter XVII).

In November 1909 the Milwaukee and UP agreed that they would share the new North Coast station in Spokane and the Milwaukee would enter Spokane from the east by building a branch from its main line at Plummer Junction to Manito, and from there it would use the UP to Spokane. West the Milwaukee would leave Spokane on the new NC Spokane-Ayers line to Marengo where it would connect with its main line. All of this was ready for operation September 15, 1914.[41]

Except for its mainline through Rosalia, the Milwaukee did not significantly enter the Palouse until it acquired the WIM in 1962. Following abandonment of its western extension, the WIM became a branch of the Burlington Northern from 1981 to 1996.[42]

D. The Spokane & Columbia River Railroad & Navigation Co.[43]

The SCRRN was a projected railroad on the western periphery of the Palouse Country. The NP and ORN perceived it as a threat and when it was acquired by Robert Strahorn, as part of his North Coast scheme, it became part of a mystery and possibly a larger threat.

The Eastern Washington Railroad (EWA) was incorporated December 5, 1904, to build a railroad from Ringgold, on the Columbia River north of Pasco, via Connell northeast to Fletcher, approximately 63 miles. It was reported on the 30th that 39 miles had been surveyed and grading was in progress. In late December the EWA inquired whether the NP had 66-pound steel rails or other weights they wished to dispose of for construction from Connell to Fletcher. The EWA also desired a connection at Connell and a supply of cars. There was concern that supplying rail might be seen by the ORN as a violation of their agreement. Hannaford informed Elliott in early January that the line would draw traffic from the NP mainline. He was told that businessmen in Connell and farmers along the route were liberally subscribing stock and donating right-of-way. In late January J. C. Stubbs of the UP traffic department wrote D. Miller, the CB&Q liaison between the NP and ORN:

> I am informed the Messrs. E. W. Swanson and W. S. Foster of the Farmers' Grain & Supply Co., Spokane, are the incorporators and promoters, and state if the line be narrow gauge they will charge nominal rate of about 5¢ per sack on wheat from shipping points to Connell, where they expect to erect a large warehouse to be served by both the N.P. and O.R.& N....If broad gauge, the N.P. and O.R.& N. are expected to compete in getting their cars on the line to secure the wheat which the Farmers' Grain & Supply Co. will control—estimated about 2,500,000 bu. per annum. The farmers, it is understood, have been asked to subscribe $75,000 in shares of $100 each, the Supply Co. to subscribe the balance, $125,000, making total of $200,000 with which to build and equip the road... the farmers desire the road built, but are loath to subscribe, believing the line would not pay expenses, as after the wheat had moved there would be practically no other traffic. The general opinion appears to be that the road will not be constructed, the route being through a hilly country and fuel would be an expensive item.

The NP and ORN agreed to discourage the proposal. Elliott wrote Miller early in February, "I gave them no encouragement, and said very plainly that we were opposed to the enterprise; that it was unnecessary at this time, and that when that section of the country needed a branch road we expect to build it."[44]

The EWA chief engineer estimated that the 59 miles from the Columbia River in Franklin County to Fletcher, Adams County, would cost $10,654 per mile and that its grades would compare favorably with other railroads in eastern Washington. "A conservative estimate of wheat to be handled by this road...will not be less than 7,000,000 bushels." On June 12, 1905, the EWA was reincorporated as the Spokane & Columbia River Railroad & Navigation Co. (SCRRN). It was reported in mid-July that a contract was awarded to Nelson Bennett, and grading had begun and was to be completed by October 1.[45]

The NP agent at Connell reported in late June that Foster had advised him that they were having track material, ties, and culvert material, etc., shipped from Chicago by W. E. Dorwin & Co. As far as the agent could ascertain their surveyors were about 10 miles west of Connell working toward the Columbia River. In early July the NP did not find any grade stakes between Connell and Fletcher. It was estimated that in 1905 the NP would lose 1,850,000 bushels out of 4,375,000 between Connell and Ritzville, and the ORN would lose 558,000 bushels out of 1,450,000 between Sulphur and Washtucna. Elliott thought if these figures were accurate the NP should consider a spur into the area. Miller reported to Elliott a few days later that W. E. Dorwin of Chicago was inviting bids to be delivered from August 1 to 5 to Connell for 6,000 tons rails, one 40-ton locomotive, 12 flat cars, and 50 box cars. NP third vice president C. M. Levy was told by the ORN that it would not make a connection at Connell. "If this little road was built and had a connection with the O.R.& N. and ourselves, there would be a good deal of danger in the situation, unless there was a very definite understanding and agreement on the subject between the O.R.& N. and Northern Pacific." Elliott telegraphed that he wanted to find out whether the "parties are really going to build railroad.... I doubt the wisdom of letting this independent road be in there even with understanding with other parties." The same day Elliott wrote UP's Kruttschnitt that the NP and UP should control the road if it were built. It might push to a connection with the SIE. He wondered whether the UP would object to the NP putting in surveyors and getting right-of-way? Kruttschnitt responded that the UP had no objections to the proposed NP action "with the understanding that the ultimate ownership and operation of the road shall be joint with the O.R.& N. Co." Levy received a report in early August that the line was located between Connell and Fletcher and about 25 percent cross-sectioned. The contracts for right-of-way stipulated standard gauge to be completed not later than October. The estimated cost was $14,000 per mile or $450,000. No contracts for grading had been let and teams that were there earlier were taken away. "The farmers are very dissatisfied at the withdrawal and would welcome any bonafide R. R. company."

In early August Swanson and Foster stated that the road would not be built that year because of the inability to secure rails. Also the ORN and NP had added an arbitrary increase of $11.20 per ton on steel rails. Later in the month Foster said they hoped to be ready to lay rails in December and have the road completed by March 1.[46]

Levy in mid-October wrote Elliott that he and Henry M. Richards, president of the Washington Water Power Company, had decided on a plan: a Spokane bank official would inform Swanson that the Power Co. expected to build from Spokane to compete with the SIE, but did not want to reveal the plan. Richards reported back that Swanson and Foster thought they had the line financed by Twohy Bros., but after considering the matter turned them down. Swanson claimed to have a contract with a New York bond house which would take the bonds at 85 cents and supply the funds for 25 miles when the SCRRN stockholders had graded and bridged the 25 miles. The stock and bonds had been issued. Most of the right-of-way contracts had expired. Richards wrote, "Rutter [the banker] thinks the Swanson outfit are very full of enthusiasm but not much else and that the farmers would leave them in a bunch to take up with railroad people of experience who would build the road." Elliott reacted, "it seems desirable that we should control this enterprise if it is really going to be built. It does, however, seem to me that it is an unnecessary piece of railroad construction, and perhaps if we could get a hook on it...we could have a little work done, and in that way side track the enterprise."

Levy wrote Elliott November 8 that Richards informed him that a contractor who had expected to grade the line, concluded that neither Swanson nor Foster had any money; he would not do the work. They now proposed to build an electric line from Spokane to the Columbia River. Levy thought the line was more of a threat to the NP than the ORN. He suggested the safest course was for the NP to build a line from Connell to Fletcher or take the chance that Swanson and Foster would be unable to get sufficient support for their line. According to press reports, work started November 11 with about 40 teams under a contract for grading 63 miles. The first 26 mile section from Ringgold on the Columbia River to Connell to be completed by April 1, 1906, and the remainder by December 31. The railroad would be 133 miles from the

Columbia River to Spokane and initially enter Spokane on the Washington Water Power Co. The Spokane NP superintendent learned that,

> the Company has been financed through the contracting firm of...[Eldenbel] Construction Co. of New York; that the agreement provides for the construction company furnishing all track material and rolling stock necessary and taking the bonds of the railway in settlement, with the proviso that the railway company is to do the necessary grading and bridging and as soon as twenty-five miles of grading bridging have been completed the construction company is to immediately track it; further that the railway company has made an arrangement for $60,000.00 with which to do the grading.[47]

The NP was informed December 13 that the SCRRN had 140 teams and about 200 men grading east of Connell and claimed that eight miles had been graded. A contract for 10 miles of grading west of Connell to the river had been let and the contractor thought the line would be completed from Fletcher to the river by April 15. A few days later Swanson said if a reasonable traffic agreement could be made with the NP at Connell they would not build to the Columbia. The people furnishing the money insisted that they build to the river so as not to be at the mercy of a connection at Connell. Elliott informed Levy that the NP would be surveying from Spokane to Connell. "As soon as we make active preparations, getting right of way, and making ready to grade, I should think the Farmers' road would die."

In early January 1906, SCRRN officials denied any connection with the Milwaukee. Reports had been damaging to the railroad in that farmers were willing to donate land to the SCRRN, but not the Milwaukee. In a letter to Levy, January 10, Richards said that Swanson and Foster had inquired where the Washington Water Power Company would connect with the SCRRN to bring it into Spokane. Reports in mid-January said that between 200 and 300 teams were at work both east and west of Connell and that the NP had two parties locating a line between Connell and Spokane. Levy learned the 23rd that Swanson claimed to have absolute title to the SCRRN and all he wanted was the cash actually paid, salaries for Foster and himself for the time devoted at $250 per month, that the road would be built and he would retain the town sites. It was reported to Levy February 7 that the farmers in the area told the NP engineer that Swanson was about at the end of his rope. The *Review* reported that Swanson said, "I feel that I can positively say that the road will be complete by the end of the present year." The NP resident engineer reported that 13.5 miles of grading were practically finished. "Very light work, looks more like skid road than railway profile but grade...does not exceed 1.5% grade and is skinning just over surface to get enough out of cuts to make fill." No preliminary surveys were made and "when they thought they needed a curve they put it in, consequently plenty of them. These curves are not spiraled.... This road is not being built for operation by same people. It is being built for a money making proposition as...promoters have entire control of it. It looks to me like the one that offers the best price gets it. I may be mistaken in this but hardly think I am." A representative of the Eldenbel Construction Co. claimed that the line would be completed to Spokane by the end of the year. NP Chief Engineer Darling reported to Elliott, March 18, 1906, that Foster claimed that "Swanson et al outfits have sold out to Strahorn or the North Coast (NC) people in New York, who were to put up bonds for Swanson's work and failed to do so." Foster claimed to have gotten $15,000 cash out of it.[48]

On March 20 it was reported that Robert E. Strahorn had purchased the right-of-way and equipment of the SCRRN for $30,000. Included was 53 miles of right-of-way, 36 miles of roadbed and bridges between Connell and Berry City, and "considerable" grading between Ringgold and Connell. Strahorn March 21 "denied most emphatically" that he had brought the line. On March 27 he again denied that he or the North Coast Railroad (NC) had purchased the SCRRN. He thought the rumors might have come about because they had investigated the road. Among the reasons the NC would not buy the road were its "excessive grades, bad alignment, and its light construction, what there is of it, is nearly all wrong for our uses." He hoped help could be found for the promoters, who "struggled along against great odds on slender resources until they seem to be simply at the end of their string." On March 29 Strahorn purchased the SCRRN in his name. How much was paid is uncertain: the ICC valuation reports note "Recorded money outlay" at $34,000. The NC account books show that as of April 30, 1906, Strahorn had withdrawn $45,092 on account of the SCRRN; Asay writes that the amount was $48,000 cash; and the *Review* in April said the amount was about $80,000. Gill claims Strahorn bought the property for the proposed Marengo-Benton City line of the NC. Strahorn in mid-April suspected fraud and had surveyors seeking a line east of Connell which would reduce the grade from 2 to 1 percent. Surveys were also being made from Ringgold toward the Big Bend country.[49]

On April 6 Darling wrote Elliott that someone had bought the SCRRN, and while most of the forces had been withdrawn engineers were "revising the line and putting it in better shape." Little grading had been done west of Connell but grading to Berry City was well along. Darling thought the NP should endeavor to control the line as a branch feeding the mainline at Connell. An early April 1906 NP map shows the SCRRN from Ringgold to Berry and NP surveys following the ORN out of Connell and then branching in three different places north to Rock Creek. The remainder of the SCRRN story is in the next section on the North Coast Railroad.

E. The North Coast Railroad in the Palouse[50]

On September 28, 1905, Robert E. Strahorn and others incorporated the North Coast Railway (NC). The charter contained no projections, but on December 18 the charter was amended to increase the capital stock from one million to $25 million and projected a line from Seattle to Walla Walla. The *Review* reported in October that Strahorn said the NC would build from Kiona, Washington, east to the coast via North Yakima and Cowlitz Pass, and grading had begun in the Natchez Valley west of N. Yakima. Strahorn denied knowing whether NC was part of a transcontinental system; "the men back of him in New York could give this information." All he knew was that he was to build 250 miles of road centered on North Yakima.[51] The activities of the NC covered a wide area in Washington State; here the focus will be primarily on the activities in and adjacent to the Palouse.

According to Asay, sometime between September 1905 and the following January, Edward Harriman secretly retained New York banker Harvey Fisk & Sons to acquire the NC without revealing UP's involvement. Fisk encouraged Strahorn to sell the railroad and on January 25 Strahorn offered to sell the NC for $100,000 plus expenses. As Asay writes, "There wasn't much to the North Coast except the survey and the grandiose plans. On paper the company looked a lot like many other blue-sky railroad projects in the western states. Maybe this was a virtue to Harriman.... Fisk signed the contract without quibbling." Strahorn in New York, January 31, 1906, said,

> The road will be built on its own rails from Tacoma to Walla Walla and continued to Spokane. I do not admit that it is backed by Harriman, Gould or the Canadian Pacific, but it has all the backing it wants. The North Coast is to be considered a local railroad build to handle the rich local traffic of Washington. It will cross Cowlitz pass and run through North Yakima and the Spokane branch will leave the main line near Pasco and run parallel to the Northern Pacific.

Strahorn on February 7 was instructed to buy terminal property at North Yakima. According to Asay, "This may have been the key to the deal: Harriman wanted to get into Yakima...without arousing NP's ire, which he was trying at the same time to secure rights over the NP's Portland-Tacoma line.... Kruttschnitt warned Harriman: 'As soon as NP learns (Strahorn) has backing, the immunity he has enjoyed as a smallfry beneath their notice will cease and steps will be taken to thwart him in every possible way.'" A few days later Strahorn said he did not understand why other railroads "or the public should be so desperately concerned about our connections or finances, or why this persistent effort to tie us up to some one of these roads. We feel that we are much stronger in our independent position so long as we are able to finance the matter, which we hope to succeed in to the end." As Gill writes,

> In this development of the North Coast Mr. Strahorn became the man of mystery to the keen eyed and keen scented railroad men of the Northwest, for it was determined to maintain with the utmost secrecy the connection of the Union Pacific with the road. So it became the 'mysterious North Coast,' and so remained until in November, 1910, the reorganization of the O. R. & N.... Every effort was made to find out where the Spokane Sphinx got his money and where he got his directions for the building the road, but so thorough had been the preparations that not even the Chief Engineer knew for whom the road was being built."[52]

As related in the above section on March 29 Strahorn purchased in his name the SCRRN. NP Chief Engineer Darling wrote President Elliott April 8:

> Following definite information regarding Spokane & Columbia River Railroad, first promoted by Swanson, President People's National Bank Spokane; money was to have been furnished by Edelbaum [sic] Construction Co. New York; four miles graded southwest of Connell and about 90% graded from Connell to Berry City; New York people failed to put up the money; Swanson gave Strahorn an option on work and Strahorn was afterwards offered $5,000.00 to release bond but refused. Strahorn took up option and has paid $25,000.00 down cash, part of it his personal check on Traders National Bank Spokane, part of it paid through Seaboard National Bank, New York.

> Party who told me thinks it Seaboard but not absolutely sure; also says have every reason to believe it is O. R. & N. scheme. Strahorn and his attorney Williams of Spokane go to Portland every two weeks. Line is being revised to get lower grade; object of present owners to connect with O. R. & N. at Winona with branch from Berry City, north through Ritzville to Davenport; from Connell west through Ringgold bar to Mabton, connecting with North Coast line through Cowlitz Pass; papers say North Coast has let contract Kiona to Mabton.[53]

On April 12 Strahorn authorized a statement that the NC would cross the NP at Connell, that the surveys had been made from Ringgold Bar to Fletcher and from Kiona to Ringgold Bar surveys were underway. By May both Kruttschnitt and General Solicitor William W. Cotton were confused about what was going on with SCRRN: the former to the latter, "I have lost thread of these badly mixed up transactions." Cotton responded, "What are your plans for this railroad? I am in the dark and can't adequately supervise Strahorn's spending." The NC Trustees in April accepted a location map, Connell to Berry City, 31.9 miles of which 24.5 miles from Connell were a revision of the SCRRN. NC surveyors in May were working north from Berry City. On May 18 a temporary receiver was appointed for the SCRRN. The NC trustees in August accepted a location map from the east bank of the Columbia River to Connell, 26.65 miles.[54]

Cotton discovered the North Coast Railway was not properly incorporated and needed to be reincorporated and the surveys remade. As a result the North Coast Railroad (NC) was incorporated April 14, 1906. Strahorn said October 1 that the NC expected to connect with the Milwaukee southwest of Spokane, the ORN and NP at Connell, the Chicago & Northwestern on the Snake River at the mouth of the Salmon River, the Canadian Pacific at Spokane and the Western Pacific south of Portland or on a line north from Winnemucca. "For any and all of these lines we can offer more advantages over important sections of our road in the way of lower grades and easier curvature than they can otherwise get."[55]

The NC trustees from January to December 1907 accepted location maps on the Palouse branch: from Spokane southeast along Hangman Creek to Tekoa, 41 miles. In late March NC engineers said that the maximum grade on the Palouse branch would be 0.6 percent compared with 2.0 percent on other lines. The maximum curvature would be four degrees compared to 10 to 12 degrees for other roads. By mid-May it was reported in the *Chronicle* that right-of-way deeds for most of the line had been filed in Spokane and Whitman Counties.[56]

M. L. Burkhart bought up the notes that farmers had given to the SCRRN and sold them to David Gross. Burkhart said on April 9, 1907, "that the farmers can not escape payment and may as well save the expenses of a lawsuit." Many farmers believed they would not have to pay unless the railroad was built. For each share purchased there was only an entitlement to $100 worth of transportation. They could not fall back on any tangible property the company acquired. "The impression has gained ground that E. W. Swanson and other promoters...never had a serious intention of building a railroad line, but that it was an ordinary promotion scheme to get money from farmers' pockets by making a show of construction through a territory where railroads are badly needed. Mr. Burkhart, however, declares his faith in the good intentions of the promoters and says that if it had not been for the financial difficulties of Mr. Swanson, which compelled him to sell the interests of the company to Mr. Strahorn of the North Coast, the line would have been completed." An entry was made in the NC journals June 30, 1907, that $59,227 settled all disputes and paid accounts on the SCRRN; this included vouchers of $36,495 for that June and thus probably does not include the $45,092 recorded over a year earlier.[57]

In September 1907 a railroad was buying property in Spokane between Howard and Monroe streets. When questioned, Strahorn would not say whether the NC was involved, but he did not conceal his satisfaction that the buying had progressed for nearly two week before it was published.[58]

It was reported in July 1908 that NC surveyors were working from the SCRRN right-of-way possibly toward Hooper. On July 25 the NC filed 114 deeds, worth approximately $1 million, within the city limits of Spokane. The *Review* said, "It would be well nigh impossible to secure another such position so near the business center and well inside of all existing stations without an outlay which would be absolutely prohibitive." It was pointed out that the expensive features of the NC were two Columbia River bridges, costing about a half a million each, the high and long bridge across the Snake River on the Walla Walla-Spokane line, about eight miles in the Palouse canyon descending to the Snake River which would cost close to $200,000 per mile, and a three mile tunnel between the Tieton and Cowlitz Rivers in the Cascades. The system was projected at 701 miles with terminals at Spokane, Seattle, Portland, Walla Walla, and Davenport. The distances between terminal points were shorter than other railroads and the Cascade Mountains grade was a maximum of 1.25 percent and 6 degree maximum curves as against 2.2 percent and 10 degree curves of other lines. The estimated cost was about $40 million.[59]

It was officially announced May 25, 1909, that the GN and UP would use the NP's line from South Tacoma to over the Columbia River bridge at Vancouver and the NP line would be double tracked. It had been intimated that such an agreement would end NC activity. Strahorn in Yakima said, "if the Hill-Harriman agreement meant the end of the North Coast road it was unfortunate that the railroad interests involved had not notified him as, since the agreement had been reached, the North Coast has ordered 75 miles of steel rails to be used in this valley."[60]

By mid-November 1908 construction began on the Palouse branch beginning near the junction of Marshall and Hangman Creeks toward Waverly. This was probably more show than serious business, but in 1909 work became more serious. Surveys began March 1, 1909, and continued until at least March 14, 1910. In late August 1909 a $400,000 contract was awarded for 10 miles of rock work on Hangman Creek. In the 10 miles would be five tunnels through solid rock aggregating a distance of one mile. Work commenced November 1 on the concrete contract, $165,000 for the first 20 miles. Nineteen miles of grading was done from November 1909 to the following July. The Lewiston *Morning Tribune* believed December 18, 1909, that because the NC was doing permanent work on the Palouse line it left "no doubt that his [Strahorn] road and the Pittsburg & Gilmore, who are running a line down the Salmon river to Lewiston, are auxiliaries of a single parent company and that company is the Chicago & Northwestern." The UP was also involved because the NC and UP seemed to operate in harmony. The *Deary (ID) Enterprise* in January 1910 reported that the NC was surveying from Lewiston on the north bank of the Clearwater River to the mouth of the Potlatch River, up the river to Kendrick, up Pine Creek crossing the WIM (probably about Deary) to meet the line from Tekoa. By late January NC surveyors had been in the Deep and Crane Creek area (near Potlatch) for four months and several tunnels had been surveyed at the heads of the two creeks to connect the drainages of Hangman Creek and the Palouse River. The survey from Tekoa to Lewiston was completed February 12, 1910.[61]

On March 2, 1910, the NC filed an amended charter projecting a line from its Seattle-Spokane line in Spokane County via Tekoa to Lewiston, about 131 miles. The amendment dropped mention of Farmington which had been in an earlier amendment. By mid-April 1910 NC had filed maps on the north side of the Clearwater River from opposite NP roundhouse in Lewiston to Arrow Junction, up the Potlatch and a short distance up Bear Creek just above Kendrick. The *Review* commented that the line was up the hillside from the Potlatch River avoiding the flooding problems of the NP. At least 17 Palouse branch maps out of at least 143 maps were adopted by the NC trustees between February 1906 and December 1910.[62]

NP President Elliott received a report October 18, 1910, that the NC was surveying between Juliaetta and Kendrick. Elliott had been told by UP President Robert S. Lovett to take up NC matters with the UP Director of Maintenance & Operation Julius Kruttschnitt. Elliott asked Kruttschnitt whether the NC was doing the surveying. Kruttschnitt responded on the 20th that "some months ago" instructions had been issued to withdraw all parties, but he learned from Strahorn that NC surveyors were there temporarily because they were not needed elsewhere, and he wired Strahorn that the parties were to be withdrawn at once, which was done. This correspondence is of interest because it indicates that before it was publicly known, the NP knew that the NC was controlled and financed by the UP. The NP may have learned of the UP-NC connection in the negotiations that lead to the incorporation of the Camas Prairie Railroad November 4, 1909 (see chapter XVI).[63]

On November 23, 1910, the UP chartered the Oregon-Washington Railroad & Navigation Co. (OWRN) to consolidate the UP holdings west of Huntington, Oregon; this included acquiring the ORN and the NC. The *Review* with a large headline reported the 24th that the OWRN articles showed that the NC was owned by the UP. "This is not only a big milestone in one of the most unique, carefully planned, and brilliantly executed operations in railroad history, but it is far more important in its bearing upon the transportation interests of the whole northwest, both on account it easily being the largest railway corporation ever formed in this field and on account of the revelation of the vast provision being made for new work in all parts of Washington and Oregon and in the Spokane country especially." The newspaper lauded that Spokane would now be 60 miles closer to Portland and 65 miles closer to Walla Walla and it also noted in text and map the proposed and partially graded line from Spokane to Lewiston via Tekoa, but failed to note that the latter was not included in the 11 NC lines listed in the OWRN charter, a list the newspaper included in its report. In mid-December Strahorn, now a vice president of the OWRN, said that the NC would carry on the construction work.[64]

On December 23 the trustees of the NC sold to the OWRN most of its property for $7,550,000.[65] No NC line was in operation on the date of the transfer. Specifically excluded from the NC transfer was the projected Palouse branch, from the Spokane city limits to Lewiston,

Idaho, its franchises, right to be a corporation, and cash on hand. A portion of the SCRRN, Ringold to Connell and east to the Spokane-Ayer line, was conveyed.[66] On December 28 the OWRN filed in Spokane the transfer of $65,540,000 of property located in Washington State. The largest transfer was the ORN; the second largest the NC.[67]

Apparently the NC continued work on the Palouse branch because the Oregon *Journal* of February 22, 1911, reported that the NC was buying property from Nez Perce Indians on Potlatch Creek and on June 13, 1911, the NC filed application for right-of-way down Potlatch Creek and Clearwater River to the west boundary of the Nez Perce Indian Reservation, east of Lewiston. Elliott wrote UP President Lovett June 19 inquiring what this meant, pointing out that the Camas Prairie line partially paralleled the proposed NC line.[68] No part of the Palouse branch was completed.

Palouse & Lewiston Branches, 1901–1910

The Spokane-Lewiston passenger train, December 21, 1900, encountered a washout two miles above the mouth of the Potlatch River. About 200 feet of track was destroyed. A heavy rain February 15–16, 1901, damaged every bridge between Troy and Kendrick. Between Juliaetta and Kendrick the line was in places under water, four bridges were out, and considerable roadbed gone. Bear Creek at Troy "was a raging torrent." The first train since the 15th arrived in Lewiston the 25th. Regular service was restored two days later on temporary track. On March 2 the Spokane train returned to Lewiston because a pile bridge five miles south of Juliaetta had been damaged by a sudden flood. "The washout is where the longest washout occurred two weeks ago, took out nearly 700 feet of heavy rock embankment. It was repaired by the construction of a long piling bridge."[1]

In March two bridge crews were at work. Roadmaster A. B. Ford said,

> all the bridges on this stretch of road will be placed on concrete piers, past experience having shown that no other form of pier will withstand the fierce rush of the waters of Bear creek and the Potlatch. An effort will be made to give the stream a larger waterway, of even grade, and as straight as it can be constructed in the narrow canyon. Where the grade is constructed in the bottom of the canyon it will be strengthened by being rock ballasted, each side of the grade being riprapped with large stones. The riprapping will be made much less steep than that put in previously.
>
> The repair of the portion of the track between Juliaetta and Potlatch [Junction],...is the greatest problem that the company has to solve in this region. The track here for a long distance runs on an embankment build along what used to be the high water channel and for that matter it is still the high water channel, the water have taken out fully 600 feet of this embankment.

In April wash outs were still being filled between Juliaetta and Potlatch Junction. NP Chief Engineer McHenry planned to avoid the annual washouts between the two points by the using bundles of brush wired together and weighted down with heavy stones placed as buffers or wing dams to divert the water away from the grade. In many places the grade would be raised and heavy riprap on a gentle slope piled higher than the grade would be used to protect the embankments. The 1901 NP Annual Report stated, "As a result of disastrous floods...it has been found necessary to provide Howe truss spans for three crossings of the Potlatch River and nine crossings of Little Bear Creek."[2]

In mid-March three train loads of immigrants were en route to Whitman County. Other train loads of immigrants followed. The rush of home seekers continued into the fall.[3]

The 1901 the wheat crop yield per acre in Washington was the highest ever and "the quality of the grain was never better." It was estimated that the crop in Washington would be 25 million bushels (10 million in the Palouse), and additions from Idaho and Oregon would bring the total to at least 35 million bushels. By the end of September grain shipments encountered a shortage of cars on the NP which persisted into early November. In a week in mid-October at least two million bushels of grain were sold in Whitman County.[4]

On August 26, 1901, President Mellen requested "a careful survey made of the line from Marshall...to Lewiston...with a view to the improvement of alignment and grades.... I want to replace all bridges and permanent structures, and bring the line up to a first class branch line, in every way." In September new Chief Engineer W. L. Darling went over the line and commented, "It seems quite impracticable to do anything in the way of radical improvements in grades." Recommendations and estimates were made in December; included were line changes, grade reductions (primarily to reduce grades in the direction of loads, east bound, to 0.7 percent), and improvements such as replacing 56 pound rail with 66 pound steel rail, bank widening and sag raising, ballasting, extra passing and house tracks, fencing and cattle guards, and replacing bridges with permanent structures or filling, for a grand total of $1,754,323. He pointed out that the line would probably be nothing more than a branch and so the main problem was to get the local tonnage to the main line in the cheapest manner. "The main question in improving this line is as to what direction the traffic will be handled; whether north to the main line or south to the Clearwater and thence via river route to Wallula: And again it depends upon whether the cut-off to Ellensburg is constructed." Most of the difficulties and operating expense could be avoided by building a new line of approximately 35 miles with 0.5 percent grades both ways between Rosalia and Sprague, saving 24 miles of haul and reducing elevation gain to about 350 feet. The line would cost $630,000 and on the basis of five trains a day save $686,000. If the line to Ellensburg was built 75 percent of the business would go over the new line. A line from Spangle to Cheney, 9.26 miles, would save 8.4 miles and 350-foot descent and a 250-foot ascent, and with 0.5 percent grades both ways, it would cost $209,800. Another matter to look into would be to use or parallel the ORN line from Pullman to Moscow "rather than try to improve our present line, which it is almost impracticable to do on account of the heavy hill... and the very bad alignment" He noted that it would eliminate an elevation gain out of Moscow of 140 feet. After Darling's revisions the estimate for improvements, without any new routes, was a maximum of $822,191. In 1905 Chief Engineer Pearson in response to an inquiry, wrote that there were no immediate plans for a line from Rosalia or Spangle to Sprague.[5] The available authorizations for expenditures through 1905 show construction of passing sidings and trestle filling, but little realignment and profile work outside of Troy to Potlatch Junction

On November 3, 1901, two freight trains collided at Rosalia. The local train was standing on the main track with the engine detached for switching. No one flagged for the train. An extra wheat train pulled by two engines could not stop. The crew jumped and were not hurt. The wheat train crashed into the rear of the local freight. The caboose and two cars were smashed into kindling, and both engines piled in a heap. The engines jammed into a corner of the depot and the building caught on fire, but was soon extinguished. "No blame is attached to the train crews, as they were apparently unable to stop their heavily loaded battering ram." On the 10th a new hill engineer lost control of a returning helper engine almost immediately after leaving Howell. He and the fireman jumped below Howell, and neither was injured. People in Troy saw the engine come through town a few minutes after nine o'clock with every wheel throwing off sparks. The engine left the rails four miles above Kendrick, nearly nine miles after being abandoned by its crew. It ran on the ties for about 200 feet before the engine and tender ran into a rocky bank in which they were buried for half of their width. In mid-January 1902 a freight from Spokane was ditched two miles east of Joel when two furniture cars loaded with lumber jumped the track.[6]

In early November 1901 more than 300 men were attempting to protect the road from flooding between Troy and Potlatch Junction. High water was hampering work on improvements. Extensive dredging was being done at the mouth of the Little Potlatch with the hope that the new channel would carry the waters of the Little Potlatch in times of extreme flood, "when the stream rises from four to six feet within two hours." Two miles above Potlatch Junction 75 men were blasting away the east hillside (the railroad was on the west side) to construct a new channel for the river. Riprapping above Kendrick along Little Bear Creek had been completed and the crew moved to Juliaetta to build a stone dike to protect the yard and depot grounds. When improvement work ended in early February the roadmaster said that $95,000 in labor costs had been incurred, most of it between Troy and the mouth of the Potlatch River.[7]

NP eastern Washington branches in 1901 experienced a high volume of agricultural and lumber products. According to Superintendent F. W. Gilbert, fruit, hops, and horse shipments were up and the wheat crop was almost 50 percent better than in any previous year. During 1901 the NP hauled 218 carloads of cattle from Lewiston and up to 1,000 carloads from the Clearwater country. In February the receipts for freight received at Pullman were 132 percent higher than a year earlier while shipments from Pullman were up more than 300 percent. In November 1902 twenty cars of stock were loaded at Garfield, seven over the NP and remainder on ORN. Stockmen in the area said they would not ship over the NP until it put in a scale at Garfield. If the NP treated them as the ORN did, they would divide their shipments between the two roads.[8]

The Whitman County wheat crop for 1902 was over eight million bushels, more than the entire state of Oregon. The NP at Rosalia shipped the most wheat, 757,000 bushels, and St. John on ORN was second at 670,000. Palouse, one of the few points in the county which handled more grain in 1902 than 1901, received 300,000 bushels of wheat. The 1903 wheat crop was down from 1902. Rosalia led all other points in the Palouse with 550,000 bushels.[9]

A conductor on a Genesee branch train was arrested for blocking a Pullman street crossing for 13 minutes; the town ordinance allowed only three minutes. "Frequent complaints of this character have been made recently." The NP brought several suits in January 1903 in Kendrick for right of way violations. The railroad claimed a right of way of 100 feet on either side of the center of the main track. The defendants claimed that when the town was platted the right of way was fifty feet on either side. The railroad served notice two years earlier and was willing to make long-term leases at a nominal rent.

The offer was ignored. In June 1902 the railroad served notice for the property to be vacated. No attention was paid and hence the suits. The three mills on the Potlatch River above Kendrick had in early March 1903 about two million feet of logs ready for sawing. In late March a brick yard was put in east of the NP Moscow depot.[10]

On October 25, 1903, the second engine of a northbound freight double header jumped the track at Pullman Junction, and ran on the ties for some distance, as the train rounded the curve at the wye. The derailed engine was slightly damaged, but six boxcars loaded with grain and fruit were badly wrecked. The initial report said the brakeman was "somewhat bruised." He subsequently sued the railroad for $15,000 for injuries he suffered when jumping from the engine. He claimed he could no longer work. In mid-March 1904 track two miles north of Kendrick washed out, with fifty feet of track hanging in the air. A transfer was made between passenger trains. On June 11, 1904, a runaway gravel train demolished the 80-foot truss bridge across Lapwai Creek at Spalding. Four cars were reduced to splinters, but no one was badly injured. In late July, 11 freight cars burned at Pullman Junction; tramps probably started a fire for supper.[11]

President Elliott traveled the P&L in July 1904, and found that the line between Lewiston and Marshall was "not quite as good as it should be for the business, which is growing all the time.... The Genesee branch is all right." Ballasting between Pullman and Howell was ordered August 1. The gravel would come from near Marshall.[12]

In August 1904 the division engineer examined the line between Moscow and Howell for possible improvements. He reported that the higher summits were unavoidable, but there was some chance to shorten the line and lessen curvature. He thought a 1 percent grade southbound and slightly less northbound were possible. "North of Moscow it looks probable that a light grade line could be had to Whelan, cutting out six miles in a distance of sixteen, by taking the main line out of Pullman. I believe it will profitable to develop this at some time." In October 1905 the division engineer reported that from Spangle to Whalen grade reduction would require occasional high crossings of ravines. He said that probably a line could be run from Moscow to Spangle on a grade not exceeding 0.5 percent if the line was built directly from Moscow to Whalen. From Moscow to Howell it was possible to have a line which would not exceed 1 percent grades in either direction by cutting summits and filling in sags—nine miles of heavy reconstruction. "Bridge 170 should be filled or a parallel line built immediately east thereof."[13]

In September 1904 30 men had been working on the Kendrick hill for two months and would continue until snow. The approaches to five bridges between Kendrick and Troy were filled and protected by rock dikes. A short distance south of Troy two bridges were removed, track straightened, and the channel of the creek moved to where the roadbed had been. South of Kendrick two miles of new rail was laid and new rail and ties were being placed on the hill. A new bridge would span the creek at Spalding.[14]

Correspondence in 1905 and 1906 indicates that the P&L was being prepared for the use of S-4 (4-6-0) and F-1 (2-8-0) power. All the pile bridges, if they were in good condition, and had sufficient stringers, would accommodate both kinds of power. Bridge 49 across South Pine Creek, consisting of two 48-foot pony trusses, was good for class D-3 (2-6-0), but not S-4 and F-1. It was announced September 5, 1906, that the NP would overhaul the entire road bed of the P&L from Lewiston to Moscow. Better grades would be established and heavier rail laid to make the operation of heavier engines and longer trains possible.[15]

On July 22, 1905, the Moscow local freight backing from Potlatch Junction to the yards, about a mile, was hit by an extra train bound for Spokane. A brakeman was injured. The Lewiston bound passenger train was delayed in arriving at Lewiston from 3:20 p.m. to about 7 p.m. A brakeman was run over by an engine at Moscow on the 26th.[16]

In past years most of the grain at Pullman had gone by the ORN, but in 1905, most was going via NP because of higher prices paid at NP terminal points. The warehouses on the NP were full of sacked grain, but the warehouses on the ORN had little grain. The price of wheat at Pullman was 1.5 cents higher than at Colfax and some wheat which would ordinarily go to Colfax went to Pullman. The NP had difficulty moving all the 1905 Palouse wheat crop; as a result it was piled on the ground at elevators.[17]

Because of the creation of the new town of Potlatch east of Palouse, the NP in November 1905 changed the name of Potlatch Junction to Clearwater Junction to avoid confusion. To avoid confusion with another town called Clearwater above Stites, the junction was changed to Arrow Junction in June 1906. In late November the Moscow city council increased the charge to the NP for water from $25 to $75 per month. In the summer the railroad hauled water from Moscow to the Troy tank. Three years earlier the town council agreed to provide water to the NP for $25 provided that the company made Moscow a division point, but no contract was signed.[18]

In the early morning of March 27, 1906, a car of gasoline and kerosene on local train No. 59 was destroyed at

Rosalia. The fumes from a leaky tank were ignited by the flame from a brakeman's lantern. The car was detached from the train, and only the tracks and cans were left after the fire went out. The concern was that the lumber yard of the Potlatch Lumber Co., the Farmers Grain & Supply Co.'s warehouse, the Interior Warehouse Co. and Grant Smith & Co.'s warehouse would be swept away, but rain prevented it.[19]

On July 24, 1906, J. W. Kettenbach, of Lewiston, accompanied by his wife, mother, chauffer, and mechanic left Moscow at 6:35 a.m. "in a heavy touring car of between 40 and 50 horsepower." The Moscow-Spokane train left Moscow at its scheduled 7:00 a.m. "The car was overtaken between Palouse and Garfield at a point where the wagon road parallels the railroad for several miles. There the race started. It was exciting and the passengers in the train manifested the liveliest interest cheering the driver when he gained with the big machine spinning along the road at a 25 miles an hour clip." The train reached the crossing a mile from Garfield first, but the car soon over took the train and arrived at Garfield first. "Between Garfield and Spangle the race was pilot to dashboard, the passengers saying it was the most finest bit of jockeying they ever saw outside a race track." Beyond Spangle the tracks and road parted. The car arrived at Hotel Spokane five minutes before the train arrived at the depot at its scheduled 11:30.[20]

The Washington State Railroad Commission, September 18, 1906, ordered connections between the NP and the ORN at Connell, Farmington, Oakesdale, and Pullman. The NP appeared willing to do so for one-half the cost, but the ORN declined. The commission ruled May 13, 1907, that ORN, SIE, and NP were required to make physical connections at Oakesdale and Garfield, between the ORN and NP at Pullman, Connell, and Farmington, and between the SIE and NP at Rosalia. The fine for failure was $250 per connection per railroad per day. On June 20 the ORN filed objections to the orders claiming that the commission went beyond its powers. "Regarding connections," the ORN argued, "it would be absolutely impossible for the roads to agree as to dividing the costs." The railroad denied that Connell, Pullman, and Farmington were important shipping points or entitled to better facilities than they then enjoyed. The railroad commission in September again ordered connections. In addition to the preceding connections, the ORN and SIE were ordered to connect at Waverly, Thornton, and Colfax. Connections between the NP and SIE at Rosalia and Palouse were not ordered because the railroads did not cross at grade, nor intersect, nor terminate at or near such stations. (Later the NP and SIE did make connections at both of those places. Also the NP and ORN later connected at Garfield because the Weyerhaeuser interests wanted a connection for WIM traffic.) The ORN appealed to the Washington State Supreme Court that the penalties were excessive, "thus making it necessary to comply with the orders of the commission rather than resort to the courts for a decision as to the validity and reasonableness of the orders."[21]

The *Review* had in the same issue, August 12, 1906, conflicting reports of an accident on the P&L: the head lines were "Train Wrecked at Burning Bridge...two cars destroyed in fire" and "Halts Train on the Brink Northern Pacific Escapes a Wreck near Eden." The reports differed as to whether the occurrence was north or south of Garfield, the train was from Moscow or going toward Moscow, if there was damage to rolling stock, and whether the bridge was a "culvert" or 40 feet long. They did agree that a track structure was on fire as a passenger train approached. The *Herald* said that three miles north of Garfield a passenger train was stopped as a result of a burning bridge. While an accident was averted, "As it happened, the tank car [engine tender], baggage and mail and smoking coaches were precipitated over the bank and burned. No one was injured." On December 5, 1906, engineer Thomas Brand and newly promoted engineer Thomas Richart were killed at Cedar Creek and the engines were "good for little else than scrap iron." Brand was the engineer on the passenger train due 11:55 a.m. at Pullman. Richart's train was running light to Spokane after service on the WIM. His train backed into the siding at Cedar Creek, but the fireman who had opened the switch failed to close it. Brand's train ran through the open switch at 30 miles per hour. Application of the emergency brake was too late to reduce the speed of his train. Both engineers were probably killed instantly. This reminded a reporter that Brand had saved his fireman in a wreck 17 years earlier. None of the passengers were seriously injured. The mail and baggage cars were derailed and "badly splintered." A tramp who had been riding on the blind and put off the train at Garfield thanked the train men for saving his life.[22]

In the fall of 1906 there was a car shortage. There was also a shortage of both coal and wood, which was in part caused by the car shortages. This caused raids at various locations on cars carrying coal. The NP said in mid-December that floods had cut it off from its coal mines at Roslyn and was itself running out of coal, but was distributing coal for private use. In mid-December grain growers charged that the grain car shortage was caused by the NP using over 4,000 of the 8,000 cars allocated for grain for flour shipments. In the meantime a million bushels of wheat were rotting on platforms at NP stations. On the ORN it was reported that 1,100 cars of grain were at Portland waiting to be unloaded. Late in December the NP, ORN, and GN began moving grain in larger quantities and the NP was allowing the use of idle cars for the storage of grain. In January the ORN confiscated commercial coal for use on mail trains. The ORN and GN annulled freight trains for the lack of fuel and the NP was getting near to the same action. In early February ORN river traffic on the Snake was tied up because of the lack of fuel and a shortage of cars to unload the boats. The car shortage still existed in mid-March. The coastal millers appealed in March to the Washington State Railroad Commission for relief from the

> deliberate policy on the part of the railroads to discriminate against the millers in favor of through freight. The shortage [of cars] has become so serious...that the millers are facing tremendous losses and damage suits because they can not fill their orders.
>
> ...There are now stored in warehouses in the Palouse and Big Bend countries more than 10,000,000 bushels of wheat, all of which should have been moved by this time.
>
> All of this wheat has been paid for and the farmers have received their money for it. But where do we stand with millions of dollars tied up in what we can't move? The railroad officials told us last Saturday that the very best they can promise us in the future is 1500 cars a month. The average load for one car is 1000 bushels. At that rate it would take us seven months to move the wheat now ready for milling. In four months there will be a new crop coming on.
>
> ... Even when we do get cars at the mills and unload them we are not allowed in many cases to use them for shipping our flour and feed. The railroad tacks a "bad order" card on the car and it is moved to a sidetrack. There it joins other cars reserved in alike manner until sometimes there are strings of one hundred cars awaiting the arrival of one of the steamships from the orient. As soon as a big ship gets in the cars are found to be in good order with great rapidity. Cars we should have had are used to haul through freight from the orient to the east, while the local shipper can wait until the road can get other cars for his needs.[23]

In early April 1907 more cars for wheat shipments were available. "Several full trainloads of wheat went out in the last few days for Tacoma. Many of the cars were ordinary flat cars, on which the sacked wheat was piled and covered with tarpaulins. Cattle cars and coal cars are used for wheat shipments." But there was a shortage of men to load the cars at 25 cents per hour.[24]

Snow and floods reduced railroad operations in the winter of 1907. The ORN was particularly hit. The NP put an additional coach on its Lewiston-Spokane train. In order to make good time the grill car was to be taken off at Moscow and waited for the return train. "This will not interfere in any way with the number of meals which can be served on either train and will make a light haul over the heaviest of the grades."[25]

The February 1, 1907, estimate for laying 72-pound rail, widening banks and ballasting from Rosalia to Plaza was about $175,000. Provision had been made in 1905 for strengthening bridges to carry S-4 power, but the track still needed work as did bridge 170 and the grade revisions had not been done. The division engineer recommended that a comprehensive plan be made for revising the line from Palouse to Spangle and from there build a line to the Portland & Seattle Railway near Cheney. Darling responded "I have no doubt but that a portion of the line, at least from Spangle to Palouse, and possibly to Marshall, will be maintained as a first class line."[26]

On August 7, 1907, passenger train No. 10 bound for Spokane, trying to make up time, was wrecked about two miles north of Cedar Creek when it hit a thresher engine at a grade crossing on an obscured curve. The threshing outfit was completely demolished and its engineer and fireman seriously injured. The locomotive engineer, Elmer Vetter, told the fireman, E. Nelson, to jump. Both were less seriously injured. The engine went down the embankment and the tender was turned over and four of the six coaches were derailed and badly damaged, but not overturned, and the track was torn up for a considerable distance. All the injured passengers were expect to recover. The wreck was at the same place as one the previous spring in which two engineers were killed and two engines damaged. A passenger train to Genesee, about 2:30 p.m., August 24, was caught near Leon in a cloudburst, which tore out about 300 feet of track. The train returned to Uniontown.[27]

In September 1907 the SIE Garfield agent claimed that the road got 90 percent of the freight and 95 percent of the passenger business between Garfield and Spokane. The state grain inspector estimated that the 1907 wheat crop would be 40,845,000 bushels on 2,000,000 acres. Whitman county's share would be 8,250,000 bushels on 375,000 acres, in both categories the most of any county. The wheat raised in the state would bring $33,000,000, farmers receiving $26,000,000, on wheat averaging 82.5 cents per bushel.[28]

Troy in late September had insufficient cars for over 4,000 cords of wood. Only three cars of apples had been shipped from Pullman by late October when 50 cars were expected. Grain warehouses were used to store apples awaiting shipment. In 1908 Whitman County had 4,794 acres in fruit trees, nearly half in apples.[29]

On November 2, 1907, a light engine and the yard engine collided in Pullman. The light engine was running to Kendrick. The switch engine, returning to the depot pushing an empty wood rack in front and pulling a loaded coal car, met the light engine just south of the Pullman depot in the deep rock cut on the sharp curve where it was impossible for the engineers to see ahead more than a few feet. Two brakemen riding the wood rack were thrown off suffering major injuries. The wood rack between the two engines was destroyed. Damage to the engines was not serious. On December 2 a double headed freight train from Lewiston crashed into the Genesee bound passenger train at Pullman Junction. The pilot and headlight of the lead engine were knocked off and the trucks knocked from under the passenger car. Several passengers were slightly injured and all badly shaken up. On the 5th the Washington State Railroad Commission issued a complaint against the NP and scheduled a hearing on an order to compel the railroad to establish a block system or device for protection between Pullman Junction and Pullman. The commission charged that because the road ran from Pullman Junction to the city through a cut and a very crooked down grade, trainmen could not see the main line at the station, resulting in a number of collisions. December 14, two miles south of Moscow, six cars in the center of a freight train jumped track and ran on the ties a half mile before toppling over. The cars were loaded with oats for the coast. The track was torn up for several hundred feet and six cars destroyed. The Lewiston and Spokane trains were delayed and passengers transferred around the wreck.[30]

Late December 1907 the NP announced that it would build a combination depot at "Joseph" (post office named "Spalding"). The depot would be the transfer point for the P&L and the Grangeville and Clearwater branches in place of Lewiston or North Lapwai. Earlier the NP planned a transfer station at Arrow Junction but abandoned it with the construction of the Grangeville branch.[31]

In 1907 the ORN, in connection with Washington State College, ran a very popular farm demonstration train in eastern Washington. The NP in collaboration with the college began running such a train in the Palouse and Big Bend regions in June 1908. In 1910 the fourth NP agricultural demonstration train left Pullman with five cars and several college faculty members. The trains received considerable coverage in the *Gazette*. In 1908 the U.S. Department of Agriculture credited Washington State with 1.5 percent of the total wheat acreage in the United States. Kansas had the largest wheat acreage at 19.1 percent of the total. The value of Washington wheat per acre averaged $17.77 in the past 10 years, in Kansas, $11.06. Washington's average exceeded every other state by at least $5.00 per acre.[32]

The principal assistant engineer wrote Chief Engineer Darling February 5, 1908, that the NC location at Marshall "appears to me to be as good as can be done." He recommended that the Cheney to Spangle line be built. A P&L to a mainline connection at Cheney would be an improvement over the connection at Marshall; level grade vs. 0.4 percent grade, more room for expansion, less curvature, shorter distance, and less rise on west bound traffic. Regarding passenger business, "if no attempt be made to compete with electric lines at Cheney, Rosalia, etc., it can be operated from Cheney, saving main line mileage between Spokane and Cheney, or, if competing for business, will give addition[al] service between Spokane and Cheney, principal competitive points." He believed that the NC would "agree to pay $50,000 to $75,000 to get rid of our layout at Marshall...this scheme should be carried out at net cost of $175,000.00."[33]

Mid-March 1908 the P&L was again flooded along the Potlatch River. "At many points the water is said to be higher than in 1900, when the Palouse branch was out of commission 40 days, when the loss amounted to more than $1,000,000. Since that time the track has been protected by much riprap, but heavy loss is unavoidable. That no trains will be operated for days is shown by the orders issued to agents to receive no perishable freight." Three days later passengers were transferred around a washout north of Arrow. Severe flooding in the Clearwater region occurred again in early June. The P&L Clearwater bridge was thought to be in danger of breaking loose. The same month the NP ordered replacement of 56 pound rail between Pullman and Howell with 72 pound rail. In the late fall 1908, the NP made extensive improvements between Moscow and Arrow Junction in anticipation of the opening of the Lewiston-Pasco line. It was expected that all grain traffic to tidewater from south of Garfield would go through Lewiston. About 15 million bushels each season were expected through Lewiston. Heretofore the congestion at Kendrick during the heavy shipping season had been considerable. Only a half dozen cars (probably per engine) could be hauled up Kendrick hill.[34]

Levy announced in Lewiston July 23, 1908, signing of a contract for completion before December 31 of a new depot at Lewiston. The depot would have offices for the new joint line from Riparia to Grangeville on the second floor. The estimated cost was $35,000 for the building

The first Lewiston (combination) depot, two-story 24′ x 46′, one-story 40′ x 130′, was built in 1898, photographed c. 1910. It became the Lewiston freight depot in approximately 1909 when a passenger depot was built. It was moved in about 1984 and burned shortly after. At right is the 1898 two-stall engine house. *Photograph PG 71-20 (Eaton Family Photo Album), Special Collections & Archives, University of Idaho Library.*

and $25,000 more for occupancy. The 1909 NP annual report in the capital account added $49,066 for the Lewiston passenger depot, yard, and tracks. The Lewiston depot was the most impressive built on the P&L.[35]

Special Agent Sam Cone was sold beer and whisky on a buffet parlor car while it was on the Nez Perce Reservation. It was expected that the car would be seized on its next trip to Lewiston and the porter arrested. The NP withdrew the buffet parlor car and substituted a café parlor and thereby thwarted the government's intention of seizing the offending car. The liquor chests henceforth were locked while on the reservation.[36]

In 1909 the Troy Lumber and Manufacturing Co., with more than 50 men employed, was expected to eclipse 1908's record of six million feet of lumber. The mill put out all grades of lumber and manufactured bank, store, and office furniture. The mill owners had planned to move the mill to Lewiston, but the town agreed to their demands to build a new school and to vote saloons out. In late June the farmer's association in Genesee decided to buy the site of the recently burned flour mill and erect a 60 x 150-foot warehouse.[37]

In February 1909 the price of some varieties of wheat reached above $10 a bushel in the Palouse, possibly an all-time record. Both the NP and ORN said there would be no car shortage to move the 1909 bumper grain crop. By early October 800,000 bushels of grain had been delivered to or shipped from Palouse [City] and another 600,000 bushels were accounted for by other stations within six miles of Palouse. Oats were 50 percent of the grain in that area. In December there was a shortage of cars on the ORN's Palouse lines. The switchmen's strike in Spokane prevented the transfer of foreign cars to the ORN and the cars the railroad could get were sent to Lewiston to get as much of the Camas Prairie business as possible during the tie up.[38]

On May 19, 1909, the State Railroad Commission met in Pullman and heard complaints about inadequate facilities at the depot and other matters, all of which the NP said it would remedy. The matter of connecting the ORN with the NP at Pullman was discussed, and "the Northern Pacific people expressed willingness to connect the tracks at once, but the O. R. & N. refuses to allow the connection saying 'If we do we will get to do the switching charges and the Northern Pacific will haul the freight and get the freight charges.' The matter rests there, but the commission expressed a determination to force connection if the law will allow it." In June the Commission ordered additional NP improvements in Pullman, but none of the improvements were made as of mid-January 1910. The following April 8 a front page cartoon in the *Herald* showed Death with the caption,

"'Washout of Schupfer Gulch about 1909, transferring baggage from one train to another.' Juliaetta." So reads the caption with the photograph. A search of various maps and documents did not find Schupfer Gulch, but it is probably between Kendrick and Arrow along the bank of the Potlatch River. The engine is NP 340, 4-6-0, Class E-3, built by Baldwin in 1889. *Photograph 9-3-10, Latah County Historical Society.*

The Lewiston, Idaho, Camas Prairie Railway/NP/UP passenger depot built in 1909, still in place in 2018. It appears that the depot was not yet in service and the bricks for paving the street are still stacked. It was built as a two story 38' x 62' & 6' x 18'; one story 30' x 84' with a covered platform 30' x 41' brick. *Photograph PG 90-BK10-14C, Clifford M. Ott Collection, Special Collections & Archives, University of Idaho Library.*

The flood at Pullman in March 1910, with the Washington State College student-built bridge across South Palouse River. The view is from the west side of the river, which flows from right to left in the image. The wreckage of an ORN bridge is on the far side of the river under the east end of the bridge. The second NP depot in Pullman is in the background, built in 1902, 32' x 160', located about 600 feet west (toward the viewer) of the site of the first NP depot. The third NP depot, still extant, was built in 1916 on the site of this depot. *Photograph 78-156, Manuscript and Special Collections, Washington State University Library.*

"Death, which has been lurking at the Northern Pacific crossing of Kamiackum street, has been driven away by the order of the State Railroad Commission, establishing an electric alarm there."[39]

On November 2, 1909, at 7:30 p.m., the Genesee train ran into the rear of an extra train hauling hogs near Pullman Junction. Engine No. 51 on the extra train was pushing and it was knocked into the caboose which contained seven men who were with the hogs. They were injured by the caboose being wrecked and by broken steam lines on No. 51. No trainmen were injured. The tracks were torn up. On the 3rd the passenger train leaving Lewiston at 3:30 p.m. derailed three miles east, the engine turned at right angle to the track, derailing the mail and baggage cars. "When the engine left the rails Engineer McGilvery applied the emergency brakes with such steadiness that not a passenger was thrown from his seat." The passenger cars were pulled back to Lewiston.[40]

Improvements on the P&L continued in 1909. Near Howell a big cut was made in a hill avoided by the old route. The company was spending more than $200,000 on roadbed. The Clearwater bridge was strengthened in anticipation of heavier trains.[41] Five new families would come to Pullman as the result of a December 13 schedule which had the Genesee trains laying over in Pullman rather than Genesee.[42]

Beginning mid-January 1910 the railroads in the Northwest suffered from flooding and numerous washouts. The P&L did not operate and no ORN trains were in or out of Riparia in two days. Colfax was hit the hardest and Pullman, beginning March 1, had heavy losses. Lewiston was practically isolated and business suspended. The ORN trestle at Pullman was destroyed. The ORN gave the county the timbers from the Howe truss bridge in Pullman after it landed on Main Street. The track between Kendrick and Juliaetta was blocked by numerous slides and the Little Potlatch bridge was not safe. An NP freight train was derailed five miles below Plaza due to soft roadbed and eight feet of mud buried an ORN engine north of St. John. The losses in Whitman County were "conservatively" estimated at $2 million. The NP losses were considered light compared to the ORN losses (for the latter see chapter XVII). College boys at Pullman

A train, probably No. 10, to Spokane, entering Plaza, Washington. The note on the back says "This is a picture of the train coming from the south during the snow taken from the porch of your house." It was postmarked Plaza, 3/14/1910. *Photograph 032531, Bancroft Library, University of California, Berkeley.*

aided greatly, including a suspension bridge across the Palouse River. The estimated cost of damage on the P&L and Genesee branches was $8,025, and the estimated cost of work to prevent future washouts was $14,600.[43]

A car of oats got away from Plaza April 13 and headed down hill with three men on board. The agent at Rosalia was warned, but the afternoon passenger train for Spokane had already left. The agent telephoned a farm north of Rosalia and the farmer's wife flagged down the train. The train was apparently backing up when struck by the freight car. The engineer and a passenger were injured. The three men on the car were not injured. The engine was slightly damaged and the car demolished. The train was delayed about two hours.[44]

In mid-September 1910 there were slides on either side of Arrow Junction In the same month, for the first time Palouse grain was passing through Lewiston daily en route to Riparia. In late October two brakemen on the Genesee branch were arrested for stealing flour, and six of the 11 bags were recovered. On November 12 the NP ran a special train from Pullman to Spokane for the University of Washington-Washington State College football game. Over the years the NP ran many such trains, as well as trains for students from home to college and back. Double tracking from Yardley (Spokane) to Marshall, which P&L trains used, was completed in November.[45]

The Whitman County auditor reported for 1910 that the county had 575 miles of railroad, 493 miles of main track, and 82 of side track, at a total assessed value of $9,947,267 (the county's total assessed value was $37,881,856). The NP had 107 miles, all former S&P except eight miles of main track on the Snake River branch, 93 miles of main track, and 14 miles of side track, at a total assessed value of $1,270,251. The NP's main track was assessed at $13,075 per mile and the side track at $3,653 per mile. The ORN had the largest mileage in the county, 298, with 266 miles of main track and 32 miles of side track, and largest assessed value, $5,465,898.[46]

The Clearwater bridge, No. 202, built in 1898 of wood Howe trusses, had by October 1910 become "old and weak for the power that is being used." Immediate remedial work needed to be done and the bridge needed to be replaced. A report June 19, 1913, said: "there have been no renewals of members except ties, we have been compelled to hold it up for the power we have been using for the past year or more, with false work which was recently carried away by high water, compelling us to use light power at present, and it seems almost imperative that we have the new structure completed before the high water next spring." The bridge was replaced in 1914.[47]

Conclusion

In general our history of the S&P and its competitors has been brought up to 1910. No major construction followed and then it was three branches of the NP's Idaho Division.[1] Authorizations for expenditures are available into the 1960s and they show continuing capital expenditures for track, bridges, facilities, and minor additions and retirements. The line received heavier rail, including some welded rail.[2] Both in the steam and diesel eras the NP ran a six-days-a-week, round-trip from Spokane to Lewiston, primarily hauling forest products, as well as local freights. This continued well after the passenger trains disappeared. When the NP merged into the Burlington Northern in March of 1970 both the Palouse & Lewiston and Genesee branches were intact and operating. At the same time, with a minor exception all the ORN and Spokane & Inland Empire (SIE) lines were also intact and operating.

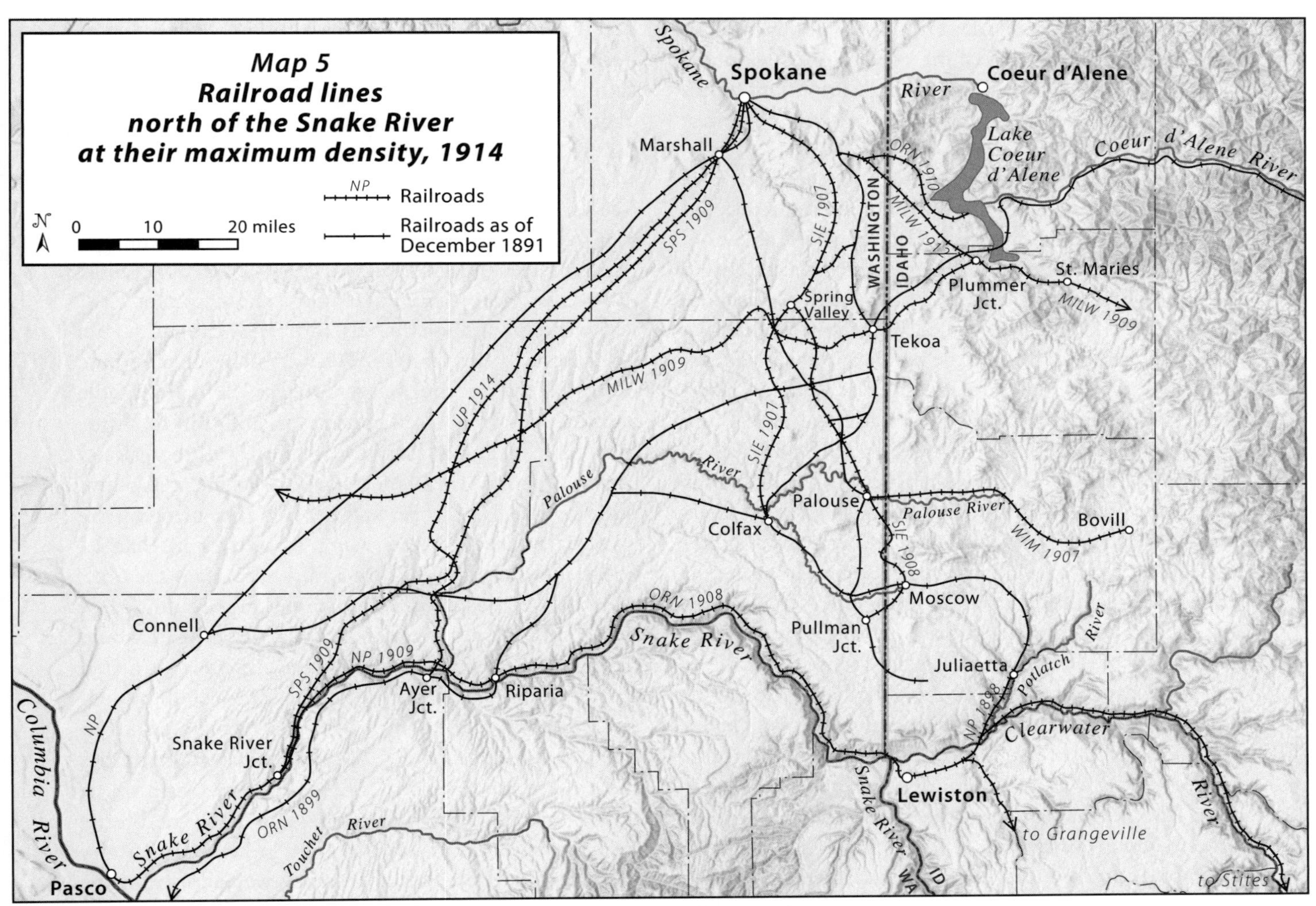

Mileage of the railroads north of the Snake River more than doubled between 1891 and 1914. *Map by Mike Bartenstein, Mike Walker, 1998, and Philip Beach. Drawn by Chelsea Feeney, www.cmcfeeney.com.*

Were the railroads overbuilt in the Palouse, and why was most of the Palouse trackage gone prior to 2017? It has been argued that in many instances United States railroads were overbuilt; railroad mileage and facilities were not justified by available traffic. If they were overbuilt, economic resources were wasted. The foregoing chapters contain many instances of S&P/NP and ORN/UP officials worrying about and trying to avoid overbuilding while at the same time running numerous, often competitive, surveys for additional route miles. Most of these extensions were not built, but commitment in some cases is evident in the purchase of rights of way.

The following discussion pertains only to "the Palouse railroads": the S&P/NP (all lines); ORN/UP (all lines north of the Snake River); and SIE (all lines south of Spokane). The following lines that touched the Palouse, but were not important Palouse grain carriers and were built for other purposes are: NP mainline, Pasco to Spokane; Spokane Portland & Seattle; UP, Ayer Junction to Spokane; Milwaukee; and Washington, Idaho & Montana (WIM). The latter was not a particularly important source of grain traffic, but was an important source of forest product traffic.

At first glance it appears that the Palouse railroads were overbuilt. By the end of 1908 the Palouse railroads had approximately 699 miles in the Palouse; see Table C-6. The Whitman County auditor reported for 1910 that the county had 493 route miles of railroad; the Palouse railroads had 431 of those miles, 87 percent of the total county route miles.[3] Most of the significant towns had two or three of the Palouse railroads: all three were in Oakesdale, Garfield, and Moscow; two were in Rosalia (S&P and SIE plus Milwaukee), Palouse (S&P and SIE plus WIM), Farmington (S&P and ORN), Thornton and Colfax (ORN and SIE), Pullman (S&P and ORN), and Lewiston (S&P and ORN and also the CSP which was jointly owned by the NP and UP and became another important source of forest product traffic). Only the NP's Genesee branch and Lewiston extension above the Clearwater River and the ORN's lines west of Colfax were without direct competitive pressure. In 1910 Lewiston had a population of 6,043; the remainder of the mentioned towns had a total population of 13,973 (unincorporated Thornton not recorded). Whitman County, Washington, the heart of the Palouse that includes all the towns mentioned except Lewiston and Moscow, had a population of 33,280 in its 2,159 square miles (15.2 persons per square mile). While Whitman County had grown during the railroad building era (it had a population of 10,390 in 1883), it was still thinly populated.[4]

But for the Palouse railroads, passengers and merchandise were subsidiary traffic. They were built to haul grain, particularly wheat, and agricultural supplies. Furthermore, except for the ORN's Rockford-Spokane line, which was built near the end of ORN construction on the Palouse Plateau, they were not initially built to be trunk roads, but the ORN from Riparia via Colfax to Spokane and the S&P from Lewiston to Spokane became trunk lines. The Whitman County auditor's report of 1910 shows 941,671 acres of improved farm land in the county and another 286,927 acres of unimproved farm lands. The value of farm land and improvements on that land was $20,761,855 while town lots and their improvements were only $3,326,395.[5]

When the initial railroad construction took place, 1884–91, the Palouse was very much in a state of development and thus initial traffic volume, if it were available, would not be a very good indicator of over-development. We do have S&P traffic information for seven years in the 1890s and early 1900s (see Table C-1). The number of bushels of grain are officially reported; the author's calculation estimates the number of tons and cars. The amount of grain traffic is substantial, more so when we recognize that we do not have similar information for the ORN, which had more mileage in the Palouse than the S&P (see Table C-6). The magnitude of the grain crop varied year to year. The table clearly shows that the volume of grain trended upward over the years reported. A report in 1903 said "the Whitman County wheat crop for 1902 was over eight million bushels, more than the entire state of Oregon."[6] Note that the 1902 harvest began after June 30, 1902, and was thus was reported as 1903 on the table and includes grain from counties in addition to Whitman. The S&P and ORN carried nearly all the Palouse grain crop, so the ORN must have carried in excess of five million bushels of wheat and other grains, bringing the total grain carried by the two railroads to more than 12 million bushels in 1902.[7] In addition to grain the S&P and ORN carried flour from the mills in the Palouse (see note 9 for volumes in tons for S&P). Other years would have been similar. "The state grain inspector estimated that the 1907 wheat crop would be 40,845,000 bushels on 2,000,000 acres. Whitman County's share would be 8,250,000 bushels on 375,000 acres, in both categories the most of any county."[8] There was some grain traffic not captured by the two railroads: grain that went directly from farms to flour mills and grain grown in proximity to the Snake River; both alternatives were limited by the feasibility of transporting grain by teams in wagons over dirt roads.

Table C-1

Number of Bushels, estimated tonnage and cars, of Grain Shipped by S&P, 1894–1903.[9]

Year Ended June 30	Wheat			Other Grains		
	Bushels	Est. Tons	Est. Car Loads	Bushels	Est. Tons	Est. Car Loads
1894	NA	75,165	2506	NA	NA	NA
1897	3,472,300	104,169	3472	172,400	NA	NA
1898	5,557,600	166,748	5558	350,900	7004	234
1899	3,934,990	118,050	3935	613,000	13,112	437
1900	3,656,500	109,695	3657	687,205	11,824	394
1902	5,835,960	175,079	5836	1,946,720	39,019	1301
1903	4,889,400	146,682	4889	2,324,170	47,278	1576

Sources for bushels: 1894: MHS, 134.F.38.F #3226; 1897: statistical report used to prepare the NP 1897 Annual Report; NP Confidential Reports, 1898, 194, 206–07; 1899, 26–7; 1900, 28–9; 1902, 30; 1903, 39.

While grain was the most important traffic source, it was the not the only traffic on the Palouse roads. Again unfortunately we only have fragmentary evidence for the S&P and none for the ORN. Table C-2 shows the amount of commercial coal moved over the S&P in roughly the same time frame as grain above. Again the trend is upward. There would have been some additional coal for use by the NP.

Table C-2

S&P Commercial Coal Shipments, year ending June 30, 1896–1902

Year	Tons & % of NP	Revenue & % of NP	Est. Cars
1896	523 NA	NA	17.4
1897	1374 5.9%	$4,762 NA	45
1898	2,690 4.0%	$8,981 6.2%	89.7
1899	4001 5.4%	$13,585 9.3%	133.4
1900	5186 NA	NA	173
1901	5570 NA	NA	185.7
1902	7571 NA	NA	252.4

Source: NP Confidential Reports, 1898 (for 1896 & 1897), 115; 1899 (for 1898 & 1899), 113; 1900, 128. The estimate of total cars calculated by author at 30 tons per car.

Table C-3 shows the total freight traffic on the S&P for six years around the turn of the twentieth century. Nearly all of the grain traffic (and forest products traffic) would have been in the "Freight Forwarded." In 1903 the freight forwarded included 146,682 tons of wheat, 47,278 tons of other grains (Table C-3), and 3,900 tons of flour (note 9) for a total of 197,860 tons of the 244,644 tons (Table C-3) or 81 percent of the forwarded tons on the S&P in 1903. In 1898 grain and flour represented 87 percent of the tons forwarded. Except for 1899 the tons forwarded were over twice the tons received. Both tons forwarded and received show a generally upward trend. The S&P was built to haul grain and that is what it did.[9]

Table C-3

Spokane & Palouse Railway Total Freight Forwarded from and Received at Stations, year ending June 30, 1898–1903

	Freight Forwarded & Percent of NP System Total		Freight Received & Percent of NP System Total	
	Tons	Earnings	Tons	Earnings
1898	202,343 4.1%	$724,098 4.2%	53,360 1.1%	$243,892 1.4%
1899	182,790 3.1%	609,157 3.2%	97,494 1.7%	424,534 2.2%
1900	184,168 2.6%	552,894 2.5%	87,690 1.2%	355,143 1.6%
1901	215,931 2.5%	799,592 3.5%	62,647 0.07%	301,440 1.3%
1902	234,539 2.1%	1,068,612 3.6%	82,005 0.07%	413,875 1.4%
1903	244,644 1.9%	838,460 2.6%	107,780 0.08%	538,261 1.6%

Sources: NP Confidential Reports: 1898, 196; 1899, 226; 1899 & 1900, 248; 1901 & 1902, 252; 1903, 312.

Table C-4 shows the passenger business of the S&P. While Passenger revenues were well below that of freight they were close to the same proportions of total NP system numbers and revenues as was freight.[10]

Table C-4

Spokane & Palouse Railway Total Number of Passengers and Revenue from Passenger Services.

	Number of Passengers & Percent of NP System Total	Revenue Passenger Services & Percent of NP System Total
1898	53,891 3.8%	$77,466 2.2%
1899	74,984 4.4%	114,156 3.0%
1900	79,721 3.8%	136,834 2.8%
1901	81,689 2.9%	130,326 2.4%
1902	103,179 2.8%	162,808 2.4%
1903	131,920 3.0%	197,857 2.5%

The NP did a study of the average yearly earnings of its branches in 1921–23. The P&L had the fourth highest station earnings of 59 branches. See table C-5.

Table C-5

Average earnings per route mile and 2017 equivalent for P&L, Genesee, and the Snake River branches (Riparia to Snake River Junction).

Branch	1921–23	Earnings per route mile	2017 equivalent
P&L	$2,202,169	$15,854 (138.9 miles)	$32,819,504 ($236,282)
Genesee	319,222	11,566 (27.6 miles)	4,757,450 ($172,371)
Snake River	101,505	2,475 (41 miles)	1,512,756 ($36,896)[11]

In the author's opinion these numbers for the S&P are impressive. The Genesee branch was more dependent on grain and community earnings than the P&L which had also forest products, but on average not quite as good grain lands. The much poorer showing of the Snake River branch reflects the NP's preference at the time of sending traffic to Marshall (see chapter XVIII); also there was very little, if any, local traffic.

A large volume of business does not itself demonstrate that the branch was profitable after operating costs and fixed costs, i.e. bond interest, are both included in determining profitability. A full treatment of profit and loss of a branch line would also include the revenues that the main line received from traffic interchanged with the branch line. There is evidence the S&P made a profit for the NP. The NP annual reports for June 30, 1888 and 1889 show deficits for the S&P of $12,765 and $65,589, but mainline revenues from interchange with S&P were $339,191 and $664,392 respectively. The NP assistant general auditor wrote General Manager J. W. Kendrick January 18, 1894, that if the S&P was given equally favorable terms as other branches, "there would be no difficulty about their earnings meeting operating expenses and fixed charges. This is notably the case with the Spokane & Palouse Railroad."[12] The 1896 report for the S&P says that the interchange earnings for 1895 were $600,000. "There is no doubt that the Spokane & Palouse is a very valuable feeder to the Northern Pacific, and if it were not already built, I would strongly recommend the construction of a line serving that territory."[13] This was before there was significant amounts of forest product traffic; a higher proportion of the latter traffic probably went east than grain traffic which went mostly to the west coast; a longer haul east generated more revenue per car or per ton than the short haul on grain. The forest product traffic continued to grow through most of the twentieth century to the point that on the branch specific motive power was dedicated to that traffic and a symbol (i.e., identified as to origin and terminal) freight train from Lewiston to Minot was created by the Burlington Northern.[14]

What about the ORN? We do not have even fragmentary evidence comparable with that on the S&P. The Portland elites were certain that the ORN, free from NP control, was essential to the well-being of Portland. While they exaggerated, they were correct. To free itself from dependence on the Central Pacific/Southern Pacific for reaching tide water the UP was anxious to gain and maintain control of the ORN. For the UP, the ORN was both the completion of a trunk line to the coast, and eventually to Spokane, and a source of traffic from the Palouse. (To have data comparable to the S&P data the trunk line traffic, particularly between Huntington and Portland, and traffic from the other branches south of the Snake River, would have to be separated from the Palouse traffic.) But much of the acquired traffic was short mileage to Portland; according to the UP president the ORN did not provide much long distance east bound traffic at Huntington. Once the UP had control through the lease, the UP president argued that the ORN profits were insufficient to cover the costs of the lease. In 1893 when the UP went into receivership, $12 million of its $20 million floating debt incurred from the purchase of a majority in ORN stock, which James J. Hill thought was well watered. Daggett, a neutral observer, wrote that, "The immediate problem was the floating debt, swollen to unwieldy proportions by the acquisition of branch lines, and in particular by the purchase of the [ORN]."[15] The failure of the UP to pay the interest on the ORN bonds, required by the lease, precipitated the bankruptcy. Hill turned down an opportunity to acquire the ORN, with its much desired Palouse lines, because it was poorly built, as well as his position, whether he actually believed it, that he could build a better line much more cheaply.

Even before receivership ended, the UP system was buying ORN stock and soon came to control the ORN again. The UP before and after bankruptcy refused to share any control of the ORN with the NP, even with the possibility of sharing the NP line to Puget Sound. How much of this resistance was associated with the trunk line aspect of the ORN and how much with the Palouse traffic cannot be said. The author's opinion is that at least in the long run the UP saw the ORN as a valuable investment, but that could be for reasons having little to do with Palouse traffic. But it is also my opinion that with time there was adequate traffic to be had in the Palouse to support both the S&P and ORN Palouse branches.

Table C-6 provides a list of routes built by the three Palouse railroads. Prior to 1907 the S&P and ORN built 455 miles in the Palouse. The S&P's branch to Farmington was redundant in that Farmington was on the ORN's line to Spokane and the two NP terminals were only six miles apart; almost immediately after construction the S&P Farmington railroad yard started contracting by removal of the wye at Farmington in 1893, and shrinkage of trackage continued for the whole life of the branch. The ORN's line to Waverly was unsuccessful when the sugar mill at Waverly was unsuccessful, and it was only five miles from ORN's Spokane line. Removal of these two lines reduces the pre-1907 total to 444 miles. The ORN in 1895 ceased operating the Washtucna to Connell line portion of the Connell to Colfax line, about 30 miles. The line had been very important prior to the ORN building the Riparia to La Crosse line. In 1901-04 the ORN restored the line from Washtucna to Connell. The ORN's position was it restored the line because traffic had developed there. But was it actually to interfere with the NP, which had shown interest in having a line from Pullman to Connell, or to thwart an irrigation project which would benefit the NP? The ORN refused for many years to put in a connection with the NP at Connell. Without traffic data it is impossible to know whether the traffic justified the reconstruction, but it did remain for almost 80 years. If this 30 miles had not been restored, the pre-1907 mileage would be reduced to 414 miles, sufficient to adequately serve the Palouse.

Two lines were built after 1907, the ORN's Riparia to Lewiston in 1908 and the NP's Riparia to Snake River Junction in 1909. These two lines are not in the Palouse, but below it in the Snake River Canyon on the north bank. They are included here because their construction is treated in the text. The NP's line, which was to be a western outlet for Lewiston/Clearwater and possibly Palouse traffic, was never as important as anticipated at the time of construction. If the NP had had 20-20 foresight it is unlikely that the costly line would have been built. Its 41 miles can be eliminated from the table bringing the NP/ORN mileage down to 373. The ORN's line, while not strictly a Palouse line, was and is important and remains in service, although all of it was moved or raised with the construction of the Snake River dams in the 1950s and '60s. In 1959 the United States acquired the Snake River Junction to Riparia roadbed to build the Lower Monumental Dam on the Snake River. The NP then used the UP tracks from Wallula to Riparia. Ultimately this line in the 1980s received all the NP traffic that had moved from Lewiston/Clearwater area toward Spokane (see below).

Even with much uncertainty, it seems reasonable to argue that prior to the SIE in 1908, the Palouse was not over built with railroads and that the S&P and ORN were a successful oligopoly.

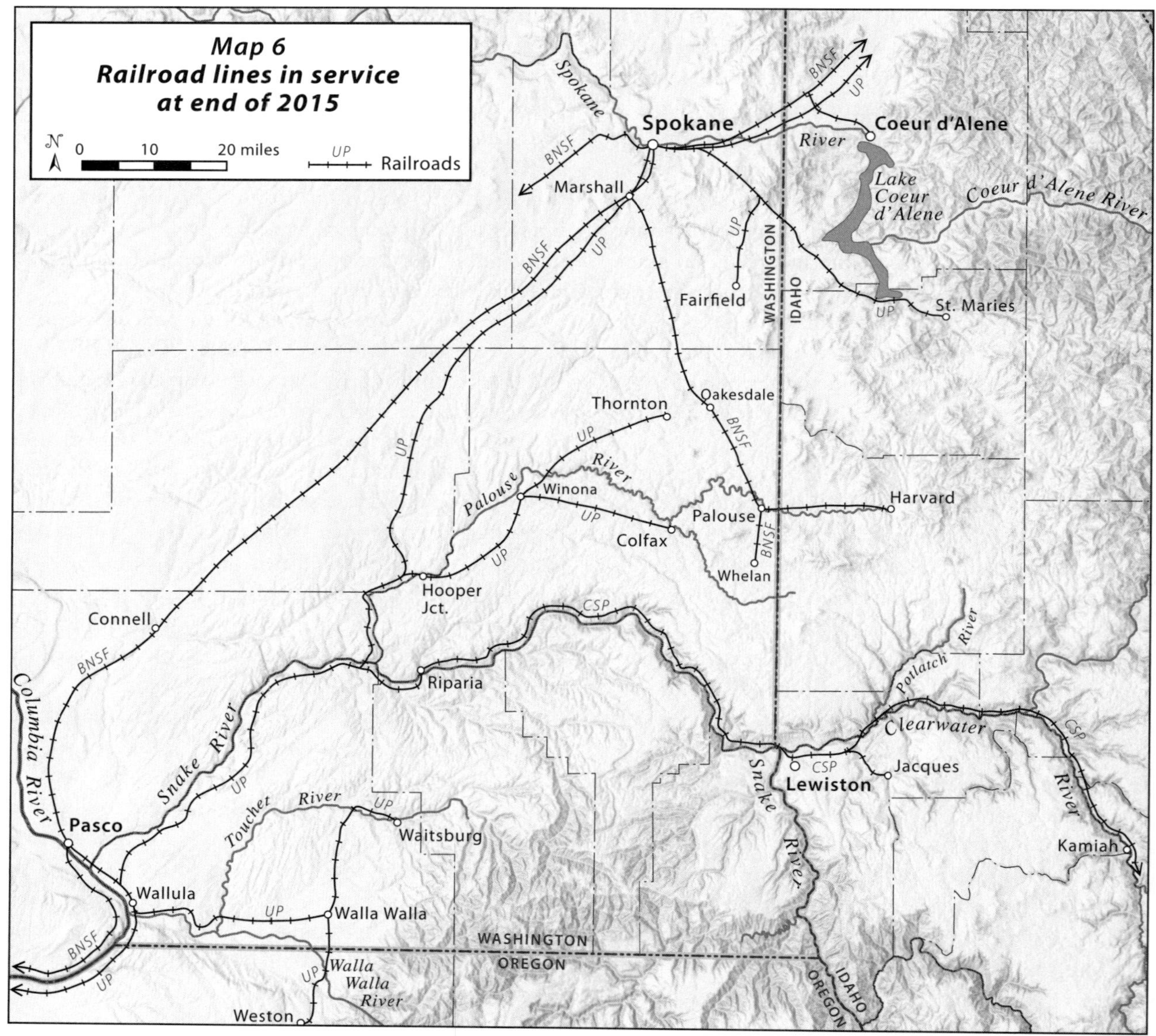

The massive reduction in mileage of southeastern Washington railroads between 1914 and 2015 is apparent in comparing Map 5 and Map 6. *Map by Mike Bartenstein, Mike Walker, 1998, and Philip Beach. Drawn by Chelsea Feeney, www.cmcfeeney.com.*

Table C-6

Approximate Route Miles in the Palouse by the Three Palouse Lines.[16]

Constructed Miles (year of operation)		Operated Route Miles (end of calendar year)		
S&P/NP/BNSF		1967	1992	2017
Marshall to Pullman Jct.	77 (1888)	77	76	66
Pullman Jct. to Genesee	27 (1888)	27	27	0
Belmont to Farmington	6 (1891)	0	0	0
Pullman Jct. to Arrow	47 (1891/98)	47	0	0
Arrow to Lewiston	15 (1898)	15	15	15
Riparia to Snake River Jct.	41 (1909)	0	0	0
Total	213	166	118	81
ORN/UP				
Connell to Colfax	89 (1884)	89	52	47
Colfax to Moscow	28 (1885)	28	28	0
Colfax to Farmington	27 (1886)	27	0	0
Farmington to Rockford	34 (1888)	34	7	7
Rockford to Spokane	27 (1889)	27	27	27
Riparia to La Crosse	25 (1888)	25	0	0
Winona to Seltice	48 (1889)	48	32	32
Fairfield to Waverly	5 (1899)	0	0	0
Riparia to Lewiston	7 (1908)	72	72	72
Total	355	350	218	185
Subtotal of S&P and ORN	455 (1907)	516	336	266
SIE/GN/BNSF				
Total	131 (1908)	125	0	0
Grand Total	699 (1909)	641	336	266

Unlike most interurban lines, the SIE's Palouse lines were built to haul grain freight.[17] The SIE paralleled both the S&P and ORN. Most of its route miles were within five miles, generally feasible for wagon haulage, of one or both of the other two lines and it did not develop any new territory; thus all of its traffic could have gone to either the S&P, the ORN, or both. Both the S&P and ORN did suffer from car shortages and insufficient capacity at terminals, but there is no reason to believe that the SIE would be immune to these problems. The Palouse lines of the SIE were not financially viable as an independent company and when controlled by the GN, interchange revenue offset the operating losses of the line.[18] With the completion of the SIE the Palouse was overbuilt.

Table C-6 shows that 58 miles were eliminated between 1909 and the end of 1967, but by the end of 1992, 25 years later, 363 miles of the 699 miles present in 1909 were gone. And at the end of 2017 only 266 miles of the 699 miles of 1909 remained, with 87 of those miles accounted for by lines now cut off from the Palouse—the Riparia to Lewiston line, never a strictly a Palouse line, and the Arrow to Lewiston line. Most of the remainder only exist because the State of Washington purchased them. Why did most of the Palouse lines disappear?[19]

The Palouse lines were built in the late nineteenth and very early twentieth centuries; this meant light rail, small steam engines, box cars of modest capacity, car shortages, and blockades (cars could not be unloaded at grain terminals in a timely manner), and numerous passenger and freight trains serving many small farms and communities which were, except for those close to navigable water, dependent on railroads for all transportation beyond modest distances. At the same time the forest products industry was growing to provide longer hauls and year-round traffic.

Since World War II farms have become fewer and larger, the grain crops have become greater per acre and harvested in a shorter period of time, and farms employ fewer people. Communities that were along the rail lines have for the most part either disappeared or declined in population,[20] and those that remain have become less dependent on railroads as roads have been improved and trucks have become larger. As long as boxcars were used to haul grain, the Palouse railroads suffered from boxcar shortages caused by eastern railroads failing to return cars to western railroads in a timely manner.[21] Railroads no longer had a near monopoly in moving the grain crops; large trucks, which in some cases have transported grain from the Palouse to tide water, have been joined by barges enjoying slack water on the Columbia and Snake Rivers. The trucks and barges have been supported by large public infrastructure investments and in the past by the Interstate Commerce Commission favoring trucks and barges when railroad rates threatened them. Railroads also lost the inbound traffic because of fewer people and road transportation. What remains of the outbound short distance grain traffic is seasonal and of low profitability. At the same time the long haul forest products have declined. The abandonment of the S&P line from Arrow eastward has cut off the S&P from the forest products in Lewiston and the Clearwater country. Before the abandonment the BN shifted most of the remaining traffic away from the line to Marshall to the mostly water level line to Wallula.

The short seasonal harvest time can be mitigated to some extent by spreading the traffic over more months by the construction of large grain storage facilities capable of serving unit trains. Unit trains with large covered hopper cars can also reduce railroad transportation costs, increasing railroad competitiveness with trucks and barges, but require a considerable investment in cars and infrastructure. Marc Entze notes, "[R]ailroads were slow to purchase covered hoppers for grain shipments, in part because of the expense, but primarily because they were poor fits with the existing country elevator system…but as late as 1976 the Burlington Northern and Union Pacific combined owned just 17,093 cars; the 1978 harvest of more than 134 million bushels from the Pacific Northwest filled nearly two and half times that many covered hoppers." Entze goes on, "The inability of the railroad to respond to the huge increases in agricultural production, a nearly impossible task with existing infrastructure, led to increased barge competition, but trucks and barges were a *symptom* of rail decline, not the *cause*.…A 1978 survey of grain shippers in the Pacific Northwest found that 'rail car availability' was the most often mentioned problem. Most shippers estimated that the delays in obtaining freight cars ranged from two to four weeks." In the 1970s railroads purchased more covered hoppers than any other type of freight car. But at around $43,000 per large capacity covered hopper, efficient utilization became important. A shipment of grain from eastern Washington generated a few hundred dollars, but from the mid-west to the Pacific Coast the car could generate as much as $2,000 per trip. "With the cost to upgrade the light rail branch lines far exceeding the revenue potential, boxcar to covered hopper transition contributed to the abandonment of numerous branch lines."[22]

The Staggers Act of 1980 changed railroad regulation from protecting communities and businesses, making it difficult to abandon railroad lines, toward protecting railroads by making it easier to abandon lines. The ease of abandonment, coupled with a pessimism about the future of railroads, did not offer strong incentives to explore opportunities which might have retained trackage. The Latah County Grain Growers, after losing rail service at other locations, had plans to remodel the elevators at Joel on the former S&P for unit train loading. But as the plans were finalized the BN served notice of its intent to abandon the Arrow to Moscow line where Joel was located. The grain growers "almost found themselves with a unit train elevator, but no railroad."[23] If there had been better communication and coordination, perhaps the former S&P lines would still include not only Joel, but Moscow and Pullman, the two largest towns in the Palouse. Unit train facilities have been installed at several locations in the Palouse: on the former S&P in 2017, including a 110-car facility at McCoy and 26-car facilities at Spangle, Oakesdale, and Fallon; and on the former ORN, 25-car or more capacity at Thornton, Willada, Endicott, and Fairfield.[24] Except for Fairfield, the unit train facilities are located on short line railroads which acquired portions of lines that the major railroads sought to abandon.

If the story of the decline of the S&P can be told in one train, it is Nos. 661 and 662, the "High Ball," long scheduled freight six days a week between Yardley (Spokane) and Lewiston. Its purpose was to connect traffic off the CSP, including the big Potlatch lumber and paper mill at Lewiston, with the transcontinental mainline at Spokane. In the 1930s its power was Class W, 2-8-2's. In the 1950s the power was Class W-3, 2-8-2's, three on the Kendrick-Howell grade and two from Howell to Spokane. The aggregate tonnage rating of three W-3s on the 2.4 percent Kendrick-Howell grade was 2,250 tons.[25] The crew went to Lewiston in the evening and back the next afternoon. In the 1960s GP-9 diesels were assigned to the High Ball in order to make a round trip within the 16-hour rule to connect with a transcontinental freight train in the morning at Spokane. In the 1970s the BN began to move the CSP and Lewiston traffic to the Riparia-Wallula line. In April 1981 the High Ball was discontinued with its traffic moved to the Wallula line. Shippers north of Moscow were serviced two days per week, which meant the end of time sensitive traffic. In August 1981 the big Potlatch Lumber Co. mill at Potlatch closed. Only the Bennett Lumber Co. mill at Princeton on the WIM remained tributary to the P&L where in the past there had been several on-line lumber mills, plus those interchanged onto the line. The BN filed to abandon the Moscow to Arrow line March 1984, and abandonment occurred a year later. In June 1984 the Genesee branch, dependent on the seasonal grain harvest, was abandoned. Aside from the Bennett mill, the former S&P lines were left with little to no long-haul traffic, diminishing local traffic, and the seasonal grain harvest. As of January 2018 the P&L was operating only to Fallon.[26]

Entze's summary of the situation for the former S&P and former ORN lines remains the same in 2018 as when he wrote in 2010.

> The cause of the abandonments was not simply the change in legislation with the Staggers Act—although the streamlined abandonment process was an important factor—but a culmination of factors that included farm policies, branch lines with outdate track structures, the elimination of local agencies that exacerbated problems with car shortages, competitive transportation, and the railroads' desire to increase their rate of returns and thus do away with the low density, seasonal branch lines. These factors were in play and began [to] effect the region in the 1970s, but they gained momentum during the lean years of the mid-1980s.[27]

Situations change with time, but we should not forgot that there were several decades in which the NP and UP branch lines in the Palouse were very important to their owners and to the people and businesses they served.

Appendix I

The Spokane & Palouse Railway

1. Finance and Construction Costs.

Sometime after March 1912 but before 1916, the NP created a detailed cost of construction: Marshall to Idaho State Line, $2,376,289; State Line to Genesee, $168,492; Pullman Jct. to Idaho State Line, $460,577; State Line to Lewiston, $2,990,768; and Belmont to Farmington, $99,562; for a total of $6,095,688. In its 1916 report to the ICC the NP claimed total S&P construction costs as approximately $2,625,000 or $2,709,000 depending on how it is read. The ICC's report on the NP valuation gives the original construction cost as $2,898,463 ($84,766,082 in 2016 dollars); $1,669,313 by the S&P and $1,229,149 by the NP. On August 31, 1896, the date the NP Railroad was succeeded by the NP Railway, the funded debt of the S&P was $2,984,000 consisting of (1) first-mortgage sinking fund 6 percent bonds (Washington division), dated May 1, 1886, due May 1, 1936, $1,766,000 and (2) first-mortgage 5 percent bonds (Idaho division), dated October 1, 1890, due October 1, 1940, $1,218,000. The NP held $2,976,000 of the bonds and subsequently acquired $5,000 additional.[1]

2. Physical Plant.

A. Physical Inventory of P&L, Genesee, and Farmington Branches, c. 1912.[2]

Reporting Category	Branches					
	Palouse & Lewiston		Genesee		Farmington	
	#	Estimated Cost	#	Estimated Cost	#	Estimated Cost
Right of Way & Station Grounds (acres)	2058	$1,697,043	376	$112,836	73	$14,658
Grading (all aspects)		1,617,807		156,075		20,272
Steel Bridges	0	0	0	0	0	0
Wooden Bridges						
Combination & Howe Trusses	22	148,800	0	0	0	
Length	2228'		0		0	
Pile and Frame, Length	7604'	72,312	1319'	11,758	330	2898
Culverts		84,892		11,461		4884
Rails: Branch Lines, miles	138.76	616,729	27.5	121,223	5.88	24,808
Rails: Yards, Sidings & Spur tracks, miles	23.27	100,759	4.54	20,137	0.39	1711
Total Line length, miles	162.03		32.04		6.27	
Ballast, cu. Yds.	123,795	81,705	0		0	
Earth Ballast, miles	79.5	36,570	32.04	14,738	6.27	2884
Passenger & Comb. Depots, frame	16	53,750	5	13,698	1	2202
Freight Houses, Frame	3	14,389	0		0	
Lunch Buildings	1	782	0		0	
Stock Yards	13	8281	4	2090	1	232

(continued on next page)

Engine Houses, frame/Total # Stalls	2/4	5633	1/2	1803	0	
Water Stations	10	29,504	2	6989	0	
Coal Platforms	5	2576	1	721	0	
Section Houses/Bunk Houses	10/8	15,397	2/0	3708	1/0	1186
Tool Houses/Track Scales	13/2	4005	2/0	237	0/0	
TOTAL ESIMATED COST (all the categories on the form)		$5,367,056		$629,069		$99,562

Grand Total Estimated Cost: $6,095,687 ($148,672,292 in 2014[3]). As reported in Chapter XV, the ICC's valuation of the NP in 1927 states that the construction cost of the S&P was $2,898,463[4] ($70,694,220 in 2014). To some extent this is an apples-oranges comparison, but the over two-to-one ratio raises a question about the validity of one or both of these estimates. On the other hand, in 2014 it would not be possible to build the three branches for a hundred fifty million dollars.

For allowable freight rates the ICC included the valuation of real estate owned by the railroad which was essential to the operation of the railroad. In rate cases, land owned by the NP for right of way and station grounds, 1,103.55 acres, from Marshall to the Idaho State boundery (line to Lewiston) was valuated at $300 per acre, $331,065 total. In 1909 the NP had its land and improvements in Oakesdale, Palouse, and Pullman appraised; the total for 44.71 acres was $276,545. The recommendation in 1911 was that the remaining land remain at $300 per acre, which gave a total of $594,197 for the right of way and station grounds for that segment of the P&L. The valuation for Pullman to State Line on the Genesee branch had been $200 per acre in the rate cases; the recommendation was that the 280.68 acres be raised to $300, thus a valuation of $84,204. From State Line to Genesee the 95.44 acres were valued at $300 per acre for a total of $28,632. In rate cases, the 954.64 acres land for right of way and station grounds from State Line to Lewiston was valued at $400 per acre, $381,856 total, in two cases and in another case at $933,986 because Lewiston was given a separate valuation of $575,778. Appraisals, including improvements, done at Lewiston and Moscow in 1909, valued at Moscow at $64,795 and at Lewiston at $864,913. The 1911 recommendation was these appraisals be accepted and the remaining 865.69 acres be reduced to $200 per acre, giving a total valuation of $1,102,846 for the line. The valuation of the Farmington Branch was 73.29 acres at $200 per acre, for a total of $14,658.[5] As can be seen in the 1925 table below the NP land valuation increased from 1911, but the ICC was well below the 1911 recommendations.

A valuation dated December 28, 1909, placed estimated cost of reproduction of the line between a thousand feet east of the east headblock of the wye at Joseph and the connection with the bridge approach track at Lewiston at $1,275,879.[6]

In 1925 the NP filed a protest with the ICC regarding its proposed reproduction costs for branch lines:[7]

Branch	**Northern Pacific Reproduction Cost**			**ICC Reproduction Cost**		
	As of 12/31/24	Land, NP Value	Total	As of 6/30/17 + Work to 12/31/24	Land, ICC Appraisal	Total
P&L	$7,338,536	$1,228,978	$8,567,514	$4,927,196	$502,509	$5,429,705
Genesee	960,652	94,491	1,055,143	656,341	34,223	690,564
Farmington	197,481	23,799	221,280	134,210	8305	142,515

While the two tables cannot be directly compared because the first is based on the estimated cost of construction and the second on the cost of reproducing the branches in 1924, they nevertheless continue to show that the railroad and the Interstate Commerce Commission came to significantly different conclusions.

B. Alignment and Profile, Marshall to Lewiston and Pullman Jct. to Genesee. By 1900 all major construction on the S&P was completed.

Divisions & Miles	Alignment			Level Line Miles	Profile: Ascending Grades			Profile: Descending Grades		
	Number of Curves	Aggregate Length Curved Line Miles	Aggregate Length Straight Line Miles		#	Sum of Ascents Feet	Aggregate Length Miles	#	Sum of Descents Feet	Aggregate Length Miles
[a]Marshall to Lewiston 138.41	423	60.83	77.58	11.29		2321 (USGS)	51.12		3716 (USGS)	76.24
[b]Pullman Jct. to Genesee 27.52	54	10.80	16.72	6.30	22	479	17.00	6	186	4.22
[b]Belmont to Farmington 5.94	14	1.60	4.34	0.10	2	168	5.00	1	50	0.84

a Alignment and profile calculations for Marshall to Lewiston made by David C. Beach from NP 1924 Profile. Alignment and profile reports for Marshall to Lewiston in 1903 Confidential Report are unreliable, see below.] USGS: United States Geological Survey.

b NP Confidential Report, 1903, 359.

"Ascending" and "descending" grades are from the perspective of a train traveling westward, toward Lewiston. The gross descent from Howell, NP 2735', to Arrow, NP 750', is 1985'. The June 30, 1892, report to the Interstate Commerce Commission gives the sum of the descents from Pullman Jct. to Juliaetta as 2011.5', consistent with the foregoing, also consistent are the reports to ICC in 1893, 1895-96 which give the sum of descents from Marshall to Juliaetta as 3442'. The 1903 Confidential Report has the sum of the descents as 1768' and the sum of the ascents as 1908', making Lewiston higher than Marshall (NP Condensed Profile, 1/1/66, gives the Marshall elevation NP 2134' and Lewiston NP 666'; reporting Marshall 1468' higher). (NP reports to the Washington State Railroad Commission c. 1905 are similarly inaccurate.) In 1908 there was a realignment of a little over a half mile between MP 95 and 96 which reduced both ascending and descending grades. The curves from Marshall to Lewiston add to 39.15 complete circles.

Westward from Marshall at 2134' (all the elevations in this paragraph are NP) the line ascends from the Spokane River drainage onto the Palouse Plateau and in about 15 miles summits at 2553' into the Pine Creek/Palouse River drainage. It then descends to cross North Pine Creek at 2187'. It then crosses three summits arriving at the town of Palouse, MP 59, 2440', on the Palouse River. From there it crosses two summits and a long descent into Pullman mile 75.9, 2357'. Westward from Pullman Jct. the line crosses a summit and enters Idaho, shortly beyond Moscow it crosses a summit into the Potlatch River/Clearwater River drainage and then crosses two additional summits before reaching the summit at Howell, 2731' the highest point on the S&P. At Howell the descent from the Palouse Plateau begins to Vollmer (Troy) on a 2.2% compensated grade, from Vollmer to Kendrick the descent is mostly 2.4 % compensated grade and from Kendrick to Arrow (Potlatch Jct.), mile 123.7, at 750', the descent along the Potlatch River is continuous but varies below one percent. The continuous descent follows the Clearwater River to Lewiston at 666'.[8]

C. Ruling Grades Spokane to Genesee.

Spokane to Genesee (Westward).		Genesee to Spokane (Eastward).	
Stations	Percent Grade	Stations	Percent Grade
Yardley (Spokane) to Marshall	1.1	Genesee to Colton	0.5
Marshall to Cheney	1.0[a]	Colton to Johnson	1.1
Marshall to Pullman	1.4	Johnson to Pullman	Down
Pullman to Johnson	0.8	Pullman to Belmont	1.1
Johnson to Colton	1.3	Belmont to Oakesdale	0.5
Colton to Genesee	0.5	Oakesdale to Spangle	1.0
		Spangle to Marshall	0.6
		Marshall to Yardley (Spokane)	1.0

Source: Idaho Division Special Instructions No. 1, 7/2/1933.

a Not a S&P ruling grade, over two miles of 1.0% grade westward from Marshall to Cheney. There were recurrent proposals to connect the S&P directly to Cheney to avoid this grade against the grain traffic.

Pullman to Lewiston

Pullman to Lewiston (Westward).		Lewiston to Pullman (Eastward).	
Stations	Percent Grade	Stations	Percent Grade
Pullman to Howell	1.7	Lewiston to Arrow	0.7
Howell to Lewiston	Down	Arrow to Kendrick	0.8
		Kendrick to Troy	2.4
		Troy to Howell	2.2
		Howell to Pullman	1.5

D. Farmington Branch, Grade and Curvature as Reported May 17, 1933.

Belmont to Farmington (timetable west)*, Wash. 5.89 miles									
Ruling Grade: West 1.5%; East 1.3%									
Miles of Grade-									
	Level	.3	.4	.5	.7	1.2	1.3	1.4	1.5
West	.1	.6	2.7	.3	.3	.6		.1	.4
East							.8		
Maximum Curve 10 degrees									

Miles of Tangent and Curves							
Tangent	2°	3°	4°	6°	7°30'	8°	10°
4.33	.39	.09	.10	.60	.06	.20	.12
Total Degrees of Curvature West: Right 196° Left 240°							

Additional Track Data (from Profile: June 15, 1907):
Twelve curves.
Timetable west: Two ascending grades, 165.5 feet sum of ascents, 5.03 aggregate length in miles.

The elevation of the Farmington Branch at the junction with the S&P/P&L was 2528 feet, with grades up to 1.5% a summit of 2601 feet was reached in a little over a mile and after descending 0.8 miles on a 1.3% grade there was a continuous moderate ascent to Farmington at 2639 feet. The 1907 profile shows six bridges, all trestles. The sharpest curve was near the summit.

E. Spokane & Palouse Railway Bridges.[9]

From Marshall to Belmont, mile post 44, including the wye at Belmont, 91 numbered bridges were built. All but one of these were trestles (generally labeled "piling"), the exception was Bridge 49, South Pine Creek, mile 28.5, from east to west it was 195' piling, 2 50' Howe trusses, 45' piling. The Howe truss bridges probably came from another location (see Mohr's letter, April 23, 1886, in the text). Some of the trestles were over a hundred feet in length (MHS 134.L.18.8. F, Construction Profile)).

From Belmont to Genesee bridges were numbered from No. 93 (no bridge No. 92 given) west of MP 44 to bridge No. 155 west of MP 91, 62 bridges were built, from there to the end of the track at Genesee there were an additional nine unnumbered bridges. Most of the bridges were trestles (generally labeled "piling"), a few over a hundred feet in length. There were three Howe truss bridges over the Palouse River between MP 56 and MP 59: bridge No. 120, east to west 153' piling, 100' Howe truss, 227' piling; bridge No. 122, 52.7' piling, 161.25' Howe truss, 20' piling; and bridge 123, 130' piling, 100' Howe truss, 130' piling (Construction Profile).

From Pullman Jct. to Juliaetta the Construction Profile shows 38 bridges, all trestles, but additional bridges were built over the years. Between 1890 and 1968 at least 57 sites had bridges. The ten Bear Creek bridges, between Troy (Vollmer) and Kendrick, between MP's 99 and 108, were presumably originally all trestles (the four shown on the Construction Profile were trestles). Because of repeated flood damage at least nine, and probably all ten, and the Middle Potlatch Creek bridge west of Kendrick, were replaced about ten years later with Howe Truss bridges. Between 1913 and 1916 six of the former ten Bear Creek Howe Truss bridges were replaced with steel girders and between 1927 and 1932 the remaining four were similarly replaced. The new bridges, some with additional length remained in place in 1968. In 1968 the total steel girder length in the ten bridges was approximately 900 feet. The middle Potlatch Creek bridge Howe Truss was replaced in 1926 with a steel bridge.

Several of the original trestles were over a hundred feet long. Two note worthy trestles were Nos. 24 and 28. No. 24 (subsequently Bridge #170 and when shortened #170.1, later #95) in mile 18, about a mile west of Howell was according to Van Arsdol in 1891 a two deck trestle 878' in length costing $8975, subsequent correspondence said it was forty to fifty feet high. Beginning in 1904 there is correspondence about its replacement. About 1906 a concrete arch was built for the stream under it, about 1908 the bridge was filled except for a 52' three span pile trestle near the east end of the former bridge. In 1951 it was rebuilt as a 79' five span pile trestle with a height of 18' for a roadway. No. 28 (subsequently Bridge #174, later #171 and #98) in mile 21 just north of Troy, was according to Van Arsdol a two deck trestle 495' in length costing $4615. In 1902 authorization was made to fill 150' and construct a 36" culvert. The bridge was rebuilt several times and in 1930 was built as a 26' I-Beam with a four span pile trestle, total length 81' and in 1942 it was rebuilt as a three I-Beams and 96' in length over Idaho State Highway 8.[10]

From Juliaetta to Lewiston, from 1898 to 1968 there were at least twenty bridge sites. Except for the Clearwater River and Lapwai Creek bridges, all the initial bridges were trestles. The original Clearwater Bridge, #202.3, later renumbered 126, consisted of five 155' Howe Trusses and one 200' Howe draw span plus trestle approaches at both ends (975' plus trestles).[11] By 1910, "The condition of the bridge is such that something must be done now . . . ." False work was put in place to stabilize the bridge, but in 1913 much of the false work washed out. Some consideration was given to replacing the bridge with a new timber bridge which would accommodate 2-6-2 power. In 1914, the bridge was rebuilt with three 140' and one 116' steel spans from the Lewis River Bridge on the Tacoma Division plus two new 126' steel truss spans and three 75' deck plate girders (1040' total) for a net cost of $108,544.[12]

The trestles over the Little Potlatch Creek, Rock Creek/Deering Creek (NP names, USGS; "Howard Gulch") and the Lapwai Creek's 80' Pony Span were replaced with steel bridges in 1926, 1935 and 1916 respectively.[13]

F. Stations and Spurs: Distances, Elevations and Selected Facilities.

First Column: Mileage to the nearest tenth of mile, but changes less than 0.3 miles generally not given.
Second Column: Selected facilities. All depots are "combination depots" (passenger & freight) unless other wise noted. Shelter sheds are typically only passenger. All included "Legends" are given if they appear, irrespective of date.
Third and fourth Columns: Dates of changes in miles and name. The earliest and the last year station listed in sources (end of tables) except that no date later than 3/3/1970 given, date of NP merger with Burlington Northern. Bracketed dates indicate existence there prior to date given.
Fifth Column: Elevations rounded up or down to whole feet and selected grades ("ascending grades" against west bound traffic toward Lewiston and Genesee).

Marshall to Lewiston (Built 1886–1888, 1890–1891, 1898)
Spokane and Palouse Railway (1886–2/1899); NP Idaho Division:

Palouse & Lewiston Branch (1899–1911); 4th Sub. . . (1/1912–1932); 6th sub. . . (1932–1970 [last ETT 8/1//68];
Arrow to Lewiston, Campus Prairie Railroad (1933–); Moscow to Arrow embargoed 1983, scrapped 1997.

Approximate miles from Marshall.	Station and Spur names. Legend: W, water; C, coal; O, scales; T, turntable; Y, wye.	Earliest available year.	Last available year listed prior to 3/4/1970.	Elevation in feet.
-9.0	Spokane Depot			NP 1931', U.S. 1922'
0	Marshall [Junction] Spokane County, Washington WCY Depot 1886–1942. Water Station 1886-?.	1883	3/3/1970	NP 2134', U.S. 2123'
2	Marshall [State] Quarry Spur	1909	1917	1.65%, mile 1.6 to 3.2
4	Lumber Spur	1901	1901	
5.4	Dynamite	1907	1954	
11.3	Spangle W Depot 1886–1967, One story 24x75' frame. Water station 1886.	1887	3/3/1970	2430'
12.8	County [Infirmary] Spur Cospur Spur Academy Spur Shelter Shed in 1907 & 1950, 5'x12' frame.	1894 1913 1946	1894 1945 1969	
13.3	Highway Spur	1928	1928	
13-15	Fellows	Construction Profile	Only on Profile	Mile 14.8, 2553' summit between Spokane & Palouse rivers' drainages
15.7	Freedom Spur Shelter Shed 1918–1943, 8'4"x24'4.	1910	1959	
19.8	Plaza Depot 1905–1950 still in place; one story 16x48' frame.	1888	3/3/1970	2359'
21.9	Hardman's	Construction Profile	Only on Profile	
23.4	North Pine	1902	1950	2187' Pine Creek

25.3	Boundary between Spokane and Whitman counties, Distance Schedule, 1950.			
26.7	Rosalia W Depot 1886–1978, One story 24x84', frame, 1920 sewer installed, 1922 toilet installed. Section House 1886–1976, One and one half story 20x26', with one story addition 13x26; frame, 1953 toilet installed. 1886: tool house –1978, water tank and pump house –1939.	1887	3/3/1970	2224'
28	Broadview Spur	1909	1919	
28.8	Donahue	1902	1963	
31.9	McCoys [McCoy's] McCoy	1897 1915	1915 3/3/1970	2407, 1.1-1.2% ascending grade mile 31.2 to 34.1 to 2550'
34.9	Unnamed Bros. Spur Flaig Spur	1894 profile 1920 profile 1926	Only on Profile Only on Profile 3/3/1970	
37.3	McCoy's Spur	1896 Distance Schedule	Only on Distance Schedule	
37.6	Oakesdale Depot 1886–1983, One story 24x67', frame, 1903 extended to 105'. Water station 1886–?	1887	3/3/1970	2465'
38.4 38.5	ORN/UP Crossing, Distance Schedule 1950 SIE/GN Crossing, Distance Schedule 1950 Both 38.2 miles on 1908 Employee Timetable	1886 1907/8	3/3/1970 3/3/1970	
40.3	Kelley's Spur Duckworth Spur	1900 1916	1915 1952	
42.9	Belmont WCY Depot 1886–1953, One story, 24x84' frame, 1953 was 25x64'; shelter shed 1953–? 9.4'x16'. Wye 1887–1920. 2 stall engine house 1886–? Water station 1886–1959. Coal Platform 1887–1959 12x150'.	1886	3/3/1970	2508'
43.8	End of Construction, 1887.			2610' summit mile 45.6, 1.1% descending grade to mile 47.1
47.2	Eden	1891	3/3/1970	2532' 1.5% ascending grade to 2563' summit, mile 47.8 to 48.2, 1.1% descending to mile 49.6
49.5	Garfield Depot 1887–1969, One story 20x81' frame, 1892 moved.	1888	3/3/1970	2494'
49.9	ORN/UP & SIE/GN crossings	[1950] Distance Schedule	3/3/1970	1.5% ascending grade to 2605' summit, mile 50.2 to 51.6, 1.1% descending grade to mile 56.1
53	Amador, Cedar Creek, Cedar Spur all written in different hand on Profile	Profile 1894	Only on Profile	
53	Cedar [Creek] Spur	1896	1903	
53	Cedar Creek Shelter Shed 1911–1943 9x14' frame	1897	1950	1st crossing Palouse R. mile 56.5, 2nd crossing mile 58
58.5	Sawmill Spur	Distance Schedule 1896	Only on Distance Schedule	3rd crossing mile 58.9

59	Palouse City Palouse WO Depot 1887–?, one story 20x108', frame, 1892 extension = 158', 1942 remove 50', 1965 remove 45'=20x63'. Interchange with WIM to SIE. Water tanks 1887–1950, 1950–1957.	1888 1897 [1893]	1893 3/3/1970	NP 2440', U.S. 2431' 0.8 to 1.3% ascending grade to 2685' summit, mile 59.1 to 61.4, 1.1% descending grade to mile 65.4, Four Mile Creek
65.7	Four Mile Fallons [Fallens] Fallon	1888 1893 1889	1896 1915 3/3/1970	2495'
66.6	W. A. Tate Spur Tate Spur Titus Spur	[Profile 1894] 1930 1932	[Only on Profile] 1932 1936	
67.1	Madson Spur	1954	3/3/1970	1.5% ascending grade to 2615' summit, mile 67.5, 1.1 descending grade, to mile 69.1, mostly continuous descending grade to Pullman
70.4	Branham Whelan Wheelan Depot 1887–1917, One story 20x108' frame, 1899 unused. Shelter Shed 1919–1927?, 8x22'.	1888 1901 Freight Conductor's Record	3/3/1970 Only on Record	2519'
73.7	Palmerton Harvey Spur [Kitzmiller] Pullman Spur	Profile 1894 1903	1903 Agent's Record 1947	
75.6	Pullman WYC 1st Depot 1888–1902, 80'8"x20' frame. 2nd Depot 1902–1916, 32x160' frame about 600' west of 1st depot; more "suitable and convenient location at competitive point." 3rd Depot 1916–2018 still in place, One story 25x50', 25x46', and 36x63' with covered platform 20x25', and basement 25x33', brick on location of 2nd depot. Water Station 1887–1959, two different locations. Coal platform, 1902–1927, 17x28' frame with derrick. Coaling dock 1928-1957.	1888	3/3/1970	NP 2357, U.S. 2348
76.2	Enos Spur	1896 Distance Schedule	Only on Distance Schedule	
76.4	UP Crossing	[1950] Distance Schedule	3/3/1970	
77.1	Pullman Junction Y	1893	3/3/1970	2379' Continuous ascending grade up to 1.75% to 2669' summit from mile 77.1 to 81.8
78.9	Busbey's Spur	1897	1912	
79.7	[Side Track]	1896 Distance Schedule	Only on Distance Schedule	
80.7	Sunshine Telegraph office reported 1890.	1893	3/3/1970	2580'
82	Material Yard	1901 Freight Conductor's Record	Only on Conductor's Record	1.5% descending grade from mile 81.9 to 83.7
84.2	State Boundary, Whitman County, WA and Latah County, ID			
85	Hagon & Cushing Co. Spur Hagen Spur	1894 Profile 1912	Only on Profile 1930	

85.9 8.8	Moscow WTC Depot 1891–1950, Two story 24x28' One story 24x112' frame, converted to freight house 1937[?] destroyed by fire c. 1950. Passenger Depot 1937–1965, One story brick Tudor style, two end wings each 28'3"x35' & one intermediate sec 26'6"x30', NP & OWRN each owned 1/2 undivided interest. Freight depot 1951–?, 28x56' & bay 4x8.5' brick. Coal Platform 1903–1926 21x99'. Water station 1904–1955. Turntable 1903-1939, 64' deck plate girder	1891 1897 ETT #3	3/3/1970 Only Instance	2575' 1.75% ascending grade mile 88.8 to 90.25 to 2736' summit (from Palouse R. drainage to Potlatch R.), 1.5% descending grade to mile 91.6
92.3	Joel Depot 1890?–1944, One story 24x33' frame. Shelter Shed 1944–? 9.5x14.3'.	1893	3/3/1970	2609'
93	Cornwall No evidence of station or spur, but cited in surveys.			
96	Rock Spur	1901 Freight Conductor's Record	Only in Conductor's Record	
96.5 19.5	Howell T Telegraph office reported 1890. Turntable: 1899, 56' Turntable, no record of removal; 1902 or 07, 64' deck plate girder, built 1902 removed 1939. 1907 plans drawn for coal dock, to reduce amount of coal hauled to Lewiston, no record of construction.	1893 1897 ETT #3	3/3/1970 Only Instance	2732', 2735' highest point S&P. 2.2% descending grade mile 96.8 to 99.4
99.1	Troy Brick Yard Spur	1913	1947	
99.5 99.4	Vollmer W Depot, 1890–?, two story 24x24' one story 24x31' frame, 1960 retire 2nd story 24x24'. Water station, 1890–1931. Name changed 1903 to Troy W	1891 1903	1903 3/3/1970	2473'
100	Vollmer Log Spur Troy Log Spur	1900 1909	1909 1917	Mile 99.9 1st crossing Bear Cr.
100.2	Equation			NP from Marshall 2431' = NP to mile 117.5 2355' = U.S. 2423'
101.4	Brown's Spur	1900	1902	2.4% descending grade mile 101.4 to mile 110.6
103.3	Clarence Spur	1911	1914	
103.5	Gil's Spur	1901	1902	
105.5	Adams Bovard	1903 1910	1910 3/3/1970	 1745'
106.1 105.9	Rock Spur	1904 1939	1915 3/3/1970	
106.8	Clyde Clyde Spur	1894 Profile 1900	Only on Profile 1937	Mile 107.7 10th crossing Bear Cr.
108 108	Allen's Spur Clyde	1901 Freight Conductor's Record 1903 Officers, Agents, etc.	Only on Conductor's Record Only on Officers, Agents, etc.	
110.8	Kendrick Grain Cos. Spur	1894 Profile	Only on Profile	Continuous descending grade mile 110.6 to mile 123
111	Kendrick WCT Depot, 1891–?, Two story 24x24', one story 24x33' frame, 1921 frame addition 5.2'x14.4', 1960 retire 2nd story. Water Station, 1890–1957. Turntable 1891–1907, 56' deck Pl. girder. Two stall engine house 1890. Coal platform 1890–1926, 18'x100' with 8'x8' extension.	1891	3/3/1970	1144' Mile 114.5 crossing Middle Potlatch R.

115	Juliaetta Depot, 1891–1978 burned, Two story 24x24' one story 24x36' frame, 1943 remove one story frame freight room and second story living room portion, one story 24x36 frame	1891	3/3/1970	1009'
115.1	Holbrook's Spur	1894 Profile	Only on Profile	
117.1	End of Construction, 1891			
117.5	Latah- Nez Perce counties boundary Equation			NP from mile 100.2 979' =NP to Lewiston 926', = U.S. 996' Mile 118.9 crossing Little Potlatch Cr.
123.5	Potlatch Junction Potlatch Clearwater Junction Arrow (Y gone 1928 washout, restored 1930, removed 1935)(W gone 1931). Shelter 1899,10x14' frame. Depot 1917–?, One-story 22'x44'frame. Water station 1915. Turntable 1930, place 80' turntable, no work done. Beginning 1933: Arrow to Lewiston Governed by CSP.	1900 1901 Freight Conductor's Record 1905 1906	1905 Only on Conductor's Record 1906 3/3/1970	750'
124	Arrow Storage Spur	1912	1928	Mile 126.1 crossing Clearwater R.
126.5 126.8	Lapwai Junction Renamed Joseph Y Shelter shed 1921–?, frame 12.4 x 20.3. Beginning 1910: Joseph to Lewiston Governed by CSP. Renamed Spalding Y	1900 1907 1927	1907 1927 CSP	 734'
127.4	North Lapwai Depot 1898–1933, Two story 24x24' one story 24x31', frame	1899	CSP	731'
128.5	[Platform]	1917 Engineering Report	1927 Retired AFE	
132.4	(Lewiston Yard Limit Sign) 1950 Distance Schedule			
133.4	Gurney 1910 Porter's renamed Gurney	1910 1917 Officers, Agents, etc.	CSP	
134	Haynes Forebay (formerly Gurney)	1903 Officers, Agents, etc. 1950 Distance Schedule	CSP CSP	
134.5	Porters (see Gurney at 133.4)	1900	1910	
135	Potts (Pott's) Spur	1900	1902	
135.6	Water Co. Spur Water Works East Lewiston Water Station 1915–1957. Coal dock 1915–1956. Round House 1915 8 stalls, 90' deep brick. Turntable 1915 85' plate girder.	1900 1901 Freight Conductor's Record 1950 Distance Schedule	1912 CSP CSP	

136.9 137.5	Lewiston WCT Passenger (2nd) depot 1909-to date, two story 38x62' & 6x18'; one story 30x84' with covered platform 30x41' brick. Combination (1st) depot 1898-1984 two story 24x46; one story 40x130' frame; became freight depot 1909[?] Two stall engine house 1898-removed Turntable 1898-removed, 56' Coal platform	1911 1898	3/3/1970 1910 (1911)	NP 666', = U.S. 736'
138	End of Construction, 1898			
138.9	End of Branch	[1950] Distance Schedule		
	Clarkston (no track) Depot 1910 30.4'x48.4' sold 1937			

Belmont to Farmington (Built 1890)
Spokane and Palouse Railway (1890–2/1899); NP Idaho Division:

Farmington Branch (1899–1911); Farmington Branch 6th Subdivision (1/1/1912–1921); 5th Subdivision 1921–1932; part of the 6th Subdivision, Palouse and Lewiston Branch (1932–1960); branch abandoned 1961.

Approximate miles from Marshall & Junction with P&L mainline	Station and Spur names. Legend: W, water; C, coal; O, scales; T, turntable; Y, wye.	Earliest available year.	Last available year listed if prior to 3/3/1970.	Elevation in feet.
43.8 & 0.0	Palouse & Lewiston Branch Head Block connection to Farmington Branch, 1950 Distance Schedule			2528'
45.7 & 2.0	Hayfield Spur Condensed Profiles 1931 & c. 1949 have mile 2.7.	1909	1952	
4.5	UP Crossing	1890	1961	
6.1 5.8 5.6 0.27	Farmington Y Depot 1890–1931, two story 24x24, one story 24x31', frame. Wye 1890–1893. (Employee timetables do not agree with 1896 & 1950 distance schedules nor with author's calculations from Farmington Station maps of incremental track changes, 1890 to 1961.) To connect a 0.02 spur to P&L mainline, remove remainder of branch.)	1890 End of construction 1896 Distance Schedule End of Branch, 1950 Distance Schedule 1961	1961	2637'

Pullman Junction to Genesee (built 1887–1888)

Spokane and Palouse Railway (1887–2/1899); NP Idaho Division: Palouse & Lewiston Branch (1899–1911);
Genesee Branch, 7th subdivision (1/1/1912–1921); 6th sub. . . (1921–1932); 7th sub. . . (1932–1970 [last NP ETT 8/18/1968]. Branch abandoned 1984.

Approximate miles from Marshall & Pullman Jt.	Station and Spur names. Legend: W, water; C, coal; O, scales; T, turntable; Y, wye.	Earliest available year.	Last available year listed if prior to 3/3/1970.	Elevation in feet.
77.3 & 0.0	Pullman Junction Y Palouse & Lewiston Branch Head Block connection to Genesee Branch, 1950 Distance Schedule.			NP 2379 = U.S. 2372
78.9 & 1.8	Busbey' Spur Busbey Spur Busbeys	1897 1896 Distance Schedule; 1913 1901 Freight Conductor's Record	1912 3/3/1970 Only on Conductor's Record	
82.1 & 5.0	Staley Shelter Shed 1887–1928, 16x24', frame.	1888	3/3/1970	NP 2527 = U.S. 2515
84.4 & 7.3	Chambers Shelter Shed 1907–1941 14x20' frame. Chamber's renamed Chamber, 1915 (1917, Officers, Agents, etc.)	1888	3/3/1970	
87.0 & 9.8	Johnson's Siding Johnson Siding Johnsons "New" depot 1902, one story, 20x81' frame. Johnson's renamed Johnson, 1915, (1917, Officers, Agents, etc.)	1888 1888 1891 1908 1915	 1908 1915 3/3/1970	2636' 1.0-1.5% ascending grade from mile 9.9 to 11.1 to summit 2715', 1.1% descending grade to mile 11.3
92.2 & 15	Colton W Depot 1888–1975, One story 20x108'; frame, 1944 remove 20x37' middle section—remodeled to 20x71', joined 50 & 21 end portions, 1959 lumber from Uniontown depot used to add two rooms for living quarters. Water station 1887–1951.	1888	3/3/1970	2553' Continuous ascending grade to Genesee
94.9 & 17.8	Uniontown Depot 1888–1959 one story 20x71' frame, 1959 lumber from depot used at Colton depot.	1888	3/3/1970	2567'
97.3 & 20.2	Leon Shelter Shed 1916-? still in place 1950, 8x22'; frame.	1889	3/3/1970	2591'
20.4	Boundary between Whitman County, WA and Nez Perce County, ID.	1950 distance schedule		
104.1 & 27 27.5 27.6	Genesee WCY Depot 1888–? one story 20x116' frame. Water station 1887–1957. Coal platform 1888. End of Branch	1888 1896 Distance Schedule 1950 Distance Schedule	3/3/1970	NP 2672' = U.S. 2660'

Sources: Dates: NP Idaho Division Employee Timetables (most timetables prior to 16A 6/20/01 not available, only three missing after 16A); BN 3/3/70, first Burlington Northern Employee Timetable, entries for BN indicate that station or spur existed that date, no subsequent dates in table; Public Timetables used to supplement missing Employee Timetables; Agent's Record, Agent's Record of Seals, Applied, Removed and Issued, August 15, 1903, Circular #40. Faculties: Mostly Authorizations for Expenditures (AFE's), also contemporary correspondence and 1917 Revised Engineering Report (dates corrected by AFE's and correspondence). Elevations and Bridges: Condensed Profile Palouse & Lewiston Branch, 1/1/65, Farmington Branch, c. 1949, and Genesee Branch, 1/1/64, and Pocket List of All Bridges, 1935. Other sources in table.

3. Motive Power, 1886–1910.

The table below contains the engines that are recorded in photographs, newspapers and NP documents up to, and including, 1910. Undoubtedly there were many engines on the S&P not appearing in the available sources. Nevertheless the table does give an indication of many of the classes of engines that worked on the S&P during the early years. The engine numbers are those recorded on the S&P; many engines were renumbered before and after the years recorded here. Most of the engine classes, wheel arrangements, and built dates are from two books by Schrenk and Frey, 2010 and 2013.

Spokane and Palouse Locomotives: The NP sold four engines to the S&P in 1886 and repurchased in 1887. Except for S&P 1, researchers have not found the NP numbers of the other three engines.

NP#	Class		Blt.	Years recorded
2	M	2-10-0	1886	1908
9	B-2	4-4-0	1871	1888
51	F-1	2-8-0	1889	1909
55	F-1	2-8-0	1889	1906
70	F-1	2-8-0	1888	1888
94	F-1	2-8-0	1891	1909
100	C-2	4-4-0	1883	1903
146	F	2-8-0	1883	1898
181	C-2	4-4-0	1882	1890, 91, 92
191	C-2	4-4-0	1883	1891
192	C-2	4-4-0	1883	1887, 92
223	C-2	4-4-0	1882	1887
270	C-2	4-4-0	1883	1887, 91
202	P	4-6-0	1898	1900
310	B-2	4-4-0	1880	1890
313	B-2	4-4-0	1880	1899
338	E-3	4-6-0	1889	1900
340	E-3	4-6-0	1889	1909
342	E-3	4-6-0	1889	1891
343	E-3	4-6-0	1889	1896
345	E-3	4-6-0	1890	c. 1908
361	E-1	4-6-0	1888	c. 1904
363	E-1	4-6-0	1888	1899
364	E-1	4-6-0	1888	1899
365	C-6	4-4-0	1884	1902
375	E-2	4-6-0	1888	1902
383	E-2	4-6-0	1888	1899
446	E-1	4-6-0	1888	1890, 92
449	E-1	4-6-0	1888	1890
467	D-3	2-6-0	1889	1891
504	D-2	2-6-0	1888	1896
521	D-2	2-6-0	1888	1891
652	B	4-4-0	1887	1904
671	B	4-4-0	1887	1906
673[a]	B-1	4-4-0	1889	c. 1908
676[b]	C-19	4-4-0	1887	c. 1899
698	C-3	4-4-0	1882	c. 1890, 99
700	C-3	4-4-0	1883	c. 1898, 99

S&P#	Remarks
1	Re-lettered NP 36 when sold back to NP. Class A-1, 4-4-0, built 1872.
2	
3	There is a photograph of a S&P engine on the Spokane Falls & Idaho, 1886. John Wood, based on magnification, writes that it is possibly S&P engine 3 (communication 10/8/16). Lorenz Schrenk, NP engine authority, writes that it appears to be an NP class A-1 Baldwin, see #1 above (communication 10/9/16).
4	

a Built for Oregon & Washington Territory Railroad, #6, retained number on Washington & Columbia River Railway, purchased from WCR 7/1/1907 by NP and renumbered (information provided by Jan Taylor and Bill Venable).

b Built for Montana Union Railway, #2, purchased from MU 7/1/1898 by NP and renumbered (information provided by Jan Taylor).

Appendix II

The Columbia and Palouse Railroad

1. Finance and Construction Costs.

The Tripartite Contract stated that the C&P was to be financed by the OT, built by the NP for the benefit of the ORN. For reasons related in Chapter II the NP turned the C&P over to the ORN in June, 1884. President Coolidge reported to the ORN Executive Committee on March 24, 1884, that all the C&P stock, except that held by the directors, had been received from the OT. The ORN purchased the C&P for $2,489,520 ($26,400 per constructed mile) which included securities having a par value of $3,829,000, consisting of $1,000,000 in capital stock and $2,829,000, $30,000 per 94.3 constructed miles, in first mortgage six percent gold bonds dated July 2, 1883, due October 1, 1923. The securities had been acquired by the OT to compensate the OT for construction expenditures of C&P; the 1934 ICC UP Valuation Report gives the C&P construction costs by the OT as $1,935,779. The 1884 ORN Annual Report, issued in October, listed as assets the acquired C&P stocks and bonds plus additional construction costs ($70,435) for a total of $2,559,955 or $27,147 per mile.[14] The OT had paid in advance the interest on the bonds for two years at six percent. The additional cost may have been for buildings and raising the roadbed at Washtucna Lake plus ORN costs not paid by the O&T.

From August 1, 1884, when service to Colfax resumed, to December 31, 1886, the ORN operated the C&P, as a separate corporation, through stock ownership. On that date the C&P was physically complete at 144.8 miles; from Connell to Moscow, 117.32 miles, and Colfax to Farmington, 27.48 miles (142.44 in Washington and 2.36 in Idaho, 40.25 miles of line in Washington had iron rails, the remainder steel). From January 1, 1887 the C&P was operated under lease to the ORN, which was assigned to the Oregon Short Line Railway until September 6, 1910. The C&P Directors July 27 authorized conveyance of all C&P property to the ORN which in turn on December 23 sold it to the Oregon-Washington Railroad & Navigation Co.[15] The books of the C&P at the time of the sale showed an investment of $4,852,967 in road, including land. The C&P owned no equipment.[16]

2. Physical Plant.

A. Length.

The original construction mileage is 143.8 which was broken down in the report to the ICC as follows (corrections added another mile): Connell to La Crosse 53.12 (53.08); La Crosse to Colfax 35.68; Colfax to State Line 26.2; State Line to Moscow 1.6 (2.36); and Colfax to Farmington 27.2 (27.48); Total 143.8 (144.8). (Gill 1916, 5); ICC 1934, 271 plus author calculations.[17]

B. Alignment and Profile.

Divisions & Miles	Alignment			Level Line Miles	Profile: Ascending Grades			Profile: Descending Grades		
	Number of Curves	Aggregate Length Curved Line Miles	Aggregate Length Straight Line Miles		#	Sum of Ascents Feet	Aggregate Length Miles	#	Sum of Descents Feet	Aggregate Length Miles
Connell to Moscow 117.32 miles	211	33.05	84.27	19.55	172	2428	80.41	28	755	17.36
Colfax to Farmington 27.45 miles	67	13.06	14.42	2.42	41	738	23.62	2	56	1.44

Source: The 1907 Annual Report to the ICC on the C&P, p. 73.

C. Track and Road Way.

In the summer of 1899, the OR&N replaced the iron rails between Colfax and Pullman with fifty-six pound steel. The next summer the iron rails from Pullman to Moscow were replaced. By the end of August, 1899, steel for a new OR&N bridge across the South Palouse River in Colfax was on site. The bridge would replace a Howe Truss bridge on the main line just north of the old Colfax depot. The bridge at Elberton was being torn down and replaced by a steel bridge.[18]

D. Stations and Spurs, Distances, Elevations and Facilities.[a]

Palouse Junction/Connell to Farmington.
(Connell to Kahlotus reconstructed 1904)
(Connell to Hooper Junction abandoned 1979)
(Colfax to Farmington abandoned 1991)

Approximate miles from Connell.[b]	Station name and depots (all combination depots unless otherwise noted).[c]	Earliest available year.[d]	Last available year listed if prior to 12/10/1978.[e]	Elevation in feet.[f]
0.0	Palouse Junction (Jct. with NP) Connell[k] 1-story 22'x66' frame 1886, replaced 1978, still exists 2009. 1-story approx.16'x20' metal c. 1978.	1884 1889	1887	832
1.9	Curry	1931		832
6.8	Sulphur	1884/1885		755
10.6	Estes	1910		827
15.5	Kahlotus 1-story 22'x61' frame c. 1900, retired 1963.	1884		892
19.0	Wacota	1931	1968	
23.6	McAdam[s]	1910	1963	
28.1	Franklin County/Adams County			
29.4	Washtucna 1-story 22'x61' frame c. 1900, retired 1963.	1884/1885	1968	991
35.0	Palouse Falls	1931	1933	
37.2	Hooper Jct.[i] 2-story 24'x30' and 1-story 22'x60' frame 1914. Jct. with UP Spokane/Ayers line.	1914		1035
37.8	Palouse River Crossing Adams County/Whitman County			1049
38.2	Hooper[i]	1884		1057 Ascending 1.28% ruling grade to Pampa.
44.7	Gordon	1938		1164
48.3	Pampa	1884/1885		1339
49.4	Benner	1931	1933	
52.9	La Crosse Jct. (Jct. with Riparia line) La Crosse 2-story 22'x68' frame 1888. 1-story approx. 50' addition c. 1900; destroyed by fire 8/23/10.[h] 2-story 24'x31' and 1-story 24'x51' frame, 1911,[i] retired 1972. 1-story 20'x48' metal, 1972, still exists 2009.	1889 1910	1891	1473
56.3	Union Flat Creek Crossing			1472
59.5	Sutton	1886		1536

63.5	Winona Jct. (Jct. with Tekoa line) Winona 2-story 24'x42' and 1-story 24' 24'x51' frame 1908, retired 1971.	1889 1900	1891	1482
64.1-67.6	Between miles 64.1 and 82.7 eight [plus] crossings of Rebel Flat Creek			1487-1631
69.3	Endicott 1-story 22'x78' frame 1883, retired c. 1976.	1884		1594
76.2	Lee Harbin Thera	1900 1909 1910	1909	1863
79.8	Diamond[s] 1-story 22'x61' frame 1901, retired by 1957.	1886		2025
83.8	Mockonema	1889		2120
86.2	Crest	1884/1885	1963	2264 Approximately a mile each of 2.4% & 3.0% descending.
88.3	S. Fork Palouse River Crossing			1949
88.6	SIE/GN Crossing			
88.7	Colfax[j] 1-story 24'x130' frame 1883, [burned January, 1899], work commenced on the Colfax depot, fourth class, 118'x22' (PG 11/28/84, 3), converted to freight house by 1904. [25'x96' 1899 depot, new freight house 1906], Passenger depot 1-story 24'x144' frame by 1904, retired by 1977.	1884		1945
94.7	Clear Creek Crossing			2063
94.8	Glenwood	1889		2065
101.0	Elberton 1-story 22'x69' frame 1886, retired by 1957.	1886		2174
101.7	N. Fork Palouse R. Crossing			2196 Approximately three miles, 1.38% ascending.
102.1-105.8	Five crossings Silver Creek			
106.4	Garfield 1-story approx. 22'x70' frame 1886, rebuilt or retired by 1906. 1-story 22'x113' frame by 1906, retired c. 1978.	1886		2457
106.8	S&P/NP Crossing			
107.3-109.4	Two crossings Silver Creek			
109.9	Walters	1931		2519
114.7	S&P/N.P. Crossing	1891	1961	
115.8	Farmington It has four living rooms up stairs, for the agent (WWDJ 9/24/86). 31-story 22'x129' frame 1886, retired 1971. Connects to Spokane and Wallace lines via Tekoa.	1886		2617

Colfax to Moscow. Abandoned 1997, 2004

Approximate miles from Connell.[b]	Station name. (all combination depots unless otherwise noted).[c]	Earliest available year.[d]	Last available year if prior to 12/10/1978.[e]	Elevation in feet.[f]
88.7	Colfax	1884		1949
88.8-91.7	Two Crossings S. Fork Palouse River			1948-2033
93.2	Risbeck	1909		2080
94.5-94.8	94.3 end of construction 12/31/83 Two Crossings S. Fork Palouse River			2109-2120
96.3	Riverside Pravin	1889 1910	1900	 2152
96.8-97.0-98.2	Three Crossings S. Fork Palouse River Mouth of Four Mile Creek opposite side of Palouse R. between 2nd and 3rd crossings			2161-2171-2181
98.4	Shawnee	1886		2183
99.4-100.6-101.2	Three Crossings S. Fork Palouse River			2204-2220-2228
101.4	Guy Albion 1-story 18'x40' frame 1906, retired by 1976.	1886 1916	1910	 2233
101.8-102.0	Two Crossings S. Fork Palouse River			
103.1	McAvoy	1931	1938	[2254]
104.0	S. Fork Palouse River Crossing			2270
104.4	Armstrong	1931	1959	[2275]
105.5	S. Fork Palouse River Crossing			2294
107.4	Pullman 1-story 22'x113' frame 1886 (includes 20' extension c. 1900), retired 1938-39. 1-story 30'x154' brick & frame 1938, retired c. 1976, still exists.	1886		2329
107.7-107.9-108.1	Three Crossings S. Fork Palouse River			
108.3	S&P/NP Crossing	1891		
108.9	Whitlow	1901,[g] 1931		2378
109.9	Holland	1931	1953	
112.8	Garrison	1889	1948	2489
114.9	Whitman County, WA/Latah County, ID			
116.8	Moscow[1] Connections to S&P/NP and S&IE/GN 1-story 31'x124' frame 1885, converted to freight house, retired 1983. 2-story joint NP-OWR&N union depot 35'x85' built 1938, retired 1965.	1886		2560
117.2	End of Track			2571

a A "station" may be only a side track or spur without a depot. Sources: NP public timetable 10/1/1884; OR&N, OWR&N and UP employee timetables 3/8/1885 to 12/10/1978: 1885, 1886, 1887, 1889, 1890, 1891, 1910, 1931, 1932, 1933, 1938, 1942, 1943, 1947, 1948, 1950, 1951, 1956, 1959, 1963, 1968, 1978; Washington State Department of Transportation line abandonment, 1979, 1991; UP condensed profile 1/1/1977; Official Guide 1901 (tt 1900); 1910 (tt 1909); 1916 (tt 1916); 1926 (tt 1925); 1930 (tt 1929); 1941 (tt 1941); 1945 (tt 1945); 1946 (tt 1946); 1954 (tt 1954); 1957 (tt 1956); 1964 (tt 1963).

b All distances are approximate from Connell. Over time the mileage given in the timetables was measured from Connell, La Crosse, Portland, Umatilla and Ayer, but here all are calculated from Connell.

c Original name, as it appears in earliest available year, with any subsequent changes by date. Unless otherwise noted, depot histories from Carter (2009b, 125-26).

d Because not every timetable is available, it is possible that the station existed prior to the year given. On the opening of the C&P in January, 1884, only Endicott and Colfax were not prepay stations, whether the others showing a 1884 date had an agent is unknown. Palouse Jct. is in the NP 1884 timetable, but may have been also a prepay station (PG 1/4/84, 3). The date for Risbeck is from PH 7/30/09, 1, which said the station was being built; the earliest available timetable date is 1931.

e If the cell is blank the station appears in the employee timetable 12/10/1978. Official Guides were used only for extending the last date.

f Where available elevations and grades from UP Condensed Profile 1/1/1977, except Washtucna and ruling grade from Hooper to Pampa (Lewty 1987, 119).

g Mentioned in PH 8/31/01, but not 1910 timetable.

h SR 8/24/10, 6.

i CG 8/25/11, 1: almost completed.

j Newspaper accounts in brackets (SR 1/8/99, 12; 5/6/99, 5; 10/20/99, 5; 3/7/06, 16).

k The history of depots at Connell is unclear. The history of the C&P/OR&N/UP depots in the chart above are from Carter, 2009b. Newspaper reports follow: Originally the OR&N built a depot at Connell and the NP used it jointly. When the OR&N withdrew the NP bought the depot (SR 9/14/04, 12); In late August, 1905, it was reported that the OR&N would soon build a new depot at Connell, it would be 75x25 feet and contain freight, express and passenger rooms plus living apartments for the agent (SR 8/26/05, 12). NP Connell depots: 1 story 22'x148' frame 1907, retired 1945; 1 story 12'x45' brick, 1945, still existed 2009 (Carter 2009b, 91).

l Asay 2014, 318, 376; MHS 134.I.B.12.F; NP AFE 293-65; Lecompte 1988, 25. Sanborn maps suggest that 1885 depot was about 100' longer.

Notes

Introduction

1. The principal works on the history of the NP, UP, S&P, ORN, and C&P in the Palouse are Lewty 1987 and 1995, and Asay 1991. Lewty's work is a sound introduction, but does not have the detail of this work and makes far less use of corporate records and contemporary publications. Asay's work focuses on the ORN as a whole with the Palouse being a secondary concern, nearly ignores the relationship with the NP in the Palouse and very briefly treats the C&P.

2. Meinig 1968, 10. Meinig, the standard work on the Columbia Plateau, provides a very good account of the settlement and development of the Palouse country. Also see Duffin 2004 for an account of the development of agriculture in the Palouse; his account of railroad development is not entirely accurate. By 1880, the three counties with the largest populations in Washington Territory were in the Palouse region: Walla Walla (8,683), Whitman (7,079), and Columbia (7,074). The three accounted for almost a third of the territory's total population (WWU 8/21/80, 3).

3. SR 4/10/08, 5; 6/3/08, 14; 6/17/08, 6; 6/22/08, 8; 6/23/08, 10; PH 7/8/10, 1; CG 3/26/09, 1 (and others); PH 4/18/08, 3. Given that the price of wheat varied by only a few cents per bushel from place to place, the $5.00 per acre is an indirect measure of the high productivity of the Palouse.

I: Railroad Beginnings in the Palouse Country, 1864–83

1. 13 U.S. Stat. 365, 7/2/64; 16 U.S. Stat. 378, 5/31/70; Hedges 1930, 20–21, 29, 47ff; Lewty 1987, 5. In addition to Hedges and Lewty other accounts of the formation and early construction of the NP are found in Smalley 1883, Renz 1980 and Lewty 1995.

2. A history of the OSN is found in Asay 1991, chapter 1, and in Johansen & Gates 1967; Gill 1914, 2–29; MHS, 137.J.9.10.F; Trimble 1914, 127; Meinig 1968, 226.

3. MHS, 134.I.5.8.F; Renz 1980, 30; Ficken 2002, 89.

4. An offer to sell the OSN to the NP was made at least as early as 1/23/66 (Gill 1914, 36).

5. MHS, 137.J.9.10.F; Gill 1914, 107; Villard 1904, 286–87; NP Papers; Smalley 1883, 188.

6. For accounts of the early NP surveys in the Clearwater and Salmon Rivers, see Baird 2003 and Eastwick 1999. NP 1906 Surveys; Renz 1980, 58–59. For evidence of the Colfax route, see LT 5/30/79, 2.

7. Lewiston, Idaho, at the junction of the Snake and Clearwater rivers, was founded in 1861 to serve the Orofino mining district on the Clearwater. Its settlement breached a treaty with the Nez Perce Indians (Bancroft 1890, 238). NYT 5/25/79; NP Papers, Smalley 1883, 158.

8. LT 5/9/79, 2; 7/18/79, 2; 8/29/79, 2; LT 9/5/79, 1, 2; 11/28/79, 2. Surveyors for the Idaho, Clearwater & Montana Transportation Co. in 1881 discovered in the vicinity of Lolo Pass a marker by T. P. Roberts, Chief of Party, NP, October 29, 1871 (LT 9/15/81, 4). This confirms that the NP had information on Lolo Pass prior to McCartney's survey and why his search south of Lolo was sensible. Also in October 1879, T. R. Tannatt, Henry Villard's General Eastern Agent wrote Villard that he had talked to Henry L. Abbott, of the U.S. Corps of Engineers, on lease to the NP, and was told "no practical pass through the Coeur d'Alene and Bitter Root Mountains could be found giving entrance to the 'Westward' to either the North or South Fork, of the 'Clearwater'" (WSU, Cage 4545).

9. NP Papers; NP 1933; PG 3/5/80, 4.

10. PG 11/24/77, 4; PG 11/17/77, 4.

11. Villard 1944, 65.

12. PG, 6/29/78, 4; 1/24/79, 4. Confusion and errors exist regarding the place names on the Snake River from the mouth of the Tucannon River to Riparia. The ORN line from Walla Walla reached the south side of the Snake River at "Tucannon"— the mouth of the Tucannon River known both as Grange City (Sec. 3; T.12N; R.37E) and Tucannon Junction or Grange City Junction (not a junction until the 1899 completion of the line from Wallula to a junction with the line from Walla Walla). To the east, up river, from Grange City are the Texas Rapids (in both Sec. 36; T.13N; R.37E and Sec. 31; T.13N; R38E), a barrier to navigation in low water; above the rapids navigation to Lewiston was possible most of the time. The ORN built east from Grange City approximately

five miles to Texas Ferry (Sec. 30; T.13N; R.38E) or South Texas. Texas Ferry was also known as Texas City or Riparia, the two names being attached to both sides of the Snake River. On the north side of the Snake, Riparia was at the mouth of Alkali Flat Creek. The names Texas Ferry and Texas City were dropped and Riparia was identified as being either "North" or "South." Generally "Riparia" without the adjectives is a reference to North Riparia. Riparia, being upstream from the rapids, allowed the railroad to bring cargo for steamboats to Lewiston. For the use of various place names see as examples: Gill 1916, 47, 75; Asay 1991, 61, 329; Hitchman 1985, 110, 252, 300, the latter includes errors. On November 28, 1907, it was announced that, "All obstructions will be removed from Snake river at Texas rapids by the end of the present navigation season.... With the removal of the obstructions, the most serious bar to open navigation of the Snake river will have been removed, and a long step taken toward an open river to the sea" (SR 11/29/07, 5). With the opening of Lower Monumental Dam in 1969, Texas Rapids ceased to be an obstacle to navigation. The construction of that dam necessitated the removal of the original bridge at Riparia and the construction of a new bridge about a mile downriver from the mouth of the Tucannon River. With the construction of that dam and three others, the Snake River has slack water navigation from its mouth to Lewiston. Dams built on the Columbia River provide slack water from the Snake River to Portland. The dams on the two rivers and large trucks ended most of the grain traffic on the railroads south of the Snake River, in south Whitman County, and in Latah and Nez Perce Counties in Idaho.

13. WS 7/79, 194.

14. There are numerous accounts of the rise, fall, re-emergence and withdrawal of Villard from railroad affairs in the Pacific Northwest, included: Asay 1991; Buss 1977; de Borchgrave 2001; Ficken 2002; Hedges 1930; Lewty 1987 & 1995; Villard 1904 & 1944; and Winks 1991. Villard was in Buss' view a "transatlantic entrepreneur" who "was the single most effective person encouraging export of German capital to America during the late nineteenth century" (Buss 1977, 255, 261).

15. Accounts of the WW&CR and Dorsey Baker are found in Lewty 1987, Baker 1934, and Mills 1950.

16. Cited in Schwantes 2008, 64.

17. The UP was dependent on the Central Pacific for reaching the Pacific Coast. UP officials realized that they were at the mercy of the Central Pacific, which would shortly be able to divert eastward traffic to the new Southern Pacific 'Sunset Route." As a result they encouraged Villard and built the Oregon Short Line to connect with the ORN (Rigdon 1954, 96).

18. WWU 10/4/79, 3.

19. References to charter documents mentioned are found in "References" under "Railroad Charter Documents." No further citation will be given to charter documents.

20. OHS, 299, Exec. Com. Rec. p. 38. Craghead on Villard and Portland: "the Portland business elite welcomed him as an insider; and in turn, he became a patron rarely equaled and never exceeded" (Craghead 2016, 10).

21. Ficken 2002, 137; Lewty 1987, 42.

22. LT 6/20/79, 2; 6/27/79, 2; 8/15/79, 2; Hedges 1930, 62.

23. Winks 1991, 225–26, 242; NP Papers.

24. ST 9/4/79, 3; PG 10/31/79, 2; 12/26/79, 2 & 1; LT 12/19/79, 2; PG 1/23/80, 2; 3/5/80, 2; 2/13/80, 4.

25. Baker, box 44/f327.

26. PG 2/13/80, 3; 2/27/80, 1; 3/12/80, 3; 4/16/80, 3.

27. WSU, Cage 4545; NP Papers. In addition to the WSU collection there is a biography of Tannatt: Woodward, 2006.

28. PG 6/25/80, 3; PG 7/23/80, 3; RG 8/20/80, 448, 449; PG 8/20/80, 3. As constructed the westward grade out of Colfax was approximately a mile each of 2.4 percent and 3.0 percent (Lewty 1987, 119; UP 1977).

29. Whitman College, 40/95/27 also Multnomah County Library, 0-385 0695.

30. PG 9/10/80, 2; WWU 1/29/81, 2; 6/18/81, 3; RW 7/23/81, 713.

31. Both lines were turned over to the operating department April 15, 1882 (Renz 1978, 20).

32. Villard 1944, 88; Winks 1991, 226, 243; Baker, Box 26/f244; NP Papers.

33. Ainsworth 1992, 15.

34. Traffic Contract, 1880, 23, 22; OHS, 299, Exec. Com. Rec. p. 86 (also OHS, 2017); NP Papers; Rigdon 1954, 1988, 1990–91. The only examples that Rigdon gives of the NP management not adhering to the contract are building the Cascade branch and building "by indirection" south of the Snake. The Cascade branch was not precluded by the contract or the supplementary 1882 contract. The charge that the NP built south of the Snake by "indirection" is debatable. Regarding the north bank line, Villard said later (1944, 89): "We made the concession relative to the north-bank line on the presumption that it would never be built." Rigdon (96) also writes, "Villard made certain traffic contracts between the Northern Pacific and the Navigation Company; they were one-sided, in the Northern Pacific's favor, giving it an arbitrary constructive mileage division on interchanged traffic through Wallula, and requiring the O. R. & N. to pay the Northern Pacific 5 per cent of its gross earnings on that traffic, and to bear the entire cost of the interchange at Wallula." He is correct, the traffic agreement was favorable to the NP, but it was Villard who sought the contract and the concessions to the NP can be seen as enticements to get an agreement which Villard, more than Billings, wanted.

35. Villard sought to increase the NP's difficulties in the Cascades by acquiring right of way across the Cascades via Snoqualmie Pass with the purchase in October 1880, of the Seattle and Walla Walla Railroad & Transportation Co. which in November 1880 he reincorporated as the Columbia and Puget Sound Railroad (Buss, 1977, 114; LT 10/15/80, 2, report from Seattle says that T. R. Tannatt purchased the line for Villard). Armbruster

(1999) has an account of the Seattle & Walla Walla. Whether Villard sought to use the S&WW against the NP or to prevent the S&WW from crossing the Cascades is according to Hedges 1930, 65–67, unclear. Villard also dealt with the possibility of a Columbia River line: using maps acquired during the traffic agreement negotiations, he directed his agents in the spring of 1881 to buy up parcels which would give him control of essential strips and thereby forestall construction (Winks 1991, 246; Hedges 1930, 78).

36. Hedges 1930, 73.

37. Winks 1991, 244; Ainsworth, 1992, 15; SR 11/13/00, 6.

38. Hedges 1930, 82–85; NYT 12/24/80, 2; Villard 1904, 296; Villard 1944, 90, 1; Gill, 1914, p. 205; WWU 1/8/81, 3; 4/9/81, 2; RA, June ??, 1881, 364; Oregonian as quoted in Buss 1977, 124; NYT 3/24/81; 5/20/81; Villard 1944, 93; NYT 9/16/81; Renz 1978, 3. There are a number of accounts of the "blind pool" and Villard's gaining control of the NP, including Hedges 1930, chapter IV; Lewty 1987, chapter 7; Renz 1980, 75–77; Buss 1977, chapter 5; Winks 1991, chapter 22. William Endicott, one of Villard's closest advisors, thought it unwise to buy a controlling interest in the NP. He wrote Villard, February 6, 1881, "Our true policy…is instead of gobbling up the Northern Pacific to be in good condition to be gobbled." Villard wrote back on the 12th, "You may think me a rash fellow but sometimes rashness of this kind is really the greatest prudence" (Buss, 1977, 119, 120). For an account of Villard's actions and influence on Washington Territory see Ficken 2002.

39. ST 3/10/81, 2; LT 4/21/81, 2 & 4/28/81, 1.

40. Klein 1987, 560; Villard 1944, 92; C&F Vol. 33, 12. OT Annual Report, 1883, said that the OT owned 162,792 shares of NP common and 151,300 shares of preferred. The total constituted 34.894 % of the total NP shares, "sufficient for continued control of the Company." The OT owned 128,535 shares of ORN, more than an absolute majority of the stock.

41. Buss 1977, 129; Hedges 1930, 80–81, 86–87. The letter to Oakes is at the MHS.

42. NP Papers, Executive Committee 9/30/81.

43. Hedges 1930, 88–97; Villard's Portland address is in LT 11/3/81, 1.

44. A newspaper clipping 10/12/81 in WSU, Cage 65 box 5 (emphasis added); LT 10/20/81, 2; Ficken 2002, 150–51.

45. ST 3/10/81, 2; SFC, 6/29/81, 4 (also in RG 7/1/81, 367); RG 8/12/81, 446; RW 8/20/81, 808. The 6/30/81 ORN Annual Report said that as of 7/1/81, Texas Ferry to Union Flat, 26 miles, was graded.

46. The Palouse lines were: Crossing of the Snake River to the mouth of Rebel Flat (Jct. with Elk Creek Branch), 38 miles; the mouth of Rebel Flat to Colfax, 26 miles; Elk Creek Br., 16 miles; Colfax and Pine Creek Br., 39 miles; and Colfax to Moscow, 26 miles (p. 8). The first two were allowed under the 1880 agreement. I have not located Elk Creek, but it may be Cottonwood Creek. A Pine Creek branch of 39 miles would probably terminate north of Rosalia, thus north of any direct feasible route to Farmington.

47. Bancroft Library, Banc P-B 220.

48. The charter is found LT 8/4/81, 2; LT 4/27/82, 2. It was a survey for the IC&MT which found the 10/29/71 Lolo Pass marker of the NP's T. P. Robert survey (LT 9/15/81,4).

49. Lewty 1987, 81; Gill 1916b; PG, 10/7/81, 2; 10/21/81, 3; 10/28/81, 3 & 11/4/81, 2; LT 11/3/81, 2 & 12/22/81, 1. The bridge contract of July 3, 1881, was cancelled in January 1882. The 1883 ORN Annual Report map shows a projected line from Texas Ferry to Lewiston. While ORN service to Texas Ferry began December 1881, the ORN did not begin railroad service to Lewiston until July 1908.

50. PG 11/25/81, 3.

51. Gill 1916, 47; NP 1933.

52. LT 1/5/82, 1.

53. The next year's ORN Annual Report (6/30/83) contains a map showing a line from Grange City to Lewiston via Marengo on the Tucannon River. Into the next century the ORN surveyed numerous times in the hills south of the Snake River hunting for a suitable route to Lewiston. None was found.

54. MHS, 137.H.3.1.B; 132.I.4.7; PG 8/3/83, 2; WWU 8/25/83 3. A March 16, 1899, letter from NP Chief Engineer McHenry to NP President Mellen reported that the Chief Engineer's office had surveys on the north bank of the Columbia River from 1873 to 1882 (MHS, 134.I.5.8.F).

55. Asay 1991, 39; MHS, 137.J.10.1.B.

56. Villard had a deep interest in promoting settlement, see Hedges 1930, chapter VI; Villard 1904, 295–96. Mickelson 1993 is a general account of the NP's land sales.

57. See Beach 2013 for an exceptional case of litigation on the S&P.

58. WWU 11/15/79, 2; 11/29/79, 2; 2/21/80, 2; 2/28/80, 2; 7/3/80, 3; 12/4/80, 2 & 4; 12/11/80, 2; 1/1/81, 2; 2/5/81, 2; Commissioners 1881. Other newspapers of the time are unavailable, but probably the Union was not the only newspaper used. A good source on land sales in the Palouse is Fahey 1986, 25–29. A more general history of the NP's land sales see Cotroneo 1966; despite its title it does have a history prior to 1900.

59. Mickelson 1993, 28.

60. Villard organized the Oregon Improvement Company in October, 1880 (Villard 1904, 85).

61. NP Papers. These lands became a source of controversy. On September 20, 1887, Elijah Smith, as the president of the Oregon Improvement Co. (he was at the time also president of the O&T and ORN), wrote NP President Harris that there was a shortage of lands conveyed under the contract of October 20, 1880. The alleged shortage occurred because the actual survey of the land found that certain tracts were smaller than recorded by the U.S. Government survey. Harris' position was that if the quantities of land conveyed were short by the government survey the NP was to compensate with land or pay $2.60 per acre for the shortage. "[A]ny excess or shortage of that quantity as ascertained by actual

survey is not to be taken into consideration. The sale was by the acreage, according to the government survey, and no other." Furthermore, Harris, wrote the making up of any deficiency referred to the entire quantity and not to any parcel or parcels (MHS, 137.H.11.1.B).

62. MHS, 137 H.3.6.F.

63. NW October, 1888, 29; February 1889, 33; Fahey 1986, 19.

II: The Columbia and Palouse Railroad to 1886 and the Fall of Villard

1. PG, 2/3/82, 3; 2/24/82, 3.

2. WS 3/82, 58. "Endicott," named after William Endicott, Boston investor and Villard associate, was started about this time by the Oregon Improvement Co. Endicott is on land bought by the Oregon Improvement Company (OI) from the NP. Lewty 1987, 117; PG, 5/19/82, 2, 3; 5/26/82, 2.

3. NP Papers; Contract 1882, 1, 2. In December 1898 an NP Committee in negotiations with the UP/ORN over division of territory in the interior discovered the agreements of 1880 and 1882. The committee used these agreements to refute the ORN claim "that the N. P. should never go into Colfax, the equitable right of the O. R. & N. Co. to Colfax and the rest of the Palouse country, based on prior occupation, being superior in its opinion to those of the Northern Pacific!" See chapter XV.

4. Tripartite Contract, 1882; also in C&F Vol. 34 (6/3/82), 637 and LT 7/6/82, 1. The common explanation why the NP could not build branch lines under its own name has been that its charter did not allow it. Questions have been raised as to whether this was true. Jerry Masters and William Bursack researched the matter extensively and concluded that the NP was indeed constrained in building branches under its own name and that only after the reorganization of the company in 1896 could the NP build branches without forming separate companies to do so (communication from Masters, September 2008).

5. C&P Charter; Gill, 1916, 5; Hitchman 1985, 54; OHS, Gill 1591 B.6.F.11, and 299, Box 131, C&P Record, 22–24.

6. OT 1882 Annual Report, 4, 6; RA 8/24/82, 473; NP 1882 Annual Report.

7. LT 4/19/83, 2; 5/3/83, 2; 5/10/83, 2; Allen 1990, 219–20. Allen's account is based on the contemporary story in the Lewiston *Teller*, but is not faithful to that story. The story is also inaccurate in the Lewiston *Morning Tribune* of April 21, 1984. The most important differences between the account published in 1883 and retellings is the later versions say that Villard did not leave the boat or meet with anyone but his agent in Lewiston. The *Teller* followed closely the OSL surveys down the Snake River.

8. OHS, Gill 1591 B.6 F11 and OHS, 299, Box 131, C&P Record, 38–57.

9. Tripartite Contract, 1883, numerous pages; Gill 1916, 90. The OT Annual Report, June 30, 1883, explained that $20,000 per mile in the original Tripartite Contract had to be modified because of higher construction costs. The report goes on to say that the NP and ORN were each responsible for half of the $30,000 per mile for the interest and the sinking fund. The bonds were to be "held in trust to assure the payment of the principal and interest of the bonds, and a harmonious joint ownership and other benefits" (OT 1883 Annual Report, 10–11).

10. Lewty 1987, 117; PG 7/14/83, 2 & 3; SFC, 7/25/82, 2.

11. MHS, 137. H.3.6.F; RW 11/25/82, 1117; PG 2/9/83 3.

12. MHS, 137.H.4.2.F.

13. OHS, 299, Box 131, C&P Corporate Records, 30–32; OHS, Gill 1591 B.6.F.11; NARA-P; MHS, 137.H.3.10.F.

14. WWU 4/7/83, 2; PG 6/22/83, 3; 6/29/83, 2.

15. MHS, 137.H.4.1.B & 137.H.4.2.F. See Appendix to this chapter for track laying record.

16. PG 7/6/83, 3; 7/13/83, 3; WWU 7/21/83 3, reported both of these stories.

17. PG 7/13/83, 3.

18. Jackson 2005, 80; PG 8/31/83, 3; communication from Edith Erickson, 3/6/2006.

19. PG 8/3/83, 3; 8/10/83, 3; 8/17/83, 3. The C&P Trustees on November 19 approved maps southward from Plainview Junction, 32.09 miles, approximately the distance of the line built to Moscow. OHS, 299, Box 131, C&P Record, 76–84; OHS, Gill 1591 B.6 F.11.

20. MHS, 137.H.3.7.B; PG 8/24/83, 3; WWU 9/29/83, 3.

21. MHS, 137.H.4.2.F; 137.H.4.1.B.

22. PG 10/19/83, 2, 3.

23. PG 11/16/83, 3; WWU 11/24/83, 3; WWU 12/8/83, 3; RW 11/24/83, 1214; OHS, 299, Box 85, Executive Committee Minutes, 126–30. Ceasing construction was also probably connected to the sale of the C&P to the ORN, see below.

24. PG 1/4/84, 1, 2, 3; 1/11/84, 1.

25. PG 1/18/84, 3; MHS, 137.H.4.5.B.

26. Gill 1914, 212; MHS, 137.H.4.2.F; PG 1/25/84, 3.

27. PG 2/1/84, 3.

28. Daggett 1908, 273–74; PG 8/3/83, 2; LT 8/23/83; PB 8/31/83, 1; NYT 9/21/83; Hedges 1930, 110. Hedges cites a letter from William Endicott Jr. to Villard, August 31, 1881, protesting the promise of large dividends on OT stock.

29. Baker, Letter Book 51; Box 84/f596.

30. The diary entries are very terse with little elaboration. The diary goes on: December 13: "All day again at O & T meeting [?]... Villard has feathered his nest." Billings was very concerned about the price of his OT stock. December 24: "the more I reflect, the more I believe Villard to be a scoundrel" (BFA).

31. Baker, Letter Book 51, 437–39, 475.

32. Baker, 8993 vol. 48.

33. OHS, 299, Box 85, ORN Executive Committee Minutes, 124–25, 134.

34. Villard's resignation letter to the ORN was dated 12/30/83 and was accepted by the ORN Directors on 1/2/1884. At the same meeting a 2 percent dividend was declared. OHS, 299, Box 85, Executive Committee Minutes, 132–33; OHS, Gill 1591.B6.F40; NYT 12/18/83, 2; Lewty 1987, 109–10; Asay 1991, 41.

35. NP Papers; NYT 1/5/84; Renz 1978, 3; RG 1/11/84, 38. A good account of "Henry Villard's Downfall" is chapter 11, Lewty 1987; also see Renz 1980, 102–07; Buss 1977, chapter VI; RG 1/4/84, 13; Buss 1977, 159.

36. NYT 3/21/84; Asay 1991, 42, 53; Renz 1978, 3, 4; NYT 1/18/84; Hedges 1930, 133; Renz 1980, 135. Wright had a large stake in the NP and had been president from April 1875 to May 1879, when Billings became president. For Harris' reputation see RG 1/25/84, 67–68 and Overton 1965, 161.

37. RG 1/4/84, 18; RA 1/10/84, 30.

38. MHS, 137.H.4.3.B; Gill, 1916, 89; NYT 1/11/84, also RG 1/18/84; OHS, 299, Exec. Com. Rec., 137.

39. OHS, 299, Box 85, Executive Committee Minutes, 135; RA 9/16/86, 516; Meinig 1968, 269 also 6/30/84 ORN Annual Report. At the time the NP sold the land to Villard it was verified to be 148,890.42 acres, see chapter I.

40. Baker Letter Book 51, 493–95.

41. Coolidge's letter of resignation 7/10/84 is found in E. Smith 1889b, 23–25.

42. Athearn 1976, 324; MHS, 137.I.19.2.F #18; Asay 1991, 41. Morison's findings are pertinent to subsequent events. He found the construction accounts showed $8,034,877 spent on the 211 miles from Portland to Wallula, $38,080 per mile, an extraordinary amount for the times. Asay 1991, 42, says the result of the report was the lowering of the construction transportation charge to a cent per ton mile and the firing of Chief Engineer Hans Thielsen effective March 14, 1884. Thus the ORN with its high costs on poor construction and inflated net earnings during construction would need to keep its rates as high as possible to pay for both dividends and financial charges.

43. NP Papers. The July 1, 1883, supplement was a traffic contract modifying the October 20, 1880, contract giving recognition that the NP was about to complete its transcontinental line.

44. MHS, 137.H.4.4.F; 137.I.19.6.F.

45. MHS, 137.I.19.6.F, 137.H.10.9.B & 137.H.4.3.B; Gill 1916, 5. Gill in another place records that trains were withdrawn February 4 on account of washouts and the submerging of the line by Lake Washtucna (OHS, Gill 1591 B6.F41), but that is probably an error. Oakes is in error as to the location of the flood. The town of Washtucna is 29.4 miles from the junction, but there is no lake there. Kahlotus is 15.5 miles from the junction; at about mile 16.5 is Lake Kahlotus, formerly named "Washtucna Lake." (A small pond or lake just east of Lake Kahlotus is still named "Washtucna Lake" according to a recent USGS Kahlotus map.) An NP map from 1882, updated to 1906, shows Washtucna Lake where the present Lake Kahlotus is located (MHS, 132.1.4.4). Available Oakes communications in March 1884 are all from St. Paul—he did not personally observe the flood that month, possibly never. Probably Oakes was told the flood was at Washtucna Lake, whether the mileage was included in the message is unknown, but if it was not, it is likely that Oakes found Washtucna on a distance schedule of some kind and assumed that Washtucna and the lake were in the same general area and so informed Harris. The Washtucna Coulee runs from about the town of Washtucna to Palouse Junction.

46. MHS, 137.H.10.9.B; 137.I.19.6.F.

47. MHS, 137.I.19.6.F & 137.H.10.9.B.

48. OHS, 299, Exec. Com. Rec., 145; ICC 1934, 271; Gill 1916, 6; MHS, 137.I.19.2.F #19; NYT 10/19/84, 2; ORN 1884 Annual Report; MHS, 137.H.4.10.F; NP Papers. See Appendix II for additional details on C&P financing.

49. MHS, 137.I.19.6.F; 137.H.4.4.F; 137.H.10.9.B.

50. PG 5/2/84, 3; 5/16/84, 3; WWU 5/3/84, 4 (the issue with opinion).

51. MHS, 137.H.4.4.F; NP 1887 Annual Report, 56.

52. PG 7/4/84, 3; 7/11/84, 3; 7/18/84, 3 & 8/1/84, 3; WWU 10/11/84, 1.

53. Quoted in Buss 1977, 89.

54. WWU 2/3/83, 2.

55. Gill 1914, 211.

56. OT vs. NP, affidavits 1887, 43. Frederick Billings' diary of the transfer period, while not mentioning the transfer, does give some support to the author's theory and Harris' testimony. Billings was concerned about the Cascade branch construction. On January 4 he mentions Villard's resignation but nothing about C&P. January 8: "Better make Harris Pres" (BFA).

57. Hedges 1930, 133.

58. MHS, 137.H.4.3.B & 137.I.19.6.F. "Constructive mileage" is the actually mileage multiplied by some number or some section is counted as a certain number of miles rather than its actual miles, e.g., the Snake River bridge. Constructive miles are used to achieve a certain return which is desired for whatever reason or to compensate for more than average construction and maintenance costs, e.g. a bridge. As we will see, manipulation of mileage plays a role in NP-GN-UP/ORN negotiations for nearly the next three decades.

59. MHS, 137.I.19.6.F; 137.H.10.9.B; NP Papers; NP 1933. According to Harris' deposition in 1887, see above, the NP agreed April 5, 1884, to abrogate the Tripartite Contract.

60. PG 11/28/84, 3; WWU 12/13/84, 3; PG 1/2/85, 3; WWU 1/31/85, 3.

61. MHS, 137 H.10.10.F; 137 H.4.6.F.

62. PG 6/26/85, 2, 3.

63. PG 10/30/85, 3; WWU 10/24/85, 3.

64. OHS, Gill 1591 B.6 F.11; MHS, 137 10.10.F; MHS, 137.H.4.7.B; OHS, 299, Box 131, C&P Record, 98–104.

65. MHS, 137.H.10.10.F; 137.H.4.10.F; OHS, 299, Box 141, C&P Journal, 35.

66. MHS, 137.H.10.10.F; NP Papers. The Oakes' letter and memorandum of May 24th have not been found.

67. MHS, 137.H.4.9.B.

68. PG 5/4/83, 3; 9/19/84; Lecompte 1988, 23.

69. PG 4/24/85, 2; 5/22/85, 4.

70. PG 7/3/85, 3; Lewty 1995, 22; Lecompte 1988, 23. The WWJ (10/29/85, 3) reported the subsidy as two dollars a ton.

71. PG 7/24/85, 3. In his report to the ICC Gill (1916, 5, 7) said that construction began August 18 by the ORN in the name of the C&P, but the contemporary newspaper reports indicate construction began before August 1. Most of the grading was done by the ORN. Freight was assessed at rate of 1 [cent] per ton mile on material and supplies. Wages were as follows: Extra Gang Foremen $75, $80 and $90; white laborers $1.75, 2.00, 2.25, 2.50; Chinese 80 cents; about half the force was Chinese. The tools were leased from the Oregon Construction Company (OHS, Gill 1591 B.6.F.41).

72. PG: 7/31/85, 3; 8/7/85, 3; 8/14/85, 3; 8/21/85, 2; 8/28/85, 3; WWDJ: 8/5/85, 3; 9/14/85, 3.

73. PG 9/18/85, 3; OHS, Gill 1591 B.4. F.1; Lecompte 1988, 24–25; PG 10/2/85, 3; Gill 1916, 5. The report to the ICC gives the opening date to Moscow as October 1, 1885.

74. WWDJ: 10/29/85, 3; 2/17/86, 3; 2/18/86, 3; 1/27/86, 2; PG 12/11/85, 3.

75. PG 10/9/85, 1 & 3; 10/16/85, 2; 10/30/85, 3. Apparently there was also a meeting on the 16th, see chapter III.

76. Lewty 1995, 30; PG 11/13/85, 3; 11/20/85, 3; 12/4/85, 3.

77. MHS, 137 H.4.7.B.

78. OHS, Gill 1591 B4 F3; MHS, 136 K.12.3.B; 137.H.4.8.F.

79. WWDJ 3/12/86, 3; PG: 3/19/86, 3; 4/16/86, 3.

80. OHS, 299, Exec. Com. Rec., 214; Gill 1916b.

81. OHS, Gill 1591 B.4.F.4.

82. WWDJ 5/19/86, 3. Concerning George W. Hunt see chapters IV, VIII, XIII.

83. PG 5/21/86, 3; WWDJ 5/22/86, 1; PG 5/28/86, 3. Gill 1916, 5, gives the beginning of construction as "June" 1886.

84. PG: 6/4/86, 2, 3; 6/11/86, 2, 3; 6/18/86, 1; WWU 6/19/86, 3.

85. PG 6/25/86, 3; WS May 1887, 125.

86. WWDJ 7/1/86, 3; PG 7/2/86, 3.

87. PG 7/23/86, 3; 7/30/86, 1; Lewty 1995, 31–32; PG 8/13/86 3.

88. PG 8/27/86, 3; 9/3/86, 3; 9/24/86, 3; WWDJ 9/24/86, 3.

89. Gill 1916, 5; OHS, Gill 1591 B.6.F.41; OHS, 299, Exec. Com. Rec., 334 & Gill 1916b.

90. WWDJ 11/23/86, 2; PG 12/3/86, 3.

III: The Northern Pacific Prepares to Return to the Palouse, 1885–86

1. PG 2/20/85, 4; SER: 7/1/85, 2; PG 10/16/85, 2; OHS, Gill 1591 B4.F1.

2. SR: 10/12/85, 2; 10/13/85, 2; 10/27/85, 2. The PG 10/30/85, 3, reported a meeting on the 24th at Palouse City (see chapter II on construction of the Farmington Branch).

3. MHS, 137.H.4.6F #3821.

4. SER: 10/27/85, 1; 10/28/85, 2; 10/31/85, 1; 10/30/85, 3; 11/11/85, 1, 2.

5. Lewty 1995, 27; WWDJ 11/2/85, 3, 1; PG 11/6/85, 3, 2; 11/20/85, 3; MHS, 137.H.4.6.F B/3632. There is also reference to the survey in MHS, 137.H.4.6.F C/3821.

6. SER 11/12/85, 3. Wright was the son of C. B. Wright, NP director and former president.

7. MHS, 137.H.4.7.B M/3800.

8. Philadelphia was the home of C. B. Wright Sr. It was filed in Washington Territory December 3, 1885. The formation of the EW was reported in PG 11/20/85, 2; WWU 11/21/85, 3.

9. From charter document and S&P 1916. Thomas H. Brents and Miles C. Moore of Walla Walla were said to be among the early supports of the railroad. E. J. Brickell of Spokane Falls and Watson C. Squire of Olympia were also later said to be incorporators (O&T vs. NP, affidavits 1887).

10. O&T vs. NP, affidavits 1887. Correspondence at the time, including Oakes' letter in the following text, support the claim that Harris did not direct the formation of the EW.

11. MHS, 137 H.4.7.B.

12. SMR 11/19/85, 4.

13. NP Papers also MHS 137 H.4.7.B; MHS, 137.10.10.F.

14. MHS, 137.H.4.7.B M/3630; MHS, 137.10.10.F.

15. MHS, 137.H.4.7.B M/3800; MHS, 137.10.10.F.

16. SMR 11/25/85, 1.

17. OHS, Gill 1591 B4 F1.

18. MHS, 137 H.4.7.B & 137 10.10.F. The matter of the Coeur d'Alene country is treated in chapter VII.

19. MHS, 137 H.4.7.B. I have substituted place names for range and township numbers in my paraphrase.

20. MHS, 137 10.10.F; 137 H.4.7.B.

21. MHS, 136 K.12.3.B & 137.H.4.8.F. Alexander's suggestions on lines from Oakesdale to Colfax and from Union Flat via Penawawa Canyon to the Snake River would be renewed periodically for the next 20 years, but were not built. His estimate: Marshall to Genesee via Palouse City and Pullman, 113 miles at $11,229 per mile, $1,268,877; Penawawa Division, 39 miles at $11,436, $446,000; Colfax branch, 20 miles, at $14,800, $296,000; total, 172 miles, $2,010,877.

22. NP Papers.

23. NP Papers; MHS 136, K.12.3.B. Subsequent communications indicate that the terminal point was section 26, Township 19 North, Range 44 East, at the junction of McCoy and Spring Creeks, about a mile south of Oakesdale and four miles north of Belmont.

24. SMR 2/21/86, 2.

25. MHS, 137.10.10.F; S&P charter. Oakes was NP vice president and general manager and was brought to the west coast by Villard. Wright senior was a Philadelphia financier and railroad promoter who was an early backer of the NP, on the NP board of directors beginning in 1870, was NP president 1875 to 1879, and had large investments in the Tacoma area and was a strong advocate for building the Cascade branch. Wright Jr., the son of C. B. Wright, was president of the Rio Grande and Eagle Pass RR, and was active in Pacific Northwest railroads. Bennett was a railroad construction contractor who did extensive work for the NP; his most famous accomplishment would be the construction of Stampede Tunnel on the NP Cascade branch. Cannon, born in 1837, was a founder of Spokane Falls, banker, merchant, lumber manufacturer, and at the time Mayor of Spokane Falls. He would shortly become the first president of the S&P. Mohr, born 1849 in Ohio and educated as a civil engineer in Germany, would become the Engineer in Charge of the S&P. Newbery was long active in railroad matters in the Spokane area. Jorgensen resided in Walla Walla.

26. MHS, 137.H.10.10.F.

27. Curtiss 2014, 35.

28. MHS, 136.K.12.3.B.

29. MHS, 137.H.19.1.B; S&P 1916. The dates of the meetings is uncertain. The file date is 3/8/86, but the document refers to the trustee meeting which did not occur until the 9th. The Trustees did not have a quorum on the 8th because of the absence of Jorgensen.

30. SMR 3/10/86, 2. The same story was in WWDJ 3/11/86, 3 and SFR 3/13/86, 1. A shorter version was in PG 3/19/86, 3.

31. MHS, 137.H.4.8.F. Emphasis in the original.

32. UMT, 128/370/512; PG 3/26/86, 2.

33. MHS, 137.H.10.10.F & 137.H.4.8.F. Anderson's comment that Mohr and Cannon thought they should be paid, because neither they, nor others, received stock in the company, may be touching on unhappiness regarding the NP gaining full control of the S&P. See terms of Newbery, Mohr, and Cannon agreement in next paragraph.

34. MHS, 136.K.12.3.B contains a copy of the agreement, but it is dated 10/26/86, which must be incorrect.

35. MHS, 137.H.4.8.F; 137.H.10.10.F.

36. On April 23 the *Gazette* carried a similar story from Palouse City, but it ended on an even more uncertain note. PG 3/19/86, 3; 4/23/86, 3.

37. MHS, 137.H.19.6.F; 137.10.10.F.

38. SMR 3/27/86, 2, 3.

39. MHS, 137.H.4.8.F; 137.H.10.10.F; 137.J.14.4.F.

40. MHS, 137.H.4.8.F; 137.H.10.10.F; 137.H.4.9.B.

41. Lease, 1886; NP Papers; NW Sept., 1886, 24; Lease, 1887. The NP board of directors, April 21, 1887, corrected what was called "a clerical error," changing the mileage of the S&P from 43 miles to about 110. A "Supplementary" lease dated June 1, 1887, corrected the error and was filed at Spokane and New York respectively on June 1 and 21, and at Colfax January 30, 1888.

42. O&T vs. NP, affidavits 1887; Mohr to Harris, 7/27/86, MHS, 137.H.4.10.F; MHS, 137.H.10.10.F; Mortgage, 1886; MHS, 137.H.19.1.B.

43. Stock Trust Agreement, 1886.

44. MHS, 137.H.10.10.F.

IV: Lease Negotiations, 1881–87

1. From newspaper clipping 10/12/81 in WSU, Cage 65, box 5; WWU 2/3/83, 2.

2. WWU 2/9/84, 2; PG 3/7/84, 2; 3/28/84, 2 & 3; 5/2/84, 3.

3. WWU 6/7/84, 2; 10/25/84, 4.

4. WWU 1/24/85, 2; 1/31/85, 4.

5. WWJ 6/11/85, 3.

6. MHS, 137.H.4.1.B; NP Papers.

7. NP Papers.

8. RG 2/15/84, 138; MHS, 137.H.4.3.B; 137.I.19.6.F.

9. Hedges 1930, 134; Asay 1991, 41; Oregonian assessment found in Lewty 1995, 1–2.

10. MHS, 137.H.10.10.B; PG 4/4/84, 4. The editorial appears in WWU 3/29/84, 4. That issue of the *Union* devotes a good deal of space to Portland control of the interior.

11. Gill 1916b; NP Papers; OHS, 299, Exec. Com. Rec. p. 154; MHS, 137.H.10.9.B.

12. Gill 1916b; Asay 1991, 42, 48; Klein 1987, 561.

13. PG 7/25/84, 1, 3; WWU 7/26/84, 2 (also found in PG 8/1/84, 2); WWU 8/9/84, 2.

14. MHS, 137.H.4.3.B; NP Paper. The action of board on the 9th was modified in the minutes of 9/17/84.

15. NP Papers & MHS, 137.H.4.5.B; Hedges, 1930, 135–36. See Hedges (pp. 136–42) for OT attempts to divert the NP from the Cascade Branch by involving it in stopping the Central Pacific's control of the Oregon and California and by stopping construction by securing an injunction against the Cascade Branch. The Teller was convinced that in addition to preventing the Cascade branch the joint lease was pushed by Portland to prevent the OSL from building down the Snake River to Lewiston, e.g. see LT 3/25/86, 2.

16. WWU 10/11/84, 3.

17. MHS, 137.H.10.9.B.

18. MHS, 137.H.4.5.B; 137.H.10.9.B; Agreement 1885.

19. Asay 1991, 42; Gill 1916, 47–48.

20. PG 12/5/84, 2; WWU 12/13/84, 4.

21. MHS, 137 H.10.10.F.

22. NP Papers; Lewty 1995, 1–3; MHS, 137.H.10.10.F.

23. Rigdon 1954, 1993.

24. NP Papers.

25. Rigdon 1954, 1991–92; MHS, 137.10.10.F; Asay 1991, 48; WWU 6/6/85, 4; 6/13/85, 3 (Philadelphia story also in PG 6/19/85, 2).

26. MHS, 137.H.10.10.F; NP Papers; WWU 6/27/85, 3; NYT 6/24/85, 2.

27. WWU 6/27/85, 4; WWJ 7/3/85, 2.

28. NYT 8/2/85, 2. A Harris letter to Wright August 8 suggests that he did not, at least "officially," become aware of Wright's circular until about the time of the *Times* report (MHS, 137.H.10.10.F).

29. NP Papers; MHS, 137.H.10.10.F; WWJ 7/29/85, 3.

30. NP Papers; WWJ 9/1/85; WWU 9/5/85. On July 20, 1885, Wright wrote Dorsey Baker asking for his proxy (Whitman 40/95/5).

31. NYT 9/16/85, 2; NP Papers; NYT 9/18/85; Hedges 1930, 140–41. Interestingly, Smith's letter is certified as a true copy of a resolution passed by the OT Executive Committee on September 18.

32. MHS, 137.H.10.10.F; Adams quoted in White 2011, 187; WS December 1885, 354; NW December 1885, 11.

33. Hedges 1930, 135; also RG 10/1/86, 681; SMR 10/15/86, 3. Klein (1987, 561) has a similar view on the ORN's "myopic policy on through business."

34. Hedges 1930, 142; WWU 1/30/86, 4; PG 2/12/86, 2; WWU 3/6/86, 3.

35. Athearn 1976, 325; Klein 1987, 561–63; Rigdon 1954, 1993–94; MHS, 137 H.10.10.F.

36. WWU 6/19/86, 3; PG 6/18/86, 1, 4.

37. WWJ 6/23/86, 3; PG 6/25/86, 2; WWU 6/26/86, 4; 7/3/86, 2 (the Gazette expressed a similar view, 7/9/86, 2).

38. Grenville Dodge Papers, Iowa State Archives.

39. Gill 1916b; NP Papers; RG 11/19/86, 804.

40. Klein 1987, 563–64; Asay 1991, 51; OHS, Gill 1591 B4 F5; MHS, 137 H.10.10.F (has a copy of the letter dated 11/7/86, but this must be an error).

41. OHS, Gill 1591 B4 F5.

42. MHS, 137 H.10.10F; OHS, Gill 1591 B4 F5; Rigdon 1954, 1999–2000.

43. NP Papers.

44. MHS, 137 H.10.10.F; 137.H.5.1.B.

45. NP Papers; MHS, 137.H.11.1.B. Placing operating costs into construction costs meant they went into the debt of the company and inflated the net revenues of the ORN, thereby justifying higher dividends. Harris wrote Cheney on the 14th enclosing Brookman's analysis, "by which you will see, he estimates a very much larger deficit than it has been supposed would accrue."

46. MHS, 137.H.11.1.B; OHS, Gill 1591, B4 F7; PG 1/14/87, 1; WS Feb., 1887, 184; WWJ 3/9/87, 2; SR 3/12/87, 3; 3/28/87, 1.

47. OHS, 299, Exec. Com. Rec., 323 & Gill 1916b; Rigdon 1954, 1995–97; WWJ 11/28/86, 3.

48. OHS, 299, Exec. Com. Rec., 276–92; OHS, Gill 1591 B4 F7. "Investigating Committee" refers to Congressional investigations of UP.

49. OHS, 299, Exec. Com. Rec., 276–92; ORN 1887, 2–3, 7, 10, 13–14, 15, 19; Lewty 1995, 5; Rigdon 1954, 97, 1998.

50. WWJ 4/26/87; PG 4/29/87, 3; Daggett 1908, 237; Asay 1991, 52. Given the ORN's directors' loyalty to Portland the UP's control of the navigation company was incomplete and would cause problems for the UP and the NP.

51. NP Annual Report, 1887, 56.

52. OWT 1916; Lewty 1995, Chap. 7; MHS, 137 H.10.10.F; 137.H.11.1.B; OHS, Gill 1591 4 F3. Adding to the ORN/UP concerns about an NP invasion south of the Snake River were surveys that NP Chief Engineer Adna Anderson in October 1886 ordered to be carried out by Spokane & Palouse Engineer in Charge Paul F. Mohr. On February 23, 1887, the NP engineer's office in St. Paul received Mohr's 29-page printed report of surveys and reconnaissances done in November. Included were numerous surveys south of the Snake River (MSH 137.H.10.10.F; 136.K.12.3.B).

53. MHS, 137.H.4.9.B.

V: The S&P Begins Construction: Marshall to Belmont, 1886–87

1. MHS, 136.K.12.3.B & 137.H.4.8.F. The contract was approved by the NP Executive Committee after May 20 (137.H.10.10.F).

2. PG 4/23/86, 4, 3; OHS, Gill 1591 B 4 F3. The valuation report to the ICC states that construction began April 9, 1886 (S&P 1916). Here after, unless otherwise cited, Mohr's correspondence is from UMT, 128/370/512.

3. MHS, 137.H.4.8.F; 137.H.10.10.F.

4. Many of the dates of construction progress come from the construction profiles found in MHS, 134.L.18.8.

5. PG 5/7/86, 3, 2; 5/14/86, 3; SR 5/22/86, 2.

6. PG 5/28/86, 2; Hitchman, 1985, 213.

7. MHS, 137.H.10.10.F.

8. SR 6/6/86, 2; also in PG 6/11/86, 4; SR 6/20/86, 3; Erickson 1983, 10.

9. MHS, 137.H.4.9.B; 137.H.10.10.F; 137.H.4.8.F.

10. MHS, 136.K.12.3.B.

11. UMT, 128/370/514. Except for NP #36 which was S&P #1 (SFR 8/1/4/87, 6, 3), the identity of the remaining three NP engines remains a mystery. They were sold back to the NP in 1887, see chapter VI.

12. MHS, 137.H.4.8.F #B/4583; 137.H.10.10.F, Vol. 37. See chapter appendix for a table of track laying completions.

13. Curtiss 2014, 362; PG 7/30/86, 3; 8/6/86, 3; WS, 258.

14. MHS, 137.H.4.8.F; 137.H.10.10.F.

15. SR 9/1/86, 6 (also 9/2/86, 5); MHS, 137.H.4.10.F; 137.H.10.10.F; NP 1933; S&P 1916. Anderson wrote 8/1/87 that it was turned over to operating department on 11/1/86 (MHS, 137.H.6.6.F #57).

16. MHS, 137.H.10.10.F & 137.H.4.9.B.

17. SR 9/29/86, 4.

18. PG 10/1/86, 1; WWU 10/9/86, 3).

19. MHS: 137.H.10.10.F; 137.J.14.4.F & 137.H.4.8.F; PG 12/17/86, 4.

20. UMT, 128/370/514.

21. MHS, 136.K.12.3.B.

22. MHS, 137.H.5.1.B; SR 2/4/87, 4; PG 2/18/87, 3; SR 8/27/87, 5; PG 3/2/88, 3; 3/16/88, 3.

23. MHS, 137.H.11.1.B; MHS, 137.H.4.10.F.

24. MHS, 137.H.6.6.F.

25. SR 8/21/87, 5.

26. MHS, 137.H.11.1.B.

VI: The S&P Extends to Genesee, 1886–88

1. MHS, 137.H.10.10.F; 137.H.4.9.B.

2. OHS, 299, Exec. Com. Rec., 229–30; MHS, 137.H.10.10.F; 137.H.4.8.F; PG: 12/3/86, 3.

3. UMT, 128/370/514.

4. PG 12/10/86, 3; 12/17/86, 3; UMT, 128/370/514; NP Papers.

5. UMT, 128/370/514.

6. OHS, Gill 1591 B.4.F.7; PG 1/21/87, 3.

7. UMT, 128/370/514. Mohr's letter contains details of alternative routes in the vicinity of Palouse City.

8. The route selected avoided a long and high trestle across the Palouse River at Palouse City that would be required by the alternative routes. MHS, 136.K.12.3.B; 137.H.5.2.F; 137.H.11.1.B.

9. PG: 2/11/87, 3; 2/18/87, 3; 3/4/87, 3; 3/11/87, 3.

10. Mohr 1887, 4–5, 10, 12, 17. See chapter IX for early Penawawa surveys.

11. OHS, Gill 1591 B.4.F.7. The route from Endicott toward the Coeur d'Alene district was built in 1888–89.

12. PG: 3/11/87, 3; 3/25/87, 3.

13. NP Papers; MHS, 137.H.4.10.F; 137.H.11.1.B; SR 3/19/87, 2; PG 3/25/87, 3.

14. MHS, 137.H.4.10.F; 137.H.11.1.B; 136.K.12.3.B.

15. PG 4/1/87, 3; 4/8/87, 3; WWJ 4/1/87, 1.

16. WWJ 4/13/87, 3; OHS, Gill 1591.B4.F7; LT 4/21/87, 3. The valuation report to the ICC stated that construction began on the extension to Genesee, May 1, 1887 (S&P 1916).

17. MHS, 137.H.5.2F? The Gazette reported (4/29/87, 3) that the ORN had been securing right-of-way from Pullman to Genesee and was dealing liberally with the owners.

18. MHS, 137.H.11.1.B; 137.H.6.6.F # 57.

19. PG 5/27/87, 3; MHS, 136.K.12.3.B; Construction Profile; PG 5/6/87, 3.

20. Unless otherwise noted the Spokane Falls investigation is from MHS, 137.H.6.6.F.

21. MHS, 137.H.5.2.F; 137.H.11.l.B.

22. MHS, 137.H.5.1.B.

23. The sources for this dispute are MHS, 137.H.5.2.F #M7049; 137.H.11.1.B; NP Papers.

24. MHS, 137.H.4.10.F; MHS, 137.H.5.2.F #M7049.

25. OHS, Gill 1591.B4.F8. It was reported that the Palouse Land Company had sold holdings from 140 to 640 acres in the vicinity of Diamond on the C&P/ORN northwest of Colfax (CG 1/15/04, 7). With the announcement that the Spokane & Inland Empire was to build south from Spokane, D. T. Ham, president of the Palouse Land company and for 21 years a dealer in Palouse realty, said: "This line is coming at a time when our company is about closed out of Palouse lands and it will necessitate a reinvestment if I am to get a direct benefit from it" (CG 12/16/04, 1). The author has found no evidence to support the allegations against the land company.

26. NP Papers.

27. MHS, 137.J.14.4.F; Lease 1887, 2.

28. PG 5/27/87, 3; 6/3/87, 3; 6/10/87, 3; 6/24/87, 3; SR 7/9/87, 3.

29. OHS, Gill 1591, B.4.F.8; 299 Exec. Com. Rec., 305–09; Gill 1591 B.6.F.11; Gill 1916b; also in OHS, Gill 1591 B.6.F.40; 299, Exec. Com. Rec. Vol. 2, 29. See chapter II for additional charter changes and activities of C&P. See chapter VIII for the other Potter recommendations.

30. NYT 5/27/87, 5; RA 6/3/87, 388; RG 6/3/87, 376; 7/15/87, 477; Renz 1980, 136–37; SR 6/9/87, 3; MHS, 137.H.11.1.B; Lewty 1995, 33. The deposed defendants in the suit testified, among other things, that the business and affairs of the S&P were not "managed, directed, shaped or controlled" by the NP; that the S&P constructed its own railroad to Belmont and was constructing its own railroad south of Belmont; that the financial and lease arrangements between the NP and S&P were similar to arrangements made earlier by the OT and NP with other branch line companies including the C&P; the only contract the NP entered into with the S&P was the lease; that the S&P was financed by its own bonds and not the NP; that Elijah Smith, President of the OT, was informed of everything done by the directors of the NP and no protest or objection was made; that the OT sought through its control of the ORN to divert traffic off the C&P to the ORN at Riparia and to the OSL and UP; and that the S&P will secure for the NP traffic west and east. With respect to the September stockholders election, from July 9, 1887, to the time of the election the OT was a holder of record of 6,120 shares of NP common stock and no preferred stock. At the election Elijah Smith was present and under a power of attorney for the OT voted 1,980 shares of NP preferred stock and 6,120 shares of common stock. The stockholders at that meeting unanimously adopted a resolution approving the directors having caused branch lines to be built by local corporations and leased, and authorized the directors to take such actions in the future (OT vs. NP, affidavits 1887). Most likely in June, Harris wrote Oakes in cipher advising him that in the OT suit, "Newbery, Cannon and Mohr have made affidavit that in the fall of 1886 you came to Spokane Falls…and while there they laid before you their plan for building the Spokane & Palouse, and explained it to you and represented to you that the road would traverse a rich agricultural country and bring large business to Northern Pacific, and they informed you that they were about to organize a corporation to build the road and invited you to become one of the incorporators,

and thereupon you consented to take an interest in the road. I inform you of this that you may have it in mind when making your affidavit" (MHS, 137.H.11.1.B). In this same time period there were on-going negotiations among the NP, UP and ORN over the disposition of the OWT; see chapters IV and VIII.

31. MHS, 137.H.11.1.B, 137.H.5.2.F, 137.H.4.10.F; 137.H.5.1.B. Vollmer was for many years an important banker, merchant, and entrepreneur in Lewiston and earlier had been an agent for Villard in Lewiston. Later he was the S&P's representative in Lewiston. "Mr. Vollmer had the original contract for building the road from Pasco to Spokane at the time the Northern Pacific first started construction work in that vicinity, and ever since then he has been heavily interested in the road. At one time during the 80s he held the balance of power, and New York financiers kept the wires to Lewiston hot trying to get Mr. Vollmer's proxy, his proxy resulted in the election Henry Villard as president of the road." This is part of a report that Vollmer had, after the stock distribution from the Northern Securities Co. settlement, sold his NP stock to buy NP 3 percent bonds. (SR 3/23/05, 14). His name will appear in later chapters. A biography is found in NI 1903, 137–38.

32. PG 7/8/87, 3.

33. MHS, 137.H.5.1.B; 137.H.11.1.B; 136.K.12.3.B also 137.H.5.2.F; 137.H.4.10.F; 137.H.5.1.B.

34. RG 7/15/87, 477; RA 7/15/87, 496; MHS, 137.H.11.1.B.

35. MHS, 137.H.11.1.B; 137.H.4.10.F.

36. PG 7/29/87, 3; WWJ 8/1/87, 3; Profile.

37. MHS, 137.H.5.1.B; 137.H.11.1.B. See appendix of this chapter for a record of track laying.

38. SR 8/6/87, 1; 8/14/87, 6. The record of the numbers of the other three engines has not been found.

39. PG: 8/19/87, 3; 9/2/87, 3; 9/9/87, 3.

40. PG 9/16/87, 3; Lewty 1995, 34; MHS, 136.K.12.3.B; Joint Facilities 1929; OHS, 299, Box 131, 151–59.

41. MHS, 137.H.11.1.B; 136.K.12.3.B; 137.H.5.1.B.

42. PG 9/23/87, 3; 9/30/87, 3; MHS, 132.I.8.8.F.

43. PG: 10/7/87, 3; 9/30/87, 3; 11/25/87, 3. See page 160 for a photograph of the water tank and pump house about a half mile south of the depot, rather than on Missouri Flat near the depot. A subsequent water station was near the depot.

44. Messages hereafter from Mohr, unless otherwise specified, are in MHS, 132.I.8.8.F.

45. MHS, 137.H.11.1.B; 137.H.4.10.F; RA 11/4/87, 778.

46. MHS, 137.H.5.1.B. An account of the Slaght land cases from 1887–1907 is in Beach 2013.

47. PG 11/18/87, 3; 11/25/87, 3; WWJ 12/19/87 3; PG 12/30/87, 3.

48. MHS, 137.H.5.2.F.

49. MHS, 137 H. 5.1.B; 137.H.11.1.B; 136.K.12.3.B.

50. The sources for the Genesee controversy are WWJ 7/30/87, 3; PG 8/5/87, 3; MHS, 137.H.5.3.B; 137.H.6.6.F #2383; 137.H.11.1.B; 132.I.8.8.F; and NP Papers.

51. MHS, 137.H.5.1.B; 137.H.11.1.B.

52. MHS, 137.H.5.2.F; 137.H.11.1.B; Lewty 1995, 34.

53. MHS, 137.H.11.1.B; 137.H.5.1.B; 137.H.5.3.B; PG 1/13/88, 3.

54. MHS, 137.H.11.1.B; 137.H.5.2.F; 137.H.5.3.B.

55. MHS, 137.H.11.1.B; 137.H.5.3.B.

56. MHS, 137.H.11.1.B; 137 H.5.2.F.

57. MHS, 137.H.5.3.B; 137.H.6.6.F #2383 Special Papers #75. The value of the lots was Garfield $5000; Palouse City $15,000; Four Mile $500; Whelan $500; Pullman $5000; Staley $500; Colton $1500; Uniontown $1500; and Genesee $10,000.

58. MHS, 137.H.5.2.F; 137.H.11.1.B.

59. Unless otherwise indicated all Wrightman correspondence is found at UMT, 128/370/513.

60. MHS, 137.H.5.2.F; H.11.1.B.

61. PG 3/16/88, 3; WWJ 3/20/88, 3.

62. WS 4/88, 221; LT 5/3/88, 1; SR 3/30/88, 4.

63. MHS, 137.H.5.2.F; 137.H.11.1.B; SR 3/30/88, 3; 137.H.5.3.B; 137.J.14.4.F.

64. SR 5/17/88, 3; PG 5/11/88, 2.

65. MHS, 136.K.12.3.B; 137.H.19.1.B.

66. PG 6/1/88, 3; 6/15/88, 3; WWU 6/16/88, 1.

67. MHS, 137.H.11.1.B; NP Papers.

68. NP Annual Report 1888, 66.

69. Reproduction of the original order in *The Spokane Star News*, May 21, 1875 1. Thanks to Bob West for sending the clipping. The engine number is not included in the order nor in the newspaper. The order with additional information also in SR 7/10/10, 7D. Engineer Bowman began engineer service on the NP, October 13, 1883, and continued on the Palouse line until 1906; in 1910 he was still an NP engineer. Conductor Garvin was in 1910 the general yardmaster at Spokane.

70. A scheduled train ran between Marshall Jct. and Belmont and several scheduled trains between Marshall Jct. and Spokane Falls. "12" means "do you understand" or "advise that you understand" and "13" means "I understand" (personal communications 5/14 & 17/2014 from Dave Sprau, former NP dispatcher). "FPW" is probably the initials of the Idaho Division Superintendent, F. P. Weymouth, at Sprague.

71. SMR 7/11/88, 4.

72. WWU 8/25/88, 3; RR 9/22/88, 551.

73. Oakesdale Breeze 9/20/88; LT 10/4/88, 4; PG 10/12/88, 3; SR 10/24/88, 3; 11/8/88, 2; PG 11/9/88, 3; 12/14/88, 3.

74. The S&P Trustees meeting in Tacoma 4/23/92 stated that J. W. Kendrick was appointed chief engineer, 12/3/88, not re-elected by oversight. "[H]ereby is elected Chief Engineer of the S&P Ry Co., to serve until his successor be appointed...that all acts heretofore performed and done by the said J. W. Kendrick, acting as Chief Engineer, of the Company, by and the same are hereby ratified and confirmed." C. H. Prescott who had been ORN general manager became NP second vice president in 1888. MHS, 137.H.11.1.B; 137.J.14.4.F; Renz 1978, 4.

75. PH 12/1/88, 1; SR 12/28/88, 3.

76. PH 3/2/89, 2; Weis 1994, 72.

VII: ORN Projection and Expansion in the Palouse, 1884–90

1. This account of the WI is in the context of its relationship to the Palouse; for a more extended accounts of the railroads in the Coeur d'Alene mining district, see Lewty 1995, chapters 9 & 10 and Wood 1983.

2. MHS, 137.H.4.3.B.

3. MHS, 137 H.4.7.B; OHS, Gill 1591 B4 F1.

4. MHS, 137 H.4.7.B. D. P. Thompson was referred to as president of the Oregon Construction Co. and as president of The Commercial National Bank of Portland. MHS, 137 10.10.F and also OHS, Gill 1519 B.4 F.1; MHS, 137 H.4.7.B.

5. MHS, 137 H.4.7.B.

6. OHS, Gill 1591; B.4 F1, F3, F4; MHS, 137 H.4.8.F.

7. UMT, 128/370/512; MHS, 137.H.6.6.F; PG 6/25/86, 4. "Break bulk" refers to transferring freight from one form of transportation or container in order for the freight to proceed to its destination.

8. MHS, 137.H.6.6.F; 137 H.4.9.B; UMT, 128/370/512. Corbin was a Montana and later Spokane entrepreneur (Fahey 1965, 4).

9. PG 7/9/86, 2.

10. Gill 1914, 214.

11. Fahey 1965, 29–57; CRN 1916; Wood 1983, 183.

12. MHS, 137.H.6.6.F.

13. MHS, 137.H.4.8.F; 137 H.4.10.F; 137.H.10.10.F.

14. The SFI was originally incorporated in Montana as the Spokane and Idaho (SR 10/28/86, 6). The company was leased to the NP October 1, 1887. Newbery on a S&P letterhead, April 18, 1887, informed Hauser that he had been elected trustee and vice president of the SFI. NP Papers; PG 9/3/86, 3; NP, 1933; Fahey 1965, 33–56; Wood 1983, 183.

15. OHS, Gill 1591, B4 F5; PG 9/3/86, 3; WWU 10/16/86, 3.

16. OHS, Gill 1519 B4 F5.

17. UMT, 128/370/514.

18. OHS, Gill 1591 B4 F5.

19. Hill Library, R-10, 207–8. The "Manitoba" was leased to the Great Northern Railway January 31, 1890 (Hidy 2004, 73). OHS, Gill 1591 B4 F7; NW May 1887, 26.

20. UMT, 128/370/514; OHS, Gill 1591 B.4.F.7.

21. MHS, 137.H.5.2.F; UMT, 128/369/12; S&P 1916.

22. MHS, 137 H.5.1.B; 137 H.11.1.B; OHS, Gill 1591 B.4.F.8; MHS, 137.H.5.2.F. No evidence in NP sources has been found for a Rosalia to Coeur d'Alene route. Gill claims that the ORN, anticipating that the NP would join the OSL lease of the ORN, made no move to construct extensions in eastern Washington and northern Idaho, but Elijah Smith was annoyed that the NP exercised no such restrain and in June 1887, Truax was directed to locate a line in the Coeur d'Alene area and to start grading at strategic points (Gill 1914, 216). Perhaps people on the scene jumped the gun and began grading earlier than June.

23. WSU, Van Arsdol, Cage 103, 1.

24. Lewty 1995, 108.

25. WWJ 7/19/87, 1; 8/6/87, 1; PG 8/5/87, 3; WSU Cage 103, box 1; SR 8/20/87, 6; WWJ 9/13/87, 1; LT 9/22/87, 2.

26. OHS, 299, Exec. Com. Rec., 334–79. The joint lease negotiations are examined in chapter VIII.

27. Wood 1983, 27–28, 183, 184; OHS, Gill 1591 B.6.F.40.

28. NP 1933; NP Papers; MHS, 137.H.11.1B; Fahey 1965, 39–57; Wood, 1983, 183–84; OHS, Gill 1591 B4 F14. Wood gives the date of the lease as September 14, 1888.

29. RA 6/14/89; OHS, Gill 1591 B4 F15; Gill 1916, 85, 86.

30. Spokane Falls was incorporated in 1881 and renamed Spokane in 1891 (Phillips 1971, 134–35).

31. SR 12/15/86, 4; PG 5/4/88, 3; MHS, 137.H.5.3.B; 137.H.11.1.B; Hedges 1930, 174–75. See chapter VIII for more details.

32. Gill 1916b; PG 12/21/88, 2; OHS, Gill 1591 B6.F.40, 41; PG 6/8/88, 3; 8/17/88, 3; Lewty 1995, 125.

33. SR 11/10/88, 2; WS May 1889, 279, also PG 5/3/89, 3; Lewty 1995, 126; SR 5/4/89, 3; PG 6/28/89, 3; SR 5/11/89, 1; RA 6/14/89; SR 9/11/89, 5. Curtiss 2014, 287, has the date of incorporation as April 24, 1889.

34. OHS, Gill 1591 B4 F15; Lewty 1995, 126; SR 10/5/89, 3.

35. The ORN Board of Directors declared January 8, 1890, that the WI lines from Farmington to Spokane Fall, 59.9 miles, and from Tekoa to St. Joe, Idaho, 23 miles, and the proposed extension to Mullan, 65 miles, were constructed by the ORN at its expense under the Oregon Short Line lease of January 1, 1887, as modified November 7, 1889. The WI was operated under lease by the OSL from December 15, 1888 to July 31, 1889, and by successor Oregon Short Line & Utah Northern to October 12, 1893; operated by receivers of the UP October 13, 1893 to July 3, 1894 and by E. McNeill ORN Receiver July 4, 1894 to August 17, 1896. The Reorganization Committee said the mortgaged debt of the WI was $4,447,500. It was deeded July 18, 1896, to the Purchasing Committee of the Reorganization Committee of Oregon Railway and Navigation Co.; deeded to the Oregon Railroad and Navigation Company August 17, 1896; and deeded to Oregon-Washington Railroad & Navigation Company December 23, 1910. OHS, Gill 1591 B.6.F.40; Gill 1916, 85, 86; ORN Reorganization.

36. Gill 1916, 40; Meinig 1968, 473.

37. See note 12, chapter I, regarding place names at Texas Ferry (aka South Riparia) and Riparia (aka North Texas Ferry).

38. WWU 10/24/85, 3; PG 10/30/85, 3; WWJ 11/9/85, 3.

39. Gill 1916b; OHS, 299, Exec. Com. Rec., 229–30; PG 12/17/86, 3.

40. PG 1/14/87, 1; WWJ 1/18/87, 3; 3/18/87, 3.

41. OHS, Gill 1591, B.4.F.8; OHS, 299 Exec. Com. Rec., 305–309; OHS, Gill 1591 B.6.F.40; PG 7/1/87, 3; WWU 9/24/87, 2; Lewty 1995, 9.

42. OHS, 299, Exec. Com. Rec. Vol. 2, 20–21; OHS 1591.B6.F40.

43. MHS, 137.H.5.2.F; 137.H.11.1.B.

44. OHS, Gill 1591.B.4.F11; PG 4/20/88, 3; WWU 4/21/88, 3; Gill 1914, 218.

45. OHS, 299, Exec. Com. Rec. Vol. 2, 20–21; HS Gill 1591 B.6.F.40; Lewty 1995, 124.

46. PG 6/1/88, 3; 6/8/88, 2, 3; 6/22/88, 3; WWU 6/2/88, 3; 6/9/88, 3; 6/23/88, 3.

47. PG 7/27/88, 3; WWU 7/28/88, 3; OHS, Gill 1591 B.6.F 40.

48. PG 8/10/88, 3; WWU 8/18/88, 3; 8/25/88, 3; Lewty 1995, 12; PG 8/31/88, 3.

49. Gill 1916, 47 & 48; Gill 1914, 219; Lewty 1995, 122; Gill 1916b. Probably not included in the September 30 expenditure is $100,901 paid by the ORN to the Oregon & Transcontinental Co. for grading done by the O&T prior to the completion of the C&P (ICC 1934, 271). The February estimated cost for the permanent Riparia bridge was $387,289 (OHS, 299, Exec. Com. Rec. Vol. 2, 20–21, 29). The bridge was not completed before September 30; how much of the bridge cost was included on that date is unknown.

50. PG 1/11/89, 3; 1/25/89, 3; SR 2/21/89, 1; WWU 2/23/89, 3.

51. Lewty 1995, 124; PG 1/18/89, 3; 2/15/89, 2; 5/3/89, 2; 6/21/89, 2.

52. PG 4/12/89, 3; Lewty 1995, 123; Asay 1991, 61.

53. Lewty 1995, 124; SR 12/27/89, 3; OHS, Gill 1591 B4 F15; OHS, 299, B85; OHS, Gill 1591 B.6.F.40; UP 1977; Gill 1916, 45. The only other line built by the ORE was from La Grande to Elgin, Oregon, in 1890, 20.89 miles. The ORE had an aggregated indebtedness to the ORN for construction of $1,753,608 (ICC 1934, 268).

54. RG 5/28/09, 1145; SR 10/19/10, 8.

VIII: The Joint Lease and the Arbitration Contract Negotiations, 1887–89

1. MHS, 137.H.11.1.B.

2. NYT 8/28/87, 2; WWU 9/3/87, 4; WWJ 9/8/87, 2; 9/19/87, 4; PG 9/23/87, 2; WWJ 10/10/87, 4; 11/14/87, 2.

3. MHS, 137.H.11.1.B; NP Papers—report of committee for conferring with UP, July 21, 1887.

4. OHS, Gill 1591, B.4.F.8; OHS, 299 Exec. Com. Rec., 305–09; also in OHS, Gill 1591 B.6.F.40.

5. Gill 1914, 216; Asay 1991, 53.

6. WWJ 6/7/87, 3; 8/3/87, 1; 8/16/, 1; 9/5/87, 2; Hedges 1930, 147–50; Renz 1980, 137; Klein 1987, 568; Gill 1914, 216; Asay 1991, 53. Also see *New York Tribune* 5/20/89 interview with Villard.

7. Adams to Colgate Hoyt, 8/19/87 in Rigdon 1954, 2002–03.

8. WWU 9/3/87, 2; WWJ 9/20/87, 3.

9. NW 10/87, 28; NYT 9/16/87, 2; Lewty 1995, 6; PG 9/23/87, 2; WWJ 9/23/87, 4; PG 9/30/07, 3; Hedges 1930, 150–51; Buss 1977, 179ff; Villard 1904, 324, 327–328.

10. OHS, Gill 1591 B4 F9; NP Papers; WWU 10/8/87, 3; PG 10/7/87, 3; LT 10/13/87, 4.

11. Rigdon 1954, 2003–05; Klein 1987, 569.

12. NP Papers; OHS, Gill 1591 B4 F9.

13. MHS, 137.H.11.1.B.

14. WWJ 12/1/87, 3; Rigdon 1954, 2008–09; MHS, 137.H.11.1.B; NP Papers.

15. Rigdon 1954, 2008–09; Hedges 1930, 156–58.

16. Gill 1916b; Rigdon 1954, 2009–2010.

17. NP Papers. LT 4/12/88, 2, contains provisions of the lease related to division of the territory.

18. Rigdon 1954, 98, 2010.

19. SR 1/25/88, 2; WWJ 2/16/88, 2; WWU 2/18/88, 2, 3; LT 2/23/88, 2. Also see Hedges 1930, 160.

20. Rigdon 1954, 2011–2013; Baker 8993/54/366; Klein 1987, 570.

21. The NP directors February 16 revised the amount for the WI to $70,000. NP Papers; OHS, 299, Exec. Com. Rec. Vol. 1, 334–383 & Vol. 2, 10; Gill 1914, 218.

22. Rigdon 1954, 2014–17.

23. OHS, 299, Exec. Com. Rec. Vol. 2, pp. 2–7, 10; Rigdon 1954, 2017–19, 2013; Klein 1987, 570.

24. OHS, Gill 1591.B4.F11.

25. Rigdon 1954, 2019–20; Klein 1987, 570 & Gill 1914, 220½.

26. RG 3/9/88, 163, 157–58.

27. Hedges 1930, 166–67. Allen C. Mason of Tacoma in an advertisement in Walla Walla *Union Weekly* (7/7/88, 1) claimed that the costs from Tacoma to the Pacific per vessel were $2,000 to $4,000 less than from Portland to the Pacific and this resulted in wheat being worth three to five cents more per bushel at Tacoma than at Portland. According to *The Northwest Magazine* (March 1888, 21) the *Oregonian* stated the difference was $4,000.

28. Hedges 1930, 167–71; Rigdon 1954, 2021. Hedges drew his account of the meetings from "Report of Committee," *Oregonian*, April 10, 1888. There is a lengthy earlier account of the Oregon delegation taken from the *Oregonian* in the Walla Walla *Weekly Union* (3/31/88, 2).

29. NP Papers.

30. OHS, Gill 1591.B4.F11; Klein 1987, 571.

31. MHS, 137.H.5.3.B; WWU 3/31/88, 2 (This issue is a particularly rich with articles on the joint lease and development of the OWT).

32. WWU 3/24/88, 2; 4/14/88, 3; NP 1933; WWJ 6/2/88, 3; SFMR 5/13/88, 4; SR 5/22/88, 3.

33. Rigdon 1954, 2021–22; MHS, 137.H.5.3B.

34. NP Papers; Hedges 1930, 172–73; LT 5/3/88, 4.

35. MHS, 137.H.5.3.B; NP Papers; 137.H.11.1.B; Hedges 1930, 174–75; Rigdon 1954, 2022; OHS, 299, Exec. Com. Rec. Vol. 2, 36; OHS 1591.B6.F40. See chapter VII for an account of the ORN's proposed Palouse lines.

36. Rigdon 1954, 2025–27; Hedges 1930, 176–78, 182 note 89; Klein 1987, 571–72; Klein nd, 100; Villard 1904, 329; WWU 6/2/88, 3.

37. NP 1933; Shipments were calculated from Hedges 1930, 143; Ficken 2002, 2.

38. MHS, 137.H.11.1.B; 137.H.5.3.B; NP Papers (June 21, 1888). Rigdon 1954, 98, attributes the withdrawal of the UP from the joint lease to the refusal by the NP to recognize the understanding allowing the UP to build down the Snake River to Lewiston.

39. WS June, 1888, 343.

40. Klein 1987, 571–72; Rigdon 1954, 2026; Hedges 1930, 176–78; NW July, 1888, 21; WWU 6/30/88, 4.

41. SR 7/28/88, 1; 7/29/88, 4; PG 8/3/88. The Walla Walla *Weekly Union* (8/4/88, 3 & 4) reported the suit and commented that "several New York stock gamblers" had sued and "These stock gamblers should go hang themselves. By the way, when did a New York City judge obtain jurisdiction of affairs in Washington Territory."

42. Rigdon 1954, 2027–36; Hedges 1930, 178–81; Klein 1987, 572–73; SFMR 6/19/88, 1; & Klein nd., 100. Bancroft writing in 1888 and believing that the joint lease had gone into effect July 1, 1888, wrote: "It is not clear to me what was Villard's motive for wishing to join in the U. P.'s lease. The motive of that company, which the Central Pacific had kept out of California, in desiring to come to the Pacific coast is easy to comprehend. The O. R. & N. erred, in my judgment, in yielding the control of the best railroad property on the northwest coast to a company with the standing of the U. P. The Southern Pacific will show its hand in competition soon or late, and will build more feeders than the U. P., while the N. P., on the other side will make the most of its reserve rights, thus narrowing down the territory of the leased road" (Bancroft 1888, 749, n. 6).

43. Hedges 1930, 181–82; see WWWU 6/23/88, 3 for officers of and directors of ORN, OT, and OI.

44. MHS, 137.H.11.1.B; NP Papers.

45. Rigdon 1954, 2037–39.

46. NP Papers; RR 8/25/88, 492; PG 8/10/88, 2; RR 9/8/88, 520.

47. RR 9/22/88, 551; C&F Vol. XLVII, 690 & 745; Rigdon 1954, 2023–25; Decision of Ives et al. vs. Elijah Smith et al. & NYT 7/28/88, 2.

48. NYT 9/21/88, 2; NP Papers; PG 9/28/88, 2.

49. Rigdon 1954, 2039–40; Hedges 1930, 183–4; Klein 1987, 574.

50. Rigdon 1954, 2040–41; NP Papers.

51. Klein 1987, 574; Klein nd, 101.

52. PG 12/14/88, 2; Lewty 1995, 14; C&F January 1889 Vol. 48; RR 12/15/88, 717; NP Papers; MHS, 137.H.11.1.B; NYT 2/22/89, 2. Lewty is correct in his view that the arbitration agreement was an attempt by Villard to rescue the OT from its debt; see below.

53. Hedges 1930, 185–88; a report of the details of the contract appeared SR 2/28/89, 3 & WWU 3/2/89, 2; C&F May 25, 1889, 700.

54. Hedges 1930, 188–90; C&F May 25, 1889, 700–701.

55. MHS, 137.H.11.1.B; Klein 1987, 575.

56. PH3/2/89, 3; WWU 3/9/89, 4; LT 3/14/89, 2.

57. Rigdon 1954, 2042–43. A 5 percent rental would strengthen UP finances, which was a potential threat to the NP, and reduce OT income.

58. NYT 4/8/89, 2; 5/16/89, 2.

59. ISHS box 70.

60. Rigdon 1954, 2044–47; C&F May 25, 1889, 698, 702; Hedges 1930, 190–91. The C&F copy is in Villard's Second Affidavit in the Elijah Smith suit (below). Neither the Rigdon nor the C&F copies are a complete copy of the text of the letter.

61. Rigdon 1954, 2049–50, emphasis in the original.

62. NP Papers; MHS, 137.H.11.1.B.

63. Rigdon 1954, 2047–48; Klein 1987, 576.

64. NP Papers; PH 5/11/89, 3. There is no indication in the minutes that the Villard substitute was voted upon.

65. Rigdon 1954, 2050–51; Lewty 1995, 15; Hedges 1930, 194; ISHS box 70; C&F May 25, 1889, 695; Gill 1914, 221, 222.

66. ISHS boxes 184, 70.

67. C&F 5/18/89, 663; RA 5/17/89, 324; C&F 5/25/89, 696–700 (the issue has a lengthy report on the case, pp. 693–702, which contains an account of Villard's interpretation of events preceding the suit—the report also appeared in NYT 5/22/89, 2). Hedges 1930, 193ff has an account of the struggle to control the OT.

68. Hedges 1930, 196–199; MHS, 137.H.11.1.B.

69. ISHS box 70.

70. ISHS box 70; Rigdon 1954, 2057–58. The by-laws of the ORN, as amended in 1884, allowed a minority of the stock to elect.

71. NYT 5/21/89, 5. Also in *New York Tribune*, May 20, 1889.

72. E. Smith 1889a, 3, 4, 5–6, 10; E. Smith 1889b, 1–2. See chapter II for Smith's statements on Villard's resignation in 1883 and the condition of the OT at that time.

73. Rigdon 1954, 2061, 2067–68; MHS, 137.H.11.1.B.

74. Rigdon 1954, 2053; Villard 1904, 332; Lewty 1995, 17; NYT 5/19/89, 5 also has an account of events up to that point.

75. C&F 6/1/89, 730; Rigdon, 2059.

76. ISHS box 70; Rigdon 1954, 2054–57; Hedges 1930, 199–200.

77. ISHS box 70; Rigdon 1954, 2059–61.

78. Hedges 1930, 201 (the *Oregonian* quotation is also on this page); Klein 1987, 576–79 has an account of the negotiations; SR 6/14/89, 3, 1.

79. Rigdon 1954, 2062–64; ISHS box 70; NYT 6/18/89, 2; C&F 6/22/89, 828.

80. Rigdon 1954, 2065–67; Hedges 1930, 201–02; SR 6/20/89, 5.

81. Hedges 1930, 202–03, *Oregonian* 6/15/89. Also see LT 6/20/89, 2 for text of speech and questions.

82. MCL, 0-385 S64t.

83. OHS, Gill 1591, B6, F40; Asay 1991, 56.

84. RG 7/5/89, 446.

85. ISHS box 70.

86. ISHS boxes 184 & 70.

87. Rigdon 1954, 2068–70. Adam's admission of failing to abide by the decision of the UP's in a traffic matter and the UP's aggression in Puget Sound traffic may be related to the sale of through tickets to Puget Sound noted in this chapter above.

88. Rigdon 1954, 2070–71; ISHS box 70.

89. NYT 9/20/89, 2; 10/18/89, 5; 6/15/94, 2; SR 10/18/89, 1; Renz 1980, 167.

90. NP Annual Report, 1889, 24.

91. Gill 1914, 224 & 225.

92. Rigdon 1954, 99, 567; RA 11/8/89, 744; UP 1889, 12, 11; Daggett 1908, 237–38; Gill, 1916, 51, 52, 114; WWS 12/29/90, 2. The OSL&UN was an August 1, 1889, consolidation of the OSL with several other UP companies. The wheat rate issue is found in Oakes to Hannaford and Oakes to Adams 11/17 & 18/1890 (MHS, 137.H.11.2.F).

93. Hedges 1930, 210–11; Villard 1904, 335–36. While the NP was never Villard's most favored railroad, he had a great influence on the development and financial affairs of the NP. In the writer's opinion the NP would have been better off without him. Prior to Villard the NP had secured the financial backing necessary for constructing the transcontinental line without the complexities of Villard's financial and operational schemes, which were directed at protecting the ORN, not the wellbeing of the NP. The transcontinental line would have been built, perhaps more slowly, but probably better and at less cost. His initial strategy of railroad consolidation in the Pacific Northwest failed because of poor management, particularly financial which was supposedly

his strength. It also failed because it rested largely on his personal involvement rather than on institutional ties which might have outlasted him. His later attempts to bring about consolidation, probably doomed to failure from the beginning, stood no chance of success after he had antagonized the other major players. In many respects he was a "great" man, but "greatness" did the NP little good. The trackage agreement which Harris and Adams worked on might have succeeded if Villard had not been trying to protect the OT. But Hedges may be correct, it was not possible to reach any agreement. I wonder where Hedges saw the "grass-covered railway tracks," perhaps west end of the C&P? Villard's influence over the affairs of the NP diminished as his North American Company, successor to the OT, reduced its stock holdings in the NP from about 40 percent of the stock to probably less than 20 percent in 1891 (WWS 7/9/91, 2).

94. Rigdon 1954, 100.

95. WS 3/15/1890, 344–45 provides a contemporary view of the situation.

IX: Early Projections of the S&P to Colfax and Penawawa, 1885–92

1. PG 7/17/85, 3; MHS, 137.H.11.1.B; UMT 128/370/514.

2. MHS, 138.E.2.4, map 66. The title of the map is, "Map Showing Reconnaisance [sic] made by O. Wolford C. E. in Eastern Washington T. in November 1885." MHS, 136 K.12.3.B; 137.H.4.8.F; PG 7/9/86, 2; MHS, 137.H.4.9.B; PG 7/30/86, 3; 8/6/86, 3.

3. MHS, 137.H.10.10.F & 137.H.4.9.B. See chapter IV for a fuller report of the correspondence; UMT 128/370/514; Lewty 1995, 32.

4. Mohr 1887, 4–5, 10, 12, 17. The 29.75 miles along the Snake River he estimated at $16,000 per mile, the 35 miles from the foot of Penawawa to S&P at $14,000.

5. MHS, 137.H.11.1.B; 137.H.5.1.B; NP Annual Report 1887, 67.

6. SR 2/14/89, 1; PG 2/15/89, 3; 3/8/89, 3; SR 6/25/89, 1; PG 8/16/89, 3; 9/6/89, 3; 12/6/89, 3; SR 12/11/89, 5; PG 12/13/89, 2, 3; 12/20/89, 3.

7. WWU 7/6/89, 1; 11/23/89, 3.

8. WSU cage 103, box 1; MHS, 136.K.13.1.B; NARA-P. On August 20, 1891, McHenry wrote Kendrick that he had found an estimate prepared by Van Arsdol and revised by Huson: "Oakesdale to Colfax; Main Line 25 miles; sidings 2.2 miles; total 27.2 miles. Total cost to complete, $279,782, or an average per mile of $15,191." He thought there was an underestimate on earth work by 20 percent (MHS, 137.H.5.8.F).

9. The small amount of increase in production is trifling; it does not make a compelling case for construction unless the NP would receive a large share of the total production. This the farmers imply in their desire to obtain nearer transportation: "we have been compelled to haul our grain to the Snake River over very steep and rocky roads or haul a greater distance north and east to the [ORN] road." MHS, 137.H.5.5.B; 137.H.5.7.B.

10. WSU cage 103, box 1; Reference to the maps and profile are found in letter Division Engineer to McHenry, 1/10/1899 and to Van Arsdol 1/13/99 (UMT 128/290/3). MHS, 137.H.5.5.B, 137.J.14.4.F; 137.H.11.2.F.

11. PG 5/16/90, 2, 3; WS 5/10/90, 598; PG 5/30/90, 2; 6/6/90, 3.

12. MHS, 137.H.5.5.B; 137.H.5.6.F.

13. PG 1/23/91, 2.

14. Curtiss 2014, 1; PH 11/4/38 (in Dubaur Scrapbooks); WSU Cage 103, 1.

15. MHS, 137.H.5.8.F.

16. SR 3/15/92, 3; PG 3/18/92, 1, 6; 3/25/92, 1; SR 3/27/92, 6; PG 4/1/92, 1; WSU Cage 103, 1.

17. WSU Cage 103, 1; PH 11/4/38 (in Dubaur Scrapbooks).

18. S&P 1916, 372.

X: The S&P and ORN Consider Routes to Lewiston, 1885–92

1. SR 1/23/89, 4; PG: 2/1/89, 3; 3/15/89, 3; 2/15/89, 2; 3/8/89, 3.

2. MHS, 137.H.11.1.B; Joint Facilities 1929, 8-A-162; PG: 4/18/90, 3; 4/25/90, 2; 6/27/90, 5; 3/1/89, 3; SR 5/4/89, 3; PG: 6/21/89, 2; 8/16/89, 3; 8/23/89, 2; 11/22/89, 3; 12/6/89, 3; 12/20/89, 3; 2/22/89 3.

3. Provisional Contract, 1889.

4. PG 7/5/89, 3; 8/6/89, 3.

5. NP Annual Report, 1889, 29–30.

6. PG 12/13/89, 2; SR 12/31/89, 6; PG 1/10/90, 3.

7. MHS, 137.H.11.1.B.

8. LT 6/16/87, 1.

9. PG 5/27/87, 3; OHS, Gill 1591 B.6.F.11 and charter; NARA-P.

10. MHS, 137.H.5.3.B; 137.H.11.1.B.

11. WWU 4/7/88, 1; MHS, 137.H.5.2.F; 137.H.11.1.B; 137.H.4.10.F.

12. MHS, 132.I.5.5 box 4, map 313–15.

13. UMT 128/370/513. This reference continues for the Wightman correspondence until the end of 1888. Details of surveys are in the reference.

14. WWU 8/11/88, 3.

15. LT 9/13/88, 2; 10/4/88, 2.

16. MHS, 137.11.1.B.

17. PG 11/16/88, 2; PH 11/10/88, 1; SR 1/26/89, 1; PG 2/1/89, 3; SR 2/5/89, 1.

18. MHS, 136.K.12.4.F. July 25, 1889, Huson sent an annual report of 1888 and 1889 to Kendrick which summarized the S&P surveys (MHS, 136.K.12.4.F, 9–10).

19. The station at the head of Bear Creek became "Vollmer" and subsequently "Troy." The location of the second station is not known. The third station became "Adams," renamed "Bovard," but never amounted to much. The fourth station became "Kendrick" after the NP's chief engineer. Cornwall did not realize the importance Huson predicted. A mile west of Cornwall is Joel which did achieve some modest importance.

20. MHS, 137.J.14.4.F; 137.H.11.1.B; 136.K.12.3.B.

21. MHS, 136.K.12.4.F.

22. The map shows ORN projected lines: from Waverly on the Farmington-Spokane line to Spangle; from Moscow to Cornwall with a line to Genesee and another down the Middle Potlatch to Juliaetta and thence to Lewiston.

23. MHS, 137.H.5.5.B.

24. MHS, 136.K.13.1.B; 137.H.5.7.B.

25. MHS, 136.K.13.1.B; 137.H.5.7.B also 137.H.11.2.F; NP Papers.

26. MHS, 137.H.19.1.B; MHS, 137.H.5.7.B also 137.H.11.2.F. A supplemental mortgage executed by the S&P to correct a clerical error stating that Marshall to the Snake River was 43 miles, was never executed by The Farmers' Loan and Trust Company because the error was "immaterial."

27. MHS, 137.H.5.7.B.

28. Unless otherwise cited the sources for the Idaho Transit are: A Lewiston newspaper article of August 7, 1903, found in MHS, 137.I.15.4.F and NI 1903, 79. Both contain interviews with Vollmer. The charter for the company is found in Kendrick's 1/30/90 letter to Oakes (MHS, 137.H.5.5.B).

29. MHS, (misplaced).

30. LT 11/15/88, 2.

31. MHS, 136.K.12.4.4.

32. WS March, 1889, 164; MHS, 136.K.13.1.B.

33. MHS, 137.H.11.1.B; 137.H.5.1.B; 136.K.12.3.B; PG 11/4/87, 3.

34. WWU 7/28/88, 3; PG 8/3/88, 4; Lewty 1995, 124; PG 4/12/89, 3.

35. NW Dec., 1892, 45; also SR 10/18/92, 7, described probably the same tramway, but located it at the "old Bowman farm."

XI: S&P Operation, Lewiston Extension Construction, 1890–93, and the Farmington Branch, 1890–1910

1. SR 1/3/90, 5; 1/4/90, 5; 1/5/90, 3; 1/7/90, 5; 1/9/90, 5; 2/6/90, 3; PG 1/17/90, 3; 1/24/90, 3; WWU 1/22/90, 3.

2. PH 3/1/90, 1; SR 5/18/90, 7.

3. NP Papers. Incorporation was reported in RG 6/13/90, 427; SR 6/3/90, 2.

4. SR 7/25/90, 7; PG 7/18/90, 2; PH 7/12/90, 1.

5. PG 8/1/90, 1.

6. Mortgage 1890a; MHS, 137.H.19.4.F; NP Papers; Mortgage 1890b: S&P 1916; MHS, 134.H.9.1.B.

7. SS 9/11/90, 3; 9/21/90, 2; 9/25/90, 8; PG 9/26/90, 3; SS 10/1/90, 3; PH 10/4/90, 7; 10/25/90, 1.

8. SR 11/6/90, 4; 11/12/90, 4.

9. MHS, 137.H.11.2.F; SR 11/29/90, 1. Between June 30, 1889, and June 30, 1890, the NP increased its box car inventory from 6,394 to 7,832, NP Annual Report, 1890, 82.

10. UMT, 128/369/7; SR 11/27, 1; 11/28/90, 1; PH 11/29/90, 7; SR 12/11/90, 2; 12/2/90, 8; 12/18/90, 11; PG 12/19/90, 1; SR 12/23/90, 2.

11. MHS, 137.H.5.6.F (Mellen letter 12/20/90); PG 12/26/90, 1; WWU 1/8/91, 3; WWS 12/29/90, 3; MHS, 137.H.5.8.F.

12. PG 1/16/91, 3; SR 1/16/91, 5; PH 2/21/91, 2; 5/9/91, 1; 6/19/91, 2.

13. SR 3/22/91, 8; WWU 4/15/91, 3; SR 5/22/91, 7.

14. SR 7/11/91, 1; 7/15/91, 5; 8/4/91, 5; LT 7/16/91, 1; PH 7/17/91, 1.

15. SR 8/30/91, 4; 10/18/91, 2; PG 10/28/91, 2.

16.

To Eastern Terminals	146,429,104 lbs	Revenue $732,685.92
To Seattle	36,533,838	103,938.51
To Tacoma	237,523,206	664,439.03
To Portland	5,052,264	15,847.66
Totals	425,538,412	$1,516,911.12

MHS, 137.H.5.8.F.

17. NP Annual Report 1891, 16.

18. PH 11/6/91; SR 11/7/91, 2; WWU 11/8/91, 4; SR 11/10/91, 5; 11/28/91, 3.

19. SR 12/8/91, 2; 12/29/91, 7.

20. NW June, 1892, 19; MHS, 137.H.6.1.B; "Tacoma's Wheat Record." *New West*, 12/3/92, 41; PG 3/11/92, 1.

21. PN 8/19/92, 1; SR 9/25/92, 6.

22. PN 11/18/92, 6.

23. SR 6/26/93, 2; 7/26/93, 8; 8/7/93, 1; 10/8/93, 2; 10/25/93, 1; 11/8/93, 3.

24. SR 1/26/90, 3, 4.

25. PH 3/1/90, 7; SR 3/18/90, 1, 7; LT 4/24/90, 1; 5/8/90, 1; 5/15/90, 1.

26. UMT, 128/286/1; PH 4/19/90, 1; SR 4/27/90, 12.

27. MHS, 137.H.19.1.B; 137.J.14.4.F; 137.H.5.5.B; 137.H.11.2.F; NP Papers; MHS, 136.K.13.1.B; 137.J.14.4.F. The bids ranged from Donald, Smith & Howell's $478,622 to $603,064. The bids covered work only; materials were to be furnished by the company. In addition to right of way work and bridges, track laying and surfacing, the bids included: two third-class combination two story depots; five second-class combination two story depots; one telegraph office; six first-class section houses; four water tanks and pump houses; a six-stall brick round house; a two-stall engine house; and two 60-foot turntables.

28. LT 5/8/90, 1; WSU cage 103, box 1; UMT, 128/369/1; 128/370/515.

29. UMT, 128/286/4.

30. LT 5/29/90, 1; MHS, 137.H.5.5.B; 137.H.11.2.F; UMT, 128/369/1; 128/286/2; LT 6/5/90, 1; WSU cage 103, box 1.

31. PH 6/7/90, 7 (the construction profiles also indicate that grading began east of Moscow in June, MHS, 134.L.18.8.F).

32. LT 6/12/90, 1; UMT, 128/370/515; SR 6/20/90, 10; UMT, 128/286/2.

33. MHS, 137.H.5.7.B.

34. UMT, 128/370/515; 128/286/2.

35. LT 6/26/90, 1; PG 7/4/90, 6; MHS, 136.K.13.1.B. The WWU on 6/26/90, 4, correctly reported the change, but the PG 6/27/90, 5 still said the line would be out of Whelan.

36. UMT, 128/370/515; 128/371/516; MHS, 137.H.11.2.F. Moore was the son-in-law of Dorsey Baker of Walla Walla and the last Washington Territorial Governor.

37. Unless otherwise cited the Tammany Creek railroads' stories come from communications from Thornton Waite and from Konen 1975. LT 2/13/90, 2; 4/24/90, 1; PH 11/15/90, 7; UMT, 128/371/518; 128/371/516; 128/286/4; LT 6/5/90, 1; 6/12/90, 1; 7/3/90, 1; PG 6/20/90, 1.

38. UMT, 128/286/2; LT 6/26/90, 1; 7/3/90, 1; SS 9/16/90, 5; SS 9/23/90, 2. NP 1906, shows an ORN survey from Garfield east to approximately were Harvard, ID, is now located. From Harvard there is a route south to connect with Bear Creek. BLM maps do not show a survey.

39. LT 7/3/90, 1; SR 7/11/90, 2; UMT, 128/286/3; 128/370/515; 128/369/1; SR 7/25/90, 7; PG 7/25/90, 3.

40. UMT, 128/370/515; 128/371/516; 128/369/1; 128/369/2.

41. UMT, 128/371/516; Construction Profile, MHS, 134.L.18.8.F. Construction included an early use of a track laying machine (Renz 1980, 148).

42. UMT, 128/371/516; SR 9/11/90, 7; UMT, 128/286/4; SS 9/14/90, 2.

43. MHS, 137.H.11.2.F; 137.H.5.5.B; UMT, 128/369/4; 128/371/516.

44. PH 10/11/90, 7; SR 10/23/90, 5; UMT, 128/371/516; LT 10/30/90, 1; UMT, 128/371/518; WWS 10/30/90, 3; PG 11/7/90, 3.

45. MHS, 137.J.14.4.F.

46. PH 11/15/90, 7; 11/29/90, 7; UMT, 128/371/518; 128/286/4; SS 12/27/90, 3.

47. MHS, 137.H.5.7.B; UMT, 128/372/521.

48. UMT, 128/371/522; 128/368/1; 128/372/521; LT 2/26/91, 1 also in PG 3/6/91, 4.

49. UMT, 128/372/521; MHS, 136.K.13.1.B.

50. UMT, 128/368/2; 128/372/521.

51. UMT, 128/368/2; 128/372/521; 128/372/523; 128/372/524; 128/368/5; LT 4/23/91, 1; Renz 1980, 148; LT 5/7/91, 1; 12/31/91, 8; Lewty 1995,174.

52. PH 4/18/91, 1; UMT, 128/368/2; 128/372/521; PH 5/9/91, 1.

53. MHS, 137.H.11.2.F; LT 5/14/91, 1.

54. UMT, 128/372/523; 128/368/3.

55. MHS, 136 K.13.1.B; UMT, 128/372/523.

56. UMT, 128/368/3; 128/372/523.

57. LT 6/25/91, 1; 7/2/91, 1; UMT, 128/368/4.

58. MHS, 137.H.5.8.F; 137.H.11.2.F & 137.H.5.8.F; UMT, 128/368/4.

59. UMT, 128/372/523, except for January 1892, the document gives the monthly dates as 1890, but it is clear that they should be 1891.

60. UMT, 128/372/523; 128/368/4; WWS 8/18/91, 3.

61. UMT, 128/368/5; 128/372/524.

62. MHS, 137.H.11.2.F; SR 3/15/92, 3; 3/16/92, 6; 4/6/92, 7; LT 3/17/92, 1; 3/31/92, 1.

63. MHS, 137.H.5.10.F; Farmers' 1894, 181.

64. SR 12/12/92, 8; MHS, 137.I.14.9.B; 137.H.6.3.B; SR 5/21/93, 4.

65. Erickson, 1983, 34; Hitchman, 1985, 88; Paul Curtiss 10/28/08.

66. MHS, 137.H.5.5.B; WSU cage 103, box 1.

67. MHS, 137.H.5.5.B. Tannatt's letterhead: T. R. Tannatt. Civil and Mining Engineer and Real Estate Agent. (Late General Land Agent Oregon Railway and Navigation Company.) Farmington Townsite Agent." He owned a large hardware store in Farmington and was the former mayor of Walla Walla. Tannatt also wrote Oakes in December that G. W. Truax, WI President, had said that the OR&N would in the spring build from Farmington through the Deep Creek country to Lewiston and the Camas Prairie.

68. MHS, 137.H.11.2.F; 136K.12.3.B; PG 7/4/90, 3; 8/1/90, 3; UMT, 128/369/2.

69. MHS, 136.G.8.1.B; UMT, 128/371/516; SR 8/12/90, 6; UMT, 128/286/2; NP Papers; MHS, 137.H.5.5.B; MHS, 137.J.14.4.F.

70. SS 9/9/90, 7; 9/16/90, 5; UMT, 128/371/516; 128/369/5; PG 10/31/90, 1; UMT, 128/371/518; PG 11/28/90, 3; UMT, 128/371/518; 128/286.4.

71. The *Review* said it was turned over to the operating department December 2 (SR 12/9/90, 3). NP 1933 has the date as the 10th. S&P 1916. MHS, 136.G.8.1.B; author's calculation of cost per mile.

72. MHS, 137.H.19.6.F; UMT, 128/371/518; 128/372/521; 128/372/523; PG 2/6/91, 3.

73. UMT, 128/372/521; 128/368/3.

74. SR 6/28/91, 10; PG 7/3/91, 3.

75. MHS, 137.H.6.2.F; 137.H.11.2.F; 137.H.5.10.F. As of June 3, 1895, $2,570 of the subscription remained uncollected. (MHS, 136.K.12.3.B).

76. UMT, 185/vol. 338/branch line reports; MHS, 137.I.15.3.B #2171.

77. MHS, 137 E.5.9.B #1344; SR 6/21/07, 11; 10/22/08, 10. AFE's 61–19 (1918) and 131–21 (1921) reference a OWR&N connection at Farmington, but no subsequent AFE was found mentioning the connection nor does the connection appear on any available map. Also no interchange of freight cars at Farmington is reported on H. H. Copeland's Interchange tables for 1925 and 1931 or on data in the NP President's subject files on cars forwarded for 1925, 1926, 1942, 1945, and 1948.

78. SR 8/27/07, 11. The "Farmer's Warehouse Co." is the largest warehouse shown on the 1917 Farmington Station Map. A similar movement in the Walla Walla area was reported in April 1908. Farmers there expected to erect six warehouses. (SR 4/18/08, 6; 4/22/08, 5).

79. SR 8/19/90, 3, 2; 8/23/90, 8.

XII: James J. Hill, the Great Northern, and the Palouse to 1894

1. LT 11/24/87, 2; 3/22/88, 2; 6/21/88, 2; 8/2/88, 2; PG 3/9/88, 2; SR 10/24/89, 1; JJH.

2. Gill 1914, 225; SR 9/19/90, 1; PG 12/5/90, 2.

3. PG 5/15/91, 1; RA 5/23/91: p. 416. Clark was a Spokane property manager (Fahey 1981, 4). In 1885 Clark corresponded with NP President Harris about a Palouse railroad; see chapter III. Newbery was involved with the S&P and Spokane & Northern; see chapters III & V.

4. Correspondence, Paul Curtiss; SR 9/15/91, 1; NYT 10/29/91; also in RA 11/6/91 & WWU, 10/30/91, 1.

5. SR 5/31/92; 8/16/92, 5; PG 2/19/92, 1; Malone 1996, 139–40, 146; Lewty 1995, 160–61.

6. SR 4/5/93, 8; PG 4/7/93, 5; 4/14/93, 6; PH 4/7/93, 1; MHS, 132.E.7.2.F. An 1895 GN map (Historic Map Library CD) shows a GN line from Spokane to Portland via Wallula.

7. Pyle 1917, I, 336; Hedges 1930, 204–05; Villard 1904, 335–36; Martin 1976, 372–73.

8. Klein 1987, 581; Kirkland 1965, 121; Agreement 1890; Asay 1991, 64; Klein 1987, 582–83; ISHS box 70; Klein 1987, 630–31; Athearn 1971, 355; NW Jan., 1891, 38; Klein 1987, 645.

9. WWU 4/4/90, 1; PG 9/18/91 5; 3/11/92, 3; SR 3/18/92, 3; 5/27/92, 4; 6/4/92, 1; WWU 5/25/92, 4.

10. Pyle 1917, I, 456.

11. SR 11/26/92, 6; 12/30/92, 1; 2/24/93, 2; 3/8/93, 2; 3/19/93, 3; 6/26/93, 8; 11/8/93, 1; WWS 3/6/94, 2; 4/6/94, 3; CG 5/25/94, 3; SR 5/22/94, 1; 7/29/94, 2; 12/19/94, 6; 12/28/94, 6.

12. Martin 1976, 435–36; Overton 1965, 229–31.

13. SR 2/20/1892, 2; also WWU 2/23/92, 1; WWU 11/9/89, 3.

14. SS 10/5/90, 1; 10/7/90, 1; also in WWS 10/7/90, 3; 10/25/90, 3; SR 11/6/90, 6. According to Overton 1965, 229, the CB&Q in the early 1890s made a series of surveys "to such points as Helena, Montana, and The Dalles in Oregon." Neither the OWT nor Hunt are in the book's index.

15. SR 10/8/90, 8; 10/9/90, 4; 10/9/90, 3; SS 10/10/90, 4; SR 10/19/90, 2; JJH-R-15.

16. MHS, 137.H.6.6.F, Special papers #74.

17. SR 2/26/91, 2; MHS, 138.H.6.8.F; 132.E.19.9.B; WWU 3/4/91, 1; MHS, 137.6.6.F, Special Papers #74.

18. Seattle *Telegraph* 3/5/91, 2; also WWU 3/7/91, 4; 3/8/91, 4; SR 2/20/1892, 2; also WWU 2/23/92, 1.

19. SR 3/5/91, 8.

20. SR 5/1/91, 1; WWU 5/1/91, 1, 4; WWS 5/1/91, 3; 6/2/91, 3.

21. OWT 1916; W&CR 1916.

22. For histories of the SLSE see Armbruster, 1999, chapter 9 and Lewty 1995, chapter 11.

23. SR 2/16/87, 4; LT 8/4/87, 1; 10/13/87, 2.

24. SR 3/30/88, 3; 4/8/88, 3; Lewty 1995, 132.

25. Both were 4-4-0's built by Rhode Island in August 1888; "Cannon" was SLSE No. 11 (1st) and "Mohr" was No. 12 (1st), Armbruster 1999, 139.

26. SR 5/13/88, 4; 9/16/88, 4; 5/11/88, 3; 5/22/88, 3; NP 1933; Lewty 1995, 132–38; Meinig 1968, 274.

27. PG, 5/25/88, 2. A report said that the SLSE would build to Helena, MT, to meet the Manitoba (SR 2/11/90, 1).

28. SR 12/15/88, 1; Ruffner 1889, 219.

29. PG 10/24/89, 1; 10/25/89, 4; WS 11/2/89, 226; SR 11/21/89, 6.

30. SR 2/19/90, 6; 2/21/90, 5; 2/26/90, 3; 3/9/90, 1; Klein 1987, 581–82.

31. Hill in Spokane, September 14, 1891, was reported to have said that the SLSE "resembled a toboggan slide in places and must have been built as a real estate proposition" (SR 9/16/91, 5). Lewty 1995, 139, 149–50, 158–59; SR 4/2/90, 12; JJH R-14, 659.

32. Armbruster 1999, 137 n46; Hedges 1930, 204; SR 6/10/90, 3; 6/11/90, 2; 6/12/90, 1; 6/26/90, 2; 7/22/90, 2; 9/25/90, 1. The *Review's* story on the 22nd said the annual rent was $800,000, Renz 1980, 142, said the rent was $300,000. I have used the Armbruster amount because it is the most credible. Renz gives the stock purchase as $45 per share, $2,335,000 of $4,150,000 outstanding. SR 7/29/90, 3; 9/21/90, 1; Lewty 1995, 140; SR 6/6/91, 8.

33. WWU 3/15/92, 1; Gill 1914, 228, 229; Armbruster 1999, 139–40.

34. NYT 2/19/93, 11; 3/1/93, 2.

35. J. A. Phillips, III, in TellTale (email) February 8, 2007.

36. SR 8/20/89, 2; 9/5/89; 4/1/90, 7 also NYT 4/5/90, 2; WWS 11/21/90, 3; PG 12/19/90, 4.

XIII: The Palouse Railroads during the Northern Pacific Receivership, 1893–96

1. SR 9/27/92, 3; NYT 10/21/92, 3; 2/19/93, 11, see comments in the report on the SLSE in chapter XII, also SR 10/21/92, 2.

2. Villard's financial mismanagement, which was apparent to the New York *Times* in spring 1892, was a repeat of his failures in the early 1880s. See for examples, NYT 5/15/92, 5; 10/5/93, 8; 5/5/94, 2; Renz 1980, 170, 181–82.

3. Hidy & Hidy, 21–28; SR 8/16/93, 1; Renz, 1980, 148, 179; SR 10/13/93, 3.

4. NYT 6/22/93, 3; 8/16/93, 5; 8/17/93, 3; 10/8/93, 12; 10/20/93, 3; 10/21/93, 3; 10/29/93, 16; 11/4/93, 5; 12/29/93, 8; 9/9/94, 2; 9/11/94, 1; 9/15/94, 5; 10/16/94, 3 & 6/28/95, 10; WWU 8/16/93, 1; SR 10/16/94, 1 & 10/17/94, 1; Lease, 1894; Daggett 1908, 289–93. More detailed accounts of the bankruptcy can be found in Daggett 1908, Lewty 1995, and Renz 1980. Campbell 1938, 59–60, says that two suits were brought against Villard, neither were concluded.

5. SR 12/26/93, 2.

6. Daggett, 1908, 296–310, has an account of the working out of the reorganization of the NP. SR 5/19/95, 1; 5/21/95, 2, 5; 5/29/95, 3; 6/5/95, 5.

7. SR 8/10/95, 6; 3/31/96, 1; Daggett, 1908, 298–302.

8. Memorandum of a Conference 4/2/96, Hill papers; Dissolution 1900; Daggett, 1908, 303–7; Hidy & Hidy, 21, 17; Martin 1976, 455–57; Malone 1996, 181–82; NYT 4/10/97, 11.

9. SR 4/28/96, 1; 5/3/96, 3; 5/14/96, 2; 8/23/96, 2; NYT 7/26/96, 7; C&F 6/6/96, 1041; Gill 1914, 234; Renz 1978, 5–7; Renz 1980, 191–93.

10. Lease, 1894; ICC 1929, 709; S&P 1916; C&F 12/9/93, 880; 4/28/94, 736; 8/4/94, 192; NYT 9/9/94, 2; 6/2/96, 10; MHS, 137.I.14.10.F; 134.F.38.F; Farmers' 1894, 239.

11. MHS, 137.I.14.9.B #279; 134.I.4.13.B; 137.I.14.10.F; Renz 1980, 148.

12. SR 11/7/95, 8; PH 11/9/95, 5; MHS, 134.I.4.13.B; PH 11/16/94, 1; SR 11/16/94, 1; 3/25/95, 1; 4/11/95, 1.

13. SR 10/17/95, 4.

14. UMT, 185/vol. 338/branch line reports. The capitalization and mileages given in the report are the same as the June 30, 1896, report to the ICC.

15. The details of duplication costs are: Marshall Jct. to Genesee, 104.507 miles at $15,000, $1,567.605; Belmont Jct. to Farmington, 6.084 miles at $12,000, $73,008; Pullman to Juliaetta, 20 miles at $15,000, $300,000, 13 miles at $35,000, $455,000 and 7.5 miles at $18,000, $135,000 for a combined total of $890,000 for the Pullman to Juliaetta section. The $35,000 per mile would be in the Bear Creek Canyon and the $18,000 in the Potlatch Canyon.

16. Darling's and the division engineer's comments can be found in MHS, 134.F.6.7.B #1063 and 134.I.9.6.F #2012.

17. McHenry wrote another report on the S&P two years later, March 18, 1898. The brief report restates some of the earlier report (MHS, 134.I.4.14.F).

18. MHS, 134.F.38.F #3226.

19. SR 3/20/94, 4; 6/6/94, 1.

20. SR 7/1/94, 2; 7/6/94, 1; 7/15/94, 5; PH 7/13/94.

21. PH 6/22/94; SR 8/22/94, 3; 10/2/94, 3; PH 9/7/94, 1; SR 3/26/95, 3; 6/13/95, 5.

22. SR 4/7/95, 1, 4; 4/8/95, 3; 4/13/95, 3; 4/14/95, 5; 4/15/95, 1; 4/17/95, 5; 4/30/95, 6. (The Spokane & Palouse Land Co. was named as claimant on the Cannon estate, SR 7/27/95, 3.)

23. SR 9/26/95, 8; 10/18/95, 1; 11/16/95, 3; 12/6/95, 8.

24. LT 11/21/95, 1; SR 11/19/95, 1.

25. SR 12/25/95, 8.

26. PH 2/8/96.

27. PH 7/11/96.

28. SR 10/9/96, 5.

29. SR 10/16/96, 1; 10/17/96, 6 & 7; 10/18/96, 7; 10/22/96, 6; 11/12/96, 6; 12/1/96, 6; LT 11/26/96, 1; SR 11/26/96, 6; 1/27/96, 8.

30. The first four paragraphs: Mercer 1985, 51; Athearn 1976, 371; NYT 12/7/93, 2; Rigdon 1954, 279; Daggett 1908, 237; Asay 1991, 69; SR 8/12/94, 1; 8/24/94, 2; 8/30/94, 1; 1/3/95, 1; 6/11/95, 1; 6/12/95, 2; NYT 11/10/94, 6; 2/5/95, 15; 5/29/95, 10 & 6/11/95, 15; Klein 1989, 18–19 WWS 3/30/94, 3; also SR 3/29/94, 1; Gill 1914, 229, 230, 232, 234; CG 6/1/94, 4; WWS 6/25/94, 3.

31. NYT 8/24/95, 7; 7/11/96, 6; 8/22/98, BR1; Asay 1991, 73; Gill 1914, 234–35; Gill 1916, 6, 40, 44, 45, 51, 52 & 86 114; CG 7/24/96, 2; ORN 11/25/96; ORN Annual Report 1897, 5.

32. Trottman 1966, 261; SR 12/7/96, 8.

33. Asay 1991, 70; WWS 7/13/94, 3; SR 7/21/94, 4; 7/23/94, 4; 8/6/94, 1; 8/12/94, 1; 8/28/94, 4; WSJ 9/6/94, 1.

34. SR 4/3/95, 1, 4; 4/7/95, 6; 4/8/95, 4; 5/14/95, 4.

35. SR 6/5/95, 5; CG 1/31/96, 5.

36. WSJ 9/1/96, 1.

XIV: Completion of Lewiston Extension and the Demise of the S&P, 1897–1900

1. SR 1/1/97, 15; MHS, 134.I.4.13.B; Ficken 2007, 229; SR 7/28/97, 1; 8/4/97, 5; 8/12/97, 1; 8/13/97, 3; 9/4/97, 6; 3/6/98, 8; NP Confidential Report, 1898, 194, 206–07.

2. SR 7/24/97, 6; 8/22/97, 1; CG 8/6/97, 1; SR 8/18/97, 6; CG 8/20/97, 1; 12/17/97, 3. In April the NP reported that the value of the S&P main track at $2500 a mile, total $213,102 and side track at $1,000 a mile, $11,125; depots and building were valued at $5400, office furniture $700 and real estate $105; and rolling stock at $81,153; and the total for all property was $311,675, or a blanket value of $3655 per mile. The ORN reported a total value of its property in Whitman County as $984,262 on 194.9 miles of main track and other property or $4794 per mile (PH 5/1/97).

3. LT 10/29/97, 1.

4. MHS, 134.I.5.5.B.

5. MHS, 137.J.14.4.F; 137.H.19.1.B; MHS (from the legal department to chief engineer).

6. SR 2/19/98, 3; 3/22/98, 6; NP Confidential Report, 1898; Gill 1916, 40; SR 8/7/98, 16; 9/27/98, 3.

7. NP 1933.

8. SR 10/26/98, 3; 11/1/98, 5; 5/2/99, 5. Also there were R. P. O. cars on the ORN: Spokane, Walla Walla & Portland; Spokane

& Pendleton; Wallace & Tekoa; and rural routes on the ORN: Moscow & Colfax; and Seltice Junction & Winona.

9. NP 1933.

10. PH 12/17/98, 1.

11. SR 12/15/98, 5; 12/17/98, 4; 12/19/98, 3; 12/29/98, 3.

12. SR 1/20/99, 5; 1/22/99, 5; 1/25/99, 5; 5/2/99, 5; 5/12/99, 5.

13. S&P 1916; ICC 1929, 500, 707; SR 3/1/99, 5.

14. SR 4/13/99, 5; 4/14/99, 1; PH 4/15/99, 1; 4/22/99, 1.

15. SR 9/14/99, 3.

16. SR 10/11/99, 5; 10/18/99, 3; 10/25/99, 5; 11/1/99, 5.

17. Ficken 2007, 253; MHS, 137.D.5.4.F #575.

18. SR 12/16/99, 1; 12/17/99, 2; 12/19/99, 3; 12/26/99, 8. Bain was promoted to engineer 10/20/99 (courtesy of Jan Taylor).

19. PH 1/20/00, 1.

20. UMT, 178.99.6; SR 1/14/00, 1, 5; 1/15/00, 1; 1/16/00, 1, 5; 1/17/00, 5; 1/18/00, 5.

21. SR 1/15/00, 5; 1/20/00, 5; 1/23/00, 5; 1/24/00, 5.

22. UMT, 128/307/2.

23. SR 1/30/00, 5; 2/7/00, 5; 2/9/00, 5; 2/14/00, 5; 2/28/00, 5; 3/1/00, 5; 3/9/00, 5; 3/11/00, 8.

24. MHS, 137.B.20.20.5.B; SR 3/31/00, 12; 4/27/00, 8; Profile 1899; Annual Report, 1900, 29.

25. SR 6/2/00, 8; 6/10/00, 8; 6/18/00, 8; AFE 1183–99.

26. SR 5/27/00, 8; 6/8/00, 5. The Washington State Railroad Commission ordered permanent connections between the NP and ORN in several places in the Palouse (see chapter XX), but no evidence has been found of Idaho making a similar order.

27. CG 8/10/00, 2; SR 12/1/00, 6; 12/28/00, 4; PH 1/12/01.

28. MHS, 137.H.18.2.F; LT 12/24/97, 1; PH 12/18/97; MHS, 134.I.4.13.B.

29. MHS, 137.B.20.5.B, #155?. That the letter was found in the NP Presidents subject files indicates that NP officials were aware of Mohler's thinking.

30. MHS, 134.I.4.13.B #95; 137.B.20.5.B #155; 136.K.12.7.B #107; 136.G.8.1.B; SR 1/23/98, 1.

31. LT 1/28/98, 2; 2/11/98, 1; 2/25/98, 3.

32. PH 2/26/98; SR 3/8/98, 3; MHS, 134.I.4.13.B #95; LT 3/18/98, 1.

33. MHS, 134.I.4.13.B #95; LT 5/13/98, 1.

34. LT 6/17/98, 3; 7/1/98, 2; 7/22/98, 1 (which has the first train over the bridge on the 20th); MHS, 134.M.I5.B.

35. MHS, 134.I.4.13.B #95.

36. SR 9/3/98, 5; 9/11/98, 6; LTR 9/25/38; MHS, 134.I.4.13.B #95. NP 1933 also has October 1, 1898, as the first day of operation.

37. MHS, 134.I.4.13.B #95.

XV: The Northern Pacific, James J. Hill, and E. H. Harriman and the Snake River Country, 1897–1901

1. There is a voluminous literature on the Hill-Harriman conflicts, but most of it gives primary attention to events outside of the Snake River country. If the Snake River country is mentioned, it is prologue to a larger story (for example, see Hofsommer 1991). In this work the Snake River country conflicts are the story.

2. NYT 1/13/97, 13; Gill 1914, 236; Memorandum 1927; Hidy & Hidy, 21:24; Hidy 2004, 94, 132; a copy of the agreement is attached to a letter from Adams to Winter 2/17/97, MHS, 137.B.20.6.F #170.

3. Klein 1989, 72; SR 9/12/97, 1; 10/13/97, 1; 10/16/97, 1; 10/19/97, 1.

4. Martin 1976, 477–84; SR 4/14/97, 2.

5. SR 4/8/97, 1; 4/30/97, 1; 5/1/97, 6; 5/16/97, 14; NYT 4/30/97, 11; Hidy & Hidy, 21:19–20.

6. Gill 1914, 236; Klein 1989, 73; Hidy & Hidy, 21:25. Later when Mohler was president of the UP, he wrote to Hill July 2, 1912, on the announcement of Hill's retirement from active involvement in the GN, it "brings home forcibly to me the valuable instructions I received under you in an Official capacity, which has had much to do with what little Success I have attained in the Profession since" (MHS, 20.E.3.4).

7. JJH.

8. In some correspondence the date is given as August 6. The agreement is found MHS, 137.C.8.1.B #276 and 137.B.15.16.F and JJH; Memorandum 1927; Hidy & Hidy, 21:25; Hidy 2004, 94; Gill 1914, 237; NP Confidential Report, 1898. The NP and ORN in the same spirit entered into an agreement, November 1, 1897, covering business in the Coeur d'Alene country.

9. JJH #3118. Not all of the letter from Mohler to Heidelbach can be read. In his letter to Hill, Mohler presented statistics on

curvature from Omaha to Portland: The degrees of curvature per mile, UP 17.5, OSL 20.5 and ORN 83.4.

10. Hidy & Hidy 21, 19–20; NYT 8/13/97, 9; SR 8/13/97, 5. Coster was also on both the ORN and OSL boards of directors.

11. SR 9/17/97, 5; 9/21/97, 1.

12. MHS, 137.C.8.1.B #276; JJH. Some of the letters are found in both places.

13. For information on Harriman see Klein 1989 and 2000; Mercer 1985. SR 6/1/97, 6; 6/15/97, 6; 6/16/97, 2; 11/2/97, 1; Memorandum 1927, 14–15; Gill 1914, 236–37; NYT 8/22/98, BR1; Klein 1989, 48–49; Klein 2000, 152; SR 10/13/98, 2. Harriman's improvement program lead to significant efficiency improvements. See Mercer 1985 57ff, and Currie.

14. SR 2/14/98, 3; MHS, 134.I.5.5.B #95.

15. Lorenz Schrenk, unpublished draft "The Washington & Columbia River Railway Company," nd, 4; Renz 1978, 197; SR 2/22/98, 1; 2/25/98, 2. Renz erroneously has the date of purchase as March 4.

16. JJH; MHS, 137.C.16.7.B #421; Memorandum 1927, 10–13.

17. MHS, 137.C.16.7.B #421.

18. Asay 1991, 121; SRV charters.

19. UMT, 128.286.6; SR 3/15/98, 1; MHS, 134.I.5.5.B & 137.C.19.7.B #495; 137.C.19.7.B #495E.

20. JJH.

21. JJH also MHS, 137.D.5.4F; MHS, 137.C.16.7.B #421; Memorandum 1927, 10–13.

22. MHS, 137.C.19.7.B #495.

23. MHS, 137.C.19.7.B #495.

24. MHS, 137.D.5.4.F.

25. Hidy & Hidy, 21:27; JJH; MHS, 137.C.16.7.B #421.

26. JJH.

27. Klein 1989, 76.

28. MHS, 137.C.16.7.B #421. The undated fourth memorandum and an accompanying table, which appears to be from the same time period, contain a series of leases and trackage involving the GN and UP as well as the ORN and NP. What is proposed is more complex and far more extensive than the other three memoranda and therefore even less likely to be the basis of a settlement (MHS, 137.C.19.7.B #495).

29. MHS, 137.C.19.7. #495.

30. JJH.

31. Martin 1976, 483–85; Klein 1989, 76–77; Klein 2000, 154–56.

32. MHS, 137.B.15.16.F 1–13.

33. Correspondence 1898, 1–4; JJH (Hill letter press book microfilm).

34. UMT, 128/286/6.

35. CWV and CSL charters; MHS, 134.I.5.6.F #477.

36. MHS, 137.C.16.7.B #421; 137.C.19.7.B #495.

37. Correspondence 1898, 17–19.

38. MHS, 137.C.19.7.B #495.

39. SR 11/19/98, 1; 11/20/98, 1; 11/22/98, 5.

40. MHS, 137.C19.7.B #495.

41. SR 11/24/98, 5; 11/26/98, 5; NYT 11/27/98, 3; SR 11/29/98, 5.

42. MHS, 137.C19.7.B #495. Thanks to Gary Miller for a copy of the 25th memorandum. The CSL and WCR did file for additional lines on December 5, 8, and 13, see above.

43. MHS, 137.C.19.7.B #495.

44. SR 12/9/98, 5; 12/12/98, 5; 12/13/98, 5.

45. RA 12/16/98, 921. A longer version of his statement appears in SR 12/15/98, 1 and NYT 12/15/98, 8, also typed copies MHS, 137.B.16.13.B & 137.C.19.7.B #495. SR 12/16/98, 5.

46. SR 12/17/98, 5; 12/24/98, 5; 12/28/98, 4.

47. UMT, 128/286/6. The lines were: 1. Clearwater line from mouth of Potlatch River to a point opposite mouth of Cottonwood Creek in Camas Prairie; 2. From this point to Camas Prairie Bench; 3. From North Lapwai to best terminal point south of Lawyer's canyon; 4. From most convenient connection with Palouse and Lewiston Line westerly along and across Penawawa Creek to a connection with line on south bank of Snake River; 5. From a convenient junction with this line via Colfax to Oakesdale; 6. From Riverside to Waitsburg; 7. From Eureka Flat Branch easterly to best terminal point on west bank of the Tucannon; 8. From Lewiston to Riparia.

48. SR 12/27/98, 1; CG 12/30/98, 1; SR 12/30/98, 5.

49. MHS, 137.C.19.7.B, italics in the original.

50. JJH.

51. MHS, 137.C.19.7.B #495.

52. WSJ 1/13/99; SR 1/21/99, 5; LTR 1/20/99, typescript WSU Cage 103, 1; SR 1/20/99, 5.

53. Mercer 1985, 54–55; Klein 1989, 73; SR 3/9/99, 5; 3/10/99, 5.

54. MHS, 137.D.5.4.F #575 also 137.C.19.7.B #495.

55. MHS, 134.I.5.8.F; MHS, 134.I.5.7.B #511.

56. MHS, 134.I.5.6.F #477; UMT, 128.286.6 also 128.316.409.F; NP Confidential Report, June 30, 1899.

57. Klein 1989, 77–78; MHS, 137.D.5.4.F #575.

58. SR 4/15/99, 1; SR 4/17/99, 5.

59. SR 4/22/99, 5; 4/29/99, 5; 5/3/99, 5.

60. MHS, 137.C.19.7.B #495, emphasis in original. A joint interest in Dayton to Covello (south of the Snake River) did exist for a short period.

61. MHS, 137.C.19.7.B #495; Klein 2000, 181–186; SR 5/30/99, 1.

62. SR 6/16/99, 5; LTR 7/1/99, 1 also WSJ 7/17/99; RG 7/14/99, 515.

63. MHS, 137.C.19.7.B #495.

64. SR 7/2/99, 5; NI 1903, 80–81.

65. MHS, 137.C.19.7.B #495.

66. NYT 7/14/99, 1; 7/16/99, 3; SR 7/15/99, 5; 7/16/99, 8; RA 7/21/99, 548. By the time of the ORN annual meeting in September 1902, the OSL owned all but 150 shares of the 350,000 common shares of the ORN (SR 9/5/02, 1).

67. Gill 1914, 238; Hidy & Hidy, 21:29; Hill Papers; Klein 1989, 78.

68. MHS, 137.C.19.7.B #495; WSJ 7/31/99.

69. SR 8/4/99, 8; MHS, 137.C.19.7.B #495; Klein 2000, 158, 210; Truce Agreement; Asay 1991, 79–80ff; SR 8/11/99, 1 & 5; 8/16/99, 5; JJH; also Hidy & Hidy, 21:48; SR 8/18/99, 5; *Oregonian* quote from NI 1903, 81.

70. Klein 1989, 78; Klein 2000, 157–58; Daggett 1908, 257; Trottman 1966, 279; MHS, 137.B.20.6.F #170; SR 8/27/99, 3; 8/28/99, 1; NYT 9/8/99, 9; Mercer 1985, 54–55.

71. A somewhat longer version of the article is found in Beach, 2015. SR 8/30/99, 5; 6/4/00, 8. From July 1 to November 1, 1899, the gross earnings of the GN were $11,093,672 and those of the NP $11,738,117 (SR 11/25/99, 5).

72. JJH; Hidy & Hidy, 21:30; Pyle 1917 II, 41–46; Klein 1989, 79.

73. MHS, 134.I.5.6.F #477; SR 10/7/99, 5.

74. MHS, 137.C.19.7.B #495; SR 10/10/99, 1, 5.

75. JJH; NP 1933. There were several stories and editorials in the *Review* in the summer and fall, 1899, which speculated or reported that Hill would or had taken over the WC.

76. MHS, 137.D.5.4.F #575.

77. NP 1933; SR 11/18/99, 1; MHS, 134.I.5.6.F #477; SR 12/25/99, 5.

78. JJH. Coster forwarded Mellen's response to Hill. SR 12/24/99, 3; 1/11/00, 5; 1/12/00, 5.

79. MHS, 137.B.15.16.F also 137.C.20.1.B #495 & 137.C.19.7.B #495–B; also Memorandum 1927, 20–21; Gill 1916, 75.

80. MHS, 137.C.19.7.B #459–B; 134.I.5.6.F #477; 134.F.2.14.F; UMT, 128/312/7.

81. SR 1/20/00, 5; 1/21/00, 1; 1/25/00, 5. A report from New York January 24 made a similar argument about UP interests; the ORN's movement into the Clearwater was a local matter, which could be sacrificed to the larger interests of the UP (CG 1/26/00, 4).

82. NI 1903, 82.

83. SR 2/6/00, 5; 2/7/00, 5.

84. MHS, 137.D.5.4.F #573.

85. Probably MHS, but no identification.

86. NYT 3/21/00, 7; Hidy & Hidy, 21:48–49.

87. JJH; Adams and Mellen letters are probably MHS, but no identification.

88. JJH. (Both Klein 1989, 94 and Martin 1976, 485 read the date of the letter as July 31, 1900; it appears to me that it is July 21.)

89. SR 8/6/00, 8.

90. NYT 11/8/00, 11; SR 11/11/00, 12; 11/16/00, 10.

91. Dissolution 1900; SR 10/23/00, 10; 11/18/00, 1; 11/22/00, 10; 11/23/00, 6.

92. NYT 11/13/00, 3; SR 11/13/00, 1, 3, 6, 7, 9.

93. SR 12/22/00, 1; 1/5/01, 8.

94. MHS 137.D.5.4.F #575; JJH.

95. SR 3/7/01, 10; 3/16/01, 12.

XVI: Conflict and Agreement, 1901–1910

1. Martin 1976, 485–91, 494–523; Malone 1996, 203–25; Klein 1989, 95–111, 148–49; Klein 2000, 212–39, 308–16; Mercer 1985, 88–103; Meyer 1906; Renz 1980, 209–15; Pyle 1917 II, 103–87; SR 6/2/01, 8. In a lengthy statement in December 1901, Hill explained why the actions of himself and associates to prevent the NP coming under the control of the UP was in best interests of the Northwest (SR 12/22/01, 1) A report of Hill's statement to the Interstate Commerce Commission in Chicago is found SR 1/25/02, 1 & 2/11/02, 10, and Harriman's SR 1/26/02, 1. Mellen, in St. Paul testimony in a suit against the Northern Securities Company, said that the NP had not taken part in the formation of the company (SR 10/24/02, 1). In June 1903 it was reported that Mellen supported the "trust buster" Theodore Roosevelt

and would give $10,000 to his 1904 campaign for reelection (SR 6/7/03, 1). A copy of the Metropolitan agreement is in JJH.

2. Martin 1976, 464; SR 6/12/01, 10; 12/27/01, 3.

3. SR 7/13/01, 10; NW 9/01. It was reported in October 1905 that the NP had decided again to build the Lind-Ellensburg cut-off (SR 10/28/05, 1), but it was never built.

4. SR 8/10/01, 1; 2/6/02, 10.

5. MHS, 137.C.19.7.B #495; JJH; SR 5/21/02, 1 & NYT 5/21/02; SR 5/28/02, 10.

6. MHS, 137.C.19.7.B #495.

7. JJH; MHS, 137.C.19.7.B.

8. OHS, Gill 1591.B.5.F.8.

9. MHS, 137.C.19.7.B #495 also 134.I.5.11.B #603; OHS, Gill 1591.B.5.F.8.

10. OHS, Gill 1591.5.F.8.

11. SR 7/22/02, 10; 7/25/02, 10; 8/4/02, 1; 8/6/02, 10; MHS, 137. C19.7.B; JJH.

12. SR 9/30/02, 12; 10/12/02, 13.

13. MHS, 20.C.6.3; JJH.

14. MHS, 20.D.3.2. The unresolved issues included: the matter of traffic from the W&CR using the ORN from Wallula to Portland; the use by the ORN of the NP's line via Pasco between Wallula and Puget Sound points; and the question of per diem or other compensation to be paid by the Northern Pacific for the use of ORN cars.

15. SR 11/19/02, 10; 12/10/02, 12; OHS, Gill 1591 5.8.

16. SR 7/11/02, 1; 7/14/02, 4; 10/14/02, 12; 3/24/03, 1; Derleth 2002, 171; Gill 1914, 244, 255.

17. MHS, 137.B15.16.F.

18. MHS, 137.D.2.F #972. The line was a predecessor of the Spokane & Inland Empire Railway and was not controlled by the ORN (see chapter XX).

19. SR 7/5/03, 9; 7/7/03, 12; 7/16/03, 12.

20. In 1906 the OWI acquired SRV's partially constructed right of way east of Riparia (Gill 1916, 72).

21. JJH. In another letter of the same date, October 8, 1903, Mellen outlined to Adams improvements which the NP should make, "if the Northern Pacific is to be permitted to work out its own destiny...and if the great amount of business now seeking its lines for transportation is to be accommodated, and the property not used to divert business to the lines of its less prosperous neighbor, the Great Northern, then what I have outlined to you will be absolutely necessary...nothing but the most culpable mismanagement, management with the intention, not of promoting the interest of this property, but of operating the same to the benefit of its neighbor, can ever make the securities of the Northern Pacific Railway Company other than highly attractive to people wanting railway investment" (from Jerry Masters).

22. SR 10/22/03, 14; Hidy & Hidy 23, 1–3; Mellen had become a director of New Haven 9/19/03 (SR 9/20/03, 9); NYT 12/3/03; SR 12/24/03, 13.

23. Gill 1914, 242; SR 3/30/04, 14; SR 9/7/06, 9.

24. MHS, 137.I. 15.3.B #2171; 137.C.19.7.B, #495E.

25. MHS, 137.B.15.16.F, "UP Agreements 1881–1904"; MHS, 20.D.3.2; Hidy & Hidy, 22, 14.

26. MHS, 137.I.15.2.F #1582; 137.C.20.1.B #495; 137.C19.10.F #495M F-4.

27. SR 5/14/05, 2–9; MHS, 137.C.20.1.B, #495; 134.I.8.4.F; also OHS, Gill 1591.B.5.F.10; SR 5/27/05, 14; NP 1905 Annual Report, 12; SR 8/3/05, 14. Gill in his report to the ICC said construction began September 1905 (Gill 1916, 72).

28. Hidy & Hidy, 22, 16–18; Gill 1914, 243–44; SR 9/11/05, 10; 6/15/10, 3. While it was known by September 21, 1905 (see SR 9/21/05, 1), it was not officially revealed until May 8, 1906, that Harriman was behind both the WP and CV which were building on the 1897 surveys of G. W. Hunt which had been sold in 1898 to ORN President Mohler (Gill 1914, 248). The CV was incorporated in 1899.

29. SR 9/25/05, 1; 10/22/05, 9.

30. There is no comprehensive history of the NC, though Asay 1991 does have some history. For the Strahorn-Harriman relationship, see Beach 2012. NP President Elliott was informed by the UP of its connection to the NC at least several weeks before the public, see chapter XIX. Among others the OWRN acquired the ORN, NC, OWI, and SRV. It completed lines begun by the NC: Attalia to N. Yakima, 98.07 miles, opened March 24, 1911, and Ayer Junction (on Snake River) to Spokane, 104.30 miles, opened September 15, 1914. UP President R. S. Lovett said that a reason for the new corporation was that the ORN mortgage limited it to $25 million in bonds which was inadequate for construction of new lines and thus forced the creation of separate corporations which were operated as a unit and whose stock was held by the UP.

31. SR 10/25/05, 1; WSJ 10/25/05; SR 11/2/05, 1; MHS, 137.B.15.16.F; Truce Agreement, 18, 19.

32. SR 1/2/06, 14; MHS, 137.D.20.3.B, #1127G; 137.I.15.3.B, #27.F.12.

33. MHS, 137.C.20.1.B, #495.

34. WSJ 3/12/07, 1; Gill 1914, 250; NYT 3/5/07, 1; 3/23/07; 4/3/07; 4/4/07; 10/19/07; MHS 134.I.8.10.F #1690.

35. MHS, 137.D.20.3.B #1127G.

36. Gill 1914, 251; the Pacific and Idaho Northern Railway Co. over several years built north from the Boise area; SR 9/15/07, 15;

9/17/07, 2; 9/25/07, 7; 10/2/07, 8; 10/23/07, 12; 10/24/07, 20; 2/1/08, 8.

37. SR 4/14/08, 10; 5/3/08, 2; 6/7/08, 5; 6/14/08, 3A.

38. Gill 1916, 72; SR 10/1/08, 13; 10/6/08, 8; 11/13/08, 18; 10/14/08, 5.

39. SR 10/31/08, 8; NP 1933; SR 2/18/09, 18; 3/28/09, 1; 3/30/09, 1.

40. Gill 1914, 257; SR 8/5/09, 8. Gill has no record of the MIP in his 1916 report to the ICC; NP 1933; NP Annual Report 1909, 6, 15; SR 5/26/09, 11; NYT 5/27/09; 6/6/09; WSJ 9/9/09; Gill, 1914, 256; Asay 1991, 109–10.

41. MHS, 134.I.9.1.B #1874; SR 7/15/09, 8; 7/23/09, 8; 8/23/09, 8.

42. SR 11/5/09, 8; NP Annual Report 1910, 17; Gill 1916, 2–3 (mileage as of June 30, 1916); IDSHS Ms 563. The UP's NP stock—held by the OSL—was sold by the end of 1909 (Renz 1980, 215).

43. Memorandum 1927, 21–24.

XVII: The Columbia & Palouse Railroad and the La Crosse Gateway, 1887–1980

1. Gill, 1916; OHS, Gill 1591 B.6.F.11; OHS, 299, Box 131, C&P Record, 124–30.

2. PG 6/24/87, 3; WWU 6/25/87, 4 has a longer version.

3. PG 6/3/87, 3; WWDJ 6/1/87, 3; OHS, Gill 1591, B.4.F.8 and OHS, 299 Exec. Com. Rec. pp. 305–09; also in OHS, Gill 1591 B.6.F.40. Other recommendations are treated in chapters VI and VIII.

4. OHS, Gill 1591 B.6.F.11; OHS, 299, Box 131, C&P Record, 131–145 and amended charter; NARA-P.

5. MHS, 137.H.5.1.B.

6. A copy of the handwritten letter is in the author's files. Its source is lost, probably MHS or OHS (Gill).

7. Hitchman 1985, 54.

8. PH 11/17/88, 1; 11/24/88, 1; PG 10/9/91, 1; SR 10/11/91, 9.

9. Gill, 1916, 6.

10. MHS [?]; UMT, 185/vol. 338/branch line reports. More on the report is in chapter XV.

11. MHS, 137.C.16.7.B #421, #471; Memorandum 1927, 14–15; MHS, 137.D.5.4.F.

12. MHS, 134.I. 5.5.B; 134.I.5.5.B; PH 6/4/98, 1; 6/18/98, 1; CG 6/17/98, 8; SR 6/30/98, 3; CG 7/1/98, 1.

13. Hidy & Hidy, 21:27; JJH; SR 7/7/98, 3; MHS, 137.C.16.7.B #495.

14. MHS, 134.I.5.5.B, the estimate is also found in MHS, 136.G.8.1.B; McHenry to Mellen also found MHS, 137.C.16.7.B #495; McHenry to Bihler 6th, also in UMT 178/81/1; MHS, 134.I.5.6.F #464.

15. MHS, 137.C.19.7.B #495.

16. SR 1/25/99, 5; 1/26/99, 5; 4/5/99, 5; UMT, 128/286/6.

17. SR 1/8/99, 12; 1/12/99, 3; PH 1/28/99, 1; SR 2/3/99, 5; 2/7/99, 5; 3/17/99, 5; 5/6/99, 5; 5/9/99, 5; 6/17/99, 5; 8/17/99, 5; 9/20/99, 5; 10/20/99, 5; 10/21/99, 5; 12/28/00, 10.

18. SR 7/2/99, 5 also RW 7/8/99, 762; MHS, 137.C.19.7.B #495; PH 9/23/99, 1; 9/30/99.

19. SR 9/29/99, 5; 11/22/99, 5; 11/25/99, 5; 12/12/99, 5; 5/16/00, 8. The move to Winona did not occur.

20. SR 3/29/00, 8; 5/22/00, 8; 10/28/02, 12.

21. CG 5/18/00, 3; also SR 5/15/00, 8.

22. SR 4/7/01, 9; 6/16/01, 1; 7/18/01, 5. Gill, 1916, 6; Gill 1914, 239, 240. Gill wrote that the line had all but disappeared except for the rails and that restoration of service required "substantial expenditures in the way of repair to tracks and grade." No evidence has been found of a "Hartersville" on the C&P.

23. SR 3/9/03, 10; 3/10/03, 6; 3/16/03, 4.

24. SR 7/23/04, 11; 7/30/04, 12; CG 12/30/04, 2; 1/27/05, 1.

25. SR 6/8/03, 6 (accounts of earlier proposals are in WWU 1/24/92, 1; 4/14/92, 4; 1/4/93, 4); CG 12/30/04, 2; 1/27/05, 1.

26. SR 8/13/04, 2; 8/17/04, 1, 6; PH 8/20/04; SR 8/28/04, 10.

27. SR 7/31/04, 9; MHS, 137.C.16.7.B #420 (some in 137.I.15.3.B #2171).

28. SR 9/8/04, 12; 10/8/04, 14.

29. SR 10/24/04, 7; PH 11/19/04, 2; SR 2/13/05, 3; MHS, 137.I.15.2.F, file #1582; 134.I.7.13.B #1416.

30. CG 3/31/05, 1; 4/7/05, 7.

31. SR 4/22/05, 1; 4/23/05, 9; 4/29/05, 2; 5/3/05, 13; 11/20/05, 9; 4/2/06, 6.

32. Lewty 1987, 121; Gill 1914, 242. A brief account of the proposal is in Oberst 1978, 64–65.

33. SR 1/28/06, 9; 1/29/06, 4.

34. SR 1/11/06, 1; 1/19/06, 16; SC 1/12/06; SR 1/19/06, 16.

35. MHS, 137.C.16.7.B #420.

36. SR 10/20/08, 18; Railroad Commission of Washington: 1st report 6/23/05–12/31/06, 95, 25; 10th 12/1/19–11/30/20, 10; NP 1949, 75; UP 1954.

37. SR 2/22/07, 6 also CG 2/22/07, 6; SR 3/14/07, 18. If there was a relocation it did not create a significant change in mileage.

38. SR 5/2/07, 5; 5/7/07, 2; also CG 5/24/07, 5; SR 5/25/07, 5; 6/1/07, 5.

39. Chee 1954, 29; SR 5/26/07, 5A; 7/29/07, 6; 8/9/07, 5; PH 5/25/07, 1; 8/10/07, 1; MHS, 137.D.20.3.B #1127; 137.D.20.3.B #1127G; SR 11/5/07, 20.

40. SR 8/4/07, 1, 4; 9/14/07, 5; CG 9/20/07; 6/12/08, 9.

41. SR 11/24/08, 9; 11/28/08, 18; 12/8/08, 8.

42. SR 2/10/09, 18; 3/8/09, 8.

43. CG 7/2/09; 5/12/11, 2; Carter 2009, 62. The SIE was a Spokane company which came under the influence of J. J. Hill; see chapter XVIII.

44. CG 10/29/09, 1.

45. SR 12/2/09, 8; 12/6/09, 8; CG 12/3/09, 1; PH 12/9/09, 1; SR 12/9/09, 18.

46. SR 12/18/09, 8; 12/17/09, 8; OHS ms 299 box 88; Gill 1914, 254; CG 12/17/09, 1, 1; SR 12/22/09, 8; 12/23/09, 8; PH 12/24/09, 1; 12/31/09, 1.

47. SR 12/22/09,8; MHS, 134.I.10.11.B #1665; PH 12/31/09, 1.

48. CG 1/14/10, 1; MHS, 137.E.14.5.B #1603.

49. SR 1/28/10, 8; PH 3/4/10, 1; 3/11/10, 1; 3/18/10, 1, 5; 5/27/10, 3; CG 3/11/10, 3; 3/25/10, 1; 4/8/10, 5; 9/1/11, 1; 10/20/11, 1; 10/27/11, 1.

50. MHS, 137.E.14.5.B #1603; 137.E.5.9.B #1340.

51. Gill, 1916, 5–6, 90.

52. PH 1/13/11, 1.

53. MHS, 137.C.16.7.B #420 (includes SR 11/11/12 and Colfax *Commoner* 11/15/12); MHS, 138.H.4.5.B E-52.

54. Lewty 1987, 121; Gill 1916; Gill 1914, 242; OHS, Gill 1591 B.6.F.41; UP 1948; WSDOT.

55. Currie 2007, 134, 139, 303; Robert W. Downing (retired BN vice chairman and chief operating officer) personal communication 4/7/2009. Downing shared Currie's assessment that "It soon became clear that this had been a bad decision because a great deal of money soon had to be spent to upgrade the Northern Pacific line" (139). Downing also did not accept the rumored reasons for abandoning the SPS route along the Snake River, i.e., deteriorating bridges and slides; he said he did not know of problems with the bridges and the SPS successfully dealt with the slides by grooming the slopes once a year.

XVIII: Projections, Surveys, and Construction, 1886–1913

1. MHS, 134.I.5.5.B #95; UMT, 128/290/3; Gill 1916, 75.

2. CG 9/25/98, 1; 11/11/98, 1; SR 11/21/98, 3; 11/24/98, 5; 11/27/98, 3; 12/5/98, 5; 12/9/98, 5; 12/31/98, 5; CG 12/30/98, 4.

3. UMT, 128/290/3. The letter is also in MHS, 134.I.5.11.B #454.

4. WSU Cage 103, 1; UMT, 128/303/1; 128/286/6; SR 2/3/99, 5; MHS, 134.I.5.6.F #477.

5. SR 2/7/99, 5; 2/9/99, 5; 2/11/99, 5. A February 15 NP telegram supports the newspaper reports: The ORN had parties on Spring Creek and Penawawa Creek, "obviously designed to embarrass our Company as routes would be comparatively useless to them" (MHS, 134.I.5.6.F #477).

6. UMT, 128/316/409F; 128/290/3; 128/286/6; 128.316.409.F; 128/316/412; MHS, 134.I.5.11.B #596; 134.I.5.6.F #477; SR 2/19/99, 5; 2/20/99, 5; 2/23/99, 5; 2/25/99, 5; 3/1/99, 5; 3/4/99, 5; 3/6/99, 5; 3/11/99, 5; 3/17/99, 5; 3/24/99, 5; 3/27/99, 5.

7. MHS, 134.I.5.6.F #477.

8. SR 3/24/99, 5; 3/27/99, 5; 4/5/99, 5.

9. UMT, 128/316/412; MHS, 137.C.19.7.B #495.

10. MHS, 134.I.5.11.B #596; 136.G.8.1.B; 137.C.19.7.B #495; NP Confidential Report, 1900, 15, 17; UMT, 128/290/3 & MHS, 134.I.5.14.B; MHS, 134.I.4.13.B.

11. PH 7/23/04, 1; SR 7/17/04, 11; 4/15/06, 10; MHS, 137.C.16.7.B #420; 137.I.15.3.B #277; 134.H.9.1.B, 155.

12. Unless otherwise indicated the NP source for this section is MHS, 134.I.5.5.B #452.

13. LT 4/21/87, 3. In April 1887 Van Arsdol made a reconnaissance from Yakima to Riparia. The *Teller* report may be of an extension of the reconnaissance or a related survey (WSU 103.1).

14. WWJ 5/7/87, 3; 9/17/87, 3; 10/13/87, 3; WWU 10/22/87 2; 11/8/87, 3; PG 12/9/87, 3; also in WWU 12/17/87, 3.

15. OHS, 299, Exec. Com. Rec. Vol. 2, 20–21; OHS, 1591.B6.F40; OHS, Gill 1591.B4.F11; PG 2/1/89, 3.

16. Asay 1991, 121; MHS, 134.I.5.5.B; 137.C.19.7.B #495.

17. MHS, 137.C.19.7.B #495; MHS, 137.J.14.4.F; 134.I.5.11.B; 136.G.8.1.B; UMT, 178/81/1.

18. MHS, 137.C.19.7.B.

19. MHS, 137.B.20.5.B #155; 134.I.5.5.B #448; PH 12/3/98, 1.

20. PH 11/26/98.

21. CG 11/25/98, 3; Gill 1916, 72; SR 11/29/98, 5; LTR 1/14/99 in WSU Cage 103, 1; SR12/10/98, 5. Nelson Bennett and H. S. Huson had contracts for the Wallula-Lewiston line. Bennett constructed NP's Stampede Tunnel and graded much of the S&P line including yards at Lewiston. Huson had been a division engineer for the NP.

22. UMT, 128/303/1; SR 12/29/98, 5; UMT, 128/290/3.

23. SR 1/11/99, 5; 1/17/99, 5; LTR 1/28/99, WSU Cage 103, 1. The report to the ICC says that the SRV began construction on the north bank of the Snake River from Riparia to Lewiston in January 1899 (Gill 1916, 72, 75).

24. SR 2/12/99, 8; UMT, 128/301/1; 128/316/409F; 128/286/6; 128/316/412; 128/303/1; 128/316/412; MHS, 137.C.19.7.B #495.

25. SR 3/13/99, 5; MHS, 134.I.5.6.F #477; MHS, 137.C19.7.B #495.

26. UMT, 128/303/1; 128/303/1; MHS, 137.C.19.7.B #495; UMT, 128/286/6; 128/316/412; MHS, 137.C.19.7.B; 134.I.5.6.F #477; SR 5/22/99, 5; 5/27/99, 5.

27. UMT, 128/303/1; 128/316/412; 128/286/6; 128/316/412.

28. UMT, 128/316/412; MHS, 134.I.9.1.B #1874; SR 7/2/99, 5; LTR 7/1/99, 1.

29. UMT, 128/303/1; 128/316/412; 128/317/416; (some newspapers reports in UMT files); SR 7/12/99, 5; 7/27/99, 5; 7/31/99, 8; 8/12/99, 5; 9/9/99, 5; 9/30/99, 5; PH 9/30/00; OHS, Gill 1591.B.6.F.47; Gill 1916, 72, 75.

30. SR 8/20/99, 3; 9/3/99, 3; 9/30/99, 5; 10/10/99, 5; 11/13/99, 5; Gill 1916, 75. The line was operated by the ORN through stock ownership of the SRV from December 1, 1899, to June 30, 1907, and under lease from July 1, 1907, to December 23, 1910. On that date the property was deeded to the Oregon-Washington Railroad & Navigation Company.

31. MHS, 134.I.5.11.B #603 & 137.C.19.7.B #495E without table. Some of the 70 miles of right-of-way from Lewiston to Riparia was purchased in 1899 and 1900 by the CSL (CSL 1916).

32. SR 12/25/99, 5; 1/11/00, 5; PH 2/10/00, 1.

33. UMT, 128.303.1; MHS, 137.C.19.7.B #495. A letter (2/11/04) contains a profile from Hunt's Junction via Pleasant View to Grange City dated 2/10/04. The distance is a little over 60 miles; the constructed distance to Pleasant View is little less than 42 miles. Hunt's Junction's elevation is 302 feet, the highest elevation is at mile 40, 1426 feet, from approximately mile 42.5 to 52.25 and from approximately mile 55 to Grange City the descent is 1.32 percent compensated grade. (MHS, 137.C.19.7.B #495 also 134.I.5.11.B, #614).

34. MHS, 134.I.5.11.B also 137.C.19.7.B #495; 1900 NP Confidential Report, 16, 17, 18. The lines were Lewiston to Grange City, Grange City to Pleasant View, Pullman to Penawawa, Potlatch branch, Lapwai branch (Culdesac to Nez Perce), Camas Prairie branch, and east of Dayton. The latter was WCR and remainder CSL.

35. MHS, 137.C.19.7.B, #495E & 134.I.5.11.B, #614; SR 7/12/04; 7/13/04, 12; 7/14/04, 12.

36. SR 9/12/05, 14; OHS, Gill 1591.B.6.F.47; Gill 1916, 72, 75; SR 6/3/06, 9A; 6/8/06, 14; 7/17/06, 14; 8/17/06, 16; 12/13/06, 6. The OWI was incorporated by the ORN August 8, 1903.

37. SR 10/23/06, 18; RA 11/2/06, 558; Gill 1914, 246; SR 1/7/07, 14.

38. SR 6/30/07, 10A; 8/3/07, 10; 8/9/07, 18; 10/5/07, 6; 11/7/07, 18; 12/9/07, 13; 3/31/08.

39. SR 5/28/09, 5; 5/29/09, 11; 5/30/09, 8.

40. Gaertner 1990, 6, 11–26; Grande 1992, 192; Austin & Dill, 1996, 125; MHS, 134.I.9.1.B #1874; NP 1933; NP Condensed Profile, 1970; OHS, Gill 1591.6.F8, 7/20; SR 2/3/06, 1; 3/31/06, 1; 4/16/06, 12; 9/14/06, 6. A measure of the dominance of Marshall over the Snake River Branch would be a comparison of the net revenue ton miles on the two lines. Unfortunately only three years, 1931, 1935, and 1939, are available. In those three years approximately 292,961 net revenue ton miles moved over the Riparia to Snake River Junction line (41 miles), while 1,093,410 moved over the Belmont to Marshall line (43 miles). Because the two mileages are similar the comparison is not significantly distorted by distance (H. H. Copeland & Son). In 1959 the United States acquired the Snake River Junction to Riparia roadbed to build the Lower Monumental Dam on the Snake River. The NP then used the UP tracks from Wallula to Riparia.

41. SR 12/16/10, 7; MHS, 134.I.17.14.F; 134.H.9.1.B, 124.

42. MHS, 137.C.20.1.B #495P.

43. NP 1933; Whitman College Archives.

44. UMT, 128/312/7; MHS, 137.B.15.16.F. The other three lines were from Mission Creek on the Lapwai Branch, from Culdesac, and from Stites on the Clearwater.

45. For a history of the L&SE and related lines see Konen 1975 and also Butler 1978 and Riegger 1986.

46. SR 4/5/03, 4; 5/27/03, 4; 6/23/03, 4; 5/15/05, 1; 5/18/05, 1; PH 5/20/05.

47. MHS, 134.I.6.9.B #1143; 134.I.7.6.F #1396; 137.C.19.7.B. In 1911 the NP reported owning 1.10 acres, valued at $110, on the Tammany Creek Line (MHS, 134.H.9.1.B, 102).

48. SR 3/2/06, 14; 3/4/06, B3.

49. MHS, 134.1.7.6.F #1396; NP 1906; CSL 1916, 420–21. A February 1906 map of NP surveys shows a line from Lewiston to Lake Waha and the Ilo-Nez Perce right of way.

50. SR 2/11/08, 16; 6/26/08, 9; 7/21/08, 16.

51. Konen 1975; SR 7/17/08, 16; 7/25/08, 16; 8/21/08, 16; 6/8/10, 5; 6/10/10, 5; 6/25/10, 3; 8/25/10, 8; CSL 1916, 420–21.

52. Konen 1975; Butler 1978; MHS, 137.C.19.7.B #495G.

53. MHS, 134.I.12.1.B #3789; 137.E.2.5.B #1225.

54. Burg 2003, has an account of the white pine belt and the Moscow and Eastern as well as the Washington, Idaho and Montana Railway. Petersen 1987, also covers the same ground.

55. PG 5/27/87, 3; 9/6/87, 2; SR 4/27/90, 12; PG 7/18/90, 2.

56. SR 5/12/95, 6; CG 1/29/97, 4.

57. SR 3/39/97, 3; 4/1/97, 3; 5/8/97, 3.

58. MHS, 134.I.5.5.B #95; Burg 2003, 9, 10; UI MG 139 WI&M IV; SR 11/7/97, 3. This "Vollmer" was located on upper West Fork of Bear Creek in Latah County, Idaho. It was named after Lewiston banker and merchant John P. Vollmer "who foreclosed on notes during the 1893 depression, and [the community] decided to hold an election to choose a new name. As the story goes, a Greek working for the railroad set up a barrel of liquor at the poll site and offered all the liquor one wanted if he voted for Troy, the most illustrious name in history and literature. The results [9/6/1897] were 29 votes for Troy and 9 for Vollmer" (Boone 1988, 380). The NP did not change the name of the station to "Troy" until 10/25/1903. The other "Vollmer" referred to earlier in the chapter was located on the Camas Prairie in Lewis County, Idaho, and was named after the same person. The name of that "Vollmer" was changed to "Craigmont."

59. SR 1/23/99, 5; MHS, 137.C.19.7.B #495D; SR 2/1/99, 5; 2/4/99, 5, 8; 2/8/99, 5; UMT, 128/286/6; SR 2/17/99, 5; MHS, 134.I.5.5.B #437.

60. SR 3/5/99, 5; MHS, 137.C.19.7.B #495; SR 3/11/99, 5; 3/20/99, 5; 3/25/99, 5; MHS, 134.I.5.6.F #477.

61. UMT, 128/286/6; 128/316/412; MHS, 134.I.5.6.F #477.

62. SR 5/6/99, 5; MHS, 134.I.5.5.B #437; SR 5/21/99, 8.

63. UMT, 128/286/6; SR 7/8/99, 5; 7/17/99, 5; 7/18/99, 5; 8/14/99, 8; UMT, 128/316/412.

64. SR 7/24/99, 1; 8/3/99, 3; 8/6/99, 3.

65. MHS, 134.I.5.5.B #437.

66. MHS, 134.I.5.11.B #615; 137.C.19.7.B #495 & 495D; 134.I.5.5.B #437; UMT, 128/317/416.

67. MHS, 134.I.5.5.B #437; 134.I.5.11.B #615.

68. Burg 2003, 11; Petersen 1987, 20.

69. RA 4/26/01 (reported as Moscow & Idaho, but names are the same as names on the 1899 charter of M&E); PH 5/25/01; SR 11/20/01, 4; 12/3/01, 4; 1/11/02, 4; 1/21/02, 4; 5/24/02, 5; 5/30/02, 4; 6/1/02, 7; 9/27/02, 4; 3/11/03, 4; 7/12/02, 1; 9/8/02, 3; 2/13/03, 3; 2/17/03, 4; 2/20/03, 8; 3/6/03, 3.

70. RA 7/24/03; RA 7/29/04; 8/?/04; SR 10/21/03, 13. In the Moscow offices of the M&E was a map dated 5/10/05 "Moscow & Eastern Survey Bear Creek to Bovill" which contains a branch toward Potlatch (UI MG 139).

71. The NP agent at Moscow reported in August 1906 that ORN officials looked over M&E documents that month (MHS, 137.14.5.B).

XIX: New Railroads in the Palouse, 1901–1910

1. Histories of the predecessors and successors to the Spokane & Inland Empire Railroad: Carter 2009; Fahey 1994, chapter 4; Grande 1997, chapter 8; Mutschler 1987; Hilton & Due 1960, 389–90; ICC 1927.

2. SR 12/11/03, 1; Map SR 12/17/03, 9; CG 12/18/03, 2 reports on the backers and additional proposed routes; SR 3/1/04, 14 has a detailed report of the preliminary survey from Colfax to Spokane.

3. Mutschler 1987, 191; SR 1/9/04, 7.

4. SR 8/29/04, 5 & 7; 9/12/04, 7; 11/15/04, 1; 2/24/05, 9; 3/12/05, 9.

5. JJH 132.E.14.4.B, #4034-F7.

6. PH 1/21/05, 1; CG 1/27/05, 2, 4, 6; 2/10/05, 2; 2/17/05, 2; SR 3/19/05, 9; CG 3/31/05, 1; 4/7/05, 7; SR 4/7/05, 14; CG 4/14/05, 1; 4/28/05, 2; 5/19/05, 1.

7. MHS, 137.E.6.3.B, # 1375. There is also a June 10, 1905, letter—probably from Elliott—attempting to discourage investment in Graves' road. "It is a bad scheme for our interests, and, in my judgment, will be a bad scheme for anyone to put money into because the territory cannot support three railroads" (MHS, 137.E.5.9.B, #1340).

8. MHS, 137.E.5.9.B #1340; JJH.

9. PH 10/7/05, 1; CG 9/29/05, 1; 10/6/05, 2; 10/20/05, 2; Mattson.

10. MHS, 137.E.2.5.B #1231; Truce Agreement, 20.

11. SR 12/3/05, 11A; 1/10/06, 1; 1/24/06; CG 1/26/06, 1, 2; 3/9/06, 2.

12. JJH 132.E.14.4.B, #4034; Grande 1997, 376.

13. Except for newspaper references which are cited separately, financial transactions and related material here and below are drawn from: Carter 2009, 8–14; Grande 1997, 377, 389; JJH; MHS, 137.C.19.7.B #495G; 137.E.6.3.B #1375; 137.E.14.5.B #1603; 137.E.14.6.F #1604–2; Fahey 1994, 69, 71, 72; Hidy & Hidy, 22–25; Hilton & Due 1960, 389–90; Patrick Hiatte to Jerry Masters, 8/12/12. ICC Reports, Volume 124, March July, 1927, Finance Docket 6014, "Acquisition of Lines by Spokane, Coeur D'Alene & Palouse Ry." Decided April 21, 1927, 355–62.

14. SR 1/27/06, 4; 2/2/06, 16; 2/3/06, 13; 3/10/06, 1; 3/27/06, 16; PH 4/7/06, 4; SR 4/20/06, 9; 4/25/06, 16; 5/4/06, 16; MHS, 134.I.8.9.B #1665. The SIE was allowed to build and maintain a bridge over the NP north of Rosalia at no expense to the NP and the grade crossings of the NP at Oakesdale and Garfield were to be maintained and protected at the expense of the SIE (Joint Facilities 1929). At Garfield the SIE passed over the ORN.

15. SR 7/25/06, 16; 8/9/06, 14; 8/17/06, 16; CG 9/7/06, 7; SR 10/12/06, 18; 10/23/06, 5.

16. SR 9/5/06, 7; MHS, 137.E.5.9.B #1340; 137.14.B.B. The *Herald* reported in mid-July 1907 that the SIE "has purchased the branch of the O. R. & N. between Colfax and Moscow and that it will be equipped for electric cars" (PH 7/13/07, 1).

17. JJH 132.E.14.4.B, #4034; SR 10/18/07, 20; 2/6/08, 10. Miller was perhaps ignorant of Hill's investing in the SIE.

18. UI MG 183; SR 12/9/06, 7A; 12/21/06, 8; SR 1/23/07, 18; 1/18/07, 11; 1/28/07, 14.

19. SR 1/9/07, 1; MHS, 137.E.14.5.B; 137.E.5.9.B #1340.

20. SR 7/8/07, 14; CG 7/12/07, 1; CG 8/2/07, 2; 10/4/07, 1; PH 12/14/07, 2; SR 2/3/08, 5; 3/26/08, 18.

21. MHS, 137.E.5.9.B #1340; SR 2/9/08, 5A; 2/11/08, 16; MHS, 137.C.19.7.B 495G; SR 6/26/08, 9; 7/16/08, 16; 7/21/08, 16; MHS, 137.C.6.3.B; SR 9/14/08, 6; 9/17/08, 16.

22. SR 1/14/09, 20; 4/8/09, 9; 4/4/09, 10A; 6/15/09, 9; PH 4/9/09, 1; SR 6/17/09, 8.

23. SR 2/10/10, 8.

24. SR 10/29/09, 1; 10/31/09, 4A.

25. SR 1/15/10, 8.

26. MHS, 137.E.5.9.B #1340 also 137.E.14.5.B #1603.

27. SR 10/29/09, 1. Howard Elliott, then the NP chairman, in a memorandum, April 19, 1926, placed the loss to the NP at $5,772,730. This cost does not included the lost revenue of the NP (and the ORN). All of the area served by the SIE was tributary to either or both the NP and ORN (Patrick Hiatte to Jerry Masters, 8/12/12). As with the S&P's Farmington Branch, investment in the SIE was an economic waste, except for possibly the GN's mainline revenues.

28. The major work on the WIM is Burg 2003.

29. SR 3/30/03, 4; 4/23/03, 4; 5/8/03, 4. 6/8/03, 4; Burg 2003, 22; MHS, 134.I.4.14.F #178; SR 10/20/03, 12; 11/10/03, 13; UI MG139.331.

30. MHS, 137.I.15.2.F #1582; 137.D.10.10.F #767; 137.C.20.1.B #495.

31. MHS, 137.D.10.10.F #767.

32. SR 5/6/05, 1; 11/15/05, 5; JJH; MHS, 137.D.10.10.F #767; Burg 2003, 28.

33. MHS, 137.D.10.10.F#767.

34. Burg 2003, 37, 59; SR 6/7/06, 16; 6/9/06, 5; SR 9/16/06, 12C.

35. MHS, 134.I.9.13.B; 137.D.10.10.F #767; Burg 2003, 74; SR 1/22/10, 8; 5/27/10, 8; 6/14/10, 5.

36. MHS, 137.E.6.3.B #1375; personal correspondence from Thomas Burg 1/25/2012.

37. A general history of the CM&SP is Derleth 2002.

38. SR 1/28/06, 1; 3/17/06, 10; 3/21/06, 1; 3/29/06, 1.

39. SR 9/1/06, 1; 10/11/08, 10A; 10/31/08, 8; CG 12/25/08.

40. Gill, 1914, 255; SR 10/17/09, 9A; CG 10/1/09; SR 10/1/09, 9; 10/6/09, 11; CG 11/12/09, 1; MHS, 137.E.14.5.B #1603; CG 1/14/10; SR 1/23/10, 8A; Deary *Enterprise* 2/4/10; Burg 2003, 79; SR 5/24/10, 8.

41. Asay 1991, 129.

42. See Burg 2003, chapters 13 to 15.

43. NP reports and correspondence are in MHS, 137.E.2.5.B #1231, 134.I.8.1.B, and 134.I.8.10.F.

44. Gill 1916, 14; RA 12/16/04, 876; 12/30/04, 943.

45. OHS, Gill 1591.B.5.F.11; Gill 1916, 14; RA 7/14/05, 55.

46. SR 8/26/05, 12.

47. SR 11/12/05, 9; Spokane *Chronicle*, 11/11/05, 1; RG 11/24/05, 107; 12/22/05, 201.

48. Spokane *Chronicle* 1/6/06; SR 2/9/06, 16; SR 2/19/06, 12; 3/15/06, 1. According to Gill, at the end of 1905 "18 miles of completed grade had been constructed from Connell toward Fletcher, a distance of 33 miles. No more had been done on account of lack of funds to prosecute it, when Mr. Strahorn bought the property" (Gill 1914, 243).

49. SR 3/20/06, 1; 3/22/06, 9; 3/28/06, 7; 4/6/06, 6; 4/10/07, 6; 4/15/06, 10; Gill, 1916, 76; ICC 1934, 284; OHS, 299/Vol. 136, 158; Gill 1914, 243; Asay 1991, 122–23.

50. There is no comprehensive history of the North Coast Railway/Railroad.

51. Gill 1914, 201–02, 208; SR 10/12/05, 16; 10/28/05, 16; 10/31/05, 1. Beginning almost 30 years earlier and for several years Strahorn was employed by the Union Pacific to do literary and advertising work. For several years Strahorn was located in Caldwell, Idaho, as general manager of the Idaho & Oregon Improvement Co., which owned town sites along the route of the Oregon Short Line.

52. Asay 1991, 121–22; Gill 1914, 243. ICC 1934, 284–85: Harvey Fisk and Sons advanced to the North Coast Railway $85,900, of which $38,310 was found to be applicable to the property owned by the OWRN. The difference of $47,590 might be what Strahorn received for the franchise (SR 2/1/06, 1; 2/11/06, A11). For a more extensive account of the Strahorn-Harriman relationship, see Beach 2012. Included in the latter is Strahorn's (1942) account of his first meeting with Harriman.

53. MHS, 137.E.2.5.B #1231 and 134.I.8.10.F. E. W. Swanson listed on a letterhead of The State Bank of Washington, Spokane, as president and director. Darling's intelligence so early in the game is interesting. An investigation of the Seaboard National Bank might have revealed the Strahorn-Harriman connection. How much officials of the ORN knew of this arrangement is unknown; perhaps nothing until the lines were merged in 1910, but in any case it was a Harriman scheme independent of the ORN.

54. SR 4/13/06, 16; Asay 1991, 122–23; OHS, 299, Vol. 34 or Box 100; SR 5/14/06, 12; 5/19/06, 9; 5/20/06,9A; 5/29/06, 16.

55. Asay 1991, 122; OHS, 299/box 100; SR 10/2/06, 8.

56. OHS, 299, Vol. 34 or Box 100; SR 3/21/07, 11; the *Chronicle* report in MHS, 137.D.19.9.B #1127B.

57. SR 4/10/07, 6; OHS, 299 Vol. 5, 12.

58. SR 9/22/07, 9A.

59. SR 7/22/08, 8; 7/26/08, 1A, 1B.

60. SR 5/26/09, 11; 6/2/09, 2.

61. SR 11/17/08, 16; 8/24/09, 1; 11/3/09, 9; OHS, Gill 1591.136. F29. *Tribune* article in MHS, 137.D.19.9.B #1127B. The *Deary Enterprise* 1/21/10; SR 1/28/10, 8.

62. OHS, 299, Vol. 34 or Box 100; MHS, 137.C.20.1.B #495; SR 4/7/10, 8.

63. MHS, 137.D19.9.B #1127B.

64. SR 11/24/10, 1; 12/21/10, 8. Spokane would only be closer to Portland and Walla Walla when the Spokane-Ayers line, begun by the NC, was completed in 1914.

65. OHS, 299 Vol. 87, 9; Gill, 1916, 29. Eleven lines of the NC were conveyed. The most important were the partially constructed Attalia to North Yakima and Spokane to Ayer Junction, both of which were completed by the OWRN and opened to traffic on March 24, 1911, and September 15, 1914, respectively. The Spokane to Ayer Junction was built to a very high standard and largely paralleled the Spokane, Portland & Seattle Railway. In addition to the Palouse Branch, the Wallula-Walla Walla line, the surveys east of Walla Walla, and the surveys west of North Yakima and south of the Attalia-North Yakima line were not conveyed.

66. The total cost of the NC to 12/23/10 was $8,455,006 (OHS, 299 Vol. 5, 181). How much of the cost of the property not sold should be attributed to the Palouse Branch is unknown, but is likely to be significant given that some construction occurred on the branch whereas little or no construction took place on the other unsold property.

67. SR 12/29/10, 7.

68. MHS, 137.C.19.7.B #495G; 137.D.19.9.B #1127B.

XX: Palouse & Lewiston Branches, 1901–1910

1. SR 12/22/00, 8; 2/17/01, 1; 2/20/01, 10; 2/26/01, 10; 2/28/01, 10; 3/3/01, 12.

2. SR 3/21/01, 4; 4/13/01, 10; 4/25/01, 12.

3. SR 3/17/01, 8. Immigrants to the Palouse see SR 4/28/01, 4; 10/17/01, 1; 4/29/02, 5. The estimate for immigrants for Washington in 1902 was 44,000 (SR 4/20/02, 1).

4. NYT 9/1/01, 1; SR 9/27/01, 4; 10/15/01, 1; 11/5/01, 4; 10/22/01, 4.

5. All references to the proposed improvements are in MHS, 134.F.6.7.B #1063 (also in 137.B.20.5.B #155). The 1901 Annual Report said that 87 percent of the NP branch line mileage in 1901 was laid with 56-pound rail. Darling wrote Mellen April 23, 1903: "The country between Rosalia and Sprague has already been examined, and favorably reported on.... I would recommend a reconnaissance being made [Rosalia]...to Connell in order to have the information regarding character of country at hand, but I believe if it ever becomes necessary to serve the country West of Cow Creek that it can be done more economically by a stub line from Ritzville southeasterly down Cow Creek for 15 to 18 miles."

6. SR 11/12/1901, 4; 11/14/01, 4; PH 11/9/01; 11/16/01; 1/18/02.

7. SR 11/6/01, 10; 12/1/01, 9; 2/10/02, 8.

8. SR 11/18/01, 8; PH 1/11/02; SR 2/11/02, 4; 12/12/02, 4; 3/6/02, 12. The Revised Engineering Report of June 30, 1917, shows a four ton scale at the stock yard in Garfield.

9. SR 1/1/03, part 5, 2 & 1; 1/6/03, 4; 11/22/03, 18.

10. SR 2/19/03, 4; 1/30/03, 4; 3/2/03, 4; 3/26/03, 4.

11. SR 10/26/03, 10; PH 10/31/03, 1; 12/19/03, 4; SR 3/11/04, 14; PH 6/18/04; 7/30/04, 1.

12. MHS, 137.I. 15.3.B #2171; SR 8/3/04, 12.

13. MHS, 134.F.6.7.B #1063; MHS, 134.I.9.6.F #2012. Bridge 170, between Joel and Howell, was 879 feet long and as high as 40 feet, and was eventually filled.

14. SR 9/26/04, 10.

15. MHS, 134.F.6.7.B #1063; SR 9/6/06, 16. NP 1935, shows that in 1914 four 30-foot i-beam bridges were installed at bridge 49.

16. SR 7/23/05, 4; 7/27/05, 5.

17. SR 9/30/05, 4; 12/13/05, 16.

18. SR 11/20/05, 5; 11/24/05, 4. "Potlatch Jct." remained at least until employee timetable #25 6/4/05; in timetable #27 6/2/07 it was "Arrow Jct." (no employee timetables are available between the two dates). Public timetable July 1906, has "Clearwater Jct." on both the timetable and the regional map, but the main map has "Potlatch Jct."; April 1907 and May 1907 have "Arrow" in the timetable, "Clearwater Jct.," in the regional map, and "Potlatch Jct." on the main map.

19. SR 3/28/06, 6.

20. SR 7/25/06, 7.

21. Railroad Commission of Washington: 1st report 6/23/05–12/31/06, 95, 25; MHS, 137 E.5.9.B #1344; SR 6/21/07, 11; 10/22/08, 10; PH 9/14/07, 1. See chapter XVII for additional information about the Connell connection.

22. SR 8/12/06, 9A & 1B; PH 8/18/06, 2; 12/8/06, 1; SR 12/10/06, 9. The tramp was probably riding between the engine tender and the first car.

23. SR 10/23/06, 18; 10/25/06, 5; 10/27/06, 7; 11/25/06, 14A; 12/3/06, 1; 12/7/06, 1; 12/16/06, 4B; 12/18/06, 1; 12/20/06, 5; 12/28/06, 16; 12/30/06, 7B; 1/8/07, 7; 1/9/07, 1; 1/17/07, 7; 2/6/07, 6; 3/15/07, 20; 3/31/07, 9C (and many others).

24. SR 4/13/07, 5; 4/24/07, 5; 4/30/07, 1.

25. SR 2/27/07, 6.

26. MHS, 134.F.6.7.B # 1063.

27. SR 8/8/07, 1; CG 8/9/07, 2; PH 8/10/07, 1; SR 8/25/07, 1.

28. SR 9/13/07, 18; CG 10/25/07, 1.

29. SR 9/30/07, 6; 10/25/07, 6; 11/18/07, 6; 4/12/08, 6C.

30. PH 11/2/07, 1; SR 12/3/07, 6; 12/6/07, 11; 12/15/07, 5A.

31. SR 12/28/07, 5. "Lapwai Jct.," renamed "Joseph" November 17, 1907, never had a depot. North Lapwai was a mile west and had a depot from 1898. It and Arrow served as the transfer points. In 1909 Joseph received a 5'x6' frame register booth and in 1921 a 12.4'x20.3' frame shelter shed. "Joseph" was renamed "Spalding" in 1927.

32. SR 4/10/08, 5; 6/3/08, 14; 6/17/08, 6; 6/22/08, 8; 6/23/08, 10; PH 7/8/10, 1; CG 3/26/09, 1 (and others); PH 4/18/08, 3.

33. MHS, 134.1.9.11.B.

34. SR 3/17/08, 1; 3/20/08, 18; 6/5/08, 1; PH 6/27/08, 4; SR 11/20/08, 20; 2/11/09, 18.

35. SR 7/24/08, 16. A valuation dated December 28, 1909, estimated cost of reproduction of the Lewiston depot at $50,081 (MHS, 134.I.8.4.F).

36. SR 9/1/08, 5; 9/25/08, 6.

37. SR 1/31/09, 6A; 7/3/09, 6.

38. PH 2/12/09, 1; SR 7/2/09, 8; 7/12/09, 8; 10/3/09, 9C; 10/4/09, 6; 12/30/09, 9.

39. PH 5/21/09, 1; 1/21/10, 5; 4/8/10, 1.

40. PH 11/5/09, 1; SR 11/3/09, 5; 12/14/09, 5.

41. SR 11/3/09, 8. A Condensed Rail Chart, June, 1916, shows 72 pound rail between Pullman and Howell (MHS, 137.B.20.6.F #171). A NP Condensed Profile and Track Chart, July 1922, revised January 1, 1931, shows 72 pound rail from Marshall to Lewiston. This *Review* article claimed heavier rail was put in between Pullman and Howell.

42. PH 12/17/09, 1. The schedule change was for the mixed train, not the passenger train which continued to originate at Genesee.

43. PH 3/4/10, 1; 3/11/10, 1; SR 1/23/10, 6A; 1/24/10, 1; 1/26/10, 5; 2/16/10, 6; 2/21/10, 1; 2/24/10, 1; 3/1/10, 9; 3/2/10, 5 & 8; 3/4/10, 1; 3/6/10 2A & 5A; 3/9/10, 5; CG 3/25/10, 1; MHS, 137.D.4.5.B #528.

44. SR 4/14/10, 5.

45. SR 9/18/10, 6; 9/17/10, 8; PH 10/28/10, 1; 11/11/10, 1; SR 11/22/10, 5.

46. SR 11/2/10, 10; CG 1/20/11, 6. The state tax commission found that there were 5,725 miles of steam railroad track in the state in 1910. King County had the most at 618 miles. The assessed value of Whitman County farm land in 1909 was $13,280,933, an increase in six years of over five and half million dollars. There were 943,106 acres of improved farm land and 284,366 acres of unimproved.

47. MHS, 134.I.10.7.B #2833; NP 1935.

Conclusion

1. We shall continue to refer to it as the Spokane & Palouse (S&P) because that encompasses all three branches. If the reader is uncomfortable about retaining the S&P designation, just substitute Northern Pacific (NP or BN/BNSF). Our subject is now generally referred to as the Palouse & Lewiston (P&L) which was technically only the branch from Marshall to Lewiston.

2. Rail weight is a surrogate for maintenance and improvements. In 1970 just prior to BN merger the P&L branch had 26 miles of 100 and 112 lb rail, 92 miles of 90 lb rail and 19 miles of 85 lb rail; the Genesee had 27 miles of 90 lb; in both cases this covered the entire length of the branch's main track. In 1977, the UP had on average somewhat heavier rail from Hooper Jct. to Spokane via Colfax. Sources: NP Condensed Profile, 1/1/70 and UP condensed Profile 1/1/77.

3. CG 1/20/11, 6.

4. Meinig 1968, 515–16; Nesbit & Gates 1946.

5. CG 1/20/11, 6.

6. SR 1/1/03, part 5, 2 & 1.

7. This estimate was derived from 1903 on Table C-1: 4,889,400 + 2,324,170 + 5,000,000 = 12,213,540 bushels (see note to the table for tons and cars calculations). In the prior chapters are a number of statements in the press that the ORN was receiving a majority of the grain brought to a particular station—whether true or not the statements imply that the ORN was competitive with S&P. See note 9 for tons of flour for 1902 and other years and one season of fruit shipped by P&S.

8. SR 9/13/07, 18; CG 10/25/07, 1.

9. Wheat tons and car loads calculated by author based on 60 lb. per bushel, 2000 lb. per short ton, and 30 tons capacity per car. Other grains include oats (32 lb./bushel), barley (48 lb./bushel), rye (56 lb./bushel), and flax (56 lb./bushel)—the calculation of tons of other grains is an aggregation of each grain's weight in lbs. per bushel. The "est. car loads" is probably an underestimate because most cars were less than 30-ton capacity. In 1899 30-ton cars were only about a quarter of the total freight cars owned by the NP; the same year half of the UP cars had a 30-ton capacity (White 1993, 198). Because the total number of bushels for each grain varies from year to year the relationships among bushels, tons, and cars, unlike wheat, varies from year to year. The Confidential Reports also contain tons of flour shipped: 1898, 1990 (66 cars); 1899, 2033 (68 cars); 1900, 3075 (1,025 cars); 1902, 2,772 (92 cars); 1903, 3,900 (130 cars). In the 1901 season S&P moved 264 cars of fruit.

10. The terminologies of "revenue" and "earnings" of the passenger business and freight business differ, we are treating them as interchangeable, which NP seems to do in other contexts.

11. MHS, 137.C.15.1B. The 1921–23 average earnings for the Farmington Branch were $347.

12. MHS, 134.F.38.F. Accompanying the letter is a table showing that the S&P rates for merchandise to Tacoma and merchandise and grain to Portland were all below 40 percent of the rates for the same mileage as for the Washington & Columbia River branch of the NP. On the grain rates per ton on the same 536 main line miles to Portland, the W&CR branch line miles rates were higher between 4.3 times (on 53 branch miles) and 43 times (on 5 branch miles) than the rate on the S&P. Both branches had strong ORN competition.

13. UMT, 185/vol. 338/branch line reports. The capitalization and mileages given in the report are the same as the June 30, 1896, report to the ICC.

14. Thanks to Mark Entze for pointing out the symbol freight.

15. Daggett 1908, 237.

16. Mark Entze and Thomas Hillebrant helped me account for the abandonments.

17. Hilton & Due 1960, 389: "The [Palouse] lines were…designed primarily for freight service from the beginning. The rolling Palouse wheat country was very unpromising territory for an interurban in terms of passenger traffic, but offered potential freight business.… Freight service was emphasized from the first, with a number of standard boxcars bought when the road was built, and interchanged with the steam roads." From 1905 to 1907 the SIE bought 375 freight cars (160 flats, 205 box, and 10 stock) (Carter 2009, 91). Recall Hill's efforts to gain access to the Palouse without building a railroad line. He gained access with a traffic contract with the SIE in 1907 and by 1909 he had acquired a controlling interest in the SIE and the GN purchased the line in 1927 (Carter 2009, 2).

18. Carter 2009, 5–14. The forest products traffic that the SIE acquired from the WIM at Palouse was certainly more profitable to the GN than the grain traffic.

19. I am particularly in debt to Marc Entze in the following discussion, from his Ph.D. dissertation (Entze 2010) and numerous exchanges of emails.

20. The only major exceptions to disappearance or declined population in the Palouse are Pullman and Moscow which are both university towns. Their growth can be largely attributed to increase in student and staff populations. Neither town now has a railroad when once they had the S&P and ORN and in Moscow the addition of the SIE.

21. How much of the shortage was caused by western railroad under investment is hard to determine, but it is clear that it was not the sole cause of the problem; eastern railroads did not own sufficient box cars for their needs and made up for their under investment by retaining western railroad's box cars; the NP in the early 1960s had available the equivalent of only 62.3 percent the boxcars it owned, the GN had only 53 percent, while the Pennsylvania had on its lines equivalent of 137.4 percent of the boxcars it actually owned, the New Haven, 164.8 percent, and the Reading 182.2 percent (Entze 2010, 155–56). A virtue of covered hoppers was

that the eastern railroads had less need for them, so did not retain them (the same was true of center beam flat cars for lumber replacing regular flat cars and box cars).

22. Entze 2010, 173, 230–32.

23. Entze 2010, 258.

24. Information on unit train facilities from Marc Entze, email 1/18/18.

25. See Beach 2007 for an account of a trip on the High Ball.

26. Email communications with Entze January 2018; Bud Cain interview by Beach 7/5/95; "Operating Information for Idaho Division Collected for J. W. Barriger, RFC" c. 1936, Barriger Collection, Mercantile Library; Burg 2003, 341; see Beach 2007.

27. Entze 2010, 222.

Appendices I and II

1. S&P 1912; S&P 1916, 373; ICC 1929, 556, 707-710.

2. This appendix is based on Form 97, 3-12 P, pp. 159-62, 191-96 (MHS 134.H.9.1.B). It is organized by Interstate Commerce Commission valuation sections and was probably prepared in anticipation of, or for, the 1917 report to the ICC. There is no indication as to the date it was prepared, but some of the reporting is prior to 1917, e.g., no steel bridges were reported, but at least ten steel bridges, including the Clearwater River bridge, were built prior to 1916, but not prior to 1912; and all of the depots are recorded as frame structures, but two depots, Pullman, built 1916, and Lewiston, 1909, were "Passenger Stations, Brick or Stone" (the Pullman and Lewiston depots were recorded as brick in the Engineering Report to the ICC of June 30, 1917). I have combined the forms into the three branches of the NP's Palouse lines. Not all the reporting categories separately stated in the appendix.

3. http://www.davemanuel.com/inflation-calculator.php.

4. ICC 1929, 556, 707-710.

5. MHS 134.H.9.1.B, pp. 97-99,124-127.

6. MHS 134.I.8.4.F.

7. MHS 134.I.17.4.F #6618.

8. NP Condensed Profile and Track Chart, Jan. 1, 1966.

9. This is not a comprehensive account of the S&P bridges. It seeks to give a general accounting of bridges in the original construction and what the author views as significant changes. For more detailed accounts see NP 1935 and NP 1968.

10. Construction Profile (MHS 134.L.18.8); 1894 Track Profile; 1932 Track Profile; Authorizations for Expenditures; NP Bridge lists 1935 & 1968; MHS 134.F.6.7.B #1063; UMT 128/372/521.

11. MHS 134.I.10.7.B #2833 has a drawing of the bridge.

12. MHS 134.I.10.7.B #2833; 134.M1.5.B.

13. Construction Profile (MHS 134.L.18.8); 1894 Track Profile; 1932 Track Profile; Authorizations for Expenditures; NP Bridge lists 1935 & 1968; MHS 134.F.6.7.B #1063; UMT 128/372/521.

14. Whether the OT bought the bonds at par or at discount is not known, but discounts were common. Also whether in initiating the financing Villard and associates received a discount is not known, but was likely. In any case the OT now had nearly two and half million dollars to apply to its debt. Because the par value of the bonds owned by the ORN equaled the miles certified, it is unlikely that there were more than a few, if any, bonds owned by others. OHS, 299, Exec. Com. Rec., 145; ICC 1934, 271; Gill 1916, 6; MHS 137.I.19.2.F #19; NYT 10/19/84, 2; OR&N 1884 Annual Report; MHS 137.H.4.10.F; NP Papers.

15. C&P 1907 Annual Report to the ICC; Gill, 1916, 5-6, 90.

16. This total includes the $3,829,000 in bonds and stock sold by the OT to the OR&N in 1884. The remainder of the investment, $1,023,967, consisted of nonnegotiable debt of the ORN for construction: $840,265 from five miles east of Colfax to Moscow and from Colfax to Farmington; $100,901 from La Crosse to Riparia, subsequently completed by the ORN; and $82,801 of mostly finance charges. Thus the attributed construction costs of the C&P, excluding finance charges and La Crosse to Riparia, were $2,846,479 ($1,935,779+70,435+840,265, $19,658 per mile for 144.8 miles). La Crosse to Riparia is excluded because it was built by the OR&N under its own name and was legally never part of the C&P. (ICC 1934, 271; plus author calculations.)

17. 143.8 miles is the original construction mileage which was broken down in the report to the ICC as follows (corrections added another mile): Connell to La Crosse 53.12; La Crosse to Colfax 35.68 (35.64); Colfax to State Line 26.2; State Line to Moscow 1.6 (2.36); and Colfax to Farmington 27.20 (27.48); Total 143.8 (144.8). (Gill 1916, 5).

18. SR 7/12/99, 5; 7/25/99, 5; 10/6/00, 10; 8/30/99, 5; 9/20/99, 5.

References

Documents

Agreement 1885. *Agreement between the Union Pacific Railway Company Oregon Short Line Railway Company and the Northern Pacific Railroad Co. Dated April 14th, 1885.*

Agreement 1890. *Agreement between the Oregon Short Line and Utah Northern Railway Company and the Great Northern Railway Company, covering joint ownership of the Portland & Puget Sound Railway. Dated October 13, 1890.*

Commissioners 1881, United States. *Spokane Falls, Washington Territory November 4th 1881.* Library of Congress, from Jerry Masters.

Construction Profile, Construction Profiles of the S&P (MHS 134.L.18.8.F).

Contract 1882. *Supplementary Contract. The Oregon Railway & Navigation Company and Northern Pacific Railroad Co. Dated August 17th, 1882.* (MHS H2791 N795 N8 #129).

Copeland, H. H. & Son, New York. *Northern Pacific Ry. Freight Traffic Density by Divisions and Direction.* Various dates. *Northern Pacific Ry. Traffic Interchanged,* 1925 and 1931.

Correspondence 1898. *Correspondence re Northern Pacific and Oregon Railroad and Navigation Company, October-November, 1898* (MHS 137.C.19.7.B).

C&P 1907. Annual Report to the ICC.

CR&N 1916. NP Valuation filing with the ICC on the corporate history of the Coeur d'Alene Railway and Navigation Company. (MHS 134.H.9.1.B).

CSL 1916. NP Valuation filing with the ICC on the corporate history of the Clearwater Short Line Railway Company. (MHS 134.H.9.1.B).

Dissolution 1900. *Dissolution of the Voting Trust of the Northern Pacific Railway Company. November 12, 1900.*

Farmers' 1894. *The Farmers' Loan and Trust Company against Northern Pacific Railroad Company et al.* Circuit Court of U.S., Eastern District of Wisconsin (MHS 138.H.20.3.B).

Gill 1916, Frank B. *Oregon-Washington Railroad & Navigation Company Report to the Interstate Commerce Commission, Corporate History as Required by Valuation Order No. 20, June 30, 1916.*

——1916b. *Notes from Minutes of Meetings of Stockholders, Directors and Executive Committee [OR&N].* February, 1916. OHS, Gill Collection, Mss 1591, Box 6, Folder 40.

ICC 1927. Interstate Commerce Commission Reports, Volume 124, March July, 1927, Finance Docket 6014, "Acquisition of Lines by Spokane, Coeur D'Alene & Palouse Ry." Decided April 21, 1927. pp 355-362.

ICC 1929. Interstate Commerce Commission, Vol. 25, Valuation Reports, February-May, 1929. Northern Pacific Railway Company. Washington, D.C.: GPO, 1929

ICC 1934. Interstate Commerce Commission, Vol. 44, Valuation Reports, June-July, 1933, Union Pacific, Oregon-Washington Railroad & Navigation Company, GPO, 1934, pp. 213-321.

Joint Facilities 1929. Photographs included in the document taken 1927-29. From collection of Daniel Cozine.

Lease, 1886. *Lease. Spokane and Palouse Railway Company to Northern Pacific R. R. Company. Dated May 1st, 1886.* MHS HE 2791 N 795 N8.

Lease, 1887. *Indenture Supplementary to Lease Spokane & Palouse Rwy. Co. to Northern Pacific R. R. Co. Dated June 1, 1887.* MHS HE 2791 N 795 N8.

Lease, 1894. Three leases of November 17, 1894 between Farmers' Loan & Trust Company, Receivers for the Northern Pacific and the Spokane & Palouse Railway. MHS HE 2791 N795 N8 No. 301.

Memorandum 1927. St. Paul, Minn., October 24, 1927 in NP President's subject file 137.C.19.7.B #495-B. Author unknown.

Mohr 1887, Paul F. *Report Upon surveys and Reconnaissances for different projected lines of Railway in Umatilla County, Oregon and Walla Walla, Columbia and Whitman Counties, Washington Territory, with estimates of cost of construction, and approximate estimates of tonnage and earnings . . ."* undated, but date stamped February 23, 1887, NP Engineers Office St. Paul, Minn. (MHS 136.K.12.3.B)

Mortgage, 1886. *Mortgage Spokane and Palouse Railway Company to The Farmers' Loan and Trust Company, Dated May 1st, 1886.* MHS HE 2791 N 795 N8.

Mortgage, 1890a. *Northern Pacific and Idaho Railroad Company. First Mortgage.* June 2, 1890. (MHS)

Mortgage, 1890b. *Spokane and Palouse Railway Company Idaho Division to The Farmers' Loan and Trust Company. Dated October 1, 1890.* (MHS HE 2791 N795 N8 No. 99)

Northern Pacific 1907. *Northern Pacific Railway Co. v. Slaght, 205 U.S. 122 (1907).*

NP AFE, Authorizations for Expenditures in the NPRHA collection.

NP 1894. Track Profile. Dates originally drawn: S&P: 1894: MP 0-117; 1899: MP 117.5-138.6, corrected on later dates. NP 1898: Genesee Branch.

NP 1896, *NP Distance Schedule, Idaho Division, 9/1/1892, rev 4/1896.*

NP 1906. *Surveys and Reconnaissances of N. P. Ry. in Washington 1882* [Map, contains some OR&N and electric routes up to 1906, but NP appears to be to 1882]. Office of Chief Engineer, St. Paul MN February 15, 1906. MHS 132.I.4.4.

NP 1907. Track Profile Farmington Branch, June 15, 1907 (with two notes from 1922).

NP 1917. *Revised Engineering Report as of June 30, 1917.*

NP 1922. *Branch Line Data, Idaho Division.* May, 1922.

NP 1932. Track Profile. Dates originally drawn: P&L: 1932: MP 0-80, 100-120; 1924: MP 80-100; 1933: MP 120-138; Genesee Branch: 1924: MP 0-27; Farmington Branch: 1907: MP 0-6; corrected on later dates.

NP 1933. *Index Diagram and Original Track-laying Record.* Office of Chief Engineer, March 15, 1933.

NP 1935. *Pocket List Showing All Bridges Owned or Maintained . . . by the Northern Pacific Railway,* Bridge Engineer, 1935.

NP 1961. Track Profile, P&L partial MP 114-124.

NP 1968. *Pocket Bridge List,* Bridge Engineer, March 6, 1968.

NP 1949. *Table of Distances,* January 21, 1949; Effective February 24, 1949.

NP 1950. *NP Idaho Division, Distance Schedule,* nd, notes 1946-53.

NP Agent, *Lists of Officers, Agents, Stations,*[etc.]: 7/1/07.

NP Annual Reports to Stockholders, 1877, 1881-1885, 1887-95, 1896 "Official Statement", 1897 (including "Official Reports" and "Statistics" used in preparation of the First Annual Report), 1898-1900.

NP Condensed Profiles and Track Charts, various dates.

NP *Confidential Reports and Statistics.* June 30, 1898-1900, 1902, 1903. Thanks to Lorenz Schrenk for making these available.

NP Employee Timetables and Special Instructions, Idaho Division 8/2/1885 to 8/18/68 unless otherwise noted.

NP Hearings, 1925. *Hearings before the Joint Congressional Committee on the Investigation of the Northern Pacific Railroad Land Grants, exhibits, Part 1a.* 1925.

NP Papers, *Northern Pacific Railway Company Papers.* Part I, 1864-1922, Series A. University Publications of America, Inc., MHS 1984, Microfilm. These include minutes of the Board of Directors, Executive, Finance and Land Committees, and receivers. It also includes minutes and reports of special committees and miscellaneous documents. The organization and dates for the citations are in the text.

NP Public Timetables, various dates.

The Official Guide of the Railways . . ., various dates.

OHS, C&P or OR&N. Stock holders, directors, and executive committee minutes. OHS collection 299.

OR&N Annual Reports, June 30, 1881-85, 88, 97, 98 (MHS 137.J.10.1.B; OHS 025935 and MCL 0-385 0689).

OR&N 1887, *Indenture of Lease, January 1st, 1887, between Oregon Railway & Navigation Company and Oregon Short Line Railway Company and Union Pacific Railway Company.* April 25, 1887, New York.

OR&N Reorganization. *Amended Plan and Agreement for the Reorganization of the Oregon Railway & Navigation Company's System,* nd (MHS 137.J.10.1.B).

OR&N 11/25/96. Memorandum (OHS 299, 101).

OR&N/OWR&N/UP Employee Timetables, various dates.

O&T, Annual Reports, June 30, 1882; 1883 (MHS 137.7.H.2.F & 137.J.11.2.F; 1883 also in NW August, 1883, 14).

O&T vs. NP, affidavits 1887. No. 4152, *The Oregon and Transcontinental Company, versus Northern Pacific Railroad Company,* in the Circuit Court of the United States, Southern District of New York [1887], Affidavits on behalf of the Defendant, New York, 1887 (MHS 137.J.11.2.F).

O&WT 1916. NP Valuation filing with the ICC on the corporate history of Oregon & Washington Territory Railroad (MHS 134.H.9.1.B).

Powers 1901. *Powers v. Slaght, 180 U.S. 173 (1901).*

Provisional Contract 1889, *Provisional Contract. Spokane and Palouse Railway Company with Northern Pacific Railroad Company, Dated February 15th, 1889.* (MHS

Sanborn Fire Insurance maps, various dates and places, as indicated in the text.

S&P Reports to Interstate Commerce Commission.

S&P 1912. NP estimate of S&P construction costs on Form 97, 3-12 P (MHS 134.H.9.1.B).

S&P 1916. NP Valuation filings with the ICC on the corporate history of Spokane & Palouse Railway (MHS 134.H.9.1.B).

Stock Trust Agreement, 1886. *Stock Trust Agreement between The Stockholders, Spokane and Palouse Railway Co., Northern Pacific Railroad Co., and The Farmers' Loan and Trust Co., Trustee. Dated July 1st, 1886.* (MHS HE 2791 N 795 N8).

E. Smith 1889a. *Elijah Smith and Edward R. Bell against The Oregon and Transcontinental Company and others. Oregon and Transcontinental Record of the Recent Injunction Proceedings Facts for the Stockholders. Henry Villard, Charles L. Colby, Colgate Hoyt, New York May 24, 1889.* (MCL 0 385 067r).

E. Smith 1889b. *Elijah Smith in Reply to Statements Published by Mr. Henry Villard, May, 1889. To the stockholders of the Oregon and Transcontinental Company.* The statement is dated May 31, 1889, New York. (MCL 0-385 S64).

Supplementary Contract, 1882. *Supplementary Contract, The Oregon Railway & Navigation Company and Northern Pacific Railroad Co., Dated August 17th, 1882.* (MHS H2791 N795 N8 #129).

Traffic Contract, 1880. *Traffic Contract, the Oregon Railway & Navigation Company and Northern Pacific Railroad Co., Dated October 20th, 1880.* (OHS, 2017, Box 6).

Tripartite Contract, 1882. *Tripartite Contract Between the [blank], the Northern Pacific Railroad Company and the Oregon and Transcontinental Company,* [1882] (Bancroft pHE 2791 N8T7).

Tripartite Contract, 1883. *Tripartite Contract Between The Columbia and Palouse Railroad Comp'y, The Northern Pacific Railroad Company, The Oregon Railway and Navigation Comp'y, and the Oregon and Transcontinental Company,* 7/10/83. (MHS HE 2791 N795 N8 No. 2).

Truce Agreement. *So-Called "Truce Agreement" between Union Pacific and Northern Pacific, Affecting Construction of New Line in Common Territory, Eastern Washington and Northern Idaho.* Source unknown. Appears to be a UP/OR&N document (but may come from Hill papers). Contains copies of correspondence from 8/7/99 to 11/7/05 plus memorandum of agreements from 1897 to 1905. 21 pages.

UP 1889. *Report of the Union Pacific Railway Company.* December 31, 1889.

UP 1948. Union Pacific Historical Society, *Union Pacific Railroad System Employee Timetables, Vol., February 29, 1948.* Cheyenne, WY, 2000.

UP 1954. Union Pacific Railroad, *Freight Interchange Map of the United States,* 1954.

UP 1977. Union Pacific condensed profile 1/1/1977.

W&CR 1916. NP Valuation filings with the ICC on the corporate history of the Washington & Columbia River Railway (MHS 134.H.9.1.B).

Washington State, The Railroad Commission, Annual Reports.

WSDOT. Washington State Department of Transportation , "Washington Railroad Abandonments." [Dates are "Decision Date"]

Railroad Charter Documents

Bitter Root Railroad Company: Oregon 72116 (9/9/07).

Camas Prairie Railroad Company: Oregon (11/4/09—from MHS 134.K.17.3.B).

Clearwater Short Line Railway Company: Idaho 894(a) (11/26/1898), 894(a?) (12/5/1898), 894(b) (11/26/1898), 894 (12/13/1898), 894(h) (12/23/1899), 894(i) (8/6/1903), 894 (6/2/1909), 894 (6/24/1909), 2/19/1910.

Clearwater Valley Railroad Company: Oregon, 11/2/1898, 12/27/98, 3/16/99, 12/2/99.

Columbia and Palouse Railroad Company: Washington Territory, 0191 (6/29/1882), 0220 (11/28/1882), 0375 (7/16/1883), 0699 (8/17/1887).

Eastern Washington Railway Company: Washington Territory, 0553 (11/15/1885 [12/3/1885]), 0577 (3/1/1886).

Lewiston and Southeastern Railway Company: Idaho 2612 (6/7/90).

Moscow and Eastern Railroad [Railway]: Idaho C3009 (4/1/1897), C3007 (7/15/1899).

Montana, Idaho & Pacific Railroad Company: Idaho 6245 (4/26/1909).

North Coast Railroad Company: Washington State, 17812 (4/14/06), 19452 (12/15/06), 24780 (2/27/09), 27313 (12/18/10).

North Coast Railway: Washington State, 16644 (9/28/05), 17032 (12/18/05).

Northern Pacific and Idaho Railroad Company: Washington State, 455 (6/4/1890).

Oregon Railroad and Navigation Company: Washington State, 1037F (11/21/1898, Oregon 7/16/96), 3350F (7/6/1910, includes Oregon 4/17/1901).

Oregon Railway and Navigation Company: Washington Territory, 028F (8/27/1879), 037F (8/22/1882), There was also supplement articles filed in Oregon October 11, 1887, see WWJ 10/13/87, 3.

The Oregon Railway Extensions Company: Washington Territory, 616F (5/29/1888); Washington State, 143F (2/26/1891), 451F (4/9/1890).

Oregon and Transcontinental Company: Washington Territory, 372F (8/22/1882), 373F (8/24/1882).

Oregon-Washington Railroad and Navigation Company: Oregon, 15366 (11/23/1910).

Oregon, Washington and Idaho Railroad Company: Washington State, 1664F (9/1/1903).

Pacific and Idaho Northern Railway Company: Idaho 3386 (2/14/1899), 3386e (5/18/1910).

Payette Valley and Northern Railway Company: Idaho 12/6/1893.

Seattle, Boise and Salt Lake Railway Company: Idaho 12/9/1890.

Snake River Valley Railroad Company: Washington State, 901F (3/5/1898, OR March 3rd), 1056F (1/18/1899, OR 12/27/1898), 1204F (5/8/1900, OR 12/6/1899), 2089F (1/10/1906, OR January 9th), 2105F (2/1/1906, OR January 27th).

Spokane and Palouse Railway Company: Washington Territory, [Eastern Washington 0577 3/1/1886], 0326 (6/13/1887); Washington State, 7096 (6/21/1898); Idaho, 8/4/90, 11/21/90, 9/11/91, 3/22/98, 5/23/98.

Union Flat Railroad Company: 16681 [state?] (12/16/09).

Washington and Idaho Railroad Company: Washington Territory, 0619 (7/7/1886), 0284 (11/10/1886), 0332 (7/2/1887), 0831 (9/3/1888), 01443 (7/30/1889).

Weiser, Idaho and Spokane Railway Company: Idaho 2/16/1897.

Books, Articles and Manuscripts

Ainsworth 1992, Walt. "Portland, the NP, and Henry Villard." *The Mainstreeter.* Vol. 11, No. 2 (Spring, 1992), 11-20.

Allen 1990, Margaret Day. *Lewiston Country: An Armchair History.* Nez Perce County Historical Society, 1990.

Armbruster 1999, Kurt E. *Orphan Road: The Railroad Comes to Seattle, 1853-1911.* Pullman WA: Washington State University Press, 1999.

Asay 1991, Jeff. *Union Pacific Northwest: The Oregon-Washington Railroad & Navigation Company.* Edmonds, WA: Pacific Fast Mail, 1991.

Athearn 1976, Robert G. *Union Pacific Country.* Lincoln NE: University of Nebraska Press, 1976.

Austin & Dill, 1996, Ed & Tom. *S.P. & S.: The Spokane Portland & Seattle Railway.* Edmonds, WA: Pacific Fast Mail, 1996.

Baird 2003, Lynn and Dennis, eds. *In Nez Perce Country: Accounts of the Bitterroots and the Clearwater after Lewis and Clark.* Moscow ID: University of Idaho Library, 2003.

Baker 1934, W. W. *Forty Years a Pioneer: Business Life of Dorsey Syng Baker, 1848-1888.* Seattle, WA: Lowman & Hanford Co., 1934.

Bancroft 1888. Hubert Howe. *The Works of. . ., Volume XXX, History of Oregon, Vol. II. 1848-1888.* San Francisco: The History Company, Publishers, 1888.

——1890. *The Works of. . ., Volume XXXI, History of Washington, Idaho, and Montana, 1845-1889.* San Francisco: The History Company, Publishers, 1890.

Beach 2007, Philip F. "Highballing the Palouse and Lewiston Branch." *The Mainstreeter,* Vol. 26 No. 2 (Summer, 2007), 4-18.

——2012. "Robert Strahorn: The Spokane Sphinx and the Union Pacific's Secret Railroad." *The Streamline,* Vol. 26 No. 4 (Fall, 2012), 12-35.

——2013. "The Slaght Land Cases in Palouse City, Wash., 1887-1907." *The Mainstreeter,* Vol. 32 No. 4 (Winter, 2013), 19-21.

——2015. "James J. Hill, Charles S. Mellen: Who Was in the Bottle and Who was Sitting on the Cork?". *The Mainstreeter,* Vol. 34 No. 1 (Spring, 2015), 16-22.

Boone 1988, Lalia. *Idaho Place Names: A Geographical Dictionary.* Moscow, ID: U. of Idaho Press, 1988.

Burg, 2003, Thomas E. *White Pine Route: The History of the Washington, Idaho and Montana Railway Company."* Coeur d'Alene, ID: Museum of North Idaho, 2003.

Buss 1977, Dietrich G. *Henry Villard: A Study of Transatlantic Investments and Interests, 1870-1895.* Ph.D. dissertation, Claremont Graduate School (reprinted by Arno Press, New York, 1978).

Butler 1978, W. Daniel. "The Nezperce Railroad War" in Don L. Hofsommer, ed., *Railroads in the West.* Manhattan KS: Sunflower University Press, 1978, pp. 21-27.

Campbell 1938, E. G. *The Reorganization of the American Railroad System, 1893-1900.* New York: Columbia University Press, 1938.

Carter 2009, Clive. *Inland Empire Electric Line: Spokane to Coeur d'Alene and the Palouse.* Coeur d'Alene, ID: Museum of Northern Idaho, 2009.

Carter 2009b, Clive and Ann. *Washington State Railroad Depots.* Hudson, WI: Iconografix, 2009.

Chee 1954, Bruce B. *The Development of Railroads in the State of Washington 1860 to 1948.* 2nd ed., 1954. Unpub. Manuscript. [MHS 137.E.4.10.F #1289-96.

Cochran 2011, Barbara F. *Seven Frontier Women and the Founding of Spokane Falls.* Edited by Suzanne and Tony Bamonte. Spokane: Tornado Creek Publications, 2011.

Cochran 1970, John S. "Economic Importance of Early Transcontinental Railroads: Pacific Northwest. *Oregon Historical Quarterly* (71: 27-98, March, 1970).

Cotroneo 1966, Ross Ralph. *The History of the Northern Pacific Land Grant 1900-1952.* Dissertation University of Idaho, 1966. Published by Arno Press, New York, 1979.

Currie 2007, Earl J. *James J. Hill's Legacy to Railway Operations.* Privately printed.

Curtiss 2014, Paul D. *No More Bells, Nor Whistles: Washington State Railroads.* [Pasco WA]: Washington State Railroads Historical Society, 2014.

Daggett 1908, Stuart. *Railroad Reorganization.* Reprinted New York, NY: Augustus M. Kelly, Publishers, 1967.

de Borchgrave 2001, Alexandra Villard & John Cullen. *Villard: The Life and Times of an American Titan.* New York: Doubleday, 2001.

DeLorme 1992. *Idaho Atlas & Gazetteer.* Freeport, Maine: DeLorme Mapping, 1st ed., 1992.

——1995. *Washington Atlas & Gazetteer.* Freeport, Maine: DeLorme Mapping, 3rd ed. 2nd printing, 1995.

Derleth 2002, August. *The Milwaukee Road: Its First Hundred Years.* Iowa City: University of Iowa Press, 2002 (originally published 1948).

Dubaur Scrapbooks, micro film, University of Washington archives.

Duffin 2004, Andrew P. "Remaking the Palouse: Farming, Capitalism, and Environmental Change, 1825-1914." *Pacific Northwest Quarterly* (95: 194-204, Fall, 2004).

Eastwick 1999, Philip G. *Report of the Northern Pacific Railroad's Survey of the North Fork of the Clearwater River in 1871.* Moscow ID: University of Idaho Library, 1999.

Entze 2010, Marc A. *Deconstructing the Countryside: Agriculture and Railroad Abandonments in the Pacific Northwest Wheat Belt, 1900-1990.* Unpublished Ph.D. dissertation, Washington State University, 2010.

Erickson 1983, Edith E. *Whitman County: From Abbieville to Zion.* Colfax, WA: University Printing, N.D. [1983].

Fahey 1965, John. *Inland Empire: D. C. Corbin and Spokane.* Seattle, WA: University of Washington Press, 1965.

——1981. "When the Dutch Owned Spokane." *Pacific Northwest Quarterly* 72 (Jan. 1981), ff 2.

——1986. *The Inland Empire: Unfolding Years, 1879-1929.* Seattle, WA: University of Washington Press, 1986.

——1994. *Shaping Spokane: J. P. Graves and His Times.* Seattle, WA: University of Washington Press, 1994.

Faith 1990, Nicholas. *The World the Railways Made.* New York: Carroll & Graf Publishers, 1990.

Ficken 2002, Robert E. *Washington Territory.* Pullman, WA: Washington State University Press, 2002.

——2007. *Washington State: The Inaugural Decade, 1889-1899.* Pullman, WA: Washington State University Press, 2007.

Gaertner 1990, John T. *North Bank Road: The Spokane, Portland & Seattle Railway.* Pullman, WA: Washington State University Press, 1990.

Gill 1914, Frank B. "An Unfinished History of Transportation in Oregon and Washington in the form of contributed articles to the 'Pacific Semaphore' with some supplementary notes . . . ." Portland, OR, 1914, 1920 (unpublished manuscript in UWS).

Grande 1992, Walter R. *The Northwest's Own Railway: Spokane, Portland & Seattle Railway and its Subsidiaries.* Volume One, The Main Line. Portland, OR: Grande Press, 1992.

——1997. *The Northwest's Own Railway: Spokane, Portland & Seattle Railway and its Subsidiaries.* Volume Two, The Subsidiaries. Portland, OR: Grande Press, 1997.

Hedges 1930, James Blaine. *Henry Villard and the Railways of the Northwest.* Yale University Press, 1930 (reprinted by Russell & Russell, New York, 1967).

Hidy & Hidy, Ralph W. & Muriel E. Unpublished manuscript on the history of the Great Northern Railway.

Hidy 2004, Ralph W. et al. *The Great Northern Railway: A History.* Minneapolis, MN: University of Minnesota Press, 2004 (Originally published 1988).

Hilton & Due 1960, George W. & John F. *The Electric Interurban Railways in America.* Stanford, CA: Stanford University Press, 1960.

History 1889. *History of the Pacific Northwest-Oregon and Washington.* Vol. II. Portland, OR: North Pacific History Co., 1889.

Hitchman 1985, Robert. *Place Names of Washington.* Tacoma, WA: Washington State Historical Society, 1985.

Hofsommer 1991, Don L. "For Territorial Dominion in California and the Pacific Northwest: Edward H. Harriman and James J. Hill." *California History.* Spring, 1991, pp. 31-45, 135-136.

Howard & Co., Publishers. *Oregon and Washington Territory: A General Description.* Portland, OR, 1883.

Jackson 2005, Brenda K. *Domesticating the West: The Re-creation of the Nineteenth-Century American Middle Class.* Lincoln: U. of Nebraska Press, 2005.

Johansen & Gates 1967, Dorothy O. & Charles M. *Empire of the Columbia: A History of the Pacific Northwest.* 2nd edition, New York: Harper & Row, 1967.

Kerr 1968, K. Austin. *American Railroad Politics, 1914-1920; Rates, Wages, and Efficiency.* Pittsburgh, PA: University of Pittsburgh Press, 1968.

Kirkland 1965, Edward Chase. *Charles Francis Adams, Jr. 1835-1915 The Patrician At Bay.* Cambridge, MA: Harvard University Press, 1965.

Klein 1986, Maury. *The Life and Legend of Jay Gould.* Baltimore: The John Hopkins University Press, 1986.

——1987. *Union Pacific: The Birth of a Railroad 1862-1893.* New York: Doubleday, 1987.

——nd. *Source Notes for Union Pacific: Birth of a Railroad 1862-1893.* Distributed by the Union Pacific Museum, Omaha, NE, nd.

——1989. *Union Pacific: The Rebirth 1894-1969.* New York: Doubleday, 1989.

——2000. *The Life & Legend of E. H. Harriman.* Chapel Hill, NC: University of North Carolina Press, 2000.

Konen 1975, John D. "The Johnson Line: The Story of the Nezperce Railroad and its Predecessors." *Inland Empire Rail Quarterly*, Vol. 2, 1; Spring, 1975, pp. 3-11.

Lecompte 1988, Janet. "When the Railroad Came to Moscow." *Latah Legacy,* Winter, 1988, 21-28.

Lewty 1987, Peter J. *To the Columbia Gateway: The Oregon Railway and the Northern Pacific, 1879-1884.* Pullman WA: Washington State University Pres, 1987.

——1995, *Across the Columbia Plain: Railroad Expansion in the Interior Northwest, 1885-1893.* Pullman, WA: Washington State University Press, 1995.

Malone 1996, Michael P. *James J. Hill; Empire Builder of the Northwest.* Norman OK: University of Oklahoma Press, 1996.

Martin 1976, Albro. *James J. Hill and the Opening of the Northwest.* New York: Oxford University Press, 1976.

——1988. "Charles Henry Coster" in Robert L. Frey, ed. *The Encyclopedia of American Business History and Biography: Railroads in the Nineteenth Century.* New York: Facts on File, 1988.

Mattson, James J. NP, GN & UP corporate histories, unpub.

Meinig 1953, Donald William. *The Walla Walla Country: 1805-1910 A Century of Man and the Land.* Unpublished Ph.D. dissertation, University of Washington, 1953.

——1968, D. W. *The Great Columbia Plain; A Historical Geography, 1805-1910.* Seattle, WA: University of Washington Press, 1968.

Mercer 1985, Lloyd J. *E. H. Harriman: Master Railroader.* Boston: Twayne Publishers, 1985.

Meyer 1906, Balthasar Henry. *A History of the Northern Securities Case.* Madison, WI: Bulletin of the University of Wisconsin No. 142, 1906.

Mickelson 1993, Sig. *The Northern Pacific Railroad and the Selling of the West.* Sioux Falls, SD: The Center for Western Studies, 1993.

Mills 1950, Randall V. *Railroads Down the Valleys: Some Short Lines of the Oregon Country.* Palo Alto, CA: Pacific Books, 1950.

Morrisey 1997, Katherine G. *Mental Territories: mapping the inland empire.* Ithaca, NY: Cornell University Press, 1997.

Mutschler 1987, Chas. V. et al. *Spokane's Street Railways: An Illustrated History.* Spokane, WA: Inland Empire Railway Historical Society, 1987.

Neill 1977, Judge Thomas. *Incidents in the Early History of Pullman and the State College of Washington.* Fairfield, WA: Ye Galleon Press, 1977.

Nesbit & Gates 1946, Robert C. & Charles M. "Agriculture in Eastern Washington." *Pacific Northwest Quarterly.* 37:269-302 (Oct,, 1946).

New West "Tacoma's Wheat Record." 12/3/92, 41.

NI 1903. [Guy Senter?] *An Illustrated History of North Idaho Embracing Nez Perces, Idaho, Latah, Kootenai and Shoshone Counties State of Idaho.* Western Historical Publishing Co., 1903.

Nolan 1983, Edward W. *Northern Pacific Views: The Railroad Photography of F. Jay Haynes, 1876-1905.* Helena, MT: Montana Historical Society Press, 1983.

NW 1883, "Second Annual Report of the Board of Directors of the Oregon and Transcontinental Co." August, 1883, pp. 14-16.

NW 1884, "Official Record." January, 1884, pp. 17-18.

Oberst 1978, Walter A. *Railroads, Reclamation and the River, A History of Pasco.* Pasco, WA: Franklin County Historical Society, 1978.

Overton 1965, Richard C. *Burlington Route: A History of the Burlington Lines.* New York: Knopf, 1965.

PNQ. "Two Railroad Reports on Northwest Resources" 37: 175-191 (July, 1946).

Petersen 1987, Keith C. *Company Town: Potlatch, Idaho, and the Potlatch Lumber Company.* Pullman, WA: Washington State University Press, 1987.

Peterson 1966, Robert L. "The Idea of the Railroads: Regional Economic Growth." *Oregon Historical Quarterly.* (67: 101-123, June, 1966).

Phillips 1971, James W. *Washington State Place Names.* Seattle: U. of Washington Press, 1971.

Poor's 1887, Henry V. Poor. *Manual of the Railroads of the United States for 1887.* New York, 1887.

Pyle 1917, I & II, Joseph Gilpin. *The Life of James J. Hill.* Garden City, NY: Doubleday, Page & Company, 1917, two volumes.

Relf, 1917, R. H. Assistant Secretary Northern Pacific Railway, for summaries of NP records for ICC

Renz 1978, Louis T., compiler, *The Northern Pacific Railroad Data Tables.* Walla Walla WA, 1978.

——1980, *The History of the Northern Pacific Railroad.* Fairfield, WA: Ye Galleon Press, 1980.

Riegger 1986, Hal. *The Camas Prairie: Idaho's Railroad on Stilts.* Edmonds, WA: Pacific Fast Mail, 1986.

Rigdon 1954, Paul. *Historical Catalogue Union Pacific Historical Museum.* Council Bluffs, IA: Union Pacific Museum, 1954.

Robertson 1991, Donald B. *Encyclopedia of Western Railroad History, Volume II, The Mountain States.* Dallas, TX: Taylor Publishing 1991.

——1995, *Encyclopedia of Western Railroad History, Volume III, Oregon Washington.* Caldwell, ID: Caxton Printers, 1995.

Ruffner 1889, W. H. *A Report on Washington Territory.* New York: Seattle, Lake Shore & Eastern Railway, 1889.

Schrenk & Frey 2010, Lorenz P. & Robert J. *Northern Pacific Pioneer Steam Era.* Minneapolis, MN: Monad Publications, 2010.

——2013, *Engines of Growth, 1887-1905.* Minneapolis, MN: Monad Publications, 2013.

Schwantes 1993, Carlos A. *Railroad Signatures across the Pacific Northwest.* Seattle: University of Washington Press, 1993.

Schwantes 2008, Carlos A. & James P. Ronda. *The West the Railroads Made.* Seattle, WA: U. of Washington Press, 2008.

Smalley 1883, Eugene V. *History of the Northern Pacific Railroad.* New York: Putnam's Sons, 1883 (reprinted by Arno Press, New York, 1975).

Smart 1954, Douglas. "Spokane's Battle for Freight Rates." *Pacific Northwest Quarterly,* Vol. 45, 19-27 (January 1954).

Strahorn 1911, Carrie Adell. *Fifteen Thousand Miles by Stage.* New York: G. P. Putnam's Sons, 1911.

Strahorn 1942, Robert E. *Ninety Years of Boyhood.* Manuscript in Strahorn Library, College of Idaho, Caldwell, Idaho, 1942 (microfilm thereof).

Taylor 1998, Bill & Jan. *The Butte Short Line: The Construction Era 1888-1929.* Missoula MT: Pictorial Histories Pub. Co., 1998.

——1999, *The Northern Pacific's Rails to Gold and Silver: Lines to Montana's Mining Camps – Volume I: 1883-1887.* Missoula MT: Pictorial Histories Pub. Co., 1999.

——2008, *The Northern Pacific's Rails to Gold and Silver: Lines to Montana's Mining Camps – Volume II: 1888-1898.* Missoula MT: Pictorial Histories Pub. Co., 2008.

Trimble 1914, William Joseph. *The Mining Advance into Inland Empire.* Madison, WI, 1914 (reprinted by Ye Galleon Press, Fairfield, WA, 1986).

Trottman 1966, Nelson. *History of the Union Pacific: A Financial and Economic Survey.* New York: Augustus M. Kelley, Publishers, 1966.

Villard 1904, Henry. *Memoirs of Henry Villard: Journalist and Financier 1835-1900.* Vol. II, 1863-1900. Westminster: Archibald Constable & Co., Ltd., 1904.

——1944, *The Early History of Transportation in Oregon.* Eugene OR: University of Oregon, 1944 (reprint by Arno Press, New York, 1981).

Weis 1994, Viola Owen Geisler. *Uniontown: Its Beginning, Its Centennial.* Weis 1994.

White 1993, John H. Jr. *The American Railroad Freight Car: From the Wood-Car Era to the Coming of Steel.* Baltimore: The Johns Hopkins University Press, 1993.

White 2011, Richard. *Railroaded: The Transcontinentals and the Making of Modern America.* New York: W. W. Norton & Co., 2011.

Winks 1991, Robin W. *Frederick Billings: A Life.* New York: Oxford University Press, 1991.

Wood 1983, John V. *Railroads Through The Coeur d'Alenes.* Caldwell, ID: Caxton Printers, 1983.

Woodward 2006, Doris. "Thomas and Elizabeth Tannatt, Serving the Inland Northwest With Vision and Integrity." *The Pacific Northwesterner,* Vol. 50, #1 7-38 (April 2006).

Index

Illustrations in italics.

Note: Activities of subsidiary railroads are in many cases found in the entries of their superior railroad companies; this follows the practice, generally without explanation, of contemporary primary sources and newspapers.